Traversing the Ethical Minefield

EDITORIAL ADVISORS

ASPEN CASEBOOK SERIES

Traversing the Ethical Minefield

Problems, Law, and Professional Responsibility

Third Edition

Susan R. Martyn

Stoepler Professor of Law and Values
Distinguished University Professor
University of Toledo College of Law

Lawrence J. Fox

Partner, Drinker Biddle & Reath
George W. and Sadella D. Crawford
Visiting Lecturer in Law, Yale Law School

Wolters Kluwer
Law & Business

Published by Wolters Kluwer Law & Business in New York.

Wolters Kluwer Law & Business serves customers worldwide with CCH, Aspen Publishers, and Kluwer Law International products. (www.wolterskluwerlb.com)

To contact Customer Service, e-mail customer.service@wolterskluwer.com, call 1-800-234-1660, fax 1-800-901-9075, or mail correspondence to:

Wolters Kluwer Law & Business
Attn: Order Department
PO Box 990
Frederick, MD 21705

Printed in the United States of America.

1 2 3 4 5 6 7 8 9 0

ISBN 978-1-4548-0814-5

Library of Congress Cataloging-in-Publication Data

Martyn, Susan R., 1947-
   Traversing the ethical minefield : problems, law, and professional responsibility / Susan R. Martyn, Lawrence J. Fox. — 3rd ed.
       p. cm.
   ISBN 978-1-4548-0814-5 (alk. paper)
   1. Legal ethics — United States. 2. Attorney and client — United States. I. Fox, Lawrence J., 1943- II. Title.

KF306.M37 2013
174'.30973 — dc23

2012034432

SUSTAINABLE FORESTRY INITIATIVE

Certified Sourcing
www.sfiprogram.org
SFI-01234

SFI label applies to the text stock

About Wolters Kluwer Law & Business

Wolters Kluwer Law & Business is a leading global provider of intelligent information and digital solutions for legal and business professionals in key specialty areas, and respected educational resources for professors and law students. Wolters Kluwer Law & Business connects legal and business professionals as well as those in the education market with timely, specialized authoritative content and information-enabled solutions to support success through productivity, accuracy and mobility.

Serving customers worldwide, Wolters Kluwer Law & Business products include those under the Aspen Publishers, CCH, Kluwer Law International, Loislaw, Best Case, ftwilliam.com and MediRegs family of products.

CCH products have been a trusted resource since 1913, and are highly regarded resources for legal, securities, antitrust and trade regulation, government contracting, banking, pension, payroll, employment and labor, and healthcare reimbursement and compliance professionals.

Aspen Publishers products provide essential information to attorneys, business professionals and law students. Written by preeminent authorities, the product line offers analytical and practical information in a range of specialty practice areas from securities law and intellectual property to mergers and acquisitions and pension/ benefits. Aspen's trusted legal education resources provide professors and students with high-quality, up-to-date and effective resources for successful instruction and study in all areas of the law.

Kluwer Law International products provide the global business community with reliable international legal information in English. Legal practitioners, corporate counsel and business executives around the world rely on Kluwer Law journals, looseleafs, books, and electronic products for comprehensive information in many areas of international legal practice.

Loislaw is a comprehensive online legal research product providing legal content to law firm practitioners of various specializations. Loislaw provides attorneys with the ability to quickly and efficiently find the necessary legal information they need, when and where they need it, by facilitating access to primary law as well as state-specific law, records, forms and treatises.

Best Case Solutions is the leading bankruptcy software product to the bankruptcy industry. It provides software and workflow tools to flawlessly streamline petition preparation and the electronic filing process, while timely incorporating ever-changing court requirements.

ftwilliam.com offers employee benefits professionals the highest quality plan documents (retirement, welfare and non-qualified) and government forms (5500/ PBGC, 1099 and IRS) software at highly competitive prices.

MediRegs products provide integrated health care compliance content and software solutions for professionals in healthcare, higher education and life sciences, including professionals in accounting, law and consulting.

Wolters Kluwer Law & Business, a division of Wolters Kluwer, is headquartered in New York. Wolters Kluwer is a market-leading global information services company focused on professionals.

For Our Grandchildren

Vivienne Reece
Juliet Maeve
William Henry
Roger Edward

Summary of Contents

Contents

PART II: LAWYERS AND CLIENTS: FIDUCIARY DUTY

PART III: LAWYERS AND JUSTICE: THE LIMITS OF ADVOCACY

PART IV: LAWYERS AND SOCIETY: THE PROFESSION

Chapter 15: Professional Regulation   563

Preface

This book represents a unique collaboration between a law professor with extensive academic experience (Susan Martyn) and a long-time practitioner who teaches law students and has dealt with most of the issues in this book (Larry Fox). We suspect that our casebook is unlike many you have encountered so far in law school, so we begin your study by introducing you to our pedagogical goals as well as several distinctive features of the book you are about to use.

Overall, we intend these materials to accomplish four goals. First, we seek to engage you in a fascinating and dynamic subject. Second, we expect to teach you the rapidly expanding law governing lawyers. Third, we want to remind you of the need to pay careful attention to facts and context. Fourth, we invite you to recognize good lawyering, or the need to develop practical ethical judgment, a task that often may require lawyers to do more than simply comply with the law. To achieve these goals, we provide you with a combination of short problems, professional code provisions, interesting cases, short stories, and a series of continuing notes that introduce and develop themes in the material.

The Problems

The short problems that introduce each section of the book ask you to evaluate the actions of a hypothetical law firm, Martyn & Fox. Each set of problems is followed by citations to the relevant rules of professional conduct and sections of the Restatement of the Law Governing Lawyers found in your rules supplement. You should prepare for each class by formulating answers to the problems after considering these provisions along with the relevant cases and other materials in the book.

As you address the dilemmas faced by Martyn & Fox, you will discover that the firm is capable of great inconsistency. At times, the lawyers at Martyn & Fox may seem wise and capable. On other occasions, you will wonder at their fallibility. In many situations, you may identify with their confusion and angst. Most often, the firm can be rescued from disaster by sage advice.

We intend these problems to promote all of our pedagogical goals, so you should expect to approach them on several levels. First, we hope they will engage you in interesting issues faced by modern lawyers. Second, we want them to motivate you to study the relevant provisions in various lawyer codes, the Restatement of the Law Governing Lawyers, and the cases and other materials that explain and construe them. Third, we anticipate that the relative brevity of each problem will lead you to conclude that the answer "depends on" additional facts that might change the advice you offer Martyn & Fox. We invite you to articulate your assumptions and to anticipate how additional facts might change your answer. For example, does it matter whether Martyn & Fox is a two- or two-hundred-person law firm? Whether it focuses primarily on litigation or transactional work? Whether its practice is located in a rural area or a major city? Whether the lawyer is a partner or an associate? Whether Martyn & Fox's client is an individual or an entity? How much Martyn & Fox's client can pay?

Finally, once you get into the law that governs the situation described in a problem, you will discover occasions when Martyn & Fox has a range of options. In these instances, you should identify the discretion ceded to the lawyer's individual moral conscience and articulate how you believe that discretion should be exercised. Here, we hope to assist you in developing practical ethical judgment as well as learning the law.

The Cases

Most people new to this subject are surprised at the vast array of cases that explain and expand on the professional code provisions and other remedies that make up the law governing lawyers. We offer you a rich assortment of these cases, emphasizing those decided in the past decade. Each of the seventy-two cases in this book has been edited for clarity. We use ellipses or brackets to indicate omissions from the court's opinion, but omitted citations and footnotes are not identified.

The Short Stories

The five short stories in this book offer you the opportunity to engage in a difficult issue of legal ethics from the viewpoint of the lawyers confronting the situation. Larry wrote each these stories as chapters in his books, *Legal Tender: A Lawyer's Guide to Handling Professional Dilemmas* and *Raise the Bar: Real World Solutions for a Troubled Profession*. We have included these vignettes to offer you a break from traditional law study and an alternative way to learn some substantive law. Primarily, however, we intend these excerpts to show you the human face of some of the legal issues raised in the story. The extended detail of the story will enable you to understand more fully the context in which the lawyer must make a practical ethical judgment.

The Continuing Notes

Unlike the note material in most casebooks, the twenty-nine notes in this book are short essays organized around five general themes. These notes detail important background law relied on in the law governing lawyers, further explanation of a case or series of cases, and an opportunity to explore a topic at an accessible but more advanced level. They also serve as occasions to connect and integrate the basic ideas and themes that the courts have woven throughout the law governing lawyers.

The first set of continuing notes, entitled **Lawyers' Roles**, makes explicit the often-unnoticed roles lawyers assume when they represent clients, with particular emphasis on the balance of power in the professional relationship. Six notes on this theme appear throughout the book:

In these notes we identify various client-lawyer relationships and examine the legal risks created by each of these roles. We consider both philosophical issues, such as whether a lawyer who serves a client also can serve the interest of justice, and personal matters, such as the effect of various client-lawyer relationships on the personal and professional happiness and success of the lawyer. We hope these notes prod you to think about why some of the lawyers who became the subject of cases in this book got into trouble, as well as encourage you to consider the kind of lawyer you want to be.

The second series of continuing notes, entitled **The Law Governing Lawyers**, encompasses six notes:

Here, we explore the fiduciary obligations lawyers assume when they say "yes," or agree to represent clients and the remedies provided by the cases and materials when these obligations are ignored. We emphasize the difference and connections between professional discipline and the other legal consequences that can flow from lawyer malfeasance, such as disqualification, malpractice, and fee forfeiture.

In the third group of notes, entitled **The Bounds of the Law**, six notes explain when lawyers may or must say "no" to clients, because of the applicability of other law that imposes a limit on the lawyer's advocacy.

In these notes, we explore the vast law of fraud, the ever-expanding criminal law, procedural sanctions, and the impact of the Constitution on the regulation of lawyer conduct. Each of these bodies of general law has been read into the professional codes to create an explicit boundary beyond which lawyers tread only at great risk both to themselves and to their clients.

The fourth series of continuing notes, entitled **Practice Pointers**, offers you practical advice about how to avoid or mitigate the legal consequences raised by the problems, cases, and other materials. Here we showcase six topics:

The final set of notes focuses on **Lawyers and Clients** in five common practice settings. Here, we examine specialized legal regulation of the client's rights and responsibilities, which in turn shapes, enhances, and also can limit a lawyer's advocacy on behalf of the client.

The Combination

Overall, we intend the problems, rules, cases, stories, and continuing notes in this book to serve as a guide to identifying, understanding, and avoiding the minefields and mistakes that the lawyers in these materials have confronted. We also hope you enjoy this study as much as we have enjoyed preparing it.

Susan Martyn and Larry Fox
November 2012

Acknowledgments

We could not have completed this casebook without the accumulated wisdom of hundreds of lawyers who have taught and refined our understanding of these issues. In particular, we thank our colleagues who served as reporters and advisors to the American Law Institute's Restatement (Third) of The Law Governing Lawyers and those who served with us on the ABA Ethics 2000 Commission. We also are indebted to many at the ABA Center for Professional Responsibility, who provided us with information about recent developments exactly when we needed it.

The two of us first met in 1987 in a windowless conference room at the American Law Institute during a meeting of the advisors to the Restatement of the Law Governing Lawyers. These meetings clearly are an acquired taste. The Reporters to Restatement projects circulate a draft weeks before each meeting, then sit on a raised dais facing a semicircle of twenty-five or thirty judges, professors, and lawyers to defend each section, comment, and example line by line, usually for several days at a time. Only the good will and good humor of the participants can make such a process bearable, and we soon found that we were providing large doses of both for each other. From our thirteen-year sojourn with the ALI, a broad friendship developed that also took us into new adventures, including CLE programs and the ABA's Ethics 2000 project in which we both served as Commissioners to undertake a stem-to-stern review of the ABA Model Rules of Professional Conduct.

For us, nothing has been quite like our work on this volume. After Larry returned from a stay in Ithaca, Susan learned of the problems he had developed for his Professional Responsibility course at Cornell Law School and decided they could form the backbone of a casebook. Susan selected and edited the cases, organized the materials, and wrote the continuing notes in the book while teaching the materials to students at Toledo, Marquette, and George Washington Law Schools. Larry contributed to the third edition while teaching at Harvard and Yale Law School. Susan wrote the essay materials with irreverent but helpful editorial critiques from Larry, which more than occasionally led to another conversation that benefited us both. In short, we could not have completed this book without each other, and we both feel free to blame the other for the flaws that remain.

The faculties and students at seven law schools—Cornell, George Washington, Harvard, Marquette, Yale, the University of Pennsylvania, and the University of Toledo—contributed to these materials by consulting, arguing, and correcting many of our mistakes. Others across the country also commented on and helped us formulate our ideas. Special thanks to Susan Becker, Kathleen

Clark, Ben Cooper, James Caruso, David Caylor, Roger Cramton, Richard Dooley, Mark Harrison, Leslie Griffin, Susan Daicoff, Stuart Green, Geoffrey Hazard, Barbara and Charles Hicks, Jack Kircher, Andy Kaufman, Margaret Love, Judith Maute, Nancy Moore, Mitt Regan, Ellyn Rosen, Tom Morgan, Lee Pizzimenti, Jack Sahl, Jack Sammons, Becky Stretch, Robert Tuttle, William Van Alstyne, Brad Wendel, and Leah Wortham. We also received able research assistance from Breanne Democko and Christine McIntyre.

Our ideas never would have taken shape without the capable, cheerful, and knowledgeable assistance of Bea Cucinotta.

Susan would not have had the time to devote to this project without a sabbatical leave granted by the University of Toledo and the assistance of the Eugene N. Balk Fund, which provided the funds to carry out most of the research in the continuing notes. Larry never would have been able to develop the problems if it were not for the invitation from Charles Wolfram to escape practice and teach at the Cornell Law School.

Finally, our thanks to the following for permission to reproduce all or portions of their work:

Oxford University Press, IN THE INTERESTS OF JUSTICE: REFORMING THE LEGAL PROFESSION by Deborah L. Rhode (2000). 2,488 words from pp. 49-79. By permission of Oxford University Press, Inc.

Philadelphia Bar Association Professional Guidance Committee, Opinion 2010-6

Professional Ethics Committee for the State Bar of Texas, Opinion 583 (2008)

The University of Chicago Press, *The Edge of Meaning* by James Boyd White, pp. 223-226. © by the University of Chicago, all rights reserved. Published 2001.

Part I

Introduction

Most other law school courses are designed to improve your ability to assist your clients in achieving their goals by articulating their interests, asserting their rights, and defending their positions. Only in this course are you provided with the tools to recognize your own obligations and professional responsibilities, the limitations on your own conduct, and your rights as a lawyer, an officer of the legal system, and a citizen. Our experience indicates that many legally educated professionals (practicing lawyers and academics) are less than fully aware of some of the most crucial concepts covered in this course. Our purpose is to ensure that this will not be the case for you.

Chapter 1

Lawyers, Role, and Law

A. Lawyers and Role

Problems

1-1. Should Martyn & Fox file a claim on behalf of a client after the statute of limitations has expired? What if we are fairly sure the opposing party will not be represented?

1-2. During negotiations, a lawyer for the buyer agrees on behalf of his client to pay an extra $50,000 because, the lawyer observes, "the land is zoned for ten lots." Martyn & Fox, representing the seller, knows that the lawyer is mistaken. Should Martyn & Fox close the deal without correcting the mistake?

1-3. Should Martyn & Fox advise its client to sign an agreement in a divorce case that settles property division and child support when the opposing lawyer mistakenly believes that alimony can be negotiated later, but we know that the law will bar such a claim? What if the opposing lawyer is a best friend? Has not handled many divorces?

1-4. Should Martyn & Fox tell a client the chances of her getting caught doing something illegal, for example, deducting the cost of a child's wedding as a business expense? How about the chances of getting caught withholding a document in response to a legitimate request for production of documents?

Consider: Model Rules Preamble and Scope
Restatement of the Law Governing Lawyers § 1

Monroe H. Freedman & Abbe Smith
Understanding Lawyers' Ethics
pp. 8, 45, 46–47, 54, 62–63, 68, 69, 70–71, 72–74 (4th ed., LexisNexis 2010)

. . . In expressing the distinctive feature of ethics in the legal profession, we would identify the client not as "this other person, over whom I have power," but as "this other person whom I have the power to help." In this view, the central concern of lawyers' ethics is not how my client "can be made as good as possible."[29] Rather, it is how far I can ethically go—or how far I should be required to go—to achieve for my clients full and equal rights under law.

Shaffer thinks of lawyers' ethics as being rooted in moral philosophy, while we think of lawyers' ethics as being rooted in the moral values that are expressed in the Bill of Rights. . . .

Can you be a good lawyer and a good person at the same time? The question implies that serving your clients competently and zealously will require you to violate your personal morality in at least some instances. At the heart of that issue is whether it is the lawyer or the client who should make the moral decisions that come up in the course of the representation. As it is frequently put: Is the lawyer just a "hired gun," or must the lawyer "obey his own conscience, not that of his client?" . . .

In an influential article,[6] [Professor Richard] Wasserstrom recalls John Dean's list of those implicated in the Watergate cover-up. Dean placed an asterisk next to the names of each of the lawyers on the list, because he had been struck by the fact that so many were lawyers. Wasserstrom concludes that the involvement of lawyers in Watergate was "natural, if not unavoidable," . . . [the] "likely if not inevitable consequence of their legal acculturation." Indeed, on the basis of Wasserstrom's analysis, the only matter is why so many of those on John Dean's list were *not* lawyers. What could possibly have corrupted the non-lawyers to such a degree as to have led them into what Wasserstrom sees as the uniquely amoral and immoral world of the lawyers? "For at best," Wasserstrom asserts, "the lawyer's world is a simplified moral world; often it is an amoral one; and more than occasionally perhaps, an overtly immoral one."

Wasserstrom considers "role-differentiated behavior" to be the root of the problem. As he says, the "nature of role-differentiated behavior . . . often makes it both appropriate and desirable for the person in a particular role to put to one side considerations of various sorts—and especially various moral considerations—that would otherwise be relevant if not decisive." Illustrative of how Wasserstrom thinks lawyers should make moral considerations relevant is his suggestion that a lawyer should refuse to advise a wealthy client of a tax loophole provided by the legislature for only a few wealthy taxpayers. If that case were to be generalized, it would mean that the legal profession can properly regard itself as an oligarchy, whose duty is to nullify decisions made by the people's duly elected representatives. . . .

Nevertheless, Wasserstrom suggests that lawyers should "see themselves less as subject to role-differentiated behavior and more as subject to the demands of *the* moral point of view."

But is it really that simple? Is there a single point of view that can be identified as "the" moral one that everyone accepts? . . .

---

29. *See* Thomas Shaffer, *Legal Ethics and the Good Client*, 36 Cath. U. L. Rev. 319, 320 (1987).
6. Richard Wasserstrom, *Lawyers as Professionals: Some Moral Issues*, 5 ABA Human Rights 1 (1975).

In day-to-day practice, the most common instances of amoral or immoral conduct by lawyers are those occasions in which lawyers preempt their clients' moral judgments. That occurs in two ways. Most often lawyers assume that the client wants her to maximize his material or tactical position in every way that is legally permissible, regardless of non-legal considerations. That is, lawyers tend to assume the worst regarding the client's desires, and act accordingly. Less frequently, a lawyer will decide that a particular course of conduct is morally preferable, even though not required legally, and will follow that course on the client's behalf without consultation. In either event, the lawyer fails in her responsibility to maximize the client's autonomy by providing the client with the fullest advice and counsel, legal and moral, so that the client can make the most informed choice possible. . . .

One of the essential values of a just society is respect for the dignity of each member of that society. Essential to each individual's dignity is the free exercise of individual autonomy. Toward that end, each person is entitled to know his rights with respect to society and other individuals and to decide whether to assert of those rights through the due processes of law.

The lawyer, by virtue of her training and skills, has a monopoly over access to the legal system and knowledge about the law. Consequently, the lawyer's advice and assistance are often indispensable to the effective exercise of individual autonomy.

The attorney acts both professionally and morally in assisting clients to maximize their autonomy, by counseling clients candidly and fully regarding the clients' legal rights and moral responsibilities as the lawyer perceives them, and by assisting clients to carry out their lawful decisions. The attorney acts unprofessionally and immorally when she deprives clients of autonomy, by denying them information regarding their legal rights, by otherwise preempting their moral decisions, or by depriving them of the ability to carry out their lawful decisions. . . .

Closely related to the concept of client autonomy is the lawyer's obligation to give "entire devotion to the interest of the client, warm zeal in the maintenance and defense of his rights and the exertion of [the lawyer's] utmost learning and ability."[1] This ethic of zeal is a "traditional aspiration" that was already established in Abraham Lincoln's day, and zealousness continues today to be "*the* fundamental principle of the law of lawyering," and "the dominant standard of lawyerly excellence."

Client autonomy refers to the client's right to decide what her own interests are. Zeal refers to the dedication with which the lawyer furthers the client's interests. The ethic of zeal is, therefore, pervasive in lawyers' professional responsibilities, because it informs all of the lawyer's other ethical obligations with "entire devotion to the interest of the client." . . .

The obligation of "entire devotion to the interest of the client [and] warm zeal in the maintenance and defense of his rights" is not limited to the role

---

1. ABA Canons of Prof. Ethics 15 (1908).

of the lawyer as advocate in the courtroom. . . . It is important to remember, however, that any lawyer who counsels a client, negotiates on a client's behalf, or drafts a legal document for a client must do so with an actual or potential adversary in mind. When a contract is negotiated, there is a party on the other side. A contract, a will, or a form submitted to a government agency may well be read at some later date with an adversary's eye, and could become the subject of litigation. The advice given to a client and acted upon today may strengthen or weaken the client's position in contentious negotiations or in litigation next year. In short, it is not just the advocate in the courtroom who functions in an adversary system, and it is not just the client currently in litigation who may both require and be entitled to "warm zeal in the maintenance and defense of his rights." . . .

We want to emphasize, however, [that] the lawyer's decision to accept or to reject a client is a moral decision for which the lawyer can properly be held morally accountable. Indeed, there are few decisions a lawyer makes that are more significantly moral than whether she will dedicate her intellect, training, and skills to a particular client or cause. . . .

One of the most important considerations in deciding to accept or reject a client is that the lawyer, in representing the client, might be required to use tactics that the lawyer finds offensive. . . .

The proper solution to the lawyer's moral objections to using such tactics, however, is not for the lawyer to take the case and then to deny the client his rights; rather, the lawyer should refuse to take the case. . . .

[A]ny decision to turn down legal business for moral reasons has to be balanced against the effect that decision might have on one's ability to earn a living. To recognize that there are moral concerns on both sides of the issue serves to emphasize that the choice can be an extremely difficult one. . . .

Turning down clients on moral grounds (as distinguished from suggesting moral considerations to a client) can be costly and therefore can require considerable courage. However, the decision of whether to represent a client is the point at which the lawyer has the most scope for exercising autonomy. Once you have committed yourself to serve as your client's zealous representative, your ability to act on conscientious grounds is, and should be, significantly limited.

Deborah L. Rhode

In the Interests of Justice: Reforming the Legal Profession

pp. 49–79 (Oxford University Press 2000)

The Advocate's Role in the Adversary System

My first legal case was almost my last. It brought home Dostoevski's definition of an advocate as "a conscience for hire." And it made me wonder about putting mine on the market.

The insight came when I was interning at the Washington, D.C., public defender's office after my first year in law school. Two of the office's juvenile clients had stomped an elderly "wino" to death, just for the fun of it. They confessed to my supervising attorney and to the arresting officer; indeed, they appeared somewhat proud of their accomplishment. However, the police committed a number of constitutional and procedural violations in obtaining the confession and other inculpating evidence. My supervisor was able to get the case dismissed on what the public would consider a "technicality." He also was proud of his accomplishment. The clients were jubilant and unrepentant. I had no doubt that the office would see them again. Nor did I doubt that I was utterly unsuited to be a criminal defense lawyer. I wasn't sure I was ready to be a lawyer at all.

Now, with the benefit of a quarter-century's hindsight, I think both my supervisor and I were right. He was providing an essential and ethically defensible safeguard for constitutional values. And I was right to feel morally troubled by the consequences. I had assisted a process that sent the wrong messages to guilty clients: some lives are cheap; a gifted lawyer can get you off.

This is one of the "hard cases" in legal ethics. Its moral tensions arise from deeply rooted conflicts in America's commitments to both individual rights and social responsibilities. This conflict plays out in many law-related contexts, and legal ethics is no exception. When lawyers straddle these cultural contradictions, the public both demands and condemns their divided loyalties. Defense of disempowered clients and unpopular causes earns lawyers their greatest respect but also their sharpest criticism. The clash between lawyers' responsibilities as officers of the court and advocates of client interests creates the most fundamental dilemmas of legal ethics. All too often, the bar has resolved this conflict by permitting overrepresentation of those who can afford it and underrepresentation of everyone else. The result is to privilege the profession's interests at the expense of the public's. . . .

The Premises of Partisanship

The standard ethical justifications for the advocate's role rest on two major premises. The first assumption, drawing on utilitarian reasoning, is that an adversarial clash between opposing advocates is the best way of discovering truth. The second assumption, based on individual rights, is that morally neutral partisanship is the most effective means of protecting human freedom and dignity. Both claims unravel at several key points.

The truth-based rationale for the advocate's role assumes that the "right" result is most likely to occur through competitive presentations of relevant law and facts. As a report by the Joint Conference of the American Bar Association and the Association of American Law Schools emphasized, only when a decision-maker "has had the benefit of intelligent and vigorous advocacy on both sides" can society have confidence in the decision. This faith in partisan process is part of a broader worldview that underpins America's basic social and economic institutions. Robert Kutak, chair of the ABA commission that drafted the Model Rules of Professional Conduct, observed that our commitment to the advocate's role in an adversarial framework reflects "the same deep-seated values we place on competition" in other contexts.

A second defense of neutral partisanship involves the protection of rights and the relationships necessary to safeguard those rights. Here again, the priority we give to personal liberties is rooted in more general cultural commitments. In a highly legalistic society, preservation of personal dignity and autonomy requires preservation of access to law. . . . The legal profession has no special claim to righteousness and no public accountability for their view of justice. By what right should they "play God" by foreclosing legal assistance or imposing "their own views about the path of virtue upon their clients"? . . .

And if advocates were held morally accountable for their clients' conduct, less legal representation would be available for those most vulnerable to popular prejudice and governmental repression. Our history provides ample illustrations of the social and economic penalties directed at attorneys with unpopular clients. It was difficult enough to find lawyers for accused communists in the McCarthy era and for political activists in the early southern civil rights campaign. Those difficulties would have been far greater without the principle that legal representation is not an endorsement of client conduct.

These rights-based justifications of neutral partisanship assume special force in criminal cases. Individuals whose lives, liberty, and reputation are at risk deserve an advocate without competing loyalties to the state. Ensuring effective representation serves not only to avoid unjust outcomes but also to affirm community values and to express our respect for individual rights. Guilt or innocence should be determined in open court with due process of law, not in the privacy of an attorney's office. The consequences of an alternative model are readily apparent in many totalitarian countries. Where defense lawyers' role is to "serve justice," rather than their clients, what passes for "justice" does not commend itself for export. Often the roles of counsel for the defendant and the state are functionally identical and the price is paid in innocent lives. A case in point involves China's celebrated prosecution of the Gang of Four following the Cultural Revolution of the 1960s. The attorney appointed to defend Mao Tse Tung's widow chose not to honor his client's request to assert her innocence or to conduct any investigations, present any witnesses, or challenge the government's case. According to the lawyer, such advocacy was unnecessary because "the police and the prosecutors worked on the case a very long time and the evidence they found which wasn't true they threw away."

This country has had similar experiences when the crime has been especially heinous or the accused has been a member of a particularly unpopular group. To take only the most obvious example, for most of this nation's history, southern blacks accused of an offense against a white victim stood little chance of anything approximating zealous advocacy or a fair trial. Despite substantial progress, racial and ethnic bias in legal proceedings remains common, as most Americans and virtually every bar task force agree. The risk of abuse is significant in other contexts as well. Perjury, fabrication of evidence, and suppression of exculpatory material by law enforcement officials remain pervasive problems. Such abuses were present in some two-thirds of the sixty-odd cases involving defendants facing the death penalty who recently have been exonerated by DNA evidence. . . .

Although these rationales for zealous advocacy have considerable force, they fall short of justifying current partisanship principles. A threshold weakness is the bar's overreliance on criminal defense as an all-purpose paradigm for the lawyer's role. Only a small amount of legal work involves either criminal proceedings or civil matters that raise similar concerns of individual freedom and governmental power. An advocacy role designed to ensure the presumption of innocence and deter prosecutorial abuse is not necessarily transferable to other legal landscapes. Bar rhetoric that casts the lawyer as a "champion against a hostile world" seems out of touch with most daily practice. The vast majority of legal work assists corporate and wealthy individual clients in a system that is scarcely hostile to their interests. When a Wall Street firm representing a Fortune 500 corporation squares off against understaffed regulators or a victim of unsafe practices, the balance of power is not what bar metaphors imply.

A similar problem arises with traditional truth-based justifications for neutral partisanship. Their underlying premise, that accurate results will emerge from competitive partisan presentations before disinterested tribunals, depends on factual assumptions that seldom hold in daily practice. Most legal representation never receives oversight from an impartial decision maker. Many disputes never reach the point of formal legal complaint, and of those that do, over 90 percent settle before trial. Moreover, even cases that end up in court seldom resemble the bar's idealized model of adversarial processes. That model presupposes adversaries with roughly equal incentives, resources, capabilities, and access to relevant information. But those conditions are more the exception than the rule in a society that tolerates vast disparities in wealth, high litigation costs, and grossly inadequate access to legal assistance. As a majority of surveyed judges agreed, a mismatch in attorneys' skills can distort outcomes; a mismatch in client resources compounds the problem. In law, as in life, the haves generally come out ahead. . . .

For similar reasons, the bar's traditional rights-based justifications offer inadequate support for prevailing adversarial practices. Such justifications implicitly assume that clients are entitled to assistance in whatever the law permits. This assumption confuses legal and moral rights. Some conduct that is socially indefensible may remain lawful because adequate prohibitions appear unenforceable or because decision-making bodies are too uninformed or compromised by special interests to impose effective regulation. An ethic of undivided client loyalty in these contexts has encouraged lawyers' assistance in some of the most socially costly enterprises in recent memory, the distribution of asbestos and Dalkon Shields, the suppression of health information about cigarettes, and the financially irresponsible ventures of savings and loan associations. . . .

Autonomy does not have intrinsic value; its importance derives from the values it fosters, such as individual initiative and responsibility. If a particular client objective does little to promote those values, or does so only at much greater cost to third parties, then the ethical justification for zealous advocacy is less convincing. . . .

Professional Interests and Partisan Practices

Whatever their inadequacies in serving the public interest, prevailing adversarial practices have been reasonably effective in serving professional interests. They permit all the justice that money can buy or a client who can afford it, and they impose few responsibilities on those who cannot. . . .

The Price of Partisanship

Yet these financial and psychological comforts come at a price. The avoidance of ethical responsibility is ultimately corrosive for lawyers, clients, and the legal framework on which they depend. For many practitioners, the neutral partisan role undermines the very commitments that led them to become lawyers. . . . The submersion of self into a role too often leaves the advocate alienated from his own moral convictions. When professional action becomes detached from ordinary moral experience, the lawyer's ethical sensitivity erodes. The agnosticism that neutral partisanship encourages can readily spill over into other areas of life and undercut a lawyer's sense of moral identity. . . .

Neither lawyers' nor clients' long-term interests are served by eroding the institutional frameworks on which an effective rule of law depends. Taken to its logical extreme, a professional role that gives primary allegiance to client concerns can undermine the legal order. Yale law professor Robert Gordon gives an example: "[T]ake any simple case of compliance counseling; suppose the legal rule is clear, yet the chance of detecting violations low, the penalties small in relation to the gains from noncompliance, or the terrorizing of regulators into settlement by a deluge of paper predictably easy. The mass of lawyers who advise and then assist with noncompliance in such a situation could, in the vigorous pursuit of their clients' interests, effectively nullify the laws." . . .

The bar has similar responsibilities concerning core cultural values. Norms like good faith, honesty, and fair dealing are essential for efficient markets and effective regulatory systems. These values depend on some shared restraint in the pursuit of short-term client interests. Legal processes present frequent opportunities for obstruction, obfuscation, and overreaching. An advocacy role that imposes few practical constraints on such behavior erodes expectations of trust and cooperation. These expectations are common goods on which clients as a group ultimately depend. In the short term, free riders can profit by violating norms that others respect. But these values cannot survive if deviance becomes a routine and acceptable part of the advocate's repertoire. Over the long run, a single-minded pursuit of clients' individual self-interests is likely to prove self-defeating for clients as a group. . . .

An Alternative Framework

An alternative framework for the advocate's role . . . would require lawyers to accept personal responsibility for the moral consequences of their professional actions. Attorneys should make decisions as advocates in the same way that morally reflective individuals make any ethical decision. Lawyers' conduct should be justifiable under consistent, disinterested, and generalizable principles. These moral principles can, of course, recognize the distinctive needs of lawyers' occupational role. . . .

[U]nlike the bar's prevailing approach, this alternative framework would require lawyers to assess their obligations in light of all the societal interests at issue in particular practice contexts. . . . Respect for law is a fundamental value, particularly among those sworn to uphold it. Adherence to generally accepted rules also serves as a check against the decision maker's own bias or self-interest. . . .

Most ethical dilemmas arise in areas where the governing standards already leave significant room for discretion. Individual attorneys can decide whether to accept or withdraw from representation and whether to pursue certain tactics. In resolving such questions, lawyers need to consider the social context of their choices. They cannot simply rely on some idealized model of adversarial and legislative processes. Rather, lawyers must assess their action against a realistic backdrop, in which wealth, power, and information are unequally distributed, not all interests are adequately represented, and most matters will never reach a neutral tribunal. The less confidence that attorneys have in the justice system's capacity to deliver justice in a particular case, the greater their own responsibility to attempt some corrective. . . .

[T]he [position] . . . most compatible with the contextual ethical framework proposed here, seeks ways of advancing justice without violating formal prohibitions. Lawyers taking this position may pursue a result that is morally but not substantively justified as long as they refrain from illegal conduct such as knowing presentation of perjury or preparation of fraudulent documents. . . .

. . . [T]he aim of this alternative framework is for lawyers to make the merits matter and to assess them from a moral as well as a legal vantage. Not all poor clients would be entitled to unqualified advocacy. But neither would factors like poverty be irrelevant if they affect the justice of a particular claim. Of course, in a profession as large and diverse as the American bar, different lawyers will make different judgments about what is in fact just. Although such judgments should be defensible under accepted ethical principles, their application will necessarily reflect individuals' own experiences and commitments. . . . But the framework proposed here does not demand that lawyers reach the same results in hard cases. It demands rather that lawyers recognize that such cases *are* hard and that they call for contextual moral judgments. . . .

Lawyers' Roles:
The Client-Lawyer Relationship

Close your eyes and try to imagine yourself as a lawyer meeting a prospective client for the first time. First, how do you envision your client? Will you be representing an individual? An organization? A government? Second, how do you decide whether to undertake this representation? Will you consider the nature of the matter? The client? Whether and how much the client can pay? The effect of this legal representation upon society as a whole? Third, assuming you decide to handle the matter, what will you do for the client? Do you imagine yourself as a legal technician who will execute the client's instructions? A guardian of the rule of law whose job it is to explain the legal realities of the situation to the client? How much will you interact with your client? Finally, imagine the place where this meeting occurs and what it conveys about the answers to these questions.

In this series of notes entitled "Lawyer's Roles," we will examine these questions, focusing on the way that lawyers articulate their own sense of role in relation both to clients and the legal system. Professors Freedman, Smith, and Rhode all believe that the lawyer's personal sense of morality, as well as the lawyer professional codes, should foster a distinct model of the client–lawyer relationship.[1]

Professors Freedman and Smith endorse what has been labeled the "dominant," "standard," or "adversary" ethic. This view emphasizes that lawyers have fiduciary duties to represent clients zealously, motivated by and focused on the client's values and goals. Legal rights exist to protect human autonomy, which is essential to human dignity.[2] Lawyers do the right thing by serving what is essentially human in others. Justice is defined in terms of the legal rights granted to citizens. The legal system protects and reinforces the individual decisions that people are best able to make for themselves, rather than any competing version of social welfare or outcome.

To a philosopher, this view is "relentlessly deontological," that is, focused on the duties of lawyers in relation to clients, rather than on any particular outcome those relationships create.[3] The lawyer's morality depends primarily on her role as an advocate, which in turn requires two primary virtues. The lawyer must be simultaneously neutral (because her client's interests should prevail) and partisan (to promote those interests). Once this occurs, the lawyer should not be held accountable for the client's goals or conduct. Amoral advocacy becomes the guiding norm of the adversary ethic.[4]

Commentators have characterized this view in a number of colorful ways.[5] A lawyer who adopts some form of the dominant or adversarial ethic has been labeled "client-centered," as well as called an "amoral instrument," "hired gun," "plumber," "puppet," or "prostitute." This lawyer strongly advocates client interests but in doing so can overidentify with clients and lose the independent judgment necessary to provide proper legal advice.

Professor Rhode criticizes the neutral partisanship this role seems to require. She opts instead for a public-interest ethic that would hold lawyers

---

1. *See also* Neil Hamilton & Verna Monson, *The Positive Empirical Relationship of Professionalism to Effectiveness in the Practice of Law,* 24 Geo. J. Legal Ethics 137 (2011) (emphasizing the need for self-reflection over an entire career and empirical research on the impact of law firm culture on lawyer behavior).

2. *E.g.,* David Luban, *Legal Ethics and Human Dignity* (Cambridge U. Press 2007).

3. Timothy P. Terrell, *Turmoil at the Normative Core of Lawyering: Uncomfortable Lessons from the "Metaethics" of Legal Ethics,* 49 Emory L.J. 87 (2000); Stephen L. Pepper, *The Lawyer's Amoral Ethical Role: A Defense, a Problem, and Some Possibilities,* 1986 Am. Bar Found. Research J. 613.

4. *See* David Luban, *Lawyers and Justice: An Ethical Study* at xx (Princeton U. Press 1988).

5. *See* James E. Moliterno, *Ethics of the Lawyer's Work* 129-130 (2d ed., West 2003); Symposium, *Client Counseling and Moral Responsibility,* 30 Pepp. L. Rev. 591 (2003).

morally accountable for the consequences of their actions. She agrees with Professors Freedman and Smith that deontological or rights-based justifications have special force in criminal cases, where individuals can be overwhelmed by governmental power. But she questions why lawyers should apply the same ethic to powerful interests like wealthy individuals and large corporations. She also defines justice in terms of distributive fairness rather than individual rights, meaning that lawyers should consider the social harm they help clients foist on unrepresented persons or interests.

A philosopher might label Professor Rhode's view teleological or utilitarian; that is, focused on the ultimate goal or consequences of individual client-lawyer relationships. According to this view, lawyers cannot rely on their social role alone to escape moral accountability;[6] rather, they should assess the consequences of each legal representation to determine whether it served some larger conception of the public interest. This lawyer ultimately will need to accept personal moral responsibility for distributive fairness, or "justice in the long run."[7]

Commentators note that this view can represent another extreme, and have labeled it in equally colorful ways as "directive," "traditional," "authoritarian," "moralist," or "parentalist." Expert lawyers, familiar with the legal system, might presume they know what is best and act as authorities in all aspects of the relationship. These lawyers can underidentify with clients and can assume a judgelike perspective, ignoring fiduciary duties that demand advice, obedience to client instructions, and zealous advocacy.

Lawyers as Instruments

Instrumental lawyers tend to focus on providing individual client representation and adversarial advocacy. Some pride themselves in representing almost any client who seeks their assistance, on the theory that every point of view deserves legal representation. Others, like Professors Freedman and Smith, emphasize that lawyers should exercise moral judgment about which clients to represent.[8]

Once they agree to take on a representation, instrumental lawyers rightly recognize fiduciary duties of control, competence, communication, confidentiality, and conflict of interest resolution to clients.[9] But their preference for client autonomy might tempt them to suppress their own moral judgment and cede all authority to the client in the process. Single-minded loyalty to a client then becomes transformed into a narrow-minded, unquestioning devotion to that client's will. The client's value system controls the representation, and the lawyer escapes any moral accountability for either the outcome or the means employed.

---

6. Arthur Isak Applbaum, *Ethics for Adversaries: The Morality of Roles in Public and Professional Life* 257-259 (Princeton U. Press 1999).

7. *See* William H. Simon, *The Practice of Justice; A Theory of Lawyers' Ethics* 53-76 (Harvard U. Press 1998).

8. Monroe H. Freedman, *A Critique of Philosophizing About Lawyers' Ethics,* 25 Geo. J. Legal Ethics 91 (2012).

9. David A. Binder, Paul B. Bergman, Susan C. Price, & Paul R. Trembly, *Lawyers as Counselors: A Client-Centered Approach* 9-11 (2d ed. West 2004).

Lawyers who prefer an instrumental view of their role see only one limit to client advocacy: the bounds of the law and the legal system itself. Yet these legal bounds might be unclear to an instrumental lawyer because law itself could be viewed as a malleable means to pursue the client's desires. If the legal system exists to promote individual welfare, then law can be envisioned primarily as a process that provides clients with a means to challenge or take advantage of the existing order.[10]

Instrumental lawyers view the social fabric as relatively strong, capable of withstanding most challenges to the existing limits or bounds of the law or other majoritarian interests. At the same time, however, focusing primarily or exclusively on client interests might cause them to lose opportunities to explain a legal or moral boundary to clients or to discover a client's true intention. Worse, these lawyers can become blind to a clear legal limit that could subject the client and the lawyer to severe sanctions. The result could be serious harm to others as well as to the client and the lawyer.

Professor Wasserstrom warns that assuming such role-differentiated behavior also can transform a lawyer's entire personality. Lawyers who see their role in instrumental terms might be unrelenting and unwilling to compromise, even when the client seeks settlement. Lawyers who live an amoral professional life might be tempted to assume an amoral personal existence as well. Such lawyers also could incorporate those qualities deemed essential to accomplishing their task, such as competitive, aggressive, ruthless, and pragmatic behavior rather than cooperative, accommodating, compassionate, and principled action.[11]

Lawyers as Directors

Directive lawyers tend to focus on their roles as officers of the legal system and members of a profession. They are generally accustomed to relying on their own judgment and tend to lean on their own personal values in deciding which clients to represent and how to represent them.

Once they agree to take on a representation, directive lawyers nod to basic fiduciary duties, but primarily regard themselves as legal experts capable of determining how to handle the matter with little client consultation. Their preference for legal solutions might tempt them to underidentify with clients, who they see as lacking the lawyer's experience and judgment or as too emotionally close to the matter to consider the short- and long-term consequences of their decisions. The lawyer's legal expertise then can transform into a moral judgment about the proper outcome for a client. Here, the lawyer cedes little authority to the client, and the lawyer's values can control the representation.

Lawyers who believe they know more than their clients also might find it relatively easy to impose limits on client advocacy. The lawyer's own view of the law and its limits can be seen as an objective datum not subject to argument or

---

10. Of course, this statement vastly oversimplifies the complexity of various philosophies of law, which may shape any lawyer's practice. *See* Gerald B. Wetlaufer, *Systems of Belief in Modern American Law: A View from Century's End*, 49 Am. U. L. Rev. 1 (1999).

11. Richard Wasserstrom, *Lawyers as Professionals: Some Moral Issues,* 5 Hum. Rights 1 (1975).

modification. Directive lawyers might envision the legal system as a means to promote social order and stability, and the law as the categorization of principles, rules, and procedures that shape client expectations.[12] Those who define their role as conciliatory, for example, might pressure a client to settle or compromise when the client wishes to vindicate an important right. They are apt to see law as necessary to preserve a relatively thin social fabric that easily could unravel without constant tending by lawyers.

But focusing on morally preferred legal outcomes could prevent a directive lawyer from seizing an opportunity to challenge a legal rule or apply it in a different context. More extreme is the tendency of some directive lawyers to limit client advocacy by imposing their own social agenda on the client's matter. Even worse, knowing what is best might be confused with preferring a lawyer's own personal agenda (often a monetary goal) over the client's interests. The client then becomes an object to be used to pursue the lawyer's goals, rather than a subject who deserves individual respect. If this occurs, lawyers who believe they know best can become blind to basic fiduciary duty, which requires them to consult and obey client instructions.

Like instrumental lawyers, directive lawyers can assume personality characteristics that permeate the lawyer's life. Directive lawyers might be judgmental, controlling, even patronizing and overbearing in their professional and personal life. They also might be impatient and have trouble listening to others. Such lawyers also could share the pragmatism of instrumental lawyers, but they often will prefer tangible legal standards to individual facts or emotional feelings that are less clearly articulated.

Lawyers as Collaborators

Most lawyers intuitively steer clear of extreme instrumental or directive behavior. They heed both fiduciary duty and the limits or bounds of the law.[13] Such a lawyer can be characterized as a "collaborator,"[14] "translator,"[15] "wise counselor,"[16] teacher,"[17] "statesman,"[18] or "friend."[19] Collaborative lawyers see the professional role

---

12. Professor Wetlaufer attributes this view to those who have faith in the fairness and legitimacy of the existing social order, including legal formalists, natural law proponents, and positivists, as well as the legal process and law and economics schools of thought in this group. Wetlaufer, *supra* note 10, at 61-63, 72.

13. W. Bradley Wendel, *Lawyers and Fidelity to Law* 2-7 (Cambridge U. Press 2010).

14. Robert F. Cochran, Jr., John M. A. DiPippa, & Martha M. Peteres, *The Counselor-at-Law: A Collaborative Approach to Client Interviewing and Counseling* (2d ed., Lexis-Nexis 2006).

15. Clark D. Cunningham, *The Lawyer as Translator, Representation as Text: Towards an Ethnography of Legal Discourse,* 77 Cornell L. Rev. 1298 (1992).

16. Lon L. Fuller & John D. Randall, *Professional Responsibility: Report of the Joint Conference of the American Bar Association and the Association of American Law School,* 44 ABA J. 1159, 1161 (1958).

17. William F. May, *Beleaguered Rulers: The Public Obligation of the Professional* (Westminster John Knox Press 2001).

18. Anthony T. Kronman, *The Lost Lawyer: Failing Ideals of the Legal Profession* (Harvard U. Press 1993).

19. Thomas L. Shaffer & Robert F. Cochran, Jr., *Lawyers, Clients, and Moral Responsibility* 44-54 (West 1994); Stephen R. Morris, *The Lawyer as Friend: An Aristotelian Inquiry,* 26 J. Legal Prof. 55 (2002). *But see* Charles H. Fried, *The Lawyer as Friend,* 85 Yale L.J. 1060 (1976).

as an opportunity rather than a problem,[20] creating enough professional distance to offer objective advice, while fostering a relationship that enables the client to articulate the ends and means of the representation. Clients are seen as best able to make decisions for themselves, but they need the expertise and perspective of lawyers to consider fully both their own interests and the effect of their decisions on others.

Philosophically, this model of the client-lawyer relationship acknowledges both a deontological and a utilitarian view, but also can rely on a virtue ethic[21] or a relational ethic of care.[22] Collaborative lawyers adopt a deontological viewpoint because they respect and see it as their duty to promote the individual autonomy of each client. Collaborative lawyers also care about the utilitarian legal and nonlegal consequences of a client representation, both for the client and those whom the client might affect. Beyond professional duties and client rights, many collaborative lawyers also exhibit character traits such as empathy and compassion to discern the client's full scope of interests. In deciding how to proceed, this means that the lawyer weighs heavily the significant obligation to favor the client's interests, as articulated by the client.

To enable clients to articulate their interests, collaborative lawyers believe that they should work with clients in the representation, pay attention to context, but neither dominate nor be dominated by a client's values. The relationship itself is participatory,[23] deliberative, or collaborative. At the same time, collaborative lawyers care about integrating personal and professional morality, which could lead them to question, or even challenge, the goals of the representation as well as the client's values. Lawyer and client might even be characterized as friends who "wrestle with and resolve the moral issues" in the representation.[24] Individual clients should be respected as subjects, not treated as objects, although entity clients might be more objectified.

Lawyers as collaborators recognize the law itself as more than formless process, but less than categorical command. They understand that many legal norms are definitive and can dictate some of the representation. At the same time, they appreciate the fact that applicable legal norms might conflict and that law must be applied to individual circumstances.[25] Overall, they view law as deeply embedded with moral norms that address some of the most significant

---

20. William H. Simon, *Role Differentiation and Lawyers' Ethics: A Critique of Some Academic Perspectives,* 23 Geo. J. Legal Ethics 987 (2010).

21. Daniel Markovits, *A Modern Legal Ethics: Adversary Advocacy in a Democratic Age* (Princeton U. Press 2008); Christine Parker & Adrian Evans, *Inside Lawyers' Ethics* (Cambridge U. Press 2007); Fred C. Zacharias, *Integrity Ethics,* 22 Geo. J. Legal Ethics 541 (2009).

22. *See* Barbara Glesner Fines & Cathy Madsen, *Caring Too Little, Caring Too Much: Competence and the Family Law Attorney* 75 UMKC Law Rev. 965 (2007); Stephen Ellmann, *The Ethic of Care as an Ethic for Lawyers,* 81 Geo. L.J. 2665 (1993).

23. Douglas E. Rosenthal, *Lawyer and Client: Who's in Charge?* (Russell Sage Foundation 1974).

24. Shaffer & Cochran, *supra* note 19, at 42-54.

25. *E.g.,* Alexander A. Guerrero, *Lawyers, Context, and Legitimacy: A New Theory of Legal Ethics,* 25 Geo. J. Legal Ethics 107 (2012).

issues in human existence. They understand and value the contribution of these norms to the social welfare, but remain willing to challenge existing majoritarian interests when those interests do not respect the individual rights of a client. In short, collaborative lawyers seek to act as translators of the moral norms of the law to their clients, as well as translators of their client's moral interests back to the legal system.[26]

Collaborative lawyers believe that they assume joint moral accountability with their clients for the representation. They feel free to express their own moral and legal judgment, but remain subject to the client's final determination of which interests to pursue, within the limits of the law. They attempt to steer clear of directive thinking by focusing on fiduciary duties to their clients, and they try to avoid instrumental thinking by being aware of the limits or bounds of the law. They listen to clients but also refuse to exclude their own personal values from a client's representation.

In practice, individual lawyers can fall anywhere on a spectrum between instrumental and directive behavior. Many lawyers borrow from all three models to assess their role obligations. As you study the materials in this book, consider how the lawyers involved characterized their roles. If a lawyer ended up in trouble, think about whether that lawyer's view of his role contributed to the problem. As you assess what the lawyers in these cases and materials did well or poorly, you will begin to formulate your own tentative concept of the kind of role and relationships you want to establish with your clients.

B.   Lawyers and Law

As we examine the law governing lawyers, we will encounter two very interesting dimensions. First, this is a typical law school class, which examines a great variety of substantive law. Second, the "ethics" in legal ethics indicates that both this course and the law governing lawyers address moral questions and afford room for moral discretion.

▧ The Law Governing Lawyers:
Sources of Law

In this series of notes entitled "The Law Governing Lawyers," we consider the substantive standards, remedies, and sanctions embedded in the various strands of law that, taken as a whole, constitute the law governing lawyers. Professional responsibility or legal ethics is the study of what is required for a lawyer to provide a professional service to another. The law governing lawyers regulates this relationship and creates obligations to the legal system that act as limits on a lawyer's conduct on behalf of a client. The law governing lawyers also provides for a variety of remedies when lawyers violate professional norms.

---

26. *See* Lawyer's Roles: *Zealous Representation Within the Bounds of the Law, infra* p. 297

Sources of Law

The law governing lawyers includes two vast bodies of law, the applicable rules of professional conduct enacted by the highest court in each jurisdiction, and general common law and statutes applied to lawyers. The Restatement (Third) of the Law Governing Lawyers (2000) brings these two bodies of law together. Although each body of law imposes its own legal consequences, they have developed in parallel paths and cross-fertilized each other over the past century.

Rules of Professional Conduct Lawyers are the only professional group licensed and regulated by the judicial rather than the legislative branch of government. The highest state court in each jurisdiction adopts Rules of Professional Conduct that govern lawyer conduct after admission to the bar.

In the past century, the American Bar Association (ABA) has promulgated various model professional codes and recommended them to the highest courts in each jurisdiction.[27] Each state and federal court in turn has enacted its own version of an official set of professional rules, usually in the form of court rules. Violation of a rule provision subjects a lawyer to professional discipline, with sanctions ranging from private or public reprimand to fines, suspensions, and permanent disbarment from legal practice.[28] Disciplinary proceedings are usually administrative in nature, require a high burden of proof (clear and convincing evidence), and allow for an appeal to the highest state court.[29]

The idea of lawyer professional rules began as an annual series of lectures on legal ethics by retired Judge George Sharswood, at the University of Pennsylvania Law School in the mid-nineteenth century.[30] His essays influenced the development of the first ABA-recommended set of professional rules in 1908, the Canons of Professional Ethics ("Canons"), which was then officially adopted by nearly every jurisdiction in this country. The ABA Model Code of Professional Responsibility ("Model Code," or "CPR") superseded the Canons in 1969. Again, nearly every jurisdiction followed the ABA's recommendation, replacing the Canons with the Model Code. The Model Code retained the aspirational language of the Canons in statements called Ethical Considerations (ECs), and added black-letter mandatory standards called Disciplinary Rules (DRs).

In 1983, the ABA recommended that the Model Rules of Professional Conduct ("Model Rules") replace its Model Code. The Model Rules significantly expanded the provisions of the Model Code and changed its structure to mirror other uniform codes: black-letter rules followed by comments. To date, all but a

---

27. The ABA is a private organization of lawyers. At any given time, one third to more than one half of licensed U.S. lawyers are members.
28. RLGL § 5, *ABA Standards for Imposing Lawyer Sanctions* (1986).
29. *See, e.g., ABA Model Rules for Lawyer Disciplinary Enforcement* (1996).
30. George Sharswood, *An Essay on Professional Ethics* (5th ed., T & J. W. Johnson & Co. 1884). Sharswood's essays were influenced by David Hoffman's "Resolutions in Regard to Professional Deportment" in *A Course of Legal Study Addressed to Students and the Profession Generally* 752-775 (2d ed., J. Neal 1836).

few jurisdictions have adopted their own version of the Model Rules, including amendments recommended in 2002 by the ABA Ethics 2000 Commission.

When lawyers are unsure about the meaning or applicability of a rule provision, they can ask a local, state, or national bar association for an ethics opinion or call an ethics hotline for advice.[31] Unless written by an official disciplinary agency, ethics opinions are advisory; that is, they are not binding on courts. However, courts that subsequently disagree with an ethics opinion rarely discipline a lawyer for following a committee's advice.[32]

The substantive provisions of these various lawyer codes have evolved in a slow, hundred-year process by applying general legal and moral concepts found in other bodies of law to lawyer behavior. For example, First Amendment principles shaped the law of lawyer advertising and solicitation, the law of agency delineated a lawyer's obligations to avoid conflicts of interest, the evidentiary attorney-client privilege informed duties of confidentiality, contract law dictated some of the law on lawyer fees, and competence duties were borrowed from tort law.

General Law The common law that influenced the drafting of lawyer codes has applied general legal concepts and rules to lawyer conduct in an evolving common law process over the past two centuries. In civil cases, the common law has been called on to address issues such as fiduciary duties, the formation of a client-lawyer relationship, fee arrangements, malpractice liability for professional errors, and the attorney-client privilege. In criminal cases, the constitutional rights of defendants have shaped prosecutorial obligations of fairness, as well as the standards of competence for defense counsel. Most of these cases sought civil and criminal remedies apart from, and in addition to, professional discipline, such as civil liability, reversal of a criminal conviction, disqualification, and fee forfeiture. In cases that seek these judicial remedies, courts often rely on lawyer codes to assist them in articulating common law principles, and the appropriate standard of behavior in a civil or criminal case. This explains the general rule that violation of a lawyer code provision may be "evidence of breach of the applicable standard of conduct" in a civil suit or motion to disqualify.[33]

In practice, lawyers increasingly worry about these other consequences that follow from the breach of obligations to clients, third parties, and tribunals, such as the threat of a malpractice suit, nonclient reliance on an opinion letter, or discovery abuse. For example, lawyers can be held liable in tort to clients for malpractice or breach of fiduciary duty. They are accountable to nonclients for misrepresentation and can be subject to monetary sanctions for violating procedural rules (such as Federal Rule of Civil Procedure 11 or 26). Moreover, judges now exercise their power to "fire" lawyers representing clients by disqualifying them if the lawyer's conduct threatens to taint a trial process, or enjoining them

---

31. *See* Peter A. Joy, *Making Ethics Opinions Meaningful: Towards More Effective Regulation of Lawyer's Conduct*, 15 Geo. J. Legal Ethics 313 (2002).
32. *See, e.g.,* Morrell v. State, 575 P.2d 1200 (Alaska 1978).
33. Model Rules, Preamble and Scope ¶ 20; RLGL § 52(2).

from continuing representation. Courts also dismiss claims and defenses, grant new trials, deny the admission of evidence, exercise their contempt power, sanction and fine lawyers, and order fee forfeiture.[34]

Multiple consequences   The parallel development and influence of the lawyer codes and general civil and criminal law applied to lawyers can result in multiple legal consequences for the same conduct. For example, because the lawyer codes incorporate some general legal obligations (such as competence or confidentiality), as well as some general legal prohibitions (against fraud or frivolous lawsuits), lawyers who are professionally disciplined also could suffer criminal or civil accountability for the same conduct, or vice versa.[35]

Learning the Law Governing Lawyers

Understanding the sources of the law governing lawyers will help you analyze the rest of the problems in this book. In preparing your answers to these problems, notice whether a question asks you about professional discipline or other remedies. If it asks only about professional discipline, then the answer should be found in the ABA Model Rules of Professional Conduct.

Most of the problems in this book will ask more generally whether a lawyer "may" or "should" take a specific action. In that case, you should refer both to the relevant lawyer code sections and to the general law applied to lawyers, including the cases and other materials that follow each set of problems as well as the applicable sections of the Restatement of the Law Governing Lawyers (RLGL).[36] When you move beyond the lawyer codes, remember that you are examining other legal remedies that might exist, or other consequences that

---

34. RLGL § 6.

35. *E.g., In re Halverson,* 998 P.2d 833 (Wash. 2000) (lawyer who had sexual relationship with client suspended from practice for six months, five years after he settled a civil suit by the client for a "substantial sum"); *People v. Sichta,* 948 P.2d 1018 (Colo. 1998) (lawyer convicted of security and wire fraud disbarred); *Dodrill v. Exec. Dir., Comm. on Prof. Conduct,* 824 S.W.2d 383 (Ark. 1992) (lawyer who filed repeated frivolous complaints and motions in bankruptcy court violated FRCP 11; held in criminal contempt and suspended for one year); *In re Perl,* 407 N.W.2d 678 (Minn. 1987); *Gilchrist v. Perl,* 387 N.W.2d 412 (Minn. 1986) (lawyer who employed opposing party's adjuster on other matters suspended from practice for one year and forfeited some or all of $705,000 fee to 128 plaintiffs in Dalkon Shield litigation); *In re Conway,* 301 N.W.2d 253 (Wis. 1981); *Ennis v. Ennis,* 276 N.W.2d 341 (Wis. App. 1979) (lawyer who represented wife in divorce against former client/husband disqualified from further representation of wife, denied fee award, and publicly reprimanded).

36. This usage parallels the use of the term "may" in the Multistate Professional Responsibility Examination, where "may" "asks whether the conduct referred to or described in the question is professionally appropriate in that it:

   a. would not subject the lawyer . . . to discipline; and
   b. is not inconsistent with the Preamble, Comments, or text of the ABA Model Rules of Professional Conduct . . . ; and
   c. is not inconsistent with generally accepted principles of the law of lawyering."

might befall an errant lawyer or law firm, such as civil or criminal liability, litigation sanctions, fee forfeiture, or disqualification by a court.

In seeking legal answers to the problems confronting Martyn & Fox, you will realize that the law in this course, unlike much of the law you study in law school, directly addresses your own personal concept of what it means to be a lawyer in modern society. In traversing the law governing lawyers and the choices of the lawyers involved in these materials, try to identify the moral discretion inherent both in the rules and in the answers you articulate. At the same time, you should feel free to question the moral choices that Martyn & Fox lawyers contemplate, as well as the rules that govern their conduct.

Ultimately, the stories of lawyers that run throughout this book should help you consider which examples you wish to follow. We see the law governing lawyers as a map that will help you understand your professional responsibilities and avoid the ethical minefields that await you in law practice. At the same time, we see the "ethics" in legal ethics as an integral part of the lawyer's practical moral wisdom, which is essential to make modern law practice meaningful. We hope that as you study the law governing lawyers your explorations also will help you map out the kind of lawyer you want to be.

Chapter 2

Judicial and Professional Regulation of Lawyers

This chapter focuses on two aspects of the inherent power of the judicial branch of government to regulate the practice of law: admission to practice and professional discipline.

Few give a second thought to the special power that a law license provides. Yet only lawyers can "practice law," by launching lawsuits, issuing subpoenas, demanding documents and testimony and appearing in courts on behalf of clients, drafting legal opinions and legal documents without which transactions would not be consummated and the wheels of commerce would not turn smoothly, and by giving legal advice and offering moral suasion that promotes private respect for the law and its requirements. The fact that lawyers regularly exercise all these powers—and others—should enhance our appreciation and respect for the fact that a law license grants these powers exclusively to members of our profession.

A. Bar Admission

Problem

2-1. Martyn & Fox represent Mary Moore, who is about to graduate from law school.
   (a) Should Moore be denied admission to the bar because she included as text, and without attribution, seven direct quotations, three from cases and four from law review articles in a seminar paper in law school?
   (b) What if Moore pleaded guilty to drunk driving five years ago and again last year?
   (c) What if Moore owes $250,000 in student loans, has $25,000 in credit card debt, and has no job?

(d) What if Moore believes in Aryan supremacy and has announced plans to become General Counsel to the KKK White Council?

Consider: Model Rules 8.1, 8.4

In re Application of Converse

602 N.W.2d 500 (Neb. 1999)

Per Curiam.

Paul Raymond Converse appeals a decision of the Nebraska State Bar Commission (Commission) denying his request to take the July 1998 Nebraska bar examination. Converse claims that the decision of the Commission should be reversed because the Commission rested its denial of Converse's application, at least in part, upon conduct protected by the First Amendment to the U.S. Constitution and, in the alternative, that Converse's conduct did not constitute sufficient cause under Nebraska law for denying his application on the ground of deficient moral character. For the reasons that follow, we affirm the decision of the Commission. . . .

[As part of the application process, Converse's law school dean certified that he had completed law school and checked "yes" when asked whether the Bar Examiners should inquire further regarding his moral character, which triggered a Commission hearing revealing the following facts.]

After the completion of his first semester at the University of South Dakota Law School, Converse sent a letter to then assistant dean Diane May regarding certain issues . . . that he had had with his fall classes, closing that letter with the phrase, "Hope you get a full body tan in Costa Rica." . . .

After he received a grade he believed to be unjustified by his performance in the appellate advocacy course, Converse wrote letters to May and to the USD law school dean, Barry Vickrey, requesting assistance with an appeal of that grade. In addition to writing letters to Vickrey and May, Converse also sent a letter to the South Dakota Supreme Court regarding the appellate advocacy course professor's characterization of his arguments, with indications that carbon copies of the letter were sent to two well-known federal court of appeals judges. . . . Despite all such correspondence, Converse testified at the hearing that no formal appeal of the grievance was ever filed. Converse's grade was never adjusted.

The evidence showed that following the grade "appeal," Converse prepared a memorandum and submitted it to his classmates, urging them to recall an "incident" in which yet another professor lashed out at him in class, and to be cognizant of the image that incident casts "on [that professor's] core professionalism" prior to completing class evaluations. Converse also wrote a letter to a newspaper in South Dakota, the Sioux Falls Argus Leader, regarding a proposed fee increase at the USD law school. Converse immediately began investigating the salaries of USD law professors and posted a list of selected professors' salaries on the student bulletin board, as well as writing a letter that accused Vickrey of trying to pull a "fast one."

Converse's next altercation at the USD law school involved a photograph of a nude female's backside that he displayed in his study carrel in the USD law library. The picture was removed by a law librarian. In response to the removal of this photograph, Converse contacted the American Civil Liberties Union (ACLU) and received a letter indicating that his photograph might be a protected expression under the First Amendment. Once again, Converse went to the student newspaper to alert the student body of the actions of the law school authorities, accusing them of unconstitutional censorship.

Converse redisplayed the photograph once it was returned by the law librarians. Vickrey received several complaints about the photograph from other students, classifying Converse's behavior as "unprofessional and inappropriate." Upon Converse's redisplay of the photograph, Vickrey sent him a memorandum explaining that the picture would not be removed only because Vickrey did not want to involve the school in controversy during final examinations. Converse testified that he redisplayed the photograph in order to force the alleged constitutional issue. . . .

The Commission also heard testimony regarding Converse's attempt to obtain an internship with the U.S. Attorney's office in South Dakota. Converse arranged for the internship on his own, only to have his request subsequently rejected by the law school. Upon receiving his denial, Converse sent a complaint to all of USD's law school faculty members. Vickrey testified that Converse's internship was rejected because he failed to comply with the law school's procedures regarding internships. Converse then contacted the chairperson of the law school committee of the South Dakota State Bar Association with his complaint, expressly referring to Vickrey as being "arrogant." There is no indication of a response from the chairperson in the record.

The issue next considered by the Commission was that of various litigation threatened by Converse. Converse indicated that he would "likely" be filing a lawsuit against Vickrey for violations of his First Amendment rights. Converse was also involved in a dispute with other law students, in which he threatened to file a lawsuit and warned the students that all lawsuits in which they were involved would need to be reported to proper authorities when they applied to take a bar examination. Further, Converse posted signs on the bulletin board at the law school denouncing a professor, in response to the way in which Converse's parking appeal was handled, and then went to the student newspaper to criticize the process and those involved in that appeal.

One of the final issues addressed by the Commission in its hearing was that of a T-shirt Converse produced and marketed on which a nude caricature of Vickrey is shown sitting astride what appears to be a large hot dog. The cartoon on the shirt also contains the phrase "Astride the Peter Principle," which Converse claims connotes the principle that Vickrey had been promoted past his level of competence; however, Converse admits that the T-shirt could be construed to have certain sexual overtones. Converse admitted that the creation of this T-shirt would not be acceptable behavior for a lawyer.

In response to not being allowed to post signs and fliers at the law school, Converse sent a memo to all law students in which he noted to his fellow students that his "Deanie on a Weanie" T-shirts were in stock. In that same memo, Converse included a note to his schoolmates:

> So far 4 causes of action have arisen, courtesy Tricky Vickrey. [He then listed what he believed the causes of action to be.] When you pass the SD Bar, if you want to earn some atty [sic] fees, get hold of me and we can go for one of these. I've kept evidence, of course.

Vickrey asked Converse not to wear his T-shirt to his graduation ceremony, and Converse decided that "it would be a better choice in [his] life not to go to that commencement." Converse acknowledges that Vickrey's request was made in a civil manner.

The evidence also revealed that prior to law school, Converse, in his capacity as a landlord, sued a tenant for nonpayment of rent and referred to the tenant as a "fucking welfare bitch." At the hearing, in response to questioning from the Commission, Converse testified at great length as to how he tends to personally attack individuals when he finds himself embroiled in a controversy.

After the Commission notified Converse on December 18, 1998, that he would not be allowed to sit for the Nebraska bar examination, Converse appealed the adverse determination to this court pursuant to Neb. Ct. R. for Adm. of Attys. 15 (rev. 1996). . . .

Converse first assigns as error that the Commission's determination should not stand because it is based in large part upon speech that is protected by the First Amendment. Thus, the threshold question we must answer is whether conduct arguably protected by the First Amendment can be considered by the Commission during an investigation into an applicant's moral character and fitness to practice law. We answer this question in the affirmative.

There are four U.S. Supreme Court cases that provide particular guidance with respect to this issue. In Konigsberg v. State Bar, 366 U.S. 36 (1961), the bar applicant argued that when the California bar commission forced him to either answer questions about his affiliation with the Communist Party or to face the repercussions of not being certified as possessing the required moral character to sit for the bar, the commission violated his First Amendment rights. The Supreme Court disagreed, [and] . . . balanced the effect of allowing such questions against the need for the state to do a complete inquiry into the character of an applicant and concluded that questions about membership would not chill association to the extent of harm caused by striking down the screening process. *Id*. The Court held that requiring the applicant to answer the questions was not an infringement of the applicant's First Amendments rights. . . .

Converse conceded at oral argument that the Commission's decision cannot be based solely on an applicant's exercise of First Amendment freedoms but that it is proper for the Commission to go behind the exercise of those freedoms and consider an applicant's moral character. That is exactly what was done by the Commission in the instant case. An investigation of Converse's moral character is not a proceeding in which the applicant is being prosecuted for conduct arguably protected by the First Amendment, but, rather, "an investigation of the conduct of [an applicant] for the purpose of determining whether he shall be [admitted]." . . .

Were we to adopt the position asserted by Converse in this case, the Commission would be limited to conducting only cursory investigations of an applicant's moral character and past conduct. [I]n Law Students Research Council v. Wadmond, 401 U.S. 154 (1971), [the majority] noted that the implications of such an attack on a bar screening process are that no screening process would be constitutionally permissible beyond academic examination and an extremely minimal check for serious, concrete character deficiencies. "The principal means of policing the Bar would then be the deterrent and punitive effects of such post-admission sanctions as contempt, disbarment, malpractice suits, and criminal prosecutions." . . .

We conclude that the Commission properly considered Converse's conduct as it reflects upon his moral character, even if such conduct might have been protected by the First Amendment. . . .

Converse next contends that the Commission violated his due process rights by not making him aware of all of the "charges" against him in these proceedings. . . .

There is no question that "[a] state can require high standards of qualification, such as good moral character or proficiency in its law, before it admits an applicant to the bar . . . . " Schware v. Bd. of Bar Examiners, 353 U.S. 232, 239 (1957). The Court has also stated that it must be "kept clearly in mind . . . that an applicant for admission to the bar bears the burden of proof of 'good moral character' a requirement whose validity is not, nor could well be, drawn in question here." Konigsberg v. St. Bar, 366 U.S. 36, 40-41 (1961). "If at the conclusion of the proceedings the evidence of good character and that of bad character are found in even balance, the State may refuse admission . . . . "

With that in mind, we commence our analysis with the standards for moral character required for admission to the Nebraska bar as set out in our rules governing the admission of attorneys. Neb. Ct. R. for Adm. of Attys. 3 (rev. 1998) governs this situation, which provides in pertinent part:

> An attorney should be one whose record of conduct justifies the trust of clients, adversaries, courts, and others with respect to the professional duties owed to them. A record manifesting a significant deficiency by an applicant in one or more of the following essential eligibility requirements for the practice of law may constitute a basis for denial of admission. In addition to the admission requirements otherwise established by these Rules, the essential eligibility requirements for admission to the practice of law in Nebraska are:
>
> (a) The ability to conduct oneself with a high degree of honesty, integrity, and trustworthiness in all professional relationships and with respect to all legal obligations; . . .
>
> (c) The ability to conduct oneself with respect for and in accordance with the law and the Code of Professional Responsibility; . . .
>
> (j) The ability to conduct oneself professionally and in a manner that engenders respect for the law and the profession.

Under rule 3, Converse must prove that his past conduct is in conformity with the standards set forth by this court, and the record in this case compels the conclusion that he has failed to do so.

We considered an appeal of a similarly situated bar applicant in In re Appeal of Lane, 544 N.W.2d 367 (Neb. 1996). *Lane* involved an individual seeking readmission to the Nebraska bar whose past included confrontations with law school faculty, the use of strong and profane language with fellow students at his bar review course, the use of intimidating and rude conduct directed at a security guard at the place where he was taking his bar review course, and some controversial interactions with females. We held that, taken together, "these incidents show that Lane is prone to turbulence, intemperance, and irresponsibility, characteristics which are not acceptable in one who would be a counselor and advocate in the legal system," and we upheld the denial of his application.

We explained in . . . *Lane* that the "requisite restraint in dealing with others is obligatory conduct for attorneys because 'the efficient and orderly administration of justice cannot be successfully carried on if we allow attorneys to engage in unwarranted attacks on the court [or] opposing counsel. . . . Furthermore, "'an attorney who exhibits [a] lack of civility, good manners and common courtesy . . . tarnishes the . . . image of . . . the bar . . . .'" . . . We held in . . . *Lane* that "abusive, disruptive, hostile, intemperate, intimidating, irresponsible, threatening, or turbulent behavior is a proper basis for the denial of admission to the bar." . . .

The evidence in this case shows that Converse's numerous disputes and personal attacks indicate a "pattern and a way of life which appear to be [Converse's] normal reaction to opposition and disappointment." *See Lane*. The totality of the evidence clearly establishes that Converse possesses an inclination to personally attack those with whom he has disputes. Such inclinations "are not acceptable in one who would be a counselor and advocate in the legal system."

In addition to Converse's tendency to personally attack those individuals with whom he has disputes, his pattern of behavior indicates an additional tendency to do so in arenas other than those specifically established within the legal system. This tendency is best exemplified by observing Converse's conduct in situations where there were avenues through which Converse could have and should have handled his disputes, but instead chose to mount personal attacks on those with whom he had disputes through letters and barrages in the media. . . .

Converse is 48 years old, and his actions cannot be excused as isolated instances of youthful indiscretions.

Taken together with the other incidents previously discussed, the evidence clearly shows that Converse is prone to turbulence, intemperance, and irresponsibility; characteristics which are not acceptable in one seeking admission to the Nebraska bar. . . . In light of Converse's admission that such conduct would be inappropriate were he already an attorney, we reiterate that we will not tolerate conduct by those applying for admission to the bar that would not be tolerated were that person already an attorney. . . .

The record before us reflects that the Commission conducted such an inquiry and, at the conclusion thereof, correctly determined that Converse possessed a moral character inconsistent with one "dedicated to the peaceful and reasoned settlement of disputes," *see* 401 U.S. at 166, but, rather, more consistent with someone who wishes to go outside the field of law and settle disputes by mounting personal attacks and portraying himself as the victim and his opponent as the aggressor. Such disruptive, hostile, intemperate, threatening, and turbulent conduct certainly reflects negatively upon those character traits the applicant must prove prior to being admitted to the Nebraska bar, such as honesty, integrity, reliability, and trustworthiness.

The result might have been different if Converse had exhibited only a "single incident of rudeness or lack of professional courtesy," *see* In re Snyder, 472 U.S. 634, 647 (1985), but such is simply not the case. The record clearly establishes that he seeks to resolve disputes not in a peaceful manner, but by personally attacking those who oppose him in any way and then resorting to arenas outside the field of law to publicly humiliate and intimidate those opponents. Such a pattern of behavior is incompatible with what we have required to be obligatory conduct for attorneys, as well as for applicants to the bar. . . .

We conclude that the Commission's determination to deny Converse's application was correct. . . .

B.   Professional Discipline

Problems

2-2.   Martyn discovers that a valuable and brilliant associate has been charging a client for phantom travel expenses, thereby generating money that he has used to fund a gambling addiction. To make matters worse, the client has filed a bar complaint against Associate. Martyn tells Fox not to worry because Associate has repaid the money and joined Gambler's Anonymous. May Fox accept Martyn's advice?

2-3.   Fox told Associate, who was counsel of record in a matter, not to appear in court because he wanted to "take care of the matter," even though Fox was not admitted to practice in the state in question. When the judge questioned Associate's absence, Fox replied that Associate had a medical emergency that prevented her appearance. The next day, Fox told Associate: "The judge wants to verify your absence. Just send a letter to the court backing me up—nobody has to know."

2-4.   Client hires Martyn & Fox to get back her $25,000 retainer from her former lawyer. Client explains: "That bum charged me $10,000 for incompetent work and won't refund the rest of my $15,000." Martyn writes a demand letter to client's former lawyer that includes the following:

"My hope is to avoid an ethics investigation for you. If you do not return my client's $25,000 within 14 days, it is likely my client will file a disciplinary complaint."

Consider: Model Rules 5.1, 5.2, 8.3, 8.4
           RLGL § 5

People v. Walker

2011 Colo. Discipl. LEXIS 32

William R. Lucero, Presiding Disciplinary Judge, Gail C. Harriss, Hearing Board Member, Dean S. Neuwirth, Hearing Board Member. . . .

I. SUMMARY

Respondent converted over $22,000.00 from twelve clients by failing to return their retainers after he neglected to perform agreed-upon work. His neglect of most of those matters was so pronounced as to amount to abandonment. Respondent's major depressive disorder, however, was principally responsible for his misconduct. In light of Respondent's demonstrated mental disability and other mitigating factors, the Hearing Board determines that a three-year suspension is warranted in this matter. . . .

On February 24, 2010, the People filed a complaint alleging that Respondent violated Colo. RPC 1.3, 1.4(a), 1.15(b), 1.16(a)(1), 1.16(d), and 8.4(c). . . .

III. FINDINGS OF FACT AND RULE VIOLATIONS . . .

This case involves extensive misconduct with respect to fourteen client matters. Because Respondent has stipulated to this misconduct, the facts of each matter are presented here in an abbreviated form. . . .

Shannon Boerger Matter . . . Shannon Boerger ("Boerger") hired Respondent in November 2008 to represent her in a contempt action against her ex-husband. She paid Respondent a $3,000.00 retainer. Respondent neglected her case by taking nearly three months to file the contempt motion. He failed to prepare and timely submit exhibits prior to the contempt hearing and then failed to appear for the hearing, resulting in the postponement of Boerger's trial. Boerger was subsequently unable to reach Respondent. Respondent abandoned Boerger and failed to return either her file or any portion of her retainer, thereby converting unearned legal fees. Through these actions, Respondent violated Colo. RPC 1.3 (requiring lawyers to act with reasonable diligence and promptness), 1.4(a) (requiring lawyers to communicate with clients about their matters), 1.16(a) (requiring lawyers to withdraw from representation if continued representation will result in violations of the Rules of Professional Conduct), and 8.4(c) (requiring lawyers to refrain from conduct involving dishonesty). . . .

The Colorado Attorneys' Fund for Client Protection paid a total of $22,707.00 to Respondent's clients to reimburse them for Respondent's conversions.

IV. SANCTIONS

The American Bar Association *Standards for Imposing Lawyer Sanctions* ("ABA *Standards*") . . . *Standard* 3.0 mandates that, in selecting the appropriate sanction, the Hearing Board consider the duty breached, the injury or potential injury caused, Respondent's mental state, and the aggravating and mitigating evidence.

Duty: Respondent violated the duties he owed to fourteen clients. He failed to uphold some of the most fundamental obligations of a lawyer, including the obligations to act with loyalty and honesty towards clients. By failing to properly terminate his representation of clients, he also violated duties he owed as a professional.

Injury: Respondent caused serious injury or potential injury to his clients. His abandonment of his clients' cases caused delay in those matters and jeopardized the clients' interests. In some instances, Respondent's failure to attend hearings on his clients' behalf appears to have led to adverse judicial rulings. Moreover, Respondent converted over $22,000.00 in client funds, in some cases depriving clients of money they needed to hire another lawyer. By failing to appear at scheduled hearings, Respondent also caused harm to the court system by wasting judicial resources. Finally, Respondent's misconduct negatively influenced the public's perception of the legal profession.

Mental State: Respondent stipulated to the mental state required to support each rule violation alleged by the People in this matter. In doing so, Respondent admitted that the gravamen of his misconduct—his abandonment of clients and his conversion of client funds—was knowing.

ABA *Standard* 3.0–Aggravating Factors . . .

Dishonest or Selfish Motive—By converting funds from clients, Respondent benefitted at his clients' expense. Respondent's conversion permitted him to continue to pay his own bills while in some cases depriving his clients of the opportunity to hire an attorney to pursue or defend their interests.

Pattern of Misconduct—Respondent engaged in the same rule violations with respect to numerous clients.

Multiple Offenses—In the client matters underlying this proceeding, Respondent violated multiple rules of conduct.

ABA *Standard* 3.0–Mitigating Factors . . .

Absence of a Prior Disciplinary Record—Respondent has not previously been subject to discipline for violations of the Rules of Professional Conduct.

Personal and Emotional Problems—Respondent testified that prior to his misconduct he suffered from a variety of personal and emotional problems, such as his divorce, the death of a pet dog, and significant medical issues, including surgeries.

Timely Good Faith Effort to Make Restitution—As of the date of the sanctions hearing, Respondent had paid a total of $60.00 in restitution, made in six installments. This sum may represent a significant effort on Respondent's part in light of his now minimal income. But given the large amount of funds Respondent converted, the Hearing Board finds that this mitigating factor merits minimal weight.

Full and Free Disclosure to Disciplinary Board or Cooperative Attitude toward Proceedings—Although Respondent initially did not respond to letters from the People, Respondent became more cooperative as his mental and emotional status improved. The Hearing Board gives considerable weight to Respondent's decision to facilitate the resolution of this matter by admitting to the rule violations alleged by the People.

Remorse—Respondent testified that he regrets his misconduct. His psychotherapist also testified that Respondent has demonstrated remorse and has assumed responsibility for his actions. Accordingly, the Hearing Board finds Respondent to be genuinely remorseful for his misconduct.

Mental Disability—ABA *Standard* 9.3(i) provides that a mental disability or chemical dependency is a mitigating factor when:

(1) there is medical evidence that the respondent is affected by a chemical dependency or mental disability;

(2) the chemical dependency or mental disability caused the misconduct;

(3) the respondent's recovery from the chemical dependency or mental disability is demonstrated by a meaningful and sustained period of successful rehabilitation; and

(4) the recovery arrested the misconduct and recurrence of that misconduct is unlikely. . . .

The Hearing Board heard extensive testimony from three mental health experts, a friend of Respondent, and Respondent himself regarding Respondent's mental condition. The testimony shows that Respondent entered a state of depression starting in 2008, which significantly worsened during the spring and summer of 2009. During the summer and fall of 2009, he attempted to commit suicide twice and was committed to a mental hospital on three occasions. . . . Respondent continued to suffer from significant depression through the beginning of 2010, during the period when Respondent lived temporarily with his brother in Texas. Through therapy and the use of medications, Respondent's condition improved, and he returned to Colorado later that year. . . .

[Two other experts who treated respondent testified that] respondent has made significant strides in treating his depression and a relapse is unlikely as long as Respondent continues to "take care of himself," . . . [and] respondent is unlikely to engage in further misconduct if he continues to "learn" and to "grow."

The expert testimony that Respondent's misconduct would have been unlikely but for his severe depression demonstrates that Respondent suffered from a mental disability and that a direct causal connection exists between that disability and Respondent's misconduct. In addition, the expert testimony shows that Respondent has largely been rehabilitated through weekly therapy sessions since January 2010 and that recurrence of misconduct is unlikely. Even as of the summer of 2010, Dr. Wortzel found that the disabling aspects of Respondent's depressive episode no longer persisted and that he appeared to be "restored in terms of functional abilities." . . .

Sanctions Analysis Under ABA *Standards* and Case Law

Under the ABA *Standards*, the presumptive sanction for Respondent's misconduct is disbarment. ABA *Standard* 4.11 provides that disbarment is typically warranted when a lawyer knowingly converts client property and thereby causes injury or potential injury. Similarly, ABA *Standard* 4.41 provides that disbarment is generally appropriate when a lawyer causes serious or potentially serious injury to a client by knowingly failing to perform services for a client, engaging in a pattern of neglect with respect to client matters, or abandoning the practice.

The Colorado Supreme Court likewise has held that, except where significant mitigating factors apply, disbarment is the appropriate sanction for knowing conversion of client funds in violation of Colo. RPC 8.4(c). Where a lawyer's conversion of client funds is coupled with abandonment of the client, it is all the more clear that disbarment is the presumptive sanction. The Colorado Supreme Court, however, has cautioned that mitigating factors merit close examination and may in some cases warrant a departure from the presumption of disbarment.

Here, Respondent's misconduct occurred during the time period when Respondent was suffering from a mental disability, and his most serious misconduct—conversion of client funds and abandonment of clients—occurred while Respondent was experiencing a severe mental disability. As a result, we find that Colorado Supreme Court case law supports Respondent's argument that his mental disability justifies a sanction less severe than disbarment under these circumstances. . . .

The Colorado Supreme Court held in People v. Lujan that a lawyer whose mental disability caused her to steal from her law firm did "not deserve to be disbarred."[20] In that case, the lawyer suffered a head injury requiring surgery when she was involved in a serious automobile collision in Egypt. Although she initially had no memory of the accident, she later recalled that she had been sexually assaulted on the side of the road just after the accident. Upon returning to the practice of law, she began to submit falsified charges to her law firm, using the money she obtained through the fraudulent charges to purchase clothes costing in excess of two thousand dollars a month. She was diagnosed with major depression and obsessive compulsive disorder, which she subsequently controlled through the use of medication. The hearing board determined, after considering expert medical testimony, that "the respondent's obsessive compulsive disorder caused the misconduct" and that this mitigating factor should be accorded the greatest weight because the lawyer's misconduct was solely attributable to her disability. The Colorado Supreme Court upheld the imposition of a year-long suspension.

In People v. Boyer, the court approved a conditional admission of misconduct and imposed a 180-day suspension upon an attorney who engaged in sexual relationships with two clients, drove while drunk, lied to a police officer, and used cocaine.[27] The court found that such misconduct typically would warrant a longer suspension, but the respondent's lack of prior discipline, his full and free disclosure to disciplinary counsel, his remorse, and a bipolar personality

---

20. 890 P.2d 109, 110 (Colo. 1995).
27. 934 P.2d 1361, 1362-63 (Colo. 1997).

disorder, which was exacerbated by alcohol and chemical dependency and which substantially contributed to the misconduct, justified a reduced sanction. . . .

The Hearing Board also draws guidance from other jurisdictions' decisions, including those cited in the comment to ABA *Standard* 9.3(i). In several of those decisions, courts have determined that the severity of a lawyer's misconduct was not sufficiently mitigated by a mental disability to overcome a presumption of disbarment, or that disbarment was appropriate because the attorney had the capacity to refrain from misconduct. But our review of disciplinary case law identified far more examples of cases in which a demonstrated mental disability or chemical dependence warranted a departure from the presumptive sanction, including in cases involving such egregious misconduct as the conversion of client funds. . . .

Finally, . . . we briefly address Respondent's argument in his written supplement to oral closing argument that "[s]anctions applied after a period of disability for conduct occurring during that period of disability may be illegal under the terms of the Americans with Disabilities Act" ("ADA").[36] The Colorado Supreme Court previously held that the ADA did not preclude it from suspending a lawyer who suffered from depression while chronically neglecting client matters and misusing client funds.[37] The court followed decisions from the Florida and Oklahoma supreme courts holding that, even if a mental disability is a cause of attorney misconduct, attorneys who commit serious misconduct are not qualified to serve as members of the bar, and no "reasonable modifications" can be made for such individuals.[38] In other words, otherwise qualified attorneys with mental disabilities that prevent them from meeting the essential requirements of their work are not entitled to protections under the ADA. Accordingly, we reject Respondent's argument that the ADA bars the imposition of disciplinary sanctions in this matter.

V. CONCLUSION

Respondent's conversion of funds from twelve clients and his wholesale abandonment of client matters is an example of the most serious misconduct in which an attorney can engage. Such extensive misconduct not only has harmed Respondent's clients but also has brought disrepute upon the legal profession. Yet sanctions for attorney misconduct may be tempered where, as here, the evidence

---

36. The ADA offers protections to a "qualified individual with a disability," meaning "an individual with a disability who, with or without reasonable modifications to rules, policies, or practices, . . . or the provision of auxiliary aids and services, meets the essential eligibility requirements for . . . the participation in programs or activities provided by a public entity." 42 U.S.C. § 12131(2).

37. *People v. Reynolds*, 933 P.2d 1295, 1305 (Colo. 1997). In *Reynolds*, the respondent's depression did not qualify as a mitigating factor under ABA *Standard* 9.32(i) because he had not been fully rehabilitated.

38. *See Fl. Bar v. Clement*, 662 So. 2d 690, 699-700 (Fla. 1995); *State ex rel. Okla. Bar Ass'n v. Busch*, 919 P.2d 1114, 1119-1120 (Okla. 1996); *see also In re Marshall*, 762 A.2d 530, 539-40 (D.C. 2000) (holding that an attorney's disbarment did not constitute discrimination based upon his disability and observing that the ADA does not require authorities to accommodate a disabled individual by overlooking violations of the law); *Cincinnati Bar Ass'n v. Komarek*, 702 N.E.2d 62, 67 (Ohio 1998) ("The ADA does not prevent disciplinary authorities from disbarring an attorney with a bipolar disorder who had misappropriated client funds.").

establishes that a professionally-diagnosed mental disability was principally responsible for the attorney's misconduct and where the evidence also shows that treatment and monitoring will allow the attorney to successfully resume his professional duties. Under the particular facts of this case, the Hearing Board finds that the sanction for Respondent's misconduct is appropriately lowered from the presumptive sanction of disbarment to a three-year suspension.

Kentucky Bar Association v. Helmers
353 S.W.3d 599 (Ky. 2011)

JOHN D. MINTON JR. . . .

The Board of Governors of the Kentucky Bar Association has recommended to this Court that Respondent, David L. Helmers, . . . who was admitted to practice law in Kentucky in 1997, . . . be permanently disbarred from the practice of law as a result of six ethical violations. . . .

Respondent worked for the law firm of Gallion, Baker, and Bray as a clerk during law school and subsequently as an associate after being admitted to the Bar in 1997. He worked almost exclusively on researching potential claims for injuries arising from the use of the diet drug Fen-Phen. In 1998, a class action (hereinafter referred to as the *Guard* case) was filed in the Boone Circuit Court against American Home Products (AHP) consisting of plaintiffs who alleged they were injured by Fen-Phen. The plaintiffs signed contingent fee contracts with William Gallion, Shirley Cunningham, Melbourne Mills, Jr., and Richard Lawrence for representation. The contingent fee contracts provided that the attorneys were entitled to fees equaling 30% to 33.3% of any recovery in addition to expenses. Respondent, working under Gallion's supervision, spent countless hours on the *Guard* case. In fact, Respondent served in many occasions as a contact person for the plaintiffs and opposing counsel.

In 2001, the Boone Circuit Court ordered the parties to mediate. Respondent attended the mediation, along with Gallion, and took notes. Respondent also signed the final settlement agreement, which gave an award of $200,000,000 to the plaintiffs. The settlement was contingent on the decertification of the class action claims. It also required that unless 95% of the plaintiffs sign a release by a certain date, the settlement could be terminated by AHP. How the settlement award would be allocated among the various plaintiffs was the responsibility of their attorneys, including Respondent. Respondent subsequently appeared with Gallion, Chesley, and Cunningham in the Boone Circuit Court to decertify the class action and dismiss the case. The judge granted their request.

After the dismissal, Gallion instructed Respondent to prepare a schedule setting the monetary amount that each of the settling plaintiffs would receive. Respondent's work in the preliminary stages of the case made him the most knowledgeable of the plaintiffs' attorneys on the relative damages sustained by each plaintiff. Respondent created the schedule and presented it to AHP for approval.

Gallion then instructed Respondent to meet with many of the settling clients. Following Gallion's instructions, Respondent met with thirty-nine clients and obtained their releases.

When meeting with the individual clients, Respondent presented a proposed settlement amount, and led the client to believe that the settlement award offer came straight from AHP. He did not inform them that their attorneys (including himself) had decided how much their individual monetary award would be, that the individual client's case was just one of 440 cases that had been settled for an aggregate sum of $200,000,000.00, that the class action had been decertified and dismissed by the Boone Circuit Court, or that $7,500,000 of the settlement fund was being held to indemnify AHP against certain other claims.

Furthermore, Respondent had been instructed by the other attorneys to offer each client an amount substantially below the amount assigned to that client in the predetermined allocations that AHP had approved. If the client refused the initial offer, he or she was presented with a larger offer at a later date. This continued until the client agreed to the settlement, and simulated from the client's perspective, an actual settlement negotiation with AHP. The clients were never informed by Respondent that they could entirely refuse the offer and were not provided copies of the documents they signed. Additionally, Respondent told many of the clients that if they spoke to others about their settlement award, they could face a penalty assessment of $100,000.

Apparently, Gallion had misinformed Mills about the true terms of the settlement, and in early 2002, Mills discovered that the total settlement award was $200,000,000 and not $150,000,000 as Gallion had told him. To assuage Mills, Gallion instructed Respondent to make a second distribution of settlement money to the clients. Respondent set up meetings with the clients he had previously met with and presented them a letter stating that the trial court had authorized a second distribution. This letter also revealed to clients for the first time that an unspecified amount was being held in escrow to indemnify certain third parties, if necessary. Respondent also asked if the plaintiffs would object if some of the undistributed award money was given to charity. A donation to the "Kentucky Fund for Healthy Living, Inc." in the amount of $20,000,000 was made.[4]

Because of their actions in the *Guard* case, most of the attorneys with whom Respondent worked have been disbarred. See Gallion v. Ky. Bar Ass'n, 266 S.W.3d 802 (Ky. 2008); Kentucky Bar Association v. Cunningham, 266 S.W.3d 808 (Ky. 2008); Kentucky Bar Association v. Mills, 318 S.W.3d 89 (Ky. 2010).

In February 2002, the KBA Inquiry Commission opened an investigative file on Respondent. This investigation led to an Inquiry Commission complaint in October 2005. Respondent was subsequently charged with the following eight ethics violations.

○ Count One charged that the Respondent was guilty of violating [Rule] 1.4(b) "by failing to inform his clients in the Guard case of relevant information, including but not limited to: the amount of the total aggregate settlement offer from AHP; the process that had been used to determine the amount that each of the clients would receive; the options available to the client in the event that participation in the aggregate settlement was refused by the client;

---

4. The Kentucky Fund for Healthy Living, Inc. paid board of directors consisted of Gallion, Mills, and Cunningham.

the fact that the small amount of money left over after the second payment to clients was actually over $20 million; accurate information as to how and why the second distribution occurred; and by instructing or allowing others to give his clients inaccurate information about multiple aspects of the case."

○ Count Two charged that the Respondent violated [Rule] 1.8(g) "by, including but not limited to: failing to explain to his clients that AHP had agreed to an aggregate settlement of the claims of 440 clients and the total amount thereof; failing to explain that the settlement agreement stated that the attorneys would determine the amount that each client would receive from the aggregate settlement; failing to disclose or explain the proposed allocations in the settlement agreement; failing to communicate the amount of the total settlement from AHP to his clients; or failing to obtain the informed consent of his clients to participate in an aggregate settlement."

○ Count Three charged that the Respondent violated [Rule] 2.1 "by failing to exercise independent professional judgment in the settlement distribution process or by failing to render candid advice to his clients during the representation, including advice relating to their participation in the aggregate settlement."

○ Count Four charged that the Respondent violated [Rule] 5.2(a) "by violating Rules of Professional Conduct in part at the direction of Gallion, Cunningham, and/or Chesley."

○ Count Five charged that the Respondent violated [Rule] 5.3(b) "by failing to appropriately supervise non-lawyer staff persons in order to ensure that their conduct was compatible with his ethical duties in their dealing with the clients and discussions about settlement matters."

○ Count Six charged that Respondent violated [Rule] 8.4(a) "by violating the Rules of Professional Conduct by knowingly assisting the other lawyers, non-lawyers working for the lawyers, and the Boone Circuit Judge to violate the Rules of Professional Conduct."

○ Count Seven charged that Respondent violated [Rule] 8.4(c) "by, including but not limited to: deceiving his clients into accepting the individual settlement amounts offered; deceiving clients about their claims even after demand for more specific accounting; misrepresenting to the Boone Circuit Court that his clients had agreed to donate a substantial portion of the total settlement received from AHP to charity; failing to inform the Boone Circuit Court that the attorneys had contingent fee contracts with all their clients which set a specific fee; misrepresenting the amount of attorneys' fees paid to the lawyers relative to the payments to the clients; failing to disclose to clients that "extra funds were being held for various contingencies, or even that such contingencies existed; or providing, or assisting in providing false or misleading information to the Boone Circuit Court about the fees and expenses, as well as the manner in which the settlement had been reached with the clients."

○ Count Eight charged that the Respondent violated [Rule] 5.1(c)(1) in that "The Respondent is fully responsible for any conduct of the lawyers in the Guard litigation, including Shirley Cunningham, William Gallion, Melbourne Mills, and Stanley Chesley, that he ratified with knowledge of their conduct by virtue of [Rule] 5.1(c)(1)."

The Trial Commissioner held a hearing and determined that Respondent should be found guilty of Counts One, Two, Three, Four, Six, and Seven. His report recommended that Respondent be suspended from the practice of law in this Commonwealth for a period of five years. The Trial Commissioner expressly noted that Respondent was not the mastermind of the scheme, that he was subordinate to Gallion, Cunningham, and Mills, and that he cooperated with the criminal investigation into the matter. The Board of Governors of the Kentucky Bar Association by a vote of eleven to five decided to consider the matter *de novo* instead of accepting the Trial Commissioner's recommendation. After oral arguments, the Board of Governors by a vote of sixteen to zero found Respondent guilty of Counts One, Two, Three, Four, Six, and Seven and not guilty of Counts Five and Eight. By a vote of eleven to five,[5] the Board recommended that Respondent be permanently disbarred from the practice of law in Kentucky and that he pay all costs associated with this action. . . .

We are aware that Respondent has had no other disciplinary issues raised against him. We are aware that Respondent was a young law student when he first began working for Gallion, and that Gallion was then a well-regarded and reputable attorney. We are aware that as a new attorney working with Gallion, Cunningham, and Mills, Respondent was inexperienced, impressionable, and may have been influenced, and perhaps even led astray, by those more seasoned lawyers. But, we cannot ignore the fact it takes no technical expertise or experience in the settling of class action lawsuits, or any sophisticated understanding of the rules of ethics to know that Respondent's course of conduct, personally and directly deceiving his clients, some of whom had been egregiously injured, was wrong. That he did so at the direction of his employer does not permit us to overlook the serious deficiency in character revealed by the facts before us.

In light of the serious ethical violations committed by Respondent, permanent disbarment from the practice of law in Kentucky is reasonable. . . .

Thus, it is ORDERED that:

1) Respondent, David L. Helmers, is adjudged guilty of violating [Rules] 1.4(b), 1.8(g), 2.1, 5.2(a), 8.3(a), and 8.3(c) and is hereby permanently disbarred from the practice of law in Kentucky. Respondent thusly, may never apply for reinstatement to the Bar under the current rules;

2) Respondent in accordance with SCR 3.390, shall notify all Courts in which he has matters pending and all clients for whom he is actively involved in litigation and similar matters, of his inability to continue representation;

3) Respondent shall immediately cancel and cease any advertising activities in accordance with SCR 3.390;

4) In accordance with SCR 3.450, Respondent is directed to pay all costs associated with these disciplinary proceedings in the amount of $39,673.53, for which execution may issue from this Court upon finality of this Order.

All sitting. All concur.

---

5. The five members voting against permanent disbarment instead voted to suspend Respondent from the practice of law for five years as recommended by the Trial Commissioner.

A Lawyer's Duty to Report Professional Misconduct of Other Lawyers and Judges

Kentucky Bar Association Ethics Opinion E-430 (2010)

Introduction

. . . [Rule] 8.3 [imposes an obligation on] Kentucky lawyers . . . to report certain types of ethical misconduct of other lawyers and judges. The obligations imposed by the rule are designed to preserve the integrity of the profession and to assure public confidence in the judicial system. Because the legal profession has the privilege of self-regulation it has the corresponding responsibility of assuring that the profession's high standards are respected. Rule 8.3 reflects that privilege and responsibility.[3]

In many circumstances, lawyers are in the best position to know of another lawyer's misconduct and to minimize its consequences to others. Not only do lawyers know the standards by which lawyers and judges are expected to conduct themselves, lawyers also work closely with them and may be the first ones actually to observe the acts of misconduct. In many cases, the victim of the misconduct may not even be aware of it. As officers of the legal system, lawyers must take the affirmative responsibility to assure that both the bench and bar maintain the highest standards, and to assure that those who do not conform to these standards are disciplined. It is only by taking an active role in the disciplinary process that the profession is deserving of the public's trust and confidence.

The reason for the reporting obligation is summarized in the Preamble to [the] Rules of Professional Conduct:

> [12] The legal profession's relative autonomy carries with it special responsibilities of self-government. The profession has a responsibility to assure that its regulations are conceived in the public interest and not in furtherance of parochial or self-interested concerns of the bar. Every lawyer is responsible for observance of the Rules of Professional Conduct. A lawyer should also aid in securing their observance by other lawyers. Neglect of these responsibilities compromises the independence of the profession and the public interest which it serves.

Many questions have been raised about the rule's application. . . . This opinion is designed to provide a framework for that analysis. In questionable cases, lawyers should seek further advice from their District Member of the Ethics Hotline.

I. Under what circumstances does Rule 8.3 impose a duty to report professional misconduct of others? . . .

Before a lawyer has an obligation to report the conduct of another lawyer or judge, the following specific conditions must be met:

---

3. ABA Formal Op. 04-433 (2004).

■ The reporting lawyer must "know" of the violation.

■ In the case of a lawyer, the violation of the Rules of Professional Conduct must raise "a substantial question as to the lawyer's honesty, trustworthiness or fitness as a lawyer in other respects."

■ In the case of a judge, the violation of the Rules of Judicial Conduct must raise "a substantial question as to the judge's fitness for office."

■ The information that serves as the basis of "knowledge" must not be "protected by Rule 1.6 or other law" nor have been "receive(d) in the course of participating in the Lawyer Assistance Program [KYLAP] . . ."

If the above conditions are met, and none of the exceptions discussed below apply, then the lawyer with "knowledge" must report. If the misconduct raises a substantial question as to a lawyer's honesty, trustworthiness or fitness, the report must be made to Bar Counsel. . . . If the misconduct raises a substantial question as to a judge's fitness for office, the report must be made to the Judicial Conduct Commission. The duty to report to Bar Counsel or the Judicial Conduct Commission is independent of any other reporting obligations, such as a lawyer's obligation to report perjury to a tribunal under [Rule] 3.3(a)(3). Lawyers cannot satisfy their obligations under Rule 8.3 by advising the tribunal of misconduct or by making a referral to KYLAP. The duty to report is an individual duty. It is not satisfied because a report has been made to another person or by another lawyer.

II. When does a lawyer "know" a violation has occurred?

Before a lawyer's duty to report is triggered, the lawyer must "know" of the violation [as] . . . is defined by [Rule] 1.0 [f] (Terminology) . . . :

The standard is an objective one. As the Louisiana Supreme Court recently observed:

> A lawyer will be found to have knowledge of reportable misconduct, and thus reporting is required, where the supporting evidence is such that a reasonable lawyer under the circumstances would form a firm belief that the conduct in question had more likely than not occurred. As such, knowledge is measured by an objective standard that is not tied to the subjective beliefs of the lawyer in question.[7]

In order to trigger the reporting requirement, absolute certainty is not required; but mere suspicion is insufficient to trigger the reporting requirement. While lawyers cannot turn a blind eye to obviously questionable conduct, as a general rule they do not have a duty to investigate. However, there may be circumstances where another rule or principle of law may impose an independent duty to investigate. For example, under [Rule 5.1], a supervising lawyer who suspects a subordinate lawyer is engaging in unethical conduct would have a duty to investigate further. Similarly, an independent duty to investigate misconduct might arise under [Rule] 1.5, which permits the division of fees between unrelated lawyers,

---

7. *In re Riehlmann,* 891 So.2d 1239, 1247 (La. 2005).

but requires the lawyers to assume joint ethical and financial responsibility for the representation, as if they were partners. . . .

If lawyers have doubt as to their duty to report, any reasonable doubt should be resolved in favor of reporting. It is then up to the appropriate authority . . . to follow-up and determine if an investigation should go forward or if the matter should be terminated.

III. What constitutes a "substantial question" within the meaning of Rule 8.3?

Both Rule 8.3(a), applicable to lawyers, and Rule 8.3(b), applicable to judges, use the term "substantial question." . . .

The intent of these two provisions is to require reporting of serious violations. [The committee cites Rule 8.3, Comment [2].]

Thus, not every violation must be reported. For example, an isolated failure to respond to a discovery request in a timely manner may be a violation of [Rule 3.4 (c)], which states that the lawyer shall not fail to comply with the rules of the tribunal. However, Rule 8.3 would not normally require the reporting of this violation because it does not involve a substantial violation of the rules reflecting on the lawyer's trustworthiness, honesty or fitness.

It would be impossible to list all of the situations in which a lawyer would be obligated to report. Clearly any conduct that would result in disbarment or suspension must be reported. Typical examples of conduct which have led to disbarment or suspension . . . include theft, conversion, abandonment of clients, credit card fraud, perjury, tampering with evidence, comingling of client funds, fraud, failure to act with reasonable diligence or keep client reasonably informed, mishandling of trust accounts, refusal to return unearned fees, and failing to take appropriate action to protect the client upon withdrawal or termination. . . .

Although most situations which require reporting involve dishonesty and untrustworthiness, Rule 8.3 also contains a catch-all provision, which requires reporting when conduct raises a substantial question as to the lawyer's "fitness in other respects . . . ." Reported examples include breach of a confidentiality agreement, egregious conflicts of interest, improper contact with jurors, and misconduct by a suspended lawyer. The catch-all provision may also apply to chronic neglect. Examples include situations in which a lawyer has repeatedly, and without explanation, missed court dates, failed to comply with court orders or failed to honor deadlines imposed by the court or the rules. In addition, any conduct which results in a contempt order by the court would normally fall within the catch-all provision and trigger the duty to report.

Misconduct, particularly neglect of duty, often arises when a lawyer is suffering from some kind of impairment. Impairment may arise as a consequence of senility, dementia, alcoholism, drug addiction, substance abuse, chemical dependency or mental illness. While not all impairments must be reported, any impairment that materially affects the fitness of the lawyer or the judge must be reported, unless one of the exceptions described below applies.

IV. Does a lawyer have a duty to report conduct unrelated to the practice of law or to judicial duties?

. . . Although most of the duties under the Rules of Professional Conduct relate to the representation of clients, some do not. [Rule] 8.4, especially subsections (b) and (c), may involve behavior unrelated to the practice of law. Specifically, the Rule provides that it is professional misconduct to "commit a criminal act that reflects adversely on the lawyer's honesty, trustworthiness or fitness as a lawyer . . . " or "engage in conduct involving dishonesty, fraud, deceit or misrepresentation." . . . Thus, for example, a lawyer could be disciplined for fraud in connection with the sale of a personal residence, falsification of documents for personal use, or embezzlement from a non-profit organization with which the lawyer does volunteer work. All of these examples raise a substantial question as to the lawyer's honesty and trustworthiness. Similarly, a lawyer would have a duty to report a judge who engaged in the activities described above, because they would raise a substantial question as to the judge's fitness for office. Whether a lawyer has a duty to report activities unrelated to the practice of law or judicial responsibilities will depend on the nature of the act and the circumstances under which it was committed. Clearly, theft, fraud or other serious misrepresentation, even when unrelated to professional activities, must be reported.

V. Does a lawyer have a duty to report information protected by [Rule] 1.6 . . .?

Rule 8.3 provides [that] a . . . lawyer may not, without the client's consent, report misconduct of another if the knowledge is based on information protected by Rule 1.6. In the context of Rule 8.3, the lawyer's duty of confidentiality takes precedence over any obligation to report misconduct.

Having recognized the exception for knowledge protected by Rule 1.6, two points must be made. First, the rule specifically authorizes the client to consent to disclosure, thus permitting the lawyer to report. "Informed consent" is defined by the Rule 1.0(e) [Terminology] . . . Reporting is designed to protect the public and lawyers are encouraged to discuss possible waiver and reporting with their clients, especially where the public faces a serious risk of harm. . . .

In addition to the exception for information protected by Rule 1.6, Rule 8.3 (c) does not require disclosure of information obtained while participating in a lawyer assistance program. . . . This reporting exception does not relieve a lawyer who is not a staff member or volunteer from reporting an impaired lawyer or judge whose conduct raises a substantial question as honesty, trustworthiness or fitness. The rule attempts to balance the goal of assisting impaired lawyers by providing a confidential support network, with the need to protect the public. . . .

VI. Does a lawyer have a duty to self-report his or her own misconduct or that of an associate?

Rule 8.3 requires a lawyer to report certain misconduct of "another lawyer" or "judge." As a general rule, a lawyer does not have to self-report. This is not to say that a lawyer should not self-report and in some circumstances it may be the best course of action.

However, self-reporting is required under SCR 3.453, which provides that lawyers must report discipline from other jurisdictions, including federal court. In addition, SCR 3.166 requires a lawyer who has pleaded "guilty to a felony, including a no contest plea or a plea in which the member allows conviction but does not admit the commission of a crime, or is convicted by a judge or jury of a felony, in this state or in any other jurisdiction" to self-report.

A lawyer's obligation under Rule 8.3 may require a lawyer to report a partner or associate. This may have consequences for the reporting lawyer, but there is nothing in the rule to suggest that the duty to report does not extend to one with whom the reporting lawyer is or was associated. For example, if a lawyer knows that another lawyer in the firm falsified material documents for trial, the lawyer is obligated to report that misconduct unless one of the exceptions applied.

VII. Does a lawyer have a duty to report a suspended or disbarred lawyer?

A lawyer who has been suspended is still subject to application of certain Rules of Professional Conduct. If a suspended lawyer engages in unprofessional conduct, including the unauthorized practice of law, then a lawyer who knows of that misconduct has a duty to report. It is particularly important to report suspended lawyers who have engaged in misconduct because they may ultimately apply for reinstatement. One of the primary considerations on the application for reinstatement will be whether the suspended lawyer complied with the terms of suspension, and the rules during the period of suspension.

A disbarred lawyer is no longer a lawyer, and not subject to the Rules of Professional Conduct. . . . The Kentucky Bar Association has no authority over a disbarred lawyer's general conduct, but it does have the authority to investigate unauthorized practice and initiate proceedings. If a lawyer is involved in a matter in which a disbarred lawyer is engaged in the unauthorized practice of law, the failure to report the unauthorized practice of law could result in the lawyer's violation of [Rule] 5.5(a), which prohibit a lawyer from assisting another in the unauthorized practice of law. . . . The interests of both the public and the profession are best served by reporting the disbarred lawyer who is engaged in the unauthorized practice of law. . . .

IX. Is the reporting lawyer immune from civil or criminal liability?

A lawyer who makes a report in good faith is immune from civil or criminal liability or disciplinary action by the bar . . . .

X. What are the procedures for reporting a violation and when must the report be made?

. . . The purpose of the rule is to permit Bar Counsel or the Judicial Conduct Commission to begin an inquiry into the alleged misconduct. Thus, the reporting lawyer should report the facts underlying the belief that there is a substantial question as to the reported lawyer's honesty, trustworthiness or fitness as a lawyer or the reported judge's fitness for office. Reporting the facts underlying the belief further demonstrates the reporting lawyer's good faith basis for making the report. . . .

It is clear that an anonymous report does not comply with the rule and affords no protection to the reporting lawyer.

The rule does not address the question of when one must make the report. Because the purpose of the rule is to protect the public, under most circumstances the report should be made within a reasonable time after discovery. There may be cases in which a report might have a detrimental impact on the reporting lawyer's client. This might be the case where there are on-going relationships between the client and the lawyer who has engaged in misconduct. Assuming that the information came to the reporting lawyer in the course of the representation of the client, it would be protected by Rule 1.6; absent client consent, the lawyer could not report. To the extent that the client's interests are not protected by the Rule 1.6 exception, it is the view of the Committee that where an immediate report would have a detrimental impact on the client, the lawyer may delay reporting to protect the client's interests. The lawyer would be well served to document any discussions with the client and the reasons for delaying the reporting. . . .

Conclusion

Under amended Rule 8.3, a lawyer does not have a duty to report every known violation of the rules, but must report those that underlie the core values of the profession: honesty, trustworthiness and fitness. . . . It is not easy to file a report against a fellow lawyer or judge, particularly if the reporting lawyer has a personal relationship with the lawyer or judge or knows of some unfortunate circumstances involving either. Nevertheless, the Rules require lawyers to report lawyers and judges who have engaged in serious misconduct. A lawyer's obligation to the profession and to the public outweighs any personal reservations the lawyer may have about reporting another lawyer or judge. Again, it is not the lawyer's duty to determine another lawyer's or judge's guilt, but merely to make the report so that the appropriate disciplinary authorities can make that determination.

The Law Governing Lawyers: *Admission and Discipline*

The materials in this chapter illustrate aspects of the system of professional licensure and discipline that form the backbone of the professional regulation of lawyers. *Converse* illustrates that bar applicants bear the burden of proving the requisite character and fitness; *Helmers* and *Walker* indicate that once licensed, bar counsel bears the burden of proving a professional code violation. Courts have inherent power to regulate the practice of law. They do so by establishing substantive and procedural requirements for professional admission and discipline.

Becoming a Licensed Lawyer

Most states require those who seek bar admission to satisfy five criteria: age, education or experience, examination, the taking of an oath, and good moral character.

To facilitate consideration of character and fitness to practice law, bar applicants are required to complete a lengthy questionnaire that canvasses relevant topics related to these criteria.[1] Court rules, like those relied on in *Converse*, focus on general criteria such as honesty, respect for law, and the ability to act professionally. The inability to act honestly can be evidenced by a criminal record, civil judgment,[2] academic misconduct, or neglect of professional or financial obligations.[3] Bar examiners treat any lack of candor in the bar admission application itself as equally serious.[4] The ability to act professionally in a manner that engenders respect for law and the profession can be evidenced by letters of reference, by reports of law school administrators, or the absence of a history of drug or alcohol dependence or mental illness or successful treatment for these conditions.[5]

In deciding whether an applicant has met the necessary criteria, courts assess how these factors predict future ability to practice.[6] They often also consider

---

1. Applicants have a continuing obligation to update their bar applications until they gain bar admission. *E.g., In re Strzempek*, 962 A.2d 988 (Md. 2008) (bar applicant who failed to disclose guilty plea to driving under the influence that occurred after he submitted bar application denied admission for failure to timely report).

2. *E.g., In re Application of Chapman*, 630 N.E.2d 322 (Ohio 1994) (consent decree in civil action by State Attorney General against bar applicant alleging deceptive and unconscionable sales practices in connection with a business demonstrated recent pattern of highly questionable and outright illegal behavior that justified rejection of bar applicant; renewed application that would demonstrate substantial change in applicant's conduct may allow for admission at a later date).

3. *E.g., In re Griffin*, 943 N.E.2d 1008 (Ohio 2011) (bar applicant with $170,000 in student loans and $16,500 in credit card debt denied admission because he worked only part time, had made no payments on any debt, and had no plans to begin repayment; neglect of financial obligations is conduct constituting "a record manifesting a significant deficiency in the honesty, trustworthiness diligence, or reliability of an applicant."); *In re Steffen*, 261 P.3d 1254 (Ore. 2011) (filing for bankruptcy alone not enough to deny bar admission, but bar is entitled to inquire about details of bankruptcy, with an eye to determining whether it was triggered by "extraordinary hardship" or arose from "selfishness, a disregard of fiscal and moral responsibilities, or other irresponsible conduct," which would suffice to deny bar admission); *In re Stewart*, 240 P.3d 666 (Okla. 2010) (bankruptcy discharge precludes consideration of debt in lawyer's application for bar license under 11 U.S.C. § 525(a)).

4. *E.g., Radtke v. Bd. of Bar Examrs.*, 601 N.W.2d 642 (Wis. 1999) (lawyer who misstated material fact on his bar application about his earlier plagiarism did not satisfy character and fitness requirement).

5. *E.g., In re Ralls*, 849 N.E.2d 36 (Ohio 2006) (two DUI convictions during law school combined with failure to accept responsibility for alcohol abuse precluded applicant from admission until he demonstrated sustained period of compliance with alcohol treatment programs); *In re Covington*, 50 P.3d 233 (Or. 2002) (three years of sobriety not enough time to establish that applicant's past abuse of drugs and alcohol would not recur).

6. Courts use similar criteria in assessing reinstatement after suspension or disbarment. *E.g., Milligan v. Bd. of Profl. Resp.*, 301 S.W.3d 619 (Tenn. 2009) (suspended lawyer failed to show moral qualifications to practice law required for reinstatement, measured by honesty, remorse,

whether past conduct would have violated a professional code requirement if the candidate had been licensed at the time. If so, the applicant usually will not succeed in showing the requisite character and fitness to practice law.[7] Most obvious are prior criminal convictions, where applicants must show rehabilitation to be admitted.[8] Less obvious are troubling patterns of behavior, like those in *Converse*, which indicate disruptive characteristics that probably will cause future trouble with clients, opponents, and tribunals.[9]

Converse also illustrates how courts respond when confronted with First Amendment challenges. Bar admissions officials may ask about membership in specific associations, so long as such a membership is relevant to fitness to practice.[10] On the other hand, a question that asks candidates to list memberships in all organizations during law school is overbroad and not rationally related to the ability to practice law.[11] For example, in a fairly recent Illinois Bar admission case, applicant Matthew Hale readily admitted that he headed an organization

---

positive conduct during suspension, and detailed character testimony from witnesses who know the specifics of the lawyer's misconduct and payment of disciplinary costs).

7. *E.g., In re Mustafa*, 631 A.2d 45 (D.C. App. 1993) (because applicant's conduct if undertaken by a lawyer would have resulted in disbarment for at least five years, applicant should wait for a similar period of time from proven misconduct before good moral character can be established).

8. Courts look to the timing, number, and nature of the convictions as well as the applicant's recognition of the wrongfulness of the conduct and change in behavior over a period of time since the criminal activity. *In re R.M.W.*, 428 F. Supp. 2d 389 (D. Md. 2006) (adopting uniform procedure and criteria for applicants with prior criminal convictions); *In re Hamm*, 123 P.3d 652 (Ariz. 2005) (no person ever convicted of first-degree murder has been able to make the extraordinary showing of good moral character for bar admission); *In re Prager*, 661 N.E.2d 84 (Mass. 1996) (16 years of marijuana use, international smuggling, and living as a fugitive not outweighed by 7 years of a credible work history and successful completion of probation and law school, but applicant could reapply in 5 years).

9. Lawyers have been disbarred for conduct strikingly similar to Converse's. *See, e.g., Off. of Disc. Counsel v. Baumgartner*, 796 N.E.2d 495 (Ohio 2003) (lawyer who "repeatedly harmed her client's interests, manipulated the legal system, and publicly accused dozens of people of criminal wrongdoing" and whose "actions were done as a means to retaliate against anyone who defied her" disbarred). *See also Grievance Admin'r. v. Fieger*, 719 N.W.2d 123 (Mich. 2006), *cert. denied*, 127 S. Ct. 1257 (2007) (lawyer who castigated appellate judges in radio broadcasts, calling them Nazis and "three jackass Court of Judges," and announcing that they deserved anal violation publicly reprimanded).

10. *Law Students Civ. Rights Research Council, Inc. v. Wadmond*, 401 U.S. 154 (1971) (upholding an inquiry into whether the applicant specifically intended to further an organization's advocacy of violent overthrow of the government while a member of the organization); *Schware v. Bd. of Bar Exam'rs. of N.M.*, 353 U.S. 232, 246-247 (1957) (Communist Party membership prior to World War II could not be used as the basis to infer moral unfitness to practice law because such past membership had no rational connection to evil purposes or illegal conduct); *Konigsberg v. St. Bar of Cal.*, 366 U.S. 36, 52 (1961) (state can inquire about current Communist Party membership and can deny bar admission to an applicant who refused to answer, because of the state's interest "in having lawyers who are devoted to the law in its broadest sense, including . . . its procedures for orderly change").

11. *Baird v. St. Bar of Ariz.*, 401 U.S. 1 (1971) (overturning a general inquiry not connected to knowing membership); *In re Stolar*, 401 U.S. 23 (1971) (overturning inquiry that asked whether applicant has been or is a member of any organization that advocates the overthrow of the government of the United States by force).

called the World Church of the Creator, which did not sanction violence, but called for white racial supremacy and the use of political power to provide for the deportation of all other races, including Jews, blacks, and other "mud races" so that the United States could then become a "white race"–only country. He claimed he would follow the law until he could change it by peaceable means. A hearing panel focused on Hale's conduct, rather than his beliefs, denying him admission because he had admitted he would follow the Rules of Professional Conduct "only when he felt like it." They held that he was "absolutely entitled to his beliefs, but at the same time the public and the bar are entitled to be treated fairly and decently by attorneys."[12]

The Supreme Court also has invalidated two licensure requirements — citizenship and residency — on constitutional grounds. It barred citizenship requirements for lawyers on Equal Protection grounds, holding that the state could not prove a compelling interest that would overcome the strict scrutiny required by the Fourteenth Amendment to protect resident aliens.[13] It overturned residency requirements under the privileges and immunities clause in Art. IV, § 2 of the Constitution, concluding that the state could require lawyers to be familiar with local law, obey the jurisdiction's professional codes, participate in *pro bono* work, or be available to appear in court, but could not use residency as a surrogate for such restrictions.[14] The same principles were applied to federal court residency requirements in *Frazier v. Heebe,* where the Court exercised its inherent power to invalidate a local district court residency requirement.[15]

The net result of these decisions is that states remain free to impose admission requirements on residents and nonresidents alike, so long as the prerequisites do not favor resident lawyers.[16] Several courts also have upheld similar prerequisites to *pro hac vice* admissions (to represent a client with tribunal permission in one particular matter).[17]

---

12. W. Bradley Wendel, *Free Speech for Lawyers*, 28 Hastings Const. L.Q. 305 (2001). The Illinois Supreme Court refused to hear the case on appeal, but one justice dissented, characterizing Hale's conduct as "open advocacy of racially obnoxious belief." *In re Hale*, 723 N.E.2d 206 (Ill. 1999). Since being denied bar admission, Hale has been convicted of soliciting the murder of a federal judge. Natasha Korecki & Frank Main, *Supremacist Gets 40 Yrs.; Hale Given Maximum for Trying to Have Judge Murdered, Chicago Sun-Times* (Apr. 7, 2005).

13. *In re Griffiths*, 413 U.S. 717 (1973).

14. *Piper v. S. Ct. of N.H.*, 470 U.S. 274 (1985). *See also Barnard v. Thorstenn*, 489 U.S. 546 (1989) (invalidating similar residency requirements in the Virgin Islands); *S. Ct. of Va. v. Friedman*, 487 U.S. 59 (1988) (invalidating residency requirements as a condition of admission on motion).

15. *Frazier v. Heebe*, 482 U.S. 641 (1987).

16. *E.g., Tolchin v. S. Ct. of N.J.*, 111 F.3d 1099 (3d Cir. 1997) (upholding a requirement that lawyers maintain a local bona fide office and attend continuing legal education courses).

17. *See, e.g., Paciulan v. George*, 229 F.3d 1226 (9th Cir. 2000) (residents not admitted to the bar not allowed to appear *pro hac vice*); *Mowrer v. Warner-Lambert Co.*, 1998 U.S. Dist. LEXIS 12746 (E.D. Pa. 1998) (local counsel of record required for *pro hac vice* admission); ABA Model R. on Admission by Motion (2012) *available at* http://www.abanow.org/wordpress/wp-content/files_flutter/13442860792012AM_105E.pdf.

Professional Discipline

Once admitted to the practice of law, lawyers become subject to Rules of Professional Conduct, violation of which can result in professional discipline.

Over the past 40 years, state and federal courts have extensively reformed the substance of these Rules of Professional Conduct, updated the procedures for disciplinary enforcement, and implemented guidelines to standardize disciplinary sanctions. The result has been more extensive discipline for a wider variety of professional misconduct. At the same time, because professional discipline continues to reach only a small fraction of client and third-party complaints, other remedies, such as malpractice, fee forfeiture, disqualification, and procedural sanctions also have expanded to fill the regulatory void.

The Emergence of Modern Disciplinary Systems

Professional disciplinary procedures are *sui generis*, neither civil nor criminal in nature.[18] The potential for loss of professional license is less serious than loss of liberty, but a more severe penalty than civil damages. These realities explain why the Supreme Court has required procedural due process guarantees such as notice of the charge,[19] and the right to invoke a Fifth Amendment privilege against self-incrimination in disciplinary proceedings.[20] At the same time, the Fifth Amendment protection against double jeopardy does not apply because the purpose of a disciplinary proceeding is not to punish the lawyer, but to protect the public.[21] The unique nature of the process further justifies the use of a jurisdiction's rules of civil procedure and evidence, a requirement of clear and convincing evidence, adjudication by judges or other lawyers rather than a jury, and a right to appeal a hearing committee decision.[22] The Supreme Court also has applied the *Younger* abstention doctrine to state disciplinary proceedings, requiring federal courts to refrain from considering constitutional challenges to pending state proceedings that afford the lawyer an opportunity to present the constitutional issues.[23]

---

18. ABA Model R. for Law. Disc. Enforcement, R. 18(A) (1999).

19. *In re Ruffalo,* 390 U.S. 544 (1968) (lawyer entitled to notice of charge in disbarment proceeding). The adequacy of due process in a state disciplinary proceeding also determines whether a federal court can impose reciprocal discipline for the same conduct without plenary review. *See Selling v. Radford,* 243 U.S. 46 (1917); *Ruffalo,* 390 U.S. at 550; *In re Edelstein,* 214 F.3d 127 (2d Cir. 2000).

20. *Spevack v. Klein,* 385 U.S. 511 (1967) (lawyer cannot be disbarred for properly invoking the Fifth Amendment privilege against self-incrimination in disciplinary proceeding). A federal court has added the constitutional right to clear and convincing evidence, *In re Medrano,* 956 F.2d 101 (5th Cir. 1992).

21. *See, e.g., In re Cardwell,* 50 P.3d 897 (Colo. 2002); *In re Caranchini,* 160 F.3d 420 (8th Cir. 1998); *In re Brown,* 906 P.2d 1184 (Cal. 1995); *Disc. Counsel v. Campbell,* 345 A.2d 616 (Pa. 1975).

22. ABA Model R. for Lawyer Disc. Enforcement, *supra* note 18, R. 11 and R. 18.

23. *Middlesex County Ethics Comm'n. v. Garden St. Bar Assn.,* 457 U.S. 423 (1982).

Today, continual improvements in state and federal disciplinary proceedings[24] mean that professional staff now administer lawyer discipline, usually as part of an official court agency.[25] Many states now conduct public disciplinary hearings,[26] and most grant immunity to complainants.[27] The ABA's Center for Professional Responsibility administers a National Lawyer Regulatory Data Bank, which has enabled jurisdictions to share information about public lawyer regulatory sanctions and thus enhance reciprocal discipline (sanctions based on prior discipline in another jurisdiction).[28] *Walker* illustrates state court acceptance of the ABA Model Rules for Lawyer Disciplinary Enforcement and Standards for Imposing Lawyer Sanctions, which have encouraged uniform procedures and expanded the range of sanctions. One example is interim suspension, which now routinely occurs for conviction of a serious crime or where serious harm to the public is threatened, such as by a lawyer who abandons a law practice.[29] A few jurisdictions have expanded the scope of professional regulation even further by making law firms as well as individual lawyers subject to disciplinary sanctions.[30]

The scope of public protection has been further expanded by the judicial branch's addition of complementary agencies, such as client protection funds, fee arbitration, mediation of malpractice complaints, law practice assistance, and substance abuse counseling.[31] These additional agencies address issues that

---

24. *E.g., In re Jaffe*, 585 F.3d 118 (2d Cir. 2009) (court disbarred lawyer rejecting disciplinary committee's recommendation that lawyer be allowed to resign to avoid reciprocal discipline).

25. Courts also rely on their inherent power to discipline lawyers, *e.g., In re Lehtinen*, 564 F.3d 1052 (9th Cir. 2009) (bankruptcy courts have inherent power to suspend lawyers from practicing before the court). Federal agencies may require additional admission and disciplinary standards. *See, e.g.,* FTC Rules of Practice, 16. C.F.R. Parts 0-5.

26. *Landmark Commun. Inc. v. Va.*, 435 U.S. 829 (1978) (state law that made it a crime to disclose information about grievance proceedings violates First Amendment); *R.M. v. N.J. S. Ct.*, 883 A.2d 369 (2004) (rule that required confidentiality in grievance records unconstitutional prior restraint on free speech).

27. *State v. Rutherford*, 863 So. 2d 445 (Fla. 4th Dist. App. 2004) (absolute civil immunity for complainants did not bar criminal perjury charges).

28. *E.g., In re Demos*, 875 A.2d 636 (D.C. 2005) (lawyer stricken from the roll of attorneys in Arizona federal court for lying on bar application disbarred for the Arizona conduct in D.C.); *Gadda v. Ashcroft*, 377 F.3d 934 (2004) (federal law does not preempt state regulation of lawyers and allows for disbarment by the state of California, and reciprocal disbarment by federal board of immigration appeals, as well as Ninth Circuit); *Atty. Grievance Comm'n. v. McCoy*, 798 A.2d 1132 (Md. 2002) (lawyer disbarred in Delaware disbarred in Maryland for the same conduct).

29. ABA Model R. for Law. Disc. Enforcement, *supra* note 18, R. 19, 20; Ex parte Case, 925 So. 2d 956 (Ala. 2005) (lawyer entitled to procedural due process guarantees before interim suspension except when convicted of a serious crime or genuine emergency exists).

30. *See, e.g.,* N.Y. Rule 5.1. *See also* Ted Schneyer, *Professional Discipline for Law Firms?* 77 Cornell L. Rev. 1 (1991).

31. ABA, *A National Action Plan on Lawyer Conduct and Professionalism* 80 (1999); ABA Model R. for Law. Disc. Enforcement, *supra* note 15 at R. 1(A). For a discussion of the impact of practice assistance programs as an alternative to discipline, *see* Diane M. Ellis, *A Decade of Diversion: Empirical Evidence that Alternative Discipline Is Working for Arizona Lawyers*, 52 Emory L.J. 1221 (2003).

may be dismissed as less serious than those that warrant formal discipline; by doing so, they respond to a greater number of legitimate client complaints that cannot otherwise be addressed by the disciplinary system. The American Bar Association (ABA) recommends additional client protections, such as financial record keeping, trust account maintenance and overdraft notification, random audits of trust accounts, the maintenance of malpractice insurance, and a program of recertification.[32]

Which Lawyers Are Disciplined?

Complaints to disciplinary authorities can come from clients, judges, other lawyers, or third parties.[33] In 2009 (when the total lawyer population was 1,482,271), state disciplinary agencies received 126,696 complaints, investigated 77,832 of them, and imposed public and private sanctions against 6,769 lawyers.[34]

Longstanding commentary and empirical evidence indicates that solo practitioners and small-firm lawyers such as the lawyer in *Walker* are subject to discipline much more often than their large-firm or inside-counsel counterparts.[35] One report identified several "factors unique to the practice environment" that explain this result. First, lawyers in large firms tend to represent clients with more money and power—very often, large institutions. If these clients become dissatisfied, they have the ability to change lawyers, negotiate reduced fees, or litigate. On the other hand, clients of small-firm lawyers tend to be individuals who often lack the money or power to leverage such alternatives. They therefore may be more likely to seek the assistance of bar authorities when something goes wrong.

Lawyers in law firms also have a great deal more peer assistance available to them. Colleagues can cover for lawyers who become ill or overwhelmed. Larger firms are more likely to institutionalize procedures and policies that can prevent many violations, such as those dealing with client trust funds and conflicts of interest. Small firm lawyers might lack such support systems or office procedures. Financial and time pressures could cause missed deadlines, failure to communicate with clients, or "borrowing" from client trust accounts.

Helmers makes clear, however, that each and every lawyer in the firm who engages in misconduct is subject to discipline. Model Rule 5.1 and 5.3 further make supervisory lawyers responsible for the conduct of others when they know

---

32. *National Action Plan, supra* note 31, at 37 (1999).

33. Arthur F. Greenbaum, *The Automatic Reporting of Lawyer Misconduct to Disciplinary Authorities: Filling the Reporting Gap,* 73 Ohio St. L.J. 437 (2012).

34. ABA, Standing Comm. on Lawyer Disc., *Survey on Lawyer Discipline Systems 2009, available at* http://www.americanbar.org/groups/professional_responsibility/resources/survey_lawyer_discipline_systems_2009.html (last visited Mar. 1, 2012); Debra Moss Curtis, *Attorney Discipline Nationwide: A Comparative Analysis of Process and Statistics,* 35 J. Legal Prof. 1 (2011).

35. E.g., St. Bar of Cal., *Investigation and Prosecution of Disciplinary Complaints Against Attorneys in Solo Practice, Small Size Law Firms and Large Size Law Firm* (June 2001) *available at* http://www.calbar.ca.gov/LinkClick.aspx?fileticket=OydXJk36ys4%3D&tabid=224&mid=1534.

about the conduct and fail to take timely reasonable measures to mitigate it.[36] Helmers, the junior lawyer, argued that his reliance on his supervisors' professional judgment should not subject him to discipline under Rule 5.2. The court acknowledged that he may have been "led astray" by the direction of his "well-respected" supervisors, but found no "reasonable resolution of an arguable professional duty" in his egregious deceit of clients.

What Behavior Triggers Discipline?

The Kentucky Bar Opinion states that Model Rule 8.4(a) makes every lawyer code rule violation, as well as every attempted rule violation, grounds for professional discipline.[37] Anyone can initiate a disciplinary complaint, including lawyers, clients, and judges. Most jurisdictions also authorize disciplinary authorities to investigate matters without a request for investigation. The Rule also prohibits inducing others to violate the rules of professional conduct. For example, lawyers who use an agent to solicit cases or to make contact with a represented person have been disciplined under this provision,[38] as have those who direct others, such as legal assistants or secretaries, to commit acts that violate the professional rules.[39]

Model Rule 8.4(b), which prohibits lawyers from committing criminal acts that reflect adversely on their ability to practice law,[40] and Model Rule 8.4(c), which prohibits dishonesty, fraud, deceit, and misrepresentation,[41] also provide grounds for professional discipline. Violations of either of these provisions nearly always raise a "substantial question about the lawyer's honesty, trustworthiness

---

36. *E.g., In re Phillips,* 244 P.3d 549 (Ariz. 2010) (lawyer who delegated too much responsibility to nonlawyer employees and burdened lawyers with too much work created an environment making ethical violations practically inevitable, suspended for six months for violating Rules 5.1 and 5.3); *In re Foster,* 45 So. 3d 1026 (La. 2010) (five members of law firm's management committee who failed to adequately supervise marketing claims put on firm's website by firm employee publicly reprimanded for violating Rule 5.3); *State ex rel. Oklahoma Bar Ass'n v. Martin,* 240 P.3d 690 (Ok. 2010) (lawyer who facilitated employee's unauthorized practice by failing to supervise employee's "research center" in lawyer's office publicly reprimanded for violating Rule 5.3); ABA Formal Op. 08-451 Lawyer's Obligations When Outsourcing Legal and Nonlegal Support Services.

37. *E.g., Columbus Bar Assn. v. Ashton,* 840 N.E.2d 618 (Ohio 2006) (lawyer failed to advise clients of lack of professional liability insurance).

38. *E.g., In re Brass,* 696 So. 2d 967 (La. 1997) (lawyer who paid investigator to refer personal injury and criminal cases suspended for two and one-half years); *Emil v. Miss. Bar,* 690 So. 2d 301 (Miss. 1997) (lawyer who asked highway patrol officer to refer automobile injury cases in exchange for 15 percent of eventual settlements indefinitely suspended).

39. *E.g., In re Ositis,* 40 P.3d 500 (Or. 2002) (lawyer who directed a private investigator to pose as a journalist to interview a potential opposing party to a legal dispute suspended for 30 days); *In re Morris,* 953 P.2d 387 (Or. 1998) (lawyer who directed legal assistant to alter and file final account in a probate matter after it had been signed and notarized, suspended for 120 days); *Disc. Counsel v. Bandy,* 690 N.E.2d 1280 (Ohio 1998) (lawyer who tried to validate a will naming himself as beneficiary by requesting that his former secretary, who was not present when the will was signed, nevertheless sign it as an additional witness suspended for two years).

40. The Bounds of the Law: *Criminal Conduct, infra* p. 270.

41. The Bounds of the Law: *Duties to Nonclients, infra* p. 155.

or fitness as a lawyer"[42] and apply to lawyer conduct both inside and outside law practice.[43]

Model Rule 8.4(d), which prohibits conduct prejudicial to the administration of justice, also has been applied in a wide variety of contexts,[44] for example, to lawyers who abandon law practice without notifying clients,[45] and prosecutors who seriously misuse their discretion.[46] The Rule has provided the basis for discipline for misconduct during litigation, such as shoving another lawyer in the courtroom,[47] making court appearances while intoxicated,[48] or making insulting remarks during a deposition[49] or in a trial brief.[50] Lawyers have been uniformly unsuccessful in challenging Model Rule 8.4(d) as void for vagueness.[51]

Model Rules 8.4(e) and (f) further prohibit specific kinds of conduct that are prejudicial to the administration of justice. Model Rule 8.4(e) proscribes conduct that suggests a lawyer can obtain results by improperly influencing a

---

42. MR 8.3.

43. *E.g., Bosse's Case,* 920 A. 2d 1203 (N. H. 2007) (lawyer who falsified signatures as a real estate agent suspended for two years); *State ex rel. Okla. Bar Assn. v. Pacenza,* 136 P.3d 616 (Okla. 2006) (lawyer's deceit in sale of a home suspended for two years and one day); *In re Barrett,* 852 N.E.2d 660 (Mass. 2006) (lawyer who served as corporate executive and took company funds suspended for two years).

44 *E.g., Disc. Counsel v. Engel,* 2012 Ohio LEXIS 1262 (state government lawyer who recklessly disclosed inspector's general's confidential information engaged in conduct prejudicial to the administration of justice). Former president Bill Clinton agreed to a five-year suspension from practice for violating Rule 8.4(d), rather than the more specific dishonesty standard in Rule 8.4(c), for knowingly giving "evasive and misleading answers" in a court proceeding. Tom Brune, *No Clinton Indictment; President Makes a Deal,* Newsday A 05 (Jan. 20, 2001).

45 *E.g., In re Kendrick,* 710 So. 2d 236 (La. 1998) (lawyer who moved without notifying bankruptcy client, resulting in repossession of client's vehicles, suspended from practice for one year and a day and ordered to pay restitution); *People v. Crist,* 948 P.2d 1020 (Colo. 1997) (lawyer who left state, abandoning law practice of 60 pending cases, disbarred).

46. *In re Christoff,* 690 N.E.2d 1135 (Ind. 1997) (prosecutor and chief deputy prosecutor who renewed a long-dormant criminal investigation against another lawyer who sought the prosecutor's job suspended for 30 days and publicly admonished).

47. *In re Jaques,* 972 F. Supp. 1070 (E.D. Tex. 1997) (lawyer who, inter alia, assaulted a person and verbally abused another lawyer during a deposition suspended).

48. *In re Wyllie,* 952 P.2d 550 (Or. 1998).

49. *In re Golden,* 496 S.E.2d 619 (S.C. 1998) (lawyer who made threatening and degrading comments during two depositions publicly reprimanded); *Paramount Communications v. QVC Network,* 637 A.2d 34 (Del. 1993) (lawyer who "improperly directed the witness not to answer certain questions," was "extraordinarily rude, uncivil, and vulgar," and "obstructed the ability of the questioner to elicit testimony to assist the Court in this matter" demonstrated an "astonishing lack of professionalism and civility" warned in appendix to court decision that the court's summary contempt powers may be appropriate to address such conduct in the future).

50. *In re Abbott,* 2007 Del. LEXIS 199 (lawyer who made unfounded accusations in trial court brief that trial court might rule other than on the merits publicly reprimanded).

51. *See, e.g., Florida Bar v. Zamft,* 814 So. 2d 385 (Fla. 2002) (ex parte communication with a judge by a lawyer who did not represent either party in the matter); *In re Stanbury,* 561 N.W.2d 507 (Minn. 1997) (refusing to pay a law-related judgment and make payment on a court filing fee); *In re Stuhff,* 837 P.2d 853 (Nev. 1992) (intentionally interfering with sentencing of a criminal defendant by filing a disciplinary complaint against a judge just before the sentencing hearing); *In re Haws,* 801 P.2d 818 (Or. 1990) (failure to respond to bankruptcy trustee's inquiry and disciplinary complaint); *State of Nebraska ex rel. Nebraska Bar Ass'n. v. Kirshen,* 441 N.W.2d 161 (Neb. 1989) (failing to respond to bar complaint and properly supervise office staff).

governmental agency or official.[52] The rule also has been applied to judges who misuse their positions.[53] Model Rule 8.4(f) further prohibits lawyers from assisting judges in violating the rules of judicial conduct, for example, by making loans to judges before whom they appear.[54]

Some jurisdictions have added additional grounds for discipline to Model Rule 8.4. For example, Massachusetts and New York prohibit lawyers from engaging in "any other conduct that adversely reflects on the lawyer's fitness to practice law."[55] Colorado, California, and Florida provisions make nonpayment of child support obligations grounds for license suspension.[56]

Several jurisdictions also have enacted express prohibitions against discriminatory conduct—in a "law practice,"[57] in employment,[58] or more generally, unlawful discrimination in any context.[59] Courts have not had trouble disciplining lawyers for similar, truly outrageous conduct under the more general language of Model Rule 8.4(d), conduct prejudicial to the administration of justice.[60]

Disciplinary Sanctions

Once disciplinary counsel has met the burden of proof, disciplinary sanctions are imposed.[61] An increased range of sanctions and sanction uniformity has been encouraged by the ABA Standards for Imposing Lawyer Sanctions, relied

---

52. *Disc. Counsel v. Cicero,* 678 N.E.2d 517 (Ohio 1997) (lawyer who led prosecutor and client-defendant to believe he was having a sexual relationship with a judge after she recused herself from the case suspended from practice for one year); *Disc. Proceedings Against Bennett,* 376 N.W.2d 861 (Wis. 1985) (lawyer who, inter alia, told his client a bankruptcy matter could be handled in some "extralegal" way suspended for six months).

53. *E.g., In re Yaccarino,* 564 A.2d 1184 (N.J. 1989) (judge who contacted police and prosecutor about the arrest of his daughter and who conspired to obtain property that was the subject of a lawsuit over which he presided properly removed from office and subject to disbarment).

54. *Lisi v. Several Attys.,* 596 A.2d 313 (R.I. 1991) (lawyers who made loans to judges before whom they appeared subject to suspension and reprimand).

55. Mass. R. Prof. Conduct 8.4(h) (2007); N.Y. Code of Prof. Resp. DR 1-102(a)(7) (2007).

56. Cal. Bus. & Prof. Code § 490.5 (2007); Colo. R. C. P. § 251.8.5(b) (2007); Fla. R. Prof. Conduct 4-8.4(h) (2007).

57. Cal. R. Prof. Conduct 2-400 (2007).

58. D.C. R. Prof. Conduct 9.1 (2003). *See also* Mich. R. Prof. Conduct 6.5 (2010) (requiring lawyers to treat persons involved in the legal process "with courtesy and respect").

59. Ill. R. Prof. Conduct 8.4(a)(9)(A) (2003) (discrimination in violation of federal, state, or local law); N.Y. Code of Prof. Resp. DR 1-102(a)(6) (2007); Ohio R. Prof. Conduct 8.4(g) (2007). *See also* Minn. R. Prof. Conduct 8.4(g) (2009) (prohibiting harassment on the basis of sex, race, age, creed, religion, color, national origin, disability, sexual preference, or marital status); Tex. Disc. R. Prof. Conduct 5.08 (2009) (prohibiting lawyers from manifesting "by words or conduct bias based on race, color, national origin, religion, disability, age, sex, or sexual orientation").

60. *E.g., In re Monaghan,* 743 N.Y.S.2d 519 (App. Div. 2002) (race-based abuse of opposing counsel at a deposition was conduct prejudicial to the administration of justice and unlawful discrimination); *Florida Bar v. Martocci,* 791 So. 2d 1074 (Fla. 2001) (sexist, racial, and ethnic insults constituted conduct prejudicial to the administration of justice); *In re Charges of Unprofessional Conduct,* 597 N.W.2d 563 (Minn. 1999) (prosecutor who sought to disqualify defense counsel solely on the basis of race engaged in conduct prejudicial to the administration of justice).

61. There is no statute of limitations in disciplinary proceedings in most jurisdictions, and other defenses, such as laches or entrapment have not been successful. *See, e.g., In re Carson,* 845 P.2d 47 (Kan. 1993) (ten-year delay in disciplinary proceedings not available as a defense where no

on in *Walker*.[62] These Standards recognize a wide spectrum of sanctions, including disbarment, suspension, reprimand, admonition, probation, restitution, assessment of costs, limitation upon practice, appointment of a receiver, requiring that a lawyer take continuing legal education or retake all or part of a bar examination, and any other requirement deemed "consistent with the purposes of lawyer sanctions."[63] In determining the appropriate sanction, the Standards list four factors to be considered by a court: the duty violated, the lawyer's mental state, the actual or potential injury caused by the misconduct, and the existence of aggravating and mitigating factors.[64]

Aggravating factors include past discipline, dishonest or selfish motive, a pattern of misconduct or multiple offenses, obstruction of a disciplinary proceeding, refusal to acknowledge responsibility, a vulnerable victim, substantial experience in law practice, and illegal conduct.[65] Mitigating factors encompass personal and emotional problems, physical or mental disability, the absence of prior disciplinary violations or selfish motive, timely efforts to rectify harm, a cooperative attitude toward the disciplinary board, delay in the disciplinary proceedings, inexperience in law practice, good character and reputation, other penalties or sanctions imposed for the same conduct, remorse, and remoteness of prior offenses.[66] Advice of counsel is not a defense, but may be evidence of mitigation if the lawyer disclosed all relevant facts and followed the advice.[67]

One disability that plagues lawyers—substance abuse—has been the cause of a large number of disciplinary complaints. Here, most courts regard successful treatment for substance abuse as a mitigating factor, and failure to seek treatment as an aggravating circumstance.[68] *Walker* also illustrates how a disability can mitigate (but not prevent) a disciplinary sanction, but only if the disability caused the problem and can be accommodated to prevent it in the future.

---

prejudice to lawyer occurred); *In re Porcelli*, 397 N.E.2d 830 (Ill. 1979) (entrapment not available as a defense to a lawyer who paid a police officer to alter a client's blood alcohol report).

62. ABA, *Standards for Imposing Lawyer Sanctions* (1991).

63. *Id.* at Standards 2.1-2.8.

64. *Id.* at Standard 3.0.

65. *Id.* at Standard 9.2.

66. *Id.* at Standard 9.32.

67. *Disc. Counsel v. Levine*, 2006 Haw. LEXIS 118 (reliance on advice may be a mitigating factor, but is not a defense to practicing law while suspended from practice); *Atty. Grievance Comm'n. of Md. v. Johnson*, 876 A.2d 642 (Md. 2005) (lawyer cannot rely on advice of counsel defense or use it as mitigation when she failed to show that she disclosed all facts to her lawyer).

68. *Standards for Imposing Lawyer Sanctions* at Standard 9.32 (mental disability or chemical dependency are mitigating factors only when they caused the misconduct, have been confirmed by medical evidence, and recovery is demonstrated by a meaningful and sustained period of successful rehabilitation, which arrested the misconduct and makes recurrence unlikely).

Part II

Lawyers and Clients: Fiduciary Duty

A lawyer who represents a client agrees to carry on the matter to conclusion. To do this, the lawyer also takes on five basic fiduciary duties: client control concerning the goals of the representation, communication, competence, confidentiality, and conflict of interest resolution—what we call the 5 Cs. This part of the book explores these obligations and the various remedies available to clients if these duties are breached. Because most of these obligations do not exist until a client-lawyer relationship has been created, we begin in Chapter 3 by addressing how and when lawyers create client-lawyer relationships and their concomitant fiduciary duties. First, we take up access to justice issues created by the mismatch between lawyer choice and client need, including court appointments and service *pro bono publico* for the public good. Second, we examine the various ways that clients and lawyers create client-lawyer relationships, including voluntary choice and accidental or unexpected relationships recognized by law as imposing identical legal duties.

Chapter 3

Beginning the Client-Lawyer Relationship

A. Access to Justice

Problems

3-1. Should Martyn & Fox take on the representation of a financially strapped couple who have just been served with a notice of foreclosure on their home? An indigent person seeking to expunge a crime that stands in her way of getting a decent job?

3-2. How should Martyn & Fox respond if a housing court appoints us to represent, *pro bono,* an indigent tenant who says she is being evicted because she tried to force her landlord to repair the building she lives in?

3-3. Should Martyn & Fox ghostwrite a brief for a *pro se* litigant?

Consider: Model Rules 1.2, 6.1, 6.2, 8.4(c)

Bothwell v. Republic Tobacco Co.
912 F. Supp. 1221 (D. Neb. 1995)

Piester, Magistrate Judge.

Before me for consideration is a motion, submitted by plaintiff's appointed counsel, Paula Metcalf, seeking reconsideration and vacation of my order appointing her to represent plaintiff in this case. . . .

BACKGROUND

In March 1994 plaintiff Earl Bothwell, who at the time was incarcerated at the Hastings Correctional Center, submitted to this court a request to proceed in forma pauperis, a civil complaint, and a motion for appointment of counsel. . . .

In his complaint plaintiff alleged that he "immediately ceased" purchasing and smoking factory-manufactured cigarettes after Congress enacted the Federal Cigarette Labeling and Advertisement Act of 1969 ("FCLAA"), 15 U.S.C. § 1333 et seq, which mandated that a warning label be conspicuously placed on packages of such cigarettes. Plaintiff alleged that he thereafter switched to "roll your own" cigarettes, which were not covered by the FCLAA. . . . Plaintiff alleged that he switched to the defendants' products on the belief that, because the government had not mandated warning labels on loose tobacco and because the defendants had not voluntarily issued such warnings, those products were not harmful or hazardous. Plaintiff alleged that in 1986 he became aware that he suffered from emphysema, asthma, heart disease, and "bronchial and other respiratory diseases." He later learned that the loose tobacco products he had been using "were stronger that [sic] [factory-produced] cigarettes and were twice as harmful and deadly." . . .

DISCUSSION

In her brief in support of her motion to reconsider and vacate, Metcalf contends that my order appointing her as counsel is "contrary to law and clearly erroneous" because "a federal court has no statutory or inherent authority to force an attorney to take an ordinary civil case for no compensation."

Statutory Authority

Insofar as concerns statutory authority, Metcalf is correct. Plaintiff in this case is proceeding in forma pauperis pursuant to 28 U.S.C. § 1915(d). In Mallard v. U.S. Dist. Ct., 490 U.S. 296 (1989), the United States Supreme Court held, in a 5-4 decision, that section 1915(d) does not authorize a federal court to require an unwilling attorney to represent an indigent litigant in a civil case. In so holding, the Court focused on the language of section 1915(d), which provides that a court may "request" an attorney to accept a court appointment. . . . However, the Court in *Mallard* left open the question of whether federal courts possess the inherent power to require an unwilling attorney to accept an appointment. . . .

Inherent Authority . . .

Since its inception the federal judiciary has maintained that federal courts possess inherent powers which are not derived from statutes or rules. These inherent powers vest in the courts upon their creation . . . .

[T]he power to conscript lawyers to represent the indigent . . . exists for two primary purposes: (1) to ensure a "fair and just" adjudicative process in individual cases; and (2) to maintain the integrity and viability of the judiciary and of the entire civil justice system. These two purposes mirror the dual functions that lawyers serve in the civil justice system. First, they act as advocates in individual cases working to peacefully resolve civil disputes between citizens. Second, by their ready availability to act in that capacity, they preserve the credibility of the courts as a legitimate arm of the civil justice system. . . .

(1) "Fair and Just" Process in Individual Cases . . .

While it is established that a plaintiff has no constitutional right to counsel in a civil case, counsel nevertheless may be necessary in a particular civil proceeding to ensure fairness and justice in the proceeding and to bring about a fair and just outcome.

The American legal system is adversarial in nature. Gideon v. Wainwright, 372 U.S. 335, 344 (1963). The adversarial system has been embraced because it is believed that truth is best divined in the crucible of cross-examination and adversarial argument. Attorneys, because they are trained in the advocacy skills of cross-examination and argument, are a necessary component in a properly functioning adversarial system. Thus, the notion that the adversarial system is an effective method for ferreting out the truth presumes that both sides have relatively equal access to adequate legal assistance from those trained in the art of advocacy. . . .

If the lack of legal representation is the free choice of the unrepresented party or if it results from factors unrelated to the indigency of the plaintiff, our system is not offended. Where, however, one party is unable to obtain legal representation because of indigency, the resulting disparity of advocacy skills clearly offends the principle of "equality before the law" underlying our system. Further, a substantial disparity in access to legal representation caused by the indigency of one of the parties threatens the adversarial system's ability to produce a just and fair result.

Access to legal representation in this country is gained primarily through the private market. For the most part, the market is an effective mechanism for providing legal services to those who need them. However, the market sometimes fails to provide counsel regardless of the merits of the claims at issue. Where the person whose claims have been rejected by the private market is indigent, he or she may seek representation through a legal aid organization. However, the ability of such organizations to meet the needs of the indigent has taken a serious hit over the past fifteen years in the form of reduced funding to the Legal Services Corporation ("LSC"), the federal entity responsible for funding state and local legal aid offices. . . . Compounding the problem of legal access for the poor is the growing apathy of the private bar to the plight of many indigent litigants. The inevitable net result of these factors is that the poor, indeed most of the so-called "middle class," have less realistic access to advocacy services from lawyers. . . .

I conclude that, when indigency is the principal reason for disparate access to the civil justice system in an individual case, a federal court does possess the inherent authority to bring about a fair and just adjudicative process by conscripting an unwilling lawyer to represent the indigent party. . . .

(2) Preserving the Integrity of the Civil Justice System

The very purposes for the establishment of the judicial branch of government included the peaceful resolution of private disputes between citizens and the protection of the minority from loss of their rights to the majority, either at the ballot box or through force.

In order to be viable in delivering on these goals, a justice system must be both trustworthy and trusted. The judicial branch of our government was created powerless to enforce its own decisions; it relies on the respect of litigants for adherence to the law it declares, or, if necessary, actions of the executive branch. It is, to be sure, a living example of "the consent of the governed." To be accorded respect among the people it serves, it must be perceived as fair. If it is not trusted, it will not be seen as a legitimate means to serve its purposes of peacefully resolving disputes and protecting minority rights. . . .

Lawyers as Officers of the Court . . .

. . . Because the ready availability of lawyers is necessary to ensuring the perception, and indeed the reality, of fairness, their accessibility as officers of the court is necessary not only to the preservation of the justice system itself but to the ordered liberty of our society. . . .

Monopoly of Lawyers

A further justification which has been advanced for the view that attorneys are obligated to comply with court-ordered appointments is the monopoly theory. Under that theory, attorneys must provide legal services to indigents without compensation by virtue of the exclusive privilege they have been granted to practice law. . . .

[C]ritics claim that other groups enjoying monopolies as a result of state licensing, such as doctors, nurses, teachers, insurance agents, brokers, and pharmacists, do not bear an obligation to provide free services to the poor. While that is true, it misses the point. The practice of law—that is, the representation of others before the civil courts—is not simply a private enterprise. It is, in addition, a contribution to society's ability to manage its domestic affairs, a necessary condition of any civilized culture. Attorneys have a unique relationship to government not shared by other licensed groups. This relationship, which has been described as "symbiotic," places attorneys in "an intermediary position between the court and the public" where they are "inextricably linked to the public sector despite [their] dual position as a private businessperson."

By virtue of this special relationship between the bench and the bar, courts are dependent upon attorneys to aid in carrying out the administration of justice. While other professions also contribute to private gain and to the betterment of society's standards of living, no other group holds the exclusive key to meaningful participation in a branch of government and the protection of rights. This monumental difference between attorneys and other licensed groups justifies imposition of different conditions on the practice of the profession.

Ethical Obligation of Lawyers

An additional justification for the court's exercise of inherent power to compel representation is the ethical obligation of attorneys to provide representation to indigent litigants. . . . [The court cites Model Rule 6.1.]

While these obligations are not expressed in mandatory terms, they clearly indicate that service to the indigent is an essential characteristic of any ethical attorney. Two aspects deserve further attention.

First, these moral and ethical obligations to provide legal services to the poor do not exist merely to prompt the practicing lawyer to be a "good" person, respected in the profession. Rather, they are a recognition of the critical role of the lawyer in ensuring the fair and just adjudication of disputes, and the need for such advocacy in ensuring the existence of the system.

Second, these obligations are not self-executing. . . . It makes little sense to give only lip service to these ideals while the legitimacy of the court system is being challenged by other means of resolving private disputes. If our society is to have a legitimate civil justice system, the courts must be empowered to take necessary measures to create and maintain it. In a more genteel and public-spirited time, the mere suggestion by a court that a private attorney should provide free representation might be met with acceptance of the duty as a necessary means to ensure fairness and the justice system itself; perhaps that history contributes to the lack of mandatory requirements today. . . .

Necessity of Exercising Authority

In deciding whether to exercise the authority to compel representation I first note that a court must exercise its inherent powers "with restraint and discretion." The common thread running through inherent powers jurisprudence is the concept of necessity. Thus, while this court possesses the inherent power to compel representation of an indigent plaintiff, the power should be exercised only where reasonably necessary for the administration of justice. In other words, the appointment of counsel must be necessary to bring about a fair and just adjudicative process.

[W]hen determining whether counsel should be appointed for an indigent plaintiff, the court should consider such factors as (1) the factual complexity of the case, (2) the ability of the plaintiff to investigate the facts, (3) the existence of conflicting testimony, (4) the plaintiff's ability to present his claims and (5) the complexity of the legal issues. In re Lane, 801 F.2d 1040, 1043-44 (8th Cir. 1986). An additional factor . . . is the plaintiff's ability to obtain counsel on his own. . . .

I conclude that the plaintiff's failure to obtain private counsel was not the result of his indigency but rather a result of the "marketability," or lack thereof, of his claims. This "marketability" analysis, which I believe to be a proper additional consideration in determining whether to appoint counsel, involves . . . several steps.

The first step in the "marketability" analysis is to ask whether, realistically, there is a "market" of lawyers who practice in the legal area of the plaintiff's claims. Many indigent litigants, particularly prisoners, raise civil rights claims pursuant to 42 U.S.C. § 1983. There are relatively few private attorneys who practice in the area of civil rights. Also, there are few, if any, lawyers willing to assume cases on a contingent-fee basis where the indigent plaintiff primarily seeks forms of relief other than monetary damages, such as injunctive or declaratory relief. As a result, in many cases, there simply is no true "market" to look to when determining whether an indigent plaintiff should be appointed counsel. In such cases, there should be no further inquiry into the "marketability" of a plaintiff's claims. Rather, the appointment of counsel should rest on those other factors commonly used in determining whether to appoint counsel. *See* In re Lane, *supra.*

In cases where such a "market" of lawyers is found to exist, a second question must be addressed: Does the plaintiff have adequate access to that market? This inquiry is necessary for two major reasons. First, many indigent litigants are physically unable to access private counsel regardless of the merits of their claims. This is especially true where the litigant is incarcerated. . . . Second, there may be communication barriers of language or language skills; barriers of physical, emotional, or mental disabilities; or educational or cultural barriers that block understanding between attorney and client. . . . Where a "market" of attorneys exists but a party does not have adequate, realistic access to it, no further "marketability" inquiry is necessary because such inquiry could not yield a reliable conclusion regarding the involvement of indigence as a factor in the litigant's failure to obtain counsel. In such situations, the appointment of counsel should be analyzed using factors from In re Lane, *supra.*

If there is a market and the litigant had realistic access to it, the third step in the "marketability" analysis must be performed. That step requires an examination of the typical fee arrangements used in the particular area of the law implicated by the indigent plaintiff's complaint. Specifically, if contingent-fee or other low-cost financing arrangements are generally available in the area of law and would be feasible for the plaintiff, further examination is proper. . . .

Once it is determined that an accessible market exists, that the plaintiff has the ability to access that market, and that feasible fee arrangements are available, the final and most important step in the analysis must be performed. The court must determine whether the market's rejection of the party's claims was the result of indigency, for, as noted above, indigency is the touchstone which authorizes the court to exercise the inherent power to correct unequal access to advocacy services. There are many factors to consider when a lawyer is approached about taking a person's claims into litigation. These factors might include, but would not be limited to, the merits of the claims; the existence of precedent to support the claims; the costs of investigating the claims, handling the discovery needed to prepare the case for trial, and trying the case; the relationship of those costs to the amount of a likely recovery, discounted by the probability of recovery; the lawyer's time available to pursue the claims and the impact upon his/her other practice obligations, as well as upon those of partners or associates; the likeability of the litigant;[18] the popularity of the claims; and

---

18. While even the most despicable character is, by rights, entitled to the same access to the courts to voice his grievances as is the most attractive, wealthy, and urbane individual, the private market may exclude the former from access because of this intangible factor. It is not inappropriate for a court to consider this factor in determining whether the plaintiff's personal characteristics might have been a force behind the market's rejection of his claims.

the potential settlement value of the claims. So long as the market's rejection of the claims was based on the interplay of these and other such factors, and not on the indigency of the plaintiff, the notions of equal justice discussed above are not offended and compelling an attorney to represent that plaintiff is not necessary to the achievement of a fair and just adjudicative process.

Applying the foregoing "marketability" analysis to this case, I first conclude that there was an adequate "market" of lawyers practicing in the general area of plaintiff's claims. Plaintiff raises product liability claims, as opposed to civil rights claims under 42 U.S.C. § 1983. As such, a greater number of private attorneys were available to represent him than would be for a typical indigent litigant. The potential for joining a class action lawsuit against the tobacco companies further enhanced the "market" that was available to plaintiff. In sum, there was a realistic "market" of lawyers who could litigate the claims raised by plaintiff.

I further conclude that plaintiff had ready access to that "market" of lawyers. Plaintiff is not incarcerated nor has he alleged any other substantial barriers[20] which might have prevented him from communicating with private attorneys. He thus had the unfettered ability to communicate with private attorneys in his immediate locale and elsewhere. Additionally, many of the attorneys who work in products liability and personal injury claims do so on a contingent fee basis. . . . Under a contingent fee arrangement, there typically is no requirement that the plaintiff advance costs, although the plaintiff would remain liable for them ultimately. Thus, despite plaintiff's indigency, there were feasible fee arrangements available to plaintiff.

The foregoing factors indicate that, unlike most cases initiated by indigent litigants, there was a "market" of private attorneys for plaintiff's claims and that, unlike most indigent litigants, plaintiff had open access to that market and has, in fact, accessed that market, albeit unsuccessfully. It thus is proper to determine whether that market's rejection of plaintiff's claims was the result of his indigency.

I conclude that it was not. The mere existence of indigency as a condition of the plaintiff did not prevent him from suggesting to lawyers that they consider his claims. Rather, he has had the same opportunity as middle- or upper-class plaintiffs to subject his claims to the scrutiny of tort attorneys. That this "market" of attorneys has thus far rejected his claims is the result of factors unrelated to his indigency. Primary among these factors is undoubtedly the enormous cost of litigating claims against tobacco companies. . . .

Plaintiff asserts that most of the attorneys he contacted requested payment of a retainer which he was unable to afford. However, due to the enormous costs involved in this type of litigation and the unlikelihood of settlement, the amount of money required for an adequate retainer would likely be so great that even a middle-class or upper-middle-class citizen would be unable to afford it. As such, the rejection of plaintiff's claims was not based on his indigency, but rather

---

20. While plaintiff has alleged health problems, he presents no evidence indicating that these problems would inhibit him from seeking out counsel either in person or via telephone or mail.

on marketability factors such as the expenses involved and the unlikelihood of settlement.

Because it is the lack of marketability of his claims, as opposed to his indigency, which has prevented plaintiff from obtaining counsel, the notions of equal justice discussed above have not been offended. As such, it is not reasonably necessary to the administration of justice for this court to compel Metcalf to represent plaintiff. Accordingly, I shall not exercise this court's inherent authority to do so.

Lawyers and Clients: *Service Pro Bono Publico*

This series of notes, entitled "Lawyers and Clients," focuses on five groups of clients served by substantial numbers of lawyers. In each situation, we will examine the same three topics: First, who are the clients? Second, what is the special significance of the "5 Cs" fiduciary duties that lawyers owe this group of clients? Finally, what are the "bounds of the law" (including specialized legal regulation of the client's rights and responsibilities) that could shape or limit a lawyer's advocacy on behalf of that particular client? We begin by turning our attention to that large segment of the public served by a far too small group of lawyers: those without access to lawyers due to their modest means.

Access to justice in America remains elusive for most of the poor and much of the middle class. This concern is not new. In 1919, Reginald Heber Smith wrote that without equal access to the law, "[t]he system not only robs the poor of their only protection, but it places in the hands of their oppressors the most powerful and ruthless weapon ever invented."[1]

There are three different approaches that can be employed to address these needs. The first accepts public responsibility for access to justice, a goal that can be accomplished by creating legal rights to representation, publicly funding legal services programs, and simplifying legal procedures. The second approach focuses on a duty of individual lawyers to serve as court-appointed counsel or provide free or reduced-rate services *pro bono publico*, for the common good. *Bothwell* accepts both of these justifications, by acknowledging public judicial responsibility for counsel to preserve the credibility of the courts as a legitimate civil justice system and by appointing counsel to serve without pay when necessary to achieve justice in a particular case. The third approach stresses deregulation, which would permit unlicensed persons or institutions to provide some kinds of legal assistance. To date, none of these strategies has gone far enough in its implementation to alleviate the lack of access to justice in civil cases.

The Clients

The disparity between lawyers available to paying clients and those available to serve the poor explains why, for at least the past century, judges have exercised

---

1. Reginald Heber Smith, *Justice and the Poor, A Study of the Present Denial of Justice to the Poor and of the Agencies Making More Equal Their Position Before the Law with Particular Reference to Legal Aid Work in the United States* 9 (Carnegie Found. 1919).

their inherent power to offset this imbalance, first in criminal and then occasion-ally in civil cases.[2] In civil cases, *Bothwell* represents the modern trend, which recognizes the inherent judicial power to appoint lawyers in individual cases when necessary to ensure the principle of equality before the law.[3] Model Rule 6.2 reflects these developments by requiring lawyers to accept such appoint-ments unless the lawyers can present very weighty reasons to decline.[4]

Although America has a very good civil legal system and has no overall short-age of lawyers, the access gap between rich and poor continues to expand simply because access to lawyers is determined largely by market forces.[5] Currently, only one legal service lawyer is available to serve 6,415 eligible persons. This compares unfavorably with one lawyer for every 429 persons who are able to pay.[6] In the past two decades, private funding from foundations, charitable gifts, and state Interest on Lawyer Trust Accounts (IOLTA) programs have made up for some of the loss of federal money originally pledged to fund the Legal Services Corporation.[7] But in spite of these innovative alternative funding approaches, dozens of well-executed empirical studies conducted over the past two decades document that, even with the best voluntary pro bono programs and creatively financed legal services offices, lawyers address far less than half the legal needs of the poor.[8]

---

2. Other countries and international organizations have recognized the duty of lawyers and govern-ments to provide legal services to those who cannot afford to pay. *See* James Moliterno & George Harris, *Global Issues in Legal Ethics* 69-80 (Thomson West 2007).

3. *See also* Burke v. Lewis, 122 P.3d 533 (Utah 2005) (absent physician defendant in medical mal-practice case entitled to court-appointed counsel to preserve rights against malpractice insurer); Zimmerman v. Hanks, 766 N.E.2d 752 (Ind. App. 2002) (prison inmate had statutory right to appointed counsel in civil case).

4. *E.g.* St. ex rel. Missouri Public Defender Commn. v. Waters, 370 S.W.3d 592 (Mo. 2012) (ethics rules that require competent and diligent representation require trial judge to refrain from appoint-ing a public defender's office to represent an accused in violation of the office's administrative rule on "caseload protocol" that allows lawyers to decline further appointments when they have exceeded their capacity to take cases).

5. World Justice Project, *Rule of Law Index, available at* http://worldjusticeproject.org/sites/default/files/USA_CP.pdf (last visited June 20, 2012).

6. Legal Services Corporation, *Documenting the Justice Gap in America* 15, 22 (2009), *available at* http://www.lsc.gov/sites/default/files/LSC/pdfs/documenting_the_justice_gap_in_america_2009.pdf. In 1960 (when voluntary legal aid projects served less than 1 percent of those in need), the ratio of lawyers available to poor clients (those at or below the poverty level) was 1:120,000. By 1980, when legal services funding reached its height, the ratio had improved to 1:5,000. National Legal Aid & Defender Association, *History of Civil Legal Aid, available at* http://www.nlada.org/About/About_HistoryCivil (last visited July 12, 2012).

7. In 2009, LSC denied service to about 50 percent of those seeking representation due to inad-equate resources. *Justice Gap, supra* note 5, at 12. IOLTA funds, discussed in more detail in Chapter 12, also help fund criminal defense representation by public defender offices in many jurisdictions.

8 *Justice Gap, supra* note 5, at 18 (no more than 20 percent of legal needs of the poor are met); *See also* Rebecca L. Sandefur & Aaron C. Smyth, *Access Across America*, American Bar Foundation (Oct. 7, 2011), *available at* http://www.americanbarfoundation.org/uploads/cms/documents/access_across_america_first_report_of_the_civil_justice_infrastructure_mapping_project.pdf ("civil justice infrastructure is characterized by large inequalities both between states and within them").

Put simply, the law does not work for everyone. For those who lack resources, the rule of law is replaced by markets, power, organizations, wealth, and politics.[9] Neglected legal matters involve personal finances and consumer issues, housing and real property matters, domestic disputes, and employment-related problems.[10] Those who must seek a court intervention often appear pro se.[11] This lack of legal counsel is rendered more tragic when one is reminded of what every law student and lawyer knows: those able to obtain a lawyer get significantly better results.[12]

The 5 Cs: Fiduciary Duties

Both lawyer codes and common law impose five fiduciary duties on lawyers who agree to represent clients, regardless of the client's ability to pay. Lawyers owe clients affirmative duties of control over the objectives of the representation, communication, competence, confidentiality, and conflict of interest resolution. Several of these fiduciary obligations take on special significance in providing legal services to persons of limited means.

Control, Communication, and Competence   To provide more clients with legal services, some lawyers are experimenting with unbundling legal services, delivering legal services à la carte rather than assuming full-service representations.[13] They might, for example, help a pro se litigant with a discrete task, such as preparation of pleadings or a trial court brief, or assist a person in drafting a letter or document. Lawyers who offer unbundled services often refer to themselves as "client coaches" who perform some, but not all, aspects of a legal representation.

---

9. Gillian Hadfield, *Higher Demand, Lower Supply? A Comparative Assessment of the Legal Resource Landscape for Ordinary Americans,* 37 Fordham Urb. L. J. 129, 143 (2010).

10. ABA Consortium on Legal Services and the Public, *Legal Needs and Civil Justice: A Survey of Americans* 23 (1994). Low-income households were defined as those at 125 percent of the official U.S. poverty line or less, Moderate-income households as those just above this mark but earning less than $60,000 per year in 1992. *Id.* at 1. *Available at* http://www.abanet.org/legalservices/downloads/sclaid/legalneedstudy.pdf (last visited Nov. 29, 2011).

Over half of those persons, especially those who tried to handle the matter themselves or did nothing, were dissatisfied with the result. On the other hand, those few who did take a serious legal matter to the civil justice system reported the highest satisfaction with the result, 48 percent for low-income individuals and 64 percent for those of moderate means. *Id.* at 17-18.

11. *See, e.g.,* Richard W. Painter, *Pro Se Litigation in Times of Financial Hardship—A Legal Crisis and Its Solutions,* 45 Fam. L. Q. 45 (2011); Judith G. McMullen and Debra Oswald, *Why Do We Need a Lawyer?: An Empirical Study of Divorce Cases,* 12 J. Law and Fam. Studies 57 (2010).

12. *E.g.,* Carroll Seron, Gregg Van Ryzin, & Martin Frankel, *The Impact of Legal Counsel on Outcomes for Poor Tenants in New York City's Housing Court: Results of a Randomized Experiment,* 35 Law & Socy. Rev. 419 (2001) (legal counsel provided to poor tenants produced large differences in outcome independent of the merits of the case).

13. *See* Stephanie L. Kimbro, *Limited Scope Legal Services: Unbundling and the Self-Help Client* (ABA Law Prac. Mgt. 2012); Forrest S. Mosten, *Unbundling Legal Services: A Guide to Delivering Legal Services a la Carte* (ABA Law Prac. Mgt. 2000).

Some lawyers provide such services free of charge as part of a nonprofit or court-annexed limited legal services program or hotline.[14]

Unbundling proponents encourage lawyers to break down current legal services into discrete tasks, such as advice, legal research, fact gathering, negotiation, document drafting, or court representation. Proponents also seek to break up legal representation by issues, such as custody, visitation, property valuation (real, personal, business, investments, pensions, etc.), or insurance benefits.[15] A client then is offered a menu of these separate tasks and issues and is given the opportunity to select those that fit the client's budget, or reject those the client most thinks he or she can handle alone.

Unbundling challenges three core fiduciary duties: control, communication, and competence. First, unbundling assumes that clients will assume control over aspects of a matter typically undertaken by lawyers. Second, it therefore imposes special communication obligations on lawyers so that clients can understand the client's expanded role. Third, because unbundling means less than a full representation, the lawyer's duty of competence must be fulfilled in a unique manner. Model Rule 1.2(c) recognizes the ability of client and lawyer to agree to these limited scope representations, but only if the limitation is reasonable and the client gives informed consent.[16]

Indeed, the success of unbundling depends on a competent lawyer who is able to identify all aspects of the matter, clarify that handling less than all aspects is reasonable, and communicate "adequate information" about the risks and alternatives to unbundled service to obtain the client's "informed consent." In short, lawyers must provide competent representation with respect to those items the client cedes to the lawyer and adequate advice to the client about how to accomplish the rest.[17]

Some lawyers asked to provide certain pro bono services express concerns about their competence because they fear they lack the ability to handle a pro bono client legal matter outside of their regular practice parameters. Although such fears are much less often expressed with respect to new matters raised by

---

14. *See, e.g.,* N.C. Formal Op. 10 (2005) (Virtual Law Practice and Unbundled Legal Services). Hotlines offer effective service when callers understand what they are told to do and follow the advice given. Follow-ups with written instructions also improve client success. But certain kinds of cases, such as those dealing with government agencies and those involving family law matters, often require more extensive assistance. Special protocols are necessary for non-English-speaking callers, those with very low education levels, and those who report no income. Center for Policy Research, *Final Report—The Hotline Outcomes Assessment Study* (2002), *available at* http://www.nlada.org/DMS/Documents/1037903536.22/finalhlreport.pdf.

15. Mosten, *supra* note 12, at 50, 51.

16. MR 1.2(c); RLGL § 19 (significant differences in outcome may mean a limited service is not reasonable); *See, e.g.,* D. James Greiner, Cassandra Wolos Pattanayak, & Jonathan Hennessy, *The Limits of Unbundled Legal Assistance: A Randomized Study in a Massachusetts District Court and Prospects for the Future* 125 Harv. L. Rev. (2012) (two thirds of housing defendants given full representation retained possession of their units versus only one third of those provided unbundled limited assistance).

17. Mosten, *supra* note 12, at 29, 92-97; ABA Formal Op. 07-446 (Undisclosed Legal Assistance to *Pro Se* Litigants).

paying clients, in some cases those concerns are real. As a result, lawyers and judges aware of this situation have created a number of innovative voluntary pro bono programs, all of which provide education and support for lawyers seeking to provide competent pro bono services.[18] Similar programs encourage or require pro bono participation in law school.[19]

These voluntary pro bono projects have helped many, but they have never been enough. This is why another alternative, mandatory pro bono service, has been proposed.[20] Vehement opposition by lawyers has followed each proposal, which has led to current Model Rule 6.1's admonition that lawyers "should," but are not required to, render such service. This basic duty remains aspirational, but the text has been changed to quantify the recommended service at 50 hours per year and, in 2002, the rule was amended to add language that tiptoes close to a mandate: "Every lawyer has the professional responsibility to provide legal services to those unable to pay."

To date, mandatory pro bono service has been officially adopted by only one jurisdiction, New York, and only for one segment of the "bar"— those seeking admission to practice.[21] Proponents of mandatory rules agree with *Bothwell* that one basis for such a duty is the monopoly on the provision of legal services (including access to justice) that lawyers enjoy.[22] Most state proposals also seek to avoid begrudgingly provided forced service by including a buyout provision, which would enable an individual lawyer to make a payment to a legal services agency in lieu of personally providing legal services.

An intermediate option, mandatory reporting of pro bono activity, has been adopted in several states.[23] These reporting requirements do not require any pro

---

18. *See* Scott L. Cummings & Deborah L. Rhode, *Managing Pro Bono: Doing Well by Doing Better*, 78 Fordham L. Rev. 2357 (2010); *See, e.g., The Support Center for Child Advocates, available at* http://www.advokid.org (last visited June 20, 2012), an innovative Philadelphia-based program that provides lawyers for children who find themselves parties to family court proceedings and whose interests otherwise might go unrepresented; American Bar Association (ABA), *Death Penalty Representation Project, available at* http://www.americanbar.org/advocacy/other_aba_initiatives/ death_penalty_representation.html (last visited June 20, 2012), which has provided lawyers to hundreds of prisoners on death row who have no counsel to represent them in *habeas corpus* proceedings; Corporate Pro Bono, http://www.corporateprobono.org (last visited June 20, 2012), a program that works with in-house counsel to encourage their participation in community pro bono efforts.

19. One empirical study indicates that lawyers accustomed to pro bono service in law school offer much more pro bono service as lawyers than do students who attended law schools where pro bono was ignored or encouraged, rather than required. Deborah L. Rhode, *Pro Bono in Principle and in Practice: Public Service and the Professions* 154-165 (Stanford U. Press 2005).

20. The first mandatory pro bono proposal was made in 1980, when the ABA's Kutak Commission circulated a discussion draft of Rule 6.1.

21. *See* New York State Board of Bar Examiners, *available at* http://www.nybarexam.org/ (last visited June 18, 2012) (50-hour prerequisite for bar admission).

22. Rhode, *Pro Bono in Principle and Practice, supra* note 18, at 26.

23. *See, e.g.,* Ill. S. Ct. R. 756(f) (2007); Schwarz v. Kogan, 132 F.3d 1387 (11th Cir. 1998) (upholding the constitutionality of Florida's rule that requires a report of compliance on each annual bar dues statement with its aspirational goal of 20 hours or a contribution of $350 to a legal aid organization).

bono representation, but have, in fact, increased voluntary pro bono service.[24] It could be that reporting requirements remind lawyers that the need for pro bono legal assistance is great. It is also possible that lawyers report pro bono service because they fear peer or official disapproval or worry that the reporting requirement could become the precursor to a mandatory service requirement.

Confidentiality and Conflict of Interest Resolution   Because pro bono clients are entitled to the same measure of confidentiality[25] and loyalty[26] due all other clients,[27] private lawyers who offer pro bono services face the prospect that information from or service to a pro bono client could impose professional responsibility implications for their representation of other clients. In addition, three Model Rules address specific conflicts of interest that have arisen in pro bono service. Model Rule 6.3 allows lawyers who serve on legal services organizations' boards or projects to disregard any general adverse interests of their paying clients, but prohibits them from participating in specific decisions incompatible with their obligations to either private or legal services organization clients. Model Rule 6.4 creates similar provisions for lawyers who serve on the boards of law reform organizations. Model Rule 6.5 facilitates limited-term legal services programs, such as hotlines or help desks.[28] It encourages private lawyers to provide pro bono service to clients in these programs by temporarily suspending some conflict of interest requirements. Lawyers who, without any research, recognize a conflict with a private client cannot offer advice, but otherwise, lawyers are not required to do a conflicts check of a law firm database before rendering this assistance.

The Bounds of the Law

A number of solutions to remedy the problem of access to justice go beyond public payment and lawyer pro bono service. Many argue that legal procedures and rules that govern recurring situations should be simplified. Proposals include increased use of court personnel to assist pro se litigants, more small claims courts, more accessible ADR procedures such as mediation, or plain English regulations that simplify current complex legal provisions or remedies.[29]

---

24. Rhode, *Pro Bono in Principle and in Practice, supra* note 18, at 45.
25. MR 1.6, 1.8(b), 1.18; RLGL §§ 59, 60, 68, 87; Dep't. of Children & Family Servs. v. Shadonna, 58 Cal.Rptr. 3d 173 (Cal. App. 2007) (former client of publicly funded nonprofit law office can seek disqualification if she shows a reasonable possibility that material confidential information relating to the former representation has been obtained).
26. MR 1.7-1.10; RLGL §§ 121-135.
27. *See, e.g.,* Tenn. Formal Op. 2005-F-151 (ethical responsibilities of legal services organization lawyers in pilot program to provide limited legal services to otherwise pro se litigants in domestic relations matters).
28. Deborah L. Rhode, *Public Interest Law: The Movement at Midlife*, 60 Stanford L. Rev. 2027 (2008).
29. Deborah L. Rhode, *Access to Justice* 189-191 (Oxford U. Press 2004).

Some courts have recognized that court rules create obstacles to unbundled pro se representation.[30] Typical provisions require the lawyer who offers any assistance to a litigant to enter an appearance on behalf of a client, thereby creating a full-scale representation. FRCP 11 and state equivalents require lawyers who prepare pleadings to sign them. But a pro se litigant or a lawyer might wish to prepare a pleading that the litigant herself signs,[31] or a lawyer might wish to ghostwrite a trial court brief for a client. Some jurisdictions require lawyers to notify the court about their assistance because failure to do so is characterized as a fraudulent practice.[32] Others recognize a limited appearance, either by only requiring disclosure of the limited assistance,[33] or by exempting lawyers who perform specific tasks from any disclosure obligation.[34]

Other proposals recommend changes to current unauthorized practice rules that prevent nonlawyers from providing legal services.[35] One way to do this is to recognize the ability of nonprofits to hire lawyers to pursue their mission through direct client service.[36] Although the ABA has recommended that jurisdictional

---

30. *See, e.g.,* In re Liu, 664 F.2d 367 (2d Cir. 2011) (undisclosed ghostwriting did not violate lawyer's duty of candor to the court). Pro se representation is especially common in high-volume state courts, such as traffic, housing, and small claims, but it is increasing in other civil matters as well. *Id. See also* Winkelman v. Parma City Sch. Dist., 127 S. Ct. 1994 (2007) (parents of disabled children may pursue lawsuit and appeal on behalf of child pro se).

31. In some jurisdictions, signing a pleading indicates entering an appearance in the matter, a result neither lawyer nor client desire. Signing a pleading also triggers affirmations about fact and law checking that the client, but not the lawyer, has undertaken. *See* ABA Standing Committee on the Delivery of Legal Services, *An Analysis of Rules that Enable Lawyers to Serve Pro Se Litigants* 4 (2005), *available at* http://www.ajs.org/prose/Midwest%20Notebook%20Contents/Tab%205/Analysis%20of%20Rules%20-%20White%20Paper%20by%20ABA.pdf.

32. *E.g.,* Colo. C.R.C.P. 11(b) (2007); Wash. C.R. 11(b) (2007). *See also,* Davis v. Bacigallupi, 711 F. Supp. 2d 609, 626 (E. D. Va. 2010) ("Ghost-Writer Warning").

33. *E.g.,* Nev. R. Prac. 5.28(a) (2006) (limitations on scope of the representation must be disclosed in the first paragraph of the first paper or pleading filed); Fla. R. Prof. Conduct 4-1.2 comment (2006) (lawyer who assists a pro se litigant not required to sign document, but is required to state "prepared with the assistance of counsel"); Me. R. Prof. Conduct 3.4(i) (2007) (lawyer may file a limited appearance on behalf of a client); N.M. R. Prof. Conduct 16-303(e) (2007) (limited appearance must be disclosed to court).

34. *E.g.,* Tenn. Formal Op. 2007-F-153 (lawyers who help pro se litigants draft pleadings are not required to disclose their involvement to opponent or court so long as there is no continuing aid that will mislead others); Cal. R. Ct. 5.70(a) (2007) (lawyer who drafts documents in family law case not required to disclose involvement).

35. *See, e.g.,* Deborah L. Rhode, *Access to Justice, supra* note 28. Washington is the first jurisdiction to adopt a Limited Practice Rule for Limited License Legal Technicians, which establishes a framework for the licensing and regulation of nonlawyer licensed technicians to provide pro se customers assistance without the supervision of a lawyer in selecting and completing court forms, informing clients of court procedures and deadlines, reviewing and explaining pleadings, and identifying relevant documents necessary for a court proceeding. *See* http://www.courts.wa.gov/content/publicUpload/Press%20Releases/25700-A-1005.pdf (last visited July 12, 2012).

36. *E.g.,* Mo. Formal Op. 121 (2006) (nonprofit battered woman's shelter may employ lawyers to provide legal services to its clients so long as no fee is charged and the nonprofit does not interfere with client–lawyer relationship).

practice limitations be eased on lawyers during major disasters,[37] deregulation that would allow nonlawyers to compete with lawyers will undoubtedly continue to prove unacceptable to the practicing bar.[38] Complete deregulation might mean that nonlawyers could offer all kinds of legal assistance outside of court proceedings, such as drafting wills and tax forms, handling corporate and real estate transactions, collecting debts, and providing divorce or adoption services. Most of these measures would require reversal of current unauthorized practice restrictions, discussed in Chapter 15. On the other hand, the grudging acceptance by the legal profession of accountants and realtors who have established unique but overlapping turf with lawyers might mean that other allied professionals could one day become separately licensed or certified with distinct roles in the legal system.

The Future

So long as the "practice of law" is limited to licensed lawyers and government funds are inadequate to pay for civil legal services, lawyers will be left to shoulder the responsibility for the public's access to justice. Current voluntary pro bono efforts, although innovative, still fall far short of meeting the need for legal services. Most commentators see a continuing need for a network of alternatives.[39] Nearly all proposals see lawyer and law student pro bono work as an indispensable element of an overall plan,[40] and many argue that mandatory pro bono would not only provide more legal services to those unable to pay, but also would provide lawyers with a sense of personal and professional fulfillment that many are not able to achieve in practice.[41] Most proposals also focus on increased public funding, through federal and state grants, IOLTA, filing fee surcharges or service taxes on for-profit legal services, allocating punitive damage or unpaid class actions funds to a civil justice fund, and improved fee awards for successful poor claimants who establish entitlement to public benefits.[42] Many experts also envision simplified legal processes, ADR procedures, and the certifying of paraprofessionals.[43]

---

37. *See* ABA, *Model Court Rule Relaxing Licensing Requirements During Major Disasters* (Feb. 2007) *available at* http://www.americanbar.org/content/dam/aba/migrated/cpr/clientpro/Recom_Report_Katrina.authcheckdam.pdf; Douglas L. Colbert, *Professional Responsibility in Crisis*, 51 Howard L. J. 677 (2008).

38. *See, e.g.,* ABA, *Nonlawyer Activity in Law-Related Situations: A Report with Recommendations* (1995).

39. Roger C. Cramton, *Delivery of Legal Services to Ordinary Americans*, 44 Case W. Res. L. Rev. 531 (1994).

40. *Id.*; Deborah L. Rhode, *Access to Justice, supra* note 28; *Recommendations of the Conference on the Delivery of Legal Services to Low-Income Persons*, 67 Fordham L. Rev. 1751 (1999). On law students, *see* Equal Justice Works, http://www.equaljusticeworks.org (last visited June 20, 2012).

41. *See, e.g.,* Lawrence J. Fox, *Should We Mandate Doing Well by Doing Good?* 33 Fordham Urb. L.J. 249 (2005); Rhode, *Pro Bono in Principle and in Practice, supra* note 18, at 29-31.

42. Talbot D'Alemberte, *Tributaries of Justice: The Search for Full Access*, 25 Fla. St. U. L. Rev. 631 (1998).

43. *E.g.,* Deborah L. Rhode, *Access to Justice, supra* note 28.

To date, the simple truth is that we lack the political will to provide equal access to justice, just as we lack the political will to provide equal access to housing, health care, child care, and education. Yet the lack of access to justice differs from the lack of access to these other essential services because providing legal services nearly always depends on advocating a particular point of view that will affect at least one other person's interest. This means that lack of legal representation not only deprives the poor and middle class of access to redress for a legal wrong, but also creates the opportunity for dishonest or exploitive conduct by those in a position to capitalize on this disparity. This is why some argue that lawyers who assist paying clients in a system fraught with misdistribution of legal services have a moral obligation to either provide legal services to those who lack access or to consider the impact of their work on those without representation.[44]

Ultimately, *Bothwell* reminds us that the fairness of the legal representation provided by a largely market-driven system will be affected by the economic differences among those it serves. Because lawyers benefit substantially from this system, we cannot avoid the reality of this unequal access. As you work through the materials that follow, consider how a lawyer's role depends on a reasonably just legal system, and how lack of access to that system undermines confidence in the justice the legal system produces.

B. Actual and Implied Client-Lawyer Relationships

Problems

3-4. Should Martyn & Fox represent Credit Suisse in a case brought by descendants of Holocaust victims who deposited money in the bank before World War II?

3-5. Martyn is detailed by her commanding officer to represent Omar Abdullah before a military commission at Guantanamo. When Martyn meets with Mr. Abdullah, he tells her he wants to represent himself. Martyn explains that the rules of the commission do not permit self-representation. "You'll be better off with me," Martyn explains in some detail. Mr. Abdullah, persists. What is Martyn to do?

3-6. Fox really likes posting Q & A's on Martyn & Fox's new website. Yesterday a website visitor asked: "I really like the idea of being the sole director of a nonprofit because then I can't be fired. Can I do this?" Fox responded: "Our state nonprofit statute permits having one director, but the IRS may raise questions about tax-exempt status if the sole director is also a paid employee of the nonprofit. You might have an advisory board set your salary to minimize questions about your 501(c)(3) status. Call me with any questions." Okay?

Consider: Model Rules Scope ¶ [17]; 1.18, 6.4
RLGL §§ 14, 15

---

44. Kathleen Clark, *Legal Ethics: The Lawful and the Just: Moral Implications of Unequal Access to Legal Services,* 2 J. Inst. Stud. Leg. Eth. 289 (1999).

Togstad v. Vesely, Otto, Miller & Keefe

291 N.W.2d 686 (Minn. 1980)

PER CURIAM.

This is an appeal by the defendants from a judgment of the Hennepin County District Court involving an action for legal malpractice. The jury found that the defendant attorney Jerre Miller was negligent and that, as a direct result of such negligence, plaintiff John Togstad sustained damages in the amount of $610,500 and his wife, plaintiff Joan Togstad, in the amount of $39,000. . . .

In August, 1971, John Togstad began to experience severe headaches and on August 16, 1971, was admitted to Methodist Hospital where tests disclosed that the headaches were caused by a large aneurism of the left internal carotid artery. The attending physician, Dr. Paul Blake, a neurological surgeon, treated the problem by applying a Selverstone clamp to the left common carotid artery. The clamp was surgically implanted on August 27, 1971, in Togstad's neck to allow the gradual closure of the artery over a period of days. . . .

In the early morning hours of August 29, 1971, a nurse observed that Togstad was unable to speak or move. . . . Togstad is now severely paralyzed in his right arm and leg, and is unable to speak.

Plaintiff's expert, Dr. Ward Woods, testified that Togstad's paralysis and loss of speech was due to a lack of blood supply to his brain . . . [which] resulted from the clamp being 50% closed and that the negligence of Dr. Blake and the hospital precluded the clamp's being opened in time to avoid permanent brain damage. . . .

About 14 months after her husband's hospitalization began, plaintiff Joan Togstad met with attorney Jerre Miller regarding her husband's condition. Neither she nor her husband was personally acquainted with Miller or his law firm prior to that time. John Togstad's former work supervisor, Ted Bucholz, made the appointment and accompanied Mrs. Togstad to Miller's office. Bucholz was present when Mrs. Togstad and Miller discussed the case.

Mrs. Togstad had become suspicious of the circumstances surrounding her husband's tragic condition due to the conduct and statements of the hospital nurses shortly after the paralysis occurred. One nurse told Mrs. Togstad that she had checked Mr. Togstad at 2 a.m. and he was fine; that when she returned at 3 a.m., by mistake, to give him someone else's medication, he was unable to move or speak; and that if she hadn't accidentally entered the room no one would have discovered his condition until morning. Mrs. Togstad also noticed that the other nurses were upset and crying, and that Mr. Togstad's condition was a topic of conversation.

Mrs. Togstad testified that she told Miller "everything that happened at the hospital," including the nurses' statements and conduct which had raised a question in her mind. She stated that she "believed" she had told Miller "about the procedure and what was undertaken, what was done, and what happened." She brought no records with her. Miller took notes and asked questions during the meeting, which lasted 45 minutes to an hour. At its conclusion, according to Mrs. Togstad, Miller said that "he did not think we had a legal case, however, he was going to discuss this with his partner." She understood that if Miller changed his mind after talking to his partner, he would call her. Mrs. Togstad "gave it" a few days and, since she did not hear from Miller, decided "that they had come to the conclusion that there wasn't a case." No fee arrangements were discussed, no medical authorizations were requested, nor was Mrs. Togstad billed for the interview.

Mrs. Togstad denied that Miller had told her his firm did not have expertise in the medical malpractice field, urged her to see another attorney, or related to her that the statute of limitations for medical malpractice actions was two years. She did not consult another attorney until one year after she talked to Miller. Mrs. Togstad indicated that she did not confer with another attorney earlier because of her reliance on Miller's "legal advice" that they "did not have a case."

On cross-examination, Mrs. Togstad was asked whether she went to Miller's office "to see if he would take the case of [her] husband . . . . " She replied, "Well, I guess it was to go for legal advice, what to do, where shall we go from here? That is what we went for." Again in response to defense counsel's questions, Mrs. Togstad testified as follows:

Q   And it was clear to you, was it not, that what was taking place was a preliminary discussion between a prospective client and lawyer as to whether or not they wanted to enter into an attorney-client relationship?

A   I am not sure how to answer that. It was for legal advice as to what to do.

Q   And Mr. Miller was discussing with you your problem and indicating whether he, as a lawyer, wished to take the case, isn't that true?

A   Yes.

On re-direct examination, Mrs. Togstad acknowledged that when she left Miller's office she understood that she had been given a "qualified, quality legal opinion that [she and her husband] did not have a malpractice case."

Miller's testimony was different in some respects from that of Mrs. Togstad. Like Mrs. Togstad, Miller testified that Mr. Bucholz arranged and was present at the meeting, which lasted about 45 minutes. According to Miller, Mrs. Togstad described the hospital incident, including the conduct of the nurses. He asked her questions, to which she responded. Miller testified that "the only thing I told her [Mrs. Togstad] after we had pretty much finished the conversation was that there was nothing related in her factual circumstances that told me that she had a case that our firm would be interested in undertaking."

Miller also claimed he related to Mrs. Togstad "that because of the grievous nature of the injuries sustained by her husband, that this was only my opinion and she was encouraged to ask another attorney if she wished for another opinion" and "she ought to do so promptly." He testified that he informed Mrs. Togstad that his firm "was not engaged as experts" in the area of medical malpractice, and that they associated with the Charles Hvass firm in cases of that nature. Miller stated that at the end of the conference he told Mrs. Togstad that he would consult with Charles Hvass and if Hvass's opinion differed from his, Miller would so inform her. Miller recollected that he called Hvass a "couple days" later and discussed the case with him. It was Miller's impression that Hvass thought there was no liability for malpractice in the case. Consequently, Miller did not communicate with Mrs. Togstad further.

On cross-examination, Miller testified as follows:

Q   Now, so there is no misunderstanding, and I am reading from your deposition, you understood that she was consulting with you as a lawyer, isn't that correct?

A   That's correct.

Q   That she was seeking legal advice from a professional attorney licensed to practice in this state and in this community?

A   I think you and I did have another interpretation or use of the term "Advice." She was there to see whether or not she had a case and whether the firm would accept it.

Q   We have two aspects; number one, your legal opinion concerning liability of a case for malpractice; number two, whether there was or wasn't liability, whether you would accept it, your firm, two separate elements, right?

A   I would say so. . . .

Kenneth Green, a Minneapolis attorney, was called as an expert by plaintiffs. He stated that in rendering legal advice regarding a claim of medical malpractice, the "minimum" an attorney should do would be to request medical authorizations from the client, review the hospital records, and consult with an expert in the field. John McNulty, a Minneapolis attorney, and Charles Hvass testified as experts on behalf of the defendants. McNulty stated that when an attorney is consulted as to whether he will take a case, the lawyer's only responsibility in refusing it is to so inform the party. He testified, however, that when a lawyer is asked his legal opinion on the merits of a medical malpractice claim, community standards require that the attorney check hospital records and consult with an expert before rendering his opinion.

Hvass stated that he had no recollection of Miller's calling him in October 1972 relative to the Togstad matter. He testified that:

A   . . . [W]hen a person comes in to me about a medical malpractice action, based upon what the individual has told me, I have to make a decision as to whether or not there probably is or probably is not, based upon that information, medical malpractice. And if, in my judgment, based upon what the client has told me, there is not medical malpractice, I will so inform the client.

Hvass stated, however, that he would never render a "categorical" opinion. In addition, Hvass acknowledged that if he were consulted for a "legal opinion" regarding medical malpractice and 14 months had expired since the incident in question, "ordinary care and diligence" would require him to inform the party of the two-year statute of limitations applicable to that type of action.

This case was submitted to the jury by way of a special verdict form. The jury found that Dr. Blake and the hospital were negligent and that Dr. Blake's negligence (but not the hospital's) was a direct cause of the injuries sustained by John Togstad; that there was an attorney-client contractual relationship between Mrs. Togstad and Miller; that Miller was negligent in rendering advice regarding the possible claims of Mr. and Mrs. Togstad; that, but for Miller's negligence, plaintiffs would have been successful in the prosecution of a legal action against Dr. Blake; and that neither Mr. nor Mrs. Togstad was negligent in pursuing their claims against Dr. Blake. The jury awarded damages to Mr. Togstad of $610,500 and to Mrs. Togstad of $39,000. . . .

In a legal malpractice action of the type involved here, four elements must be shown: (1) that an attorney-client relationship existed; (2) that defendant acted negligently or in breach of contract; (3) that such acts were the proximate cause of the plaintiffs' damages; (4) that but for defendant's conduct the plaintiffs would have been successful in the prosecution of their medical malpractice claim. . . .

We believe it is unnecessary to decide whether a tort or contract theory is preferable for resolving the attorney-client relationship question raised by this appeal. The tort and contract analyses are very similar in a case such as the instant one,[4] and we conclude that under either theory the evidence shows that a lawyer-client relationship is present here. The thrust of Mrs. Togstad's testimony is that she went to Miller for legal advice, was told there wasn't a case, and relied upon this advice in failing to pursue the claim for medical malpractice. In addition, according to Mrs. Togstad, Miller did not qualify his legal opinion by urging her to seek advice from another attorney, nor did Miller inform her that he lacked expertise in the medical malpractice area. . . . [W]e believe a jury could properly find that Mrs. Togstad sought and received legal advice from Miller under circumstances which made it reasonably foreseeable to Miller that Mrs. Togstad would be injured if the advice were negligently given. Thus, under either a tort or contract analysis, there is sufficient evidence in the record to support the existence of an attorney-client relationship.

Defendants argue that even if an attorney-client relationship was established the evidence fails to show that Miller acted negligently in assessing the merits of the Togstads' case. They appear to contend that, at most, Miller was guilty of an error in judgment which does not give rise to legal malpractice. . . . However, this case does not involve a mere error of judgment. The gist of plaintiffs' claim is that Miller failed to perform the minimal research that an ordinarily prudent

---

4. Under a negligence approach it must essentially be shown that defendant rendered legal advice (not necessarily at someone's request) under circumstances which made it reasonably foreseeable to the attorney that if such advice was rendered negligently, the individual receiving the advice might be injured thereby. *See, e.g.,* Palsgraf v. Long Island R.R. Co., 162 N.E. 99 (N.Y. 1928). . . . A contract analysis requires the rendering of legal advice pursuant to another's request and the reliance factor, in this case, where the advice was not paid for, need be shown in the form of promissory estoppel. *See* . . . Restatement (Second) of Contracts, § 90.

attorney would do before rendering legal advice in a case of this nature. The record, through the testimony of Kenneth Green and John McNulty, contains sufficient evidence to support plaintiffs' position. . . .

There is also sufficient evidence in the record establishing that, but for Miller's negligence, plaintiffs would have been successful in prosecuting their medical malpractice claim. Dr. Woods, in no uncertain terms, concluded that Mr. Togstad's injuries were caused by the medical malpractice of Dr. Blake. Defendants' expert testimony to the contrary was obviously not believed by the jury. Thus, the jury reasonably found that had plaintiff's medical malpractice action been properly brought, plaintiffs would have recovered. . . .

Practice Pointers:
Engagement, Nonengagement, and Disengagement Letters

Togstad illustrates that misunderstandings between lawyers and clients can create real problems for both. Commentators recommend various types of engagement letters to remedy these potential differences. In their treatise entitled *Legal Malpractice*, Ronald Mallen and Jeffrey Smith identify four basic situations in which such a misunderstanding can occur.[1]

- The lawyer wants to decline a specific request for representation (*e.g.,* *Togstad*, p. **000**);
- The lawyer wants to specify which parties to a transaction the lawyer agrees to represent (*e.g., dePape, p.* **000**);
- The lawyer wants to prevent a claim for negligent misrepresentation (*e.g., Greycas*, p. **000**); and
- The lawyer wants to prevent reliance by unrepresented third parties who are beneficiaries of the lawyer's service to another client (*e.g., Cruze*, p. **000**).

Nonengagement Letters

The first situation involves facts like those in *Togstad*: the lawyer thinks he has declined representation, but the prospective client believes she has received legal advice. In that circumstance, a simple nonengagement letter (or website explanation) such as the one below can clarify any misunderstandings.[2] Consider how you would modify this form to address the facts in *Togstad* or Problem 3-6.

> [Letterhead]
> [Date]
> [Prospective Client]   Certified Mail No.
>   Return Receipt Requested
> Re: Potential Engagement Regarding [Matter]
> Dear [Name]

---

1. Ronald E. Mallen & Jeffrey M. Smith, *Legal Malpractice* § 2.12 (2012 ed. West).
2. Gary A. Munneke & Anthony E. Davis, *The Essential Formbook: Comprehensive Management Tools for Lawyers* 280 (ABA, L. Prac. Mgt. Sect. 2004).

Thank you for your visit today. As we discussed, although I have not investigated the merits of your matter, I do not feel it would be appropriate for [me/Law Firm Name] to represent you in your possible [matter]. In declining to undertake this matter, [I am/law firm is] not expressing an opinion on [the likely outcome of the matter].

Please be aware that whatever claim, if any, that you have may be barred by the passage of time. Because deadlines may be critical to your case, I recommend that you immediately contact another lawyer/law firm for assistance regarding your matter. [*Optional:* For your information, the telephone number of the legal referral service of the (State) Bar Association is:_____.]

Thank you again for your interest in [me/Law Firm Name]. *Optional:* We appreciate your having approached us regarding your matter. If you ever have need of legal assistance in the field of [practice concentration], we hope that you will think of us again in that context. (We enclose a copy of our brochure describing our practice in that area.)

Sincerely,

[Your Name/Firm Name]

Engagement Letters

Just as nonengagement letters can help clarify the absence of a duty to a prospective client, engagement letters are intended to prevent misunderstandings by clarifying the scope and basis for undertaking a client representation. But an engagement letter also can be used to address other issues that might arise during the course of the representation. A complete list is probably impossible to compile, but commentators offer the following topics as candidates for inclusion in an engagement letter:[3]

- Identification of the client, adverse parties, and related parties;
- Definition of the scope of the engagement;
- Description of the respective responsibilities of the client and the lawyer;
- Identification of and consents to conflicts of interest;
- Resolution of confidentiality issues, especially in multiple representations;
- Identification of goals of the representation;
- Proposed staffing, including agents of the client and lawyer;
- Methods of communication;
- Identification of third-party neutrals, such as judges, arbitrators, or mediators;
- Fee agreement and billing schedule;
- Grounds for withdrawal or termination;
- Policy on file retention; and
- Methods of dispute resolution between client and lawyer.

---

3. Mallen & Smith, *supra* note 1, at § 2.10; Munneke & Davis, *supra* note 2, at 141-144.

New York requires written engagement letters in most cases.[4] Several jurisdictions also require written disclosure if a lawyer does not carry adequate malpractice insurance.[5]

Disengagement Letters

To prevent misunderstandings at the close of a matter, commentators also recommend a disengagement letter. Disengagement letters can be helpful when a
lawyer completes a matter, decides to withdraw, is fired by the client, or leaves
a law firm and does not intend to continue work on a matter. The letter should
make clear the reason the relationship has ended, and include appropriate warnings about unfinished work and time deadlines.[6] The letter also can address
whether the client wishes the lawyer to communicate with successor counsel,
and can provide for the orderly transmission of client files and documents.[7]

Disengagement letters essentially transform a current client into a former
client and thereby limit (but, as we will see in the next few chapters, do not extinguish) the duties the lawyer continues to owe that person or entity. Although the
use of a disengagement letter can clarify the lawyer's lack of continuing obligation to the client, it is not an unmixed blessing. The lawyer may hope that the
client will call on the lawyer or the law firm for other services in the future. For
this reason, the termination letter should be clear, but also can convey a carefully crafted willingness to serve in additional matters.

The Law Governing Lawyers:
Actual and Accidental Clients

In Chapter 1, Professor Wasserstrom pointed out that lawyers engage in role-
differentiated behavior; that is, lawyers rightly favor the interests of clients over
the interests of others. Choosing to take on a client means taking on fiduciary
obligations to stay focused on the client's best interests as those interests are
refined in discussions between client and lawyer and then determined by the
client.

Actual Clients

In most situations, lawyers know who their clients are because they have expressly
agreed to represent them. No payment is necessary to establish a client-lawyer
relationship so long as both lawyer and client agree that the lawyer should

---

4. N.Y. Ct. Rules §§ 1215.1, 1215.2 (2012) (fees less than $3,000 or repeat clients in similar mat-
ters exempted). In domestic relations matters, New York requires lawyers to provide clients with
both a Statement of Client's Rights and Responsibilities and a written retainer agreement, regardless of the fee charged. *Id.* at §§ 1400.2, 1400.3.
5. *E.g.,* Cal. R. Prof. Conduct 3-410 (2012); Ohio R. Prof. Conduct 1.4(c) (2012).
6. *See, e.g.,* Gilles v. Wiley, Malehorn & Sirota, *infra* p. 488 (client stated cause of action against
former lawyers who withdrew at the last minute without adequately warning her that the statute of
limitations was about to run on her medical malpractice case).
7. Mallen & Smith, *supra* note 1, § 2.13.

provide legal services to that client.[1] Fiduciary duties automatically attach to each client-lawyer relationship once a lawyer agrees to represent a client.[2]

Accidental Clients

Increasingly, however, the law governing lawyers also has recognized what lawyers might think of as "accidental" clients—those a lawyer did not expect or identify, but those recognized by law as being owed the same fiduciary duties that lawyers owe clients they intend to represent. This chapter and the remainder of this book illustrate a myriad of situations where accidental clients may lurk.

1. Implied Client-Lawyer Relationships   *Togstad* illustrates how courts have found implied client-lawyer relationships when nonlawyers reasonably rely on legal advice or assistance. Lawyers might also find that they have accidentally taken on a client when they offer informal consults or give advice during public speeches or at social gatherings.[3] Lawyers also may find that advertising and websites can create accidental client-lawyer relationships if unknown persons reasonably rely on the information therein provided.[4] This law imposes a precontractual duty of good faith on lawyers by looking back on the matter from a reasonable nonlawyer perspective. As a result, a lawyer's memory of what was said or promised might not be the version that ultimately prevails.

2. Court Appointments   *Bothwell* instructs that client-lawyer relationships can be created involuntarily by court appointment. As an officer of the courts, lawyers have a duty to accept court appointments unless that lawyer can convince the judge that it would violate some other provision in the lawyer code, such as competence, confidentiality, or loyalty.[5]

3. Prospective Clients   When prospective clients discuss the possibility of obtaining legal services with lawyers, implied client-lawyer relationships can develop. Although prospective clients might not always become full-fledged clients,

---

1. RLGL § 14(1).

2. RLGL § 16. The duty of confidentiality attaches to prospective clients even if no lawyer-client relationship is formed. MR 1.18, RLGL 15.

3. *See, e.g.,* D. C. Bar Eth. Op. 316 (2002) (online chat rooms and listservs); Md. St. Bar Assn. Committee on Eth. Op. 2007-18 (2008) (lawyer conducting domestic relations law seminars for lay public); N. J. Ad. Comm. on Profl. Eth. Op. 712 (2008) (lawyer staffing telephone hotline); N. J. Ad. Comm. on Profl. Eth Op 671 (1993) (lawyer-volunteer at abused women's shelter); N. M. Bar Op. 2001-1 (Application of Rules of Professional Conduct to Lawyer's Use of Listserve-type Message Boards and Communications).

4. *E.g.,* ABA Op. 10-457; Mass. Bar Assn. Op. 07-01 (in absence of effective disclaimer, prospective client visiting law firm website that markets background and qualifications of each lawyer in attractive light, stresses lawyer's skill at solving clients' practical problems, and provides e-mail link for immediate communication with that lawyer might reasonably conclude that firm and its individual lawyers have implicitly "agreed to consider" whether to form client-lawyer relationship); Barton v. U.S. Dist. Ct., 410 F.3d 1104 (2005) (holding that responding to a law firm's Internet questionnaire can create a lawyer-client relationship if the respondent reasonably believed that in filling out the form, he/she was entering into a lawyer-client relationship).

5. MR 6.2; RLGL § 14(2).

Togstad illustrates how they become clients to the extent that they reasonably rely on a lawyer's legal advice. Even when lawyers make it clear that they will not take on a representation, if a lawyer offers legal advice and gains information from such a person, two duties, however limited, attach to such an encounter: competence in any advice offered and confidentiality that cloaks anything the lawyer learns.[6]

In addition to the formal prospective client-lawyer meeting, prospective clients lurk in many other circumstances as well, including:

- Beauty contests, where prospective clients essentially audition lawyers by interviewing several before deciding whom to hire.[7]
- Public speeches, where lawyers offer general legal information, but often are asked specific questions about specific facts. Especially dangerous is a response that begins with "There is no case/redress/cause of action in that circumstance," because a listener who takes no further action in reliance on such an option might fail to seek other legal help before a statute of limitations expires.
- Advertising, when lawyers offer advice about specific facts. Stating that no person should rely on this ad for advice (because every case differs, or the law provides for certain defenses, etc.) invites further inquiries, and also explains why reliance on the ad alone is not reasonable.
- E-lawyering, where lawyers offer advice or invite specific nonlawyer inquiries on websites. Lawyers who want to offer persons legal advice online should know to whom they are giving it, do a conflicts check, and otherwise comply with ethics requirements such as retainer agreements before offering the advice.[8]
- Consulting with other lawyers, where a lawyer seeks advice for a client, or advice for the lawyer in dealing with the client. In the right circumstances, either the lawyer or the lawyer's client can become clients of the consulting lawyer.[9]
- Splitting fees with other lawyers, where eligibility for payment depends on assuming "joint responsibility" for the representation.[10]
- Dealing with unrepresented persons where they seek advice or services from another person's lawyer.[11]
- Family members or social friends, where they seek and reasonably rely on legal advice.
- Limited-term pro bono service, where nonlawyers seek legal information from volunteer lawyers.[12]

---

6. MR 1.18; RLGL § 15.
7. *Id.*
8. ABA Formal Op. 10-457, *infra* p. 404. We discuss conflicts checking in Practice Pointers: *Implementing a Conflicts Control System, infra* p. 419.
9. ABA Formal Op. 97-406.
10. MR 1.5, Comment [7].
11. MR 4.3.
12. *See* Lawyers and Clients: *Service Pro Bono Publico, supra* p. 64.

4. Joint Clients Clients may cluster in groups, and lawyers may be consulted or paid by one client for the representation of two or more. The communication duty breached in *dePape* in the next chapter represents one pitfall of incorrectly identifying and inadequately responding to each and every one of such clients. An even more common problem is loyalty, or resolving conflicts of interest that nearly always lurk in joint representations. A lawyer must identify the conflict and obtain each client's informed consent to continue with the joint representation.[13] Some joint client conflicts are not consentable, which means that the lawyer must tell the parties that he or she cannot represent all of them.[14]

5. Third-Person Direction Third-person nonclients who pay for or attempt to direct the representation of a client also can tempt a lawyer to treat these third parties as if they control the representation. But in law practice, he who pays the piper does not always call the tune. For example, the mother who hires and pays a lawyer to represent her child in a juvenile court is not a client. Neither is the son who hires and pays a lawyer to write his father's will. In some situations, it might not be clear whether a lawyer has agreed to take on two clients or has agreed to represent only one, with the other paying the bill. Another variation on this theme involves agents of clients designated to communicate with the client's lawyer. Once again, the law governing lawyers imposes the burden of clarification on the lawyer, who must initiate communication to clarify the identity of the client(s) and remain loyal to the actual client, not the person paying or speaking with the lawyer.[15]

6. Insurance Defense Lawyers who are hired by insurers to represent insureds confront a situation often fraught with similar ambiguity. Typical liability policies promise to "defend" covered persons when they are sued for a covered event. The policy obligates an insurer to hire a lawyer to provide this defense. Less clear is whether a joint representation also has been created. As we shall see in Chapter 10, jurisdictions are split over whether the lawyer represents one client, the insured, or two clients, the insured and the insurer, in such a circumstance.[16] Everyone agrees that lawyers owe fiduciary duties to their client-insureds. Less clear than client identity is the extent to which lawyers may take direction from the insurer, whether client or not.

7. Organizations Lawyers who represent organizations can face dozens of accidental clients. In representing a publicly held corporation, family business, or

---

13. MR 1.7; RLGL § 130.

14. *See, e.g.,* Perez v. Kirk & Carrigan, *infra* p. 167 (employee-client had valid claim for breach of confidentiality against lawyers who represented employee and employer following employee's truck driving accident); Anderson v. O'Brien, *infra* p. 324 (lawyer who represented multiple parties in real estate transactions liable for reckless breach of fiduciary duty).

15. MR 1.8(f); RLGL § 134. *See, e.g.,* Machado v. Statewide Grievance Comm., *infra* p. 89.

16. MR 1.7, Comment [13], 1.8, Comments [11] & [12]; RLGL §134, Comment f; Paradigm Ins. Co. v. The Langerman Law Offices, P.A., *infra* p. 375; Lawyers and Clients: *Insurance Defense,* *infra* p. 381.

governmental unit, a lawyer must deal through individual agents who manage and direct the organization, but the lawyer does not necessarily represent any of these individuals.[17] In some circumstances the lawyer can represent both an employer and employee, but again, the lawyer shoulders the burden of adequate communication, protection of confidential information, and appropriate conflicts waivers. Consistent with the law governing other accidental client–lawyer relationships, the lawyer must clarify any doubtful situations, especially those where an individual might reasonably believe the lawyer represents his or her interests as well as those of the organization.[18]

8. Clients Who Morph The practice of law is dynamic, and accidental clients can occur when clients change. Individual clients marry, divorce, and die.[19] If lawyers do not notice, they might communicate with the wrong person or bring a lawsuit in the wrong name. Some clients have fluctuating capacities, which requires that lawyers evaluate their capacity before critical decisions can be made.[20] Organization clients change their personnel, governance structure, or their status, for example, by merging or filing for bankruptcy, at which point a new decision maker might reverse a prior decision.[21] The class in class actions may be represented by named plaintiffs, but class identification and lawyer loyalty can change as the matter progresses and class(es) are certified by courts.[22] Finally, when lawyers complete a representation, each client morphs from a current client to a former client, a characterization that changes, but does not extinguish, a lawyer's fiduciary duties.[23]

9. Quasi-Clients If lawyers owe fiduciary duties to clients, it seems axiomatic that they owe no such duties to nonclients. Yet some nonclients can be characterized as quasi-clients because of their relationship to clients. For example, intended third-party beneficiaries of client representations could be owed some of the same duties of competence owed clients.[24] Similarly, lawyers who represent client-fiduciaries such as trustees, guardians, corporate directors, or partners also need to be mindful of the fiduciary obligations their clients owe others.[25] Representing such a client-fiduciary requires advice about the broad scope of duty owed by the fiduciary to third parties, duties that lawyers are obliged to assist their client-fiduciaries in fulfilling.[26]

---

17. *E.g.*, Antioch Litigation Trust v. McDermott Will & Emery LLP, *infra* p. 92.
18. MR 1.13; RLGL §§ 96, 97; Sanford v. Commonwealth of Virginia, *infra* p. 316.
19. *E.g.*, In re Forrest, *infra* p. 276.
20. MR 1.14; RLGL § 24.
21. *E.g.*, Antioch Litigation Trust v. McDermott Will & Emery LLP, *infra* p. 92; In re Refco Securities Litigation, *infra* p. 241.
22. RLGL § 14, Comment f.
23. *E.g.*, Maritrans v. Pepper, Hamilton & Scheetz, *infra* p. 304.
24. *E.g.*, Greycas v. Proud, *infra* p. 145.
25. RLGL § 14, Comment f, § 51, Comment h.
26. *E.g.*, Fickett v. Superior Court, 558 P.2d 988 (Ariz. App. 1976) (lawyer for guardian owed duty of care to ward to prevent misappropriation of guardianship assets); Cruze v. Hudler, *infra* p. 149; The Bounds of the Law: *Duties to Nonclients*, *infra* p. 155.

10. Imputed Clients   Although some lawyers practice solo, most practice in association with others. The law governing lawyers imputes the obligations of one lawyer in a law firm to all other lawyers in that firm as well.[27] It also extends these law firm obligations to law firm employees, including temporary lawyers and student law clerks.[28]

Lawyers who do not share an employment relationship could nevertheless look or act like as though they have done so. For example, lawyers from different firms who intend to split a legal fee usually are required to assume joint responsibility for the representation, whether or not they work on the matter.[29] This creates a client-lawyer relationship with each lawyer. Similarly, lawyers who share office space might not share fees, but might act as a firm, by consulting on cases, using the same letterhead, or sharing file access. If so, they could be held to constitute a "firm" with imputed client-lawyer relationships.[30] Likewise, lawyers from different firms who participate in joint defense agreements might share enough confidential information that their conflicts will be imputed to each other.[31]

Conclusion

Lawyers cannot recognize or solve any legal ethics issue until they first learn to identify their clients, including those they might consider to be "accidental" clients. Accidental clients can appear when lawyers least expect them and can impose some or all of the same fiduciary duties on lawyers that intended clients can. Lawyers who understand that they must identify their clients will be in a position to avoid client-lawyer relationships they do not wish to create, and to recognize the moment when fiduciary duties attach to client-lawyer relationships they intend to undertake. In other words, the first step to addressing any legal ethics issue is to know your clients, so that you will be able to observe the 5 Cs for all legally recognized clients and, by the same token, avoid interference by those who are not.

---

27. MR 1.10; RLGL § 123.
28. MR 5.1, 5.3; RLGL § 11.
29. MR 1.5(e); RLGL § 47.
30. MR 1.0(c) and Comments [2]-[4]; RLGL § 123, Comment e. Courts differ over how these rules apply to public lawyers. *See, e.g.,* State v. Severson, 215 P.3d 414 (Idaho 2009) (whether public defender's office should be "firm" depends on a case-by-case evaluation); Duvall v. State, 923 A.2d 81(Md. 2007) (public defender's office must be treated as a "firm" for conflict of interest purposes).
31. *E.g.,* Wilson P. Abraham Constr. Corp. v. Armco Steel Corp., 559 F.2d 250 (5th Cir. 1977) (lawyer who represented codefendant in prior criminal investigation disqualified to protect nonclient's shared confidences in joint defense arrangement); Analytica, Inc. v. NPD Research, Inc., 708 F.2d 1263 (7th Cir. 1983) (law firm disqualified where co-counsel relationship gave it access to potentially relevant confidential data).

Chapter 4

Control and Communication

The agreement to represent a client includes the obligation to "proceed in a manner reasonably calculated to advance a client's lawful objectives, as defined by the client after consultation."[1] This chapter explores two of the most basic fiduciary duties that enable lawyers to meet this duty: control and communication.

The client-lawyer relationship is one of the oldest examples of an agency relationship, a fiduciary relationship that results when an agent (the lawyer) agrees to act on behalf of a principal (the client) subject to the principal's control.[2] The agreement between principal and agent confers power on the agent to act on behalf of the principal.[3] It also imposes on the agent fiduciary duties to ensure that the agent acts on the principal's behalf and subject to the principal's control.[4]

Lawyer-agents owe client-principals fiduciary duties to ensure that lawyers place their clients' interests first.[5] Fiduciary duties facilitate the client's control of the agency relationship, prevents lawyers from benefiting someone other than the client, and protects clients from lawyers who might take advantage of the trust and power reposed in them.

The recognition of a professional's legal obligation to defer to client control and to disclose information emphasizes the importance of autonomy, or self-governance. Respect for autonomy is essential to both religious and philosophical notions of respect for the dignity of the human person. We respect a human person by relying on that person's own self-determined choices.[6] Similarly, individuality is an element of human well-being.[7] Ultimately, however, the subjectivity of weighing possible consequences and the reality that

---

1. RLGL § 16 (1).
2. *Restatement (Third) of Agency* § 1.01 (2006).
3. *Id. Comment c.*
4. *Id. Comment e.*
5. *Restatement (Third) of Agency* § 8.0 Comment b (2006).
6. *See* Isaiah Berlin, *Four Essays on Liberty* 137 (Oxford 1969).
7. John Stuart Mill, *On Liberty* (Chapter IV, "Society and the Individual") (1863).

the client must live with the eventual results mean that respect for the client's wishes should reign.[8]

The key to understanding the lawyer's obligation of control and communication is to remember that the lawyer must initiate all client conversations. Failure to do so leaves a lawyer vulnerable to multiple remedies available to clients for breaching some or all of the 5 Cs. In this chapter, we explore three of these remedies: professional discipline, civil liability, and reversal of criminal convictions for ineffective assistance of counsel.

A. Control

1. Authority Between Client and Lawyer

Like other agents, lawyers have a duty to act on the client's behalf, subject to the client's right to control the objectives of the representation.[9] At the same time, most clients defer to and rely on their lawyers' expertise regarding the means to accomplish client goals. The Model Rules of Professional Conduct and the law of agency recognize three spheres of authority between client and lawyer, summarized in the following chart.

Client–Lawyer Allocation of Authority Inside the Relationship

Client's sole authority	Negotiated authority; delegated discretion	Lawyer's sole authority
Objectives, goals, and specific decisions	Means	Refuse unlawful conduct and take action before tribunals
MR 1.2(a) [objectives, decisions to settle; in criminal cases, pleas, jury trial waiver, and whether client will testify]	MR 1.2(a) [means and implied authorization], MR 1.2(b) [moral views], MR 1.2(c) [scope of the representation], MR 1.4 [initiate communication]	MR 1.2(d) [criminal or fraudulent activity], MR 1.4(a)(5) [consult about relevant limitations], MR 3.3 [Candor toward the tribunal]
RLGL § 22	RLGL §§ 20, 21	RLGL §§ 23, 25

---

8. There is also considerable empirical evidence that active client participation results in significantly better results. *See, e.g.,* Douglas E. Rosenthal, *Lawyer and Client: Who's In Charge?* 61 (Russell Sage Found. 1974) (New York City personal injury plaintiffs who actively participated in their claim got significantly better results than those who passively delegated responsibility to their lawyers).

9. *Restatement (Third) of Agency* § 1.01 (2006).

In the first sphere (the left column), clients retain sole authority to make decisions concerning the outcome of the representation, including whether and when to settle or appeal a matter, and in criminal cases, how to plead, whether to waive a jury trial, and whether to testify.[10] Clients can authorize their lawyers to make a particular decision within this sphere, but the ultimate authority of clients to decide cannot be completely ceded to their lawyers.[11]

In the second sphere (the right column), lawyers retain sole authority to refuse to perform, counsel, or assist a client's unlawful act[12] and in spite of client preferences to the contrary, lawyers also may take actions in tribunals they reasonably believe to be required by the law or court order.[13]

The third sphere of authority (the middle column) includes all other decisions not reserved solely to clients or lawyers. Here, authority is shared, and lawyers and clients can bargain for broad delegation of authority to a lawyer, close continuing consultation with a client, or some measure of each.[14]

All three spheres of authority place affirmative duties of communication on lawyers during a representation. When a client decision arises, the lawyer must promptly inform and consult with the client about the decision.[15] When a client insists on illegal conduct, the lawyer must promptly inform the client that the conduct is not permitted and must explain why.[16] In all other aspects of the representation, the lawyer must consult with the client regarding the means to accomplish the client's objectives, keep the client reasonably informed, and promptly respond to client inquiries.

2. Authority of Lawyer to Act for Client

The outcome of this consultation creates terms of the engagement or, in agency terminology, authority, which obligates lawyers to obey the client's lawful

---

10. MR 1.2(a); RLGL § 22(1). *See* D & D Carpentry Inc. v. U.S. Bancorp, 792 N.W.2d 193 (Wis. Ct. App. 2008) (a lawyer has no authority to agree to arbitrate a client's case without the client's consent).

11. *E.g.,* In re Coleman, 295 S.W.3d 857 (Mo. 2009) (lawyer whose fee agreement purported to give him sole authority to settle the client's claims suspended for one year); Compton v. Kittleson, 171 P.3d 172 (2007) (lawyer who charged hybrid fee agreement that impermissibly burdened client's exclusive right to settle case violated Rules of Professional Conduct and committed legal malpractice); Abbott v. Kidder Peabody & Co., Inc., 42 F. Supp. 2d 1046 (D. Colo. 1999) (lawyers representing 200 individual plaintiffs disqualified because of contract that gave settlement authority to a select group of plaintiffs; each individual client's approval is essential); In re Lewis, 463 S.E.2d 862 (Ga. 1995) (lawyer whose client signed a retainer agreement giving lawyer full authority to take all actions on client's behalf in a personal injury case and then settled her case without her express authority suspended for 18 months).

12. We develop this topic in greater detail in the continuing notes entitled "The Bounds of the Law."

13. *E.g.,* United States v. Chapman, 593 F.3d 365, 369 (4th Cir. 2010) (decision to accept a mistrial).

14. *E.g.,* Dunn v. Patterson, 919 N.E.2d 404 (Ill. App. Ct. 2009) (upholding lawyer's estate plan provisions intended to prevent elder abuse that required clients to obtain lawyer's or court's consent to amend or revoke documents).

15. MR 1.2(a), 1.4(a)(1); RLGL § 20(3).

16. MR 1.4(a) (5); RLGL § 20(1).

Lawyer's Authority to Act for Client Outside of the Relationship

---

	Actual Authority: RLGL § 26 Restatement (Third) Agency §§ 2.01, 2.02		Apparent Authority: RLGL § 27 Restatement (Third) Agency § 2.03
Definition	Lawyer's act within the scope of authority granted by client or client ratifies lawyer's act; RLGL § 26		Lawyer's act within scope of apparent authority due to third party's reasonable belief based on client's manifestation that lawyer is authorized; RLGL § 27
Examples	Express (specific authorization); RLGL § 26 cmt. a	Implied (express authority arising out of general delegation of power to act); RLGL §§ 26, 27	Presumed before a tribunal; RLGL § 25
Agency Power	Agent's acts designated or implied in principal's manifestations and acts necessary to achieving principal's objectives as agent reasonably understands them; Restatement (Third) Agency § 2.02		Power of an agent due to third party's reasonable belief agent has authority traceable to the principal's manifestations; Restatement (Third) Agency § 2.03
Result	Client bound by authorizing lawyer either specifically or generally to achieve an objective, unless lawyer misrepresents authority; RLGL § 30		Client not bound simply by retaining lawyer without actual or apparent authority; RLGL § 27 cmt c

---

instructions and empowers lawyers to act on behalf of the client.[17] The law of agency recognizes two basic kinds of authority that will bind the client-principal to third parties for acts taken by the client's lawyer-agent summarized in the chart above.

Actual authority includes both express authority and implied authority to act in a manner that will further the client's objectives, so long as the lawyer has reasonably consulted with the client and believes the client desires such action.[18] A lawyer also has actual authority if the client ratifies the lawyer's action after the fact.[19]

---

17. *Restatement (Third) of Agency* at § 8.09 (2006); RLGL § 21, Comment d.
18. *Id.* at Comment b; *Restatement (Third) of Agency* § 2.02 (2006); MR 1.2(a); RLGL § 21(3).
19. RLGL § 26(3).

A client also can be bound by a lawyer's apparent authority; that is, authority "traceable to the principal's manifestations" that causes another to reasonably believe the lawyer-agent had the requisite authority to act on behalf of the client.[20] Lawyers who purport to have actual or apparent authority but in fact do not either do not bind their clients,[21] or, if they do, could be liable to clients or third parties harmed as result.[22] *Machado* makes clear that professional discipline also can result when lawyers fail to clarify and heed their clients' intent.

Problems

4-1.   Plaintiff retained Fox in a personal injury case. A few weeks later, Fox proudly informed Plaintiff that he had settled the case for a tidy sum. Plaintiff replied that she would never settle for that amount and refused to sign a release. What should Fox do? Does it matter if Fox agreed to the settlement during a mandatory court-annexed mediation?

4-2.   CEO of Mega Corporation asks Martyn & Fox to draft a deed transferring vacant land owned by Mega to CEO. "It's just a liability for Mega," CEO explains. What should Martyn & Fox do?

4-3.   Martyn volunteers to represent a child in abuse and neglect proceedings. After a thorough investigation and interview with her client, Martyn determines that (a) her client has capacity to make decisions for herself; (b) it would be in the best interest of the client to go into foster care; and (c) her client wants to be returned to her home, which is surely dysfunctional but where she is not likely to suffer physical harm. What should Martyn do?

**Consider: Model Rules 1.2, 1.4, 1.13, 1.14
          RLGL §§ 20-27, 96**

Machado v. Statewide Grievance Committee
890 A.2d 622 (Conn. App. 2006)

Gruendel, J.

The plaintiff, Arthur D. Machado, an attorney, appeals from the judgment of the trial court dismissing his appeal from the reprimand issued to him by the defendant, the statewide grievance committee. . . .

---

20. *Restatement (Third) of Agency* § 2.03 (2006); RLGL § 27.

21. *See* Sarkes Tarzian, Inc. v. U.S. Trust Co., 397 F.3d 577 (7th Cir. 2005) (lawyer lacked express and apparent authority to enter into a contract because client, although sending lawyer to negotiate deal, required client's approval before entering into the final agreement).

22. RLGL §§ 27, Comment f, 30. *See generally* Grace M. Giesel, *Client Responsibility for Lawyer Conduct: Examining the Agency Nature of the Lawyer-Client Relationship*, 86 Neb. L. Rev. 346 (2007).

. . . The plaintiff is an attorney licensed by the state of Connecticut and was retained by the complainant, Scott V. Adams, to represent him in a bankruptcy proceeding. The plaintiff initially met with Adams in January, 2000, while Adams was in prison. At the meeting, Adams instructed the plaintiff to communicate with Kendra Cihocki because, as a prisoner, Adams had limited means of communication. Subsequent to the meeting, Cihocki delivered an $850 check to the defendant as a retainer for Adams' bankruptcy filing.

Thereafter, Cihocki instructed the plaintiff to obtain the release of a sales tax lien that had been placed on a business owned by Adams and Cihocki. The plaintiff provided legal services in connection with the removal of the sales tax lien and, in so doing, depleted the retainer. Shortly thereafter, Cihocki picked up the file from the plaintiff's office and retained new counsel. No funds were left to pursue Adams' bankruptcy, and the plaintiff took no further action on the bankruptcy. Furthermore, the plaintiff did not inform Adams that he no longer was pursuing the bankruptcy proceeding on his behalf.

In August, 2000, the plaintiff decided to close his office, and he released his last staff member the following month. By March, 2001, the lease on the plaintiff's office expired. During that time, Adams attempted to contact the plaintiff by telephone and mail regarding the status of his bankruptcy.[4] Adams never received a response to his telephone messages or letters.

On March 19, 2002, Adams filed a complaint with the defendant, alleging, among other things, that the plaintiff had failed to respond to letters and telephone calls made by Adams in 2000 and 2001. Adams also claimed that the plaintiff owed him [$850] because the plaintiff did not perform work on the bankruptcy as initially agreed by both parties. . . .

The plaintiff first . . . argues that Cihocki was Adams' agent and, therefore, the plaintiff was obliged to follow her orders in assisting with releasing a sales tax lien. We are not persuaded. . . .

First, in its February 14, 2003 decision, the reviewing committee found by clear and convincing evidence that "[Adams] retained the [plaintiff] to represent him in his bankruptcy." The reviewing committee further determined that Cihocki was indeed Adams' agent for the bankruptcy filing, but ceased being Adams' agent when she directed the plaintiff to release a sales tax lien on property owned by her and Adams. "The [plaintiff's] failure to abide by [Adams'] decision to file for bankruptcy and failure to consult with [Adams] regarding the change in the scope of representation from bankruptcy to release of a sales tax lien constituted a violation of rule 1.2 (a) of the Rules of Professional Conduct."

Second, the reviewing committee determined that the plaintiff did not keep Adams reasonably informed about the status of the bankruptcy. "By not informing [Adams] that his agent had instructed the [plaintiff] to change the scope of

---

4. Adams claimed that he spoke with the plaintiff's secretary, left messages, and wrote a letter to the plaintiff outlining how he wanted to proceed with the bankruptcy. The plaintiff contended that he never received any telephone calls or correspondence from Adams during that time.

representation from bankruptcy to release of the sales tax lien, the [plaintiff] violated rule 1.4 (a) of the Rules of Professional Conduct."

In his brief, the plaintiff claims that Cihocki had both actual and apparent authority[8] to redirect his actions to release the sales tax lien. The plaintiff argues that Cihocki had actual authority because Adams gave her a power of attorney and told the plaintiff to follow her instructions. The plaintiff also contends that Cihocki had apparent authority because it was reasonable for him to assume that Cihocki's authority extended to the redirection of his work to encompass the sales tax lien. In support of his contention, the plaintiff lists a number of facts, including that he "spoke to Ms. Cihocki on an almost daily basis" and "spoke with Adams at his initial meeting and at least once by telephone regarding the tax liens . . . ." He also claims that "the tax liens were among the debts to be discharged in the bankruptcy . . . ." We are not persuaded by those arguments. . . .

In the present case, . . . the reviewing committee determined that the plaintiff failed to abide by Adams' decision to file for bankruptcy and failed to inform Adams regarding the change in the scope of representation from bankruptcy to release of a sales tax lien. Indeed, the plaintiff admitted that he was mistaken in not having a new fee agreement document prepared when Cihocki asked him to do work on the tax issue.[9] . . .

The plaintiff further argues that . . . he was discharged by Adams and therefore could not have violated rules 1.2 (a) and 1.4 (a). Specifically, the plaintiff claims he was discharged when Cihocki picked up Adams' file from the plaintiff's office and retained new counsel. The plaintiff's argument is without merit.

. . . [T]he reviewing committee found by clear and convincing evidence that Cihocki no longer was Adams' agent when she directed the plaintiff to work on the release of a sales tax lien. In addition, the court noted that the plaintiff's failures to abide by Adams' decision to file for bankruptcy and to consult with Adams regarding the change in the scope of representation occurred prior to the removal of the file from the plaintiff's office. Even if the plaintiff was discharged when the file was picked up, the plaintiff already had violated rules 1.2 (a) and 1.4 (a). . . .

---

8. "Actual authority may be express or implied. . . . Implied authority is actual authority circumstantially proved. It is the authority which the principal intended his agent to possess. . . . Implied authority is a fact to be proven by deductions or inferences from the manifestations of consent of the principal . . . and [the] agent." "Apparent authority is that semblance of authority which a principal, through his own acts or inadvertences, causes or allows third persons to believe his agent possesses. . . . Consequently, apparent authority is to be determined, not by the agent's own acts, but by the acts of the agent's principal. . . . The issue of apparent authority is one of fact to be determined based on two criteria. . . . First, it must appear from the principal's conduct that the principal held the agent out as possessing sufficient authority to embrace the act in question, or knowingly permitted [the agent] to act as having such authority . . . . Second, the party dealing with the agent must have, acting in good faith, reasonably believed, under all the circumstances, that the agent had the necessary authority to bind the principal to the agent's action."

9. According to the plaintiff, Adams had signed a flat fee retainer agreement in connection with a chapter 7 bankruptcy petition.

The plaintiff's third claim is that the court improperly determined that scienter was not necessary to constitute a violation of rules 1.2 (a) and 1.4 (a) of the Rules of Professional Conduct. In Statewide Grievance Committee v. Presnick, 559 A.2d 220 (Conn. App. 1989), this court observed that a finding of bad faith or corrupt motive is not necessary to constitute a professional misconduct violation. . . .

The fact that the plaintiff may not have acted in bad faith plays no part in determining whether he violated rules 1.2 (a) and 1.4 (a) of the Rules of Professional Conduct. Therefore, regardless of the plaintiff's scienter at the time that he worked on Adams' bankruptcy, substantial evidence exists in the record that the plaintiff violated the two rules.

The judgment is affirmed.

Antioch Litigation Trust v. McDermott Will & Emery LLP

738 F. Supp. 2d 758 (S.D. Ohio 2010)

BLACK, Judge

This civil action is currently before the Court on Defendant's motion to dismiss and the parties' responsive memoranda.

Defendant McDermott Will & Emery LLP ("MWE") . . . served as company legal counsel for The Antioch Company from May 2003 until June 5, 2008. One of the purposes for which Antioch retained MWE was to provide legal expertise and advice in connection with ERISA and tax issues related to the Antioch employee stock ownership plan ("ESOP"). Marsha Matthews, a partner at MWE, helped plan and consummate a transaction that resulted in the Antioch ESOP owning 100% of Antioch's shares ("Tender Offer") . . .

The Antioch board of directors was led by [CEO] Lee and [his daughter] Asha Morgan Moran, who, individually, and through Morgan family trusts, owned 46.5% of all Antioch shares, and, therefore, stood to gain the most from the proposed transaction. Four of the remaining seven board members also owned substantial blocks of Antioch stock and consequently benefitted from the transaction. The entire board was subject to a conflict of interest.

Antioch retained financial advisor Houlihan Lokey to provide an opinion that the transaction was fair to the selling shareholders. Antioch never sought nor obtained an independent opinion as to whether the transaction was fair to the company as purchaser, nor did Antioch obtain an independent opinion regarding whether the underlying business decision to effect the transaction was prudent, and MWE never advised anyone to do so.

Plaintiff alleges that MWE knew or reasonably should have known that the Tender Offer, as a "prohibited transaction" under ERISA Sections 406 and 408, would result in violations of ERISA and tax law by both the individual directors and Antioch that were likely to result in substantial injury to the corporation and its constituents, including disqualification of the ESOP, loss of 100%

S-corporation status, and loss of tax-exempt status, resulting in significant tax liability. Plaintiff further alleges that MWE knew that the Morgans and a majority of the Board were subject to conflicts of interests with regard to the Tender Offer, but failed to advise the Board that the transaction would be voidable unless it could be shown to be fair to the corporation.

The Tender Offer, among other things, burdened Antioch with a massive increase in debt, from less than $11 million as of December 31, 2002 to more than $200 million as of December 31, 2003. Subsequently, a predictable surge in employee resignations aggravated the company's repurchase obligations, which were dictated by the ESOP and ERISA law, and drove the company deeper into debt. . . .

By early 2007, Antioch was in severe financial distress. As Antioch's financial problems mounted, rooted in the burdensome debt created by the Tender Offer, MWE failed to reevaluate the prudence of the Tender Offer, or advise the Antioch Board of potential claims against its financial advisors and conflicted directors prior to December 2007, when negligence claims and fiduciary claims against these entities could be found to have run. MWE's inaction may have precluded the company from recovering damages from these entities.

Antioch hired Houlihan Lokey to help it find a purchaser for the company. . . .

The Morgans, however, did not favor a sale to an independent outside buyer because they did not want to lose control of the company. . . . MWE advised the Morgans with respect to their retention of [their own financial advisor to explore other refinancing options]. The Antioch Board, lacking objective guidance from MWE, remained ambivalent and undecided about a clear direction for Antioch's future, continuing to allow the Morgans to pursue recapitalization alternatives while re-engaging Houlihan to explore a sale of Antioch. . . .

The preference given by Antioch to a deal designed by and for the Morgans had the effect of discouraging potential purchasers who were interested in acquiring control of Antioch. Potential purchasers knew that two directors, including the CEO and COO who effectively controlled the ESOP and also were the largest unsecured creditors of Antioch, disfavored the sale to such an extent that they were pursuing, with the Board's blessing, alternative transactions so as to maintain their own control of the business. The Antioch Board, advised by MWE, continued to allow the Morgans' efforts to interfere with the Board's/Houlihan's efforts.

In early June 2008, the company was in the late stages of an auction process run by Houlihan, working to close on a sale of the company's assets to J.H. Whitney pursuant to a signed Letter of Intent, to be achieved through a bankruptcy sale. MWE was actively involved in the process . . . .

On June 4, 2008, the ESOP Trustee exercised its right to replace Antioch's Board of Directors in order to bring the Whitney sales process to a halt and allow more time for the Morgans to accomplish their own deal. The Board was dismissed and replaced with Lee Morgan, Asha Morgan Moran, and an acquaintance of the Trustee, Robert Morris. At a meeting the next day, on June 5, 2008, the newly constituted Board fired MWE.

No sale or refinancing was achieved. Antioch filed for bankruptcy protection on November 13, 2008. [The bankruptcy trustee brought this malpractice action on behalf of Antioch against MWE]. . . .

Plaintiff asserts six claims of malpractice: (1) MWE failed to advise Antioch to obtain a fairness opinion for the Tender Offer and to avoid corporate waste; (2) MWE failed to advise Antioch about the legality and consequences of the Tender Offer under ERISA, tax laws, and Ohio corporate law; (3) MWE failed to provide legal advice to Antioch's individual directors; (4) MWE aided the majority shareholders (the Morgans) in breaches of their fiduciary duties; (5) MWE failed to advise Antioch about potential causes of action that Antioch had against its Board of Directors and its independent financial advisors; and (6) MWE failed to stop one of Antioch's shareholders from attempting to find an entity to buy Antioch.

A malpractice claim requires "(1) an attorney-client relationship, (2) professional duty arising from that relationship, (3) breach of that duty, (4) proximate cause, (5) and damages." Shoemaker v. Gindlesberger, 887 N.E.2d 1167 (2008). MWE alleges that the elements of a malpractice claim have not been stated, because MWE had no duty to protect Antioch, and, if it did, it did not breach such a duty. . . .

1. Fairness Opinion[23] . . .

Plaintiff claims that the Tender Offer was a self-dealing transaction designed by MWE and Deloitte primarily to benefit the Morgan directors/shareholders. The transaction consisted of the corporation offering to purchase all of its outstanding shares held by all shareholders except the ESOP. The Morgan family controlled 80% of the shares eligible to be purchased and expected to receive several hundred million dollars in direct consideration and savings from the transaction. . . .

Under Ohio corporation law, directors and officers owe a fiduciary duty to the corporation. Ohio Rev. Code § 1701.59. Specifically, a director must perform her duties "in good faith, in a manner the director reasonably believes to be in or not opposed to the best interests of the corporation, and with the care that an ordinarily prudent person in a like position would use under similar circumstances." Consequently, a director has a duty of good faith, a duty of loyalty, a duty of disclosure, and a duty to refrain from self-dealing.

In Ohio, self-dealing includes a director's participation in a transaction of the corporation in which the director has an interest. United States v. Skeddle, 940 F. Supp. 1146, 1150 (N.D. Ohio 1996) (self-dealing is considered a breach

---

23. Fairness opinions are "short letters that state an opinion about whether the consideration in a proposed transaction is fair" to the shareholders from a financial point of view. An investment banker usually addresses this letter to a special committee of the board of directors, which then publishes it in a proxy statement to all shareholders in accordance with securities law. Investment bankers deem a "fair" price to be one which falls "within a range of prices at which informed parties might strike a deal, but not necessarily the highest obtainable price."

of the duty of loyalty). Where a director engages in a transaction with the corporation, the transaction is voidable unless approved by a disinterested majority of the board of directors after full disclosure. Ohio Rev. Code § 1701.60. Here, Plaintiff alleges that there was no disinterested majority of the Board. In that situation, the only way to ensure that the transaction would not be voidable is for the corporation to be able to show that the transaction was actually fair to the corporation at the time it was authorized. If the Tender Offer was voided as not fair to the company, it would have serious consequences for the corporation. The ESOP would not be a qualified plan and therefore not a tax-exempt entity. As a consequence, the company would no longer be 100% owned by a tax-exempt entity and would owe substantial taxes.

Plaintiff argues that when an attorney representing a company is aware that the directors have a conflict of interest, or are engaged in self-dealing, the attorney must advise the board of directors, acting for the company, that the transaction would be voidable unless objectively shown to be fair to the company at the time it was authorized. [The court cites Ohio Rule of Professional Conduct 1.13(b)]. Plaintiff claims that although aware of the directors' conflicts with regard to the Tender Offer, and the substantial harm to the corporation if the transaction were disqualified, MWE failed to advise the Board that the transaction would be voidable unless it could be shown to be fair to the corporation. . . .

"An organizational client is a legal entity, but it cannot act except through its officers, directors, employees, shareholders, and other constituents." Ohio R. Prof. Cond. 1.13, Official Comment 1. Therefore, a corporation, acting through its board of directors, has an obligation to determine that a transaction between the corporation and its directors or officers is fair to the corporation and not prejudicially beneficial to the conflicted directors or officers. Thus, MWE had a duty to its client, the company, to ensure that the Board was not self-dealing. . . .

Accordingly, Plaintiff has alleged sufficient facts in order to state a claim. . . .

3. Whether the Tender Offer Violated Erisa and Burdened the Company With Debt Which Ultimately Forced It into Bankruptcy . . .

If MWE provided bad legal advice that caused individual directors and officers to breach their fiduciary duties under ERISA, MWE's client, the corporation, would be harmed by invalidation of the transaction. If the transaction was invalid, it would invalidate Antioch's entire capital structure and tax-exempt status.

Accordingly, Plaintiff's claim survives. . . .

5. Aiding and Abetting Breaches of Fiduciary Duty by the Morgans

The Trust alleges that MWE aided and abetted the Morgans' breaches of fiduciary duty when they pursued the Tender Offer to maximize their own interests at the expense of the corporation. MWE "counseled the Morgans on the best way to structure the transaction in order for the Morgans to maintain control and to minimize the effective powers of the ESOP trustee." MWE enabled and facilitated the conflicted transaction. MWE "participated in structuring the transaction, advising as to various alternatives and drafting the necessary documents," and MWE failed to advise the board of its duty to independently verify the fairness and prudence of the transaction, and failed to keep the board focused on the best interests of the corporation. Plaintiff also alleges that MWE enabled and facilitated the Morgans' interference with Antioch's efforts to find an independent purchaser, by advising the Morgans on their retention of separate financial advisors and by participating in a decision to give preference to a self-dealing refinancing by the Morgans, discouraging other suitors. . . .

Here, the Morgans acted in their own self-interest, and not in the interests of Antioch, when they allegedly breached their fiduciary duties. MWE assisted the Morgans "to maximize their own interests, which were in conflict with those of the corporation." Moreover, the complaint alleges that the transaction was to the detriment of the company." As a result of the transaction, Antioch's interest bearing debt rose from $10.8 million as of December 31, 2002 to $201 million as of December 31, 2003.

Accordingly, Plaintiff has alleged sufficient facts to state a claim for aiding and abetting. . . .

6. Claims Against Antioch's Directors and Financial Advisors

Plaintiff alleges that MWE committed malpractice by failing to advise Antioch about claims for "breach of fiduciary duty" that it had against the Morgans (and other directors) and about claims for "professional negligence" that it had against its financial advisors. The Trust has alleged that the Tender Offer was detrimental to the corporation and burdened it with massive debt from which it never recovered, ultimately forcing the company into bankruptcy. Plaintiff alleges that competent counsel would have at least questioned whether the company received proper independent financial advice and whether the directors avoided a close analysis of the benefits and detriments of the transaction to the company due to their own desire to gain from the transaction. . . .

Defendant claims that based on the opinions of three separate financial advisors that the $850 per-share price was fair, MWE had no basis for advising Antioch to assert causes of action against its Board for self-dealing. However, these valuations did not state that the $850 per-share was fair to the *corporation* (MWE's client). . . .

Conflicted fiduciaries do not fulfill ERISA's investigative requirements by merely hiring an expert. There is no indication that the directors meaningfully reviewed, discussed, or questioned the valuation.

7. Malpractice Arising Out of Mwe's Advice Relating to Antioch's Attempted Sale and Refinancing

MWE continued to represent Antioch in connection with the company's efforts to sell, refinance, or recapitalize itself, which spanned the period from early 2007 through June 5, 2008, the day that Antioch terminated MWE. While

Antioch had engaged Houlihan again to find a purchaser for the company, MWE helped the Morgan family hire a separate financial advisor . . . to assist in efforts by the Morgans to secure refinancing or recapitalization that would leave the Morgan family in control of the company. Plaintiff claims that despite conflicts between these two efforts, MWE failed to counsel the Board to stop this incompatible dual track approach, which was caused by the Morgans, acting in their own self-interest, rather than in the interest of the company. . . .

Plaintiff claims that these factual allegations support more than a plausible conclusion that Antioch foreclosed opportunities to sell the company to independent purchasers by pandering to the Morgans' interests. Plaintiff claims that it is plausible that a purchaser would pay more to purchase a company outright, including the right to control the company through its own directors and officers, than one would pay to provide financing or capital to others who would control the decision-making. . . .

Defendant claims that the number of financial advisors that Antioch should have retained is a business question, and Plaintiff concedes that MWE had no duty to provide "business advice" to Antioch. The Trust, however, does not allege that MWE should have provided business advice. Rather, the Trust alleges that, as company counsel, MWE should have advised the directors against self-dealing. . . .

[Conclusion]

As part of Antioch's plan of reorganization, in accordance with 11 U.S.C. § 1123(b)(3), Antioch's bankruptcy estate succeeded to and retained certain identified Litigation Claims and Business Litigation Claims . . .

The Trust was created to litigate claims in place of the dissolved estate. As a result, and consistent with fundamental bankruptcy law, the Trustee stands in the shoes of Antioch, and therefore can bring any claim that Antioch could have brought. . . .

Accordingly, . . . Defendant's motion to dismiss is denied.

B. Communication

The duty to communicate with clients is essential to every aspect of every fiduciary duty that lawyers owe clients. Clients cannot control the goals of the representation without information about feasible options. Lawyers cannot act competently unless they initiate communication with clients to understand the initial scope of the relationship and what the clients wish to accomplish. Lawyers must communicate with clients about confidentiality so that clients can decide when to disclose information. They must search for and discuss with clients potential as well as actual conflicts of interest to proceed with a representation.

Communication requires that lawyers understand three key ideas: when to speak, what to say, and who should communicate. The law governing lawyers regulates the "when to speak" obligation by identifying eight events that trigger a lawyer's duty to communicate:

Eight Events That Trigger a Lawyer's Duty to Communicate with Clients

---

1. Initially, to agree on a fee arrangement and to define the scope of the representation, both of which should be explained in an engagement letter.
2. When decisions require client consent about the objectives of the representation, such as the decision to settle or appeal a matter.[1]
3. When decisions require client consultation about the means to be used to accomplish the client's objectives, such as whether to litigate, arbitrate, or mediate a matter, stipulate to a set of facts; or whether to consult with another lawyer.[2]
4. When necessary to periodically update clients on the status of a matter, including information about important developments in the representation itself, as well as changes in the lawyer's practice, such as a serious illness of the lawyer or a merger with another law firm.[3]
5. When a lawyer makes a significant mistake in the matter.[4]
6. When a client requests information.[5]
7. When the law imposes limits on conduct that a client expects the lawyer to undertake.[6]
8. When the lawyer must obtain the client's informed consent, including when the lawyer seeks to:
   - Limit the scope of a representation.[7]
   - Obtain a waiver of a fiduciary obligation owed the client, especially confidentiality and conflicts of interest.[8]
   - Obtain a waiver of a fiduciary obligation to a prospective client.[9]
   - Provide an evaluation for use by a third person that is likely to adversely affect the client's interests.[10]

The second part of understanding the duty to communicate involves knowing how much and what kind of information to disclose. In most cases "reasonable disclosure of information" is required.[11] But when the lawyer is required to defer to a client's choice or seek the client's informed consent (#8 above), the law governing lawyers imposes a more exacting standard, which focuses on the importance of both disclosure and explanation of relevant information.[12] A client's agreement constitutes informed consent if the lawyer has communicated "adequate information and explanation" about two matters: "the material risks

---

1. MR 1.2(a); RLGL §2 2.
2. MR 1.2(a), 1.4(a)(2), 2.1; RLGL § 21.
3. MR 1.4(a)(3); RLGL § 20, Comment c.
4. MR 1.4(a)(3); RLGL § 20, Comment c.
5. MR 1.4(a)(4); RLGL § 20, Comment d.
6. MR 1.4(a)(5); RLGL § 22, Comment c.
7. MR 1.2(c); RLGL § 19.
8. MR 1.4(a)(1), 1.6-1.12; RLGL §§ 20, 60-62, 121-135.
9. MR 1.18; RLGL § 15.
10. MR 2.3; RLGL § 95.
11. MR 1.4, RLGL § 20(1).
12. MR 1.0(e) (informed consent); RLGL § 20(3). *See* Practice Pointers: *Implementing a Conflicts Control System, infra* p.419.

of and reasonably available alternatives to the proposed course of conduct."[13] Labeling this obligation "informed consent" restates the lawyer's fiduciary obligation recognized in several centuries of cases.[14]

The cases in this chapter illustrate that the third part of the duty to communicate, who should communicate, has two aspects. It seems axiomatic that lawyer and client should communicate, but either or both can designate agents for that purpose. When that occurs, the lawyer's fiduciary obligations to the client place additional burdens on the lawyer to clarify the goals and intent of the client.

In *Machado,* the client designated an agent to communicate with his lawyer, even signing a power of attorney to facilitate his bankruptcy. The case makes clear that the lawyer's continuous communications with the client's agent throughout the representation caused Machado to mistake both the client's instructions (file for bankruptcy) and the nature and scope of the agent's authority (bankruptcy or tax lien). A similar mistake occurred in the next case, in a joint client situation. In *dePape,* the law firm clearly took on two clients, the potential employer/clinic (Trimark) and Dr. dePape. But it relied on one of the two clients (the clinic) to speak for the other, misunderstanding the actual intent of the silent client. One lesson of these cases is that lawyers who rely on one client or client agent to fully express the interests of another do so at their own peril.[15]

These cases also illustrate the use of agents by law firms. In *Machado,* the client claimed that he spoke with the lawyer's agent, a secretary, outlining how he wanted to proceed. Model Rule 5.3 contemplates this delegation, so long as the lawyer makes "reasonable efforts to ensure that the nonlawyer assistant's conduct "is compatible with the professional obligations of the lawyer." This, of course, meant that Machado was bound by a client's oral message to a lawyer's agent, which in Machado's case served to reinforce the client's point that he had retained Machado for a bankruptcy alone.[16] In *dePape,* a similar communication gap occurred when the law firm sent a local immigration lawyer to assist its client at the border. It fell to this agent of the law firm to communicate to the client for the first time the nature of proposed but undesired immigration status. Both cases illustrate how an apparent lack of communication between agents of a lawyer and a lawyer can complicate a lawyer's representation of a client.

---

13. MR 1.0(e) (informed consent); RLGL § 20, Comment e.

14. *See* Susan R. Martyn, *Informed Consent in the Practice of Law,* 48 Geo. Wash. U. L. Rev. 307 (1980).

15. A similar issue occurs when clients need interpreters to speak to lawyers. N. H. Bar Assn. Ethics Comm. Op 2009-10/2 (lawyer should select interpreter who can understand and convey legal topics and client's wishes). *See also* RLGL § 70, Comment f (an interpreter is a client's agent for communication for purposes of the attorney-client privilege).

16. Note that Machado did not deny that this communication occurred but tried to avoid the issue by claiming that he never received phone calls or written communications from the client. *See also* Mich. Inf. Op. RI-348 (2010) (lawyer who delegates client communication to non-lawyer legal assistants must properly train and supervise them to provide competent advice and communication).

Problems

4-4. In representing an employer, Martyn & Fox forgot to insert a noncompete clause into an employment agreement for a new key employee, even though our client specifically requested that protection. Any problem? What if Martyn & Fox forgot to advise its client that a covenant not to compete could be included?

4-5. Client retains Martyn to handle a contract dispute with an important customer. Martyn files suit, warns Client of the risks of going to trial, is unable to settle the case, and the case ends in an adverse jury verdict. Disgruntled Client called Martyn several weeks later. "I've been talking to one of my lawyer friends. He couldn't understand why we didn't mediate this dispute. We could've gotten a great settlement and I wouldn't have lost a customer." Should Martyn have offered client the option of mediation or arbitration?

Consider: Model Rules 1.2, 1.4, 2.1
RLGL §§ 16, 20-23, 49

dePape v. Trinity Health Systems, Inc.

242 F. Supp. 2d 585 (N.D. Iowa 2003)

BENNETT, Chief Judge . . .

The plaintiff in this breach-of-contract and legal malpractice case, Dr. Gregory dePape, is a Canadian citizen who completed his medical studies and training in Canada. Thousands of miles away in the small city of Fort Dodge, Iowa, Trimark Physicians Group, Ltd. ("Trimark") [a wholly owned subsidiary of Trinity Health Systems, Inc.] sought a family physician to fill a vacancy and to meet the burgeoning needs of the Fort Dodge medical community. . . . Trimark successfully recruited Dr. dePape to fill this vacancy, and in March of 1999, Trimark and Dr. dePape, while still living and working in Canada, entered into a five-year employment contract.

As part of the contract negotiations process, the parties discussed immigration matters and the fact that Dr. dePape needed to obtain a visa for lawful entry and permission to work in the United States prior to beginning employment. In order to obtain such permission, Trimark engaged the services of a St. Louis, Missouri law firm, Blumenfeld, Kaplan & Sandweiss, P.C. . . .

On April 23, 1999, one month after Trimark and Dr. dePape entered into their employment contract, Blumenfeld held an initial conference regarding its representation of Trimark and Dr. dePape. Partners A and B of the Blumenfeld firm, [and representatives of Trimark] participated in this initial conference. Notably, Blumenfeld did not advise Dr. dePape to participate, nor did it even inform him of the conference. At this conference, Blumenfeld outlined Dr. dePape's immigration options. At the time of this conference, Blumenfeld learned (1) that Dr. dePape had a five-year employment contract with Trimark; (2) that both Dr.

dePape and Trimark expected an employment relationship that would endure longer than five years and, ideally, the entirety of Dr. dePape's medical career; and (3) that Dr. dePape had not taken a three-stage set of examinations, known as the USMLE's [United States Medical Licensing Examination], which precluded him from receiving one of the two visas available to foreign physicians—namely, the H-1B visa [the preferred method of bringing a foreign physician into the United States] . . .

After holding the initial conference, Partner A sent [Trimark] an engagement letter on April 26, 1999, confirming the parties' agreement and Blumenfeld's commitment to represent Trimark *and* Dr. dePape throughout the immigration process. . . . The engagement letter specifically states that both Trimark and Dr. dePape are Blumenfeld's clients, but Partner A sent a copy of the letter only to Trimark. . . . The engagement letter outlines Dr. dePape's immigration options; yet Blumenfeld did not send a copy to him, nor did Blumenfeld advise Trimark to forward the engagement letter to Dr. dePape, who . . . did not see the letter until preparing for this trial. . . .

. . . Blumenfeld never attempted to ascertain whether Dr. dePape would complete the USMLE's, nor did it advise Dr. dePape that completion of the USMLE's was a necessary prerequisite to obtaining an H-1B visa and would be in his best interest. . . . Dr. dePape declined that option because he held misconceptions about the length of time that it took to complete the exams. Dr. dePape believed that the USMLE's could not be completed in fewer than two years, while Partner A and Partner B testified that the process could be completed in six to eight months, [which Dr. dePape could have completed while waiting for his Iowa medical license]. . . .

[Eight months later when] Blumenfeld belatedly ascertained that Dr. dePape could not enter the country on an H-1B visa, it switched gears and began working on a TN visa. . . .

. . . Because Dr. dePape had a contract that outlasted the duration of the TN visa and was for a job that was not permitted by the visa, Blumenfeld, without consulting its clients, concocted a fictitious job title and description. Blumenfeld labeled this position "Physician Consultant" and described the duties of this position as a "community health care needs assessment." Blumenfeld did not discuss with Dr. dePape or Trimark the newly created position or the fact that Dr. dePape could not enter the United States and practice family medicine on the TN visa. . . .

. . . [W]hile Blumenfeld was billing for an H1B visa for which Dr. dePape was not qualified and preparing its sham TN application, Dr. dePape . . . worked in Canada doing locum tenens, which is temporary substitution work for vacationing physicians.

When Dr. dePape learned that he would be granted his Iowa medical license, he and Trimark . . . then worked with Blumenfeld to arrange a June 8, 2000 entry at the Peace Bridge in Buffalo, New York, which Blumenfeld chose because of its arrangement with a particular INS officer. Dr. dePape ended his lease, shipped all of his belongings and his vehicle to Fort Dodge, and terminated his locum tenens. He and his fiancée . . . flew from Vancouver to Toronto, and then rented a car to drive to Buffalo, New York. They planned to drive across the border, drop the car off at the rental station in Buffalo, and then fly to Fort Dodge, Iowa, where Dr. dePape intended to begin his new life. . . .

Because the costs of accompanying Dr. dePape to his INS interview at the Peace Bridge were prohibitively high, Blumenfeld, consistent with its usual practice, retained its local immigration lawyer, Mr. Eiss, to assist Dr. dePape. Mr. Eiss met Dr. dePape at a coffee shop near the INS office in Fort Erie, Canada on the morning of June 8, 2000. There, for the first time, Dr. dePape was shown the letter describing his position as a Physician Consultant and told that he could not work in the United States as a family physician. . . .

. . . During this short meeting, Mr. Eiss played the role of an immigration officer and asked Dr. dePape what he was planning on doing in the United States. Dr. dePape responded that he was going to be a family physician. Mr. Eiss shook his head and handed Dr. dePape the TN application letter. Dr. dePape was shocked, surprised, and outraged by the letter's description of his position and its temporary nature because, as far as he knew, he was permanently moving to Fort Dodge to be a doctor, not a temporary Physician Consultant doing a community health care needs assessment—something he had never heard about or even knew what it was. Dr. dePape was skeptical and concerned about the lawfulness of representing to INS that he intended to perform a community health care needs assessment and then return to Canada. However, Mr. Eiss convinced Dr. dePape that the community health care needs assessment was legal and only a mere technicality that would not impede him from practicing medicine. Hesitant but confident in the legal advice of his attorney, Dr. dePape proceeded with Mr. Eiss to the INS office to attempt Dr. dePape's entry under TN status.

There, the INS official interviewing Dr. dePape did not believe that Dr. dePape sought entry to perform a community health care needs assessment. When the INS official asked Dr. dePape directly why he was going to the United States, Dr. dePape truthfully answered that he intended to practice family medicine. Because the TN visa does not permit this, the INS official turned Dr. dePape away and sent him back to Canada. Mr. Eiss did not return with Dr. dePape to counsel him further.

Devastated and shocked by his failed entry and with no direction from Mr. Eiss or the Blumenfeld firm, Dr. dePape found a pay phone and called [a Trimark representative, who] advised him to wait thirty minutes and to try to enter the United States as a visitor. If he accomplished that, she instructed him to drop the rental car off at the Buffalo airport and to fly to Fort Dodge in order to work out a "plan B." Dr. dePape and his fiancée followed [this] advice, but the INS officials immediately recognized Dr. dePape. The officials not only interrogated him and accused him of being a liar, they searched his car and belongings and Dr. dePape and his fiancée felt as if they were being treated like criminals. INS again denied Dr. dePape entry to the United States, told him not to come back, and escorted him back to Canada. Dr. dePape felt helpless, humiliated, and angry.

When that entry attempt failed, Dr. dePape was literally stranded. He had no job, no home, and no possessions—not even his medical bag. Fortunately, he had a credit card with him and, at his own expense, he and his fiancée drove back to Toronto, where they paid over two thousand U.S. dollars for last-minute plane tickets back to Vancouver. Throughout this entire ordeal, there was no backup contingency plan and no advice from Blumenfeld.

Ultimately, Dr. dePape returned to British Columbia and, in his words, "restarted his life." He made several attempts to contact Trimark, [whose representative eventually] implored Dr. dePape to attempt another entry in Buffalo, New York, but he refused. She then asked if he was willing to take the USMLE's, but because he labored under the impression that the exams would have taken years to complete, he refused that option as well. Instead, Dr. dePape explored his employment options in Canada and ultimately began his own private practice in October of 2001.

Shockingly, no one at Blumenfeld ever attempted to contact Dr. dePape after his failed entry attempt on June 8, 2000. . . . [The court dismissed all of Dr. dePape's claims against Trinity and Trimark.]

D. COUNT IV: LEGAL MALPRACTICE . . .

It is well established that an attorney-client relationship may give rise to a duty, the breach of which may be legal malpractice. In a legal malpractice case, the plaintiff must demonstrate:

(1) the existence of an attorney client relationship giving rise to a duty, (2) the attorney, either by an act or failure to act, violated or breached that duty, (3) the attorney's breach of duty proximately caused injury to the client, and (4) the client sustained actual injury, loss, or damage.

In this case, there is no dispute that an attorney-client relationship (the first element) existed between Dr. dePape and Blumenfeld. . . .

1. Failure to Pursue H-1B Visa . . .

There is no question that Dr. dePape was not eligible for an H-1B visa because he had not taken the requisite examinations—the USMLE's. There is also no question that Blumenfeld was negligent when it failed to advise Dr. dePape of the consequences of not taking the USMLE's and failed to correct his misconception about the length of time the exams took to complete.

However, the record is devoid of any evidence establishing that Dr. dePape would have taken the USMLE's and become eligible for an H-1B visa if Blumenfeld had advised him to do so. Thus, this claim fails for lack of causation. . . .

2. Failure to Communicate and Advise

a. Breach of Duty . . .

"An attorney breaches the duty of care owed to the client when the attorney fails to use 'such skill, prudence and diligence as lawyers of ordinary skill and capacity commonly possess and exercise in the performance of the task which [is undertaken].'" Expert testimony is generally required to establish that an attorney's conduct is negligent, but, when the negligence is so obvious that a layperson can recognize or infer it, such testimony is unnecessary.

In this case, the plaintiff offered the deposition testimony of Bart Chavez to establish Blumenfeld's negligence. The court has reviewed Mr. Chavez's deposition, and his testimony strongly supports a finding of negligence in this case. Moreover, the court finds that Blumenfeld's breach is of the ilk that does not necessitate expert testimony because it is so obvious and outrageous that a lay person could easily recognize it without the assistance of an expert. Even in the absence of Mr. Chavez's expert testimony, which clearly identifies and articulates a standard of care that Blumenfeld failed to meet, the court is not without guidance in assessing the level of care Blumenfeld is charged with maintaining. Although violations of [the Rules of Professional Conduct] do not create a private cause of action for a client, the rules provide guidance in determining the fiduciary duty owed to a client by an attorney. . . .

Accordingly, the minimum communication Blumenfeld should have maintained with Dr. dePape is: [The court cites Missouri Rule of Professional Conduct 1.4 and Comment 5 because the defendants are admitted to practice in Missouri.]

In fact, Blumenfeld itself understands the importance of communication with its clients, and it prides itself on maintaining regular client contact. Indeed, the "letterhead" on each link of Blumenfeld's webpage advertises that Blumenfeld "recognize[s] the importance of personal contact with clients as an integral part of being a responsive firm." www.bks-law.com. . . .

That Blumenfeld breached its duty of communicating with and advising Dr. dePape does not present the court with a close call. Because Dr. dePape had no information, he indisputably lacked sufficient information upon which to make an informed decision about his immigration. A 20 minute meeting with Mr. Eiss at the border on the morning of Dr. dePape's entry attempt, which was preceded by months of silence, did not cure Blumenfeld's failure to communicate with Dr. dePape because, by that time, it was too late for Dr. dePape to make an informed decision regarding his immigration to the United States. Moreover, the only decision Dr. dePape was ever allowed to make was the one he was faced with at the border—lie and proceed with the immigration charade or tell the truth and be rejected. . . .

While there are a myriad of ways Blumenfeld could have fulfilled its obligation to Dr. dePape, there is no question that Blumenfeld's failure to communicate at all with Dr. dePape is inadequate to meet its obligation under any conceivable option. For example, Blumenfeld could have (1) sent a copy of the retention letter to Dr. dePape, (2) written Dr. dePape a follow-up letter to the initial conference explaining the requirements of the TN and the H-1B visas, (3) followed-up the written explanation with a telephone call to ensure that Dr. dePape understood the visa requirements and to answer any questions that Dr. dePape may have had, and (4) if it was not intended to be a sham, explained the community health care needs assessment to the hospital to determine if they needed or wanted it and to Dr. dePape to determine if he was ready, willing, and able to perform it. Because Blumenfeld failed to do anything to explain Dr. dePape's immigration options and their requirements and, in addition, sprung the community health care needs assessment on Dr. dePape at the border, the court finds that Blumenfeld breached its duty to communicate with and advise Dr. dePape. . . .

b. Causation

. . . "The burden of proving proximate cause in a legal malpractice action is the same as any other negligence action. To recover, the injured must show that, but for the attorney's negligence, the loss would not have occurred." As applied to this situation, the plaintiff must demonstrate that, but for Blumenfeld's failure to communicate with and advise Dr. dePape, Dr. dePape would have (1) gained entry to the United States or (2) would have chosen to pursue other employment options in Canada instead of attempting to immigrate to the United States. . . .

. . . [B]ecause of Blumenfeld's implausible interpretation of "temporary entry" and because of its exceedingly broad interpretation of the level of patient care permissible under the TN classification, the court finds that Blumenfeld attempted to perpetrate a fraud on the INS by representing that Dr. dePape sought entry to the United States as a Physician Consultant. . . .

However, this conclusion does not relieve Blumenfeld of liability because the court also finds that, had Dr. dePape been informed of his immigration options at the outset, he would have pursued other employment in Canada. Therefore, he would have been able to start his own practice or to begin work in an established practice as soon as he was licensed in Canada.

c. Damages . . .

i. Lost income. . . . The court previously found that, had Blumenfeld explained the implications of this to him, Dr. dePape would have chosen to remain in Canada and would have started his practice as soon as possible. . . .

The difference between the net income Dr. dePape could have earned during the damages period and what he actually earned is . . . $203,736.20 United States dollars in lost income.

ii. Emotional distress. . . . "Under the tort theory of negligence, there is no general duty of care to avoid causing emotional harm to another. However, where the parties assume a relationship that is contractual in nature and deals with services or acts that involve deep emotional responses in the event of a breach, [Iowa courts] recognize a duty of care to protect against emotional distress."

In this case, Dr. dePape shares a special relationship with Blumenfeld that gives rise to a duty to avoid causing Dr. dePape emotional harm. This is not the sort of legal malpractice case in which mental distress damages are not recoverable. In Lawrence v. Grinde, 534 N.W.2d 414, 422 (Iowa 1995), the Iowa Supreme Court held that a legal malpractice plaintiff could not recover mental distress damages in his legal malpractice action because his distress was too remote to be reasonably foreseeable. There, the plaintiff's attorney failed to disclose a recent settlement on a bankruptcy petition, and the United States government subsequently indicted the plaintiff for bankruptcy fraud. The plaintiff was acquitted, but his indictment and trial gave rise to considerable media coverage.

In that case, the mental distress damages sought were indistinguishable from the damages sought for the plaintiff's alleged damages to his reputation. But because the damage to the plaintiff's reputation as a result of the indictment was one-step removed from the defendant's negligent act in preparing the bankruptcy petition, the Iowa court held that the plaintiff's claim for mental distress damages failed on causation.

Here, Blumenfeld was retained to assist Dr. dePape with his immigration, but instead of assisting Dr. dePape, Blumenfeld's negligence placed Dr. dePape directly in harm's way. It should be noted that Blumenfeld would not be liable for the mental distress that might have accompanied a failed legitimate entry attempt because it would be unfair under those circumstances to hold a lawyer responsible for the independent decision of an independent governmental entity. But in this case, Blumenfeld not only failed to provide Dr. dePape with sufficient information for him to make an informed decision about his immigration, moments before the entry attempt, Blumenfeld (through Mr. Eiss) counseled Dr. dePape to lie to INS officials in order to gain entry to the United States under false pretenses.

Aside from being unethical, this conduct directly led to the INS official's decision to deny Dr. dePape's visa request and formed the basis of the INS official's accusation that Dr. dePape was a liar. . . . Thus, the emotional distress damages resulting from Blumenfeld's negligence in this case are not one-step removed, and Dr. dePape may recover for them.

The court finds that, while short-lived, Dr. dePape suffered severe and intense emotional distress. He was ambushed at the United States border, asked to perpetrate a fraud on the United States government in order to gain entry, and then sent on his way without even the courtesy of a phone call from his lawyers. At the border, INS officials degraded Dr. dePape, and he felt extraordinarily humiliated. Moreover, he had spent the past fifteen months planning to begin his professional career with Trimark and had made the arrangements to do so. . . .

Fortunately, Dr. dePape is a person of strong character and incredible integrity. While he was set back by the emotional turmoil surrounding the ambush at the border, he was able to move on and begin anew. Accordingly, the court finds that Dr. dePape is entitled to $75,000 USD for emotional distress to compensate him for the severe level of mental anguish directly caused by Blumenfeld's negligence. . . .

THEREFORE, upon consideration of the evidence and the parties' arguments, the court finds (1) that there is no basis in fact or in law to hold Trinity or Trimark liable for Dr. dePape's damages; and (2) that Blumenfeld was extraordinarily negligent in failing to inform and communicate with Dr. dePape concerning his immigration and in counseling him to perpetrate a fraud on the INS in order to gain entry to the United States; and (3) that, as a result of the damages caused by this negligence, Dr. dePape is entitled to recover from defendant Blumenfeld a total of $278,736.20 USD for his lost income and emotional distress. . . . [13]

C. Control and Communication in Criminal Defense Representation

Lawyers who represent criminal defendants face special issues about what it means to "proceed in a manner reasonably calculated to advance a client's lawful objectives, as defined by the client after consultation."[1] In *Maples*, we examine the harm that can befall a criminal defendant when a lawyer violates this foundational obligation to represent, and not to abandon a client. In *Frey* and *Lafler*, we consider specific issues about control and communication that arise in the context of appeals of criminal convictions based on an allegation of ineffective assistance of counsel.

Problems

4-6. Martyn & Fox is handling a state habeas petition for a death row inmate. Martyn thinks the trial counsel provided ineffective assistance of counsel. Martyn discusses this with her client. She explains the investigation she needs to undertake. The client listens intently but warns Martyn the one thing she may not do is talk to her client's mother. "I'll tell you what I told the other fellow. Mom's suffered enough already. I direct you not to talk to her."

4-7. Client insisted on taking the stand. The testimony was a disaster. Is Fox in trouble for letting his client take the stand? How about Fox's refusal, over the client's insistence, to cross-examine the 80-year-old victim, who, although slightly senile, left the jury in tears on direct?

4-8. Is Fox in trouble because he failed to inform a criminal defendant about a plea bargain offered by the prosecutor? What if Client told Fox, "I'll never cop a plea"? What if the defendant was eventually

---

13. The evidence in this case strongly supports an award of punitive damages against Blumenfeld. Dr. dePape was bushwhacked at the border by Blumenfeld's egregious breach of duty and its willful and wanton disregard for Dr. dePape's rights. The plaintiff did not request punitive damages in his prayer for relief, and the court recognizes its authority to award them when supported by the evidence, even in the absence of a specific prayer for punitive damages. *See* Boeckmann v. Joseph, 889 F.2d 1094 (9th Cir. 1989) (table op.) (plaintiff plead fraud and, therefore, the defendant was on notice because a finding of fraud supports an award of punitive damages).

In Iowa, the standard for punitive damages is "Whether, by a preponderance of clear, convincing, and satisfactory evidence, the conduct of the defendant from which the claim arose constituted willful and wanton disregard for the rights or safety of another." Iowa Code § 668A.1(1)(a). The court has carefully reviewed the plaintiff's initial and amended complaints but finds that Dr. dePape did not plead sufficient facts to put Blumenfeld on notice that punitive damages were at issue. Therefore, despite the overwhelming evidence to support an award of punitive damages in this case, the court will not impose them.

1. RLGL § 16 (1).

convicted and sentenced to five years, and the plea bargain would have resulted in a two-year sentence? What if Fox erroneously advised the client not to worry about pleading guilty because he would never be deported after living in the country so long?

4-9. Is Fox in trouble for failing to tell his client he once represented the victim of the alleged crime?

Consider: Model Rules 1.1-1.4
           RLGL §§ 21, 23

Maples v. Thomas

132 S. Ct. 912 (2012)

Justice GINSBURG delivered the opinion of the Court. . . .

I . . .

[A]s of 2006, 86% of the attorneys representing Alabama's death row inmates in state collateral review proceedings [worked for either out-of-state public interest groups or an out-of-state mega-firm.] On occasion, some prisoners sentenced to death receive no postconviction representation at all. . . .

This system was in place when, in 1997, Alabama charged Maples with two counts of capital murder; the victims, Stacy Alan Terry and Barry Dewayne Robinson II, were Maples' friends who, on the night of the murders, had been out on the town with him. Maples pleaded not guilty, and his case proceeded to trial, where he was represented by two court-appointed Alabama attorneys. Only one of them had earlier served in a capital case. Neither counsel had previously tried the penalty phase of a capital case. Compensation for each lawyer was capped at $1,000 for time spent out-of-court preparing Maples' case, and at $40 per hour for in-court services.

Finding Maples guilty on both counts, the jury recommended that he be sentenced to death. The vote was 10 to 2, the minimum number Alabama requires for a death. Accepting the jury's recommendation, the trial court sentenced Maples to death. On direct appeal, the Alabama Court of Criminal Appeals and the Alabama Supreme Court affirmed the convictions and sentence.

Two out-of-state volunteers represented Maples in postconviction proceedings: Jaasi Munanka and Clara Ingen-Housz, both associates at the New York offices of the Sullivan & Cromwell law firm. At the time, Alabama required out-of-state attorneys to associate local counsel when seeking admission to practice *pro hac vice* before an Alabama court, regardless of the nature of the proceeding. The Alabama Rule further prescribed that the local attorney's name "appear on all notices, orders, pleadings, and other documents filed in the cause," and that local counsel "accept joint and several responsibility with the foreign attorney to the client, to opposing parties and counsel, and to the court or administrative agency in all matters [relating to the case]."

Munanka and Ingen-Housz associated Huntsville, Alabama attorney John Butler as local counsel. Notwithstanding his obligations under Alabama law, Butler informed Munanka and Ingen-Housz, "at the outset," that he would serve as local counsel only for the purpose of allowing the two New York attorneys to appear *pro hac vice* on behalf of Maples. Given his lack of "resources, available time [and] experience," Butler told the Sullivan & Cromwell lawyers, he could not "deal with substantive issues in the case." The Sullivan & Cromwell attorneys accepted Butler's conditions. . . .

With the aid of his *pro bono* counsel, Maples filed a petition for postconviction relief under Alabama Rule of Criminal Procedure 32. Among other claims, Maples asserted that his . . . inexperienced and underfunded attorneys failed to develop and raise an obvious intoxication defense, did not object to several egregious instances of prosecutorial misconduct, and woefully underprepared for the penalty phase of his trial. . . .

Some seven months later, in the summer of 2002, both Munanka and Ingen-Housz left Sullivan & Cromwell. Munanka gained a clerkship with a federal judge; Ingen-Housz accepted a position with the European Commission in Belgium. Neither attorney told Maples of their departure from Sullivan & Cromwell or of their resulting inability to continue to represent him. In disregard of Alabama law, neither attorney sought the trial court's leave to withdraw. Compounding Munanka's and Ingen-Housz's inaction, no other Sullivan & Cromwell lawyer entered an appearance on Maples' behalf, moved to substitute counsel, or otherwise notified the court of any change in Maples' representation. . . .

There things stood when, in May 2003, the trial court, without holding a hearing, entered an order denying Maples' Rule 32 petition. The clerk of the Alabama trial court mailed copies of the order to Maples' three attorneys of record. He sent Munanka's and Ingen-Housz's copies to Sullivan & Cromwell's New York address, which the pair had provided upon entering their appearances.

When those copies arrived at Sullivan & Cromwell, Munanka and Ingen-Housz had long since departed. The notices, however, were not forwarded to another Sullivan & Cromwell attorney. Instead, a mailroom employee sent the unopened envelopes back to the court. "Returned to Sender-Attempted, Unknown" was stamped on the envelope addressed to Munanka. A similar stamp appeared on the envelope addressed to Ingen-Housz, along with the handwritten notation "Return to Sender-Left Firm."

Upon receiving back the unopened envelopes he had mailed to Munanka and Ingen-Housz, the Alabama court clerk took no further action. In particular, the clerk did not contact Munanka or Ingen-Housz at the personal telephone numbers or home addresses they had provided in their *pro hac vice* applications. Nor did the clerk alert Sullivan & Cromwell or Butler. Butler received his copy of the order, but did not act on it. He assumed that Munanka and Ingen-Housz, who had been "CC'd" on the order, would take care of filing an appeal.

Meanwhile, the clock ticked on Maples' appeal. Under Alabama's Rules of Appellate Procedure, Maples had 42 days to file a notice of appeal from the trial court's May 22, 2003 order denying Maples' petition for postconviction relief. No appeal notice was filed, and the time allowed for filing expired on July 7, 2003.

A little over a month later, on August 13, 2003, Alabama Assistant Attorney General Jon Hayden, the attorney representing the State in Maples' collateral review proceedings, sent a letter directly to Maples. Hayden's letter informed Maples of the missed deadline for initiating an appeal within the State's system, and notified him that four weeks remained during which he could file a federal habeas petition. Hayden mailed the letter to Maples only, using his prison address. No copy was sent to Maples' attorneys of record, or to anyone else acting on Maples' behalf.

Upon receiving the State's letter, Maples immediately contacted his mother. She telephoned Sullivan & Cromwell to inquire about her son's case. Prompted by her call, Sullivan & Cromwell attorneys Marc De Leeuw, Felice Duffy, and Kathy Brewer submitted a motion, through Butler, asking the trial court to reissue its order denying Maples' Rule 32 petition, thereby restarting the 42-day appeal period.

The trial court denied the motion, noting that Munanka and Ingen-Housz had not withdrawn from the case and, consequently, were "still attorneys of record for the petitioner." Furthermore, the court added, attorneys De Leeuw, Duffy, and Brewer had not "yet been admitted to practice in Alabama" or "entered appearances as attorneys of record." "How," the court asked, "can a Circuit Clerk in Decatur, Alabama know what is going on in a law firm in New York, New York?" Declining to blame the clerk for the missed notice of appeal deadline, the court said it was "unwilling to enter into subterfuge in order to gloss over mistakes made by counsel for the petitioner." . . .

Having exhausted his state postconviction remedies, Maples sought federal habeas corpus relief. . . . [T]he State urged that Maples had forever forfeited those claims [because] he did not timely appeal from the trial court's denial of his petition. . . .

The District Court determined that Maples had defaulted his ineffective-assistance claims, and that he had not shown "cause" sufficient to overcome the default. . . . A divided panel of the Eleventh Circuit affirmed. . . .

II

A . . .

Cause for a procedural default exists where "something *external* to the petitioner, something that cannot fairly be attributed to him[,] . . . 'impeded [his] efforts to comply with the State's procedural rule.'" Coleman v. Thompson, 501 U. S. 722, 753 (1991). Negligence on the part of a prisoner's postconviction attorney does not qualify as "cause." That is so, we reasoned in *Coleman*, because the attorney is the prisoner's agent, and under "well-settled principles of agency law," the principal bears the risk of negligent conduct on the part of his agent. Thus, when a petitioner's postconviction attorney misses a filing deadline, the petitioner is bound by the oversight and cannot rely on it to establish cause. We do not disturb that general rule.

A markedly different situation is presented, however, when an attorney abandons his client without notice, and thereby occasions the default. Having severed the principal-agent relationship, an attorney no longer acts, or fails to act, as the client's representative. See 1 Restatement (Third) of Law Governing Lawyers § 31, Comment 1(1998).

Our recent decision in Holland v. Florida, 130 S. Ct. 2549 (2010), is instructive. That case involved a missed one-year deadline, prescribed by 28 U.S.C. § 2244(d), for filing a federal habeas petition. *Holland* presented two issues: first, whether the § 2244(d) time limitation can be tolled for equitable reasons, and, second, whether an attorney's unprofessional conduct can ever count as an "extraordinary circumstance" justifying equitable tolling. We answered yes to both questions. . . .

In a concurring opinion in *Holland,* Justice Alito homed in on the essential difference between a claim of attorney error, however egregious, and a claim that an attorney had essentially abandoned his client. Holland's plea fit the latter category: He alleged abandonment "evidenced by counsel's near-total failure to communicate with petitioner or to respond to petitioner's many inquiries and requests over a period of several years." If true, Justice Alito explained, "petitioner's allegations would suffice to establish extraordinary circumstances beyond his control[:] Common sense dictates that a litigant cannot be held constructively responsible for the conduct of an attorney who is not operating as his agent in any meaningful sense of that word."

We agree that, under agency principles, a client cannot be charged with the acts or omissions of an attorney who has abandoned him. Nor can a client be faulted for failing to act on his own behalf when he lacks reason to believe his attorneys of record, in fact, are not representing him. . . .

B

From the time he filed his initial Rule 32 petition until well after time ran out for appealing the trial court's denial of that petition, Maples had only three attorneys of record: Munanka, Ingen-Housz, and Butler. Unknown to Maples, not one of these lawyers was in fact serving as his attorney during the 42 days permitted for an appeal from the trial court's order. . . .

The State contends that Sullivan & Cromwell represented Maples throughout his state postconviction proceedings. Accordingly, the State urges, Maples cannot establish abandonment by counsel continuing through the six weeks allowed for noticing an appeal from the trial court's denial of his Rule 32 petition. We disagree. It is undisputed that Munanka and Ingen-Housz severed their agency relationship with Maples long before the default occurred [leaving] Sullivan & Cromwell's employ in the summer of 2002, at least nine months before the Alabama trial court entered its order denying Rule 32 relief. . . . Hornbook agency law establishes that the attorneys' departure from Sullivan & Cromwell and their commencement of employment that prevented them from representing Maples ended their agency relationship with him. See 1 Restatement (Second) of Agency § 112 (1957). . . .

[T]he State argues that, nonetheless, . . . [o]ther attorneys at the firm, . . . continued to serve as Maples' counsel. Regarding this assertion, we note, first, that the record is cloudy on the role other Sullivan & Cromwell attorneys played.[8]

The slim record on activity at Sullivan & Cromwell, however, does not warrant a remand to determine more precisely the work done by firm lawyers other than Munanka and Ingen-Housz. For the facts essential to our decision are not in doubt. At the time of the default, the Sullivan & Cromwell attorneys who later came forward—De Leeuw, Felice Duffy, and Kathy Brewer—had not been admitted to practice law in Alabama, had not entered their appearances on Maples' behalf, and had done nothing to inform the Alabama court that they wished to substitute for Munanka and Ingen-Housz. Thus, none of these attorneys had the legal authority to act on Maples' behalf before his time to appeal expired. What they did or did not do in their New York offices is therefore beside the point. At the time critical to preserving Maples' access to an appeal, they, like Munanka and Ingen-Housz, were not Maples' authorized agents. . . .

Maples' only other attorney of record, local counsel Butler, also left him abandoned. Indeed, Butler did not even begin to represent Maples. . . . That the minimal participation he undertook was inconsistent with Alabama law, underscores the absurdity of holding Maples barred because Butler signed on as local counsel. . . .

Not only was Maples left without any functioning attorney of record, the very listing of Munanka, Ingen-Housz, and Butler as his representatives meant that he had no right personally to receive notice. He in fact received none or any other warning that he had better fend for himself. Had counsel of record or the State's attorney informed Maples of his plight before the time to appeal ran out, he could have filed a notice of appeal himself or enlisted the aid of new volunteer attorneys. . . .

C

. . . In the unusual circumstances of this case, principles of agency law and fundamental fairness point to the same conclusion: There was indeed cause to excuse Maples' procedural default. Through no fault of his own, Maples lacked the assistance of any authorized attorney during the 42 days Alabama allows for noticing an appeal from a trial court's denial of postconviction relief. As just observed, he had no reason to suspect that, in reality, he had been reduced to *pro se* status. Maples was disarmed by extraordinary circumstances quite beyond his control. He has shown ample cause, we hold, to excuse the procedural default into which he was trapped when counsel of record abandoned him without a word of warning. . . .

Justice ALITO, concurring.

. . . Unbeknownst to petitioner, he was effectively deprived of legal representation due to the combined effect of no fewer than eight unfortunate events: (1) the departure from their law firm of the two young lawyers who appeared as counsel of record in his state postconviction proceeding; (2) the acceptance by these two attorneys of new employment that precluded them from continuing to represent him; (3) their failure to notify petitioner of their new situation;

(4) their failure to withdraw as his counsel of record; (5) the apparent failure of the firm that they left to monitor the status of petitioner's case when these attorneys departed; (6) when notice of the decision denying petitioner's request for state postconviction relief was received in that firm's offices, the failure of the firm's mail room to route that important communication to either another member of the firm or to the departed attorneys' new addresses; (7) the failure of the clerk's office to take any action when the envelope containing that notice came back unopened; and (8) local counsel's very limited conception of the role that he was obligated to play in petitioner's representation. Under these unique circumstances, I agree that petitioner's attorneys effectively abandoned him and that this abandonment was a "cause" that is sufficient to overcome petitioner's procedural default. . . .

What occurred here was not a predictable consequence of the Alabama system but a veritable perfect storm of misfortune, a most unlikely combination of events that, without notice, effectively deprived petitioner of legal representation. Under these unique circumstances, I agree that petitioner's procedural default is overcome. . . .

Missouri v. Frye

132 S. Ct. 1399 (2012)

Justice KENNEDY delivered the opinion of the Court.

The Sixth Amendment, applicable to the States by the terms of the Fourteenth Amendment, provides that the accused shall have the assistance of counsel in all criminal prosecutions. The right to counsel is the right to effective assistance of counsel. See Strickland v. Washington, 466 U.S. 668, 686 (1984). This case arises in the context of claimed ineffective assistance that led to the lapse of a prosecution offer of a plea bargain, a proposal that offered terms more lenient than the terms of the guilty plea entered later. . . . Other questions relating to ineffective assistance with respect to plea offers, including the question of proper remedies, are considered in a second case decided today. See Lafler v. Cooper.

I

In August 2007, respondent Galin Frye was charged with driving with a revoked license. Frye had been convicted for that offense on three other occasions, so the State of Missouri charged him with a class D felony, which carries a maximum term of imprisonment of four years.

On November 15, the prosecutor sent a letter to Frye's counsel offering a choice of two plea bargains. The prosecutor first offered to recommend a 3-year sentence if there was a guilty plea to the felony charge, without a recommendation regarding probation but with a recommendation that Frye serve 10 days in jail as so-called "shock" time. The second offer was to reduce the charge to a misdemeanor and, if Frye pleaded guilty to it, to recommend a 90-day sentence.

The misdemeanor charge of driving with a revoked license carries a maximum term of imprisonment of one year. The letter stated both offers would expire on December 28. Frye's attorney did not advise Frye that the offers had been made. The offers expired.

. . . On December 30, 2007, less than a week before the [preliminary] hearing, Frye was again arrested for driving with a revoked license. . . . He pleaded not guilty [to the first charge] at a subsequent arraignment but then changed his plea to guilty. There was no underlying plea agreement. The state trial court accepted Frye's guilty plea. The prosecutor recommended a 3-year sentence, made no recommendation regarding probation, and requested 10 days shock time in jail. The trial judge sentenced Frye to three years in prison. . . .

II . . .

It is well settled that the right to the effective assistance of counsel applies to certain steps before trial. The "Sixth Amendment guarantees a defendant the right to have counsel present at all 'critical' stages of the criminal proceedings." Montejo v. Louisiana, 556 U.S. 778, 786 (2009) (quoting United States v. Wade, 388 U.S. 218, 227-228 (1967)). Critical stages include arraignments, postindictment interrogations, postindictment lineups, and the entry of a guilty plea.

With respect to the right to effective counsel in plea negotiations, . . . Hill v. Lockhart, 474 U.S. 52 (1985), established that claims of ineffective assistance of counsel in the plea bargain context are governed by the two-part test set forth in *Strickland* at 688, 694 [which requires the defendant to show "that counsel's representation fell below an objective standard of reasonableness, and "that there is a reasonable probability that, but for counsel's unprofessional errors, the result of the proceeding would have been different."] . . .

Ninety-seven percent of federal convictions and ninety-four percent of state convictions are the result of guilty pleas. The reality is that plea bargains have become so central to the administration of the criminal justice system that defense counsel have responsibilities in the plea bargain process, responsibilities that must be met to render the adequate assistance of counsel that the Sixth Amendment requires in the criminal process at critical stages. . . .

To note the prevalence of plea bargaining is not to criticize it. The potential to conserve valuable prosecutorial resources and for defendants to admit their crimes and receive more favorable terms at sentencing means that a plea agreement can benefit both parties. In order that these benefits can be realized, however, criminal defendants require effective counsel during plea negotiations. . . .

This Court now holds that, as a general rule, defense counsel has the duty to communicate formal offers from the prosecution to accept a plea on terms and conditions that may be favorable to the accused. . . .

Though the standard for counsel's performance is not determined solely by reference to codified standards of professional practice, these standards can be important guides. The American Bar Association recommends defense counsel "promptly communicate and explain to the defendant all plea offers made by the prosecuting attorney," ABA Standards for Criminal Justice, Pleas of Guilty

14-3.2(a) (3d ed. 1999), and this standard has been adopted by numerous state and federal courts over the last 30 years. The standard for prompt communication and consultation is also set out in state bar professional standards for attorneys. [The Court cites several state versions of Model Rule 1.4] . . .

III

These standards must be applied to the instant case. As regards the deficient performance prong of *Strickland*, . . . it is evident that Frye's attorney did not make a meaningful attempt to inform the defendant of a written plea offer before the offer expired. The Missouri Court of Appeals was correct that "counsel's representation fell below an objective standard of reasonableness." . . .

The Court of Appeals erred, however, in articulating the precise standard for prejudice in this context. . . . [A] defendant in Frye's position must show not only a reasonable probability that he would have accepted the lapsed plea but also a reasonable probability that the prosecution would have adhered to the agreement and that it would have been accepted by the trial court. Frye can show he would have accepted the offer, but there is strong reason to doubt the prosecution and the trial court would have permitted the plea bargain to become final. . . .

In this case, given Frye's new offense for driving without a license on December 30, 2007, there is reason to doubt that the prosecution would have adhered to the agreement or that the trial court would have accepted it at the January 4, 2008, hearing, unless they were required by state law to do so. . . .

Justice SCALIA, with whom THE CHIEF JUSTICE, Justice THOMAS, and Justice ALITO join, dissenting.

This is a companion case to *Lafler* v. *Cooper*. The principal difference between the cases is that the fairness of the defendant's conviction in *Lafler* was established by a full trial and jury verdict, whereas Frye's conviction here was established by his own admission of guilt, received by the court after the usual colloquy that assured it was voluntary and truthful. In *Lafler* all that could be said (and as I discuss there it was quite enough) is that the *fairness* of the conviction was clear, though a unanimous jury finding beyond a reasonable doubt can sometimes be wrong. Here it can be said not only that the process was fair, but that the defendant acknowledged the correctness of his conviction. . . .

In this case and its companion, the Court's sledge may require the reversal of perfectly valid, eminently just, convictions. . . .

Lafler v. Cooper
132 S. Ct. 1376 (2012)

Justice KENNEDY delivered the opinion of the Court. . . .

I

On the evening of March 25, 2003, respondent pointed a gun toward Kali Mundy's head and fired. From the record, it is unclear why respondent did this, and at trial it was suggested that he might have acted either in self defense or in defense of another person. In any event the shot missed and Mundy fled. Respondent followed in pursuit, firing repeatedly. Mundy was shot in her buttock, hip, and abdomen but survived the assault.

Respondent was charged under Michigan law with assault with intent to murder, possession of a firearm by a felon, possession of a firearm in the commission of a felony, misdemeanor possession of marijuana, and for being a habitual offender. On two occasions, the prosecution offered to dismiss two of the charges and to recommend a sentence of 51 to 85 months for the other two, in exchange for a guilty plea. In a communication with the court respondent admitted guilt and expressed a willingness to accept the offer. Respondent, however, later rejected the offer on both occasions, allegedly after his attorney convinced him that the prosecution would be unable to establish his intent to murder Mundy because she had been shot below the waist. On the first day of trial the prosecution offered a significantly less favorable plea deal, which respondent again rejected. After trial, respondent was convicted on all counts and received a mandatory minimum sentence of 185 to 360 months' imprisonment. . . .

II . . .

Even if a defendant shows ineffective assistance of counsel has caused the rejection of a plea leading to a trial and a more severe sentence, there is the question of what constitutes an appropriate remedy. . . .

Sixth Amendment remedies should . . . "neutralize the taint" of a constitutional violation, while at the same time not grant a windfall to the defendant or needlessly squander the considerable resources the State properly invested in the criminal prosecution. . . .

III . . .

Respondent has satisfied *Strickland*'s two-part test. Regarding performance, perhaps it could be accepted that it is unclear whether respondent's counsel believed respondent could not be convicted for assault with intent to murder as a matter of law because the shots hit Mundy below the waist, or whether he simply thought this would be a persuasive argument to make to the jury to show lack of specific intent. And, as the Court of Appeals for the Sixth Circuit suggested, an erroneous strategic prediction about the outcome of a trial is not necessarily deficient performance. Here, however, the fact of deficient performance has been conceded by all parties. . . .

As to prejudice, respondent has shown that but for counsel's deficient performance there is a reasonable probability he and the trial court would have accepted the guilty plea. In addition, as a result of not accepting the plea and being convicted at trial, respondent received a minimum sentence 3½ times greater than he would have received under the plea. The standard for ineffective assistance under *Strickland* has thus been satisfied.

As a remedy, the District Court ordered specific performance of the original plea agreement. The correct remedy in these circumstances, however, is to order the State to reoffer the plea agreement. Presuming respondent accepts the offer, the state trial court can then exercise its discretion in determining whether to vacate the convictions and resentence respondent pursuant to the plea agreement, to vacate only some of the convictions and resentence respondent accordingly, or to leave the convictions and sentence from trial undisturbed. Today's decision leaves open to the trial court how best to exercise that discretion in all the circumstances of the case.

Justice SCALIA, with whom Justice THOMAS joins, and with whom THE CHIEF JUSTICE joins . . . , dissenting. . . .

The Court requires Michigan to "reoffer the plea agreement" that was rejected because of bad advice from counsel. That would indeed be a powerful remedy—but for the fact that Cooper's acceptance of that reoffered agreement is not conclusive. Astoundingly, "the state trial court can then *exercise its discretion* in determining whether to vacate the convictions and resentence respondent pursuant to the plea agreement, to vacate only some of the convictions and resentence respondent accordingly, *or to leave the convictions and sentence from trial undisturbed."* (emphasis added).

[W]hy not skip the reoffer-and-reacceptance minuet and simply leave it to the discretion of the state trial court what the remedy shall be? The answer, of course, is camouflage. . . .

I suspect that the Court's squeamishness in fashioning a remedy, and the incoherence of what it comes up with, is attributable to its realization, deep down, that there is no real constitutional violation here anyway. The defendant has been fairly tried, lawfully convicted, and properly sentenced, and *any* "remedy" provided for this will do nothing but undo the just results of a fair adversarial process. . . .

In many—perhaps most—countries of the world, American-style plea bargaining is forbidden in cases as serious as this one, even for the purpose of obtaining testimony that enables conviction of a greater malefactor, much less for the purpose of sparing the expense of trial. In Europe, many countries adhere to what they aptly call the "legality principle" by requiring prosecutors to charge all prosecutable offenses, which is typically incompatible with the practice of charge-bargaining. Such a system reflects an admirable belief that the law is the law, and those who break it should pay the penalty provided.

In the United States, we have plea bargaining aplenty, but until today it has been regarded as a necessary evil. It presents grave risks of prosecutorial overcharging that effectively compels an innocent defendant to avoid massive risk by pleading guilty to a lesser offense; and for guilty defendants it often—perhaps usually—results in a sentence well below what the law prescribes for the actual crime. But even so, we accept plea bargaining because many believe that without it our long and expensive process of criminal trial could not sustain the burden imposed on it, and our system of criminal justice would grind to a halt.

Today, however, the Supreme Court of the United States elevates plea bargaining from a necessary evil to a constitutional entitlement. It is no longer a somewhat embarrassing adjunct to our criminal justice system; rather, as the Court announces in the companion case to this one, "'it *is* the criminal justice system.'" Thus, even though there is no doubt that the respondent here is guilty of the offense with which he was charged; even though he has received the exorbitant gold standard of American justice—a full-dress criminal trial with its innumerable constitutional and statutory limitations upon the evidence that the prosecution can bring forward, and (in Michigan as in most States) the requirement of a unanimous guilty verdict by impartial jurors; the Court says that his conviction is invalid because he was deprived of his *constitutional entitlement* to plea-bargain.

I am less saddened by the outcome of this case than I am by what it says about this Court's attitude toward criminal justice. The Court today embraces the sporting chance theory of criminal law, in which the State functions like a conscientious casino-operator, giving each player a fair chance to beat the house, that is, to serve less time than the law says he deserves. And when a player is excluded from the tables, his *constitutional rights* have been violated. I do not subscribe to that theory. No one should, least of all the Justices of the Supreme Court.

* * *

. . . Released felon Anthony Cooper, who shot repeatedly and gravely injured a woman named Kali Mundy, was tried and convicted for his crimes by a jury of his peers, and given a punishment that Michigan's elected representatives have deemed appropriate. Nothing about that result is unfair or unconstitutional. To the contrary, it is wonderfully just, and infinitely superior to the trial-by-bargain that today's opinion affords constitutional status. I respectfully dissent.

◼ Lawyers and Clients: *Criminal Defense*

Maples, *Frye*, and *Lafler* offer us a portal through which to glimpse the reality of criminal defense representation in America. In most criminal cases today, defendants have a constitutional right to counsel, but the dream that every person charged with a serious crime "will be capably defended . . . sure of the support needed to make an adequate defense"[1] remains illusory.[2]

The recognition of constitutional rights to defense counsel created the need for large numbers of lawyers qualified to handle criminal trials.[3] This need for

---

1. Anthony Lewis, *Gideon's Trumpet* 205 (Random House 1964).

2. Mary Sue Backus & Paul Marcus, *The Right to Counsel in Criminal Cases, A National Crisis*, 57 Hastings L.J. 1031 (2006); The Innocence Project documents 292 exonerations of convicted defendants due to subsequent reexamination of DNA evidence. *See* Innocence Project, http://www.innocenceproject.org/Content/Facts_on_PostConviction_DNA_Exonerations.php (last visited Feb. 29, 2012). The cost of this error is especially pronounced in death penalty cases. *See* Brandon L. Garrett, *Convicting the Innocent: Where Criminal Prosecutions Go Wrong* (Harv. U. Press 2011); James S. Liebman, *The Overproduction of Death*, 100 Colum. L. Rev. 2030, 2102-2110 (2000) (state and federal courts reversed 68 percent of the capital judgments they fully reviewed over the past 25 years).

3. In the late 1960s, the American Bar Association first adopted basic standards for providing defense counsel, *see, e.g.*, ABA, *Standards for Criminal Justice, Providing Defense Services* (3d ed. 1993); ABA, *Standards for Criminal Justice, The Defense Function* (3d ed. 1993).

specialized expertise has accelerated over the past few decades, as the number of those charged and convicted of crimes has increased dramatically.[4] Today, about two thirds of those accused of a felony are poor enough to qualify for appointed counsel.[5] As a result, lawyers in public defender offices often shoulder huge caseloads[6] and private appointed counsel, because of inadequate fee schedules, often face an "inherent conflict between remaining financially solvent and the defendant's need for vigorous advocacy."[7] These workload and financial pressures present a huge impediment to the provision of effective legal assistance.[8]

The Clients

Judicial recognition of a Sixth Amendment constitutional right to counsel was recognized first in some,[9] and then in all felony cases, on the ground that defense lawyers "are necessities, not luxuries," both to protect against the risk of wrongful conviction and to provide due process of law.[10] Rights to counsel in juvenile and certain misdemeanor cases followed.[11] *Frye* and *Lafler* make clear that a person accused of a crime has a right to retained or appointed counsel at all

---

4. Arrest rates (per 100,000 inhabitants) have increased from 897 in 1971 to 4,478 in 2009. *See Criminal Justice Sourcebook, available at* http://www.albany.edu/sourcebook/pdf/t432009.pdf (last visited June 21, 2012). Incarceration rates (the number of prison and jail inmates per 100,000 U.S. residents) have more than doubled, from 313 in 1985 to 748 in 2009. *Id., available at* http://www.albany.edu/sourcebook/pdf/t6132009.pdf (last visited June 21, 2012).

5. Deborah H. Rhode, *In the Interest of Justice: Reforming the Legal Profession* 61 (Oxford 2000).

6. The Sixth Amendment does not provide the basis for overturning convictions on the basis of completely inadequate institutional funding or assignment systems, United States v. Cronic, 466 U.S. 648 (1984), but a few state courts have done so, *e.g.*, State v. Pearl, 621 So. 2d 780 (La. 1993) (entire defender system not constitutionally inadequate, but lawyer who represented 70 active felony cases and had represented 418 defendants in the past seven months, entering 130 guilty pleas at arraignment, rebuttably presumed not able to provide effective assistance). *See also* Miranda v. Clark Cnty., Nev., 319 F.3d 465 (9th Cir. 2002) (en banc) (upholding civil rights action under 42 U.S.C. § 1983 for deliberate indifference to Sixth Amendment rights of defendants against county's public defender system, which assigned recently graduated lawyers to death penalty cases); *E.g.*, St.ex rel. Mo. Pub. Defender Commn. v. Waters, 370 S.W.3d 592 (Mo. 2012) (ethics rules that require competent and diligent representation require trial judge to refrain from appointing a public defender's office to represent an accused in violation of the office's administrative rule on "caseload protocol" that allows lawyers to decline further appointments when they have exceeded their capacity to take cases).

7. *Report of the Committee to Review the Criminal Justice Act, reprinted in* 52 Crim. L. Rptr. 2265, 2284-2285 (1993). *See also* Maas v. Olive, 992 So. 2d 196 (Fla. 2008) (legislature cannot constitutionally restrict capital defense lawyers' ability to petition courts for additional compensation beyond statutory fee caps).

8. *See* David Cole, *No Equal Justice* 81-89 (The New Press 1999).

9. Powell v. Alabama, 287 U.S. 45, 60 (1932) (Sixth Amendment requires counsel if fundamental unfairness would result). *See also* Johnson v. Zerbst, 304 U.S. 458 (1938) (requiring counsel in all federal criminal proceedings).

10. Gideon v. Wainwright, 372 U.S. 335, 344 (1963) (requiring right to counsel in all felony cases).

11. In re Gault, 387 U.S. 1 (1966) (requiring counsel for juvenile proceedings that may lead to commitment in state institutions); Argersinger v. Hamlin, 407 U.S. 25 (1972) (requiring counsel in misdemeanor cases where defendant is imprisoned); Alabama v. Shelton, 535 U.S. 654 (2002) (requiring counsel in misdemeanor cases where defendant receives a suspended sentence).

"critical stages" (including plea negotiations) of such proceedings.[12] In addition, a person convicted of a crime has a Fourteenth Amendment right to counsel for capital sentencing hearings and for the first appeal as of right, but not for other postconviction proceedings, as occurred in *Maples*.[13] The right to counsel includes a right to counsel of choice, but only to defendants who can afford to hire or otherwise find a lawyer willing to represent the defendant without charge.[14]

The Five Cs

The vast majority of issues about proper criminal defense representation have arisen as claims of ineffective assistance of counsel raised in criminal appeals.[15] Although the Supreme Court has always recognized that the Sixth Amendment requirement of counsel presupposed *effective* assistance of counsel, it did not provide a framework to evaluate the adequacy of counsel until 1984 when it decided Strickland v. Washington[16] and United States v. Cronic.[17] In these opinions, the Court found that the Sixth Amendment right to effective assistance of counsel included the right to a lawyer who would play "a role that is critical to the ability of the adversarial system to produce just results."[18] *Frye* and *Lafler* rely on *Strickland's* two-prong test to assess whether a defendant had been deprived of the effective assistance of counsel. The first prong, performance, requires the defendant to show "that counsel's representation fell below an objective standard of reasonableness" and parallels the duty-breach analysis in legal malpractice suits. The second prong, prejudice, requires the defendant to show "that but for counsel's errors, the result in the proceeding would have been different," parallels a "but-for" actual causation requirement, and functions like a harmless error analysis in criminal appeals.

Control *Maples* indicates that complete neglect of a lawyer's responsibility amounts to abandonment of the agency relationship itself.[19] When such a

---

12. *See also* Padilla v. Kentucky, 130 S. Ct. 1473 (2010) (right to have defense counsel to give correct advice about the immigration consequences of a guilty plea).

13. Douglas v. California, 372 U.S. 353 (1963); Ross v. Moffit, 417 U.S. 600 (1974) (no right to counsel for discretionary state appeals); Pennsylvania v. Finley, 481 U.S. 551 (1987) (no right to counsel in state habeas corpus proceedings).

14. United States v. Gonzalez-Lopez, 548 U.S. 140 (2006). An absolute right to counsel of choice is subject to several limitations: Counsel must be a member of the bar in good standing, and not subject to a conflict of interest. Wheat v. United States, 486 U.S. 153, 159 (1988).

15. Because most states limit direct appeals to issues raised on the face of the trial record, and because trial counsel often handles the appeal, most ineffective assistance of counsel claims are not raised or identified until collateral habeas corpus proceedings. Massaro v. United States, 538 U.S. 500, 504-505 (2003).

16. Strickland v. Washington, 466 U.S. 668 (1984).

17. United States v. Cronic, 466 U.S. 648 (1984).

18. *Strickland*, 466 U.S. at 685. The defendant also has the alternative of representing herself, if she knowingly and intelligently waives her Sixth Amendment right. Standby counsel can be appointed to assist the defendant. *See* Faretta v. California, 422 U.S. 806 (1975).

19. MR 1.3 Comment [4]; RLGL § 16.

relationship exists, Model Rule 1.2(a) specifically reserves three fundamental decisions to clients in criminal cases: "the plea to be entered, whether to waive a jury trial, and whether the client will testify." The Restatement and Sixth Amendment cases add the decision whether to appeal.[20] *Frye* and *Lafler* illustrate that lawyers who do not consult with clients about these personal client decisions or do not abide by the client's choice commit serious error.[21]

Communication   *Frye* relied in part on Model Rule 1.4(a), which requires lawyers to initiate communication about decisions that require the client's informed consent. *Lafler* illustrates another aspect of the communication duty: the obligation to offer correct legal advice. State courts also have found counsel ineffective for giving defective advice about fundamental personal client decisions.[22]

Frye's specific holding, that defense counsel has a duty to communicate a plea offer to the defendant, seems akin to a per se rule, meaning that no possible reason can justify violating this norm. In most cases, however, *Strickland* requires a case-by-case determination of incompetence, dictated by the particular facts and circumstances of the case.[23] *Strickland* rejected per se rules in part because they can result in rote application of a checklist approach when individualized client representation should be the goal.[24] However, the absence of per se rules gives defense counsel little incentive to honor basic fiduciary duties such as consultation and investigation, and results in most errors being labeled "strategic choices."

Competence   Criminal defense lawyers who face huge caseloads have affirmative obligations to refuse new appointments or seek leave to withdraw from existing cases to prevent abandonment and to provide competent representation.[25] *Maples, Frye,* and *Lafler* represent rare cases where clients received some form of redress for lawyer incompetence. In *Maples,* the court excused the procedural default, meaning that Mr. Maples can now raise his ineffective assistance of counsel argument in a collateral federal habeas corpus proceeding. Like the defendants in *Frye* and *Lafler,* Mr. Maples will now have to present evidence establishing both prongs of the *Strickland* test.

---

20. RLGL § 22(1); Roe v. Flores-Ortega, 528 U.S. 470 (2000).
21. *See* Ronald E. Mallen & Jeffrey M. Smith, *Legal Malpractice* § 27.15 (West 2012 ed.), Ellen J. Bennett, Elizabeth J. Cohen, & Martin Whittaker, *Annotated Model Rules of Prof. Conduct* 36-37 (ABA 7th ed. 2011); Wayne L. LaFave, Jerold H. Israel, & Nancy J. King, *Principles of Criminal Procedure: Post-Investigation* § 3.6 (West 2d ed. 2009).
22. *E.g.,* Ross v. Kemp, 393 S.E.2d 244 (Ga. 1990) ("fractured" defense by two lawyers who failed effectively to help defendant decide whether to testify); Crabbe v. State, 546 S.E.2d 65 (Ga. App. 2001) (defense counsel did not advise defendant that guilty pleas would remove the possibility of parole).
23. *See* LaFave, *supra* note 21, at § 3.7(d).
24. *Strickland,* 466 U.S. at 688. For a proposed checklist, *see* David L. Bazelon, *The Realities of Gideon and Argersinger,* 64 Geo. L. J. 811, 837-838 (1976).
25. ABA Formal Op. 06-441 (Ethical Obligations of Lawyers Who Represent Indigent Criminal Defendants When Excessive Caseloads Interfere with Competent and Diligent Representation).

The first performance prong requires defendants to identify the precise error or errors of defense counsel and then to present some kind of concession (as in *Lafler*) or specific expert testimony that those errors should not have occurred.[26] *Frye* illustrates how defendants also may rely on what the Supreme Court has referred to as evidence of a "codified standard of professional practice," which can serve as "important guides." *Strickland* instructs courts to "indulge in a strong presumption that counsel's conduct falls within the wide range of reasonable professional assistance," which invites courts to label any established error as due to a strategic decision rather than occurring because of an inexcusable lack of attentiveness or competence. If counsel errs following a reasonably complete investigation of the law and facts, deference usually wins the day. *Frye* and *Lafler* illustrate the Court's willingness to take a more careful look when the error relates to inexcusable legal or factual investigation.[27]

If defendants meet this first prong of *Strickland, Frye* and *Lafler* illustrate that they then face equal difficulty establishing but-for causation or the prejudice prong. This second prong requires the defendant to show that the professional mistake of counsel actually caused a "fundamentally unfair" conviction, sentence, or failure to appeal.[28] Courts typically find that counsel's errors are harmless and refuse to grant relief.[29] Like *Frye* and *Lafler,* most cases refuse to presume prejudice because per se rules require that the circumstances must be "so likely to prejudice the accused that the cost of litigating their effect in a particular case is unjustified."[30]

Confidentiality Criminal defense lawyers have special confidentiality obligations. With respect to candor to the tribunal, Model Rule 3.3 prohibits all lawyers from knowingly offering false evidence. Lawyers also may refuse to offer

---

26. A claim of ineffective assistance often requires an evidentiary postconviction hearing to develop more fully what happened and why. *See, e.g., Rompilla v. Beard,* 545 U.S. 374, 385 note 3 (2005).
27. *See, e.g., Padilla v. Kentucky,* 130 S. Ct. 1473 (2010) (failure of defense counsel to give correct advice about the immigration consequences of a guilty plea); Margaret Colgate Love, *Collateral Consequences After Padilla v. Kentucky: From Punishment to Regulation,* 31 St. Louis U. Pub. L. Rev. 87 (2011); *Sears v. Upton,* 130 S. Ct. 3259 (2010) (constitutionally deficient mitigation investigation in capital case).
28. *Lockhart v. Fretwell,* 506 U.S. 364, 372 (1993). *See, e.g., Glover v. United States,* 531 U.S. 198 (2001) (defense counsel's failure to group charges under federal sentencing guidelines, which increased defendant's sentence by 6-21 months, constituted prejudice).
29. *E.g., Smith v. Spisak,* 130 S. Ct. 676 (2010) (prejudicial closing argument that demonized defendant and painted graphic picture of crimes); *State v. Hongo,* 706 So. 2d 419 (La. 1998) (failure to object to an erroneous jury instruction); *Melancon v. State,* 66 S.W.3d 375 (Tex. App. 2001) (failure to subpoena alibi witness).
30. *United States v. Cronic,* 466 U.S. 648, 658 (1984). The "sleeping lawyer" cases illustrate the significant proof required to reach this threshold. When defense lawyers occasionally nap during a trial, courts have held that one episode of inattention or sleep is not enough to presume prejudice, *e.g., Fellman v. Poole,* 1994 U.S. App. LEXIS 22667. However, repeated periods of unconsciousness might become the equivalent of no counsel at all so that prejudice can be presumed, *e.g., Burdine v. Johnson,* 231 F.3d 950 (5th Cir. 2000), *rev'd en banc,* 262 F.3d 336 (5th Cir. 2001).

evidence they reasonably believe to be false.[31] The one exception is criminal defense. A lawyer who reasonably believes, but does not know, that his or her client/defendant will testify falsely must bow to the client's choice.[32] And, even when she knows the testimony is false, she may be required to permit the client to testify in an alternative narrative format.[33]

Conflict of Interest Resolution   In cases where a lawyer's conflict of interest becomes the basis for asserting ineffective assistance, the courts have faced a number of recurring situations where conflicts have been alleged, including the joint representation of co-defendants, previous representation of the victim or other significant prosecution witness, fee arrangements including payment by one co-defendant for others or potential royalties to counsel that may accrue after the trial, investigation or possible prosecution of counsel for the same crime, or counsel who might be called as a prosecution witness.[34] When the error is raised during a court proceeding, disqualification can be sought.[35]

In *Holloway v. Arkansas*,[36] the Supreme Court held that the failure of a trial judge to inquire into a multiple concurrent representation conflict was enough to presume prejudice.[37] In most situations, however, prejudice is not presumed, and defendants must show "actual" conflicts of interest that compelled defense counsel to compromise his or her duty of loyalty.[38] Courts have restricted this actual conflict category to a small list of flagrant conflicts, such as a lawyer who was implicated in the defendants' crime,[39] representation of co-defendants,[40] and a trial judge's direction to counsel to pull his punches if he wished his fee approved and future appointments from the court.[41] For the defendant who can demonstrate that an actual conflict existed, he or she need prove only that it "adversely affected" the lawyer's performance at trial instead of the usual but-for prejudice requirement.[42] In all other situations, however, the defendant

---

31. MR 3.3(a)(3); RLGL § 120.

32. *Id.* We deal with this issue in more detail in chapter 7. *See* The Bounds of the Law: *Client Fraud, infra* p. 252.

33. *See, e.g.*, Nguyen v. Knowles, *infra* p. 289.

34. LaFave, *supra* note 21 at § 3.9.

35. *See, e.g.*, State v. Veale, 919 A.2d 794 (N.H. 2007) (reviewing per se, actual conflict, and hybrid approaches to disqualification of appellate counsel).

36. 435 U.S. 475 (1978).

37. The trial judge can grant a motion to disqualify defense counsel if necessary to guarantee a fair trial. *See, e.g.*, United States v. Edwards, 39 F. Supp. 2d 716 (M.D. La. 1999).

38. Cuyler v. Sullivan, 446 U.S. 335 (1980). *See, e.g.*, Mickens v. Taylor, 535 U.S. 162 (2002) (when previous representation of the victim was not raised on the record, prejudice was not presumed even when the defendant was unaware of the conflict, and it was known by the prosecutor, defense lawyer, and the trial judge).

39. United States v. Fulton, 5 F.3d 605 (2d Cir. 1993).

40. *E.g.*, Moss v. United States, 323 F.3d 445 (6th Cir. 2003); Duvall v. State, 2007 Md. LEXIS 268 (conflict of interest found where same public defender's office represented both defendant, and, in an unrelated case, the man who the defendant claimed was the crime's true perpetrator).

41. Walberg v. Israel, 766 F.2d 1071 (7th Cir. 1985).

42. *See, e.g.*, Perillo v. Johnson, 205 F.3d 775 (5th Cir. 2000).

must fulfill the traditional *Strickland* two-prong standard, establishing both the nature of the conflict and actual prejudice.[43]

The Bounds of the Law

Reversing Convictions Although frequent allegations of ineffective assistance of counsel in criminal appeals show no sign of abating, very few defendants succeed in overturning convictions.[44] Part of this is because, like *Frye,* over 90 percent of criminal convictions result from a guilty plea, where far less scrutiny of counsel's performance is usually possible and, even when it is, courts have been especially reluctant to reverse convictions.[45] Due to the difficulty of satisfying both prongs of the *Strickland* test, very few convictions are reversed for trial error as well.[46]

Yet despite these hurdles, state and federal cases have recognized constitutional error in several categories of failings by defense counsel.[47] Most obvious is a lawyer who abandoned his client by failing to inform him that the lawyer no longer represented the client in an appeal, essentially depriving the client of any lawyer at all.[48] Similarly, when counsel is present, but fails to test the prosecution's case, for example, by conceding the defendant's guilt to the jury when the defendant consistently maintained his innocence,[49] or by a total lack of effort and explanation,[50] courts have no trouble finding a violation. Following a fact-specific inquiry, courts also have found counsel ineffective for failing to adequately investigate facts,[51] failing to find or understand relevant law,[52] giving

---

43. *See, e.g.,* Beets v. Collins, 65 F.3d 1258 (5th Cir. 1995).

44. *See, e.g.,* Eve Brensike Primus, *The Illusory Right to Counsel,* 37 Ohio N.U. L. Rev. 595 (2011).

45. Bruce A. Green, *Judicial Rationalization for Rationing Justice: How Sixth Amendment Doctrine Undermines Reform,* 70 Fordham L. Rev. 1729 (2002).

46. Several Supreme Court justices have pointed out the "impotence" of the *Strickland* standard. *See, e.g.,* McFarland v. Scott, 512 U.S. 1256 (1994) (Blackmun, J., dissenting to the denial of *certiorari*). *See also* Mitchell v. Kemp, 483 U.S. 1026 (1987) (Marshall, J., dissenting to the denial of *certiorari*).

47. This is especially true in death penalty cases. *See* Lawrence J. Fox, *Capital Guidelines and Ethical Duties: Mutually Reinforcing Responsibilities,* 36 Hofstra L. Rev. 775 (2008).

48. Fields v. Bagley, 275 F.3d 478 (6th Cir. 2001).

49. *E.g.,* Florida v. Nixon, 543 U.S. 175 (2004); State v. Carter, 14 P.3d 1138 (Kan. 2000).

50. *E.g.,* People v. Bass, 636 N.E.2d 781 (Mich. App. 2001) (defense counsel had no memory of trial, lost most of the file, and offered no reason for failing to call witnesses); People v. Spann, 765 N.E.2d 1114 (Ill. App. 2002) (defense counsel failed to challenge defective indictment, move to quash arrest or suppress evidence, give opening statement, or cross-examine the only witness against the defendant); Wenzy v. State, 855 S.W.2d 47 (Tex. App. 1993) (when not allowed to withdraw, counsel refused to take an active role in defense).

51. *E.g.,* Rompilla v. Beard, *supra* note 26; Wesley v. State, 753 N.E.2d 686 (Ind. App. 2002) (failure to get psychiatric record of victim who had a history of false accusations); In re K.J.O., 27 S.W.3d 340 (Tex. App. 2000) (failure to conduct investigation into juvenile's defense); People v. Truly, 595 N.E.2d 1230 (Ill. App. 1992) (failure to investigate and present alibi).

52. *E.g.,* Padilla v. Kentucky, *supra* note 27; Kimmelman v. Morrison, 477 U.S. 365 (1986) (mistake as to defense counsel's obligation to request discovery); Dando v. Yukins, 461 F.3d 791(6th Cir. 2006) (failure to consult an expert and investigate the validity of a duress defense based on Battered

defective advice about whether to testify or accept a plea bargain,[53] and failing to object to improper evidence or procedures.[54]

Malpractice Convicted defendants also can bring a legal malpractice action against their former lawyers.[55] Theoretically, such a case should not differ much from ordinary malpractice litigation. Yet courts have created some special doctrines that make malpractice recovery against criminal defense lawyers very difficult to secure. Consider, for example, whether the facts in *Maples, Frye,* or *Lafler* would justify a successful malpractice claim.

In such a suit, the defendant would first be confronted with the defense of governmental immunity. Although the courts agree that publicly employed lawyers such as prosecutors should be protected from suit by governmental immunity,[56] they generally do not grant such immunity to appointed counsel[57] and are split about whether public defenders share similar immunity.[58] Second, the statute of limitations must be confronted.[59]

Woman's Syndrome); Stanford v. Stewart, 554 S.E.2d 480 (Ga. 2001) (failure of appellate counsel to recognize the significance of an error in jury instructions); Pena-Mota v. State, 986 S.W.2d 341 (Tex. App. 1999) (failure to object to jury instruction resulted in a double jeopardy violation).

53. *See, e.g., Lafler, supra* p. 115, Padilla v. Kentucky, *supra* note 27.

54. Kimmelman v. Morrison, 447 U.S. 365 (1986) (failure to move to suppress due to a total failure to conduct pretrial discovery); Dawkins v. State, 551 S.E.2d 260 (S.C. 2001) (failure to object to hearsay statements of victim); State v. Scott, 602 N.W.2d 296 (Wis. App. 1999) (failure to object to prosecutor's breach of plea bargain); Alaniz v. State, 937 S.W.2d 593 (Tex. App. 1996) (failure to object to seating of a juror excused for cause); Evans v. State, 28 P.3d 498 (Nev. 2001) (failure to challenge prosecutor's remarks during penalty phase of trial); Ross v. State, 726 So. 2d 317 (Fla. App. 1999) (failure to object to improper remarks of prosecutor made during closing argument).

55. *See* Gregory G. Sarno, *Legal Malpractice in Defense of Criminal Prosecution,* 4 A.L.R.5th 273 (1992).

56. *See, e.g.,* Durham v. MeElynn, 772 A.2d 68 (Pa. 2001).

57. *See, e.g.,* Ferri v. Ackerman, 444 U.S. 193 (1979) (federal law does not immunize appointed defense lawyers); Mossow v. United States, 987 F.2d 1365 (8th Cir. 1993) (federal law does not bar malpractice suit against military lawyer). *But see* Mooney v. Frazier, 693 S.E.2d 333 (2010) (recognizing judicially created immunity against state law claims of legal malpractice derived from the appointed lawyer's conduct in underlying criminal proceedings in a federal court).

58. *See, e.g.,* Barner v. Leeds, 13 P.3d 704 (Cal. 2000) (public defenders not protected by statutory immunity for discretionary acts); Wooton v. Vogele, 769 N.E.2d 889 (Ohio App. 2001) (Ohio Tort Immunity Statute protects public defenders from suit); Dziubak v. Mott, 503 N.W.2d 771 (Minn. 1993) (public defenders protected from suit by judicial immunity). *See also* Polk County v. Dodson, 454 U.S. 312 (1981) (public defenders not state actors under 42 U.S.C. § 1983 because they act contrary to the government's interests); Miranda v. Clark Cnty, Nev., 319 F.3d 465 (9th Cir. 2003) (assistant public defender who represented defendant in a traditional role, was not a state actor, but administrative head of public defender office, who determined how resources were spent was amenable to suit under § 1983).

59. *E.g.,* McKnight v. Office of Pub. Defender, 962 A.2d 482 (N.J. 2008) (statute of limitations begins to run at the time of reversal of the conviction); *but see, e.g.,* Burnett v. South, 2007 Tenn. App. LEXIS 277 (defendant must bring malpractice suit before conviction overturned to meet "catch-22" statute of limitations that begins to run when the plaintiff reasonably should know of wrongful conduct); Gebhardt v. O'Rourke, 510 N.W.2d 900 (Mich. 1994) (statute begins to run at the time of conviction).

If these defenses could be surmounted, proof of breach of the professional duty of care would not be problematic in *Maples* or *Frye*. Both defendants could rely on the ABA Criminal Defense Standards as well as Model Rules to establish such a duty.[60] Both cases arguably fits within the common knowledge exception explained in *dePape* because both lawyers apparently breached basic fiduciary duties of control and communication. On the other hand, Mr. Lafler most likely would be required to present expert testimony regarding the duty to give accurate legal advice (as occurred in *Togstad*) about the consequences of going to trial versus accepting a plea offer.

Even if duty and breach could be established, proving causation in all of these cases would be impossible in most jurisdictions because the vast majority require the defendant to first have his conviction reversed.[61] Some jurisdictions require even more: an affirmative proof of innocence.[62] A few jurisdictions do allow alternative proof in certain cases, where (as in *Frye* and *Lafler*) the lawyer's error led to a longer sentence or lost appeal. They hold that defendant need only show that he would have accepted the plea (or appeal) if it had been presented to him.[63] In the few cases where causation can be shown, courts do not hesitate to approve recovery for emotional distress due to incarceration caused by the lawyer's negligence.[64]

Professional Discipline   Of course, a defendant who complains about incompetent defense counsel also may file a disciplinary complaint against his former lawyer. In most of the cases where discipline has occurred, the lawyer exhibited a pattern or practice of incompetence. For example, lawyers have been disciplined

---

60. ABA Standards for Criminal Justice, *Defense Function* §§ 4-5.2, 4-8.2 (3d ed. 1993); RLGL §§ 16(1), 22(1).

61. RLGL § 53, Comment d. In guilty plea cases, the issue of claim preclusion—whether the defendant's admission of guilt precludes a subsequent malpractice suit—raises a similar issue. *See, e.g.,* Mrozek v. Inta Fin. Corp., 699 N.W.2d 54 (Wis. 2005). *Cf.* Falkner v. Foshaug, 29 P.3d 771 (Wash. App. 2001) (*Alford* plea, which allowed client to plead guilty without admitting guilt, did not preclude later proof of client's innocence in malpractice action against defense counsel).

62. *E.g.,* Bloomer v. Gibson, 912 A.2d 424 (Vt. 2006); Schreiber v. Rowe, 725 So. 2d 1245 (Fla. 1999); Rodriguez v. Nielsen, 650 N.W.2d 237 (Neb. 2002) (allegation that defendant acted in self-defense does not establish actual innocence); Wiley v. Cnty of San Diego, 966 P.2d 983 (Cal. 1998); Glenn v. Aiken, 569 N.E.2d 783 (Mass. 1991); Carmel v. Lunney, 511 N.E.2d 1126 (N.Y. 1987).

63. *See, e.g.,* Krahn v. Kinney, 538 N.E.2d 1058 (Ohio 1989) (defendant need only show difference in sentence if he had known about and accepted a plea offer). *See also* Drollinger v. Mallon, 238 P.3d 1034 (Ore. 2011) (exoneration not necessary where malpractice occurs in postconviction appeal); Hilario v. Reardon, 960 A.2d 337 (N.H. 2008) (actual innocence not required for postconviction proceedings); Levine v. Kling, 123 F.3d 580 (7th Cir. 1997) (innocence need not be shown where defendant alleges error such as failure to press double jeopardy defense).

64. *E.g.,* Holiday v. Jones, 264 Cal. Rptr. 448 (Cal. App. 1989); Gautam v. De Luca, 521 A.2d 1343 (N.J. Super. 1987); Bowman v. Doherty, 686 P.2d 112 (Kan. 1984). *But see* Dombrowski v. Bulson, 2012 N.Y. LEXIS 1244.

for abandoning criminal clients,[65] failing to appear after being retained to do so,[66] and repeated incompetence in handling criminal matters.[67]

Conclusion

Most criminal defense lawyers function in a system that is underfunded and overworked. They often labor under difficult conditions where the stakes are exceedingly high. *Maples, Frye,* and *Lafler* illustrate that the law of procedural default and ineffective assistance of counsel addresses these errors, but it produces few incentives to counter many difficult circumstances. State courts have created similar and often more extensive barriers to recovery in legal malpractice cases. Professional discipline, although possible, also rarely occurs.

At the same time, the number of cases where procedural default or ineffective assistance of counsel is alleged points to continuing problems in criminal defense representation. Further, the number of cases that have granted relief despite these considerable proof burdens suggests a continuing wide range of deficient conduct that raises serious questions about whether our constitutional guarantee of adequate counsel is a truly meaningful one.

---

65. *E.g.,* In re Mohling, 2001 Ariz. LEXIS 84.

66. In re Lewis, 689 A.2d 561 (D.C. App. 1997).

67. In re Longacre, 122 P.3d 710 (Wash. 2005) (failure to communicate several plea offers and to inform client of correct sentencing ranges for various convictions); Atty. Grievance Commn. v. Middleton, 756 A.2d 565 (Md. 2000); Law. Disc. Bd. v. Turgeon, 557 S.E.2d 235 (W. Va. 2000). *See also* In re Wolfram, 847 P.2d 94, note 5 (Ariz. 1993) (courts making a finding of ineffective assistance should "look to the circumstances and determine whether there is arguably some infraction that should be called to the attention of the appropriate bar authorities.").

Chapter 5

Competence

This chapter explores competence, another basic duty that lawyers owe their clients. We emphasize here the various, yet related definitions of competence in several distinct bodies of law, as well as the multiple remedies provided by the law governing lawyers when professional duties of competence are breached.

We have already encountered some of these remedies in prior chapters. In Chapter 2, *Walker* involved professional discipline for incompetence and failure to communicate with a client. In Chapters 3 and 4, *Togstad, Antioch Litigation Trust*, and *dePape* introduced us to civil actions, such as legal malpractice and breach of fiduciary duty. We also explored the law of ineffective assistance of counsel as a constitutional remedy for incompetence in a criminal case.

The last section of this chapter addresses additional tort duties, those owed to third parties as well as clients, including the tort of misrepresentation and aiding and abetting a client's breach of fiduciary duty, also touched on in *Antioch*.

A. Knowledge, Skill, Thoroughness, and Preparation

Problem

5-1. Martyn & Fox is asked whether the firm can file an arbitration claim in the International Court of Arbitration. No one at Martyn & Fox has ever done one. At a partners' new business meeting, Fox declares, "Let's take it. It can't be that hard; we'll just follow the Federal Rules of Civil Procedure. Like playing on our own home court. Piece of cake."

Consider: Model Rule 1.1
RLGL § 16

Nebraska ex rel. Counsel for Discipline of the Nebraska Supreme Court v. Orr

759 N.W.2d 702 (Neb. 2009)

PER CURIAM . . .

FACTS

The underlying conduct in this case involves Orr's representation of Steve Sickler and Cathy Mettenbrink in connection with the franchising of a coffee shop business. Sickler and Mettenbrink had opened their first coffee shop together, Barista's Daily Grind (Barista's), in Kearney, Nebraska, in December 2001. In September 2002, Sickler met with Orr and asked whether Orr could help Sickler and Mettenbrink franchise their business.

Orr was engaged in private practice in Kearney, and his experience with franchising was limited. Orr testified that he had read franchise agreements on behalf of clients who either were or were interested in becoming franchisees, but had never represented a franchisor. Orr's role in those cases had been to generally advise clients as to the rights of a franchisor and duties of a franchisee under the agreement. Orr's experience had required him to review franchise agreements and disclosure statements, but he had not reviewed state or federal law governing franchising.

In response to Sickler's inquiry, Orr stated that he had recently reviewed a franchisee's agreement and that he believed he could "handle" the franchising of Barista's. Orr told Sickler and Mettenbrink that he would begin working on a franchise agreement, and he completed the first draft in October 2002. Orr stated that he had recently reviewed a restaurant franchise agreement and then utilized that document when drafting the Barista's document. Although he had never before drafted a franchise agreement, Orr believed it was simply "a matter of contract drafting," which he believed he was competent to do. Orr contacted an attorney in Washington, D.C., for assistance with the trademark and copyright portions of franchising, and that attorney warned Orr that franchising was a specialized field.

In December 2002, Orr drafted a disclosure statement. Orr used the disclosure statement he had recently reviewed on behalf of the previously mentioned franchisee, as well as "FTC documents," to finish the statement in January 2003. Orr's understanding was that a disclosure statement was required by the Federal Trade Commission (FTC) in order to inform the franchisee of the more important terms and conditions of the franchise agreement.

From 2003 to 2006, Barista's sold 21 franchises. In July 2004, Sickler was contacted by a banker in Colorado, inquiring on behalf of a prospective franchisee. The banker requested the "UFOC" of Barista's, and, unaware of what a UFOC was, Sickler referred the banker to Orr. Orr determined that the then-current disclosure statement of Barista's was "compliant and valid" and could be used anywhere. Sickler testified that Orr told him that the UFOC was a requirement of federal law which Barista's was "probably going to have to get" if it was "going to be selling franchises out of state."

In August 2004, Orr revised the franchise agreement and disclosure statement at Sickler's request due to problems Barista's was having with a franchisee
in Iowa. The Iowa franchisee had been provided with copies of the initial franchise agreement and disclosure statement. However, in February 2004, the Iowa
franchisee's attorney sent a letter to Sickler suggesting that Barista's had not
complied with federal disclosure requirements. . . .

In October 2004, due to an unrelated dispute, Sickler and Mettenbrink sued
the Colorado franchisees to terminate the franchises. A counterclaim was filed
alleging deceptive and unfair trade practices, violation of FTC rules, and violation of Nebraska's Seller-Assisted Marketing Plan Act. Orr's associate, Bradley
Holbrook, became lead counsel for this litigation, although Orr remained primarily responsible for the representation of Barista's. Holbrook researched Nebraska
law and discussed the case with Orr, including the fact that the Colorado franchisees were challenging the disclosure statement.

Disagreements were also ongoing with the Iowa franchisee, who eventually demanded rescission of the franchise agreement based on Barista's failure to comply with federal and Iowa disclosure laws. The Iowa franchisee's
attorney demanded that Sickler return the franchise fee and pay attorney
fees and other damages, and informed Sickler that he and Mettenbrink could
be held personally liable under certain provisions of Iowa law. Sickler then
informed Orr of the problem. Orr advised Sickler that the firm was going
to contact an Omaha, Nebraska, attorney for a second opinion. Holbrook
then contacted the Omaha attorney for a second opinion, which was provided
in a June 2005 [13-page] memorandum [detailing "numerous defects"].* . . .
Sickler and Mettenbrink . . . were ultimately informed of its conclusions and
advised by Orr not to sell any more franchises without considerable changes
to the disclosure statement.

A third version of the disclosure statement was created and used. Sickler
stated he was told that the disclosure statement was now "compliant with every
state," but Orr stated he also told Sickler that for out-of-state franchises, Sickler
should get advice from local counsel. Orr stated that before the third revision of the disclosure statement, he had been under the impression that FTC
requirements overrode state law. But he advised Sickler to obtain local counsel
because he had become aware that state law could be more stringent than federal requirements.

The Iowa franchisee filed suit in Iowa and . . . obtained personal judgments against Sickler and Mettenbrink. Barista's sold seven more franchises
using the third disclosure statement, but was notified by the FTC in November
2005 that Barista's was under investigation. Holbrook contacted an attorney
specializing in franchise law regarding the FTC investigation. The specializing

---

* In Sickler v. Kirby, 805 N.W.2d 675 (Neb. App. 2011), Sickler and Mettenbrink's claim for legal
malpractice was upheld against the Omaha firm for failing to advise them to seek the assistance
of another lawyer experienced in drafting disclosure statements, and to seek the advice of a legal
malpractice lawyer).

attorney reviewed the franchise documents of Barista's and concluded those documents—including the third disclosure statement—did not comply with FTC rules. The attorney characterized the deficiencies as "major."

Recognizing that it now had a conflict of interest, Orr's law firm withdrew from representing Sickler and Mettenbrink. The attorney specializing in franchising law continued to represent Sickler and Mettenbrink, and Barista's, with respect to the FTC issues. The FTC civil penalty has been suspended indefinitely, and will not have to be paid so long as the disclosures of Barista's are truthful. By April 2006, however, the franchising of Barista's had "virtually been shut down." Orr's law firm has paid for the revision of the franchising documents, as well as the research and second opinion obtained regarding the original franchising document.

Formal charges were filed against Orr on August 24, 2007, alleging that Orr had violated several sections of the Nebraska Rules of Professional Conduct. . . . This court appointed a referee, and after a hearing, the referee found that Orr had violated . . . [Rules] 1.1 and 8.4(a) of the Nebraska Rules of Professional Conduct.

[Rule] 1.1 provides that "[a] lawyer shall provide competent representation to a client. Competent representation requires the legal knowledge, skill, thoroughness, preparation and judgment reasonably necessary for the representation." . . .

ANALYSIS

. . . A proceeding to discipline an attorney is a trial de novo on the record. To sustain a charge in a disciplinary proceeding against an attorney, a charge must be supported by clear and convincing evidence. Violation of a disciplinary rule concerning the practice of law is a ground for discipline.

[N]o exceptions were filed in response to the referee's report. . . . We consider the finding of facts in the referee's report to be final and conclusive, and based on those findings, we conclude that the formal charges are supported by clear and convincing evidence. Specifically, we conclude that Orr violated . . . [Rules] 1.1 and 8.4(a). . . .

We have previously stated that "'the purpose of a disciplinary proceeding against an attorney is not so much to punish the attorney as it is to determine whether in the public interest an attorney should be permitted to practice.'" We also note that while Orr's conduct caused financial consequences to his clients, the Nebraska Rules of Professional Conduct "are designed to provide guidance to lawyers and to provide a structure for regulating conduct through disciplinary agencies. They are not designed to be a basis for civil liability." For those reasons, we accept the referee's recommendation of a public reprimand.

The referee explicitly found the existence of a number of mitigating factors, including the fact that Orr had practiced law for 40 years and has had no prior complaints or penalties. The referee noted that a number of clients, business and community leaders, and members of the bar sent letters of support and recommendation. Orr also has served the legal community and the community at large. And while the conduct occurred over a long period of time, only one client was involved, and Orr's misconduct was an isolated occurrence rather than part of a recurring pattern. . . .

The referee found Orr negligently determined that he was competent and did not knowingly engage in the practice of law in which he was not competent. We have found no support in the case law for a suspension for incompetence without other misconduct, such as dishonesty.

That is not to say we are unconcerned about Orr's conduct. We have said that "[i]t is inexcusable for an attorney to attempt any legal procedure without ascertaining the law governing that procedure." As a lawyer who has been practicing law for 40 years, Orr should have been aware that he was not competent to represent franchisors, and he was warned by another attorney that franchise law was a specialized area. At the very least, Orr should have done the research necessary to become competent in the area of franchise law. The fact that Orr did little or no research into state or federal franchising law until long after he first received notice that there was a problem with the franchising documents is inexcusable.

We take this opportunity to caution general practitioners against taking on cases in areas of law with which they have no experience, unless they are prepared to do the necessary research to become competent in such areas or associate with an attorney who is competent in such areas. General practitioners must be particularly careful when practicing in specialty areas. "If a general practitioner plunges into a field in which he or she is not competent, and as a consequence makes mistakes that demonstrate incompetence, the [Rules of Professional Conduct] demand that discipline be imposed . . . . "

B.   Malpractice and Breach of Fiduciary Duty

Problems

5-2.   Martyn interviewed a person about a potential personal injury case and agreed to get back to him. Two months later the same person called, leaving a message that he wanted to check on the "status of his case." Before returning the call, Martyn noted that the applicable statute of limitations on the claim had run three days earlier. What should Martyn do?

   (a) Must Martyn tell the caller that the statute has run and it's her fault?

   (b) May Martyn offer to settle the matter for $50,000?

   (c) Can Martyn be disciplined?

   (d) Can Martyn & Fox be disciplined?

   (e) Will Martyn & Fox be liable for malpractice?

5-3.   Client received a settlement of $1 million in a Ford Explorer rollover case. Martyn & Fox provided Client with tax advice regarding the receipt of such a large sum. Later, Client learned about a similar case that ended in a jury verdict of $3 million. Client sues Martyn & Fox for the difference. What if Martyn & Fox had been retained to advise Client about the advisability of the settlement?

Consider: **Model Rules 1.1-1.4**
RLGL §§ 14, 15, 52

Bayview Loan Servicing, LLC v. Law Firm of Richard M. Squire & Associates, LLC

2010 U.S. Dist. LEXIS 132108 (E. D. Penn.)

Yohn, J.

Plaintiffs, Bayview Loan Servicing, LLC ("Bayview") and its wholly-owned subsidiary IB Property Holdings, LLC ("IB"), bring this legal malpractice action against defendants, the law firm of Richard M. Squire & Associates, LLC (the "Squire Firm") and its employee M. Troy Freedman ("Freedman"). Plaintiffs claim that defendants represented them in a foreclosure action; that defendants failed to file a petition to fix the fair value of the relevant property within six months of the foreclosure sale, which is required by statute in order to pursue a deficiency judgment [collecting the difference between the total debt and the value of the foreclosed property], and that as a result of defendants' failure plaintiffs lost any right to pursue the deficiency they were owed. . . .

Defendants have now moved to dismiss for failure to state a claim. . . .

A. Counts I & II – Breach of Fiduciary Duty

Defendants argue that plaintiffs' breach of fiduciary duty claims against the Squire Firm (Count I) and Freedman (Count II) should be dismissed because a breach of fiduciary duty claim arises where a lawyer is disloyal to the client, and plaintiff has pleaded factual matter that supports at most a breach of defendants' duty of care. Plaintiffs respond that they have pleaded both breach of fiduciary duty and negligent malpractice claims. . . .

i. Negligence . . .

Under Pennsylvania law, a legal malpractice claim sounding in negligence requires the plaintiff to prove: (1) the employment of the attorney or other basis for a duty; (2) the failure of the attorney to exercise ordinary skill and knowledge; and (3) that such negligence was the proximate cause of damage to the plaintiff. The first element does not appear to be in dispute, and plaintiffs clearly have pleaded the second, but defendants assert that plaintiffs have failed to plead causation because they do not specifically allege that they would have succeeded in the underlying litigation in the absence of any breach of duty by defendants.

No doubt, to recover the lost deficiency that plaintiffs claim as damages they must show causation by proving that they would have recovered it in the underlying litigation but for defendants' negligence. Plaintiffs have alleged that the Property was sold well below market value; Peter Pugliese owed plaintiffs "in excess of $377,499.00" as a deficiency; plaintiffs instructed defendants to pursue the resulting deficiency; defendants failed to file a petition to fix fair value, which is required in order to pursue a deficiency; and as a result of defendants' "careless, negligent and reckless conduct" plaintiffs suffered damages. Plaintiffs' allegations sufficiently plead the element of causation, and thus plaintiffs have properly stated a claim for negligent malpractice.

ii. Disloyalty

. . . In Pennsylvania, "[a] cause of action may be maintained against an attorney for breach of his or her fiduciary duty to a client." "[T]he relationship between the attorney and his client is a fiduciary relationship." Maritrans GP Inc. v. Pepper, Hamilton & Scheetz, 602 A.2d 1277, 1287 (Pa. 1992). "[S]uch duty demands undivided loyalty and prohibits the attorney from engaging in conflicts of interest, and breach of such duty is actionable." "[A]n attorney who undertakes representation of a client owes that client both a duty of competent representation and the highest duty of honesty, fidelity, and confidentiality."

In the context of Pennsylvania legal malpractice, "breach of fiduciary duty" has often been understood by courts to describe a claim for breach of an attorney's duty of loyalty, rather than an attorney's duty of care. . . .

Thus, establishing a breach of fiduciary duty requires plaintiff to prove: "(1) that the defendant negligently or intentionally failed to act in good faith and solely for the benefit of plaintiff in all matters for which he or she was employed; (2) that the plaintiff suffered injury; and (3) that the agent's failure to act solely for the plaintiff's benefit . . . was a real factor in bring[ing] about plaintiff's injuries."

Plaintiffs do not appear to assert that defendants failed to file the petition intentionally, or because of divided loyalty. However, plaintiffs assert that defendants attempted to hide their lapse by failing to inform plaintiffs that they had missed the deadline for filing a petition to fix fair value, informing [the trial judge] that they did not object to marking the judgment satisfied without consulting plaintiffs, failing to inform plaintiffs that the judgment was marked satisfied, and continuing to press the deficiency claim despite knowing it was unmeritorious. These subsequent acts may constitute a failure "to act in good faith and solely for the benefit of plaintiff."

Of course, to recover on the theory that defendants' acts subsequent to their failure to file a petition to fix fair value were disloyal, plaintiffs will have to prove that such actions were "a real factor in bring[ing] about plaintiff[s'] injuries." *Id.* If there was no way to recover the deficiency once the original mistake was made, plaintiffs may be unable to recover the lost deficiency as damages under this theory of liability. At this stage, however, plaintiffs have sufficiently pleaded their claim.

B. Count IV — Breach of Contract

Defendants assert that plaintiffs have failed to plead a contract-based malpractice claim because they do not properly allege harm resulting from defendants' failure to file a petition to fix fair value. More specifically, defendants assert that plaintiffs have failed to allege that they would have been successful in pursuing a deficiency against Peter Pugliese if defendants had properly filed a petition to fix fair value. Defendants' argument is unavailing.

Although there is some degree of confusion in the relevant caselaw regarding the extent to which harm and causation are required elements of a contract-based malpractice claim,[12] to the extent they are required plaintiff has met the burden of pleading them for the reasons discussed above with respect to plaintiffs' negligence claims.

C. Count III – Negligent Supervision

. . . The Restatement (Second) of Agency § 213 (1958) has also been applied by Pennsylvania courts to impose liability on corporations for negligent supervision and hiring. . . . [I]t does not require that employees act outside the scope of their employment, and it contemplates potential concurrent liability for employers under both § 213 and *respondeat superior*. Moreover, the Supreme Court of Pennsylvania has recognized that an employer may be independently liable for negligent instructions and directions, irrespective of the relevant employee's liability. Thus plaintiffs' negligent supervision claim is not deficient for failing to allege that Freedman acted outside the scope of his employment. . . .

Whether as an alternative or an independent theory of liability, plaintiffs have pleaded sufficient facts to support their claim for negligent supervision.

D. Count V – Punitive Damages . . .

Under Pennsylvania law, "[p]unitive damages may be appropriately awarded only when the plaintiff has established that the defendant has acted in an outrageous fashion due to either 'the defendant's evil motive or his reckless indifference to the rights of others.'" A punitive damages claim "must be supported by evidence sufficient to establish that (1) a defendant had a subjective appreciation of the risk of harm to which the plaintiff was exposed and that (2) he acted, or failed to act, as the case may be, in conscious disregard of that risk."

Defendants rely on McCartney v. Dunn & Conner, Inc., 563 A.2d 525 (Pa. Super. Ct. 1989) to argue that plaintiffs have alleged facts that, at most, support a finding of ordinary negligence that does not support an award of punitive damages. However, . . . the allegations deemed insufficient in *McCartney*[13] did

---

12. Authority has diverged on the required elements of a contract-based claim for legal malpractice since the Pennsylvania Supreme Court decided *Bailey v. Tucker*, 621 A.2d 108 (Pa. 1993). *Bailey* limited the damages available in a contract-based malpractice claim to fees paid and statutory interest, but courts have reached different conclusions as to whether this limitation should apply only in the criminal context, as in *Bailey*.

13. The allegations comprised "[a defendant's] advice that plaintiff should proceed with the lawsuit despite his knowledge of plaintiff's precarious financial situation, [that defendant's] lack of preparation of the case until two weeks before trial and the defendant's involvement in litigation adverse to the plaintiff's radiology group at the same time that the defendants represented plaintiff." *McCartney*, 563 A.2d at 529, n.1.

not involve the kind of conscious wrongdoing plaintiffs allege in this case. Here, plaintiffs have not only alleged that defendants failed to make a necessary filing to prosecute their claim, but also that defendants subsequently engaged in a pattern of deliberate conduct that concealed and exacerbated that original mistake. Even if the original mistake alone is insufficient, plaintiffs' allegations as a whole provide sufficient factual content to support a plausible claim for punitive damages. . . .

▉ The Law Governing Lawyers:
Tort Liability to Clients

Bayview, Antioch Litigation Trust and *dePape* in Chapter 4, and *Togstad* in Chapter 3 all make clear that lawyer-agents who breach contracts or fiduciary duties may be liable in both contract and tort. The contract remedy usually is reserved for cases where a lawyer disobeys a clear and legal instruction of the client or acts contrary to the client's clear interests.[1] Tort remedies, of course, include intentional torts, such as fraud[2] and battery.[3] But because intentional torts are not covered by malpractice insurance, clients typically seek recovery against lawyers on a breach of fiduciary duty or malpractice theory.

Breach of Fiduciary Duty and Malpractice

In some cases, such as *Bayview,* courts identify a breach of fiduciary duty remedy to redress a lawyer's failure to observe basic fiduciary duties to act loyally; that is, solely for the benefit of the client. Courts have upheld this cause of action for failure to obey a client's instructions,[4] inform a client (*dePape*), keep client confidences,[5] or respond to and remedy conflicts of interest (*Bayview*).[6] In these situations, the client has been deprived of a basic fiduciary obligation designed to protect the client's interests,[7] and the lawyer has acted "outside the scope of authority granted by the client."[8] Some courts describe this cause

---

1. *E.g.*, Interclaim Holdings, Ltd. v. Ness, Motley, Loadholt, Richardson & Poole, 298 F. Supp. 2d 746 (N.D. Ill. 2004) (upholding compensatory damages of $8.3 million and punitive damages of $27.7 million on breach of contract theory against law firm that settled claims and released frozen assets without client's consent).

2. *See* The Bounds of the Law: *Duties to Nonclients, infra* p.155.

3. *See, e.g,* Barbara A. v. John G., 193 Cal. Rptr. 422 (Cal. App. 1983) (lawyer who told client he "couldn't possibly get anyone pregnant" liable for battery and fraud after client suffered a tubal pregnancy, which resulted in permanent sterility).

4. *See, e.g.,* Olfe v. Gordon, 286 N.W.2d 573 (Wis. 1980) (no expert testimony required to show that lawyer breached fiduciary duty to client by failing to draft a first mortgage client specifically requested).

5. *E.g.*, Perez v. Kirk & Carrigan, *infra* p. 167.

6. *E.g.*, Johnson v. Nextel Commc'ns, Inc., 660 F.3d 131 (2d Cir. 2011) (nonconsentable conflict caused by lawyer's agreement with opposing party to press clients into an expedited mass settlement).

7. RLGL § 49; Roy Ryden Anderson & Walter W. Steele, Jr., *Fiduciary Duty, Tort, and Contract: A Primer on the Legal Malpractice Puzzle,* 47 S.M.U. L. Rev. 235 (1994).

8. Kilpatrick v. Wiley, Rein, & Fielding, 909 P.2d 1283, 1290 (Utah 1996).

of action as constructive fraud because in a fiduciary relationship, the failure to communicate information that the principal is entitled to know constitutes fraud.[9] *Bayview* emphasizes the disloyalty in the lawyer's attempt to hide his own malpractice. Other courts, like *dePape,* seem to assume that breach of fiduciary duty is a species of malpractice that does not require expert testimony to show duty and breach.[10]

Most of the situations where clients seek a tort remedy do not involve such clear breaches of fiduciary duty. Instead, the client alleges a breach of the duties of care or competence—–that the lawyer should have known more, should have had more experience, or should have exercised reasonable judgment in seeking to accomplish the client's goals. These situations, such as occurred in *Togstad* and *Antioch,* commonly allege legal malpractice and usually require expert testimony.

Since World War II, both the number and complexity of malpractice cases against all professionals, including lawyers, has grown. The exact numbers are difficult to determine because insurers report claims, and too many lawyers do not carry malpractice insurance.[11] In Oregon, the only state that mandates malpractice insurance for lawyers, statistics for the past 20 years indicate that each year 8.7 to 13.2 percent of Oregon lawyers have claims filed against them.[12] Some think that the annual claims rate for lawyers is "probably closer to 20% or more."[13]

In formulating both breach of fiduciary duty and legal malpractice standards, courts rely on an extensive body of precedent.[14] To establish legal malpractice,

---

9. RLGL § 40, Comment a; *Restatement (Second) of Torts* § 551(2)(a).

10. *E.g.,* Estate of Fleming v. Nicholson, 724 A.2d 1026 (Vt. 1998) (no expert testimony necessary to establish negligence as a matter of law against lawyer who failed to inform client about a permit violation discovered during a title search on land the client wished to purchase, despite lawyer's claim that state had a nonenforcement policy concerning that type of violation). *See also* Charles W. Wolfram, *A Cautionary Tale: Fiduciary Breach as Legal Malpractice,* 34 Hofstra L. Rev. 689 (2006).

11. For example, one commentator estimates that 11 to 50 percent of lawyers do not carry malpractice insurance. Manuel R. Ramos, *Legal Malpractice: The Profession's Dirty Little Secret,* 47 Vand. L. Rev. 1657, 1672 (1994). A growing number of jurisdictions require lawyers to inform clients if they lack insurance. *E.g.,* N.H. R. of Prof. Conduct 1.17 (2012); Ohio R. of Prof. Conduct 1.4(c) (2012); R. of the S. Ct. of Va., Part 6, § IV, ¶18 (2007). Several jurisdictions also require malpractice insurance for lawyers who form professional corporations. RLGL § 58, Comment c. The European Union (EU) permits host states to impose insurance requirements on migrant lawyers. James Moliterno & George Harris, *Global Issues in Legal Ethics* 26 (Thomson West 2007).

12. Ramos, *supra* note 11, at 1678.

13. Ramos, *supra* note 11, at 1664. This estimate explains Ramos's conclusion that legal malpractice may be a "tip of the iceberg" problem, whereas medical malpractice more likely involves "a few bad apples." *See also* Manuel E. Ramos, *Legal Malpractice: No Lawyer or Client Is Safe,* 47 Fla. L. Rev. 1, 17 (1995).

14. *See* Merri A. Baldwin, Scott F. Bertschi, & Dylan C. Black, eds., *The Law of Lawyers' Liability: Fifty-State Survey of Legal Malpractice* (ABA 2012). Cases against lawyers can be traced to 1767. John W. Wade, *The Attorney's Liability for Negligence,* 12 Vand. L. Rev. 755 (1959). Those against physicians can be traced to 1374. *See* Allan H. McCoid, *The Care Required of Medical Practitioners,* 12 Vand. L. Rev. 549, 550 (1959).

for example, *Bayview, Antioch, dePape,* and *Togstad* agree that a plaintiff must prove four elements: the existence of a client-lawyer relationship, breach of a professional duty of care, causation (actual and proximate), and damages. The requirement that a plaintiff establish a relationship with the professional is an application of the *Palsgraf* rule, that the plaintiff must be foreseeable, or in other words, the one to whom a duty is owed.[15] Expert testimony is not only admissible but is almost always required to establish breach of the standard of care. Causation rules can be modified due to the special expertise of professionals or the kind of harm professional lapses can cause. Finally, proof of damages often requires more precision than that demanded by ordinary negligence cases.

Professional-Client Relationship

A breach of fiduciary duty or malpractice suit requires a showing of a professional relationship that creates a professional duty.[16] In *Bayview, Antioch,* and *dePape,* there was no dispute that an express client-lawyer relationship existed. The law firm in each case deliberately agreed to represent an identified client or clients. *Togstad* illustrates how courts also can find that implied client-lawyer relationships create duties to prospective clients when such parties reasonably rely on a lawyer's advice.[17] Most courts agree that prospective clients are limited-term clients to whom the duties of confidentiality and competence are due.[18] A limited-term implied client-lawyer relationship also has been found to exist in situations where a lawyer for one party to a transaction voluntarily provides services to other parties who reasonably rely on the lawyer's assistance.[19]

---

15. *See* Palsgraf v. Long Island R.R. Co., 162 N.E. 99 (N.Y. 1928).

16. In fact, most courts hold that a legal malpractice cause of action is not assignable to a third person. *See, e.g.,* Gurski v. Rosenblum & Filan, LLC, 885 A.2d 163 (Conn. 2005) (legal malpractice claims cannot be assigned to adversary in litigation); Rosby Corp. v. Townsend, Yosha, Cline, & Prince, 800 N.E.2d 661 (Ind. App. 2003) (client's assignment of a legal malpractice claim barred regardless of whether assigned to an adversary). Such a rule does not apply where the assignment occurs by operation of law, such as in *Antioch. See also* Parus Holdings Inc. v. Banner & Witcoff Ltd., 585 F. Supp. 2d 995 (N. D. Ill 2008) (corporation's successor in interest inherited right to sue predecessor corporation's lawyers for malpractice, including punitive damages), Parrett v. Natl. Century Fin. Enters., Inc., 2006 U.S. Dist. LEXIS 16982 (S.D. Ohio) (general rule against assignment of legal malpractice claims does not apply to bankruptcy, where debtor's representative can pursue suit for benefit of creditors).

17. These implied relationships are one example of accidental clients, discussed in The Law Governing Lawyers, *Accidental Clients, supra* p. **79**. *See, e.g.,* DeVaux v. Am. Home Assurance Co., 444 N.E.2d 355 (Mass. 1983) (secretary who spoke to prospective client and told her to write a letter asking for representation and have a physician document injuries had actual or apparent authority to create client-lawyer relationship).

18. *See* RLGL §§ 14, 15, 51(1).

19. Persons claiming such an implied client-lawyer relationship must reasonably believe that the lawyer represented their interests. *E.g.,* Kremser v. Quarles & Brady, L.L.P., 36 P.3d 761 (Ariz. App. 2001) (corporation's lawyers undertook responsibility to perfect nonclient creditor's security interest); Nelson v. Nationwide Mortgage Corp., 659 F. Supp. 611 (D.D.C. 1987) (lawyer volunteered to answer questions and explain document). *See also* The Bounds of the Law: *Duties to Nonclients, infra* p. **155**.

Duty

Plaintiffs must prove not only that a client-lawyer relationship existed, but also that it existed with respect to the acts or omissions that form the basis of a malpractice suit.[20] This rule recognizes that client and lawyer, within limits, can agree to limit the scope of representation to certain specific matters.[21] Once both the client-professional relationship and the scope of representation are established, courts require lawyers to "exercise the competence and diligence normally exercised by lawyers in similar circumstances."[22] Because jurors usually lack familiarity with what a particular professional should do, this general malpractice standard requires expert testimony to establish the required standard of care.[23] Lawyers are granted professional discretion, but only within the range of choices made by reasonably competent practitioners under similar circumstances.[24] When experts disagree (as they did in *Togstad*), the jury decides the appropriate standard of care.

The fact of state licensure of lawyers translates into the admissibility of expert testimony of any lawyer licensed to practice in that state.[25] Once qualified as an appropriate expert, an expert witness's testimony must clearly articulate the standard of care or customary practice of the profession.[26] As lawyers have focused their practices, the recognition of specialty areas also has become a component of the standard of care.[27] Lawyers have been held responsible for failing to understand the intricacies of a specialized task, or for failing to refer to a specialist who can competently provide the specialized service.[28] Specialty designations can be established by state regulations, by expert testimony, or by a lawyer who claims to practice in a specialized area.[29]

---

20. *See, e.g.*, SCB Diversified Mun. Portfolio v. Crews & Associates, 2012 U.S. Dist. LEXIS 754 (E. D. La.) (environmental due diligence not responsibility of law firm hired as bond counsel to verify legal validity of municipal bond sale); Kates v. Robinson, 786 So. 2d 61 (Fla. App. 2001) (lawyer hired only to execute a judgment not responsible for recognizing other potential defendants). *Cf.* Nichols v. Keller, 19 Cal. Rptr. 2d 601 (Cal. App. 1993) (initial lawyer consulted by injured worker had duty to advise about availability of third-party action as well as workers' compensation claim, but second lawyer, who undertook only workers' compensation case, had no duty to advise).

21. *See* MR 1.2(c); RLGL § 19.

22. *Id.*

23. RLGL § 52.

24. *Id.*, at Comment b; Equitania Ins. Co. v. Slone & Garrett P.S.C., 191 S.W.3d 552 (Ky. 2006) (lawyer can be liable for error in judgment that deviates from the standard of care); Jerry's Enters., Inc. v. Larkin, Hoffman, Daly & Lindgren, Ltd., 711 N.W.2d 811 (Minn. 2006) (lawyer must act with some level of reasonable care to be protected by honest error in judgment rule).

25. *See, e.g.*, Russo v. Griffin, 510 A.2d 436 (Vt. 1986).

26. *See, e.g.*, Childers v. Spindor, 754 P.2d 599 (Or. App. 1988) (expert witness's general discussion of deposition practice not sufficient to establish standard of care for legal malpractice).

27. Ronald E. Mallen & Jeffrey M. Smith, *Legal Malpractice,* § 19.4 (West 2007).

28. Horne v. Peckham, 158 Cal. Rptr. 714 (Cal. App. 1979) (lawyer who acknowledged the need for expertise in tax had duty to refer client to an expert practitioner or to comply with the specialty standard of care).

29. *See, e.g.*, Battle v. Thornton, 646 A.2d 315 (D.C. 1994) (absent proof that the defendants held themselves out as specialists in Medicaid fraud defense, or that jurisdiction or profession recognizes such a specialty, lawyer is required to exercise skill and care of lawyers acting under similar circumstances).

The power of professional custom also plays a role in mitigating the doctrine of negligence per se. *Antioch* and *dePape* illustrate the majority view in legal malpractice suits that such a professional rule violation is relevant and admissible to prove breach of the professional standard of care, but does not constitute negligence per se.[30] Courts often allow or require expert testimony to explain the professional rule standard and how it reflects the standard of care.[31]

Breach

Once evidence of the standard of care has been articulated, the jury then determines whether the defendant breached this standard of practice. *dePape* illustrates (but does not label) another aspect of legal malpractice cases: the common knowledge exception to the requirement of expert testimony. This exception was created to address situations where expert opinion was not necessary to help the jury understand the alleged duty and breach because the professional's error was obvious to a layperson.[32]

In legal malpractice actions, courts recognize three common knowledge exceptions for which juries do not need an expert to assess whether the lawyer failed to perform a basic duty owed to the client. The first involves breaches of fiduciary duty such as in *Bayview* and *dePape,* as well as *Perez* in the next chapter. The second group of cases involves lawyers who miss obvious statutory time deadlines, such as statutes of limitations.[33] Finally, some courts have concluded that plaintiffs do not need expert testimony to prove that lawyers should perform two basic functions: research applicable law[34] and investigate relevant facts.[35]

Causation

Once breach of a duty is established, courts require plaintiffs who allege legal malpractice to prove both actual and proximate causation. The "but-for" standard of actual causation and the foreseeable risk rule in proximate causation

---

30. Model Rules, Scope ¶ 20; RLGL § 52 (2). *See also* Lawyers and Clients: *Criminal Defense, supra* p. 118.

31. *E.g.,* Smith v. Haynsworth, Marion, McKay, & Geurard, 472 S.E.2d 612 (S.C. 1996) (bar rules intended to protect a person in the client's position or addressing the particular harm are admissible to assess the legal duty of a lawyer).

32. *E.g.,* Vandermay v. Clayton, 984 P.2d 272 (Or. 1999) (no expert testimony required to establish that lawyer should have warned client that agreement that client was signing did not include protection that client had insisted on); Valentine v. Watters, 896 So. 2d 385 (Ala. 2004) (trier of fact did not need expert to determine whether lawyer breached duty by misrepresenting his qualifications and missing a time deadline).

33. *See, e.g.,* Barnes v. Turner, 606 S.E.2d 849 (Ga. 2004) (lawyer who failed to safeguard client's security interest in the sale of a business by renewing the security interest as required by statute five years after the sale); George v. Caton, 600 P.2d 822 (N.M. App. 1979) (statute of limitations).

34. *See, e.g.,* Smith v. Lewis, 530 P.2d 589 (Cal. App. 1973) (lawyer who failed to research law, which would have indicated a potential, although unclear, client claim in a divorce).

35. *See, e.g.,* Schmitz v. Crotty, 528 N.W.2d 112 (Iowa 1995) (lawyer who failed to investigate property descriptions in valuing estate taxes after he was put on notice that they were inaccurate).

can present formidable obstacles to the former client.[36] In *dePape,* for example, plaintiff was unable to prove malpractice based on a duty of the law firm to pursue an H-1B visa because he did not establish that he would have taken the medical exams that were required to qualify for it. He was, however, able to establish that he would have started his medical practice in Canada 15 months sooner had the law firm properly informed him of his legal options. In *Antioch,* plaintiff alleged that negligent legal advice caused the legal invalidity of a trans-action, which in turn would have led to the destruction of the company's capital structure and tax-exempt status.

When a claim is based on the expiration of a time period such as a statute of limitations, plaintiffs who allege legal malpractice are required to prove the "case within a case," as was done in *Togstad.*[37] Some think this requirement unfair and argue that some sort of increased risk doctrine should be applied in such situations, earning the plaintiff a damage award without proving the case within the case.[38] A few courts recognize an alternative: the use of expert testimony to prove the value of the loss caused by the negligent lawyer measured by the settlement value of the underlying matter.[39]

---

36. *E.g.,* Ambase Corp. v. Davis Polk & Wardwell, 866 N.E.2d 1033 (N.Y. 2007) (record provides no support for plaintiff's assertion that "but for" law firm's failure to advise it properly, a large loss reserve would have been removed earlier and client would not have suffered loss of business opportunities). *But see* Williams v. Joynes, 677 S.E.2d 261 (Va. 2009) (client's failure to file suit in another jurisdiction after lawyer failed to file within statute of limitations in Virginia was not a superseding cause because intervening act of client was set in motion by the initial negligence of the lawyer).

37. *E.g.,* Minkin v. Gibbons PC, 2012 U.S. App. LEXIS 9158 (Fed. Cir.) (summary judgment appropriate in patent malpractice case where plaintiff failed to show that alternative drafting language would have resulted in valid patent); Viner v. Sweet, 70 P.3d 1046 (Cal. 2003) (case within a case proof required for errors in transactional work as well as litigation); Bevan v. Fix, 42 P.3d 1013 (Wyo. 2002) (summary judgment granted against client who proved that former lawyer breached fiduciary duty but did not allege facts indicating that the underlying divorce action would have been more favorable to him). The rule also burdens persons convicted of crimes who must have their convictions reversed or prove their innocence to establish causation. *See* Lawyers and Clients: *Criminal Defense, supra* p. 118

38. John Leubsdorf, *Legal Malpractice and Professional Responsibility,* 48 Rutgers L. Rev. 101, 149-150 (1995). *See also* Crist v. Lyacono, 65 So. 2d 837 (Miss. 2011) (lawyer's breach of fiduciary duty of loyalty may cause injury apart from the merits of the underlying case; improper to apply negligence but for standard).

39. *E.g.,* Garcia v. Kozlov, Seaton, Romanini, & Brooks, P.C., 845 A.2d 602 (N.J. 2004) (expert testimony sufficient to establish actual cause against lawyer who negligently failed to investigate accident claim and join one responsible driver); Wolpaw v. Gen. Accident Ins. Co., 639 A. 2d 338 (N.J. Super. 1994) ("expert testimony as to what as a matter of reasonable probability would have transpired at the original trial" in lieu of "suit within a suit" requirement). *Cf.* Jones Motor Co. Inc. v. Holtkamp, Liese, Beckemeier, & Childress, P.C., 197 F.3d 1190 (7th Cir. 1999) (malpractice plaintiff who alleged former lawyer's failure to make a timely jury trial request failed to prove causation using a lawyer-expert witness whose opinion of probable jury verdicts was unsubstantiated by actual verdicts in comparable cases). *But see* Leibel v. Johnson, 2012 Ga. LEXIS 564 (expert testimony on proximate cause is inadmissible and irrelevant).

Damages

Because malpractice is a species of negligence, damages must be shown.[40] For example, even if the jury determines that the plaintiff would have prevailed in a previous case, a defendant who can show that any judgment won would have been uncollectible will be relieved from being accountable for that portion of the verdict.[41] Traditionally, proving damages meant proving monetary or physical injury. Increasingly, clients who allege foreseeable emotional harm also may be able to recover from the professional who caused it.[42] For example, the court in *dePape* recognized the availability of damages for emotional harm against some lawyers, at least where their breach of fiduciary duty is egregious and directly causes severe emotional distress.[43] *dePape* also illustrates the willingness of modern cases to extend the availability of punitive damages to professionals where their conduct is grossly negligent or outrageous in character.[44] Query whether Dr. dePape's malpractice lawyers themselves committed malpractice by failing to plead punitive damages.[45]

Defenses

Professionals often allege several defenses to malpractice suits. Increasingly, they seek to implead or be granted contribution from other professionals who provided services to the client.[46] Statutes of limitations can differ for breach of contract, fiduciary duty, and malpractice, and are also commonly alleged as

---

40. Lawyer's fees expended in the negligently performed service generally are not credited to the damage amount on the theory that the plaintiff had to hire a second lawyer to remedy the mistake. RLGL § 53, Comment c; Nettleton v. Stogsdill, 899 N.E.2d 1252 (Ill. App. 2008) *appeal denied*, 910 N.E. 2d 1128 (Ill. 2009) (former client entitled to recover as actual damages fees that she would not have had to pay in the absence of former lawyer's negligence).

41. *See, e.g.*, RLGL § 53, Comment b. *Cf.* Garretson v. Miller, 121 Cal. Rptr. 2d 317 (Cal. App. 3d Dist. 2002) (plaintiff must prove that judgment would be collectible).

42. *See, e.g.*, RLGL § 53, Comment g.

43. *See also* Perez v. Kirk & Carrigan, *infra* p.167, which upheld emotional distress damages against lawyers whose breach of confidentiality caused a multiple-count criminal indictment against their client. *See also* Lawyers in Practice: *Criminal Defense, supra* p. 118. *Cf.* Long-Russell v. Hampe, 39 P.3d 1015 (Wyo. 2002) (damages for emotional distress not recoverable in malpractice case alleging negligent legal advice about child custody). *See also* Lawrence v. Grinde, 534 N.W.2d 414 (Iowa 1995), cited in *dePape*.

44. RLGL § 53, Comment h. *See also* Bayview Loan Servicing LLC v. Law Firm of Richard M. Squire & Associates LLC, *supra* p. 134.

45. Courts differ on whether clients can recover punitive damages that a lawyer negligently failed to pursue. *E.g.*, Tri-G Inc. v. Burke, Bosselman, & Weaver, 856 N.E.2d 389 (Ill. 2006) (clients cannot recover punitive damages that lawyer might have recovered if case not dismissed due to lawyer's negligence); Jacobsen v. Oliver, 201 F. Supp. 2d 93 (D.D.C. 2002) (terrorism victim in legal malpractice case could recover punitive damages if his lawyer negligently failed to raise the issue in the underlying action).

46. *E.g.*, Sheetz, Inc. v. Bowles Rice McDavid Graff & Love, PLLC, 547 S.E.2d 256 (W. Va. 2001) (predecessor and successor law firms may be joint tortfeasors); Parler & Wobber v. Miles & Stockbridge, P.C., 756 A.2d 526 (Md. 2000) (lawyer being sued by former client may implead or obtain contribution or indemnification from successor lawyer).

defenses.[47] Most courts agree that because clients depend on professionals, the statute is tolled during the time the professional-client relationship continues.[48] Most courts also apply the "discovery rule" to claims against lawyers; the statutory time period does not begin to run until the plaintiff reasonably should have discovered the elements of the cause of action.[49]

Courts follow similar reasoning when deciding whether comparative negligence should apply. A lawyer cannot claim comparative fault as a defense in a case such as *Antioch* or *dePape* where the client's failure to understand has been caused by the client's reasonable reliance on the lawyer's negligent or nonexistent explanation.[50]

Overall, courts apply fairly consistent rules to govern tort suits against lawyers. The development of this law has made malpractice suits a primary means of addressing professional incompetence. Understanding the contours of this remedy can help you avoid liability in practice.

C. Duties to Nonclients

Problems

5-4.   In giving an opinion to Cheltenham Township on the issuance of bonds to finance a shopping center, Martyn & Fox inserted the usual boilerplate: "This issuance complies with all applicable law." But in fact, Martyn & Fox forgot that there were new Internal Revenue Service (IRS) regulations governing the tax-exempt status of such special-purpose bonds, rendering these bonds taxable. Any problems?

---

47. A few states also have statutes of repose for malpractice suits, which start to run on the date of the act or omission. *See, e.g.,* Sorenson v. Law Offices of Theodore Poehlmann, 764 N.E.2d 1227 (Ill. App. 2001) (six-year statute of repose time stricture applies even where underlying acts produce injury only after that period of time). *Cf.* Stanley v. Trinchard, 579 F.3d 515 (5th Cir. 2009) (supremacy clause dictates that federal bankruptcy statute of limitations takes precedence over state statute of repose).

48. *See, e.g.,* Shumsky v. Eisenstein, 750 N.E.2d 67 (N.Y. 2001) (analogizing to the continuous treatment rule in medical malpractice cases); Lima v. Schmidt, 595 So. 2d 624 (La. 1992).

49. *E.g.,* Feddersen v. Garvey, 427 F.3d 108 (1st Cir. 2005) (discovery rule applies but did not toll the statute of limitations where client could have reasonably discerned that he suffered some harm caused by the lawyer at an earlier point in time); Neel v. Magana, Olney, Levy, Cathcart, & Gelfand, 6 Cal. 3d 176 (1971) (a cause of action for legal malpractice does not accrue until plaintiff knew, or should have known, all material facts essential to show the elements of the claim).

50. *See, e.g.,* RLGL § 54, Comment d; Pair v. Queen, 2 A.3d 1063 (D.C. App. 2010) (personal representative may recover late estate tax filing fee if attributable to reasonable reliance on lawyer's erroneous advice). On the other hand, a client who defrauded a third party was not entitled to indemnification from his lawyers because "fraudfeasors" cannot hold others liable for harm caused by their own fraudulent conduct. Trustees of the AFTRA Health Fund v. Biondi, 303 F.3d 765 (7th Cir. 2002); Clark v. Rowe, 701 N.E.2d 624 (Mass. 1988) (upholding jury verdict that client was 70 percent negligent in refinancing a loan). *See generally,* Vincent R. Johnson, *The Unlawful Conduct Defense in Legal Malpractice,* 77 UMKC L. Rev. 43 (2008).

5-5.   Martyn & Fox represented Client in negotiating and drafting a settlement agreement to end a lawsuit against Co-owner concerning jointly owned land. The agreement provided that Co-owner would transfer his share in the jointly owned parcel to Client in exchange for Client's agreement to sell the parcel and pay Co-owner one-half of the proceeds. After the agreement was signed, Co-owner transferred his interest in the property to Client. Client immediately sold the property and, with Martyn & Fox's advice and assistance, refused to turn over co-owner's one half, based on a claim that Client was owed at least that much from Co-owner on another joint venture. Co-owner threatens to sue both Client and Martyn & Fox to recover the $250,000 he claims he lost due to Client's actions. Any problem?

Consider: Model Rules 1.1, 2.3, 4.1, 8.4(c)
RLGL §§ 51, 95, 98

Greycas, Inc. v. Proud

826 F.2d 1560 (7th Cir. 1987), cert. denied, 484 U.S. 1043 (1988)

POSNER, Circuit Judge.

Theodore S. Proud, Jr., a member of the Illinois bar who practices law in a suburb of Chicago, appeals from a judgment against him for $833,760, entered after a bench trial. The tale of malpractice and misrepresentation that led to the judgment begins with Proud's brother-in-law, Wayne Crawford, like Proud a lawyer but one who devoted most of his attention to a large farm that he owned in downstate Illinois. The farm fell on hard times and by 1981 Crawford was in dire financial straits. He had pledged most of his farm machinery to lenders, yet now desperately needed more money. He approached Greycas, Inc., the plaintiff in this case, a large financial company headquartered in Arizona, seeking a large loan that he offered to secure with the farm machinery. He did not tell Greycas about his financial difficulties or that he had pledged the machinery to other lenders, but he did make clear that he needed the loan in a hurry. Greycas obtained several appraisals of Crawford's farm machinery but did not investigate Crawford's financial position or discover that he had pledged the collateral to other lenders, who had perfected their liens in the collateral. Greycas agreed to lend Crawford $1,367,966.50, which was less than the appraised value of the machinery.

The loan was subject, however, to an important condition, which is at the heart of this case: Crawford was required to submit a letter to Greycas, from counsel whom he would retain, assuring Greycas that there were no prior liens on the machinery that was to secure the loan. Crawford asked Proud to prepare the letter, and he did so, and mailed it to Greycas, and within 20 days of the first contact between Crawford and Greycas the loan closed and the money was disbursed. A year later Crawford defaulted on the loan; shortly afterward he committed suicide. Greycas then learned that most of the farm machinery that Crawford had pledged to it had previously been pledged to other lenders.

The machinery was sold at auction. The Illinois state court that determined the creditors' priorities in the proceeds of the sale held that Greycas did not have a first priority on most of the machinery that secured its loan; as a result Greycas has been able to recover only a small part of the loan. The judgment it obtained in the present suit is the district judge's estimate of the value that it would have realized on its collateral had there been no prior liens, as Proud represented in his letter.

That letter is the centerpiece of the litigation. Typed on the stationery of Proud's firm and addressed to Greycas, it identifies Proud as Crawford's lawyer and states that, "in such capacity, I have been asked to render my opinion in connection with" the proposed loan to Crawford. It also states that "this opinion is being delivered in accordance with the requirements of the Loan Agreement" and that

> I have conducted a U.C.C., tax, and judgment search with respect to the Company [i.e., Crawford's farm] as of March 19, 1981, and except as hereinafter noted all units listed on the attached Exhibit A ("Equipment") are free and clear of all liens or encumbrances other than Lender's perfected security interest therein which was recorded March 19, 1981 at the Office of the Recorder of Deeds of Fayette County, Illinois.

The reference to the lender's security interest is to Greycas's interest; Crawford, pursuant to the loan agreement, had filed a notice of that interest with the recorder. The excepted units to which the letter refers are four vehicles. Exhibit A is a long list of farm machinery—the collateral that Greycas thought it was getting to secure the loan, free of any other liens. . . .

Proud never conducted a search for prior liens on the machinery listed in Exhibit A. His brother-in-law gave him the list and told him there were no liens other than the one that Crawford had just filed for Greycas. Proud made no effort to verify Crawford's statement. The theory of the complaint is that Proud was negligent in representing that there were no prior liens, merely on his brother-in-law's say-so. No doubt Proud was negligent in failing to conduct a search, but we are not clear why the misrepresentation is alleged to be negligent rather than deliberate and hence fraudulent, in which event Greycas's alleged contributory negligence would not be an issue (as it is, we shall see), since there is no defense of contributory or comparative negligence to a deliberate tort, such as fraud. . . . Proud did not merely say, "There are no liens"; he said, "I have conducted a U.C.C., tax, and judgment search"; and not only is this statement, too, a false one, but its falsehood cannot have been inadvertent, for Proud knew he had not conducted such a search. The concealment of his relationship with Crawford might also support a charge of fraud. But Greycas decided, for whatever reason, to argue negligent misrepresentation rather than fraud. It may have feared that Proud's insurance policy for professional malpractice excluded deliberate wrong-doing from its coverage, or may not have wanted to bear the higher burden of proving fraud, or may have feared that an accusation of fraud would make it harder to settle the case. . . . In any event, Proud does not argue that either he is liable for fraud or he is liable for nothing.

He also does not, and could not, deny or justify the misrepresentation; but he argues that it is not actionable under the tort law of Illinois, because he had no duty of care to Greycas. . . . He argues that Greycas had an adversarial relationship with Proud's client, Crawford, and that a lawyer has no duty of straight dealing to an adversary, at least none enforceable by a tort suit. In so arguing, Proud is characterizing Greycas's suit as one for professional malpractice rather than negligent misrepresentation, yet elsewhere in his briefs he insists that the suit was solely for negligent misrepresentation—while Greycas insists that its suit charges both torts. . . . So we shall discuss both.

Proud is undoubtedly correct in arguing that a lawyer has no general duty of care toward his adversary's client; it would be a considerable and, as it seems to us, an undesirable novelty to hold that every bit of sharp dealing by a lawyer gives rise to prima facie tort liability to the opposing party in the lawsuit or negotiation. The tort of malpractice normally refers to a lawyer's careless or otherwise wrongful conduct toward his own client. Proud argues that Crawford rather than Greycas was his client and . . . we shall assume for purposes of discussion that Greycas was not Proud's client.

Therefore if malpractice just meant carelessness or other misconduct toward one's own client, Proud would not be liable for malpractice to Greycas. But in Pelham v. Griesheimer, 440 N.E.2d 96 (1982), the Supreme Court of Illinois discarded the old common law requirement of privity of contract for professional malpractice; so now it is possible for someone who is not the lawyer's (or other professional's) client to sue him for malpractice. The court in *Pelham* was worried, though, about the possibility of a lawyer's being held liable "to an unlimited and unknown number of potential plaintiffs," so it added that "for a nonclient to succeed in a negligence action against an attorney, he must prove that the primary purpose and intent of the attorney–client relationship itself was to benefit or influence the third party." That, however, describes this case exactly. Crawford hired Proud not only for the primary purpose, but for the sole purpose, of influencing Greycas to make Crawford a loan. The case is much like Brumley v. Touche, Ross & Co., 487 N.E.2d 641, 644-45 (Ill. App. 1985), where a complaint that an accounting firm had negligently prepared an audit report that the firm knew would be shown to an investor in the audited corporation and relied on by that investor was held to state a claim for professional malpractice. In Conroy v. Andeck Resources '81 Year-End Ltd., 484 N.E.2d 525, 536-37 (1985), in contrast, a law firm that represented an offeror of securities was held not to have any duty of care to investors. The representation was not intended for the benefit of investors. Their reliance on the law firm's using due care in the services it provided in connection with the offer was not invited.

All this assumes that *Pelham* governs this case, but arguably it does not, for Greycas, as we noted, may have decided to bring this as a suit for negligent misrepresentation rather than professional malpractice. We know of no obstacle to such an election; nothing is more common in American jurisprudence than overlapping torts.

The claim of negligent misrepresentation might seem utterly straightforward. It might seem that by addressing a letter to Greycas intended (as Proud's counsel admitted at argument) to induce reliance on the statements in it, Proud made himself prima facie liable for any material misrepresentations, careless or deliberate, in the letter, whether or not Proud was Crawford's lawyer or for that matter anyone's lawyer. Knowing that Greycas was relying on him to determine whether the collateral for the loan was encumbered and to advise Greycas of the results of his determination, Proud negligently misrepresented the situation, to Greycas's detriment. But merely labeling a suit as one for negligent misrepresentation rather than professional malpractice will not make the problem of indefinite and perhaps excessive liability, which induced the court in *Pelham* to place limitations on the duty of care, go away. So one is not surprised to find that courts have placed similar limitations on suits for negligent misrepresentation—so similar that we are led to question whether, . . . these really are different torts, at least when both grow out of negligent misrepresentations by lawyers. For example, the *Brumley* case, which we cited earlier, is a professional-malpractice case, yet it has essentially the same facts as Ultramares Corp. v. Touche, Niven & Co., 174 N.E. 441 (N.Y. 1931), where the New York Court of Appeals, in a famous opinion by Judge Cardozo, held that an accountant's negligent misrepresentation was not actionable at the suit of a lender who had relied on the accountant's certified audit of the borrower. . . .

Later Illinois cases, however, influenced by section 552 of the Second Restatement of Torts (1977), . . . hold that "one who in the course of his business or profession supplies information for the guidance of others in their business transactions" is liable for negligent misrepresentations that induce detrimental reliance. Whether there is a practical as distinct from a merely semantic difference between this formulation of the duty limitation and that of *Pelham* may be doubted but cannot change the outcome of this case. Proud, in the practice of his profession, supplied information (or rather misinformation) to Greycas that was intended to guide Greycas in commercial dealings with Crawford. Proud therefore had a duty to use due care to see that the information was correct. He used no care. . . .

There is no serious doubt about the existence of a causal relationship between the misrepresentation and the loan. Greycas would not have made the loan without Proud's letter. Nor would it have made the loan had Proud advised it that the collateral was so heavily encumbered that the loan was as if unsecured, for then Greycas would have known that the probability of repayment was slight. . . .

Proud argues, however, that his damages should be reduced in recognition of Greycas's own contributory negligence, which, though no longer a complete defense in Illinois, is a partial defense, renamed "comparative negligence." It is as much a defense to negligent misrepresentation as to any other tort of negligence. . . .

But we think it too clear to require a remand for further proceedings that Proud failed to prove a want of due care by Greycas. Due care is the care that is optimal given that the other party is exercising due care. It is not the higher level of care that would be optimal if potential tort victims were required to assume that the rest of the world was negligent. A pedestrian is not required to exercise a level of care (e.g., wearing a helmet or a shin guard) that would be optimal if there were no sanctions against reckless driving. Otherwise drivers would be encouraged to drive recklessly, and knowing this pedestrians would be encouraged to wear helmets and shin guards. The result would be a shift from a superior method of accident avoidance (not driving recklessly) to an inferior one (pedestrian armor).

So we must ask whether Greycas would have been careless not to conduct its own UCC search had Proud done what he had said he did—conduct his own UCC search. The answer is no. The law normally does not require duplicative precautions unless one is likely to fail or the consequences of failure (slight though the likelihood may be) would be catastrophic. . . . It is not hard to conduct a UCC lien search; it just requires checking the records in the recorder's office for the county where the debtor lives. *See* Ill. Rev. Stat. ch. 26, para. 9-401. So the only reason to backstop Proud was if Greycas should have assumed he was careless or dishonest; and we have just said that the duty of care does not require such an assumption. Had Proud disclosed that he was Crawford's brother-in-law this might have been a warning signal that Greycas could ignore only at its peril. To go forward in the face of a known danger is to assume the risk. But Proud did not disclose his relationship to Crawford. . . .

A final point. The record of this case reveals serious misconduct by an Illinois attorney. We are therefore sending a copy of this opinion to the Attorney Registration and Disciplinary Commission of the Supreme Court of Illinois for such disciplinary action as may be deemed appropriate in the circumstances.[*] AFFIRMED.

Cruze v. Hudler

267 P. 3d 176 (Ore. App. 2011)
modified, 274 P. 3d 858 (Ore. App. 2012)

SCHUMAN, P. J.

Plaintiffs brought this action against two defendants, Martin L. Hudler and Charles R. Markley, who allegedly defrauded them by means of an investment scheme. . . .

Plaintiffs Tyrone and Jacqueline Cruze owned development property in Oregon and listed that property with Pat Jay, a real estate broker. In early 2007, Hudler contacted Jay about purchasing some of plaintiffs' property. Hudler visited plaintiffs' Idaho home in May to discuss that prospective purchase. During the visit, Hudler described a real estate development business that he and Markley owned. Hudler represented that he was an experienced and successful real estate developer and that Markley was an "experienced lawyer." Hudler told plaintiffs that he and Markley had a portfolio of successful projects in Nevada,

---

[*] Mr. Proud was suspended from practice for one year, from May 1, 1990 to May 1, 1991. https://www.iardc.org/ldetail.asp?id=891824192.

Oregon, and California, and he invited Tyrone Cruze to come to Reno, Nevada, to see some of those projects.

On May 30, 2007, Tyrone Cruze sent Jay to Reno on his behalf to see the real estate projects and gauge how successful they were. Hudler and Markley met Jay in Reno and showed him eight real estate projects. Jay gave a positive report of the visit, and over the summer Tyrone Cruze met with Hudler and Markley at Hudler's office. During that meeting, Hudler explained that Markley, his partner, was an owner of one of the biggest law firms in Portland. Hudler also told Cruze about other successful projects that Hudler and Markley were working on, including a development with Robert Praegitzer, a businessman Cruze respected. Markley "heard everything [Hudler] said as he was sitting in the same room."

Hudler visited plaintiffs several more times in the fall of 2007 and ultimately convinced them to form a joint venture with Bridgeport Communities, LLC (Bridgeport), a limited liability company owned by Hudler and Markley, to develop plaintiffs' Oregon property. To that end, Bridgeport and plaintiffs formed four separate limited liability companies—the "JTB Equities" companies.

Bridgeport, meanwhile, also owned all of the membership interests in Covenant Partners, LLC, a company that served as the "operations manager" for Keycom, a company that, in turn, was to develop a parcel of property in Nevada known as the "Keystone Property." In March 2008, Hudler approached Tyrone Cruze about investing in Covenant. On March 19, Markley prepared a First Amended and Restated Operating Agreement of Covenant Partners, LLC, which Hudler then took to plaintiffs' home in order to finalize the investment. Hudler represented to plaintiffs that the investment was needed immediately because two loans related to and secured by the Keystone Property were in default.

The following day, Hudler and plaintiffs executed the Covenant Operating Agreement, whereby plaintiffs purchased half of Bridgeport's interest in Covenant . . . [agreeing] to pay Bridgeport $513,149—that is, half of the $1,026,298 that, according to Section 2.1.2 of the Agreement, Bridgeport had already contributed . . . Plaintiffs also agreed to loan $3,330,000 to Keycom and to make additional capital contributions. Hudler represented to plaintiffs that the loan to Keycom would be secured by a first priority trust deed on 40 acres of the Keystone Property.

Shortly after executing the Covenant Operating Agreement, plaintiffs paid the agreed $513,149 to Bridgeport, . . . a capital contribution of $160,000 to Covenant, pursuant to the agreement, and . . . plaintiffs also loaned just over $3 million to Keycom.

According to plaintiffs, their investment in Covenant was actually part of a fraudulent "Ponzi-like scheme" whereby Hudler and Markley operated businesses without profit, commingled funds of related companies, and raised new funds to repay earlier investors and hide the lack of profits. . . .

On March 19, 2008—the day that Hudler arrived at plaintiffs' house to finalize the Covenant Operating Agreement—Bridgeport's bookkeeper e-mailed Hudler a list of the balances in the accounts of Hudler and Markley's limited liability companies (as well as other accounts) showing just over $5,000. The e-mail states, "Here are the current balances in the accounts. *Am robbing Peter to pay Paul when necessary. Any update on Cru[z]e Wire?* " (Emphasis added.) . . .

Plaintiffs later discovered that . . . Hudler had made a number of inaccurate representations while courting plaintiffs. Those misrepresentations included (1) that a businessman plaintiffs respected, Robert Praegitzer, was an investor with Hudler and Markley, despite the fact that that investment relationship with Praegitzer had already been severed; (2) that Hudler and Markley owned or were in the process of acquiring certain properties in Reno that they had never owned or had been forced to sell; (3) that Hudler and Markley had contributed $1,026,298 to Covenant for entitlement costs, as represented in Section 2.1.2 of the Covenant Agreement, when that figure was actually closer to $430,000; (4) that the plaintiffs' loan of more than $3 million to Covenant would be secured by a first priority trust deed on 40 acres of the Keystone Property; and (5) that Hudler and his wife had a net worth in excess of $30 million, as shown on a financial statement that Hudler faxed to plaintiffs.

Plaintiffs' operative complaint alleged various claims against both Hudler and Markley . . . [and] [t]he trial court, in a written opinion, denied Hudler's motion for summary judgment [on all claims] but granted Markley's . . . for similar reasons—broadly, that there was no evidence that Markley himself made any misrepresentations to plaintiffs. . . .

[A. Common-Law Fraud]

We begin with plaintiffs' common-law fraud claim, because the facts relevant to that claim govern our analysis with respect to the others. In order to recover on a common-law fraud claim, a plaintiff must prove that the defendant made a misrepresentation "intended to deceive the victim or acted in reckless disregard for the truth." Riley Hill General Contractor v. Tandy Corp., 737 P.2d 595 (Ore. 1987). That is,

"the tort of deceit may still be proven if the representation is made without any belief as to its truth, or with reckless disregard whether it be true or false, and in cases where representations are made by one who is conscious that he has no sufficient basis of information to justify them." *Id.*

Although the bulk of plaintiffs' evidence, which is described above, pertains to misstatements made by Hudler, plaintiffs also alleged that Markley, as the drafter of the Covenant Agreement, affirmatively misrepresented the amount that Bridgeport had contributed to or on behalf of Covenant in Section 2.1.2 of that agreement. That section of the Covenant Agreement states, in part:

> "*Bridgeport represents and warrants to Cruze that it has previously contributed cash to or on behalf of Covenant in the amount of $1,026,298* . . . to obtain the entitlements necessary and appropriate to develop the Project . . . , which are outlined in the Keycom operating agreement . . . . " (Emphasis added.)

Plaintiffs presented evidence that the $1,026,298 figure was inaccurate, and that the actual contributions were significantly lower—closer to $430,000.

Markley, for his part, did not dispute that there was evidence in the record that the representation was false; instead, . . . Markley offered his own declaration, in which he averred,

> "I played no part in the determination or calculation of that amount, but was merely a passive recipient. I had no knowledge of how that figure was determined. I was never asked to calculate, evaluate, compare or otherwise confirm the accuracy of this figure. I merely repeated the information that I was provided, without editing it in any respect."

Markley also offered the declaration of Karen Harris, a former bookkeeper for Hudler and Markley's businesses, who averred that "Mr. Markley did not participate in the compiling or calculating of the expended dollar amounts." . . .

[P]laintiffs presented evidence that Markley, who directly or indirectly owned or managed Bridgeport and Covenant, drafted an agreement that significantly misrepresented the amount of money that Bridgeport had previously invested in Covenant. Plaintiffs also presented evidence from Harrell, who worked for Bridgeport Construction Group, that Markley had *actual knowledge* that his partner, Hudler, was "stealing" from others. According to Harrell, in July 2008, Markley told him, "Out of all the people that [Hudler] has been stealing from I can't believe he would steal from you." Markley then reportedly said to Harrell, "I was wondering how Bridgeport was staying afloat during this last winter."

Based on that evidence . . . a reasonable trier of fact could find that Markley knew that his various ventures with Hudler were in dire need of cash; that he prepared the draft of the Covenant Agreement knowing that it was part of an ongoing scheme to keep their businesses afloat; and that he participated in the scheme by preparing the agreement with reckless disregard of the falsity of the representation in the hopes that plaintiffs would agree to invest in Covenant. . . .

[B. Joint Liability for Substantial Assistance]

[P]laintiffs' second claim for relief, captioned "Joint Liability of Markley," [alleges] that Markley acted in concert with Hudler and provided "substantial assistance" to Hudler's efforts to fraudulently induce plaintiffs' investment. The claim is premised on the principle in the Restatement (Second) of Torts (1979), section 876, which "reflect[s] the common law of Oregon" with respect to the circumstances in which a person who assists another in committing a tort may be liable to the third party. Section 876 provides:

> "For harm resulting to a third person from the tortious conduct of another, one is subject to liability if he
>   "(a) does a tortious act in concert with the other or pursuant to a common design with him, or
>   "(b) knows that the other's conduct constitutes a breach of duty and gives substantial assistance or encouragement to the other so to conduct himself, or

"(c) gives substantial assistance to the other in accomplishing a tortious result and his own conduct, separately considered, constitutes a breach of duty to the third person."

In Reynolds v. Schrock, 142 P.3d 1062 (Ore. 2006), the Supreme Court explained:

"[T]his court's earlier decisions hold that a person may be jointly liable with another for substantially assisting in the other's breach of a fiduciary duty owed to a third party, if the person knows that the other's conduct constitutes a breach of that fiduciary duty. Our tort case law also makes clear, however, that, if a person's conduct as an agent or on behalf of another comes within the scope of a privilege, then the person is not liable to the third party."

One such privilege is that between attorney and client; thus, "for a third party to hold a lawyer liable for substantially assisting in a client's breach of fiduciary duty, the third party must prove that the lawyer acted outside the scope of the lawyer-client relationship." *Id.* . . .

The rule in *Reynolds* does not, on this record, entitle Markley to judgment as a matter of law. *Reynolds* involved an attorney (the same Markley) who was sued based on advice he provided to Schrock concerning a settlement agreement that Schrock executed with Reynolds. Markley did not have an equity interest in the client in *Reynolds* and was not wearing two different hats—that of investor and attorney for the company—when participating in the alleged breach of duty. Here, however, there is evidence that Markley stood to benefit from the Cruzes' investment given his ownership and management involvement in the company for which he was drafting the Covenant Agreement. *Reynolds* does not address the circumstance in which a lawyer is acting in two roles in a transaction—that of owner and that of lawyer—and we question whether *Reynolds* would ever extend to that situation. In no event, though, does *Reynolds* protect an attorney who commits fraud in that dual role. . . .

Reynolds itself recognizes that the rule "protects lawyers only for actions of the kind that permissibly may be taken by lawyers in the course of representing their clients," and common-law fraud is not among the acts that an attorney is privileged to commit. Thus, as was the case with plaintiffs' common-law fraud claim, the trial court erred in granting summary judgment on plaintiffs' claim that Markley is jointly liable for Hudler's misrepresentations.

[C. Oregon Securities Law Violations]

Plaintiffs' third claim against Markley . . . was for securities law violations. ORS 59.115(1)(b) imposes liability on a seller of a security if that person

"[s]ells or successfully solicits the sale of a security in violation of ORS 59.135(1) or (3) or by means of an untrue statement of a material fact or an omission to state a material fact necessary in order to make the statements made, in light of the circumstances under which they are made, not misleading (the buyer not knowing of the untruth or omission), and who does not sustain the burden of proof that the person did not know, and in the exercise of reasonable care could not have known, of the untruth or omission."

The liability extends, under subsection (3) of the statute, beyond just the "seller":

> "Every person who directly or indirectly controls a seller liable under subsection (1) of this section, every partner, *limited liability company manager, including a member who is a manager,* officer or director of such seller, every person occupying a similar status or performing similar functions, and every person who participates or materially aids in the sale is also liable jointly and severally with and to the same extent as the seller . . . (emphasis added)

In short, there are genuine issues of material fact as to whether Markley was a manager of a seller, Bridgeport, and whether Markley is liable for securities law violations. . . .

[D. Elder Abuse]

Consequently, the trial court also erred with respect to plaintiffs' claim based on financial elder abuse, . . . *See* ORS 124.110(1)(a) (authorizing action for financial abuse where "a person wrongfully takes or appropriates money or property of a vulnerable person, without regard to whether the person taking or appropriating the money or property has a fiduciary relationship with the vulnerable person"). . . . *See* Church v. Woods, 118, 77 P.3d 1150 (Ore. App. 2003) (conduct is "wrongful" under ORS 124.110 if it is carried out by improper means, including deceit and misrepresentation). . . .

[E. Racketeering]

Plaintiffs next contend that the trial court erred in refusing to allow them to amend their complaint to add claims against Hudler and Markley under the Oregon Racketeer Influenced and Corrupt Organizations Act (ORICO), ORS 166.715 to 166.735. . . .*

There is no dispute that plaintiffs, in their proposed ORICO claims, allege that Hudler and Markley engaged in a pattern of racketeering activity that included multiple "incidents" involving violations of ORS 165.042, which is among the racketeering activity listed in subparagraph (B). ORS 165.042 makes it a crime to "fraudulently obtain [ ] a signature if, with intent to defraud or injure

---

* As amended, ORS 166.725(7)(a) provides:

"Any person who is injured by reason of any violation of the provisions of ORS 166.720 (1) to (4) shall have a cause of action for three-fold the actual damages sustained and, when appropriate, punitive damages:

(A) If a criminal conviction for the racketeering activity that is the basis of the violation has been obtained, any rights of appeal have expired and the action is against the individual convicted of the racketeering activity; or

(B) If the violation is based on racketeering activity . . .

another, the person obtains the signature of a person to a written instrument by knowingly misrepresenting any fact." Plaintiffs' proposed ORICO claims allege that Hudler fraudulently obtained a signature on a deed by making misrepresentations, and that both defendants fraudulently obtained the signatures of Tyrone and Jacqueline Cruze on various LLC operating agreements and closing documents by way of misrepresentation. . . .

The trial court . . . should reconsider [on remand] whether to allow plaintiff to proceed on an amended complaint that includes ORICO claims based on racketeering activity of fraudulently obtaining signatures.

Reversed and remanded.

The Bounds of the Law:
Duties to Nonclients

This series of notes, entitled "The Bounds of the Law," borrows its title from a century-old ethical canon repeated in today's Model Rules: The lawyer has an "obligation zealously to protect and pursue a client's legitimate interests, within the bounds of the law."[1] In these notes, we examine several bodies of generally applicable law that limit a lawyer's representation of a client. We focus here on when a lawyer must say "no" to a client to avoid violating a legal limitation on the lawyer's own conduct. Lawyers who exceed these bounds of the law face at least three consequences: criminal accountability, civil liability, and professional discipline.

It seems axiomatic that lawyers should be accountable only to their clients. The most obvious example is the often-repeated statement that lawyers owe no duties to adverse parties.[2] Courts generally recognize that clients should receive frank advice untainted by lawyer concerns about liability to others. But at the same time, *Greycas* and *Cruze* illustrate that lawyers cannot escape generally applicable law that creates responsibility to nonclients. In *Cruze*, generally applicable statutes, such as those prohibiting elder abuse, regulating securities, and proscribing racketeering applied to the lawyer defendant. This note focuses primarily on longstanding and often overlooked common law obligations that also impose duties to nonclients, such as the law of fraud and aiding and abetting another's tort.

---

1. Model Rules, Preamble ¶ [9]. This language first appeared in Canon 15 of the 1908 Canons of Ethics, titled "How Far a Lawyer May Go in Supporting A Client's Cause" ("The lawyer owes entire devotion to the interest of the client, warm zeal in the maintenance an defense of his rights . . . [b]ut it is steadfastly to be borne in mind that the great trust of the lawyer is to be performed within and not without the bounds of the law.") and was the title of Canon 7 in the 1969 ABA Model Code of Professional Responsibility ("A Lawyer Should Represent a Client Zealously, Within the Bounds of the Law").

2. *E.g.*, Jeckle v. Crotty, 85 P.3d 931 (Wash. App. 2004); James v. The Chase Manhattan Bank, 173 F. Supp. 2d 544, 550 (N.D. Miss. 2001).

The Law of Fraud and Professional Obligation

The law of fraud permeates many of these third-party duty scenarios. *Greycas* and *Cruze* illustrate that lawyers who deliberately lie about a material fact face civil liability.[3] *Cruze* further illustrates that lawyers who assist client frauds (or fail to warn clients about fraud) also may be subject to intentional tort liability[4] statutory violations, and aiding and abetting a client's tort or breach of fiduciary duty.

Greycas also demonstrates how lawyers who lie or assist a client fraud can face the possibility of professional discipline.[5] The Model Rules include four provisions that effectively incorporate all of the law of fraud, deceit, dishonesty, and misrepresentation into a professional obligation. Lawyers can be disciplined if they make any false statement of material fact to tribunals[6] or third persons[7] while representing clients, whether or not the statement is relied on or causes harm. Lawyers also can be disciplined for any conduct (while representing a client or not) "involving dishonesty, fraud, deceit, or misrepresentation."[8]

---

3. *See, e.g.,* Hartford Accident & Indemn. Co. v. Sullivan, 846 F.2d 377 (7th Cir. 1988), *cert. denied,* 490 U.S. 1089 (1989) (lawyer liable for fraud in helping client obtain fraudulent bank loan); Bonvire v. Wampler, 779 F.2d 1011 (4th Cir. 1985) (lawyer who knowingly misrepresented client's honesty and experience liable for fraud); Fire Ins. Exch. v. Bell, 643 N.E.2d 310 (Ind. 1994) (lawyer who misrepresented policy limits liable for fraud). The lawyer's liability for intentional or reckless misrepresentation extends to all third persons who reasonably rely on fraudulent statements. *Restatement (Second) of Torts* § 531; Ultramares Corp. v. Touche, Niven & Co., 174 N.E. 441 (N.Y. 1931).

4. *See also* Givens v. Mullikin, 75 S.W.3d 383 (Tenn. 2002) (cause of action stated against lawyer for abuse of process for barraging opposing party with subpoenas, interrogatories, and a deposition seeking information that had already been turned over); Bevan v. Fix, 42 P.3d 1013 (Wyo. 2002) (cause of action stated by child who witnessed lawyer physically abuse his mother/client); Raine v. Drasin, 621 S.W.2d 895 (Ky. 1981) (lawyer liable for malicious prosecution for joining two physicians in malpractice case after reviewing records that clearly showed they had treated patient only after his injury had occurred).

5. In *dePape, supra* p. 100, the court similarly characterized the lawyer's "implausible interpretation" of the law as an attempt to perpetrate a fraud on the Immigration and Naturalization Service (INS).

6. MR 3.3(a)(1) (making false statements of fact to a tribunal). *See, e.g.,* In re Aitken, 787 N.W. 2d 152 (Minn. 2010) (lawyer forged client's signature on a plea agreement); In re Celsor, 499 S.E.2d 809 (S.C. 1998) (false notarization of client's signature); In re Chovanec, 640 N.E.2d 1052 (Ind. 1994) (lawyer who was not prepared falsely told court he was too sick to proceed).

7. MR 4.1(a) (making false statement of material fact to a third person). *See, e.g.,* In re Daugherty, 180 P.3d 536 (Kan. 2008) (lawyer lied to bank to get loan, misused loan proceeds, and fabricated a story to justify his misconduct); In re Eliasen, 913 P.2d 1163 (Idaho 1996) (debt collection lawyer lied to debtor about consequences of debt); Disc. Action Against Pyles, 421 N.W.2d 321 (Minn. 1988) (lawyer serving as escrow agent promised to pay money when account had been closed); In re Bennett, 501 S.E.2d 217 (Ga. 1998) (lawyer lied about representing a client to receive insurance settlement); Disc. of Granham, 395 N.W.2d 80 (Minn. 1986) (lawyer in a real estate transaction lied to parties about sending their deed to the county recorder's office).

8. MR 8.4(c). *See, e.g.,* Conduct of Kluge, 27 P.3d 102 (Or. 2001) (lawyer claimed he was a notary public when he knew he was not); Fla. Bar v. Schultz, 712 So. 2d 386 (Fla. 1998) (lawyer postdated and then stopped payment on a check to a travel agent); Conduct of Wyllie, 957 P.2d 1222 (Or. 1998) (imposing two-year suspension for submitting fraudulent MCLE forms and failing to cooperate with investigation); In re Porter, 890 P.2d 1377 (Or. 1995) (imposing 63-day suspension

Beyond their own conduct, lawyers can be disciplined for knowingly counseling or assisting a client's fraudulent or criminal conduct.[9] Together, these include all intentional, reckless, and negligent misrepresentations.[10] Judge Posner no doubt had this provision in mind when he referred Proud to the Illinois Disciplinary Commission.

The vast scope of the modern law of fraud reflects its common occurrence and often disastrous consequences. Liars are "free riders": persons who hope to gain an advantage from everyone else's honesty while benefiting from their own deceit.[11] Deceitful practices can undercut competition, raise the price of goods, and cause loss of confidence in the market system by diminishing trust in its mechanisms. In some cases, fraud can chill faith in individual relationships and social ties. A lawyer's advice can play a central role in avoiding these massive personal and social costs.

Although the law of fraud usually requires an affirmative misrepresentation, there are a few occasions when failure to speak can create liability as well. Fiduciary duties create obligations to disclose, which means that lawyers have affirmative duties to disclose material information to clients.[12] A duty to disclose also arises when previously true statements become untrue, misleading, or material.[13] For example, a lawyer would have a duty to disclose tax liens to a prospective purchaser at a foreclosure sale if the buyer was induced to bid by the lawyer's prior incomplete representations in that regard.[14]

Beyond tort liability and professional discipline, the law of fraud includes hundreds of state and federal criminal provisions.[15] Dishonest conduct also creates a defense to otherwise valid claims, and invalidates an otherwise lawful

---

for misrepresenting intentions to opposing counsel); In re Siegel, 627 A.2d 156 (N.J. 1993) (lawyer who defrauded his own law firm disbarred).

9. MR 1.2(d), 3.3(a)(3), 3.3(b), 4.1(b).

10. Some courts view "dishonesty" as connoting a lack of trustworthiness and integrity and therefore view it as being broader than "fraud" and "deceit." *E.g.,* In re Leonard, 784 P.2d 95, 100 (Or. 1989); In re Servance, 508 A.2d 178 (N.J. 1986) (lawyer represented investments were sound although "he knew little or nothing about them"). Other courts require that reckless or knowing misrepresentations be established to violate Model Rule 8.4(c). *E.g.,* Disc. Counsel v. Anonymous Atty. A, 714 A.2d 402 (Pa. 1998); Disc. Matter Involving West, 805 P.2d 351 (Alaska 1991).

11. Sissela Bok, *Lying: Moral Choices in Public and Private Life* 23 (Vantage Books 2d. ed. 1999).

12. *E.g.,* Baker v. Dorfman, 239 F.3d 415 (2d Cir. 2000) (lawyer who lied in his resume about the extent of his legal experience to a client liable for fraud, including compensatory, emotional distress, and punitive damages).

13. *Restatement (Second) of Torts* § 551. *E.g.,* Vega v. Jones, Day, Reavis, & Pogue, 17 Cal. Rptr.3d 26 (failure to correct partial disclosure that omitted material fact constitutes fraud to third party); People v. Rolfe, 962 P.2d 981 (Colo. 1998) (lawyer who stated that a social worker had "begun" her investigation of the matter, but failed to inform the court about the existence of social worker's letter that concluded no abuse could be substantiated, censured for violating MR 3.3(a)(1)).

14. Gerdin v. Princeton St. Bank, 371 N.W.2d 5 (Minn. App. 1985).

15. For a compilation of some of the major federal antifraud provisions (such as mail and wire fraud, securities, bankruptcy, health care, bank and tax fraud), *see* Milton Eisenberg, ed., *Lawyers' Desk Book on White-Collar Crime* 325-494 (Nat'l. Leg. Ctr. for Pub. Interest 1991). *See also Thomas H. Lee Equity Fund, infra* p. 233, and *In re Refco, infra* pp. 241.

consent in tort, property, and contract law. In short, fraud vitiates everything, even court orders and judgments.[16]

Aiding and Abetting a Client's Tort

The *Cruze* plaintiff successfully raised several other causes of action. The first, aiding and abetting a client's tort (including a client's breach of fiduciary duty), has generated quite a number of recent cases.[17] Here, the courts attempt to distinguish between competent legal advice and advocacy that knowingly assists a client tort.

When lawyers represent fiduciaries, such as executors, trustees, guardians, partners, or corporate officers, they know that their clients owe fiduciary duties of loyalty, disclosure, and honesty to the beneficiaries of their work. Lawyers become liable for the client's breach of fiduciary duty when they know about the client's breach and give substantial assistance not just to the client, but to the client's breach.[18] Substantial assistance requires something more than providing routine professional services, such as giving legal advice.[19] Some courts articulate this as requiring that the professional's acts must fall outside the scope of any legitimate employment.[20] Others require wrongful intent, bad faith, active participation in the fiduciary's breach, or collusion with one client against another.[21] However articulated, the requisite substantial assistance can be found in lawyer self-interest, breach of a statutory duty, or knowledge of or participation in serious misconduct such as a crime or fraud by the client (all of which allegedly occurred in *Cruze*).[22]

Finally, aiding and abetting a breach of fiduciary duty requires knowledge, both that the client owes fiduciary duties and, something far more difficult to prove, that the lawyer knew about the client's breach. In *Antioch Trust*, the plaintiff alleged that the company's lawyers knew about the one client's breach

---

16. *See, e.g.,* FRCP 60(b).

17. Douglas R. Richmond, *Lawyer Liability for Aiding and Abetting Clients' Misconduct Under State Law,* 75 Def. Couns. J. 130 (2008).

18. RLGL § 51(4).

19. Reynolds v. Schrock, 142 P.3d 1062 (Or. 2006) (lawyer who provided client advice to revoke her consent to settlement agreement provided legal services within the scope of the lawyer-client relationship and therefore did not provide substantial assistance); Witzman v. Lerhman, Lehrman, & Flom, 601 N.W.2d 179 (Minn. 1999) (accountant who provided routine services did not provide substantial assistance).

20. Reynolds v. Schrock, 142 P.3d 1062.

21. This seems to be the rationale in cases like *Antioch Trust, supra* p. 92. *See also* LeRoy v. Allen, Yurasek, & Merklin, 872 N.E. 2d 254 (Ohio 2007) (lawyer for close corporation who allegedly colluded with beneficiaries in preparing a will and stock transfer for elderly relative); Cacciola v. Nellhaus, 733 N.E.2d 133 (Mass. App. 2000) (lawyer for family partnership who represented one partner in a transaction that conflicted with duty to the partnership).

22. Weingarten v. Warren, 753 F. Supp. 491 (S.D.N.Y. 1990) (active assistance by trustee's lawyer of trustee's conversion); Morales v. Field, DeGoff, Huppert, & MacGowan, 160 Cal. Rptr. 239 (1979) (failure of trustee's lawyer to disclose conflict to beneficiaries of trust); Fickett v. Super. Ct., 558 P.2d 988 (Ariz. App. 1976) (lawyer for guardian knew or should have known of guardian's misappropriation of estate assets).

of fiduciary duty to the other because the law firm advised the other constituent client throughout the representation to capitulate. In *Cruze,* on the other hand, there was no direct evidence that the lawyer advised the client what to say. Here, the plaintiffs probably will have to prove constructive knowledge of the client's breach based on the lawyer's long-term business and professional relationship with Hudler and his knowledge of Hudler's past and ongoing questionable schemes.[23]

Negligence—Financial Harm

Greycas also finds lawyers liable for economic harm on a negligence theory. Here, the courts generally agree that this duty should be extended to nonclients in three circumstances.[24]

Invitation to Rely   Nonclients who do not wish to hire a lawyer may nevertheless be invited by a lawyer or the lawyer's client to reasonably rely on the lawyer's services.[25] As in *Greycas,* the client typically benefits from this invitation, often in the circumstance of providing a third party with an opinion. Note that if Proud had competently completed a UCC search, he would have discovered that his client had lied to him about the absence of liens on the farm property. His duty to his client then would have required him to inform the client of that fact, as well as the fact that he would have to disclose those liens if he wrote the letter to the lender. His client then could have decided whether it would be better to send the letter or drop the matter. Either way, the lawyer would have succeeded in satisfying his ethical obligation to the client and would not have committed any tort toward the third party.[26]

Third-Party Beneficiaries   *Greycas* demonstrates that most courts extend the client-lawyer relationship to third-party beneficiaries, those nonclients the client intends to benefit in documents created by the lawyer for the client.[27] For lawyers, the earliest cases involved situations in which a client sought the lawyer's help to make a third party the beneficiary of a will or trust. Here, courts found that the client's intent to benefit a third person created a duty of care by the client's lawyer to that third person as well. This meant that breach of a duty of care to the client, such as negligent drafting of the document, which later caused

---

23. *See, e.g.,* Chem-Age Industries, Inc., v. Glover, 652 N.W. 2d 756 (S.D. 2002) (20-year representation of client in failed business ventures created jury question of what lawyer's constructive knowledge of client's intent was).

24. RLGL § 51(1) lists a fifth category, prospective clients.

25. RLGL § 51(2).

26. MR 2.3; RLGL § 95. *See, e.g,* Banco Popular N. Am. v. Gandi, 876 A.2d 253 (N.J. 2005) (bank has cause of action for negligence against borrower's lawyer when bank relied on lawyer's opinion letter).

27. McIntosh County Bank v. Dorsey & Whitney, LLP, 745 N.W.2d 538 (Minn. 2008) (lawyer must be aware of client's intent to benefit a third party for third party to establish that it was a direct and intended beneficiary).

frustration of the testator's intent, created a cause of action by the intended beneficiary against the testator's or settlor's lawyer.[28]

On the other hand, where the parties are potential adversaries or incidental rather than intended beneficiaries, courts have refused to apply the third-party beneficiary doctrine.[29] For example, many courts refuse to impose duties to the estate beneficiaries on an executor's lawyer, reasoning that the latter are not intended beneficiaries and their interests might conflict with those of the executor.[30] Similarly, children cannot pursue malpractice actions against their parents' lawyers for negligence in obtaining a divorce.[31]

Negligent Misrepresentation *Greycas* also shows how nonclient liability can be based on either a malpractice or negligent misrepresentation theory. Liability for negligent (but not intentional) misrepresentation occurs when a lawyer completes a task, such as a UCC search, but negligently examines the wrong files or database. In that case, the lawyer would not have deliberately lied about a material fact, but his legal opinion (that no liens existed on the property) would have been based on a failure to exercise reasonable care in obtaining the information.[32]

Today, some jurisdictions continue to require privity for malpractice or "general" liability, but are willing to extend liability to third persons in negligent misrepresentation cases.[33] They reason that professionals have no duty to warn third persons, but when they undertake a duty to speak, they must do so with

---

28. *E.g.*, RLGL § 51(3); Estate of Schneider v. Finmann, 933 N.E. 2d 718 (N.Y. 2010) (estate's personal representative may sue decedent's lawyer for estate planning malpractice); Guardianship of Karan, 38 P.3d 396 (Wash. App. 2002) (minor child has cause of action against mother's lawyer who set up child's trust in a way that allowed pilfering of the estate); Lucas v. Hamm, 364 P.2d 685 (Cal. 1961) (intended beneficiaries of a will could recover from lawyer whose negligence in drafting document caused them to lose their testamentary rights). *But see* Shoemaker v. Gindlesberger, 887 N.E. 2d 1167 (Ohio 2008) (will beneficiary may not sue decedent's lawyer for negligent preparation of a deed that resulted in increased tax liability for the estate).

29. *See, e.g.*, Capitol Indem. Corp. v. Fleming, 58 P.3d 965 (Ariz. App. 2002) (surety who posted bond for an estate's conservator incidental, not intended beneficiary of services provided by conservator's lawyer); Bovee v. Gravel, 811 A.2d 137 (Vt. 2002) (bank shareholders were not beneficiaries of law firm's representation of bank); MacMillan v. Scheffy, 787 A.2d 867 (N.H. 2001) (buyers in real estate transaction unable to prove that seller's lawyer, who drafted the deed, intended to benefit them; mere fact that they were grantees under the deed was not enough).

30. *See, e.g.*, Estate of Albanese v. Lolio, 923 A.2d 325 (N.J. App. 2007); Jensen v. Crandall, 1997 Me. Super. LEXIS 72; Trask v. Butler, 872 P.2d 1080 (Wash. 1994); Neal v. Baker, 551 N.E.2d 704 (Ill. App. 1990). *But see* Perez v. Stern, 777 N.W.2d 545 (Neb. 2010) (lawyer hired by estate's personal representative to pursue wrongful death action owed duty of care to decedent's children and intended beneficiaries).

31. Connely v. McColloch, 83 P.3d 457 (Wyo. 2004).

32. *Restatement (Second) of Torts* § 552; RLGL § 51(2)(b). *E.g.*, Dean Foods Co. v. Pappathanasi, 2004 Mass. Super. LEXIS 571 (lawyers who opined that no litigation was pending against their client liable for negligent misrepresentation for failing to disclose pending grand jury subpoena).

33. *See, e.g.*, Orshoski v. Krieger, 2001 Ohio App. LEXIS 5018 (prospective buyers who relied on negligent misrepresentations of lawyer for developer concerning subdivision's restrictive covenants could sue for negligent misrepresentation, but not for legal malpractice).

care.[34] Initially, this duty extended beyond those in privity of contract with the professional only if the misrepresentation was made intentionally or recklessly.[35] Some jurisdictions have completely replaced the privity rule with one that depends solely on foreseeability,[36] but most have adopted the limited foreseeability rule of the *Restatement (Second) of Torts* § 552, which restricts liability to "a limited group of persons for whose benefit and guidance" the professional "intends to supply the information."[37]

Client Advocacy and Nonclient Responsibility

Every legal representation requires a lawyer to know the bounds of the law and communicate them to his or her client. The common law and the Rules of Professional Conduct agree that lawyers cannot lie, and if a client lies, the client's lawyer probably has to do something about it.

Lawyers who misrepresent a material fact can be held criminally or civilly accountable, or they can lose a benefit that they lied to obtain. Beyond these consequences, lawyers also can be professionally disciplined for acts of misrepresentation or dishonesty, whether they involve client representation or conduct of the lawyer apart from law practice. Lawyers who do not understand the tort obligations of clients can aid and abet their client's torts. Understanding these bounds of the law in all client representations can help you avoid suffering any or all of these adverse consequences.

---

34. *E.g.,* Rubin v. Schottenstein, Zox, & Dunn, 143 F.3d 263 (6th Cir. 1998) (en banc) (lawyer who represented seller in a securities transaction assumes a duty to provide complete and non-misleading information with respect to subjects on which he undertakes to speak under 17 C.F.R. § 240.10b-5).

35. Ultramares Corp. v. Touche, Niven, & Co., 174 N.E. 441 (N.Y. 1931).

36. *E.g.,* Molecular Tech. Corp. v. Valentine, 925 F.2d 910 (6th Cir. 1991).

37. *See, e.g.,* Walpert, Smullian, & Blumenthal, P.C. v. Katz, 762 A.2d 582 (Md. 2000) (accountant malpractice); RLGL § 51.

Chapter 6

Confidentiality

"I'm sorry—I never discuss my clients with their mothers."

A. Introduction

This chapter addresses another basic fiduciary duty: confidentiality. We begin by examining the scope of the professional duty and proceed in the next two chapters to consider exceptions to the obligation. Throughout, we refer to two bodies of law: the fiduciary duty of confidentiality, which is found in agency law and restated in the Rules of Professional Conduct, and the evidentiary attorney-client privilege and work product doctrine, which also impose a duty of confidentiality and block disclosure of client confidences in litigation. These bodies of law parallel each other, as the following table demonstrates.

Client Confidentiality

	Evidentiary Rules	Ethical/Fiduciary Obligation
Source of Law	Statutes; Common Law or Federal Rules of Evidence	Agency Law; and Model Rules 1.6, 1.8(b), 1.9, 1.18
Definition	RLGL §§ 68-77 A/C Privilege: Communications between privileged persons in confidence for the purpose of obtaining or providing legal assistance. WP Immunity: Material prepared by a lawyer for a client in reasonable anticipation of litigation. RLGL §§ 87- 89; FRCP 26(b)(3)	MR 1.6(a):Information relating to the representation of a client; RLGL § 59: Confidential Client Information
Client Consent	Waiver: RLGL §§78-81; 91-92 (implied by disclosure to any nonprivileged third person)	Client consent, express, or implied: MR 1.6(a), 1.13(c), 1.14(c); RLGL § 61-62

Exceptions		
Physical Harm	Future and continuing crime or fraud; RLGL § 82	Future serious bodily harm; MR 1.6(b)(1); RLGL § 66
Financial Harm/ Client Crime or Fraud	Future and continuing crime or fraud; RLGL §§ 82, 93	Future crime, prevent, rectify, mitigate substantial financial loss; MR 1.6(b)(2)(3); RLGL § 67
Seeking Advice	None	MR 1.6(b)(4) Lawyer self-defense; MR 1.6(b)(5); RLGL §§ 64, 65
Lawyer Self-Defense and Compensation	Lawyer self-protection; RLGL § 83	
Required by Law or Court Order	Invoking the privilege; RLGL § 86	Required by law or court order; MR 1.6(b)(6); RLGL § 63

The recognition of confidentiality as a core professional obligation arose first in cases applying the attorney-client privilege, which Wigmore dates to the seventeenth century.[1] By the twentieth century, the idea that lawyers were forbidden from disclosing client confidences also was recognized in agency law as an integral part of the fiduciary duty of loyalty that lawyer-agents owe to

---

1. Geoffrey C. Hazard, Jr., *An Historical Perspective on the Attorney-Client Privilege,* 66 Cal. L. Rev. 1061, 1069-1070 (1978).

client-principals.[2] At the beginning of the twentieth century, both the attorney-client evidentiary privilege and the agency duty of confidentiality were incorporated into lawyer codes as the obligation not to divulge confidences and secrets of a client.[3]

Throughout this legal development, client-lawyer confidentiality has been justified by both a consequential utilitarian rationale and a rights or duty-based deontological rationale. The utilitarian view usually concludes that confidentiality promotes the greatest good for the greatest number because it is essential to making the legal system work. The deontological view holds that confidentiality promotes respect for human autonomy by guaranteeing trust and privacy in the client-lawyer relationship.

Utilitarians focus on consequences and argue that to do their job, lawyers need complete and accurate facts, both about what has already occurred and what the client contemplates doing. Lacking these facts, the lawyer might either apply the wrong law or give incorrect legal advice, or both, which in turn will reduce public confidence in the legal system and in lawyers.[4] Other utilitarians disagree, arguing that confidentiality actually harms society and the legal system. Jeremy Bentham, for example, argued that the attorney-client privilege should be abolished because it obscured the truth from the courts and allowed those with something to hide to get away with unlawful behavior.[5]

Immanuel Kant argued that deontological justifications, which rest on categorical imperatives or fundamental rights, should provide the yardstick for moral accountability. Confidentiality obligations are essential to the purpose of the legal system, which exists to protect individual rights, such as the right to contract, to own property, or to obtain due process. These rights, which respect persons by protecting individual liberty and promoting respect for human autonomy, easily can become vulnerable to infringement by powerful majoritarian interests of the government or others. Law and the legal system provide the means to ensure that such infringements are prevented or redressed.

Confidentiality promotes both the individual rights of citizens and the trust that is central to a client-lawyer relationship. It is a fundamental ethical value, just as loyalty and honesty are integral to a trusting relationship. Privacy also promotes the individual rights of citizens by giving them personal space to plan and define their own meaning in life. The government should not be able to

---

2. The First Restatement of Agency included the prohibition against using or disclosing confidential information with other duties of loyalty. *Restatement (First) of Agency* § 395 (1933).

3. ABA Canons of Professional Ethics, Canon 6 (1908) provided: "The obligation to represent the client with undivided fidelity and not to divulge his secrets or confidences forbids also the subsequent acceptance of retainers or employment from others in matters adversely affecting any interest of the client with respect to which confidence has been reposed."

4. *See* Deborah L. Rhode & Geoffrey C. Hazard, Jr., *Professional Responsibility and Regulation* 64 (Found. Press 2d ed. 2007).

5. Jeremy Bentham, *Rationale of Judicial Evidence*, Vol. V, Book IX, Chapter 5, at 324 (1827). It is important to note that Bentham wrote at a time when no privilege against self-incrimination existed, so he reasoned that getting the facts from the mouth of the lawyer was no different from getting them from the mouth of the defendant. *Id.*

infringe on that private space when it is used to promote that individual's auton-omous sense of self. A lawyer's obligation not to share the information further protects the client's own defined sphere of privacy, which can become especially important when government compulsion seeks to invade it.

The cases and other materials in this chapter and the next two illustrate how both of these justifications inform professional obligations of confidentiality, as well as exceptions to the doctrine.

B. Fiduciary Duty

Problems

6-1. What a great idea Martyn has. The firm should include in our website the names of our important clients, our litigation victories, and the big deals we have handled. Most of it is a matter of public record, on file at the courthouse or in filings at the Securities and Exchange Commission (SEC), argues Martyn.

6-2. Martyn & Fox represents Disney as an undisclosed principal for the pur-pose of purchasing property to develop a new theme park. Fox thinks that this is a great time to purchase stock in Disney. Martyn suggests that the firm should purchase adjacent land, for it will surely rise in value, likely as a hotel site.

Consider: Model Rules 1.4, 1.6, 1.8(b)
           RLGL §§ 20, 59, 60

Matter of Anonymous
654 N.E.2d 1128 (Ind. 1995)

PER CURIAM.

The respondent has been charged by the Disciplinary Commission in a veri-fied complaint for disciplinary action with violating Rules 1.6(a), 1.8(b), and 1.16(a)(1) of the Rules of Professional Conduct for Attorneys at Law. . . .

As stipulated by the parties, the respondent was contacted by an individual (the "mother") in April or May of 1994 about representing her in seeking a child support arrearage due to her from the father ("father") of her minor child. She supplied the respondent with records concerning her support action and her income. Also included in these documents was information regarding the father, including the fact that he was going to receive a substantial inheritance, his sal-ary, his place of employment, and his address.

In the course of reviewing the documents supplied by the mother, the respon-dent discovered that on July 17, 1992, a judgment had been entered against the mother and father, making them jointly liable for almost $4,500 of medical and hospital debt resulting from the birth of their child. The judgment was in favor of the local county welfare department. The respondent was, at all times relevant to this proceeding, the attorney under contract to represent the local county welfare department.

The respondent contacted the mother to determine if the medical debt owed to the welfare department had been paid by either her or the father. It had not. The respondent then informed the mother that he would be unable to represent her in the case because of a conflict of interest, then forwarded her documents, at her request, to another attorney. Thereafter, the respondent received approval from the local county welfare department to file a collection suit against the father, which he did on April 26, 1994. Later, the father's counsel joined the mother as a party defendant in the collection suit. The respondent ultimately obtained a summary judgment against the mother and the father. The respondent did not withdraw from the case after the mother was joined as a party defendant.

We find that, by revealing information relating to the representation of the mother without her consent, the respondent violated Ind. Professional Conduct Rule 1.6(a). By using that information to her disadvantage without her consent, he violated Prof. Cond. R. 1.8(b). By failing to withdraw as counsel for the local welfare department during the collection suit against the mother when such representation violated the Rules of Professional Conduct, the respondent violated Prof. Cond. R. 1.16(a)(1).

The respondent and the Commission agree that several factors mitigate the severity of his misconduct. They agree that the information gained by the respondent about the mother's case was readily available from public sources and not confidential in nature. The respondent declined to represent the mother after he learned of her outstanding debt owed to the county welfare department, and advised her to seek other counsel. He did not at any time request that she sign an employment agreement, seek a retainer fee, or otherwise charge her. We see no evidence of selfish motive on the respondent's part.

The respondent's use of information gained during consultations with the mother represents misuse of information entrusted to him in his capacity as a lawyer. Such conduct not only threatens harm to the individuals involved, but also erodes the integrity of the profession. At the same time, we note that the respondent appears to have had no sinister motives. For these reasons, we accept the agreed sanction of a private reprimand. . . .

Perez v. Kirk & Carrigan

822 S.W.2d 261 (Tex. App. 1991)

DORSEY, J. . . .

The present suit arises from a school bus accident on September 21, 1989, in Alton, Texas. Ruben Perez was employed by Valley Coca-Cola Bottling Company as a truck driver. On the morning of the accident, Perez attempted to stop his truck at a stop sign along his route, but the truck's brakes failed to stop the truck, which collided with the school bus. The loaded bus was knocked into a pond and 21 children died. Perez suffered injuries from the collision and was taken to a local hospital to be treated.

The day after the accident, Kirk & Carrigan, lawyers who had been hired to represent Valley Coca-Cola Bottling Company, visited Perez in the hospital for the purpose of taking his statement. Perez claims that the lawyers told him that they were his lawyers too and that anything he told them would be kept confidential.[1] With this understanding, Perez gave them a sworn statement concerning the accident.[2] However, after taking Perez' statement, Kirk & Carrigan had no further contact with him. Instead, Kirk & Carrigan made arrangements for criminal defense attorney Joseph Connors to represent Perez. Connors was paid by National Union Fire Insurance Company which covered both Valley Coca-Cola and Perez for liability in connection with the accident.

Some time after Connors began representing Perez, Kirk & Carrigan, without telling either Perez or Connors, turned Perez' statement over to the Hidalgo County District Attorney's Office. Kirk & Carrigan contend that Perez' statement was provided in a good faith attempt to fully comply with a request of the district attorney's office and under threat of subpoena if they did not voluntarily comply. Partly on the basis of this statement, the district attorney was able to obtain a grand jury indictment of Perez for involuntary manslaughter for his actions in connection with the accident.[3] . . .

---

1. The summary judgment affidavits offered by Perez show the following with regard to Kirk & Carrigan's representations to him at the time they took Perez' statement:

Ruben Perez—"Kirk told me that they were lawyers hired by Valley Coca Cola, that they were my lawyers too, and that whatever I told them would be kept confidential. I trusted what these lawyers told me and I answered their questions."

Israel Perez (Ruben's father)—"Before beginning the questions, Kirk told Ruben that they were his lawyers, that they were going to help him, and that what they . . . learned from Ruben would be kept a secret."

Joe Perez (Ruben's uncle)—"Before Ruben gave his statement, to Kirk, Kirk told Ruben that they (the lawyers) represented Valley Coca Cola, that they were Ruben's lawyers too, and that they did not want anyone else to come in the room and to talk to Ruben. Kirk then told Ruben 'I know you are in pain, but we need to ask you these questions. Your mind would be fresh to tell us what happened. This will be kept confidential. We will get you a copy of it tomorrow. We will not give anyone a copy. It is between you and us.' Kirk and Carrigan did not say that they represented only Valley Coca Cola."

2. Among other things, Perez generally stated that he had a previous accident while driving a Coke truck in 1987 for which he was given a citation, that he had a speeding violation in 1988, that he had not filled out a daily checklist to show that he had checked the brakes on the morning of the accident, that he had never before experienced problems with the brakes on his truck and that they were working just before the accident, that he tried to apply the brakes to stop the truck, but that the brakes for the trailer were not working at all to stop the truck (the truck had two sets of brakes: the ones for the cab worked; the ones for the trailer did not and the greater weight of the trailer had the effect of pushing the entire truck, even though the cab brakes were working), that Perez did not have enough time to apply the emergency brakes, and that there was nothing the managers or supervisors at Valley Coca-Cola could have done to prevent the accident.

3. By his summary judgment affidavit offered in support of Perez, Joseph Connors stated that, in his professional opinion as a board certified criminal law specialist, if he had known that the statement had been provided and had been able to have Perez explain his lack of training or knowledge about the brake system to the grand jury, Perez would not have been indicted for manslaughter. Ruben Perez also stated in his affidavit that Valley Coca-Cola Bottling Company had not given him any instruction in brake inspection, maintenance, or use in an emergency situation.

. . . Perez asserted numerous causes of action against Kirk & Carrigan for breach of fiduciary duty, negligent and intentional infliction of emotional distress, violation of the Texas Deceptive Trade Practices Act and conspiracy to violate article 21.21 of the Texas Insurance Code. . . .

With regard to Perez' cause of action for breach of the fiduciary duty of good faith and fair dealing, Kirk and Carrigan contend that no attorney-client relationship existed and no fiduciary duty arose, because Perez never sought legal advice from them.

An agreement to form an attorney-client relationship may be implied from the conduct of the parties. Moreover, the relationship does not depend upon the payment of a fee, but may exist as a result of rendering services gratuitously.[4]

In the present case, viewing the summary judgment evidence in the light most favorable to Perez, Kirk & Carrigan told him that, in addition to representing Valley Coca-Cola, they were also Perez' lawyers and that they were going to help him. Perez did not challenge this assertion, and he cooperated with the lawyers in giving his statement to them, even though he did not offer, nor was he asked, to pay the lawyers' fees. We hold that this was sufficient to imply the creation of an attorney-client relationship at the time Perez gave his statement to Kirk & Carrigan.

The existence of this relationship encouraged Perez to trust Kirk & Carrigan and gave rise to a corresponding duty on the part of the attorneys not to violate this position of trust. Accordingly, the relation between attorney and client is highly fiduciary in nature, and their dealings with each other are subject to the same scrutiny as a transaction between trustee and beneficiary. Specifically, the relationship between attorney and client has been described as one of *uberrima fides*, which means, "most abundant good faith," requiring absolute and perfect candor, openness and honesty, and the absence of any concealment or deception. In addition, because of the openness and candor within this relationship, certain communications between attorney and client are privileged from disclosure in either civil or criminal proceedings under the provisions of Tex. R. Civ. Evid. 503 and Tex. R. Crim. Evid. 503, respectively.[5]

There is evidence that Kirk & Carrigan represented to Perez that his statement would be kept confidential. Later, however, without telling either Perez or his subsequently-retained criminal defense attorney, Kirk & Carrigan voluntarily disclosed Perez' statement to the district attorney. Perez asserts in the

---

4. An attorney's fiduciary responsibilities may arise even during preliminary consultations regarding the attorney's possible retention if the attorney enters into discussion of the client's legal problems with a view toward undertaking representation.

5. Disclosure of confidential communications by an attorney, whether privileged or not under the rules of evidence, is generally prohibited by the disciplinary rules governing attorneys' conduct in Texas. [citing Rule 1.6] In addition, the general rule is that confidential information received during the course of any fiduciary relationship may not be used or disclosed to the detriment of the one from whom the information is obtained. Numed, Inc. v. McNutt, 724 S.W.2d 432, 434 (Tex. App. — Fort Worth 1987, no writ) (former employee is obligated not to use or divulge employer's trade secrets).

present suit that this course of conduct amounted, among other things, to a breach of fiduciary duty.

Kirk & Carrigan seek to avoid this claim of breach, on the ground that the attorney-client privilege did not apply to the present statement, because unnecessary third parties were present at the time it was given. However, whether or not the Rule 503 attorney-client privilege extended to Perez' statement, Kirk & Carrigan initially obtained the statement from Perez on the understanding that it would be kept confidential. Thus, regardless of whether from an evidentiary standpoint the privilege attached, Kirk & Carrigan breached their fiduciary duty to Perez either by wrongfully disclosing a privileged statement or by wrongfully representing that an unprivileged statement would be kept confidential. Either characterization shows a clear lack of honesty toward, and a deception of, Perez by his own attorneys regarding the degree of confidentiality with which they intended to treat the statement. . . .

In addition, however, even assuming a breach of fiduciary duty, Kirk & Carrigan also contend that summary judgment may be sustained on the ground that Perez could show no damages resulting from the breach. Kirk & Carrigan contend that their dissemination of Perez' statement could not have caused him any damages in the way of emotional distress, because the statement merely revealed Perez' own version of what happened. We do not agree. Mental anguish consists of the emotional response of the plaintiff caused by the tortfeasor's conduct. It includes, among other things, the mental sensation of pain resulting from public humiliation.

Regardless of the fact that Perez himself made the present statement, he did not necessarily intend it to be a public response as Kirk & Carrigan contend, but only a private and confidential discussion with his attorneys. Perez alleged that the publicity caused by his indictment, resulting from the revelation of the statement to the district attorney in breach of that confidentiality, caused him to suffer emotional distress and mental anguish. We hold that Perez has made a valid claim for such damages. . . .

▇ Lawyers' Roles:
The Directive Lawyer and Fiduciary Duty

Viewed from the client's perspective, the lawyers in *Perez* breached all five fiduciary duties that lawyers owe clients. They ignored Mr. Perez's right to control the goals of the representation by failing to ask him about the use of his statement. They failed to recognize basic obligations to communicate with their client about key issues. They acted incompetently by failing to recognize their own clear legal obligations to Mr. Perez. They blatantly violated Mr. Perez's confidentiality by disclosing his confidences to the prosecutor without his consent. And they disregarded conflict of interest by favoring another client's interests over Mr. Perez's, and by pursuing their own interests at Mr. Perez's expense.

All of this caused incalculable damage to Mr. Perez, who was 25 years old when the accident occurred, and was just beginning to realize his lifelong ambition to be a truck driver like his father. The accident killed 21 of the 81 children on the bus, who drowned in a water-filled pit after the truck driven by Mr. Perez pushed it off the road. Following the accident, Mr. Perez spent three-and-one-half years awaiting trial on the criminal charges in a self-imposed bedroom prison as penance, never leaving his house.[1] The jury acquitted Mr. Perez on all 21 counts after only four hours of deliberation.[2]

The behavior of Mr. Perez's lawyers indicates that they somehow misconstrued their role in representing their client, thinking that they owed him none of the fiduciary duties that they assumed, even though they had promised all of them. They appear to have acted as directors, who imposed their own private judgment about the matter on a trusting, unsuspecting client, rather than agents with fiduciary duties subject to their client's instructions. Judge John Noonan calls this mindset "underidentification with a client."[3]

Fiduciary Duties

Agency law long has recognized the problem of generalized expertise: the tendency of experts to transfer their professional knowledge and expertise to a general control over all decisions and aspects of the relationship. Professionals easily can assume that professional competence equates with their overall ability to know what is best for clients. To ensure that the client's moral values control the agency relationship, lawyer-agents owe client-principals the 5 Cs to steer lawyers away from benefiting someone other than the client. These fiduciary duties also protect clients from lawyers who might intentionally or even inadvertently take advantage of the trust and power reposed in them.

Mr. Perez's lawyers first breached the two intertwined fiduciary duties of control and communication.[4] In their first meeting with Mr. Perez, there is no indication that the lawyers sought his consent to the joint representation, disclosed that certain conflicts of interest might develop, or indicated what would happen if they had to withdraw. After they discovered that conflicts might exist, it is also not clear what they told Mr. Perez about why they no longer represented him, to say nothing about seeking his consent to the lawyers' continuing representation of Valley Coca-Cola. Most obvious is their complete lack of any authorization whatsoever to disclose Mr. Perez's statement to the prosecutor.

---

1. Maggie Rivas, *Truck Driver Says He Spent Years After Bus Crash Doing Penance; He Went into Self-Imposed Exile at Home as Punishment*, Dallas Morning News, May 7, 1993, at 1A.

2. Maggie Rivas, *Trucker Absolved of Bus Deaths; '89 Alton Tragedy Killed 21 Students*, Dallas Morning News, May 6, 1993, at 1A. Mr. Perez continues to suffer from brain injuries he received in the accident that reduced his intellectual capacity to that of a fifth-grader, and he is permanently unable to work. *A Tragedy Remembered*, Dallas Morning News, Sept. 21, 1999, at 17A.

3. John T. Noonan Jr., *The Lawyer Who Overidentifies with His Client*, 76 Notre Dame L. Rev. 827, 833 (2001). *See also* David Luban, *Making Sense of Moral Meltdowns, in* Susan D. Carle, ed., *Lawyers' Ethics and the Pursuit of Social Justice: A Critical Reader*, 355 (NYU Press 2005) (characterizing the "chronic source of moral difficulty" for defense lawyers as whether assisting their "guilty" client's best interest requires hiding the truth).

4. RLGL § 20; *Restatement (Third) of Agency* § 8.11 (2006).

Mr. Perez's lawyers might have ignored their fiduciary obligations simply because they did not know about or understand them. If so, they breached a third duty, the fiduciary duty of competence.[5] If they mistakenly believed that they had the prerogative to disclose client information without consent or consultation, they either had never heard of or had never understood the meaning of either their own professional code provisions or case law that imposed these fiduciary duties on their conduct.

Fourth, these lawyers flagrantly violated their duty of confidentiality.[6] They offered to represent Mr. Perez, promised him confidentiality, encouraged him to confide in them, obtained his statement about the accident, and then turned it over to a hostile third party, the prosecutor. Mr. Perez's lawyers nodded to confidentiality (because they promised it), but they apparently did not appreciate either the scope or the long-term duration of this obligation under the professional rules and common law.[7] They seemed to understand that their initial promise of confidentiality to Mr. Perez included "privileged" communications, but somehow ignored the far broader fiduciary obligation not to use or reveal information relating to the representation without his consent.[8] Yet, even then they acted incompetently by failing to preserve the privilege, either by asking Mr. Perez's relatives to step outside during the interview, or by clarifying that their presence was necessary to effectuate his communication.[9]

Why did these lawyers make such obvious mistakes? One answer might be found in their failure to properly resolve conflicts of interest.[10] Mr. Perez's lawyers were hired by an insurance company to represent two insureds, Valley Coca-Cola and Mr. Perez. Prior to representing Mr. Perez, they no doubt believed that the interests of both clients were consistent; that is, that the accident was not the fault of either client. In his statement, however, Mr. Perez admitted to several possible violations of company policy, such as a prior speeding violation, and his failure to check the truck's brakes the day of the accident. Mr. Perez's lawyers then appeared to realize that they had a conflict of interest: protecting the interests of one client (Valley Coca-Cola) might require that they take action contrary to the interest of their other client (Perez). This may explain why they "had no further contact with him" and made arrangements for another lawyer

---

5. RLGL §§ 48-50; *Restatement (Third) of Agency* § 8.08 (2006); MR 1.1.

6. RLGL § 60; *Restatement (Third) of Agency* §§ 8.01 Comment c, 8.05 (2006); MR 1.6, 1.8(b), 1.9(a).

7. MR 1.9; RLGL § 60(1)(a) (prohibiting use or disclosure that would "adversely affect a material interest of the client" "during or after the representation of a client"). The Texas equivalent of Model Rule 1.9 was adopted October 17, 1989, about one month after the accident, and became effective January 1, 1990. Tex. Govt. Code Ann. T.2, Subt. G, App. A, Art. 10, § 9, R. 1.09 (2001). The comments to the rule indicate it was based on prior case law, including a case decided about six months before the accident where the Texas Supreme Court mandated that this rule be applied to all former client representations. *See* NCNB Tex. Bank v. Coker, 765 S.W.2d 398 (Tex. 1989).

8. MR 1.6(a), 1.8(b).

9. RLGL § 70, Comment f (allowing confidential agents if "the person's participation is reasonably necessary to facilitate the client's communication with the lawyer . . . and the client reasonably believes that the person will hold the communication in confidence").

10. RLGL § 121; *Restatement (Third) of Agency* § 5.04, 8.01-8.05 (2006); MR 1.7.

to defend Mr. Perez's interests. Yet instead of withdrawing completely from both representations, they allowed their continuing loyalty to Valley Coca-Cola to blind them to their competing, continuing confidentiality duty to Mr. Perez.

The Problem with Directive Behavior

Judge Noonan recalls a strikingly similar joint client incident that became the focus at the Senate confirmation hearings of future Supreme Court Justice Louis Brandeis.[11] Brandeis recommended that a client assign his business assets for the benefit of creditors. He did not tell the client that this assignment constituted an act of bankruptcy, or that Brandeis's law firm represented one of the creditors. Five days later, Brandeis, representing the creditor, instituted involuntary bankruptcy proceedings against the business client. Brandeis later claimed that he had been "counsel to the situation," not counsel to the clients. Compare Judge Noonan's characterization of Brandeis's conduct with the acts of the lawyers in *Perez*.

> Underidentification is here, no doubt, carried to the point of caricature. The lawyer does not remember that he took the client as a client. The lawyer does not give the client the most elementary advice about the consequences of the act the lawyer is advising him to perform. The lawyer represents another client and, acting for that client, puts his unremembered client into bankruptcy. At the heart of the situation is the lawyer's desire to abstract himself from the needs and pressures of a particular individual in order to go on and straighten out a mess. In some other world, law could be practiced in that fashion. It is not the way law has been generally practiced in ours.[12]

Perhaps Mr. Perez's lawyers believed that they too were hired "to straighten out a mess," or to direct or implement their own view of social retribution. But in failing to recognize that they were retained to provide representation to each of two clients, they made all the mistakes that Noonan attributes to Brandeis. Mr. Perez's lawyers recognized the legal significance of his failure to check the brakes, just as Brandeis knew the legal significance of the assignment for the benefit of creditors. They then transformed themselves into agents for their other client, Valley Coca-Cola, just as Brandeis became the advocate for his other creditor-client. Mr. Perez's lawyers gave his confidential statement to the prosecutor's office, just as Brandeis used his client's confidences against him to force a bankruptcy proceeding. Brandeis and Mr. Perez's lawyers each apparently assumed that their private judgment about the matter could dominate, even at the direct expense of their fiduciary duties to each client. Conveniently sacrificing one client's goals to the lawyers' view of the greater good also happened to dovetail neatly with the lawyers' own interests in continuing to represent another client.

---

11. Judge Noonan points out that this episode was far from typical, but was the "most damaging episode" that Brandeis's enemies could cull from a distinguished 30-year career in law practice. Noonan, *supra* note 3, at 829.

12. *Id.* at 833.

The Cure for Directive Behavior

The law has long recognized and imposed fiduciary duties as the cure for this misguided private judgment. The power that clients bestow on lawyers to handle a matter enables lawyers to manipulate the representation for their own or another's benefit. Fiduciary duties curb this power by guarding against both intentional and unintentional exploitation by agents.

Directive behavior is most endemic and least justified in situations like that of Mr. Perez, when lawyers represent individual clients unfamiliar with the law who are often facing serious legal consequences concerning past events. Professors Freedman and Smith focus on advocacy in litigation generally as the primary circumstance justifying zealous advocacy. Here, where clients are most vulnerable, lawyers should be most diligent in guarding against preempting their client's moral judgments.[13] This advice would have helped to avoid the harm foisted on Mr. Perez and Brandeis's business client.

In the end, Mr. Perez settled his lawsuit against his former lawyers for an undisclosed amount. He also reached a settlement of $462,619 against Valley Coca-Cola, which paid over $133 million in overall settlements to those injured in the tragedy, largely because of its failure to properly maintain the truck's brakes.[14] The result in *Perez* vividly illustrates that lawyers will be liable for tort damages when they breach fiduciary duties, regardless of their intent. On the other hand, lawyers who learn and incorporate into their practice the 5 Cs should not fall prey to professional discipline[15] or subject themselves to the civil relief afforded to clients whose lawyers betray them. They also will move toward respecting client interests and begin to think of themselves as collaborators in representing clients, rather than as authorities or judges who know best.

C. Evidentiary Protections: Attorney-Client Privilege and Work Product Immunity

Problems

6-3. At Client's request, Fox returns goods stolen by Client to the police. Now Fox is called to testify about the identity of the person who gave him the goods. What result?

---

13. *See also* Alexander A. Guerrero, *Lawyers, Context, and Legitimacy: A New Theory of Legal Ethics,* 25 Geo. J. Legal Ethics 107 (2012) (the functional value of lawyers in criminal defense is to help ensure that the State acts against individuals "only in cases in which the relevant triggering conditions actually obtain").

14. The company that manufactured the bus also paid $23 million to accident victims due to improperly designed hatches that did not allow the children to escape as water filled the bus. *Truck Driver Settles Suit from Crash That Killed 21 Schoolchildren in '89,* Dallas Morning News, May 26, 1994, at 29A.

15. Recall *e.g., Ky. Bar Assn. v. Helmers, supra* p. 35, *People v. Walker, supra* p. 30, *Machado v. Statewide Grievance Comm, supra* p. 89.

6-4. Clean Energy, Inc., operates multiple coal-fired power plants. Its CEO is concerned whether the company is meeting air quality standards. He suggests that they do an audit. The general counsel responds, "Let's have the lawyers do it. That way, it will be privileged, just in case the results are not so favorable." Clean Energy's general counsel interviews 25 employees at five different plants and later decides to hire an outside law firm to complete the investigation. "That will help secure the privilege."

6-5. In a privileged conversation, Client tells Martyn where he was on the night in question. Can Client now be compelled to testify as to his whereabouts?

6-6. The deal is complicated: something about synthetic collateralized mortgage obligations. Martyn meets with an investment banker to understand what was required for our corporate client to pursue a purchase of the CDOs. Now they want her to testify about her educational meeting. What result?

Consider: RLGL §§ 68-77
FRCP 26(b)(3)

Hughes v. Meade
453 S.W.2d 538 (Ky. 1970)

CLAY, Commissioner. . . .

Petitioner, an attorney, seeks to restrain the respondent from enforcing a contempt ruling entered against him because of his refusal to answer a question as a witness in a criminal trial. Petitioner was not a party to, nor did he represent anyone as an attorney in such proceeding.

The proceeding in which he was called as a witness was the trial of one Williams on a criminal charge involving the theft of an IBM typewriter. Petitioner had participated in the return of an IBM typewriter to the Lexington Police Department. His testimony with respect thereto, and so much thereof as is pertinent to the question presented, is as follows:

Q. "Would you tell the jury the circumstances and how you happened to deliver that typewriter?

A. "Well, a certain party called me and employed me because of, first of all, my relationship with the Lexington Police Department, which is very good, and I do entirely criminal law and know all of the policemen and members of the Police Department, and asked me if I could get some property returned without getting me involved in it.

Q. "Without getting who involved—you or him?

A. "Without getting me involved. . . . So I called Morris Carter, who was then either assistant chief or a major. I know Morris well, and I asked him, I said, 'Morris, are you all interested in getting some stolen property back?' And he said 'Yes we are,' and he said, 'What is it?' I said 'I don't know, I have no idea,' and I said, 'Morris, I don't want to get involved in this thing, I don't want to be called as a witness, all I want to do is get this taken care of.' He said, 'All right, how is it going to be delivered?' And I said, 'Well, I'm watching the cartoons.' It was Saturday morning, and I said, 'Somebody is going to leave it on my front porch,' and the shades were down and I heard a car come up and left, and I called Morris back and I said 'Morris, it's out here,' and he said, 'Okay I'll send somebody out to get it.' . . . (Officer Sparks arrived and a taped box was opened disclosing a typewriter.) . . .

Q. "You say that the certain party called you and employed you to do what you have just described and said you did, is that correct?

A. "Yes, sir.

Q. "Was this the extent of your employment?

A. "Yes, sir.

Q. "Have you been paid for that service?

A. "Yes, sir.

Q. "And I'll ask you now if you will tell us the name of the individual who employed you?

A. "I refuse to answer."

Petitioner was found in contempt of court for failure to identify the person who had called him. It is his contention that this information was a privileged communication under KRS 421.210(4), and the trial court improperly sought to compel him to disclose it. That subsection of the statute provides (insofar as pertinent):

> "No attorney shall testify concerning a *communication* made to him, *in his professional character*, by his client, or his advice thereon without the client's consent; . . . " (emphasis added.)

This statutory provision generally conforms to the common law policy and principle of attorney-client privilege (developed since 1800) and it is generally recognized in the United States. See 8 Wigmore, Evidence §2291 (McNaughton rev. 1961). This same author thus phrases the principle:

> "(1) Where legal advice of any kind is sought (2) from a professional legal adviser in his capacity as such, (3) the communications relating to that purpose, (4) made in confidence (5) by the client, (6) are at his instance permanently protected (7) from disclosure by himself or by the legal adviser, (8) except the protection be waived." . . .

. . . On the other hand, . . . [a]s said in 97 C.J.S. Witnesses §280, page 793:

> "Neither is there any privilege as to communications with reference to a matter in which the attorney acts, not in his professional capacity, but merely as an agent or attorney in fact, or in which the attorney acts merely as a depositary or as a

trustee, particularly where he has instructions to deliver the instrument deposited to a third person, or abstracter of titles."

Returning to the facts of this case, it is the opinion of the majority of the court that whether or not a bona fide attorney-client relationship existed between the petitioner and the undisclosed person, the principal transaction involved, i.e., the delivery of stolen property to the police department, was not an act in the professional capacity of petitioner nor was it the rendition of a legal service. He was acting as an agent or conduit for the delivery of property which was completely unrelated to legal representation. While repose of confidence in an attorney is something much to be desired, to use him as a shield to conceal transactions involving stolen property is beyond the scope of his professional duty and beyond the scope of the privilege.

Dean v. Dean

607 So. 2d 494 (Fla. App. 1992)

FARMER, J.

The issue raised here is whether the attorney-client privilege can be used to prevent the disclosure of the identity of a person who had previously consulted an attorney regarding the return of stolen property belonging to one of the parties in a civil case. . . .

The facts are unusual, to say the least. During the pendency of the Deans' dissolution of marriage case, the husband's place of business was allegedly burgled, resulting in the loss of two duffel bags containing various personal items belonging to husband's daughter, and from $35,000 to $40,000 in cash. Sometime after the theft, an unidentified person telephoned Krischer at his office. He related the conversation as follows:

I received a telephone call from an individual who knew that I was an attorney that was involved in the Baltes[1] matter and the individual asked me for advice with regard to returning property. I advised this person on the telephone that the experience that I have had in the State Attorney's office was that the best avenue was to turn the property over to an attorney and let the attorney bring it to the State Attorney's office or to the law enforcement. . . .

Krischer met twice and had one telephone conversation with this person. Nearly six weeks after the second meeting, the two duffel bags containing only the daughter's personal property were delivered to Krischer's office by someone who told his receptionist that he "would know what they are." No cash was

---

1. This refers to a widely publicized case in which a hit-and-run driver consulted Krischer for advice and, afterwards, Krischer asserted the attorney-client privilege when asked to disclose the name of the driver. The fact that the person consulting Krischer in this case referred to the widely publicized case when Krischer kept the identity of his contact confidential might reasonably be taken as evidencing the contact's strong interest in confidentiality.

included with the returned items. Krischer then delivered the bags to the police, telling them that they "may have some connection with" husband.

In a twist of irony, these events came to light through Krischer's former secretary, who had also by then become a client of husband's lawyer. Soon after, husband's lawyer served Krischer with a subpoena for a deposition, seeking the identity of Krischer's contact. Krischer asserted the privilege at the deposition. Husband then moved to compel the testimony. After a hearing, the trial court granted the motion. . . . Krischer's testimony makes plain the intent of his client. . . .

> "The individual called—I can expedite this if I can state a couple of things, judge. I had obviously been through this previously in another case. I was well aware of what was needed to be established in order to protect this client. I inquired of this client if that individual knew I was an attorney. That individual indicated that they did. I inquired if they were seeking legal advice. They indicated that they did. They discussed a legal problem with me. I gave them legal advice.
>
> A condition precedent to this person discussing the legal problem with me was that I not divulge their identity . . . . "

The trial judge . . . [relied on] Hughes v. Meade, 452 S.W.2d 538 (Ky. 1970). . . .

[W]e conclude that the trial court has misinterpreted the privilege and the policies underlying it. . . . It is indisputable that his contact . . . consulted Krischer as an attorney. It is indisputable that the client sought legal advice about a specific matter. It is indisputable that the specific matter concerned a crime that had already been committed, not a planned or future act which might be a crime. And it is indisputable that the client insisted on confidence.

The focus, as we have seen from the common law development of the privilege and our own Florida Evidence Code section 90.502 definition of "client," is on the perspective of the person seeking out the lawyer, not on what the lawyer does after the consultation. As we have also seen, it has long been understood that the representation of a client in a court or legal proceeding is not indispensable for the invocation of the privilege. That Krischer's client sought him out for purely legal advice was enough. Legal advice, after all, is by itself a legal service. It is not necessary to the existence of the privilege that the lawyer render some additional service connected with the legal advice. Nor, as we know, is it even necessary that the lawyer appear in court or contemplate some pending or future legal proceeding.

And even if it were, the engagement of an attorney to effect the return of stolen property should certainly qualify. Surely there is a public purpose served by getting stolen property in the hands of the police authorities, even if the identity of the thief is not thereby revealed. Here the consultation resulted in exactly that. Krischer advised his client to turn over the property to the state attorney or the police. A lawyer's advice can be expected to result in the return of the property if the confidentiality of the consultation is insured.

. . . [T]he mere fact that the consulted attorney acts as a "conduit" for the return of stolen property does not support the conclusion that the attorney has engaged in unprotected consultation with the person seeking the advice.[7] A legal service has been rendered just as surely as when the lawyer represents the accused thief in a criminal trial. . . .

Upjohn Co. v. United States
449 U.S. 383 (1981)

Justice REHNQUIST delivered the opinion of the Court. . . .

Petitioner Upjohn Co. manufactures and sells pharmaceuticals here and abroad. In January 1976 independent accountants conducting an audit of one of Upjohn's foreign subsidiaries discovered that the subsidiary made payments to or for the benefit of foreign government officials in order to secure government business. The accountants so informed petitioner Mr. Gerard Thomas, Upjohn's Vice President, Secretary, and General Counsel. Thomas is a member of the Michigan and New York Bars, and has been Upjohn's General Counsel for 20 years. He consulted with outside counsel and R. T. Parfet, Jr., Upjohn's Chairman of the Board. It was decided that the company would conduct an internal investigation of what were termed "questionable payments." As part of this investigation the attorneys prepared a letter containing a questionnaire which was sent to "All Foreign General and Area Managers" over the Chairman's signature. The letter began by noting recent disclosures that several American companies made "possibly illegal" payments to foreign government officials and emphasized that the management needed full information concerning any such payments made by Upjohn. The letter indicated that the Chairman had asked Thomas, identified as "the company's General Counsel," "to conduct an investigation for the purpose of determining the nature and magnitude of any payments made by the Upjohn Company or any of its subsidiaries to any employee or official of a foreign government." The questionnaire sought detailed information concerning such payments. . . .

On March 26, 1976, the company voluntarily submitted a preliminary report to the Securities and Exchange Commission on Form 8-K disclosing certain questionable payments. . . . A copy of the report was simultaneously submitted to the Internal Revenue Service, which immediately began an investigation to determine the tax consequences of the payments. Special agents conducting the investigation were given lists by Upjohn of all those interviewed and all who had responded to the questionnaire. . . . [but an IRS demand for the

---

7. In contrast, the attorney in Hughes testified that he had been contacted only to deliver stolen property to the police. His contact reached out for him, not because he was a lawyer, but instead because he was a good friend of many members of the police force. Unlike Krischer here, he gave no legal advice. His services amounted to a phone call informing the police that, if they were interested in the return of stolen property, they could pick it up on the attorney's front porch. Not surprisingly, the court determined that this attorney rendered no legal service, and therefore could not invoke the attorney-client privilege.

questionnaires themselves was opposed by Upjohn on the ground of privilege and work product]. . . .

Federal Rule of Evidence 501 provides that "the privilege of a witness . . . shall be governed by the principles of the common law as they may be interpreted by the courts of the United States in light of reason and experience." The attorney-client privilege is the oldest of the privileges for confidential communications known to the common law. Its purpose is to encourage full and frank communication between attorneys and their clients and thereby promote broader public interests in the observance of law and administration of justice. The privilege recognizes that sound legal advice or advocacy serves public ends and that such advice or advocacy depends upon the lawyer's being fully informed by the client. . . .

The Court of Appeals, however, considered the application of the privilege in the corporate context to present a "different problem," since the client was an inanimate entity and "only the senior management, guiding and integrating the several operations, . . . can be said to possess an identity analogous to the corporation as a whole." . . .

Such a view, we think, overlooks the fact that the privilege exists to protect not only the giving of professional advice to those who can act on it but also the giving of information to the lawyer to enable him to give sound and informed advice. . . .

In the case of the individual client the provider of information and the person who acts on the lawyer's advice are one and the same. In the corporate context, however, it will frequently be employees beyond the control group as defined by the court below— "officers and agents . . . responsible for directing [the company's] actions in response to legal advice"—who will possess the information needed by the corporation's lawyers. Middle-level—and indeed lower-level—employees can, by actions within the scope of their employment, embroil the corporation in serious legal difficulties, and it is only natural that these employees would have the relevant information needed by corporate counsel if he is adequately to advise the client with respect to such actual or potential difficulties. . . .

The control group test adopted by the court below thus frustrates the very purpose of the privilege by discouraging the communication of relevant information by employees of the client to attorneys seeking to render legal advice to the client corporation. . . .

The narrow scope given the attorney-client privilege by the court below not only makes it difficult for corporate attorneys to formulate sound advice when their client is faced with a specific legal problem but also threatens to limit the valuable efforts of corporate counsel to ensure their client's compliance with the law. In light of the vast and complicated array of regulatory legislation confronting the modern corporation, corporations, unlike most individuals, "constantly go to lawyers to find out how to obey the law". . . . But if the purpose of the attorney-client privilege is to be served, the attorney and client must be able to predict with some degree of certainty whether particular discussions will be protected. An uncertain privilege, or one which purports to be certain but results in widely varying applications by the courts, is little better than no privilege at all. The very terms of the test adopted by the court below suggest the unpredictability of its application. The test restricts the availability of the privilege to those officers who play a "substantial role" in deciding and directing a corporation's legal response. . . .

The communications at issue were made by Upjohn employees to counsel for Upjohn acting as such, at the direction of corporate superiors in order to secure legal advice from counsel. . . . Information, not available from upper-echelon management, was needed to supply a basis for legal advice concerning compliance with securities and tax laws, foreign laws, currency regulations, duties to shareholders, and potential litigation in each of these areas. The communications concerned matters within the scope of the employees' corporate duties, and the employees themselves were sufficiently aware that they were being questioned in order that the corporation could obtain legal advice. The questionnaire identified Thomas as "the company's General Counsel" and referred in its opening sentence to the possible illegality of payments such as the ones on which information was sought. A statement of policy accompanying the questionnaire clearly indicated the legal implications of the investigation. . . . It began "Upjohn will comply with all laws and regulations," and stated that commissions or payments "will not be used as a subterfuge for bribes or illegal payments" and that all payments must be "proper and legal." . . . This statement was issued to Upjohn employees worldwide, so that even those interviewees not receiving a questionnaire were aware of the legal implications of the interviews. Pursuant to explicit instructions from the Chairman of the Board, the communications were considered "highly confidential" when made, and have been kept confidential by the company. Consistent with the underlying purposes of the attorney-client privilege, these communications must be protected against compelled disclosure.

The Court of Appeals declined to extend the attorney-client privilege beyond the limits of the control group test for fear that doing so would entail severe burdens on discovery and create a broad "zone of silence" over corporate affairs. Application of the attorney-client privilege to communications such as those involved here, however, puts the adversary in no worse position than if the communications had never taken place. The privilege only protects disclosure of communications; it does not protect disclosure of the underlying facts by those who communicated with the attorney:

> [The] protection of the privilege extends only to *communications* and not to facts. A fact is one thing and a communication concerning that fact is an entirely different thing. The client cannot be compelled to answer the question, "What did you say or write to the attorney?" but may not refuse to disclose any relevant fact within his knowledge merely because he incorporated a statement of such fact into his communication to his attorney. Philadelphia v. Westinghouse Electric Corp., 205 F. Supp. 830, 831 (E.D. Pa 1962)

Here the Government was free to question the employees who communicated with Thomas and outside counsel. Upjohn has provided the IRS with a list of such employees, and the IRS has already interviewed some 25 of them. While it would probably be more convenient for the Government to secure the results of petitioner's internal investigation by simply subpoenaing the questionnaires and notes taken by petitioner's attorneys, such considerations of convenience do not overcome the policies served by the attorney-client privilege. . . .

Our decision . . . disposes of the case so far as the responses to the questionnaires and any notes reflecting responses to interview questions are concerned. . . . Thomas has testified that his notes and memoranda of interviews go beyond recording responses to his questions. To the extent that the material subject to the summons is not protected by the attorney-client privilege as disclosing communications between an employee and counsel, we must [decide whether] the work-product doctrine [applies to the] summonses.

. . . This doctrine was announced by the Court over 30 years ago in Hickman v. Taylor, 329 U.S. 495 (1947). In that case the Court rejected "an attempt, without purported necessity or justification, to secure written statements, private memoranda and personal recollections prepared or formed by an adverse party's counsel in the course of his legal duties." The Court noted that "it is essential that a lawyer work with a certain degree of privacy" and reasoned that if discovery of the material sought were permitted "much of what is now put down in writing would remain unwritten. An attorney's thoughts, heretofore inviolate, would not be his own. Inefficiency, unfairness and sharp practices would inevitably develop in the giving of legal advice and in the preparation of cases for trial. The effect on the legal profession would be demoralizing. And the interests of the clients and the cause of justice would be poorly served." . . .

. . . While conceding the applicability of the work-product doctrine, the Government asserts that it has made a sufficient showing of necessity to overcome its protections. . . .

The Government stresses that interviewees are scattered across the globe and that Upjohn has forbidden its employees to answer questions it considers irrelevant. The above-quoted language from *Hickman*, however, did not apply to "oral statements made by witnesses . . . whether presently in the form of [the attorney's] mental impressions or memoranda." As to such material the Court did "not believe that any showing of necessity can be made under the circumstances of this case so as to justify production. If there should be a rare situation justifying production of these matters, petitioner's case is not of that type." Forcing an attorney to disclose notes and memoranda of witnesses' oral statements is particularly disfavored because it tends to reveal the attorney's mental processes.[8] . . .

The notes and memoranda sought by the Government here, however, are work product based on oral statements. If they reveal communications, they are, in this case, protected by the attorney-client privilege. To the extent they

---

8. Thomas described his notes of the interviews as containing "what I considered to be the important questions, the substance of the responses to them, my beliefs as to the importance of these, my beliefs as to how they related to the inquiry, my thoughts as to how they related to other questions. In some instances they might even suggest other questions that I would have to ask or things that I needed to find elsewhere." . . .

do not reveal communications, they reveal the attorneys' mental processes in evaluating the communications. As [FRCP] 26 and *Hickman* make clear, such work product cannot be disclosed simply on a showing of substantial need and inability to obtain the equivalent without undue hardship.

While we are not prepared at this juncture to say that such material is always protected by the work-product rule, we think a far stronger showing of necessity and unavailability by other means than was made by the Government or applied by the Magistrate in this case would be necessary to compel disclosure.

In re Vioxx Products Liability Litigation
501 F. Supp. 2d 789 (E.D. La. 2007)

Eldon E. FALLON, United States District Judge.

. . . This discovery dispute has dragged on for over a year and at times has seemed hopelessly endless. Although Merck has produced over two million documents in this Multidistrict litigation (MDL), the company has also asserted attorney-client privilege as to approximately 30,000 documents which it contends need not be produced. The majority of the withheld documents are print-outs of electronic communications, primarily internal company e-mails and attachments. . . .

I. BACKGROUND

This multidistrict products liability litigation involves the prescription drug Vioxx, known generically as Rofecoxib. Merck, a New Jersey corporation, researched, designed, manufactured, marketed, and distributed Vioxx to relieve pain and inflammation. . . . Vioxx remained available to the public [from 1999] until September 30, 2004, at which time Merck withdrew it from the market when data from a clinical trial indicated that the use of Vioxx increased the risk of cardiovascular thrombotic events such as myocardial infarctions (heart attacks) and ischemic strokes. . . .

On April 25, 2007, after giving notice and allowing the parties an opportunity to be heard, the Court appointed Professor Paul R. Rice of American University's Washington College of Law as Special Master [and] requested that Special Master Rice review 2,000 representative documents, as well as approximately 600 additional documents selected by the Plaintiff's Steering Committee (PSC) and believed to be relevant to upcoming trial preservation depositions, and make recommendations as to whether or not Merck's claims of privilege should be upheld. . . .

II. SPECIAL MASTER'S REPORT

In addition to providing written recommendations on a document-by-document basis, Special Master Rice issued a twenty-one-page Report that discusses the law of attorney-client privilege both in general and in the context of this multidistrict litigation . . . , which reads as follows: . . .

B. Legal Advice Must Be the Primary Purpose

. . . It is often difficult to apply the attorney-client privilege in the corporate context to communications between in-house corporate counsel and those who personify the corporate entity because modern corporate counsel have become involved in all facets of the enterprises for which they work. As a consequence, in-house legal counsel participates in and renders decisions about business, technical, scientific, public relations, and advertising issues, as well as purely legal issues. . . .

Consequently, in the context of Merck's privilege claims we had to determine the purpose behind both the seeking of the assistance from in-house counsel and the responsive services that were rendered by in-house counsel.

This problem of determining the type of services being rendered by in-house counsel has been exacerbated by the advent of e-mail that has made it so convenient to copy legal counsel on every communication that might be seen as having some legal significance at some time, regardless of whether it is ripe for legal analysis. As a consequence, counsel is brought into business communications at a much earlier stage than she was in the past when communications were through hard-copy memoranda. This, of course, has been beneficial for corporations because the lawyers are some of the most intelligent and informed people within corporations. . . . In addition, because they are part of a word crafting profession, more often than not, they are excellent writers and editors. The benefit from this expanded use of lawyers, however, comes at a cost. This cost is in the form of differentiating between the lawyers' legal and business work when the attorney-client privilege is asserted for their communications within the corporate structure. The privilege is only designed to protect communications seeking and rendering legal services. . . .

The test for the application of the attorney-client privilege to communications with legal counsel in which a mixture of services are sought is whether counsel was participating in the communications primarily for the purpose of rendering legal advice or assistance. Therefore, merely because a legal issue can be identified that relates to on-going communications does not justify shielding them from discovery. The lawyer's role as a lawyer must be primary to her participation. . . . In addition, if a communication is made primarily for the purpose of soliciting legal advice, an incidental request for business advice does not vitiate the attorney-client privilege." . . . [12]

C. "Pervasive Regulation" Theory

Merck has argued that because the drug industry is so extensively regulated by the FDA, virtually everything a member of the industry does carries

---

12. In the few communications that were to and from Merck outside counsel . . . we assumed that legal advice was being sought and given unless the content of the communications indicated otherwise. We thought this logical inference was justified . . . [because] "on the basis of probability, some courts operate under a presumption that a client who consults outside counsel with no non-legal responsibilities to the client (e.g., holding corporate office) sought legal advice from that attorney." Paul R. Rice, 1 *Attorney-Client Privilege in the United States,* § 7.28 (Thomson West 2d ed. 1999).

potential legal problems vis-a-vis government regulators. In support of its claim, Merck submitted hundreds of pages of materials . . . in which the pervasive nature of governmental regulation was explored. . . . Through these voluminous materials, we have come to appreciate how services that initially appear to be non-legal in nature, like commenting upon and editing television ads and other promotional materials could, in fact, be legal advice within the context of the drug industry. However, that does not resolve the question of whether legal advice was the primary purpose behind comments and edits by Merck's in-house lawyers of specific scientific reports, articles accepted for publication in noted journals, and research proposals. . . .

Accepting such a theory would effectively immunize most of the industry's internal communications because most drug companies are probably structured like Merck where virtually every communication leaving the company has to go through the legal department for review, comment, and approval. . . . While we acknowledge that in many of these instances what appears not to be legal assistance may, in fact, fall within the protection of the attorney–client privilege, it was Merck's burden to successfully establish this on a document-by-document basis. . . .

When warning letters were received by Merck from the FDA, in which alleged violations of FDA regulations were cited, we accepted the argument that the company's preparation of its responses to those warnings were the equivalent of preparing pleadings in a legal proceeding. As a consequence, we recommended the granting of the privilege to (1) the attorney's drafts of those responses, (2) communications in which the attorney sought information from corporate employees in her efforts to prepare those drafts, and (3) the responsive comments solicited from the corporate employees on the drafts. Following the trigger of the warning letter, every communication to and from the attorney and among corporate employees that were primarily in furtherance of legal assistance on that matter were considered privileged, even if the initial draft of the response was prepared for the lawyer by a non-lawyer. . . .

E. The Corporation's Choices Have Consequences

The structure of Merck's enterprise, with its legal department having such broad powers, and the manner in which it circulates documents, has consequences that Merck must live with relative to its burden of persuasion when privilege is asserted. When, for example, Merck simultaneously sends communications to both lawyers and non-lawyers, it usually cannot claim that the primary purpose of the communication was for legal advice or assistance because the communication served both business and legal purposes. As a consequence, the privilege does not protect the communications. . . .

When non-legal departments of a corporation primarily concerned with technology, science, public relations or marketing make comments among themselves about matters within their corporate responsibilities, those communications are not protected by the attorney-client privilege. When lawyers make the same comments about technology, science, public relations, or marketing, a different result is not warranted unless Merck demonstrates that those comments are *primarily* related to legal assistance. When it failed to do this on a document-by-document basis, its claims were denied. Merck cannot reasonably expect judicial officers to make this assessment for it on either a document-by-document basis or universally through a presumption that everything in-house counsel comments upon is legal advice.

G. Special Master's Substantive Guidelines

1. If a memorandum was addressed solely to an attorney with apparently limited circulation and an identifiable legal question was raised by the author (whether or not it was answered by the attorney), it was found to be a classical example of when the attorney-client privilege is applicable.

2. When e-mail messages were addressed to both lawyers and non-lawyers for review, comment, and approval, we concluded that the primary purpose of such communications was not to obtain legal assistance since the same was being sought from all. . . . [W]hile the disclosure of such e-mail messages reveals the content of what had been communicated to the lawyer (and might otherwise be privileged because the single copy sent to the attorney could have been primarily for the purpose of obtaining legal assistance), revealing this information on the face of discoverable documents (these documents would be discoverable from the files of the other recipients) breaches the confidentiality of that communication to the attorneys and thereby destroys the attorney-client privilege protection. . . .

5. At the end of the messages described above, we occasionally encountered e-mail threads that were sent to others after the initial interaction with the lawyer ended. This additional dissemination of the e-mail thread was found not to be privileged when the conveyance was by a non-lawyer recipient, unless it was clear that legal advice previously obtained was being circulated to those within the corporate structure who needed the advice in order to fulfill their corporate responsibilities. When the conveyance was by the lawyer and it appeared that it was for the purpose of acquiring more information upon which more informed legal advice or assistance could be rendered, the additional conveyance and response were also found to be privileged. . . .

9. The doctrine of work product was created by the Supreme Court in Hickman v. Taylor, 329 U.S. 495 (1943). . . . When litigation was identified in the Merck sample documents, but the communications related only to things like news releases, work product claims were denied. Many of those communications, however, were still protected by the attorney-client privilege. . . .

IV. CONCLUSION

The emergence of the Internet and electronic methods of communication present significant challenges for traditional discovery practices. These challenges are exacerbated in MDL proceedings and otherwise complex cases where, because of their vastness, no one counsel can be expected to keep up with everything that transpires. . . .

When privilege is claimed on 30,000 documents, amounting to nearly 500,000 pages, as occurred in this case, the courts are severely taxed. When the task of review is shifted to outside experts, costs mount.[35] In the long run, such a situation is detrimental to the litigants, the courts, and our system of justice. Some acceptable solution must be devised, one which fully protects the rights of the litigants to claim privilege and at the same time is more feasible for the courts, less expensive for the parties, and less time consuming for everyone involved.

While this Court has experienced significant fits and starts in struggling with these issues, the sample resolution process suggested by the Fifth Circuit and ultimately employed in this case, along with the appropriate "packaging" of withheld documents, may be able to streamline such discovery disputes in future cases. It may be desirable to issue a pretrial order setting forth an appropriate method of organizing documents to be submitted for *in camera* review and establishing mandatory guidelines for the creation of a detailed privilege log that identifies the individuals that author and receive each document and explains their relationship to the document and to the party asserting the privilege. . . .

Lawyers and Clients: *Representing Organizations*

Lawyers who provide legal services to organizations face unique ethical issues because their clients are legal fictions: entities, abstractions, or amalgams of individual interests. These legal fictions range in size from large corporations and government agencies, to small partnerships and professional and family companies. Because organizations are so pervasive, nearly every lawyer will represent one sometime in his or her legal career. In fact, at least half of all lawyers in practice represent organizations on a regular basis, either as outside counsel or inside employees.[1] The in-house counsel lawyer-employee has only one client, the organization, and all financial rewards are provided by that same client, which can make it very difficult to remain objective in the face of client demands.[2]

Upjohn and *Vioxx* illustrate how lawyers who represent client-organizations must consult with a wide range of individuals who are agents of the organization: employees, officers, members, directors, trustees, agents, shareholders,

---

35. To date, Special Master Rice and Special Counsel Barriere have incurred over $400,000.00 in fees and expenses in reviewing approximately 2,500 representative documents over the course of three months. These costs have been paid equally by the parties.

1. About 61,000 lawyers (approximately 10 percent of the practicing bar) serve as inside counsel to about 21,000 profit and nonprofit private sector corporations. Assn. of Corp. Counsel, *ACC 2006 Census of In-house Counsel* (Dec. 2006), *available at* http://www.acc.com/vl/public/Surveys/loader.cfm?csModule=security/getfile&pageid=16297&page=/legalresources/resource.cfm&qstring=show=16297&title=ACC%202006%20Census%20of%20In-house%20Counsel.

2. E. Norman Veasey & Christine T. Guglielmo, *Indispensable Counsel: The Chief Legal Officer in the New Reality* 10-11 (Oxford U. Press 2012).

and the like. Each agent is a constituent of the whole, who speaks for the organization through a different role and with a distinctive view of the organization's
interests, often filtered through a personal lens.

The result in both cases, upholding and defining the scope of the attorney-
client and work product privileges for organizations,[3] also demonstrates that
courts have tailored specialized legal rules to fit more general legal policies to
an entity setting. These court decisions have produced some clarity for the organization's lawyer, but determining the proper standards for identifying the entity
client and affording the entity client the 5 Cs are obligations that continue to
perplex the best lawyers and judges.

The Clients

Model Rule 1.13(a) adopts the entity theory for all organizations, including
governments;[4] Indian tribes;[5] publicly held, professional, and closely held corporations; general and limited partnerships;[6] limited liability companies and
partnerships; nonprofits; and unincorporated associations such as trade and
community groups[7] and some unions. The entity concept assumes that an organization has a distinct legal personality apart from any individual constituent
or aggregate of individual constituents within the whole. It is borrowed from
corporate law, which recognizes corporations as distinct legal persons that can
contract, sue and be sued in their own right, and incur liability apart from that
of its owners.

Applied to legal representation, the entity theory means that the organization's lawyer represents and has a client-lawyer relationship with the entity only,
not with any constituent or group of constituents within the organization.[8] It
further recognizes that the organization must act through its "duly authorized
constituents," that these constituents are not clients, and that these constituents
(and the lawyer) easily can misconstrue the lawyer's role.[9]

---

3. The European Court of Justice has ruled that the attorney-client privilege is not available to
inside counsel because lawyer-employees are not sufficiently independent. *See* Case C-550/07,
Akzo Novel Chemical Ltd. v. European Comm'n, 2010 E.C.R. I-08301; *see also* Australian Mining
& Smelting Europe, Ltd. v. Commission, [1982] C.M.L.R. 264 (attorney-client privilege does not
protect communications between corporate officials and inside counsel).

4. We deal with government lawyers in a subsequent note. *See* Lawyers and Clients: *Representing
Governments, infra* p.426.

5. *See* David I. Gold, *I Know You're the Government's Lawyer, But Are You My Lawyer Too? An
Exploration of the Federal–Native American Trust Relationship and Conflicts of Interest,* 19 Buff.
Pub. Int. L.J. 1 (2000/2001).

6. ABA Formal Op. 91-361 (lawyer who represents a partnership represents the entity, not the
individual partners).

7. Paul R. Tremblay, *Counseling Community Groups,* 17 Clinical L. Rev. 389 (2010).

8. *E.g.,* General Nutrition Corp. v. Gardere Wynne Sewell LLP, 727 F. Supp. 2d 377 (W.D. Pa.
2010) (corporation cannot sue outside counsel for malpractice when monetary loss caused to affiliate); ABA Formal Op. 08-453 (law firm's ethics counsel usually represents the organization as a
whole, not individual-firm lawyers).

9. Lawrence J. Fox & Susan R. Martyn, *The Ethics of Representing Organizations: Legal Fictions for
Clients* 8-9 (Oxford U. Press 2009).

Misunderstanding who the lawyer represents is more likely to occur in small organizations where management and ownership are merged in the same constituents. In Chapter 4, *Antioch* illustrated that in closely held corporations and small partnerships, many lawyers deal with just one person or a small group of individuals, who manage and own the business.[10] But the problem arises in even the largest Fortune 500 companies, in part because the constituents are the people the lawyer deals with and they are often referred to as "clients." The confusion is further compounded when an organization's lawyer provides, typically on a pro bono basis, individual legal services to corporate officers and employees. In all of these circumstances, lawyers must clarify whether they represent the organization, the individual constituents, or both.[11]

Lack of clarity about client identity begins before an organization is established and has ramifications outside, as well as inside, the entity. The lawyer asked by an individual or group of individuals to establish an organization must first recognize whether the organizers are individual clients. A few jurisdictions allow lawyers and individuals to agree that the eventual entity is the only client, applying a kind of retroactive entity theory to the initial establishment of organizations.[12] According to this view, the lawyer who sets up an organization represents only the organization and not the individuals establishing it, provided the lawyer makes this fact clear from the beginning of the matter.

Representing organizations also can create "lateral dimension" problems; that is, a lawyer for one organization may be a lawyer for an affiliated company simply because one organization owns or controls another.[13] The Model Rules and the Restatement both reject an "all affiliates" and "no affiliates" approach[14] in favor of a four-factor analysis: (1) whether the nonclient is significantly controlled by the client, (2) whether financial loss or benefit to the nonclient will have a direct impact on the client, (3) whether confidential information of the nonclient will be disclosed, and (4) whether the client and lawyer have an understanding that the lawyer will not act contrary to the interests of the affiliates.[15]

---

10. Darian M. Ibrahim, *Solving the Everyday Problem of Client Identity in the Context of Closely Held Businesses*, 56 Ala. L. Rev. 181 (2004).

11. RLGL § 14, Comment f (in the absence of the lawyer's clarification, the reasonable expectations of the individual constituent, not the lawyer, will prevail).

12. *See* Jesse v. Danforth, 485 N.W.2d 63 (Wis. 1992) (physicians who retain a law firm to organize a medical corporation were not individual clients where attorney's involvement with the physicians was directly related to the corporation and the medical corporation was eventually incorporated because the entity rule applied retroactively); St. Bar of Ariz. Op. 02-06.

13. Henry Sills Bryans, *Business Successors and the Transpositional Attorney-Client Relationship*, 64 Bus. Law. 1039 (2009); Charles W. Wolfram, *Corporate-Family Conflicts*, 2 J. Inst. Stud. Leg. Eth. 295 (1999).

14. *Id.* at 328-331.

15. MR 1.7, Comment [34]; RLGL § 121, Comment d. *See also* ABA Formal Op. 95-390, a decision from which one of the authors stubbornly continues to dissent.

The Five Cs

Control Once an organization is created, organizational lawyers must under-stand who controls decision making for the entity. The organization's organic rules should identify this authority and, if they do not, the lawyer must make sure that any ambiguity is addressed by properly authorized groups or individu-als. Failure to do so can mean that the lawyer's work is not properly authorized or, worse, that the lawyer assists a constituent's breach of fiduciary duty to the organization (as alleged in *Antioch*).

As with individual clients, lawyers should accept and abide by decisions made by constituents of organizational clients even if the lawyer may believe them unwise, so long as the lawyer has exercised independent professional judgment and rendered candid advice about the matter.[16] Lawyers are not required to and should not second-guess business judgments made by an organization's agents.[17] At the same time, *Antioch* illustrates that the entity's lawyer must identify legal obligations of the client and, when clear violations arise, must not capitulate to a constituent's decision.

Communication *Anitoch* also relied on Model Rule 1.13(b), which makes plain that a lawyer who knows that an agent or constituent is violating a legal obliga-tion of the organization must not remain silent and, if necessary, must pursue the matter beyond that person or group to a higher authority in the organization, including the highest authority that can act on the matter. This means that the organization's lawyer must first communicate to the appropriate constituent that a clear violation of law has occurred or is occurring. If the constituent does not agree, referral of the matter for an independent legal opinion can help clarify the seriousness of the violation. If this confirms the lawyer's opinion but does not change the constituent's decision, then the lawyer must urge reassessment by taking clear violations of law up the authority ladder, all the way to the highest authority that can act for the organization, for example, the board of directors of a corporation. Continuing crimes or frauds require the lawyer to withdraw, and to notify the highest authority of the reason for the withdrawal.[18]

Competence Identifying an organizational client requires understanding the law that regulates the entity. Advising such a client often requires specialized legal knowledge and skill. For example, although individual persons can appear pro se in litigation, most organizations cannot be represented by nonlawyer constitu-ents.[19] Similarly, although FRCP 17(b) allows unincorporated associations to sue and be sued in their common names, federal diversity of citizenship jurisdiction

---

16. MR 2.1.

17. William T. Allen, *Corporate Governance and a Business Lawyer's Duty of Independence*, 38 Suffolk U. L. Rev. 1 (2004).

18. MR 1.2(d), 1.13(e).

19. United States v. W. Processing Co., 734 F. Supp. 930 (W.D. Wash. 1990) (the only proper representative for a corporation or partnership is a licensed lawyer, regardless of the unlicensed agent's close association with the entity); In re Global Constr. & Supply Co., 126 B.R. 573 (E.D.

requires that the association's capacity to sue or be sued be determined by state law.[20] Lawyers for organizations also must be able to advise small business owners about circumstances where the corporate veil might be pierced,[21] and advise constituents about their fiduciary duties to the organization.[22]

Beyond the body of law that regulates the organization's structure itself, lawyers for business organizations often need basic accounting knowledge to properly advise clients.[23] Organizational lawyers also must respond to increased legal regulation of business practice itself, as well as its globalization; in other words, be prepared to meet the organization's need for understanding foreign as well as domestic law.[24] Given this complex body of legal regulation, lawyers who represent organizations must know how to recognize their own lack of expertise and when to ask outside or inside counsel for assistance. Failing to do so can violate a duty of care to both the organization and to constituents who reasonably rely on the lawyer's legal advice.

Confidentiality Although *Upjohn* and *Vioxx* make clear that organizations are entitled to testimonial privileges, and Model Rule 1.13 combined with 1.6 extend confidentiality to entities, it is not always easy to understand or explain the precise scope of that obligation to clients and constituents. Of course, lawyers must communicate with constituent-agents who speak to the organization's lawyer for the purpose of receiving legal advice. But these agents easily can assume that they are speaking to "their" lawyer. This explains why a lawyer's assurance of confidentiality or privilege should include a clarification that confidentiality extends to the organization, not to any individuals within it, and that what individual constituents tell the lawyer will very likely be reported to others within the organization.[25]

The 2003 amendments to Model Rule 1.13 arose in the wake of the Enron scandal and include a grant of special discretion to an organization's lawyer to disclose confidential information outside the organization.[26] If the lawyer's efforts in pursuing a matter up the organizational ladder have failed to prevent the organization's clear violation of law, Model Rule 1.13(c) allows, but does

---

Mo. 1991) (bankruptcy petition filed by corporate president is null and void, even where corporation later retained a lawyer to represent it).

20. Charles Alan Wright, Arthur R. Miller, & Mary Kay Kane, *Federal Practice and Procedure Civ. 2d* § 1861 (West 2007).

21. Kurt A. Strasser, *Piercing the Veil in Corporate Groups*, 37 Conn. L. Rev. 637 (2005).

22. *E.g.,* American Law Institute, *Principles of the Law of Nonprofit Organizations* § 300 (Tentative Draft No. 1, 2007); Larry E. Ribstein, *Are Partners Fiduciaries?* 2005 U. Ill. L. Rev. 209 (2005).

23. Lawrence A. Cunningham, *Sharing Accounting's Burden: Business Lawyers in Enron's Dark Shadows*, 57 Bus. Law. 1421 (2002).

24. Milton C. Regan, Jr., *Professional Responsibility and the Corporate Lawyer*, 13 Geo. J. Legal Ethics 197 (2000).

25. *E.g.,* Westinghouse Elec. Corp. v. Kerr-McGee Corp., 580 F.2d 1311 (7th Cir. 1978) (law firm that represented trade association and received confidential information from member of trade association disqualified from subsequent representation against member).

26. Lawrence A. Hamermesh, *The ABA Task Force on Corporate Responsibility and the 2003 Changes to the Model Rules of Professional Conduct*, 17 Geo. J. Legal Ethics 35 (2003).

not require, an organization's lawyer to disclose information that the lawyer reasonably believes is necessary to prevent substantial injury to the organization.[27] This exception does not encompass lawyers who have been hired to investigate or defend a company against allegations of past wrongdoing. But it does allow a lawyer who, in the course of an ongoing matter, finds a clear legal violation and unsuccessfully takes the matter up the organizational ladder to disclose outside the organization when the board refuses to take remedial action that the lawyer reasonably believes is necessary to prevent substantial injury to the organization.

An organization lawyer's confidentiality obligation becomes doubly difficult in situations where lawyers are inquiring into possible wrongdoing in an organization, often pursuant to an ongoing or threatened governmental investigation. To clarify the situation, the lawyer speaking to an individual employee should make clear who he or she represents and that the conversation is privileged and confidential, but only insofar as the privilege belongs to the organization, not the individual. The company, through its duly authorized constituents, can waive the privilege, perhaps in response to a governmental demand for cooperation, and the information provided by the employee in the company's waived material could later be used by the government to provide the basis for an individual indictment.

Given this danger, lawyers who conduct corporate investigations where potential criminal liability exists read Model Rules 1.13(f) and 4.3 as requiring some kind of *Miranda* warning or explanation to employees to prevent any misunderstanding of the lawyer's role. The warning should include:

1. Identification of the lawyer, the client, and the matter;
2. Identification of the client organization's expectations (cooperate and tell the truth);
3. A basic explanation of confidentiality: that anything the employee tells the lawyer is confidential outside of the organization, but not within it, and the organization has the right to decide when and what to disclose to outsiders in litigation or otherwise;
4. An explanation that the lawyer does not (or does?) represent the employee; and
5. An explanation that the employee may retain separate counsel (including if available, the right of the employee to such counsel at the employer's expense).[28]

The federal government has precipitated the development of these corporate *Miranda* warnings by promulgating a series of internal Justice Department policies that allow consideration of an organization's willingness to waive the

---

27. Richard W. Painter, *Toward a Market for Lawyer Disclosure Services: In Search of Optimal Whistleblowing Rules*, 63 Geo. Wash. L. Rev. 221 (1995).
28. *See* Nancy J. Moore, *Conflicts of Interest of In-House Counsel: Issues Emerging from the Expanding Role of the Attorney-Employee*, 39 S. Tex. L. Rev. 497 (1998); Sarah Helene Duggin, *Internal Corporate Investigations: Legal Ethics, Professionalism, and the Employee Interview*, 2003 Colum. Bus. L. Rev. 859 (2003).

privilege as a factor in preventing criminal indictment of the organization.[29] Because indictment means sure business failure in many situations, organizations see no alternative to waiving the privilege, which means turning over all records of inside investigations by corporate counsel. Both employees and organizations oppose these governmental tactics, but so long as they persist, the organization and its employees are potentially adverse to each other. That potential triggers Model Rule 1.13(f)'s affirmative obligation to clarify who the lawyer represents, and when the employee is not represented, Model Rule 4.3's requirement that the lawyer undertake reasonable efforts to avoid misunderstanding, including the advice to seek independent counsel.

Conflict of Interest Resolution   These obligations to explain both the identity of the client and the organization's, rather than the constituent's, right to confidentiality are triggered by the fact that the interests of employee and employer may conflict. In an internal investigation of wrongdoing, for example, the lawyer hopes not to find any, but when she does, the organization may be best served by distancing itself and perhaps disciplining the "rogue" employees. Because organizations work only through agents who might not always pursue the company's interests, the potential for conflict between agent and organization permeates the representation. This explains why the lawyer must travel up the organizational ladder in communicating competently with the client. It also explains why an organization's lawyers have affirmative obligations to clarify misunderstandings.

Model Rule 1.13(g) does allow the organization's lawyer to represent constituents as well, subject, of course, to the same loyalty obligations imposed by Model Rule 1.7.[30] *Perez* offers a good example of such an initial joint representation.[31] Note that when Mr. Perez admitted failing to check the truck brakes on the morning of the accident (as required by company policy), the lawyers realized that his interests directly conflicted with those of his employer. This required the lawyers to withdraw from further representation of Mr. Perez. *Perez* illustrates that whenever this occurs, another conflict develops: The organization's lawyer

---

29. The most recent iteration is available at http://www.justice.gov/opa/documents/corp-charging-guidelines.pdf (last visited June 27, 2012). *See also* United States v. Stein (Stein IV), 495 F. Supp. 2d 390,427-428 (S.D.N.Y. 2007) (dismissing indictment against 13 corporate officials because the Department of Justice (DOJ) "deliberately or callously prevented many of these defendants from obtaining funds for their defense that they lawfully would have had absent the government's interference . . . thereby foreclos[ing them] from presenting the defenses they wished to present and, in some cases, even depriv[ing] them of counsel of their choice . . . . "); United States v. Stein (Stein II), 440 F. Supp. 2d 315 (S.D.N.Y. 2006) (DOJ's coercion and corporate employer's economic pressure on employees justified suppression of employees' statements); United States v. Stein, 435 F. Supp. 2d 330 (S.D.N.Y. 2006) (Stein I) (government violated employee's Fifth and Sixth Amendment rights by causing corporate employer, under threat of indictment, to apply economic pressure on employees to make full disclosure to the government or face firing and loss of corporate payment of legal fees).

30. *See, e.g.,* Sanford v. Commonwealth of Va., *infra* p. 316.

31. *Perez v. Kirk & Carrigan, supra* p. 167; Lawyers' Roles: *The Directive Lawyer and Fiduciary Duty, supra* p. 170.

has a Model Rule 1.4 obligation to share the co-clients' information, while, at the same time, the lawyer must protect the confidentiality of each joint client.

Increasingly, this issue is raised at the onset of a joint employee-employer representation as part of a conflict of interest waiver. The clients could decide to disclose everything to each other, or not to disclose anything shared in individual confidence with the lawyer. The waiver also can cover what happens if the lawyer must withdraw from representing one party, such as whether the lawyer may continue to represent the other (usually the employer).[32] However, even when granted initially, such a waiver will be adequate only if the conflict is consentable and each client has given informed consent after gaining a full understanding of the confidentiality obligations of the lawyer between the joint clients.[33]

Vioxx illustrates how lawyers for organizations must respond to another kind of conflict as well. They must recognize dual roles, which involve both legal advice and business judgment, such as general counsel–vice president or lawyer and board member of the entity.[34] The lawyer acting as lawyer will cloak the representation in privilege; the lawyer acting as business decision maker will not.

The Bounds of the Law

Modern organizations operate in a heavily regulated climate. This means that their lawyers must be especially sensitive to two massive bodies of law: the criminal law and the law of fraud, both of which we explore in greater detail in the next two chapters.[35] Whenever a client crime or fraud occurs, the Model Rules create lawyer obligations to clients and third parties. Organizational lawyers must understand these legal limits, not only to give competent legal advice to their clients, but also to assess their own conduct under the applicable lawyer code.[36]

Beyond professional discipline, other specialized legal requirements also shape the life of modern lawyers in some organizations. One example is the Sarbanes-Oxley Act, which parallels and makes more specific the 2003 amendments to Model Rule 1.13 for lawyers who represent public companies.[37] Both the statute and accompanying regulations require lawyers for public companies

---

32. Pa. Bar Assn. Op. 2006-200 (lawyers who contemplate representing both employer and employee should provide complete and objective disclosure of the risks and advantages of joint representation, reach an understanding about confidential information, and obtain written informed consent to the joint representation).

33. *E.g.,* ABA Formal Op. 05-436 (Informed Consent to Future Conflicts of Interest).

34. ABA Sect. of Litig., *The Lawyer-Director: Implications for Independence: Report of the Task Force on the Independent Lawyer* (1998); Susanna M. Kim, *Dual Identities and Dueling Obligations: Preserving Independence in Corporate Representation*, 68 Tenn. L. Rev. 179 (2001).

35. *See* The Bounds of the Law: *Duties to Nonclients, supra* p. 155; The Bounds of the Law: *Criminal Conduct, infra* p. 270.

36. *See also* Christopher J. Whelan & Neta Ziv, *Privatizing Professionalism: Client Control of Lawyers' Ethics*, 80 Fordham L. Rev. 2577 (2012) (examining organizational client's Outside Counsel Guidelines that shape the relationship between lawyer and client).

37. Karl. A. Groskaufmanis, *Climbing "Up the Ladder": Corporate Counsel and the SEC's Reporting Requirement for Lawyers*, 89 Cornell L. Rev. 511 (2004).

"to report evidence of a material violation of securities law" to those within the corporate family. A lawyer's duty under this law is triggered by a "reasonable belief" that a material violation of securities law or breach of fiduciary by a corporate constituent has occurred or is about to occur. When that happens, the lawyer has a duty to report the violation up the corporate ladder to the CEO, and eventually to the board of directors if appropriate action is not taken. Lawyers who violate these regulations face SEC disbarment; that is, they would lose their ability to prepare documents or otherwise appear before the SEC.[38]

Although the scope of reportable violations in this law seems to parallel Model Rule 1.13's "violation of law" language, the "evidence of" and "reasonable belief" reporting thresholds in Sarbanes-Oxley are triggered by more conduct than Model Rule 1.13(b)'s knowledge standard. Sarbanes also parallels Model Rule 1.13(d)'s discretionary disclosure provision by allowing, but not requiring, lawyers to inform the SEC of material violations to prevent or rectify them. These regulations apply to both inside and outside counsel who represent the public company in any matter (not just SEC matters) and provide for slightly different reporting procedures for subordinate and supervisory lawyers, a parallel to Model Rules 5.1 and 5.2.[39]

Conclusion

The ethical obligations of lawyers who represent organizations are complicated by the nature of organizations themselves. Legal fictions operate through agents, and agents can misunderstand their own role in the organization, the lawyer's role in representing the organization, or the organization's obligations to employees and third parties and vice versa. Lawyers can work their way through this thicket by remembering to identify their clients, clarifying this identity to their client's constituents when necessary, and providing the 5 Cs to the organizations that they represent. They also need to be aware of specialized laws that create additional or particularized bounds to their representation of certain organizational clients.

D. Express or Implied Authority and Waiver

Clients can decide for themselves whether to allow the use or disclosure of confidential information. Utilitarians note that the legal system requires information to function, and therefore, clients who wish to take advantage of the system's protections or allowances must agree as a condition of using the system to supply it with some information. Deontologists characterize client consent as the client's autonomous authorization to disclosure or use of the information. Agency

---

38. Lewis D. Lowenfels, Alan R. Bromberg, & Michael J. Sullivan, *Attorneys as Gatekeepers: SEC Actions Against Lawyers in the Age of Sarbanes-Oxley*, 37 U. Tol. L. Rev. 877 (2006).
39. Lawrence J. Fox & Susan R. Martyn, *The Ethics of Representing Organizations: Legal Fictions for Clients* 254-262 (Oxford U. Press 2009).

law rests on such a consensual foundation and protects extensions of autonomy by granting individuals the opportunity to act through others.

1. Express or Implied Authority

Problems

6-7. To make life easier and give lawyers the discretion they deserve, Martyn recommends that Martyn & Fox add the following clause to all personal injury retainer agreements. Should Fox agree?

> "Client agrees to allow Martyn & Fox to decide whether to disclose any information relating to the representation or to waive the attorney-client privilege or work product immunity whenever Martyn & Fox determines such action will promote the best interests of Client."

6-8. Martyn & Fox advised Widgets, Inc., "If you file that claim with DOD, criminal penalties will follow." Widget's general counsel replied, "That's the board's decision to assess the risk." Two weeks later, Martyn learned that Widgets had hired new counsel, who filed the false statement that Martyn & Fox warned against. What should Martyn do?

6-9. "Now that I'm selling my business," the 85-year-old patriarch tells Fox, "I want you to make arrangements to give half of the proceeds to dear Margaret. I don't know what I'd do without her." Margaret is patriarch's 30-year-old companion. What may (must) Fox do?

Consider: Model Rules 1.0(e), 1.6, 1.13(c), 1.14
RLGL §§ 61-62, 81

In re Pressly

628 A.2d 927 (Vt. 1993)

PER CURIAM.

Respondent Thomas Pressly appeals from a decision of the Professional Conduct Board recommending a public reprimand as discipline for his misconduct in violating [Rules 1.6 (a) and 8.4 (a)].

In 1989, respondent, a member of the Vermont bar since 1975, represented complainant in connection with relief from abuse and divorce proceedings. Complainant informed respondent that her husband had a history [of] alcoholism, battering, and abuse. After a hearing at which she was represented by respondent, complainant was granted a temporary order requiring her husband to refrain from abusing her, and, by stipulation of the parties, temporary custody of the couple's two children with supervised visitation by the father. About a month later, respondent filed a divorce complaint on his client's behalf. The parties negotiated an agreement under which complainant would retain temporary custody of the children and her husband would be allowed unsupervised visitation. Complainant, on respondent's advice, reluctantly agreed to the visitation provision.

At that time, complainant told respondent that she was being harassed by her husband, that his alcoholism was a continuing problem, and that she wanted the children's visits with their father to be supervised. Respondent advised her, however, that there were insufficient legal grounds to require supervised visits. Complainant continued to press respondent to help her prevent her husband from continuing unsupervised visitation, but no motion was filed seeking supervised visitation.

Near the end of August 1989, complainant told respondent her suspicions, based on consultation with a counselor, that her nine-year-old daughter had been sexually abused by the father. According to the counselor, a "yellow flag" went up when she observed several symptoms of abuse. Complainant told respondent her suspicions, the basis for them, and her plan to arrange for a doctor's appointment for the daughter, which she thought might provide needed evidence against the father. She asked that respondent not discuss her suspicions or plans with her husband's lawyer.

In response to opposing counsel's question as to why the wife continued to request supervised visitation and whether sexual abuse was an issue in the case, respondent, notwithstanding his client's request, revealed to him the suspicions of sexual abuse. Respondent then asked the husband's lawyer not to communicate this information to the husband.* The next day, opposing counsel wrote respondent stating, "I mentioned to [my client] the representation [your client] had made to you about their daughter making statements to her counselor about sexual abuse. . . . [They] are totally unfounded and he views them to be a blatant attempt on the part of [your client] to manufacture evidence to keep him away from his children."

Complainant confronted her attorney about the disclosure, and was told by respondent that he provided the information in response to questions from opposing counsel. She discharged respondent and retained new counsel. After the disclosure, complainant perceived that her husband became increasingly uncooperative, which heightened her sense of fear and anxiety and created emotional distress. . . .

In approving a public reprimand, the Board agreed that respondent, although he did not intend to harm his client, knew the disclosure he made was confidential. . . .

Whatever mental state we ascribe to respondent's conduct, he should have known not to disclose his client's confidence. He testified before the panel that

---

* Complainant's testimony indicated that she directed her attorney not to disclose anything about sexual abuse to the husband. No mention was made of the opposing counsel. Although respondent points out this distinction as being contrary to the findings, we fail to understand its significance. The only ethical way respondent could communicate about the case was through the husband's lawyer. [MR 4.2] Respondent could not reasonably expect husband's counsel to keep the wife's confidences unrevealed. Respondent acknowledged that if he had been given similar information by opposing counsel, he would have disclosed it to his client, notwithstanding a request not to do so.

he knew the information was to be held in confidence, but felt that when pressured as to why his client wanted supervised visitation, informing opposing counsel was best. When asked whether he had thought of ending the conversation with counsel by stating that an attorney-client privilege precluded him from revealing anything further, he stated "If I say that, I think I'm letting the cat out of the bag also." He understood that he should not have revealed what his client had requested him to hold in confidence. . . .

The Board gave respondent the benefit of the doubt on whether he knew that his disclosure to opposing counsel would cause his client anguish or jeopardize her case. If respondent did not actually know that his conduct would injure his client—his conduct being negligent because of his good intention (good faith) in making the disclosure—he still knew that his conduct violated a confidence. . . .

The Board found that complainant suffered "emotional distress" as a result of the disclosure, which "heightened her level of fear and anxiety . . . . " As the Board discussed,

Complainant was shocked by this news. She had relied upon respondent to protect the confidentiality of this information. She felt that Respondent had betrayed her trust. . . .

Respondent's conduct was injurious to his client to the extent that his actions caused her emotional distress. We do not find, however, that the disclosure had an adverse impact on the pending litigation although there was a potential for such injury. . . .

We adhere to the Board's recommendation. Respondent's infraction violated a core component of the attorney-client relationship, of which he, as an attorney in practice in this state for approximately sixteen years at the time of the infraction, should have been well aware. Respondent does not contend, nor does the record reflect, that his disclosure was intended or necessary to protect the child. His hope that opposing counsel would not disclose the information to the husband demonstrates naiveté, rather than any intent to simply disregard his client's confidence. Consequently, we agree with the Board that a suspension would be too harsh. On the other hand, a private admonition would unduly depreciate the violation.

The decision of the Professional Conduct Board is affirmed and its recommendation for discipline is approved. Thomas Pressly is publicly reprimanded for violation of [Rule 1.6(a)] by knowingly revealing a confidence of his client.

2. Privilege and Work Product Waiver

Problems

6-10. "Let's get the EPA off our back. Give 'em the damn notes," Clean Energy's general counsel tells Martyn & Fox. Can Martyn & Fox turn over notes of their interviews with Clean Energy employees to the Justice Department as part of a settlement on Clean Energy's behalf ?

6-11. "We're cleaning things up around here," the new CEO declaimed. "You can testify to all conversations with that pathetic old management. The SEC should know how inept my predecessor was." Can Fox testify to privileged communications with the old CEO of the client?

6-12. Martyn & Fox are ready to try the High Energy case against Arthur Touche and five former High Energy directors. Fox's secretary hands him a thick fax with a cover page that says: "To all Defense Counsel. Privileged and Confidential. Summary of Decision Quest's Jury Profile." What should Fox do? What if the fax reveals misconduct by the other side? What if the same document is sent in a plain brown envelope with a note saying, "Knew you'd find this interesting"?

Consider: Model Rules 1.0(e), 1.6, 1.13, 4.4(b)
RLGL §§ 78-81, 91-92

Swidler & Berlin v. United States

524 U.S. 399 (1998)

Chief Justice REHNQUIST delivered the opinion of the Court.

Petitioner, an attorney, made notes of an initial interview with a client shortly before the client's death. The Government, represented by the Office of Independent Counsel, now seeks his notes for use in a criminal investigation. We hold that the notes are protected by the attorney-client privilege.

This dispute arises out of an investigation conducted by the Office of the Independent Counsel into whether various individuals made false statements, obstructed justice, or committed other crimes during investigations of the 1993 dismissal of employees from the White House Travel Office. Vincent W. Foster, Jr., was Deputy White House Counsel when the firings occurred. In July, 1993, Foster met with petitioner James Hamilton, an attorney at petitioner Swidler & Berlin, to seek legal representation concerning possible congressional or other investigations of the firings. During a 2-hour meeting, Hamilton took three pages of handwritten notes. One of the first entries in the notes is the word "Privileged." Nine days later, Foster committed suicide. . . .

The Independent Counsel argues that the attorney-client privilege should not prevent disclosure of confidential communications where the client has died and the information is relevant to a criminal proceeding. There is some authority for this position. One state appellate court, Cohen v. Jenkintown Cab Co., 357 A.2d 689 (Pa. Super. 1976), and the Court of Appeals below have held the privilege may be subject to posthumous exceptions in certain circumstances. In *Cohen*, a civil case, the court recognized that the privilege generally survives death, but concluded that it could make an exception where the interest of justice was compelling and the interest of the client in preserving the confidence was insignificant.

But other than these two decisions, cases addressing the existence of the privilege after death—most involving the testamentary exception—uniformly presume the privilege survives, even if they do not so hold. . . .

The Independent Counsel . . . argues that the exception reflects a policy judgment that the interest in settling estates outweighs any posthumous interest in confidentiality. He then reasons by analogy that in criminal proceedings, the interest in determining whether a crime has been committed should trump client confidentiality, particularly since the financial interests of the estate are not at stake.

But the Independent Counsel's interpretation simply does not square with the caselaw's implicit acceptance of the privilege's survival and with the treatment of testamentary disclosure as an "exception" or an implied "waiver." And the premise of his analogy is incorrect, since cases consistently recognize that the rationale for the testamentary exception is that it furthers the client's intent. There is no reason to suppose as a general matter that grand jury testimony about confidential communications furthers the client's intent.

Commentators on the law also recognize that the general rule is that the attorney-client privilege continues after death. Undoubtedly, as the Independent Counsel emphasizes, various commentators have criticized this rule, urging that the privilege should be abrogated after the client's death where extreme injustice would result, as long as disclosure would not seriously undermine the privilege by deterring client communication. See, e.g., C. Mueller & L. Kirkpatrick, 2 *Federal Evidence* §199, at 380-381 (2d ed. 1994); *Restatement (Third) of the Law Governing Lawyers* § [77], Comment d. But even these critics clearly recognize that established law supports the continuation of the privilege and that a contrary rule would be a modification of the common law.

Despite the scholarly criticism, we think there are weighty reasons that counsel in favor of posthumous application. Knowing that communications will remain confidential even after death encourages the client to communicate fully and frankly with counsel. While the fear of disclosure, and the consequent withholding of information from counsel, may be reduced if disclosure is limited to posthumous disclosure in a criminal context, it seems unreasonable to assume that it vanishes altogether. Clients may be concerned about reputation, civil liability, or possible harm to friends or family. Posthumous disclosure of such communications may be as feared as disclosure during the client's lifetime.

The Independent Counsel suggests, however, that his proposed exception would have little to no effect on the client's willingness to confide in his attorney. He reasons that only clients intending to perjure themselves will be chilled by a rule of disclosure after death, as opposed to truthful clients or those asserting their Fifth Amendment privilege. This is because for the latter group, communications disclosed by the attorney after the client's death purportedly will reveal only information that the client himself would have revealed if alive. . . .

The contention that the attorney is being required to disclose only what the client could have been required to disclose is at odds with the basis for the privilege even during the client's lifetime. In related cases, we have said that the loss of evidence admittedly caused by the privilege is justified in part by the fact that without the privilege, the client may not have made such communications in the first place. This is true of disclosure before and after the client's death. Without assurance of the privilege's posthumous application, the client may very well not have made disclosures to his attorney at all, so the loss of evidence is more apparent than real. In the case at hand, it seems quite plausible that Foster, perhaps already contemplating suicide, may not have sought legal advice from Hamilton if he had not been assured the conversation was privileged.

The Independent Counsel additionally suggests that his proposed exception would have minimal impact if confined to criminal cases, or, as the Court of Appeals suggests, if it is limited to information of substantial importance to a particular criminal case. . . . However, there is no case authority for the proposition that the privilege applies differently in criminal and civil cases. . . . In any event, a client may not know at the time he discloses information to his attorney whether it will later be relevant to a civil or a criminal matter, let alone whether it will be of substantial importance. Balancing *ex post* the importance of the information against client interests, even limited to criminal cases, introduces substantial uncertainty into the privilege's application. For just that reason, we have rejected use of a balancing test in defining the contours of the privilege. *See Upjohn*, 449 U.S. at 393.

In a similar vein, the Independent Counsel argues that existing exceptions to the privilege, such as the crime-fraud exception and the testamentary exception, make the impact of one more exception marginal. However, these exceptions do not demonstrate that the impact of a posthumous exception would be insignificant, and there is little empirical evidence on this point.[4] The established exceptions are consistent with the purposes of the privilege, while a posthumous exception in criminal cases appears at odds with the goals of encouraging full and frank communication and of protecting the client's interests. A "no harm in one more exception" rationale could contribute to the general erosion of the privilege, without reference to common law principles or "reason and experience."

---

4. Empirical evidence on the privilege is limited. Three studies do not reach firm conclusions on whether limiting the privilege would discourage full and frank communication. Alexander, *The Corporate Attorney Client Privilege: A Study of the Participants*, 63 St. John's L. Rev. 191 (1989); Zacharias, *Rethinking Confidentiality*, 74 Iowa L. Rev. 352 (1989); Comment, *Functional Overlap Between the Lawyer and Other Professionals: Its Implications for the Privileged Communications Doctrine*, 71 Yale L.J. 1226 (1962). These articles note that clients are often uninformed or mistaken about the privilege, but suggest that a substantial number of clients and attorneys think the privilege encourages candor. Two of the articles conclude that a substantial number of clients and attorneys think the privilege enhances open communication, Alexander, *supra*, at 244-246, 261, and that the absence of a privilege would be detrimental to such communication, Comment, 71 Yale L.J., *supra*, at 1236. The third article suggests instead that while the privilege is perceived as important to open communication, limited exceptions to the privilege might not discourage such communication, Zacharias, *supra*, at 382, 386. Similarly, relatively few court decisions discuss the impact of the privilege's application after death. This may reflect the general assumption that the privilege survives—if attorneys were required as a matter of practice to testify or provide notes in criminal proceedings, cases discussing that practice would surely exist.

It has been generally, if not universally, accepted, for well over a century, that the attorney-client privilege survives the death of the client in a case such as this. While the arguments against the survival of the privilege are by no means frivolous, they are based in large part on speculation—thoughtful speculation, but speculation nonetheless—as to whether posthumous termination of the privilege would diminish a client's willingness to confide in an attorney. In an area where empirical information would be useful, it is scant and inconclusive.

. . . Interpreted in the light of reason and experience, that body of law requires that the attorney-client privilege prevent disclosure of the notes at issue in this case. The judgment of the Court of Appeals is Reversed.

Justice O'CONNOR, with whom Justice SCALIA and Justice THOMAS join, dissenting.

Although the attorney-client privilege ordinarily will survive the death of the client, I do not agree with the Court that it inevitably precludes disclosure of a deceased client's communications in criminal proceedings. In my view, a criminal defendant's right to exculpatory evidence or a compelling law enforcement need for information may, where the testimony is not available from other sources, override a client's posthumous interest in confidentiality. . . .

I agree that a deceased client may retain a personal, reputational, and economic interest in confidentiality. But, after death, the potential that disclosure will harm the client's interests has been greatly diminished, and the risk that the client will be held criminally liable has abated altogether. . . . The privilege does not "protect[ ] disclosure of the underlying facts by those who communicated with the attorney," *Upjohn, supra,* at 395, and were the client living, prosecutors could grant immunity and compel the relevant testimony. After a client's death, however, if the privilege precludes an attorney from testifying in the client's stead, a complete "loss of crucial information" will often result.

. . . Extreme injustice may occur, for example, where a criminal defendant seeks disclosure of a deceased client's confession to the offense. See State v. Macumber, 544 P.2d 1084, 1086 (Ariz. 1976). . . . Indeed, even petitioner acknowledges that an exception may be appropriate where the constitutional rights of a criminal defendant are at stake. An exception may likewise be warranted in the face of a compelling law enforcement need for the information. . . .

. . . The American Law Institute, moreover, has recently recommended withholding the privilege when the communication "bears on a litigated issue of pivotal significance" and has suggested that courts "balance the interest in confidentiality against any exceptional need for the communication." *Restatement (Third) of the Law Governing Lawyers* § [77], Comment d.

Where the exoneration of an innocent criminal defendant or a compelling law enforcement interest is at stake, the harm of precluding critical evidence that is unavailable by any other means outweighs the potential disincentive to forthright communication. In my view, the cost of silence warrants a narrow exception to the rule that the attorney-client privilege survives the death of the client. . . . Accordingly, I would affirm the judgment of the Court of Appeals. . . .

Merits Incentives, LLC v. The Eighth Judicial District Court of the State of Nevada

262 P.3d 720 (Nev. 2011)

By the Court, HARDESTY, J. . . .

FACTS AND PROCEDURAL HISTORY

Real party in interest Bumble & Bumble, LLC, manufactures and sells high-end salon products. Petitioners Merits Incentives, LLC, Ramon DeSage, and Cadeau Express, Inc. (collectively, petitioners), contracted with Bumble to distribute Bumble's products to the Wynn Hotel in Las Vegas, Nevada. . . . Bumble sued petitioners for breach of contract, fraud, and injunctive relief because of the alleged distribution of Bumble products by petitioners to entities other than those authorized by the parties' contract.

Prior to Bumble's suit against petitioners, Cadeau Express fired one of its logistics engineers, Mohamed Issam Abi Haidar. In a separate action from this one, petitioners sued Haidar, alleging that he stole "confidential and proprietary information and trade secrets." The district court in that case permanently enjoined Haidar from distributing any of the stolen information to petitioners' "customers, manufacturers, suppliers, or business partners."

Receipt of Disk from an Anonymous Third Party

After filing suit against petitioners, Bumble received an anonymous package from Lebanon at its New York headquarters on September 24, 2009. The package contained a disk and a note stating that the package should be forwarded to Bumble's counsel, John Mowbray, an attorney with Fennemore Craig, P.C., a law firm in Las Vegas. On October 15, less than one month later, Mowbray served on petitioners a supplemental NRCP 16.1 mandatory pretrial discovery disclosure (16.1 disclosure). The third of three disclosures identified a "[d]isk received by Bumble and Bumble on September 24, 2009 from an unidentified source." The 16.1 disclosure also included a copy of the disk and a copy of the envelope it arrived in, which bore Lebanese stamps and the phrase "[h]ighly [c]onfidential." On October 19, Bumble served an amended supplemental 16.1 disclosure on petitioners and provided another identical copy of the disk. At the time, petitioners did not inform Bumble that they objected to Bumble having the disk, and they did not file any motions with the court to preclude Bumble's use of the disk or its contents.

On November 6, 2009, Bumble served petitioners with a second request for production (second RFP), listing individually over 500 documents that were contained on the disk and requesting authentication and hard copies of some of the documents. Petitioners did not file their response to the second RFP until January 11, 2010, and generally objected to the request as follows:

> [Petitioners] object to this Request on the grounds that it seeks information and documents already in Bumble's possession, on the grounds that it is overbroad and unduly burdensome, on the grounds that it seeks information protected by the

attorney/client and/or attorney work product privilege, on the grounds that many of the documents on the Disk are corrupted and will not open, and on the grounds that it is vague and ambiguous in that Bumble has not identified the source of the Disk. Subject to the foregoing, [petitioners] state that they have produced all documents they have an obligation to produce in response to this Request. The documents previously produced . . . are generally responsive to this Request.

On January 27, 2010, Bumble used some of the documents from the disk to depose one of petitioners' employees, and petitioners still did not object or argue that the documents were privileged. On May 14, 2010, nearly eight months after Bumble first disclosed its receipt of the disk, petitioners first objected to Bumble's use and possession of the documents on the disk through a motion to the district court.

Petitioners' Motions Regarding the Disk

Petitioners filed a motion with the district court for the dismissal of Bumble's case with prejudice or, in the alternative, a motion to prohibit Bumble's use of misappropriated confidential and privileged documents and for disqualification of Bumble's counsel. In the motion, petitioners alleged that Mowbray received the disk from Haidar in violation of the injunction petitioners had obtained against him. Petitioners also alleged that Bumble failed to notify them for over eight months that it had petitioners' confidential and privileged documents, and that Bumble used that information "to gain a tactical advantage in [the] litigation." Bumble opposed the motion, arguing that it had produced the disk through the normal course of discovery. Bumble included with its response an expert report supporting its claim that Mowbray did not violate any of Nevada's ethical rules and that disqualification was not warranted. Petitioners replied and included a rebuttal expert report. . . .

In its findings of fact, which neither side challenges, the district court stated that, "[o]n or about September 24, 2009, [Bumble] received . . . an unsolicited package from an anonymous source." The district court also found that Bumble and its counsel "conspicuously set forth" their receipt of the disk in the NRCP 16.1 disclosure, and that "[n]either [Bumble] nor its counsel had actual knowledge of the injunction [petitioners had against Haidar]." . . .

DISCUSSION . . .

[W]e take this opportunity to adopt a notification requirement to apply to situations where an attorney receives documents or evidence from an anonymous source or from a third party unrelated to the litigation. Additionally, we also set forth factors for district courts to consider in determining whether an attorney who reviews privileged information under such circumstances should be disqualified. . . .

Mowbray Did Not Violate Any Ethical Duties . . .

At the outset, we note that both parties agree that RPC 4.4(b), which provides that "[a] lawyer who receives a document relating to the representation of the lawyer's client and knows or reasonably should know that the document was inadvertently sent shall promptly notify the sender," is not applicable here. We also agree that RPC 4.4(b) is not applicable, as written, because the disk was not inadvertently sent to Bumble and Mowbray.[3]

Petitioners' Caselaw Is Not Persuasive . . .

In Burt Hill, Inc. v. Hassan, an attorney claimed to have received documents anonymously but did not sign an affidavit to that effect, and the court found the claimed lack of knowledge regarding the delivery of the documents appeared "highly suspicious." 2010 U.S. Dist. LEXIS 7492 (W.D. Pa. 2010). In the instant case, Mowbray signed an affidavit in which he declared that he did not know the source of the disk, he produced the envelope he received the disk in, and the district court found that the disk was sent anonymously.

Three other cases petitioners cite involve the attorney's client providing the confidential documents to the attorney, rather than the attorney receiving the documents from an anonymous third party, and the attorney failing to immediately notify opposing counsel of the client's misconduct. See Maldonado v. New Jersey, 225 F.R.D. 120, 125-26 (D.N.J. 2004) (attorney's client obtained confidential letter from opposing party to its counsel, gave the letter to his attorney, and attorney did not disclose or return the document); In re Marketing Investors Corp., 80 S.W.3d 44, 46-47 (Tex. App. 1998) (attorney's client took documents from opposing party in violation of employment agreement and gave to his attorney who kept copies and refused to agree not to use documents despite a protective order); Castellano v. Winthrop, 27 So. 3d 134, 135 (Fla. Dist. Ct. App. 2010) (attorney's client illegally obtained opposing party's flash drive and attorney used information contained on it to file a motion to vacate a final order before notifying opposing counsel of receipt). . . .

In all of petitioners' cited cases discussing RPC 4.4(a) or 8.4(d), the courts found that the attorneys either played some part in obtaining an opposing party's documents or were complicit in actions used to wrongfully obtain those documents. Similarly, the emphasized language in RPC 4.4(a) and 8.4(d) demonstrates that the attorney must take some type of affirmative action, either by employing a method of obtaining evidence or engaging in certain conduct, to violate either of those rules. Mowbray did not do that here, as the district court's unchallenged findings of fact stated that the disk was sent anonymously and unsolicited, and that Mowbray had no knowledge of the injunction against Haidar.

An Attorney's Responsibility upon Receiving Documents or Evidence from an Anonymous Source or from a Third Party Unrelated to the Litigation

. . . Nevada does not have any ethical rules that govern the specific issue presented in this petition. It appears, however, that the district court applied RPC

---

3. . . . Model Rules of Prof'l Conduct R. 4.4 cmt. 2 (2007). [*See also*] ABA Comm. on Ethics and Prof'l Responsibility, Formal Op. 06-440 (2006).

4.4(b) by analogy, which requires an attorney to notify the sender if he or she receives documents inadvertently, and concluded that Mowbray met his ethical duties because he promptly notified petitioners of his receipt of the disk through an NRCP 16.1 disclosure.

We agree with the district court's reasoning; therefore, we now adopt a notification requirement to apply in situations where an attorney receives documents anonymously or from a third party unrelated to the litigation. Thus, an attorney who receives documents regarding a case from an anonymous source must promptly notify opposing counsel, or risk being in violation of his or her ethical duties and/or being disqualified as counsel. Notification must adequately put opposing counsel on notice that the documents were not received in the normal course of discovery and describe, with particularity, the facts and circumstances that explain how the documents or evidence came into counsel's or his or her client's possession.[7] In this case, Mowbray did just that through an NRCP 16.1 disclosure. Therefore, the district court correctly concluded that Mowbray fulfilled his ethical duties. . . .

The determination that Mowbray fulfilled his ethical duties does not end our inquiry concerning disqualification. The district court found that one document on the disk, a draft affidavit, was protected by the attorney–client privilege. . . . This court has not previously determined what factors a district court should consider when presented with a motion to disqualify an attorney who has received an opposing party's privileged information, yet played no part in obtaining the information.

The Supreme Court of Texas resolved a similar issue in In re Meador, 968 S.W.2d 346 (Tex. 1998). In that case, the defendant filed suit against a company and some of its employees for various claims, including allegations of sexual harassment. Another company employee took and copied certain documents from the company that were potentially relevant to the litigation. That employee later contacted the defendant because she was considering filing her own lawsuit against the company, and the defendant referred the employee to her attorney. When the employee met with the attorney, she gave him the documents she had copied. Later in the litigation, the company claimed the documents were privileged, and the trial court instructed defendant's counsel that the documents could not be used in the litigation and all copies had to be returned to the company. The district court declined, however, to disqualify the defendant's counsel, and the company appealed that decision. . . .

---

7. Although we do not adopt a cease, notify, and return rule, that does not prevent a party whose privileged information has been obtained by the opposing party from seeking the return of that information. If petitioners believed that Mowbray was acting unethically or possessed their privileged information, they should have immediately informed Mowbray of their concerns and sought return of the disk and any documents Mowbray retrieved from the disk. If Mowbray did not comply with their request, they could have sought relief from the district court in a timely manner. Despite petitioners' claim that they were in the midst of changing counsel, petitioners' counsel may have had an independent responsibility to promptly object to the use of documents provided by an anonymous source. See RPC 1.3.

The court went on to identify a nonexhaustive list of factors to aid trial courts in determining whether disqualification is appropriate:

1) [W]hether the attorney knew or should have known that the material was privileged;

2) the promptness with which the attorney notifies the opposing side that he or she has received its privileged information;

3) the extent to which the attorney reviews and digests the privileged information;

4) the significance of the privileged information; i.e., the extent to which its disclosure may prejudice the movant's claim or defense, and the extent to which return of the documents will mitigate that prejudice;

5) the extent to which movant may be at fault for the unauthorized disclosure; [and]

6) the extent to which the nonmovant will suffer prejudice from the disqualification of his or her attorney.

We now adopt these factors, and we further agree with the *Meador* court that, in exercising its judicial discretion, the district courts "must consider all the facts and circumstances to determine whether the interests of justice require disqualification." . . .

In concluding that Mowbray met his ethical duties, the district court stated:

In fact, it appears to the Court that, instead of lying in wait with the documents, [Mowbray] went out of [his] way to point out that [he] had received them and to let Defendants ascertain their provenance, giving every opportunity for Defendants to register an objection and demand return and non-use.

Additionally, the second RFP did not list the draft affidavit as one of the documents, and Mowbray filed an affidavit with the court stating that he did not review any such document. The district court did not make any findings that contradicted Mowbray's assertion that he never reviewed the document.

Applying the above factors, we agree with the district court's order denying disqualification. . . . The district court found that most of the documents on the disk were not privileged, and Mowbray stated he did not review the document the court determined was privileged. Mowbray sent petitioners' counsel a supplemental NRCP 16.1 disclosure one month after Bumble received the disk at its headquarters. Although the privileged document, a draft affidavit, may have had some significance, the district court prohibited its use, and petitioners failed to show any prejudice resulting from the affidavit's disclosure. Finally, Bumble would suffer prejudice if it had to retain new counsel because the litigation involves complex contracts and numerous entities.

Although we conclude that Mowbray's initial supplemental NRCP 16.1 disclosure of the disk was an adequate method of notification, he did not end there with his attempts to promptly notify petitioners of his receipt of the disk. Four days later, Mowbray filed an amended supplemental 16.1 disclosure with another copy of the envelope the disk arrived in. Additionally, approximately one month later, Mowbray propounded a second RFP that included a request spanning 22 pages and individually listing 503 of the documents contained on the disk. Thus, these additional steps taken by Mowbray further indicate that he was not trying to deceive petitioners or conceal his receipt of the disk from them. Therefore, we conclude that the district court did not abuse its discretion by denying petitioners' motion to disqualify Mowbray and his law firm. . . .

The Bounds of the Law:
Court Orders

Courts order all kinds of conduct to carry out their duties.[1] *Hughes, Dean, Vioxx, Swidler & Berlin,* and *Merits Incentives* in this chapter illustrate this bound of the law or legal limit that applies to both lawyers and clients. Each of these cases implicitly or explicitly recognized a court's inherent power to order conduct, such as disclosures consistent with the confines of the attorney-client privilege, or disqualification of a lawyer.[2] In Chapter 3, *Bothwell* discussed the inherent power of a court to order a lawyer to provide uncompensated representation. Lawyers must be aware of the importance of these court orders to avoid both contempt sanctions and professional discipline.[3]

The Model Rules

The Model Rules of Professional Conduct recognize the power of court orders in several key provisions. Most prominent are Model Rule 1.6(b)(6), which allows lawyers to disclose confidential information where required by a court order, and Model Rule 3.4(c), which states the lawyer's basic obligation to obey the rules of tribunals, including court orders.

These provisions recognize and integrate the legal limit of a court order into the requirement of a professional obligation.[4] They also presume that lawyers have a clear fiduciary and procedural obligation to properly raise and protect client interests. For example, lawyers have an obligation to assert the attorney-client privilege on a client's or former client's behalf whenever a nonfrivolous claim against disclosure or limitation of the scope of disclosure can be made.[5] Failure

---

1. *See* RLGL § 105. A court's inherent power does not extend to private arbitration misconduct. Positive Software Solutions Inc., v. New Century Mortg. Corp., 619 F.3d 458 (5th Cir. 2010).

2. The Law Governing Lawyers: *Losing a Client by Disqualification or Injunction, infra* p. 307.

3. In an extreme case, a court may dismiss an action for failure to comply with a court order. *See, e.g.,* Abner v. Scott Mem'l. Hosp., 634 F.3d 962 (7th Cir. 2011) (appeal may be dismissed for lawyer's untruthful certification that his brief met the word limit); Salmeron v. Enterprise Recovery Systems, Inc., 579 F.3d 787 (7th Cir. 2009) (dismissal of client's lawsuit justified by lawyer's leaking of opponent's sensitive document in contravention of court order).

4. *E.g.,* Stark Cnty. Bar Assn. v. Ake, 855 N.E.2d 1206 (Ohio 2006) (lawyer who violated several court orders during his own divorce suspended for six months); Herschfeld v. Super. Ct., 908 P.2d 22 (Ariz. 1995) (lawyer who continued to verbally assault a party opponent after being admonished to stop by the judge convicted of criminal contempt).

5. MR 1.6, Comment [13]; RLGL § 86; ABA Formal Op. 94-385.

to do so could result in legally effective waiver of the privilege by the lawyer, who a court will later characterize as acting with apparent authority as the client's agent.[6] Any harm that results from such a nonconsensual disclosure could then subject the lawyer to claims of malpractice or breach of fiduciary duty.[7]

The Contempt Power

Once a court has declared that confidential information is not privileged, the lawyer either must comply with the court order to disclose, or appeal the court's decision.[8] The clients and lawyers in *Hughes, Upjohn, Vioxx,* and *Swidler & Berlin* elected to raise claims about the privilege on appeal. Except for *Hughes,* the lawyers were completely or somewhat successful in convincing courts that the information was privileged, which resulted in reversal of the lower court's order to disclose or remand for further factual findings about the matter.

The lawyer in *Hughes* did not succeed on appeal, which meant that any further failure to disclose his client's identity would result in the enforcement of the trial court's contempt order. Judges use contempt sanctions to coerce or punish a lawyer or litigant.[9] Civil contempt occurs when a judge orders fines or imprisonment to accrue until the person in contempt complies with the court order.[10] Criminal contempt punishes refusal to comply and requires elaborate procedural guarantees, similar to those in criminal trials.[11] Occasionally, a lawyer will risk contempt by violating a court order for the express purpose of challenging its validity, scope, or meaning.[12] Usually this is done only if no other procedural avenue of appeal is open to the client.[13] In situations where procedural

---

6. RLGL § 77.

7. RLGL § 63, Comment b.

8. RLGL § 105, Comment d; Mohawk Industries, Inc. v. Carpenter, 130 S. Ct. 599 (2009) (orders to disclose are not immediately appealable under the collateral order doctrine because adverse ruling can be reviewed after final judgment).

9. *E.g.,* United States v. Moncier, 571 F.3d 593 (6th Cir. 2009) (lawyer charged with criminal contempt for obstructing judge's questioning of his client); In re Moncier, 329 Fed. Appx. 636 (2009) (lawyer suspended from practice before district court for seven years for the same conduct).

10. Courts also can sanction lawyers who use obstructive tactics to assist clients in violating court orders. *See, e.g.,* Guardianship of Melissa W., 18 Cal. Rptr. 2d 42 (Cal. App. 2002) (lawyer who helped clients evade custody order caused dismissal of client's appeal, was sanctioned $13,004 for opposing party's attorney's fees, and referred to the bar for further investigation).

11. Intl. Union, UMWA v. Bagwell, 512 U.S. 821 (1994). Criminal contempt proceeding requires proof beyond a reasonable doubt, a special prosecutor, and a jury trial for any imprisonment beyond six months. *See, e.g.,* Scialdone v. Commonwealth, 689 S.E.2d 716 (Va. 2010) (lawyer accused of offering a falsified exhibit cannot be convicted of contempt in a summary proceeding).

12. RLGL § 94, Comment e. Such a claim may be raised about the scope of the attorney-client privilege, the work product doctrine, or other evidentiary claims, such as irrelevancy or hearsay. *Id.* at § 63, Comment b. *See also* In re Grand Jury, 2012 U.S. App. LEXIS 10558 (3d Cir.) (court's order refusing to quash a grand jury subpoena for corporate documents not appealable without first suffering contempt sanctions).

13. *E.g.,* Maness v. Meyers, 419 U.S. 449 (1975) (lawyer who advised a client to refuse to obey a court order to testify to trigger immediate appellate review of the issue and to protect the client's Fifth Amendment rights could not be punished where procedural rules provided no other means to

rules provide for appeal, however, lawyers have been both held in contempt and disciplined for failing to obey the court order or properly challenging it.[14]

Court orders legally limit a lawyer's advocacy on behalf of a client, but their availability also offers lawyers the opportunity to challenge otherwise unassailable legal rules. For example, lawyers with nonfrivolous legal reasons to seek communication with jurors or represented persons may seek court approval to protect themselves against both contempt and disciplinary action.[15]

Court Orders and Client Advocacy

The lawyers in the cases discussed in this note understood that court orders, combined with a court's contempt power, could limit their duties to a client. At the same time, they vigorously advocated (often successfully) for legal recognition of their client's interests within and up to this limit of the law.

---

test the validity of the trial court's ruling and the lawyer believed in good faith that disclosure of the information tended to incriminate the client).

14. *E.g.*, Fla. Bar v. Gersten, 707 So. 2d 711 (Fla. 1998) (lawyer who refused to obey a court order that required him to give a sworn statement suspended); Disc. Action Against Giberson, 581 N.W.2d 351 (Minn. 1998) (lawyer who refused to pay court-ordered child support indefinitely suspended); Davis v. Goodson, 635 S.W.2d 226 (Ark. 1982) (contempt upheld against a lawyer who advised a client in open court to disregard a judge's order).

15. MR 3.5(b)-(c), 4.2.

Chapter 7

Confidentiality Exceptions: Physical and Financial Injury

Exceptions to confidentiality have coexisted with the obligation since its inception. If the rationales that support the obligation of confidentiality make sense, then the same policies should justify exceptions to the obligation. In other words, if preserving confidentiality promotes efficient functioning of the legal system, exceptions can be justified to promote effective operation of the system of justice. Similarly, if preserving client confidences is deemed important to promote trust or privacy in the client-lawyer relationship, exceptions can be justified where preserving client confidences creates a breach of trust or fosters misuse of the relationship to violate other legal norms. As you work your way through the next two chapters, consider these justifications for each exception. Consider further whether the addition of new exceptions over time has watered down the original rationales for confidentiality.

A. Physical Harm

Confidentiality seems less important when another human imperative, such as life itself, is at stake. Here, a utilitarian would argue that lawyers guarantee confidentiality in part to encourage clients to blow off steam, which affords lawyers an opportunity to counsel clients to abstain from vigilante justice. Occasionally this goal fails, either because the lawyer cannot talk the client out of dangerous behavior, or because the client describes the behavior of someone with whom the lawyer has no relationship. In those situations, the lawyer is justified in disclosing client confidences to promote the greater good of preserving human life and preventing injurious behavior. John Stuart Mill, for example, argued that "[a]s soon as any part of a person's conduct affects prejudicially the interests of others, society has jurisdiction over it."[1] The deontologist would argue that a client who wishes to use the relationship with her lawyer to harm someone else is

---

1. John Stuart Mill, *On Liberty*, Chap. IV (1859).

misusing a trusting relationship and therefore forfeits the client's right to trust or privacy.

1. Fiduciary Duty

Problems

7-1.   Martyn, visiting the assembly plant on an employment discrimination matter, has her meeting with the plant superintendent interrupted when an employee barges in and exclaims, "I just discovered arsenic drums in back of that old warehouse we bought last year." Plant superintendent responds, "Don't bother me. You know we've already exhausted our cleanup funds for the year." He then turns to Martyn, "Now, where were we?" How should Martyn respond?

7-2.   Client, in the course of estate planning, tells Fox that she is terminally ill. "I've talked to the folks at the Hemlock Society. As soon as I sign these papers, they're going to give me death with dignity." What should Fox do?

7-3.   A true nightmare: Our client is being sued by plaintiff for whiplash from a car accident. Our doctor's exam of the plaintiff indicates plaintiff has a life-threatening aneurysm. Neither plaintiff nor his lawyer has any idea of his condition, and the insurance company that hired us instructs that we not disclose any of this to anyone. What should Martyn & Fox do?

7-4.   May (must) Martyn & Fox disclose or testify that our client has committed a crime for which another person is now serving time? What if the innocent person is on death row? Does it matter if the client has died?

> **Consider: Model Rule 1.6(b)(1)**
> **RLGL § 66**

Hawkins v. King County

602 P.2d 361 (Wash. App. 1979)

SWANSON, A.C.J.

Michael Hawkins, acting through his guardian ad litem, and his mother Frances M. Hawkins, appeal from a summary judgment dismissing attorney Richard Sanders from an action sounding in tort. Appellants contend Sanders, court appointed defense attorney for Michael Hawkins, was negligent and committed malpractice by failing to divulge information regarding his client's mental state at a bail hearing. We find no error and affirm.

On July 1, 1975, Michael Hawkins was booked for possession of marijuana. Following his court appointment as Hawkins' defense counsel on July 3, 1975, Richard Sanders conferred with Hawkins for about 45 minutes, at which time Hawkins expressed the desire to be released from jail.

Also on July 3, 1975, Sanders talked with Palmer Smith, an attorney employed by Hawkins' mother Frances Hawkins, to assist in having Hawkins either hospitalized or civilly committed. Smith told Sanders then, and reiterated by letter, that Hawkins was mentally ill and dangerous. On July 8, 1975, Dr. Elwood Jones, a psychiatrist, telephoned and wrote Sanders and averred Hawkins was mentally ill and of danger to himself and others and should not be released from custody. Sanders represented that he intended to comply with his client's request for freedom.

On July 9, 1975, a district judge released Hawkins on a personal surety bond. At the bail hearing, Sanders did not volunteer any information regarding Hawkins' alleged illness or dangerousness, nor were any questions in that vein directed to him either by the judge or the prosecutor. Smith, Jones, and Mrs. Hawkins were informed of Hawkins' release, and all parties later met on two occasions in a counseling environment.

On July 17, 1975, about 8 days after his release, Michael Hawkins assaulted his mother and attempted suicide by jumping off a bridge, causing injuries resulting in the amputation of both legs. The Hawkinses commenced an action for damages against King County, the State of Washington, Community Psychiatric Clinic, Inc., and one of its employees on August 16, 1976, and amended the suit on November 30, 1977, to name Sanders a party defendant. Sanders filed a motion to dismiss for failure to state a claim. On June 16, 1978, the trial court granted Sanders' motion. . . .

On appeal, the Hawkinses essentially present two arguments: First, that by his failure at the bail hearing to disclose the information he possessed regarding Michael Hawkins' mental state, defense counsel Sanders subjected himself to liability for malpractice, as court rules and the Code of Professional Responsibility mandate such disclosure on ethical and legal grounds. Second, that by the same omission Sanders negligently violated a common-law duty to warn foreseeable victims of an individual he knew to be potentially dangerous to himself and others. *See* Tarasoff v. Regents of Univ. of Cal., 551 P.2d 334 (Cal. 1976).

Sanders asserts the Hawkinses have failed to demonstrate that he breached any duty owed to them. . . .

[The court examines the court rules that govern bail hearings and finds that they do not require a defense lawyer to disclose "information damaging to his client's expressed desire to be released from custody."]

We believe that the duty of counsel to be loyal to his client and to represent zealously his client's interests overrides the nebulous and unsupported theory that our rules and ethical code mandate disclosure of information which counsel considers detrimental to his client's stated interest. Because disclosure is not "required by law," appellants' theory of liability on the basis of ethical or court rule violations fails for lack of substance.

Turning then to the Hawkinses' theory of a common-law duty to warn or disclose, we note common-law support for the precept that attorneys must, upon learning that a client plans an assault or other violent crime, warn foreseeable victims. *See* Tarasoff v. Regents of Univ. of Cal., *supra*. . . . The difficulty lies in framing a rule that will balance properly "the public interest and safety from violent attack" against the public interest in securing proper resolution of legal disputes without compromising a defendant's right to a loyal and zealous defense. We are persuaded by the position advanced by amicus "that the obligation to warn, when confidentiality would be compromised to the client's detriment, must be permissive at most, unless it appears beyond a reasonable doubt that the client has formed a firm intention to inflict serious personal injuries on an unknowing third person."

Because appellants rely to a great extent upon *Tarasoff* in arguing a common-law duty to disclose, we will demonstrate that the *Tarasoff* decision is inapposite even though the facts are equally atypical and tragic. Tatiana Tarasoff was killed by one Prosenjit Poddar. The victim's parents alleged that 2 months earlier Poddar confided his intention to kill Tatiana to a defendant, Dr. Moore, a psychologist employed by the University of California. After a brief detention of Poddar by the police at Moore's request, Poddar was released pursuant to order of Dr. Moore's superior. No one warned Tatiana of her peril. The plaintiffs claimed the defendant psychologists had a duty to warn foreseeable victims. Defendants denied owing any duty of reasonable care to Tatiana. . . . The Supreme Court of California concluded that the complaint could be amended to state a cause of action against the psychologists by asserting that they had or should have determined Poddar presented a serious danger to Tatiana, pursuant to the standards of their profession, but had failed to exercise reasonable care for her safety.

In *Tarasoff*, the defendant psychologists had first-hand knowledge of Poddar's homicidal intention and knew it to be directed towards Tatiana Tarasoff, who was wholly unaware of her danger. The knowledge of the defendants in *Tarasoff* was gained from statements made to them in the course of treatment and not from statements transmitted by others. Further, the California court in *Tarasoff* did not establish a new duty to warn, but only held that psychologists must exercise such reasonable skill, knowledge, and care possessed and exercised by members of their profession under similar circumstances.

In the instant case, Michael Hawkins' potential victims, his mother and sister, knew he might be dangerous and that he had been released from confinement, contrary to Tatiana Tarasoff's ignorance of any risk of harm. Thus, no duty befell Sanders to warn Frances Hawkins of a risk of which she was already fully cognizant. Further, it must not be overlooked that Sanders received no information that Hawkins planned to assault anyone, only that he was mentally ill and likely to be dangerous to himself and others. That Sanders received no information directly from Michael Hawkins is the final distinction between the two cases.

The common-law duty to volunteer information about a client to a court considering pretrial release must be limited to situations where information gained convinces counsel that his client intends to commit a crime or inflict injury upon unknowing third persons. Such a duty cannot be extended to the facts before us. . . .

Spaulding v. Zimmerman

116 N.W.2d 704 (Minn. 1962)

THOMAS GALLAGHER, J.

Appeal from an order of the District Court of Douglas County vacating and setting aside a prior order of such court dated May 8, 1957, approving a settlement made on behalf of David Spaulding on March 5, 1957, at which time he was a minor of the age of 20 years; and in connection therewith, vacating and setting aside releases executed by him and his parents, a stipulation of dismissal, an order for dismissal with prejudice, and a judgment entered pursuant thereto.

The prior action was brought against defendants by Theodore Spaulding, as father and natural guardian of David Spaulding, for injuries sustained by David in an automobile accident, arising out of a collision which occurred August 24, 1956, between an automobile driven by John Zimmerman, in which David was a passenger, and one owned by John Ledermann and driven by Florian Ledermann.

On appeal defendants contend that the court was without jurisdiction to vacate the settlement solely because their counsel then possessed information, unknown to plaintiff herein, that at the time he was suffering from an aorta aneurysm which may have resulted from the accident, because (1) no mutual mistake of fact was involved; (2) no duty rested upon them to disclose information to plaintiff which they could assume had been disclosed to him by his own physicians; (3) insurance limitations as well as physical injuries formed the basis for the settlement; and (4) plaintiff's motion to vacate the order for settlement and to set aside the releases was barred by the limitations provided in Rule 60.02 of Rules of Civil Procedure.[1]

After the accident, David's injuries were diagnosed by his family physician, Dr. James H. Cain, as a severe crushing injury of the chest with multiple rib fractures; a severe cerebral concussion, probably with petechial hemorrhages of the brain; and bilateral fractures of the clavicles. At Dr. Cain's suggestion, on January 3, 1957, David was examined by Dr. John F. Pohl, an orthopedic specialist, who made X-ray studies of his chest. Dr. Pohl's detailed report of this examination included the following:

---

1. Rule 60.02 of Rules of Civ. Proc. provides in part: "On motion . . . the court may relieve a party . . . from a final . . . order, or proceeding for the following reasons: (1) Mistake, inadvertence, surprise, or excusable neglect; (2) newly discovered evidence which by due diligence could not have been discovered in time to move for a new trial under Rule 59.03; (3) fraud (whether . . . intrinsic or extrinsic), misrepresentation, or other misconduct of an adverse party; . . . or (6) any other reason justifying relief from the operation of the judgment. The motion shall be made within a reasonable time, and for reasons (1), (2), and (3) not more than one year after the judgment, order, or proceeding was entered or taken. . . . This rule does not limit the power of a court to entertain an independent action to relieve a party from a judgment, order, or proceeding, . . . or to set aside a judgment for fraud upon the court."

" . . . The lung fields are clear. The heart and aorta are normal."

Nothing in such report indicated the aorta aneurysm with which David was then suffering. On March 1, 1957, at the suggestion of Dr. Pohl, David was examined from a neurological viewpoint by Dr. Paul S. Blake, and in the report of this examination there was no finding of the aorta aneurysm.

In the meantime, on February 22, 1957, at defendants' request, David was examined by Dr. Hewitt Hannah, a neurologist. On February 26, 1957, the latter reported to Messrs. Field, Arvesen & Donoho, attorneys for defendant John Zimmerman, as follows:

"The one feature of the case which bothers me more than any other part of the case is the fact that this boy of 20 years of age has an aneurysm, which means a dilatation of the aorta and the arch of the aorta. Whether this came out of this accident I cannot say with any degree of certainty and I have discussed it with the Roentgenologist and a couple of Internists. . . . Of course an aneurysm or dilatation of the aorta in a boy of this age is a serious matter as far as his life. This aneurysm may dilate further and it might rupture with further dilatation and this would cause his death.

"It would be interesting also to know whether the X-ray of his lungs, taken immediately following the accident, shows this dilatation or not. If it was not present immediately following the accident and is now present, then we could be sure that it came out of the accident."

Prior to the negotiations for settlement, the contents of the above report were made known to counsel for defendants Florian and John Ledermann.

The case was called for trial on March 4, 1957, at which time the respective parties and their counsel possessed such information as to David's physical condition as was revealed to them by their respective medical examiners as above described. It is thus apparent that neither David nor his father, the nominal plaintiff in the prior action, was then aware that David was suffering the aorta aneurysm but on the contrary believed that he was recovering from the injuries sustained in the accident.

On the following day an agreement for settlement was reached wherein, in consideration of the payment of $6,500, David and his father agreed to settle in full for all claims arising out of the accident.

Richard S. Roberts, counsel for David, thereafter presented to the court a petition for approval of the settlement, wherein David's injuries were described as:

". . . severe crushing of the chest, with multiple rib fractures, severe cerebral concussion, with petechial hemorrhages of the brain, bilateral fractures of the clavicles."

Attached to the petition were affidavits of David's physicians, Drs. James H. Cain and Paul S. Blake, wherein they set forth the same diagnoses they had made upon completion of their respective examinations of David as above described. At no time was there information disclosed to the court that David was then suffering from an aorta aneurysm which may have been the result of the accident. Based upon the petition for settlement and such affidavits of Drs. Cain and Blake, the court on May 8, 1957, made its order approving the settlement.

Early in 1959, David was required by the army reserve, of which he was a member, to have a physical checkup. For this, he again engaged the services of Dr. Cain. In this checkup, the latter discovered the aorta aneurysm. He then reexamined the X rays which had been taken shortly after the accident and at this time discovered that they disclosed the beginning of the process which produced the aneurysm. He promptly sent David to Dr. Jerome Grismer for an examination and opinion. The latter confirmed the finding of the aorta aneurysm and recommended immediate surgery therefor. This was performed by him at Mount Sinai Hospital in Minneapolis on March 10, 1959.

Shortly thereafter, David, having attained his majority, instituted the present action for additional damages due to the more serious injuries including the aorta aneurysm which he alleges proximately resulted from the accident. . . . In a memorandum made a part of the order vacating the settlement, the court stated:

> "The facts material to a determination of the motion are without substantial dispute. . . .
>
> ". . . the Court finds that although the aneurysm now existing is causally related to the accident, such finding is for the purpose of the motions only and is based solely upon the opinion expressed by Dr. Cain (Exhibit 'F'), which, so far as the Court can find from the numerous affidavits and statements of fact by counsel, stands without dispute.
>
> "The mistake concerning the existence of the aneurysm was not mutual. For reasons which do not appear, plaintiff's doctor failed to ascertain its existence. By reason of the failure of plaintiff's counsel to use available rules of discovery, plaintiff's doctor and all his representatives did not learn that defendants and their agents knew of its existence and possible serious consequences. Except for the character of the concealment in the light of plaintiff's minority, the Court would, I believe, be justified in denying plaintiff's motion to vacate, leaving him to whatever questionable remedy he may have against his doctor and against his lawyer. . . .
>
> "There is no doubt of the good faith of both defendants' counsel. There is no doubt that during the course of the negotiations, when the parties were in an adversary relationship, no rule required or duty rested upon defendants or their representatives to disclose this knowledge. However, once the agreement to settle was reached, it is difficult to characterize the parties' relationship as adverse. At this point all parties were interested in securing Court approval. . . .
>
> "When the adversary nature of the negotiations concluded in a settlement, the procedure took on the posture of a joint application to the Court, at least so far as the facts upon which the Court could and must approve settlement is concerned. It is here that the true nature of the concealment appears, and defendants' failure to act affirmatively, after having been given a copy of the application for approval,

can only be defendants' decision to take a calculated risk that the settlement would be final. . . .

"To hold that the concealment was not of such character as to result in an unconscionable advantage over plaintiff's ignorance or mistake, would be to penalize innocence and incompetence and reward less than full performance of an officer of the Court's duty to make full disclosure to the Court when applying for approval in minor settlement proceedings."

1. The principles applicable to the court's authority to vacate settlements made on behalf of minors and approved by it appear well established. With reference thereto, we have held that the court in its discretion may vacate such a settlement, even though it is not induced by fraud or bad faith, where it is shown that in the accident the minor sustained separate and distinct injuries which were not known or considered by the court at the time settlement was approved, and even though the releases furnished therein purported to cover both known and unknown injuries resulting from the accident. The court may vacate such a settlement for mistake even though the mistake was not mutual in the sense that both parties were similarly mistaken as to the nature and extent of the minor's injuries, but where it is shown that one of the parties had additional knowledge with respect thereto and was aware that neither the court nor the adversary party possessed such knowledge when the settlement was approved.

2. From the foregoing it is clear that in the instant case the court did not abuse its discretion in setting aside the settlement which it had approved on plaintiff's behalf while he was still a minor. It is undisputed that neither he nor his counsel nor his medical attendants were aware that at the time settlement was made he was suffering from an aorta aneurysm which may have resulted from the accident. The seriousness of this disability is indicated by Dr. Hannah's report indicating the imminent danger of death therefrom. This was known by counsel for both defendants but was not disclosed to the court at the time it was petitioned to approve the settlement. While no canon of ethics or legal obligation may have required them to inform plaintiff or his counsel with respect thereto, or to advise the court therein, it did become obvious to them at the time that the settlement then made did not contemplate or take into consideration the disability described. This fact opened the way for the court to later exercise its discretion in vacating the settlement and under the circumstances described we cannot say that there was any abuse of discretion on the part of the court in so doing under Rule 60.02(6) of Rules of Civil Procedure. . . . Affirmed.

2. Privilege and Work Product: Client Crime or Fraud

Problem

7-5. May (must) Martyn & Fox disclose that Husband just stomped out of Fox's office, screaming, "I'm going to kill her rather than give her the Cape Cod house"? What if Dad tells Fox that's what Son just told Dad in a phone call, not ten minutes ago? What if Fox calls the police, and then is subpoenaed to testify at a grand jury proceeding considering whether to indict Dad? Son?

Consider: Model Rule 1.6(b)(1)
RLGL §§ 82, 93

Purcell v. District Attorney for the Suffolk District
676 N.E.2d 436 (Mass. 1997)

WILKINS, C.J.

On June 21, 1994, Joseph Tyree, who had received a court order to vacate his apartment in the Allston section of Boston, consulted the plaintiff, Jeffrey W. Purcell, an attorney employed by Greater Boston Legal Services, which provides representation to low income individuals in civil matters. Tyree had recently been discharged as a maintenance man at the apartment building in which his apartment was located. On the day that Tyree consulted Purcell, Purcell decided, after extensive deliberation, that he should advise appropriate authorities that Tyree might engage in conduct harmful to others. He told a Boston police lieutenant that Tyree had made threats to burn the apartment building.

The next day, constables, accompanied by Boston police officers, went to evict Tyree. At the apartment building, they found incendiary materials, containers of gasoline, and several bottles with wicks attached. Smoke detectors had been disconnected, and gasoline had been poured on a hallway floor. Tyree was arrested and later indicted for attempted arson of a building.

In August, 1995, the district attorney for the Suffolk district subpoenaed Purcell to testify concerning the conversation Purcell had had with Tyree on June 21, 1994. A Superior Court judge granted Purcell's motion to quash the subpoena. The trial ended in a mistrial because the jury were unable to reach a verdict.

The Commonwealth decided to try Tyree again and once more sought Purcell's testimony. Another Superior Court judge concluded that Tyree's statements to Purcell were not protected by the attorney–client privilege, denied Purcell's motion to quash an anticipated subpoena, and ordered Purcell to testify. . . .

There is no question before this court, directly or indirectly, concerning the ethical propriety of Purcell's disclosure to the police that Tyree might engage in conduct that would be harmful to others. As bar counsel agreed in a memorandum submitted to the single justice, this court's disciplinary rules regulating the practice of law authorized Purcell to reveal to the police "the intention of his client to commit a crime and the information necessary to prevent the crime."[1] The

---

1. The same conclusion would be reached under Rule 1.6(b)(1) of the Proposed Mass. R. of Prof. Conduct, now pending before the Justices. . . .

fact that the disciplinary code permitted Purcell to make the disclosure tells us nothing about the admissibility of the information that Purcell disclosed. . . .

The attorney-client privilege is founded on the necessity that a client be free to reveal information to an attorney, without fear of its disclosure, in order to obtain informed legal advice. It is a principle of long standing. The debate here is whether Tyree is entitled to the protection of the attorney-client privilege in the circumstances.

The district attorney announces the issue in his brief to be whether a crime-fraud exception to the testimonial privilege applies in this case. He asserts that, even if Tyree's communication with Purcell was made as part of his consultation concerning the eviction proceeding, Tyree's communication concerning his contemplated criminal conduct is not protected by the privilege. . . .

We . . . accept the general principle of a crime-fraud exception. The Proposed Massachusetts Rules of Evidence adequately define the crime-fraud exception to the lawyer-client privilege set forth in rule 502(d)(1) as follows: "If the services of the lawyer were sought or obtained to enable or aid anyone to commit or plan to commit what the client knew or reasonably should have known to be a crime or fraud." . . . The applicability of the exception, like the existence of the privilege, is a question of fact for the judge.

The district attorney rightly grants that he, as the opponent of the application of the testimonial privilege, has the burden of showing that the exception applies. . . . We conclude that facts supporting the applicability of the crime-fraud exception must be proved by a preponderance of the evidence. However, on a showing of a factual basis adequate to support a reasonable belief that an in camera review of the evidence may establish that the exception applies, the judge has discretion to conduct such an in camera review. Once the judge sees the confidential information, the burden of proof normally will be unimportant.

In this case, in deciding whether to conduct a discretionary in camera review of the substance of the conversation concerning arson between Tyree and Purcell, the judge would have evidence tending to show that Tyree discussed a future crime with Purcell and that thereafter Tyree actively prepared to commit that crime. Without this evidence, the crime of arson would appear to have no apparent connection with Tyree's eviction proceeding and Purcell's representation of Tyree. With this evidence, however, a request that a judge inquire in camera into the circumstances of Tyree's apparent threat to burn the apartment building would not be a call for a "fishing expedition," and a judge might be justified in conducting such an inquiry. The evidence in this case, however, was not sufficient to warrant the judge's finding that Tyree consulted Purcell for the purpose of obtaining advice in furtherance of a crime. Therefore, the order denying the motion to quash because the crime-fraud exception applied cannot be upheld.

There is a consideration in this case that does not appear in other cases that we have seen concerning the attorney-client privilege. The testimony that the prosecution seeks from Purcell is available only because Purcell reflectively made a disclosure, relying on this court's disciplinary rule which permitted him to do so. Purcell was under no ethical duty to disclose Tyree's intention to commit a crime. He did so to protect the lives and property of others, a purpose that underlies a lawyer's discretionary right stated in the disciplinary rule. The limited facts in the record strongly suggest that Purcell's disclosures to the police served the beneficial public purpose on which the disciplinary rule was based.

We must be cautious in permitting the use of client communications that a lawyer has revealed only because of a threat to others. Lawyers will be reluctant to come forward if they know that the information that they disclose may lead to adverse consequences to their clients. A practice of the use of such disclosures might prompt a lawyer to warn a client in advance that the disclosure of certain information may not be held confidential, thereby chilling free discourse between lawyer and client and reducing the prospect that the lawyer will learn of a serious threat to the well-being of others. To best promote the purposes of the attorney-client privilege, the crime-fraud exception should apply only if the communication seeks assistance in or furtherance of future criminal conduct. When the opponent of the privilege argues that the communication itself may show that the exception applies and seeks its disclosure in camera, the judge, in the exercise of discretion on the question whether to have an in camera proceeding, should consider if the public interest is served by disclosure, even in camera, of a communication whose existence is known only because the lawyer acted against his client's interests under the authority of a disciplinary rule. The facts of each situation must be considered. . . .

[T]he district attorney's brief [now] appears to abandon its earlier concession that all communications between Tyree and Purcell should be treated as protected by the attorney-client privilege unless the crime-fraud exception applies. The question whether the attorney-client privilege is involved at all will be open on remand. We, therefore, discuss the issue.

The attorney-client privilege applies only when the client's communication was for the purpose of facilitating the rendition of legal services. The burden of proving that the attorney-client privilege applies to a communication rests on the party asserting the privilege. The motion judge did not pass on the question whether the attorney-client privilege applied to the communication at all but rather went directly to the issue of the crime-fraud exception, although not using that phrase.

A statement of an intention to commit a crime made in the course of seeking legal advice is protected by the privilege, unless the crime-fraud exception applies. That exception applies only if the client or prospective client seeks advice or assistance in furtherance of criminal conduct. It is agreed that Tyree consulted Purcell concerning his impending eviction. Purcell is a member of the bar, and Tyree either was or sought to become Purcell's client. The serious question concerning the application of the privilege is whether Tyree informed Purcell of the fact of his intention to commit arson for the purpose of receiving legal advice or assistance in furtherance of criminal conduct. Purcell's presentation of the circumstances in which Tyree's statements were made is likely to be the only evidence presented.

This is not a case in which our traditional view that testimonial privileges should be construed strictly should be applied. A strict construction of the privilege that would leave a gap between the circumstances in which the crime-fraud exception applies and the circumstances in which a communication is protected by the attorney-client privilege would make no sense. The attorney-client privilege "is founded upon the necessity, in the interest and administration of justice, of the aid of persons having knowledge of the law and skilled in its practice, which assistance can only be safely and readily availed of when free from the consequences or the apprehension of disclosure." Unless the crime-fraud exception applies, the attorney-client privilege should apply to communications concerning possible future, as well as past, criminal conduct, because an informed lawyer may be able to dissuade the client from improper future conduct and, if not, under the ethical rules may elect in the public interest to make a limited disclosure of the client's threatened conduct.

A judgment should be entered in the county court ordering that the order denying the motion to quash any subpoena issued to Purcell to testify at Tyree's trial is vacated and that the matter is remanded for further proceedings consistent with this opinion. . . .

B. Financial Harm

No one disputes that lawyers cannot counsel or assist a client's crime or fraud. Specific exceptions to client confidentiality that allow disclosure to prevent, rectify, or mitigate financial harm caused by a client, however, continue to generate substantial disagreement among lawyers and the public, including the authors of this book. Yet, perhaps because the human willingness to lie can cause serious harm, some confidentiality exceptions exist when clients seek to use lawyers to promote fraudulent activity.

Utilitarians recognize that efficient operation of both a market economy and a democratic government requires honesty. If everyone could use a lawyer to promote the client's own illegal deception, the market system, many aspects of government, and the legal system itself would lose the confidence of its citizens. To prevent this erosion in confidence, some lawyers argue that they should be able to disclose activities of clients that seek to use the lawyer's services to perpetrate a fraud when the greater good would be promoted by disclosure. Others maintain that confidentiality remains an essential incentive for clients to disclose their plans to lawyers, who are then in the best position to dissuade clients from engaging in fraudulent activity. Focusing on trust and privacy, the deontologist would agree that clients should be encouraged to facilitate their plans through the client-lawyer relationship. They would add, however, that when the client seeks to use the relationship to violate another categorical imperative such as honesty, then the client's right to confidentiality has been lost. If the lawyer's services unwittingly have been used to further that fraud, the lawyer's duty of reparation for her own acts also comes into play.

1. Fiduciary Duty

Problems

7-6. Martyn attends an Internal Revenue Service (IRS) audit with client. The examiner asks about a $50,000 deduction for a business promotion event at the country club. "I brought all our reps together," answers client. Martyn knows it was the wedding of client's youngest daughter. Is there any obligation to correct the record? Does it matter whether we were present? Whether the lie came as a surprise?

7-7. May Martyn tell the other side that our client "won't possibly pay more than $500,000" when she has recommended that our client settle the case quickly for far more than that or face far more extensive liability? How about if Martyn tells the other side that she "isn't authorized to settle for more than $500,000," when she has settlement authority of $5,000,000?

7-8. Fox, representing seller, and based on seller's information, told buyer's lawyer that the property is zoned commercial. Just before closing, Fox learns that the property is zoned residential. Client insists no disclosure be made, asserting, "It'll kill the deal." Now what?

7-9. What may (must) Martyn & Fox do if at a celebration dinner the night before the initial public offering (IPO), the CEO tells us, "Sure glad we didn't have to disclose that letter threatening a patent infringement suit we got yesterday"? Or the CFO tells us, "I sure am glad the auditors didn't insist we footnote the $65 million in off-balance-sheet financing we arranged. How clever!"? May we withdraw? Will client have a claim against us if we do? What if we learn these things a week after the IPO?

Consider: Model Rules 1.0(d), 1.2(d), 1.6(b)(2) and (3), 1.13, 1.16, 2.1, 3.9, 4.1, 8.4(c) RLGL §§ 67, 94, 98

Lawrence J. Fox
Legal Tender: A Lawyer's Guide to Handling Professional Dilemmas
157-166 (ABA 1995)

The Opinion Letter

Forty years ago they were in the third grade at Highlands School. George was the new kid on the block, Lonnie the veteran from kindergarten. They met in the playground before school, quickly learned they both loved baseball (even the hapless Philadelphia A's), and soon found themselves as rival pick-up team captains. How many times they had used that elaborate ritual of alternately grabbing the baseball bat to determine who would choose first.

George's family's move to the suburbs five years later did not separate the boys for long, as Lonnie's folks followed them to Claymont one year later. There they found themselves teammates on the Claymont High School baseball team

(Class B Delaware High School champions in 1959), sharing both the visits to colleges and the springtime anxiety as they awaited the results of the torturous college admissions process. When both lads were accepted at Syracuse, the fact that Lonnie had also been admitted to his original first choice, Trinity College, was quickly ignored as the friends deliciously contemplated spending four more years together—two hundred miles from home. Visions of intercollegiate athletics, fraternity memberships, new friendships, and football weekends soon became reality; Lonnie and George thrived despite the harsh winters of upstate New York.

College was a total success, launching the new graduates into their first period of separation in nearly ten years; George went off to Villanova Law School and Lonnie to the business school at Northwestern. They had often discussed their differing interests into the night over coffee and even, it had to be admitted, over more than a few Genesee beers, jokingly suggesting that Lonnie might some day become George's biggest client. But this was no more than a joke designed to ease the pain of their going down different paths since, at the time, George envisioned himself as Assistant District Attorney in New Castle County, prosecuting the clients of Perry Mason.

Nonetheless, twenty years later, with George firmly established at the Wilmington office of the prestigious, old-line Philadelphia firm, Caldwell & Moore—practicing corporate law no less—Lonnie, who had risen to president and chief operating officer of the Mercury Maintenance Company, was presented with his first opportunity to send business George's way. Mercury, whose growth had been spectacular, found itself in need of major new financing. Its old law firm had recently forced the retirement of Mercury's original lawyer and board member, Lewis Stern. Thus Lonnie felt free to steer this important matter to George.

During the interim they had remained friends. Both moved to Greenville as they each rose up their respective ladders. Their children were friends, baseball had given way to golf (now played regularly at Wilmington Country Club), and the two couples socialized at every opportunity. But this was the first time they had actually worked together.

At Lonnie's initial visit, he explained the plan to George. Mercury had a series of long-term contracts to replace streetlights and traffic controls for municipalities throughout the Delaware Valley. Because of its reputation for high-quality, prompt, and low-cost service, Mercury had signed multi-year contracts with over two hundred boroughs, townships, three of the five major counties surrounding Philadelphia, and, of course, the City of Wilmington. In discussions with Integrity Bank it had become clear that these contracts were Mercury's biggest asset. Based on the cash flow stability they represented, the bank was prepared to lend significant sums to Mercury. Lonnie had negotiated the broad outline of a deal in which Mercury would receive a $5 million loan to be drawn down in equal installments quarterly across four years, permitting Mercury, as it expanded its operations into New Jersey, to purchase the additional trucks and cherry pickers that were critical to its delivery of service. He called on George to document the transaction, represent Mercury, and provide Integrity with any routine legal opinions it required.

"Protect us as best you can," Lonnie implored George, "but none of your aggressive stuff—we need this money and you know how cussedly independent these banks can be."

"You can count on me, Lonnie. I want your board to be proud of your selection of lawyers, even though I know the real reason you hired me is to make up for your stealing my Mickey Mantle rookie card. That's something that you should feel guilty about. Do you know what that would be worth today?"

"Your mom would've thrown it out with your old Lionel trains anyway," Lonnie replied.

George returned to the office, called up his friend Vince Almond at Integrity to inquire who would be "lawyering" this transaction for the bank, learned that Vince himself would be working on it, and made a date with Vince to meet within a week to discuss the matter.

The loan processing could not have been easier. The bank officials were so impressed with Mercury's success that many of the issues typically raised did not need to be addressed. Similarly, the documentation went smoothly, and George's firm was only asked to provide opinion letters on the corporate authority of Mercury to enter into the loan transaction and the enforceability of the long-term contracts, including the effect of the penalty clauses, if any of Mercury's customers attempted to terminate them early. Neither legal question was difficult, and George confidently and, if truth be told, proudly delivered each opinion—printed on crisp ivory Caldwell & Moore letterhead—to Vince at closing. This was the final step prior to the delivery of the first $300,000-plus installment to Mercury. New equipment would soon be on its way, and George could only think that his good friend Lonnie might be well on his way to being CEO of a major public corporation, now that Mercury had this assured flow of capital.

A celebratory dinner at the Hotel duPont brought the old friends, their spouses, and a few key colleagues together for one of those events where the fact that the wine bill actually exceeded the cost of the food only seemed embarrassing the next morning. The repeated toasts to all involved only confirmed what high hopes everyone present shared as they dined among the Winterthur reproductions.

It was just one year later that George got the call from Lonnie. George immediately could tell something was wrong. There was a tension in Lonnie's voice, a hesitancy in his approach, and no desire for small talk. Rather, Lonnie asked George if they could meet right away at the club. George knew this was important, but his idle speculation as to why they had to meet immediately did not include anything close to the story that unfolded.

Lonnie's face was drawn, his normally neatly combed auburn hair, now just flecked with grey, appeared a little disheveled, and he sat poised at the edge of his highback club chair, as he began his tale.

"George, it's just terrible. I don't even know what to say. We just had a meeting with the folks from Arthur Andersen, our auditors. They have uncovered a massive fraud. We don't even know how big it is. Seems our best sales representative, Arnold Plinger, has been systematically bribing township officials to get these contracts— not just to get them, but to have the contracts include a five-year term when the governing body has only authorized two or three. He even did it with New Castle County! All those contracts we thought were for five years paid Arnold a commission based on five years. Now it turns out some expire as soon as December of this year."

"How many are there?" George interrupted more to ease his anxiety than to learn any information.

"We don't know. At least twenty. Maybe more, many more. Arnold isn't cooperating. His psychiatrist has put him on sedatives and ordered him not to talk to anyone. But he has hired a lawyer, on our advice. We only know from contacting a few officials who, of course, had not admitted the bribes but have stated that their versions of the contract are only for two years or, at most, three years. Arnold had over one hundred customers, so who knows?"

"Well," George observed, silently thanking his lucky stars he had not opined on the genuineness of the contracts, "we must act in a forthright manner. Tell the bank. After all, they are about to give you guys another $300,000 in a few weeks, if I'm not mistaken. Based on our firm's opinion that those five-year contracts are enforceable according to their terms. We can't let that happen."

"We can't do that," replied Lonnie. "That's why I wanted to meet with you today. I remember way back when, how you told me that everything a client told you you had to keep confidential. I even remember you and I having a major fight over that case of the lawyer who knew his client had killed those kids in upstate New York. I said he had to tell the victims' families. You said it was unethical to do so."

"That was different," said George, realizing he was shouting. "That client wasn't the lawyer's best friend. The lawyer hadn't given an opinion to anyone."

"That's what Lewis Stern said you would say."

"When did you talk to him?" George inquired, not hiding his annoyance.

"We had a special board meeting yesterday to discuss all of this. One of the board members invited Lewis to join us—said we needed someone who knew the company better than you, someone who wouldn't panic. The board decided that Mercury had no choice but to keep this under wraps. If we tell the bank, they'll never lend us another dime and they'll demand repayment of what they've already paid. Without that $300,000 per quarter, we'd probably have to file a chapter proceeding. We've already spent that money, y'know. Anyway, Lewis told us that we should tell you what had happened so that you would understand why we were consulting him."

"Caldwell & Moore will have to resign if you go forward like this."

"He told us you would say that, too, and he agreed you would have to resign. In fact, he thought that was best. But he also told us you would not be able to tell anyone about our little problems with Arnold."

"But the bank is relying on my opinion. Certainly I can call them up and tell them they shouldn't continue to do so."

"Not according to Lewis. He says you lawyers call these 'noisy withdrawals.' The rules don't permit them when the fraud's complete."

"But you're taking down more money from the bank."

"That may be so. Otherwise, our company will die and your best friend Lonnie will be sleeping in your garage. But we aren't requiring any further services from you. In fact, you've withdrawn. But I must warn you, as Lewis instructed me, we better not hear another peep out of Caldwell & Moore . . . especially if you ever want to see any of the $100,000 we still owe you."

"You're being impossible. I better talk to Lewis myself. I'll be back to you shortly. Maybe all of this will seem less explosive with the passage of a few days. But those kind of threats will get you nowhere, Lonnie. If our friendship means anything, you'll not repeat such outrageous statements," George intoned, now almost unable to control his mixture of anger and shock.

George returned to his office and, after consulting with his most trusted colleague, Henry Gill, the conscience of Caldwell & Moore, it was agreed that he would make a personal call on Lewis the very next day. It was a meeting George did not look forward to at all. Lewis Stern was a giant at the bar. A member of the American College of Trial Lawyers, he had served for years as chairman of the Ethics Committee of the Delaware Bar Association, of which he had also been president. Jousting with Lewis on the issue of confidentiality was, at best, a formidable task.

The meeting began pleasantly enough. Lewis's office was spacious and encrusted with the memorabilia from a career of service to clients, charities, and the bar. Lewis greeted him warmly, an approach George found both welcoming and intimidating: he knew Lewis was planning to charm him into acquiescence.

"This is all very sad stuff, George. It's terrible that your friend, Lonnie, and the others at Mercury have been so injured by Arnold's unfortunate conduct. Now all we can do is make sure this doesn't snowball into a total disaster. I am sure you agree with Lonnie and the others that, despite the fact that these contracts are for a shorter time than we thought, Mercury is likely to obtain renewals of contracts because of its reputation for speedy, low-cost service."

"But not once they find out about the bribes," George rejoined. "At that point, Mercury may not be eligible even to bid on the renewals."

"That's true if you go blabbing about. But the way this is structured," Lewis continued, "no one has to find out—as long as you recognize your professional responsibility not to violate Model Rule 1.6."

"Violate Rule 1.6. I should say not. As you know all too well, because you led the opposition to the change, I am totally free to disclose this information to prevent, mitigate or rectify a client fraud in which the lawyer's services have been used."

"I know. I know. Damn ABA panicked in the face of threats from the SEC, and gave into those who would turn lawyers into cops, letting them arrest their own clients, of all things. But at least they didn't require you to disclose. It's only permissive. So you still have a chance to demonstrate your loyalty to your old friend, I mean your former friend."

George leaped at the opening Lewis had left him. "You know it isn't that easy. Our firm told the bank that these contracts were enforceable in accordance with their terms when, in fact, we didn't even have the version of the contracts with the correct number of years in front of us."

"Exactly my point," Lewis interrupted. "If you give discretion to lawyers to breach confidentiality then when lawyers are faced with difficult choices they will put their own interests ahead of their clients."

"Back then I agreed with you," George responded. "I'm not so sure now that I've been betrayed by Arnold Plinger."

"You've been betrayed! I should say not." Lewis was shaking now. "Your client has been betrayed by Arnold, and now is about to be betrayed by you. You can choose and you better choose non-disclosure." Lewis was pulling out all the stops.

"Lewis, you might be right if I had discretion. And under Rule 1.6 it appears I do. But not when you read Rule 4.1. That rule requires me to disclose to prevent assisting a client fraud. I have no choice but to disclose."

"But you are not aiding and abetting a fraud. This fraud already took place. I do not see how anything your firm does from this day forward will assist your former client in committing a fraud. Caldwell & Moore will be asked to do *nothing* having anything to do with the financial transactions—the loan, its extension, or its repayment. All of *that* will now be undertaken by others. Your firm will be completely shielded from all contact with any transaction. The only hint of Caldwell & Moore's existence in those ongoing transactions (whatever they may be) is your once-issued opinion. It simply is not necessary for you to do anything other than withdraw."

George listened carefully. The argument seemed too pat. Where was the place where the rabbit went into the hat? Then it struck him: "Lewis, I admire you greatly and your advocacy skills have never been greater. But frankly, you are wrong. This is a mandatory disclosure situation under Model Rule 4.1. That's why I must let the bank know they can't rely on my opinion."

"You're wrong again," Lewis replied. "The mandatory disclosure provisions of Model Rule 4.1 come into play only if the 1.6 exceptions allow disclosure, and disclosure is only allowed 'where reasonably necessary' to prevent a fraud that is 'reasonably certain to result in substantial financial injury' to the bank. The operative words here are 'reasonably necessary' and 'reasonably certain.' Here disclosure is not 'reasonably necessary' because your work is complete and therefore you are not assisting in a fraud. It's also not 'reasonably certain' that the bank will be harmed, because Lonnie and Mercury will find a way to get out of this mess."

"I can't believe you are telling me this. It's pure sophistry, Lewis. Your reading of 'reasonably' is far too narrow. Surely, one can assist a person in the future through work that was completed in the past. The fact that the work is completed renders the assistance no more or less helpful, or actionable, I might add, than if it were taking place at the same time as the client's conduct. It's also reasonably certain that the bank will lose its money. If you were the bank, wouldn't you want to know?"

But Lewis remained indomitable. "What you are saying is that by hiding behind an overly broad interpretation of 1.6(b), you can conjure up an obligation to contact the bank, and withdraw your opinion, and destroy your client. But the truth is all your clever argumentation about aiding and abetting cannot obscure the fact that Rule 1.6 gives you complete discretion whether to disclose. So when you do disclose, know that no one will celebrate George's observance of the rules. No, they will recognize a lawyer who breached his confidentiality commitment to his client because he put his own interests first. George, simply withdraw and give Lonnie one last chance to save his company, your once treasured client."

"If you would only persuade *your* client to do the right thing," George replied, "we wouldn't be in this pickle. And if I thought just withdrawing would accomplish the purpose, I would do that. But here I know that our silent withdrawal won't do anything. It's not like the bank is calling us up each week to find out if we are still representing Mercury. Under these special circumstances, we simply have no choice."

Now Lewis stood, pressing his palms on his mammoth desk as he leaned forward for emphasis. "You're right about no choice. But you're wrong about the result. You have no business disclosing Arnold's indiscretions to the bank. And if you do so, I can assure you that Caldwell & Moore will find itself the subject of a malpractice suit for the damages flowing from the bank's cutting off the credit and calling the loan. If you do anything other than withdraw, it will be a very sad day for all of us. Think about it, son. Think of Lonnie; think of your firm; think of your fine reputation. I know you'll do the right thing."

Stunned, George slowly rose from the chair and, without a word or a gesture, shuffled out of Lewis's office, his legs heavy and wooden, his hands clammy, his forehead beaded with sweat, and his psyche a battlefield of conflicting emotions—remorse, anger, regret, dismay. How difficult it was to be a lawyer, an ethical lawyer, the conscientious lawyer he always wanted to be.

In re American Continental Corporation/ Lincoln Savings & Loan Securities Litigation
794 F. Supp. 1424 (D. Ariz. 1992)

BILBY, District Judge. . . .
V. RULINGS PERTINENT TO INDIVIDUAL DEFENDANTS

D. Jones, Day, Reavis & Pogue

Jones Day . . . focuses its summary judgment motion on an individual opinion letter given in connection with a 1986 registration statement. . . . Jones Day generally claims that it has not engaged in conduct for which it could be held liable because lawyers are obligated to keep their clients' confidence and to act in ways that do not discourage their clients from undergoing regulator compliance reviews.

1. The Record

The record reveals the following facts concerning Jones Day's involvement with ACC and Keating.

Prior to joining Jones Day, defendant William Schilling was director of the FHLBB Office of Examinations and Supervision. In that capacity, he was directly involved in the supervision of Lincoln Savings. During the summer of 1985, he wrote at least one memorandum and concurred in another, expressing serious regulatory concerns about numerous aspects of Lincoln's operations. For example, he wrote:

> [U]nder new management, Lincoln has engaged in several serious regulatory violations. Some of these violations, such as the overvaluation of real estate and failure to comply with Memorandum R-4l(b), are the same type of violations that have led to some of the worst failures in FSLIC's history.

Later in 1985, Schilling was hired by Jones Day to augment its expertise in thrift representation. On January 31, 1986, Schilling and Jones Day's Ron Kneipper flew to Phoenix to solicit ACC's business. ACC retained Jones Day to perform "a major internal audit of Lincoln's FHLBB compliance and a major project to help Lincoln deal with the FHLBB's direct investment regulations."

During the regulatory compliance audit, which Jones Day understood to be a pre-FHLBB examination compliance review, the law firm found multiple regulatory violations. There is evidence that Jones Day knew that Lincoln had backdated files, destroyed appraisals, removed appraisals from files, told appraisers not to issue written reports when their oral valuations were too low, and violated affiliated transaction regulations. Jones Day found that Lincoln did no loan underwriting and no post-closure loan follow-up to ensure that Lincoln's interests were being protected. Jones Day learned Lincoln had multiple "loans" which were, in fact, joint ventures which violated FHLBB regulations, made real estate loans in violation of regulations, and backdated corporate resolutions which were not signed by corporate officers and did not reflect actual meetings. There is evidence that Jones Day may have tacitly consented to removal of harmful documents from Lincoln files. For example, one handwritten notation on a memorandum memorializing Jones Day's advice not to remove documents from files reads, "If something *is* devastating, consider it individually." (Emphasis in original.)

There is evidence that Jones Day instructed ACC in how to rectify deficiencies so that they would not be apparent to FHLBB examiners. Jones Day attorneys, including Schilling, testified that they told ACC/Lincoln personnel to provide the Jones Day-generated "to do" lists only to the attorneys responsible for rectifying the deficiencies, and to destroy the lists so that FHLB-SF would not find them in the files. For the same reason, Jones Day's regulatory compliance reports to ACC/Lincoln were oral. Jones Day paralegals testified that responsibilities for carrying out the "to do" lists were divided among Jones Day and ACC staff. Jones Day continued this work into the summer of 1986.

The evidence indicates that Jones Day may have been aware that ACC/Lincoln did not follow its compliance advice with respect to ongoing activities.

There are material questions of fact concerning the procedures Jones Day used—if any—to ascertain whether their compliance advice was being heeded. The testimony suggests that Jones Day partners knew ACC/Lincoln personnel were preparing loan underwriting summaries contemporaneously with Jones Day's regulatory compliance review, even though the loan transactions had already been closed. Moreover, the evidence reveals that Jones Day attorneys participated in creating corporate resolutions to ratify forged and backdated corporate records.

On April 23, 1986, Jones Day partner Fohrman wrote:

> I received Neal Millard's memo on ACC. In looking at the long list of people involved, it occurred to me that there will be times when individuals may be called upon to render legal services that might require the issuance of opinion letters from Jones, Day. As we all know, we now possess information that could affect the way we write our opinion letters and our actual ability to give a particular opinion may be severely restricted. However, this large list of individuals may not be aware of knowledge that is held by Messrs. Fein and Schilling. I would suggest that a follow up memo be issued by Ron Fein indicating that any work involving ACC which requires the issuance of opinions, must be cleared by Ron. . . .

Also in April 1986, ACC's Jim Grogan wrote to Jones Day's Kneipper, soliciting a strategy to "sunset" the FHLBB direct investment regulation. Jones Day subsequently made multiple Freedom of Information Act requests to FHLBB in furtherance of a direct investment rule strategy, for which Lincoln was billed. In a September 12, 1986 telephone conversation, Grogan allegedly told Kneipper: "Comment letters were great success FHLBB picked it up 'hook, line and sinker' . . . Charlie wants to do again . . . . "

The record indicates that the concept of selling ACC debentures in Lincoln savings branches may have originated at an April 9, 1986 real estate syndicate seminar given by Jones Day Defendant Ron Fein. There is evidence that Fein may have contributed to the detailed bond sales program outline, attending to details such as explaining how the sales would work, and insuring that the marketing table was far enough from the teller windows to distinguish between ACC and Lincoln Savings employees. The evidence indicates that Jones Day reviewed the debenture registration statement and prospectus, which is corroborated by Jones Day's billing records. As a result, in January 1987, ACC was able to assure the California Department of Savings & Loan that:

> The process of structuring the bond sales program was reviewed by Kaye, Scholer and Jones Day to assure compliance not only with securities laws and regulations, but also with banking and FSLIC laws and regulations.

Moreover, there is evidence which suggests that political contributions were made on behalf of ACC, in exchange for ACC's consent that Jones Day could "bill liberally." On June 23, 1986, Kneipper memorialized a phone conversation:

1) 1:15 p.m. Ron Kessler—in past, firm has given $amt. to PAC, has premium billed, & PAC contri. to candidate; concern that we're an out of state law

firm and that a $# in excess of $5,000.00 would look like an unusual move; Barnett and Kessler have done before; question re whether and how we can get some busi. from GOV. for this.

(2) 3:40 p.m. Jim Grogan

Ten tickets at $1,000.00 equals $10,000.00

Barr wants limits of $5,000.00/ contribution.

Agreed that we could bill liberally in future in recognition of this.

At deposition, Kneipper testified that his note—"agreed could bill liberally in recognition for this,"—"is what it appears to be." Jones Day set up an Arizona Political Action Committee ("PAC") specifically for the purpose of making a contribution to an Arizona gubernatorial candidate. The PAC was opened on September 4, 1986 and closed in December, 1986, after the contribution was made.

In June 1986, Jones Day solicited additional work from ACC. Jones Day attorney Caulkins wrote, in part:

> Rick Kneipper reports that ACC is very explicit that it does not care how much its legal services cost, as long as it gets the best. He states that Keating gave him an unsolicited $250,000 retainer to start the thrift work, and sent another similar check also unsolicited in two weeks. On the down side, he reports that he has never encountered a more demanding and difficult client, . . .
>
> It appears to Rick and to me that American Continental is made for us and we for them.

On October 28, 1986, Jones Day provided an opinion letter, required by Item 601(b) of SEC regulation S-K, for inclusion in an ACC bond registration statement. Jones Day's opinion letter stated that the indenture was a valid and binding obligation under California law. . . .

This evidence raises material questions concerning . . . [state securities law violations and common law fraud] . . .

4. Breach of Fiduciary Duty to Lincoln . . .

An attorney who represents a corporation has a duty to act in the corporation's best interest when confronted by adverse interests of directors, officers, or corporate affiliates. It is not a defense that corporate representation often involves the distinct interests of affiliated entities. Attorneys are bound to act when those interests conflict. There are genuine questions as to whether Jones Day should have sought independent representation for Lincoln.

Moreover, where a law firm believes the management of a corporate client is committing serious regulatory violations, the firm has an obligation to actively discuss the violative conduct, urge cessation of the activity, and withdraw from representation where the firm's legal services may contribute to the continuation of such conduct. Jones Day contends that it would have been futile to act on these fiduciary obligations because those controlling ACC/Lincoln would not have responded. Client wrongdoing, however, cannot negate an attorney's fiduciary duty. Moreover, the evidence reveals that attorney advice influenced

ACC/Lincoln's conduct in a variety of ways. Accordingly, summary judgment as to this claim is denied.

5. *Professional Negligence Claims*

Jones Day issued an opinion letter that was included with ACC's 1986 shelf registration statement. California authority provides that independent public accountants have a duty to those who are foreseeably injured from representations made in connection with publicly held corporations. While this duty does not extend to confidential advice which an attorney gives to its clients, it would apply where an attorney issues an SEC opinion letter to the public.

Accordingly, a question of fact remains as to whether the . . . Plaintiffs who purchased bonds issued pursuant to the November, 1986 shelf registration and amendments, were injured by the Jones Day opinion letter.

Thomas H. Lee Equity Fund V, L.P. v. Mayer Brown, Rowe & Maw LLP

612 F. Supp. 2d 267 (S.D.N.Y. 2009)

GERARD E. LYNCH, District Judge:

This is an action on behalf of . . . investment funds associated with Thomas H. Lee Partners, L.P. ("THL Partners"), a private equity firm (collectively, the "THL Funds"). Together, plaintiffs invested more than $ 450 million in Refco and acquired the majority of Refco's stock through a leveraged buy-out ("LBO") in August 2004 (the "2004 Purchase"). Following Refco's collapse in the fall of 2005, plaintiffs allegedly experienced losses in excess of $245 million. Plaintiffs bring this action against Refco's principal outside counsel, Mayer Brown, Rowe & Maw LLP ("Mayer Brown"), claiming that the law firm made numerous misrepresentations to them in connection with the LBO.

After the Supreme Court decided Stoneridge Inv. Partners. LLC v. Scientific-Atlanta, Inc., 552 U.S. 148 (2008), plaintiffs filed an Amended Complaint reasserting claims under Section 10(b) of the Securities Exchange Act of 1934, 15 U.S.C. § 78j(b), the Racketeer Influenced and Corrupt Organizations Act ("RICO"), 18 U.S.C. §§ 1961-1968, and state law claims for fraud and negligent misrepresentation. Mayer Brown now moves to dismiss all claims pursuant to Fed. R. Civ. P. 12(b)(6). The motion will be granted in part and denied in part.

BACKGROUND

In a recent decision, In re Refco, 609 F. Supp. 2d 304, (S.D.N.Y. 2009), this Court, in dismissing Section 10(b) claims brought by a putative class of plaintiff-investors against Mayer Brown and Mayer Brown senior partner Joseph Collins, discussed the fraudulent scheme of so-called "round-trip" loans in which Mayer Brown was alleged to have participated in order to conceal the true financial circumstances of the international brokerage firm Refco Inc. and its affiliated companies. The THL Funds base their allegations, in part, on the same conduct, arguing that Mayer Brown "helped effectuate" the round-trip loans that transformed Refco's uncollectible losses into receivables owed to Refco by third-parties and that Mayer Brown participated in drafting the documents, specifically the Offering Memorandum, that were used to induce investors into purchasing Refco's Bonds. The THL Funds also distinguish their claims against Mayer Brown, however, arguing that unlike the plaintiff-investors, they are seeking to hold Mayer Brown liable for the lies told directly to them throughout the due diligence process that effectuated the LBO. . . .

I. Mayer Brown's Participation in the Due Diligence for the LBO

In the fall of 2003, the THL Funds began to explore the possibility of purchasing an interest in Refco. A process of due diligence ensued, which involved a number of parties. As Refco's primary outside counsel, Mayer Brown was responsible for responding to the THL Funds' due diligence requests in connection with the projected purchase. Specifically, Mayer Brown handled the drafting and negotiating of the transactional documents, provided information directly to the THL Funds and their advisors, and coordinated access to documents and information being provided by Refco and its affiliates. Lawyers for Mayer Brown did this work while continuing to negotiate, coordinate, and provide material assistance for the round-trip loans, which they were—through their attendance at meetings and their assistance in drafting and reviewing a "Letter of Intent" for the acquisition—deliberately concealing from the THL Funds.

That concealment included both statements and conduct. Throughout the due diligence process, Collins in particular made a number of statements directly to the THL Funds and their counsel, Weil Gotshal & Manges, LLP ("Weil Gotshal"), including informing them that he had "confirmed with" or was "advised by" Refco management that there were no related-party transactions and that all material documents were being produced. As Mayer Brown knew, however, numerous related-party transactions, including the round-trip loans, were not being disclosed to the THL Funds, and documents related to those transactions were not being produced.

One such document was a copy of the so-called "Fourth LLC Agreement" a document requested by Weil Gotshal after it discovered an unexecuted copy of the document in the data room. Instead of turning over the executed document as requested, however—which in conjunction with the Proceeds Participation Agreement to which it referred would have led to the revelation of the RCHI receivables and thus Refco's true financial condition—Collins gave to the THL Funds a counterfeit Fourth LLC Agreement that omitted the incriminating information. Other documents, including the Proceeds Participation Agreement and the related "Letter Agreement" were never produced, despite the fact that those documents fell squarely within the THL Funds' diligence requests. Toward the end of the LBO process, Mayer Brown also negotiated, drafted, and reviewed the Equity Purchase Agreement (the "2004 Purchase Agreement") that contained representations that there were no related-party transactions, a fact that Mayer Brown knew to be false.

Upon completion of due diligence, plaintiffs consummated the LBO transaction in August 2004 and acquired a majority ownership interest in Refco as well as numerous seats on Refco's Board of Directors. In early October 2005 Refco's uncollectible debt became public and the company informed investors that they could no longer rely on its financial statements for the preceding four years. Refco's stock plummeted, and on October 17, 2005, Refco filed for Chapter 11 bankruptcy protection. This turn of events allegedly caused the THL Funds to suffer millions of dollars in losses.

II. Plaintiffs' Claims

Plaintiffs allege that Mayer Brown made a number of knowingly false statements directly to the THL Funds and their counsel, and that Mayer Brown conspired with other Refco principals to conceal Refco's uncollectible debt by engaging in secret related-party transactions, namely the so-called round-trip loans. Accordingly, the THL Funds argue that Mayer Brown should be held primarily liable for securities fraud under Section 10(b), either because of the misstatements they made directly to the THL Funds, or because they participated in the scheme — including coordinating the round-trip loan transactions and creating false documents — that belied Mayer Brown's representations to them during the due diligence process. . . . Finally, plaintiffs allege that they have stated claims for common-law negligent misrepresentation and fraud. Mayer Brown moves to dismiss all claims pursuant to Fed. R. Civ. P. 12(b)(6).

DISCUSSION . . .

II. Pleading a Violation of Section 10(b) and Rule 10b-5* . . .

The Supreme Court recently articulated the elements necessary to sustain a private cause of action for securities fraud under § 10(b) and Rule 10b-5:

> In a typical § 10(b) private action a plaintiff must prove (1) a material misrepresentation or omission by the defendant; (2) scienter; (3) a connection between the misrepresentation or omission and the purchase or sale of a security; (4) reliance upon the misrepresentation or omission; (5) economic loss; and (6) loss causation. Stoneridge, 128 S. Ct. at 768 (2008). . . .

Thus, in order for a defendant to be held liable for a claim brought under Rule 10b-5, a plaintiff must allege that the defendant made a false or misleading statement or omission that investors attributed to him or her, or that the defendant "participated in [a] fraudulent scheme or other activity proscribed by the securities laws." SEC v. U.S. Envtl., Inc., 155 F.3d 107, 111 (2d Cir. 1998).

III. Sufficiency of the Rule 10b-5(b) Claim

. . . Mayer Brown argues that plaintiffs' allegations are an unjustified attempt to broaden the reach of Rule 10b-5(b) to impose liability on a law firm based on the alleged falsity of its client's statements.

As this Court recently explained in In re Refco, 2009 U.S. Dist. LEXIS 21505, the starting point for this analysis is Central Bank of Denver v. First Interstate Bank of Denver, 511 U.S. 164 (1994), which held that § 10(b) imposes liability only on persons who, themselves, make a material misstatement or omission, and that there is no liability for aiding and abetting fraudulent conduct. In Shapiro v. Cantor, 123 F.3d 717 (2d Cir. 1997), the Second Circuit observed that "[i]f Central Bank is to have any real meaning, a defendant must actually make a false or misleading statement in order to be held liable under Section 10(b). Anything short of such conduct is merely aiding and abetting . . . *no matter how substantial that aid may be* . . . . " Id. at 720 (emphasis added). This requirement draws a "bright line" between the conduct of a secondary actor and that of a primary violator. To rise to the level of a primary violation, the secondary actor must not only make a material misstatement or omission, but "the misrepresentation must be attributed to the specific actor at the time of public dissemination," such as in advance of the investment decision, so as not to undermine the element of reliance required for § 10(b) liability. "Allegations of 'assisting,' 'participating in,' 'complicity in' and similar synonyms . . . all fall within the prohibitive bar of Central Bank." Shapiro, 123 F.3d at 720. . . .

[H]ere, the decisive question is whether the allegations against Mayer Brown are sufficient to show that the misstatements and omissions made by Mayer Brown can be attributed to them such that the statements on which the THL Funds relied are the statements of *Mayer Brown*. They are not. . . .

The misstatements to which the THL Funds refer are to instances prior to the 2004 Purchase in which Collins passed along statements made by Refco principals to representatives of the THL Funds. In each of these instances, plaintiffs' allegations specifically concede that Collins was simply repeating information provided by others without any endorsement or representation that Mayer Brown had, itself, verified or adopted the information provided. . . . Mayer Brown's mere association with statements made by others—here, by relaying a statement that is attributed to the authority of another—is insufficient to make a secondary actor liable under § 10(b).

Plaintiffs' insistence that the statements were made "directly" to the THL Funds does not alter this result. The issue is not who made the misstatement, but to whom the "misstatement is attributed . . . at the time of [its] dissemination." Lattanzio v. Deloitte & Touche LLP, 476 F.3d 147, 155(2d Cir. 2007). . . . For Mayer Brown to be liable, the statements on which the THL Funds purportedly relied must be the statements of Mayer Brown. When Mayer Brown says only, it had "confirmed with Bennett that . . . no other undisclosed contracts or arrangements existed," the statement that there are no such contracts or arrangements is expressly attributed to Bennett. All Mayer Brown is asserting on its own authority is that Bennett made certain assurances.

To be sure, this does not mean that Collins or Mayer Brown can convey such falsehoods, knowing that they are lies, with impunity. An innocent agent who conveys on behalf of another a message he believes in good faith to be true does nothing wrong; an agent who understands that his employer's statement is a lie, aids and abets the fraud. He remains, however, an aider and abettor under § 10(b), not a primary violator. . . .

Plaintiffs have pleaded no facts to suggest that Mayer Brown represented to the THL Funds, or that the THL Funds otherwise understood, that Mayer Brown was vetting or endorsing the information it was passing on from Refco's management. . . . To the contrary, as the complaint expressly alleges, Collins took care to distance himself and Meyer Brown from the statements; he did not report that he or Mayer Brown were stating that all the documents had been provided or that there were no related-party transactions, but that Bennett or Refco had so stated.

The sole allegation in the complaint that attempts to provide a sufficient factual basis that plaintiffs reasonably understood Mayer Brown to be speaking on its own authority throughout the due diligence process refers to Mayer Brown's longstanding representation of Refco. Plaintiffs contend that as counsel to Refco "[Mayer Brown] would be drawing on its own extensive knowledge and information built up over the many years that [the firm] had been working with Refco." This allegation is insufficient to establish a primary violation . . . because, "[u]nless [the THL Funds'] understanding is based on the [defendant's] articulated statement, the source for that understanding . . . does not matter." Even if what the THL Funds were, in fact, relying on was that an attorney would not knowingly convey the false statements of his client because doing so would violate the rules of professional conduct, the Second Circuit has already explained that "violation of [such rules] does not establish securities fraud in the civil context." Finnerty, 533 F.3d at 151.

Accordingly, Count Two of the Amended Complaint must be dismissed.

IV. Sufficiency of the Rule 10b-5(a) and (c) Claim . . .

In addition to Mayer Brown's actionable misstatements to the THL Funds and their counsel, plaintiffs posit a "scheme liability" theory based on Mayer Brown's participation in the round-trip loans that transformed Refco's uncollectible losses into receivables owed to Refco by third-parties.[12] This allegation is identical to the allegation made by plaintiff-investors in *In re Refco* and Mayer Brown seeks dismissal of this claim for precisely the same reason. Mayer Brown argues, inter alia, that the Supreme Court's decision in *Stoneridge* forecloses this theory of liability. For reasons more fully elaborated in *In re Refco*, they are correct. . . .

Here, as in *Stoneridge* and *In re Refco*, it is undisputed that plaintiffs did not know that Mayer Brown helped facilitate the fraudulent transactions. . . .

As this Court recently explained in *In re Refco*,

. . . Here the scheme to defraud was Refco's effort to hide from its investors the true state of its finances by concealing the uncollectible receivables and it was

---

12. Specifically sections (a) and (c) of Rule 10b-5 prohibit "employ[ing] any device, scheme or artifice to defraud," or "engag[ing] in any act, practice or course of business which operates . . . as a fraud or deceit upon any person" in connection with the sale of securities. 17 C.F.R. §240.10b-5(a), (c).

Refco that engaged in the deceitful practice of making the round-trip loans and reporting them in its financial statements as if they were bona fide loan transactions. However significant a role the Mayer Brown Defendants played in assisting Refco's management to engage in these transactions, and however culpable they may have been to do so with the knowledge that the transactions were ultimately designed as part of a scheme to defraud and practice a deceit upon Refco's shareholders—indeed even if the acts of Collins were, as the Government has charged, criminal—the liability that attaches to those acts is liability for aiding and abetting Refco's schemes and manipulation, not principal liability for executing schemes of the Mayer Brown Defendants' own. 2009 U.S. Dist. LEXIS 21505.

Accordingly, "even assuming the truth of plaintiffs' factual allegations and granting every reasonable inference therefrom, plaintiffs' evidence would establish only that investors relied on [Refco's] deceptive disclosures concerning transactions" in which Mayer Brown was involved." Count One of the Amended Complaint must therefore be dismissed. . . .

VI. Sufficiency of the Common-Law Negligent Misrepresentation and Fraud Claims

A. Negligent Misrepresentation . . .

The negligent misrepresentation claim is necessarily dismissed [because] plaintiffs have failed to allege, as they must under New York law, that there was a "near-privity" relationship between the parties.[16]

A near-privity relationship exists where there is: "(1) an awareness by the maker of the statement that it is to be used for a particular purpose; (2) reliance by a known party on the statement in furtherance of that purpose; and (3) some conduct by the maker of the statement linking it to the relying party and evincing its understanding of that reliance." Houbigant, Inc. v. Dev. Specialists, Inc., 229 F. Supp. 2d 208, 216 (S.D.N.Y. 2002).

Plaintiffs allege that Mayer Brown had regular, direct, and continuous contact with the THL Funds and their representatives—including face-to-face meetings, telephone conferences, email and other correspondence, and that Mayer Brown provided access to documents related to the 2004 Purchase. The THL Funds further allege that they were relying on the information provided by Mayer Brown and that "Mayer Brown knew full well" of that reliance. This argument fails because while "face-to-face conversation . . . or other substantive communication between the parties" can give rise to a duty of care, plaintiffs have alleged no facts that would support that there was "some conduct by [Mayer Brown] . . . evincing its understanding of [the THL Funds'] reliance." . . .

Mayer Brown's history with Refco, without more, does not constitute the type of "specialized expertise" that is required in order to impose a duty of care

---

16. Mayer Brown does not, on this motion, challenge plaintiffs' pleadings with respect to the other elements of the tort of negligent misrepresentation, which are "(1) carelessness in imparting words; (2) upon which others were expected to rely; (3) and upon which they did act or failed to act; (4) to their damage." Dallas Aerospace. Inc. v. CIS Air Corp., 352 F.3d 775, 788 (2d Cir. 2003).

in this context. See Doehla v. Wathne Limited, Inc., 1999 U.S. Dist. LEXIS 11787 (S.D.N.Y. Aug. 3, 1999) (dismissing a negligent misrepresentation claim against a lawyer by non-client where the lawyer did not "hold himself out to be an expert" and "reliance on [his] opinion by the third-party [was not the] 'end and aim' of the engagement of the lawyer"). If it were otherwise, every non-client would have a claim against every law firm who failed to exercise due care in the context of representing a long-standing client in a financial transaction. What Mayer Brown knew about Refco amounts to nothing more than knowledge of the particulars of the company's business and of the true situation underlying the misrepresentations pertaining to that business. . . .

Accordingly, New York law does not impose liability for negligent misrepresentations in such a context and Count Five of the Amended Complaint must be dismissed.

B. Fraud

Finally, Mayer Brown asserts that plaintiffs' common-law fraud claim must be dismissed, inter alia, because plaintiffs cannot establish that they justifiably relied on Mayer Brown's representations regarding Refco's financial condition.[17] In assessing the reasonableness of a plaintiff's alleged reliance, the court must "consider the entire context of the transaction, including factors such as its complexity and magnitude, the sophistication of the parties, and the content of any agreements between them." Emergent Capital Inv. Management, LLC v. Stonepath Group, Inc., 343 F.3d 189, 195 (2d. Cir. 2003). . . .

The gravamen of the THL Funds' claim is not that they relied on some stray remark or extra-contractual representation made by Mayer Brown. The THL Funds maintain that they relied to their detriment on the very representations that saturated the 2004 Purchase Agreement. As Mayer Brown itself argues in defending themselves against plaintiffs' federal securities law claims, the representations made by Mayer Brown to the THL Funds were, in fact, nothing more than the recitation by Collins and Mayer Brown of the representations being made by Bennett and Refco. Indeed, the critical representations by Bennett, relayed by Collins, that there were no undisclosed related-party transactions are the exact representations made in the 2004 Purchase Agreement itself that Mayer Brown now says are the only representations on which the THL Funds were entitled justifiably to rely. These representations were, according to the allegations of the complaint, known by the Mayer Brown defendants to be false and fraudulent, and the truth was concealed by a fraudulent scheme in which Mayer Brown was allegedly intimately involved. . . .

---

17. To prove common law fraud under New York law, a plaintiff must show that: "(1) the defendant made a material false statement or omission; (2) the defendant intended to defraud the plaintiff; (3) the plaintiff reasonably relied upon the representation or omission; and (4) the plaintiff suffered damage as a result of such reliance." Century Pacific, Inc. v. Hilton Hotels Corp., 528 F. Supp. 2d 206, 218 (S.D.N.Y. 2007). Claims of fraud must survive the heightened particularity requirements of Rule 9(b). See Stern v. Gen. Elec. Co., 924 F.2d 472, 476 n.6 (2d Cir. 1991).

Nothing in New York law prevents the THL Funds from suing Mayer Brown on the theory that the THL Funds relied on false representations made by Refco *that Mayer Brown, with knowledge of their falsity, helped Refco to make*, and the falsity of which Mayer Brown helped Refco to conceal.

Thus, while the THL Funds' claims under the federal securities law fail because the THL Funds cannot show that they relied on statements attributable to Mayer Brown, such that Mayer Brown is, for purposes of federal law, merely an aider and abettor of Refco's fraud, no such attribution is needed here. Under New York law, plaintiffs may sue defendants who aided and abetted a fraud. See Lerner v. Fleet Bank, N.A., 459 F.3d 273, 292 (2d Cir. 2006).[18] The Amended Complaint is replete with allegations that Mayer Brown's statements and conduct assisted the execution of Refco's fraudulent scheme, which culminated in the 2004 Purchase Agreement. Specifically, plaintiffs allege that Mayer Brown acted behind the scenes to help Refco to accomplish the concealment of the RGHI receivables by means of the fraudulent round-trip loans, and that Collins further aided the scheme by selectively producing documents and conveying Bennett's false representations, including representations that the Purchase Agreement expressly states are relied upon by the THL Funds. The Purchase Agreement's false representations, false warrantees, and false disclosures, the falsity of which the Mayer Brown Defendants are alleged to have helped conceal, and any doubts about which Collins is alleged to have helped assuage by conveying the false assurances of Bennett's and Refco, are precisely what induced the THL Funds to enter into the 2004 Purchase.

Mayer Brown's argument that it cannot be held liable for the "host of misrepresentations made *by Refco*, both during due diligence and in the Purchase Agreement," has the point exactly backwards. Mayer Brown's assistance in perpetrating the fraud at Refco, namely maintaining the illusion that there were no related-party transactions concealing Refco's uncollectible debt, is precisely the course of conduct that the 2004 Purchase Agreement memorialized and on which the THL Funds relied in entering the LBO. Mayer Brown's substantial and knowing participation in perpetrating the Refco frauds—if proven as alleged—including its help effectuating the round-trip loans that transformed Refco's uncollectible losses into receivables owed to Refco by third-parties its statements and in assisting Refco's misconduct throughout the due diligence process, all aided and abetted the fraud on which the THL Funds relied.

Finally, it is of no help to Mayer Brown that the THL Funds, in an effort to avoid application of the rule of *Central Bank* and *Stoneridge*, have carefully

---

18. To establish liability under New York law for aiding and abetting fraud, plaintiffs must prove: "(1) the existence of a fraud; (2) a defendant's knowledge of the fraud; and (3) that the defendant provided substantial assistance to advance the fraud's commission." Lerner, 459 F.3d at 292. The knowledge requirement of an aiding and abetting fraud claim is satisfied by alleging actual knowledge of the underlying fraud. Kolbeck v. LIT America, Inc., 939 F. Supp. 240, 246 (S.D.N.Y. 1996) The "substantial assistance" requirement is satisfied "where a defendant affirmatively assists, helps conceal, or by virtue of failing to act when required to do so enables the fraud to proceed." Cromer Fin. Ltd. v. Berger, 137 F. Supp. 2d 452, 470 (S.D.N.Y. 2001).

refrained from using the words "aiding and abetting" and have simply alleged a claim against Mayer Brown for fraud. "Fraud by a primary actor" and "aiding and abetting fraud" are not separate and distinct torts, but merely different ways in which a defendant can be liable for its participation in defrauding a plaintiff. . . . Plaintiffs have adequately pleaded facts stating a valid legal claim under New York law against Mayer Brown, and with the particularity necessary to survive the heightened pleading requirements of Federal Rule of Civil Procedure 9(b). Accordingly, the motion to dismiss Count Four must be denied.

CONCLUSION

For the reasons stated above, Mayer Brown's motion to dismiss is denied with respect to the claim of fraud and granted in all other respects.

In re Refco Securities Litigation
2010 U.S. Dist. LEXIS 107695 (S.D.N.Y.)

Jed S. RAKOFF, U.S.D.J.

. . . The Special Master's Report and Recommendation dated May 3, 2010 (the "May 3 Report") recommended the dismissal with prejudice of plaintiffs' RICO claim against defendant Mayer, Brown, Rowe & Maw LLP ("Mayer Brown"). The Report and Recommendation dated May 6, 2010 (the "May 6 Report") recommended the denial of defendant Collins's motion.[1] . . . Recently, however, plaintiffs settled all claims against both defendants. Nevertheless, since the motions raised some novel, if modest, issues, it is appropriate to set forth briefly, as promised, the reasons for the Court's previous [decisions], if the matter had not become moot.

Plaintiffs invested more than $450 million in Refco and acquired the majority of Refco's stock through the August 2004 leveraged buy-out. After Refco collapsed in the fall of 2005, plaintiffs allegedly lost more than $245 million. Plaintiffs alleged that defendants conspired with certain Refco insiders, in violation of § 1962(d) of the Racketeer Influenced and Corrupt Organizations Act ("RICO"), 18 U.S.C. §§ 1961-68, to violate § 1962(c) of RICO in such a way as to further the insiders' fraudulent scheme to conceal Refco's true financial condition.

On July 10, 2009, defendant Collins was convicted by a jury on five of fourteen counts relating to his participation in the Refco fraud: one count of conspiracy to commit securities fraud, wire fraud, bank fraud, and money laundering, to make false filings with the SEC, and to make material

---

1. Plaintiffs' Second Amended Complaint also asserted a claim for common law fraud against both defendants, which survived a prior motion to dismiss brought before Judge Lynch, see Thomas H. Lee Equity Fund V. L.P. v. Mayer Brown, Rowe & Maw LLP, 612 F. Supp. 2d 267, 286-89 (S.D.N.Y. 2009), and was not at issue on these motions.

misstatements to auditors; two counts of securities fraud; and two counts of wire fraud. Judge Patterson subsequently sentenced Collins principally to seven years' imprisonment.

Under section 107 of the Private Securities Litigation Reform Act ("PSLRA"), incorporated into § 1964(c) of RICO, a civil RICO claim may not be premised on conduct that would have been actionable as securities fraud unless brought against a "person that is criminally convicted in connection with the fraud, in which case the statute of limitations shall start to run on the date on which the conviction becomes final." 18 U.S.C. § 1964 (c). The parties do not dispute that the RICO claims at issue would have been actionable as securities fraud, but plaintiffs contend that the so-called "criminal conviction exception" of § 1964(c) applies not just to Collins but also to Mayer Brown, because defendant Collins was a Mayer Brown partner at the time of the relevant underlying events. However, even though, theoretically, the Government might have brought criminal charges against Mayer Brown based on the acts of its partner, it chose not to do so, and the plain language of section 1964(c) requires a person-specific conviction. In the absence of such a conviction, plaintiffs' civil RICO claim against defendant Mayer Brown is barred by the PSLRA. . . .

With respect to defendant Collins, the Court agrees with Special Master Capra that Collins's conviction is "final" and rejects defendant Collins's objection that a conviction is not final for the purposes of the criminal conviction exception until after the appeals process is exhausted. Collins has been convicted by a jury, his motion for a new trial has been denied, and judgment has been entered against him. This is sufficient to render a judgment final for virtually all collateral purposes.

Therefore, the Court turns to defendant Collins's objection that plaintiffs have failed to adequately plead a RICO claim, especially with respect to "scienter" and "continuity."

A claim that a person conspired under § 1962(d) to violate § 1962(c) by conspiracy to conduct the affairs of an enterprise through predicate acts of mail, wire, and securities fraud requires, inter alia, that the defendant "knew about and agreed to facilitate the [fraudulent] scheme," Salinas v. United States, 522 U.S. 52, 66 (1997). Plaintiffs allege that "Collins intended to further, agreed to further, and in fact did further the fraudulent schemes of the Refco Operators and w[as] aware of the existence, if not the very identity, of the other participants in the fraudulent schemes and conspiracy." Specific factual allegations from which scienter can be inferred include that "Collins was involved from the inception of [the sham loan] transactions" and directed the handling of the transaction documents, that "Bennett asked Collins for assistance in developing arguments that could be used to demonstrate to the Federal Reserve Bank of New York that RGHI had substantial net worth," and that Collins "manufactur[ed] . . . the counterfeit Fourth LLC Agreement, which Collins falsely represented to the THL Funds to be the genuine Fourth LLC Agreement." Plaintiffs' allegations are thus sufficiently detailed to establish that defendant Collins possessed the required scienter.

As for the requirement that the underlying pattern of predicate acts exhibit continuity, . . . [p]laintiffs' Second Amended Complaint details a fraudulent scheme by the Refco insiders . . . to conceal Refco's financial condition, that began "as early as 1997," and included Collins' involvement between 2000 and 2005 "in multiple facets of the 17 sham round-trip loan transactions that Bennett orchestrated to hide the RGHI Receivable and misrepresent Refco's true financial condition," before the scheme was finally exposed in 2005. The Court thus concludes that plaintiffs have sufficiently pleaded a continuous, close-ended pattern of racketeering activity.

For the foregoing reasons, . . . if the case had not settled, [the Court] would have now . . . granted Mayer Brown's motion to dismiss the RICO claim with prejudice, and denied defendant Collins's motion to dismiss the RICO claim. . . .

▓ Lawyers' Roles:
The Instrumental Lawyer and the Bounds of the Law

Viewed from a public perspective, the Jones Day and Mayer Brown lawyers in the *ACC* and *Refco* cases facilitated a massive fraud. Like other prominent law firms ensnared in client misbehavior in past decades, these lawyers appear to have misconstrued their role in the representation. Indeed, two years before Judge Bilby's decision in *ACC*, Judge Stanley Sporkin upheld the federal receivership of Lincoln Savings & Loan, concluding his opinion with these observations:

> There are other unanswered questions presented by this case. Keating (the client's CEO) testified that he was so bent on doing the "right thing" that he surrounded himself with literally scores of accountants and lawyers to make sure all the transactions were legal. The questions that must be asked are:
>
> Where were these professionals, a number of whom are now asserting their rights under the Fifth Amendment, when these clearly improper transactions were being consummated?
>
> Why didn't any of them speak up or disassociate themselves from the transactions? Where also were the outside accountants and attorneys when these transactions were effectuated?[1]

Both fiascos illustrate what can happen when lawyers overidentify with clients and fail to maintain the distance critical to evaluating a client's conduct. The *ACC* and *Refco* lawyers may have experienced the business lawyers' "chronic source of moral difficulty": assisting a client's business goal of gaining a competitive advantage required them to skate too close to the edge of the law and put other people's money at risk.[2] Lawyers who continue to advocate for such a client unwittingly, negligently, or knowingly can become an instrument of wrongdoing or an accessory to corrupt and dishonest conduct. The behavior of lawyers who

---

1. Lincoln Savings & Loan Assn. v. Wall, 743 F. Supp. 901, 919-920 (D.D.C. 1990).

2. *See* David Luban, *Making Sense of Moral Meltdowns,* in Susan D. Carle, ed., *Lawyers' Ethics and the Pursuit of Social Justice: A Critical Reader* 355 (NYU Press 2005).

do this suggests that they might view the law as a malleable means to pursue a client's objectives, rather than as a set of rules with some clear boundaries that should have shaped both their clients' and their own behavior.

The Bounds of the Law

The fiduciary relationship between principal-client and agent-lawyer is subject to one significant limitation: Neither may violate the limits or bounds of the law.[3] Both principal and agent remain responsible for the consequences of their own conduct. Agency law recognizes principal and agent as distinct, autonomous legal persons, and anticipates that they will behave accordingly.[4]

Lawyers can be put in a position of real conflict when it comes to abiding by client instructions. On one hand, fiduciary duty embedded in the Model Rules admonishes lawyers to do everything they can to help fulfill the client's goals of the representation, goals that are to be determined by the client.[5] On the other, clients can make decisions that the lawyer believes reflect bad judgment, or worse, that suggest to the lawyer that the client might be engaging in conduct that could run afoul of the law and subject the client to liability.[6] When lawyers place too much weight on the former role—simply being instruments and unquestioningly abiding by their client's instructions—they disserve the client by failing to share their independent view of the merits of the course of action, a failure that can facilitate wrongful behavior, opening their clients to potential legal consequences.[7] The *ACC* and *Refco* aftermaths illustrate that lawyers who are willfully blind to their client's actual goals also disserve themselves, by exposing themselves and their law firms to significant liability.

It is important to realize that a lawyer can be subjected to allegations of assisting client misconduct in at least three different circumstances. In the first, lawyers, like those in *Chen*, the next case in this chapter, unwittingly or innocently participate in the client's fraud by providing legal advice to a client who, unbeknownst to the lawyer, is using it to break the law. In the second, lawyers act negligently by failing to identify or act upon red flags, which, with the benefit of 20-20 hindsight, will be characterized as clear warnings that the client was engaged in wrongful conduct. The third, and most serious, involves lawyers who act recklessly or intentionally by blindly ignoring clear warning signs, or worse, purposefully assisting a client to violate the law. Everyone recognizes the last as a clear example of lawyer misconduct. But the middle example can get lawyers in almost as much trouble, and the first, unwitting involvement, requires an immediate response at the point the lawyer discovers the client's unlawful activity. In all of these circumstances, the lawyer who fails to keep the proper distance and overidentifies with the client is the lawyer who is most likely to ignore the warning signs.

---

3. RLGL § 23; *Restatement (Third) of Agency* § 1.01, Comment f(1) (2006).
4. *Id.* at Comment c.
5. MR 1.2(a); RLGL § 22.
6. MR 1.2(d); RLGL § 23.
7. Fred C. Zacharias, *Practice, Theory, and the War on Terror,* 59 Emory L. J. 333 (2009).

The collapse of ACC and Refco also illustrates how the many faces of corporate identity can have grave consequences for lawyers when an entity fails. At that point, a successor in interest, such as a bankruptcy trustee (or the receiver in ACC), reassesses the entity's best interests, with a view toward maximizing the funds available to creditors and other stakeholders.[8] In *Thomas H. Lee Equity Fund*, third-party investors who lost money when the company went bankrupt are making similar claims. And in *In re Refco Securities Litigation,* we learn that the senior Mayer Brown lawyer, Joseph Collins, subsequently was indicted and convicted of federal securities fraud in the matter, setting up both a successful civil RICO action against him, as well as his disbarment in Illinois.[9]

The Problem with Instrumental Behavior

No lawyer or law firm is invulnerable to serious allegations of complicity in client misconduct. In retrospect, what is so amazing about these cases is that very well educated and talented lawyers could allow themselves to be used by such clever and self-serving clients.[10] Of course, one explanation is always monetary, that a lawyer or large law firm faded ethically in seeking a lucrative economic opportunity.[11]

It is also possible that overidentification with a client might have been caused in part by nonmonetary considerations, such as admiration for the extreme risk-taking of the company's managers.[12] Whatever the motivations, the role assumed by lawyers in these situations enabled their clients to turn them into instruments of their wrongful conduct. In the process, the lawyers apparently lost some of

---

8. The Refco bankruptcy trustee brought such a fraud case as a kind of shareholder's derivative suit, alleging that Mayer Brown should not have obeyed certain officers of the company. *See In re Refco,* 609 F. Supp. 2d 304 (S.D. N.Y. 2009) (dismissing the cause of action based on federal securities law for the same reasons as *Thomas H. Lee Equity Fund*).

9. Collins was disbarred on consent on Sept. 20, 2010. ARDC.org, http://www.iardc.org/ldetail. asp?id=842716288, (last visited June 29, 2012). His criminal conviction was reversed due to error in instructions to a juror. United States v. Collins, 665 F.3d 454 (2d Cir 2012). A retrial is set to begin as this edition is being published.

10. In the Lincoln Savings and Loan matter, the Jones Day law firm eventually settled the public and private claims against it for $75 million. Henry J. Reske, *Firm Agrees to Record S & L Settlement: Shifting Standards Require Lawyers to Disclose More to Regulatory Agencies,* 79 ABA J. 16 (July 1993). The law firm of Kaye, Scholer, Fierman Nays, & Handler represented Lincoln on regulatory matters after Jones Day finally withdrew. It also settled with both private investors ($21 million) and the government ($41 million). Stephen Labaton, *Law Firm Will Pay a $41 Million Fine in Savings Lawsuit,* N.Y. Times, Mar. 9, 1992, at A1.

11. *See* Elizabeth Chamblis, *Whose Ethics?* in Leslie C. Levin & Lynn Mather, eds., *Lawyers in Practice: Ethical Decisionmaking in Context* 47 (U. Chicago Press 2012). This is a large part of the explanation given by Prof. Regan for the conviction of John Gellene of Milbank Tweed, who committed bankruptcy fraud while representing a large and lucrative client. *See* Milton Regan, Jr., *Eat What You Kill: The Fall of a Wall Street Lawyer* (U. Mich. Press 2004).

12. Several prominent public figures also admired Charles Keating, Lincoln's CEO, for his entrepreneurial abilities. The "Keating Five" was the derogatory moniker placed on five U.S. senators (Alan Cranston, Dennis DeConcini, John Glenn, Donald Riegle, and John McCain) whose careers were nearly ruined by their close association to Keating. *See* Richard L. Berke, *Cranston Rebuked by Ethics Panel,* N.Y. Times, Nov. 20, 1991, at A1.

their ability to evaluate objectively their client's conduct, and as a result, were implicated in the client's wrongdoing.[13]

Looking back, one might argue that a lack of moral integrity on the part of these lawyers prevented them from recognizing dangers when they materialized.[14] Although it is no doubt true that lawyers need to listen to their own moral intuition, it also appears to be the case that personal conscience can be significantly affected by implicit but often unexpressed values in social milieus, including the moral world of both clients and law firms.[15] Perhaps most at risk are law firms who represent lucrative clients engaged in significant risk-taking, often in businesses that are heavily regulated by law.[16] These risks can be exacerbated by clients or law firms who engage in generally dishonest strategies, such as blaming or shifting loss to others, or worse, covering up misconduct or bad results.[17]

The Cure for Instrumental Behavior

Professor Rhode warns that this kind of instrumental behavior is especially dangerous and misplaced in representing entities rather than individuals, and in counseling clients rather than litigating on their behalf. When a powerful enterprise's, rather than an autonomous individual's, interests are at stake, the rights-based justification for role-differentiated behavior has much less legitimacy. When lawyers counsel clients, Rhode echoes Judge Bilby's clear advice in *ACC*, pointing out that lawyers who deal with ongoing and future behavior are provided with an opportunity and an obligation to prevent, rather than justify, massive social and personal harm.[18]

Lawyers can recognize these dangers of "serious regulatory violations" by setting up an early warning system, which prompts them to assess both risky practice environments and the strength of their own counterintuitions. First, they should assess what level of risk comes with the territory—from the client's world as well as from the lawyer's practice environment. Second, lawyers should respond to risk by creating baselines for themselves that might warn about changes in the lawyer's personal judgments caused by the environment in which they practice. Professor Luban suggests you create your own, such as, "I will never backdate a document," "paper a deal I don't understand," or "do

---

13. This is the way Judge Noonan describes the transformation of another influential lawyer, Hoyt Moore, whose representation of Bethlehem Steel led him to bribe a federal judge to secure his client's goals. John T. Noonan, Jr., *The Lawyer Who Overidentifies with His Client*, 76 Notre Dame L. Rev. 827, 840-841 (2001). *See also* United States v. Stewart, 590 F.3d 93 (2d Cir. 2009) (affirming lawyer's conviction for giving material aid to terrorists).

14. *See, e.g.,* Stephen L. Pepper, *Counseling at the Limits of the Law: An Exercise in the Jurisprudence and Ethics of Lawyering*, 104 Yale L.J. 1545 (1995).

15. *See* Verna E. Monson & Neil W. Hamilton, *Ethical (Trans) formation: Early Career Lawyers Make Sense of Professionalism*, 8 U. St. Thomas L. J. 129 (2011); Milton C. Regan, Jr., *Moral Intuitions and Organizational Culture*, 51 St. Louis U. L.J. 941 (2007).

16. *See* Patrick Schmidt, *The Ethical Lives of Securities Lawyers*, in Levin, *supra* note 11, at 221.

17. Luban, *supra* note 2 at 364.

18. *See supra* pp. 10-11.

something I cannot explain to my (grandmother, father, or significant other)."[19] He also recommends noticing when you begin to blame others for your conduct, and suggests that self-doubt, rather than hubris, best approximates a lawyer's best chance to recognize a limit on his or her client's or the lawyer's behavior.[20] All of this advice is also subsumed in the mandate of Model Rule 1.2(d): Lawyers must recognize clear legal limits to permissible client behavior, inform the client, and be willing to withdraw from the representation when the client will not cease and desist.

2. Privilege and Work Product: Client Crime or Fraud

Problem

7-10. Martyn admonished client about the importance of fully disclosing all assets on a bankruptcy filing. Client failed to do so and was indicted for bankruptcy fraud. Can Martyn be forced to testify about the original warning?

Consider: Model Rules 1.6(b)(6)
RLGL §§ 82, 93

United States v. Chen
99 F.3d 1495 (9th Cir. 1996), cert. denied, 520 U.S. 1167 (1997)

KLEINFELD, Circuit Judge:

This case deals with the scope of the crime-fraud exception to the attorney-client privilege, where the attorney is innocent of any wrongdoing or guilty knowledge.

FACTS

Mr. Chen and his wife own Sunrider Corporation and operate TF Chen Products, Inc., a subsidiary of Sunrider. The companies manufacture health food and skin care products and import from Taiwan, Hong Kong, Japan, and other countries. The importation tariffs the companies pay depend on the price they declare they paid for the goods. Undervaluation may result in administrative, civil, and criminal penalties. A statutory procedure allows an importer to mitigate or avoid penalties by filing a disclosure statement before the Customs Service learns of the undervaluation independently. *See* U.S.C. §1592(c)(4).

Of course an importer also pays taxes on profits. The higher the cost of goods sold, then, other things being equal, the lower the level of income taxes. Thus, an importer saves money on tariffs to the extent the goods are cheap, but

---

19. Luban, *supra* note 2, at 369.
20. *Id.*

pays more in income tax. Conversely, the company saves money on taxes, but pays higher tariffs, to the extent its cost of goods is higher.

The Customs duties on the higher values are much less than the additional taxes which would be due based on the true values. Thus an importer can come out ahead by overpaying tariffs and underpaying income taxes, by overstating the cost of the goods imported.

Mr. and Mrs. Chen and Sunrider were indicted for conspiracy, tax evasion, and other crimes. The indictment alleged that Mr. and Mrs. Chen imported their inventory and paid tariffs based on the true invoiced price. Then Mr. Chen's sister, Jau Hwa, the comptroller of Sunrider, would prepare entirely fictional invoices on blank forms from Sunrider's Hong Kong affiliate, owned largely by the Chens and operated by Mrs. Chen's brother. The fake invoices purported to charge much higher prices for the goods. The fake invoices were then given to Sunrider's accountants to prepare trial balances, which were themselves given to Sunrider's tax preparers. Thus, tariffs would be paid on the true lower price of the goods, but taxes would be paid as though the goods had cost much more than they really did. Mr. Chen periodically instructed Jau Hwa to wire excess money to the Hong Kong affiliate's bank accounts, to maintain the fiction that Sunrider's payments were based on the fake invoices, not the real ones. Mr. and Mrs. Chen would subsequently recover the excess with the connivance of Mrs. Chen's brother. The government alleges that the Chens skimmed almost $90 million this way.

According to the indictment, the Chens eventually became concerned that IRS and Customs enforcement agents might communicate on their case and discover the difference in the claimed cost of their inventory. To protect themselves, they caused a disclosure to be made to Customs, purporting to acknowledge that they had understated their cost of goods imported. In the disclosure, they stated that the true cost of the goods was what they had reflected in their tax returns. Thus, the original Customs declarations were true, but the correcting disclosure was actually not a disclosure at all, but a fraud, intended to shield their tax evasion scheme. This scheme is entirely theoretical at this point, because nothing has yet been proven.

Mr. Chen's attorneys, Stein, Shostak, Shostak & O'Hara, filed a prior disclosure pursuant to 19 U.S.C. § 1592(c)(4) and section 162.74 of the Customs regulations stating that a review gave rise to the discovery that "certain charges relating to the imported products may not have been properly included in the entered value." A check for over $381,000 was enclosed with the disclosure. The law firm said that more money would be paid as more data were assembled revealing underpayments.

Jau Hwa eventually left Sunrider. She then gave the government materials she had taken from Sunrider's files, and gave a customs agent her account of events on which the indictment is based. The Customs agent filed an affidavit saying that according to Jau Hwa, "Marjorie Shostak [Sunrider's lawyer] proposed that Sunrider should file a disclosure with Customs." Though this affidavit does not say in so many words that Ms. Shostak knew that the disclosure would be false, and intended to hide a tax evasion scheme, the Assistant United

States Attorney argued that the differences between the initial and supplemental invoices was "substantial enough to put any reasonable professional on notice that this was, in all likelihood, a fraudulent scheme."

Joseph P. Cox had worked on the Sunrider matter for the Stein, Shostak firm; James D. Wilets was in-house Sunrider counsel. Both were subpoenaed before the Grand Jury. The Chens and Sunrider moved to quash these two subpoenas based on their attorney-client privilege. . . .

Ms. Shostak filed a declaration that her firm was employed to avoid litigation by bringing Sunrider into compliance with the Customs laws, by voluntarily disclosing supplemental payments already reported to the IRS. . . . She explained in detail the nature of the transactions and why her firm "saw nothing to suggest that a prior disclosure would further some alleged tax evasion scheme." She stated plainly that neither she nor any attorney to her knowledge had engaged in the conduct alleged by Jau Hwa, done anything to mislead Customs, or had any knowledge of or participation in any fraud on the government. Mr. Wilets and Mr. Cox also filed affidavits explaining what services they had performed on behalf of the Chens and Sunrider, stating that to the best of their knowledge neither they, the accountants, the Ernst & Young Customs group assisting with the prior disclosure, nor anyone else involved, including the Chens, had ever intended to further any tax evasion scheme or known about such a scheme. General counsel for Sunrider, Cynthia Muldrow, filed an affidavit establishing that no one had authorized Jau Hwa to take any documents with her when she left the corporation, or to disclose any attorney-client information to anyone outside Sunrider.

After considering all the evidence, the district judge . . . found "the attorneys are not involved in the involved crime," because there was not even a "prima facie case that these attorneys in any way participated in or joined the alleged criminal conspiracy." . . . The judge nevertheless denied the Chens' motions to quash the Grand Jury subpoenas, "provided the questioning is confined to matters concerning the disclosures which TFCP/Sunrider made to United States Customs in 1989–1990." The district judge expressly found a prima facie case establishing reasonable cause to believe that the Chens and Sunrider had used their lawyers to make false statements, albeit not known to the lawyers to be false, to the Customs Service. . . .

ANALYSIS . . .

The attorney-client privilege is essential to preservation of liberty against a powerful government. People need lawyers to guide them through thickets of complex government requirements, and, to get useful advice, they have to be able to talk to their lawyers candidly without fear that what they say to their own lawyers will be transmitted to the government.

Much of what lawyers actually do for a living consists of helping their clients comply with the law. Clients unwittingly engage in conduct subject to civil and even criminal penalties. This valuable social service of counseling clients and bringing them into compliance with the law cannot be performed effectively if clients are scared to tell their lawyers what they are doing, for fear that their lawyers will be turned into government informants. . . .

It is a truism that while the attorney-client privilege stands firm for client's revelations of past conduct, it cannot be used to shield ongoing or intended future criminal conduct. United States v. Zolin, 491 U.S. 554, 563 (1989). That principle is easily applied when a lawyer is retained to defend a client in a criminal prosecution or civil litigation relating to an entirely completed course of conduct. But it is difficult to apply when the lawyer's role is more in the nature of business planning or counseling or bringing the client into compliance for past wrongs, as opposed to simply defending the client against a charge relating to past wrongs. The act of bringing a client into compliance with the law ordinarily and properly engages the lawyer in an effort to assure the client is sanctioned no more harshly than the law requires. Because of the delicacy and importance of the attorney–client privilege in the counseling relationship, both the district court's task and ours are especially difficult when the United States Attorney insists upon using a person's own lawyer against him.

The government argues without citation that "where attorneys are involved in business decision-making, or, as Cox and Wilets acted here, as spokespersons for a company, they are clearly not acting as 'professional legal advisors.'" The government argues that this proposition takes the lawyers' planning for correcting understated customs declarations out of the privilege.

The lawyers in this case were "spokespersons" only in the sense that, as lawyers, they communicated their clients' positions to the government agencies dealing with their clients. They were not engaged in a public relations business separate from their law firm, as the government's term "spokespersons" may imply. For a lawyer to tell a judge, jury, or administrative agency, his client's position and the basis for it, that is, to be his client's spokesman, is a traditional and central attorney's function as an advocate. The communications between lawyer to perform this function are privileged. . . .

If a person hires a lawyer for advice, there is a rebuttable presumption that the lawyer is hired "as such" to give "legal advice," whether the subject of the advice is criminal or civil, business, tort, domestic relations, or anything else. But the presumption is rebutted when the facts show that the lawyer was "employed without reference to his knowledge and discretion in the law." . . . That the lawyers were "involved in business decision-making," as the government puts it, is irrelevant. What matters is whether the lawyer was employed with or without "reference to his knowledge and discretion in the law," to give the advice. In this case, the attorneys were employed for their legal knowledge, to bring their clients into compliance with the law in the least burdensome way possible (so far as the lawyers knew). Their communications with their client were therefore within the scope of the attorney-client privilege.

Appellants correctly argue that Jau Hwa, a past employee of Sunrider Corporation, lacked authority to waive the corporation's attorney-client privilege. . . . "The power to waive the corporate attorney-client privilege rests with the corporation's management and is normally exercised by its officers and directors." Commodity Futures Trading Commn. v. Weintraub, 471 U.S. 343, 348

(1985). "When control of a corporation passes to new management, the authority to assert and waive the corporation's attorney-client privilege passes as well." *Id.* at 349. It follows a fortiori that since a corporate employee cannot waive the corporation's privilege, that same individual as an ex-employee cannot do so. An employee must generally keep an employer's confidences. *See Restatement (Second) of Agency* § 395 (1958). The uncontradicted evidence in the record established that Jau Hwa never was given any authority to waive the attorney-client privilege. Thus, Jau Hwa's disclosures of attorney-client communications could not and did not waive the privilege.

Appellants next argue that the government improperly submitted Jau Hwa's affidavit and Agent Diciurcio's affidavit, thereby disclosing to the judge material protected by the attorney-client privilege, before the court decided that such a disclosure should be made. They are correct. The Supreme Court established in *Zolin* that the parties seeking to strip attorney-client communications of their privilege under the crime-fraud exception must satisfy the court with some showing prior to judicial in camera review of the privileged material. . . .

. . . Thus there are two steps. First the government must satisfy the judge that there is "a factual basis adequate to support a good faith belief by a reasonable person that in camera review of the materials may reveal evidence to establish the claim that the crime-fraud exception applies," and then if the judge decides this question in favor of the government, the otherwise privileged material may be submitted for in camera examination. *Id.* The government cannot show the otherwise privileged material to the judge unless and until the judge has made this preliminary judgment. . . .

In the case at bar, the United States Attorney submitted Jau Hwa's disclosures of attorney-client communications, and Diciurcio's affidavit telling more about her disclosures, without first making a prima facie showing and obtaining the court's permission. This was incorrect under *Zolin*. . . .

What is left of the case is whether the government's showing, without Jau Hwa's disclosures, was adequate to invoke the crime-fraud exception. It was. "To invoke the crime-fraud exception successfully, the government has the burden of making a prima facie showing that the communications were in furtherance of an intended or present illegality and that there is some relationship between the communications and the illegality." – The test for invoking the crime-fraud exception to the attorney-client privilege is whether there is "reasonable cause to believe that the attorney's services were utilized in furtherance of the ongoing unlawful scheme." Reasonable cause is more than suspicion but less than a preponderance of evidence. The government must submit "evidence that if believed by the jury would establish the elements of an ongoing violation."

In this case, there was reasonable cause to believe that the Chens and Sunrider were using attorneys' services to conceal income tax fraud. The government submitted copies of blank presigned invoices from Sunrider's supplier, which would facilitate the kind of fraud claimed by the government. The portions of Jau Hwa's affidavit other than her disclosures of attorney-client communications, tended to show, if true, that the company was claiming a low value of goods purchased for Customs' purposes, a high value for income tax purposes, and was proposing to make a fraudulent corrective disclosure to Customs in order to evade income taxes. The evidence, excluding the improperly submitted disclosures of attorney-client communications, further gave reasonable cause to believe that the Chens were using their lawyers to help prepare the paperwork for this fraudulent scheme, and using their prestige in the customs bar to hide it.

The district judge found that the lawyers in this case were innocent of any wrongful intent, and had no knowledge that their services were being used to trick the Customs Service or the IRS. But the lawyers' innocence does not preserve the attorney-client privilege against the crime-fraud exception. The privilege is the client's, so "it is the client's knowledge and intentions that are of paramount concern to the application of the crime-fraud exception; the attorney need know nothing about the client's ongoing or planned illicit activity for the exception to apply. It is therefore irrelevant . . . that [the lawyers] may have been in the dark." . . .

CONCLUSION

The prosecution should have followed the two-step submission procedure in *Zolin*, and did not. But that error was harmless, because the judge disregarded the incorrectly submitted attorney-client communications. The attorneys' lack of any guilty knowledge did not matter, because the privilege was the client's, and the client's misconduct sufficed to lose it, despite the lawyers' innocence of wrongdoing. The properly submitted materials established reasonable cause to believe that the Chens and Sunrider were using their lawyers as part of an ongoing scheme to evade taxes, so the district judge was within his discretion in allowing the government to compel disclosures under the crime-fraud exception.

The Bounds of the Law:
Client Fraud

In a previous note, we saw that lawyers are subject to the law of fraud and misrepresentation and need to understand this law in all its permutations to avoid suffering a number of adverse consequences.[1] *Thomas Hale Equity Fund* indicates that the law of fraud also plays a significant role in the advice that lawyers give to clients. *Chen* further illustrates that a client's fraudulent intent could create an exception to a testimonial privilege, even if the lawyer is unaware of the fraud.

Some of the most notorious corporate frauds of the past 50 years have raised similar questions about the lawyer's role in advising clients. Commenting on his late nineteenth-century law practice, former secretary of state and ABA President Elihu Root is often quoted as saying, "Half of the practice of a decent lawyer consists in telling would-be clients that they are damned fools and should

---

1. *See* The Bounds of the Law: *Duties to Nonclients, supra* p. 155.

stop."[2] This note examines the way the criminal and civil law of fraud and the lawyer codes instruct lawyers when they must identify, respond, and extricate themselves from client fraud.

The vast scope of the modern law of fraud reflects its equally frequent and widespread occurrence.[3] The lawyer's advice can play a central role in avoiding the massive personal and social costs of criminal and fraudulent activity, both to a client and to the others such as shareholders and employees of corporations and family members of individuals. Proper legal advice also can prevent injury to the economic system itself. Fraudulent practices can undercut competition, raise the price of goods, and cause loss of confidence in the market system. Potential economic actors might refrain from market transactions if they do not trust its mechanisms. This chilling effect further impedes the market and can damage social ties, many of which also depend on trust.[4]

The Model Rules

The Model Rules of Professional Conduct include five provisions, Model Rules 1.2(d), 1.13, 1.16, 3.3, and 4.1(b), that require lawyers to recognize and respond to client frauds.[5] Model Rule 1.2(d) prohibits lawyers from counseling or assisting clients in conduct that the lawyer knows to be criminal or fraudulent. Lawyers who represent organizations also are given discretion by Model Rule 1.13 to disclose violations of law to those outside the entity, but "only if and to the extent the lawyer reasonably believes necessary to prevent substantial injury to the organization."[6] Model Rule 1.16 requires lawyers to withdraw from representing clients when the "representation will result in violation of the rules of professional conduct" (such as Model Rule 1.2(d)), and allows withdrawal when "the client

---

2. Phillip C. Jessup, *Elihu Root* Vol. 1, 133 (Dodd, Mead & Co., 1938). Root was noted for his vigorous advocacy of powerful (and occasionally corrupt) individual and corporate clients, including Boss Tweed. Fred Zacharias, *Lawyers as Gatekeepers*, 41 San Diego L. Rev. 1387, 1389-1390 (2004).

3. Overall statistics concerning fraud are not available in the United States, but a comparison of several studies indicates that fraud crimes account for ten times the loss that more conventional crimes (such as burglary, robbery, and auto theft) cause. Brenda L. Nightingale, *The Law of Fraud and Related Offences* 1-24.1 (Carswell 2000). One example is the failure of Lincoln Savings & Loan, which cost taxpayers at least $2.5 billion. *Bad Day at Jones Day; A Record Payment Gets the Law Firm off the Hook in the S&L Debacle, Time,* May 3, 1993 at 23. Canadian statistics for the year 1999 indicate that over one quarter of all criminal prosecutions were for fraud-related crimes. Nightingale, *supra* at 1-21.

4 Nightingale, *supra* note 3, at 1-24.2 to 1-25.

5. Ethics opinions indicate that lawyers face this issue in a wide range of matters. *See, e.g.,* Conn. Informal Op. 93-8 (bank fraud); Ill. Op. 01-06; Texas Op. 480 (1993); Va. LEO 1643 (1995) (bankruptcy fraud); D.C. Op. 296 (2000); Maryland Op. 99-17; Va. LEO 1687 (1996) (immigration fraud); Pa. Bar Assn. Op. 98-27; Pa. Bar Assn. Op. 98-5; Pa. Bar Assn. Op. 91-22; R.I. Op. 93-1(insurance fraud); ABA Informal Op. 1490 (1982); (tax fraud); Utah Op. 06-04; Pa. Bar. Assn. Op. 91-39 (1992) (welfare fraud); Ala. Op. RO-94-08; Pa. Bar Assn. Op. 97-21 (worker's compensation fraud); ABA Formal Op. 93-375, (fraud on a court); Utah Op. 06-04 (fraud on an opposing party).

6. MR 1.13(c)(2).

persists in a course of action involving the lawyer's services that the lawyer reasonably believes is criminal or fraudulent." Model Rules 3.3 and 4.1(b) further require lawyers to disclose information where necessary to avoid knowingly assisting a criminal or fraudulent act by a client on a tribunal or third person.[7]

The Privilege and Work Product Exception

Chen illustrates that the client's use of a lawyer's services to commit a future crime or fraud also constitutes grounds for loss of the attorney-client privilege or work product immunity. Note that this evidentiary exception turns on the client's intent rather than the lawyer's knowledge about the client's goal. A client who either initially intends to use the lawyer to promote a crime or fraud, as well as a client who forms such an intention after the representation begins, can lose the privilege.

The *Purcell* court found that a lawyer's knowledge of the client's criminal intent, if learned during the course of an otherwise legitimate representation (advice about a lost job and eviction), is not enough to show that the client's purpose was to use the lawyer's advice to promote his illegality. In *Chen*, on the other hand, the lawyers appear to have been unaware of the clients' fraudulent intent. Nevertheless, if nonprivileged information shows that the clients' goal was in fact to use their lawyers' services to promote a fraud, then the privilege was lost.

Chen makes clear that duped lawyers still must claim the privilege and cannot testify until a court finds that the crime fraud exception justifies disclosure. It also raises a question about the extent to which a lawyer should investigate a client's intent.

The Lawyer's Knowledge

Model Rules 1.2(d), 1.13, 3.3, and 4.1 all hinge on the lawyer's knowledge of the client's activity (knowledge that it constitutes a fraud or crime is not required).[8] A lawyer has no duty to withdraw to avoid assisting client fraud under Rule 1.2(d) unless the lawyer "knows" about the client's conduct.[9] If the client refrains from

---

7. The duty to disclose to third persons in MR 4.1(b) (client frauds on third persons) arises only if an exception to MR 1.6 would permit disclosure, but the duty in MR 3.3(b) (frauds on tribunals) is not so limited. As we have seen in a previous note about lawyer dishonesty, MR 8.4(c) also prohibits lawyers themselves from engaging "in conduct involving dishonesty, fraud, deceit, or misrepresentation."

8. *E.g.*, Disc. Counsel v. O'Brien, 899 N.E. 2d 125 (Ohio 2008) (lawyer who counseled client to obey bankruptcy disclosure rules but nevertheless disbursed funds in client trust account while bankruptcy petition was still pending assisted client fraud); In re Headlee, 756 N.E.2d 969 (Ind. 2001) (lawyer who learned after filing suit to recover client's medical expenses that client had medical bills discharged in bankruptcy but did not inform the court or the defendant assisted client's fraud and was suspended for 24 months).

9. MR 1.0(f) defines knowledge as "actual knowledge of the fact in question, which may be inferred from the circumstances," a definition that seems to include willful blindness as well as actual subjective knowledge. *E.g.*, In re Wahlder, 728 So. 2d 837 (La. 1999) (lawyer who permitted his client to place the signature of client's wife on a settlement document and witnessed the signature when

or stops the wrongful activity after the lawyer learns of it, the lawyer will not have assisted or counseled it. However, if a prospective client expresses an intent to undertake the conduct, the lawyer will have to decline the representation to avoid violating Rule 1.2(d).

The knowledge requirement raises the question whether a lawyer who suspects but does not know of client wrongdoing should investigate further. On the one hand, not investigating seems an easy way to avoid triggering obligations found in these rules. On the other, not investigating risks later allegations of complicity, incompetent representation, and a lost opportunity for the lawyer to counsel the client in some manner that would avoid a crime or a fraud.[10] For example, the lawyer may be able to structure a transaction in an alternative way, or additional facts may create the basis for a new claim or defense in litigation. Further, the law that governs some tasks that lawyers undertake for clients requires "due diligence" on the part of the lawyer; that is, a competent investigation into the facts surrounding the transaction. Failure to meet these obligations or to explore alternatives for clients could result in discipline and civil and criminal liability.[11]

Beyond competence, anyone who contemplates questionable future behavior, including lawyers and clients, faces the problem of "hindsight bias," a cognitive distortion that causes humans to believe that the fact that a past event (like fraud) has occurred must have meant the event could (and should) have been identified in advance.[12] Lawyers should anticipate that hindsight bias is especially likely to occur in situations where they have some warning of wrongdoing and then encourage a client to push the law to its limits.[13] Finally, discovery of a client's ongoing or contemplated crime or fraud may mean that a lawyer loses a client's business, but it also affords the lawyer an opportunity to extricate herself

---

he knew wife did not personally sign the document violated MR 4.1(a) and 8.4(a) and (d)); In re Disbarment Proc., 184 A. 59 (Pa. 1936) (lawyer disbarred for knowingly participating in a numbers racket by agreeing in advance to represent the organized criminals and their henchmen regularly).

10. *E.g.,* Mahoning Cnty. Bar Assn. v. Sinclair, 822 N.E.2d 360 (Ohio 2004) (lawyer indefinitely suspended for preparing a quitclaim deed for client to client's daughter at time that lawyer knew of tax judgments against client and knew client was trying to hide assets from creditors but did not sign as the document's preparer because he felt "uncomfortable" with the transaction and suspected it might be a fraudulent conveyance).

11. *E.g.,* United States v. Benjamin, 328 F.2d 854 (2d Cir. 1964) (criminal prosecution of lawyers and accountants for aiding clients in mail and securities fraud).

12. *See* Jeffrey J. Rachlinski, *A Positive Psychological Theory of Judging in Hindsight,* 65 U. Chi. L. Rev. 571 (1998).

13. *See, e.g.,* FDIC v. O'Melveny & Myers, 969 F.2d 744 (9th Cir. 1992), *rev'd and remanded on other grounds,* 512 U.S. 79 (1994), *reaff'd on remand,* 61 F.3d 17 (9th Cir. 1995) (receiver of a failed financial institution stated a cause of action against the institution's lawyer assigned to the receiver by investors for not questioning auditors and a law firm that resigned just before the firm assisted the client in a private real estate syndication); FDIC v. Clark, 978 F.2d 1541 (10th Cir. 1992) (jury verdict against failed financial institution's outside counsel upheld for negligence in failing to investigate or inform the bank directors of claims of fraud made against the bank's president in a civil suit).

from the client misconduct before it results in massive liability or time spent justifying earlier conduct.[14]

The Duty to Withdraw

When the lawyer learns of the client's intent to begin or continue the wrongful conduct after the representation has commenced, withdrawal from the representation is mandated by Model Rule 1.16(a), because continuing to represent the client in the matter will result in a violation of Model Rule 1.2(d). If the lawyer does not "know," but only "reasonably believes" that the client's course of action is criminal or fraudulent, then the lawyer may, but is not required, to withdraw under Model Rule 1.16(b)(2).

Disclosure

Withdrawing from a representation that involves the lawyer in a client's crime or fraud may not exhaust the lawyer's obligations. Model Rules 1.13, 3.3, and 4.1 raise the question of whether the lawyer also must disclose some or all of the facts to avoid or remedy the client's fraud. With respect to frauds on tribunals, Model Rule 3.3(b) makes clear that even though the lawyer withdraws, the lawyer also must disclose if that step is necessary to avoid assisting the client's criminal or fraudulent act. Outside of tribunals, Model Rule 4.1(b) requires disclosure only if necessary to avoid assisting a client crime or fraud and then only if the facts fall within one of the confidentiality exceptions in Model Rule 1.6. Model Rule 1.13 specifically grants the lawyer for an organization discretion to disclose violations of law regardless of the availability of a Model Rule 1.6 exception where "the lawyer reasonably believes [this is] necessary to prevent substantial injury to the organization."[15]

The question of whether a lawyer should be able to disclose a client's fraud has been the subject of lively debate for over a quarter-century. Rules permitting or requiring a lawyer to disclose information to prevent or rectify a client fraud were adopted where the fraud was perpetrated on a tribunal (Model Rule 3.3), but initially were rejected where the fraud occurred outside the presence of a tribunal (Model Rules 1.6 and 4.1).

The Restatement debate resulted in the adoption of § 67, which allows a lawyer to use or disclose client information to prevent, rectify, or mitigate substantial financial loss in which the lawyer's services have been employed. In 2003, following Enron and other corporate disasters, the ABA adopted similar explicit exceptions in Model Rule 1.6(b)(2) and (3), which allow disclosure to prevent, mitigate, or rectify client acts that constitute a crime or fraud and are "reasonably certain to result in substantial injury to the financial interest or property of another and in furtherance of which the client has used or is using the lawyer's services." When adopted, these exceptions combined with Rule 4.1(b) make

---

14. *See* Lawyers' Roles: *The Instrumental Lawyer and the Bounds of the Law*, *supra* p. 243, for examples.
15. MR 1.13(c)(2).

disclosure mandatory unless withdrawal is sufficient to prevent assisting a client crime or fraud.

Ordinarily, disclosure of client information will not be necessary because a lawyer's withdrawal from a matter will be sufficient to prevent assisting a client crime or fraud.[16] One situation, however, is "especially delicate."[17] When lawyers engage in advising clients engaged in a course of conduct and discover fraud during the course of the representation, withdrawal might not be enough to prevent assisting. This is especially true in situations like "The Opinion Letter," where third parties are relying on lawyer work product previously produced. In this circumstance, the lawyer must disclose, but only to the extent reasonably necessary to prevent assisting. Model Rule comments suggest a so-called noisy withdrawal: giving notice of the fact of withdrawal and, if necessary, "disaffirming any opinion, document, affirmation, or the like."[18]

The Policy Debate

Today, jurisdictions agree that lawyers cannot knowingly counsel or assist criminal or fraudulent client activity (Model Rule 1.2(d)), that lawyers must withdraw to avoid doing so when clients refuse to stop (Model Rule 1.16(a)), and that lawyers have duties to tribunals, which may require disclosure of client confidences when fraud has occurred (Model Rule 3.3). Most jurisdictions also agree that the lawyer's disclosure obligation outside of tribunals when the client contemplates or commits fraud depends on the lawyer's assistance in the matter. (Model Rules 1.6 (b)(2) and (3), and 4.1(b)).

A minority of jurisdictions have not adopted exceptions designed to allow lawyers to warn or rectify client fraud because they maintain that fewer exceptions to confidentiality create more opportunity for lawyers to encourage full and frank communication with clients and therefore enhance the ability of lawyers to give legal advice to avoid or mitigate wrongful conduct. They also argue that "fraud" is always difficult to identify at the time it occurs, and therefore any exception to confidentiality tied to client fraud will cause lawyers to practice law defensively, erring on the side of disclosure and undermining client trust. Third, they maintain that exceptions to save human life recognize a competing value of "unique importance," where no remedy will suffice to prevent the harm.[19] Client fraud, on the other hand, usually results in monetary loss, for which clients, not their lawyers, are properly responsible. Finally, they argue that when client fraud does occur, the lawyer's withdrawal from the matter is sufficient to extricate the lawyer from the client's wrongdoing.[20]

---

16. MR 4.1 Comment [3].

17. MR 1.2 Comment [10].

18. MR 1.2 Comment [10], 4.1 Comment [3]. The language and option of a noisy withdrawal originated in an initial 1981 compromise, which placed the option in MR 1.6 Comment [15].

19. Freedman & Smith, *Understanding Lawyers' Ethics* 139 (4th ed. Lexis-Nexis 2010).

20. *Legislative History of the Model Rules of Professional Conduct: Their Development in the ABA House of Delegates* 48-49 (ABA 1987).

Lawyers and jurisdictions that support client fraud exceptions to confidentiality concede the possibility that clients might be less willing to confide in lawyers, but maintain that clients who misuse the client-lawyer relationship are not entitled to absolute confidentiality.[21] Further, they argue that the ability of the lawyer to encourage the client to act lawfully will be enhanced by a discretionary disclosure provision.[22] Finally, they argue that an exception to confidentiality dependent on the client use of the lawyer's services to perpetrate the fraud actually allows lawyers to extricate themselves from the client's acts before they otherwise might be able to respond under the self-defense exception in Model Rule 1.6.

Client Fraud and Client Advocacy

Whatever their view of the appropriate answers to these issues, lawyers do agree on several key points: First, you must be competent. This means that you must know the relevant facts and law that govern your representation of a client, including whether the activity constitutes a crime or fraud. Second, you must clearly communicate these findings to your client so that illegal activity can be avoided or stopped. Third, if you have been retained to defend a client's wrongful activity that is completely ended, you are not assisting or counseling it. Fourth, if a client seeks to use your services to assist in future or ongoing criminal or fraudulent activity, failure to withdraw will subject you to professional discipline, as well as potential civil and criminal liability. Fifth, if you represent an entity, you have special obligations to address serious legal violations with others beyond your immediate supervisor, going to higher authorities, such as corporate boards for reconsideration.[23] Finally, you need to know your jurisdiction's exceptions to confidentiality to determine whether you also have discretion or even an obligation to warn third persons.

---

21. RLGL § 67 Comment b. Professor Burt argues that the mistrust that pervades the client-lawyer relationship might actually be addressed and alleviated by more discretionary disclosure exceptions because they would force honest exploration of the basis for the mistrust. *See* Robert A. Burt, *Conflict and Trust Between Attorney and Client*, 69 Geo. L.J. 1015 (1981).

22. They also note that civil liability already exists in some cases (as it did in *Refco*), but point out that RLGL § 67(4) provides that any exercise of discretion under antifraud exceptions does not create grounds for discipline or liability.

23. MR 1.13. For public corporations, this obligation also stems from the Sarbanes-Oxley Act, 15 U.S.C. § 7245 (2006); 17 C.F.R. §§ 205.1-205.7 (2007); 68 Fed. Reg. 6296 (Feb. 6, 2003).

Chapter 8

Confidentiality Exceptions: Lawyer Interests and Compliance with Other Law

A. Seeking Advice, Self-Defense, and Compensation Disputes

When an accusation of misconduct against a lawyer has occurred, utilitarians would argue that the need for information to produce a just outcome allows lawyers the freedom to disclose the information necessary to defend against the allegation. Lawyers also are justified in seeking advice about their own conduct or in making an affirmative claim for fees, at least so long so the client has violated a legal obligation that should be redressed. The deontologist would defend the lawyer's right to seek advice and to respond to an accusation on the grounds that the lawyer deserves a chance to explain her conduct, especially when unjustly accused. Similarly, the lawyer who has provided legal services to a client deserves to be paid for those services because the client has promised to do so, and promises should be kept. In all of these situations, the personal interest of the lawyer in using confidential information often is corralled by protective orders or limitations on the permissible scope of disclosure.

Problems

Keep things hypothetical

8-1. Lawyer Wright, from another law firm, consults Martyn & Fox about her representation of Apex. She is worried that the CEO of Apex is planning a leveraged buyout of the company and is seeking advice from Martyn & Fox on Apex's nickel without disclosing CEO's true intentions. Wright wants another lawyer to hear all the details for a reality check. Fox responded instantly with "sage" advice. Okay?

8-2. Martyn & Fox is dealing with several difficult clients:

(a) Client threatens to sue Martyn & Fox for malpractice in a real estate transaction and file a grievance about the same conduct. Fox, quite upset about the scurrilous charges, wants to strike

259

back, threatening client that we will tell his wife about Client's illegitimate child. Would it matter if the opposing party in the transaction were threatening to sue us for aiding and abetting our client's "fraud"?

(b) Martyn & Fox want to sue to collect a fee. Can they disclose how difficult and irresponsible the client was? How the client repeatedly lied to the other side in negotiations?

(c) Martyn was appointed by a court to represent Defendant in a criminal case. Defendant was convicted and now wants to claim ineffective assistance of counsel on appeal. Outraged, Martyn wants to provide the prosecutor with a sworn affidavit detailing how outstanding she was.

8-3. Client fired Martyn & Fox after Martyn accused Client of fraudulent conduct in connection with certain lease transactions in which Martyn & Fox could not confirm the existence of the underlying equipment. Lawyer A, successor counsel, calls Fox to find out why such a fine firm was terminated. "Were there any disagreements?" Lawyer A asks. What if Martyn is called to testify about the lease transactions in subsequent litigation?

Consider: Model Rule 1.6(b)(4) and (5)
RLGL §§ 64, 65, 83

Meyerhofer v. Empire Fire & Marine Insurance Co.
497 F.2d 1190 (2d Cir. 1974), cert. denied, 419 U.S. 998 (1974)

MOORE, Circuit Judge:

This is an appeal by . . . plaintiffs, and their counsel, from an order of the United States District Court for the Southern District of New York . . . (a) dismissing without prejudice plaintiffs' action against defendants, (b) enjoining and disqualifying plaintiffs' counsel, Bernson, Hoeniger, Freitag & Abbey, and Stuart Charles Goldberg from acting as attorneys for plaintiffs in this action or in any future action against defendant Empire Fire and Marine Insurance Company (Empire) involving the same transactions, occurrences, events, allegations, facts or issues, and (c) enjoining Bernson, Hoeniger, Freitag & Abbey and Stuart Charles Goldberg from disclosing confidential information regarding Empire to others. Intervenor Stuart Charles Goldberg also appeals from said order.

The full import of the problems and issues presented on this appeal cannot be appreciated and analyzed without an initial statement of the facts out of which they arise.

Empire Fire and Marine Insurance Company on May 31, 1972, made a public offering of 500,000 shares of its stock, pursuant to a registration statement filed with the Securities and Exchange Commission (SEC) on March 28, 1972. The stock was offered at $16 a share. Empire's attorney on the issue was the firm of Sitomer, Sitomer & Porges. Stuart Charles Goldberg was an attorney in the firm and had done some work on the issue.

Plaintiff Meyerhofer, on or about January 11, 1973, purchased 100 shares of Empire stock at $17 a share. He alleges that as of June 5, 1973, the market price of his stock was only $7 a share—hence, he has sustained an unrealized loss of $1,000. . . . Plaintiff Federman, on or about May 31, 1972, purchased 200 shares at $16 a share, 100 of which he sold for $1,363, sustaining a loss of some $237 on the stock sold and an unrealized loss of $900 on the stock retained.

On May 2, 1973, plaintiffs, represented by the firm of Bernson, Hoeniger, Freitag & Abbey (the Bernson firm), on behalf of themselves and all other purchasers of Empire common stock, brought this action alleging that the registration statement and the prospectus under which the Empire stock had been issued were materially false and misleading. Thereafter, an amended complaint, dated June 5, 1973, was served. The legal theories in both were identical, namely, violations of various sections of the Securities Act of 1933, the Securities Exchange Act of 1934, Rule 10b-5, and common law negligence, fraud and deceit. Damages for all members of the class or rescission were alternatively sought.

The lawsuit was apparently inspired by a Form 10-K which Empire filed with the SEC on or about April 12, 1973. This Form revealed that "The Registration Statement under the Securities Act of 1933 with respect to the public offering of the 500,000 shares of Common Stock did not disclose the proposed $200,000 payment to the law firm as well as certain other features of the compensation arrangements between the Company [Empire] and such law firm [defendant Sitomer, Sitomer & Porges]." Later that month Empire disseminated to its shareholders a proxy statement and annual report making similar disclosures.

The defendants named were Empire, officers and directors of Empire, the Sitomer firm and its three partners, A. L. Sitomer, S. J. Sitomer and R. E. Porges, Faulkner, Dawkins & Sullivan Securities Corp., the managing underwriter, Stuart Charles Goldberg, originally alleged to have been a partner of the Sitomer firm, and certain selling stockholders of Empire shares.

On May 2, 1973, the complaint was served on the Sitomer defendants and Faulkner. No service was made on Goldberg who was then no longer associated with the Sitomer firm. However, he was advised by telephone that he had been made a defendant. Goldberg inquired of the Bernson firm as to the nature of the charges against him and was informed generally as to the substance of the complaint and in particular the lack of disclosure of the finder's fee arrangement. Thus informed, Goldberg requested an opportunity to prove his non-involvement in any such arrangement and his lack of knowledge thereof. At this stage there was unfolded the series of events which ultimately resulted in the motion and order thereon now before us on appeal.

Goldberg, after his graduation from Law School in 1966, had rather specialized experience in the securities field and had published various books and treatises on related subjects. He became associated with the Sitomer firm in November 1971. While there Goldberg worked on phases of various registration statements including Empire, although another associate was responsible for the Empire registration statement and prospectus. However, <u>Goldberg expressed concern over what he regarded as excessive fees, the nondisclosure or inadequate disclosure thereof, and the extent to which they might include a "finder's fee,"</u> both as to Empire and other issues.

The Empire registration became effective on May 31, 1972. The excessive fee question had not been put to rest in Goldberg's mind because in middle January 1973 it arose in connection with another registration (referred to as "Glacier"). Goldberg had worked on Glacier. Little purpose will be served by detailing the events during the critical period January 18 to 22, 1973, in which Goldberg and the Sitomer partners were debating the fee disclosure problem. In summary, <u>Goldberg insisted on a full and complete disclosure of fees in the Empire and Glacier offerings. The Sitomer partners apparently disagreed and Goldberg resigned from the firm on January 22, 1973.</u>

On January 22, 1973, Goldberg appeared before the SEC and placed before it information subsequently embodied in his affidavit dated January 26, 1973, which becomes crucial to the issues now to be considered.

Some three months later, upon being informed that he was to be included as a defendant in the impending action, Goldberg asked the Bernson firm for an opportunity to demonstrate that he had been unaware of the finder's fee arrangement which, he said, Empire and the Sitomer firm had concealed from him all along. Goldberg met with members of the Bernson firm on at least two occasions. After consulting his own attorney, as well as William P. Sullivan, Special Counsel with the Securities and Exchange Commission, Division of Enforcement, Goldberg gave plaintiffs' counsel a copy of the January 26th affidavit which he had authored more than three months earlier. He hoped that it would verify his nonparticipation in the finder's fee omission and convince the Bernson firm that he should not be a defendant. The Bernson firm was satisfied with Goldberg's explanations and, upon their motion, granted by the court, he was dropped as a defendant. After receiving Goldberg's affidavit, the Bernson firm amended plaintiffs' complaint. The amendments added more specific facts but did not change the theory or substance of the original complaint.

By motion dated June 7, 1973, the remaining defendants moved "pursuant to . . . the Disciplinary Rules . . . applicable thereto, and the supervisory power of this Court" for the order of disqualification now on appeal.

By memorandum decision and order, the District Court ordered that the Bernson firm and Goldberg be barred from acting as counsel or participating with counsel for plaintiffs in this or any future action against Empire involving the transactions placed in issue in this lawsuit and from disclosing confidential information to others.

. . . ⌜The basis for the Court's decision is the premise that Goldberg had obtained confidential information from his client Empire which, in breach of relevant ethical canons, he revealed to plaintiffs' attorneys in their suit against Empire. . . .⌟

There is no proof—not even a suggestion—that Goldberg had revealed any information, confidential or otherwise, that might have caused the instigation of the suit. To the contrary, it was not until after the suit was commenced that

Goldberg learned that he was in jeopardy. The District Court recognized that the complaint had been based on Empire's — not Goldberg's — disclosures, but concluded because of this that Goldberg was under no further obligation "to reveal the information or to discuss the matter with plaintiffs' counsel."

Despite the breadth of [Rule 1.6, Rule 1.6(b)(5)] recognizes that a lawyer may reveal confidences or secrets necessary to defend himself against "an accusation of wrongful conduct." This is exactly what Goldberg had to face when, in their original complaint, plaintiffs named him as a defendant who willfully violated the securities laws.

The charge, of knowing participation in the filing of a false and misleading registration statement, was a serious one. The complaint alleged violation of criminal statutes and civil liability computable at over four million dollars. The cost in money of simply defending such an action might be very substantial. The damage to his professional reputation which might be occasioned by the mere pendency of such a charge was an even greater cause for concern.

Under these circumstances Goldberg had the right to make an appropriate disclosure with respect to his role in the public offering. Concomitantly, he had the right to support his version of the facts with suitable evidence.

The problem arises from the fact that the method Goldberg used to accomplish this was to deliver to Mr. Abbey, a member of the Bernson firm, the thirty page affidavit, accompanied by sixteen exhibits, which he had submitted to the SEC. This document not only went into extensive detail concerning Goldberg's efforts to cause the Sitomer firm to rectify the nondisclosure with respect to Empire but even more extensive detail concerning how these efforts had been precipitated by counsel for the underwriters having come upon evidence showing that a similar nondisclosure was contemplated with respect to Glacier and their insistence that full corrective measures should be taken. Although Goldberg's description reflected seriously on his employer, the Sitomer firm and, also, in at least some degree, on Glacier, he was clearly in a situation of some urgency. Moreover, before he turned over the affidavit, he consulted both his own attorney and a distinguished practitioner of securities law, and he and Abbey made a joint telephone call to Mr. Sullivan of the SEC. . . . Finally, because of Goldberg's apparent intimacy with the offering, the most effective way for him to substantiate his story was for him to disclose the SEC affidavit. It was the fact that he had written such an affidavit at an earlier date which demonstrated that his story was not simply fabricated in response to plaintiffs' complaint. . . .

The burden of the District Court's order did not fall most harshly on Goldberg; rather its greatest impact has been felt by Bernson, Hoeniger, Freitag & Abbey, plaintiffs' counsel, which was disqualified from participation in the case. The District Court based its holding, not on the fact that the Bernson firm showed bad faith when it received Goldberg's affidavit, but rather on the fact that it was involved in a tainted association with Goldberg because his disclosures to them inadvertently violated [Rule 1.6]. Because there are no violations of [this rule] in this case, we can find no basis to hold that the relationship between Goldberg and the Bernson firm was tainted. The District Court was apparently unpersuaded by appellees' salvo of innuendo to the effect that Goldberg "struck a deal" with the Bernson firm or tried to do more than prove his innocence to them. Since its relationship with Goldberg was not tainted by violations of the [Rules of Professional Conduct], there appears to be no warrant for its disqualification from participation in either this or similar actions. A fortiori there was no sound basis for disqualifying plaintiffs or dismissing the complaint.

Order dismissing action without prejudice and enjoining Bernson, Hoeniger, Freitag & Abbey from acting as counsel for plaintiffs herein reversed. . . . To the extent that the orders appealed from prohibit Goldberg from acting as a party or as an attorney for a party in any action arising out of the facts herein alleged, or from disclosing material information except on discovery or at trial, they are affirmed.

B. Compliance with Law or Court Order: Physical Evidence

Legal obligations such as court orders, statutes, or procedural rules often require the disclosure of confidential client information. Creating an exception to client confidentiality when other law requires or allows such disclosure promotes the policy of that other law. At the same time, allowing other legal obligations to trump client-lawyer confidentiality may compromise a central justification for confidentiality, especially if the purpose of the other law does not mirror another recognized exception in the Rules of Professional Conduct.

Utilitarians might argue about the precise line to draw in creating an efficient and fair legal system, but probably would agree that court orders and procedural rules should be obeyed to promote the proper functioning of the courts. Some statutes, such as child and elder abuse disclosure provisions, also could be justified if their purpose is to protect human welfare and prevent harm. On the other hand, applying such statutes to lawyers could undermine the very essence of the promise of confidentiality, particularly as to past conduct. Similar arguments could be made about the law of fraud. Insofar as it prevents unfair use of the market or the legal system, a lawyer could be justified in disclosing client confidences to comply with the criminal or civil law of fraud. A deontologist would agree that court rules or laws designed to protect basic human freedoms are important. When a client seeks to infringe such an obligation, the client's conduct is blameworthy, which creates a valid reason for the lawyer to prevent such a misuse of others.

Problems

8-4. Client tells Martyn where he hid the stolen money. Now what? What if client hands Martyn the key to the safe deposit box where the money is stored? Can Martyn give it back? If she keeps the key, can she be forced to testify that her client gave it to her?

8-5. The town is in turmoil. Two children are missing. Client tells Fox he killed the two children and where the bodies are buried. Now what? Does it matter if the parents still hope the children are alive, they've been on television nightly, and the town has been conducting a massive search for two weeks?

Consider: Model Rules 1.6(b)(6), 3.4(a), 8.4(b)
RLGL §§ 63, 86, 119

New York Penal Law (2012)

§205.50. Hindering Prosecution; Definition of Term

. . . [A] person "renders criminal assistance" when, with intent to prevent, hinder or delay the discovery or apprehension of, or the lodging of a criminal charge against, a person who he knows or believes has committed a crime or is being sought by law enforcement officials for the commission of a crime, or with intent to assist a person in profiting or benefiting from the commission of a crime, he:

1. Harbors or conceals such person; or
2. Warns such person of impending discovery or apprehension; or
3. Provides such person with money, transportation, weapon, disguise or other means of avoiding discovery or apprehension; or
4. Prevents or obstructs, by means of force, intimidation or deception, anyone from performing an act which might aid in the discovery or apprehension of such person or in the lodging of a criminal charge against him; or
5. Suppresses, by any act of concealment, alteration or destruction, any physical evidence which might aid in the discovery or apprehension of such person or in the lodging of a criminal charge against him; or
6. Aids such person to protect or expeditiously profit from an advantage derived from such crime.

(L 1965, c 1030)

People v. Belge

372 N.Y.S.2d 798 (S. Ct. 1975), affirmed, 359 N.E.2d 377 (N.Y. 1976)

Ormand N. Gale, J.

In the summer of 1973 Robert F. Garrow, Jr., stood charged in Hamilton County with the crime of murder. The defendant was assigned two attorneys, Frank H. Armani and Francis R. Belge. A defense of insanity had been interposed by counsel for Mr. Garrow. During the course of the discussions between Garrow and his two counsel, three other murders were admitted by Garrow, one being in Onondaga County. On or about September of 1973 Mr. Belge conducted his own investigation based upon what his client had told him and with the assistance of a friend the location of the body of Alicia Hauck was found in Oakwood Cemetery in Syracuse. Mr. Belge personally inspected the body and was satisfied, presumably, that this was the Alicia Hauck that his client had told him that he murdered.

This discovery was not disclosed to the authorities, but became public during the trial of Mr. Garrow in June of 1974, when to affirmatively establish the defense of insanity, these three other murders were brought before the jury by the defense in the Hamilton County trial. Public indignation reached the fever pitch, . . . [and] the District Attorney of Onondaga County caused the Grand Jury of Onondaga County, then sitting, to conduct a thorough investigation. As a result of this investigation Frank Armani was no-billed by the Grand Jury but Indictment No. 75-55 was returned as against Francis R. Belge, Esq., accusing him of having violated subdivision 1 of section 4200 of the Public Health Law, which, in essence, requires that a decent burial be accorded the dead, and section 4143 of the Public Health Law, which, in essence, requires anyone knowing of the death of a person without medical attendance, to report the same to the proper authorities. Defense counsel moves for a dismissal of the indictment on the grounds that a confidential, privileged communication existed between him and Mr. Garrow, which should excuse the attorney from making full disclosure to the authorities. . . .

The effectiveness of counsel is only as great as the confidentiality of its client-attorney relationship. If the lawyer cannot get all the facts about the case, he can only give his client half of a defense. This, of necessity, involves the client telling his attorney everything remotely connected with the crime.

Apparently, in the instant case, after analyzing all the evidence, and after hearing of the bizarre episodes in the life of their client, they decided that the only possibility of salvation was in a defense of insanity. For the client to disclose not only everything about this particular crime but also everything about other crimes which might have a bearing upon his defense, requires the strictest confidence in, and on the part of, the attorney.

When the facts of the other homicides became public, as a result of the defendant's testimony to substantiate his claim of insanity, "Members of the public were shocked at the apparent callousness of these lawyers, whose conduct was seen as typifying the unhealthy lack of concern of most lawyers with the public interest and with simple decency." A hue and cry went up from the press and other news media suggesting that the attorneys should be found guilty of such crimes as obstruction of justice or becoming an accomplice after the fact. From a layman's standpoint, this certainly was a logical conclusion. However, the Constitution of the United States of America attempts to preserve the dignity of the individual and to do that guarantees him the services of an attorney who will bring to the Bar and to the Bench every conceivable protection from the inroads of the State against such rights as are vested in the Constitution for one accused of crime. Among those substantial constitutional rights is that a defendant does not have to incriminate himself. His attorneys were bound to uphold that concept and maintain what has been called a sacred trust of confidentiality.

The following language from the brief of the amicus curiae further points up the statements just made: "The client's Fifth Amendment rights cannot be violated by his attorney. . . . Garrow, although constitutionally privileged against a requirement of compulsory disclosure, was free to make such a revelation if he chose to do so. Attorney Belge was affirmatively required to withhold disclosure.

The criminal defendant's self-incrimination rights become completely nugatory if compulsory disclosure can be exacted through his attorney."

. . . In the case at bar we must weigh the importance of the general privilege of confidentiality in the performance of the defendant's duties as an attorney, against the inroads of such a privilege on the fair administration of criminal justice as well as the heart tearing that went on in the victim's family by reason of their uncertainty as to the whereabouts of Alicia Hauck. In this type situation the court must balance the rights of the individual against the rights of society as a whole. There is no question but Attorney Belge's failure to bring to the attention of the authorities the whereabouts of Alicia Hauck when he first verified it, prevented bringing Garrow to the immediate bar of justice for this particular murder. This was in a sense, obstruction of justice. This duty, I am sure, loomed large in the mind of Attorney Belge. However, against this was the Fifth Amendment right of his client, Garrow, not to incriminate himself. If the Grand Jury had returned an indictment charging Mr. Belge with obstruction of justice under a proper statute, the work of this court would have been much more difficult than it is.

There must always be a conflict between the obstruction of the administration of criminal justice and the preservation of the right against self-incrimination which permeates the mind of the attorney as the alter ego of his client. But that is not the situation before this court. We have the Fifth Amendment right, derived from the Constitution, on the one hand, as against the trivia of a pseudo-criminal statute on the other, which has seldom been brought into play. Clearly the latter is completely out of focus when placed alongside the client-attorney privilege. . . .

It is the decision of this court that Francis R. Belge conducted himself as an officer of the court with all the zeal at his command to protect the constitutional rights of his client. Both on the grounds of a privileged communication and in the interests of justice the indictment is dismissed.

C. Compliance with Law or Court Order: Practice Before a Tribunal

1. Representations of Fact and Law

Problems

8-6. Judge Smith calls Martyn into chambers. "Tell me your client's bottom line." Client authorized Martyn to offer $50,000. "$25,000," Martyn stammers, proud of her tough negotiating stance.

8-7. If Martyn & Fox's client lies about her name in a criminal case, what should we do?

8-8. Fox was retained by estate executor, the testator's daughter, to probate an estate, and he discovered substantial amounts of estate money unaccounted for. He confronted the executor, who admitted that she paid the money to her nephew for college expenses, even though the nephew had been disinherited under the will. Fox promptly informed the probate judge. Is Fox in trouble?

Consider: Model Rules 1.0(m), 1.6(b)(6), 3.3, 3.4, 8.4(c) and (d)
Model Code of Judicial Conduct, Rule 2.9 (A)(4)
RLGL §§ 63 and 120

People v. Casey
948 P.2d 1014 (Colo. 1997)

PER CURIAM.

A hearing panel of the supreme court grievance committee approved the findings and the recommendation of a hearing board that the respondent in this lawyer discipline case be suspended for forty-five days from the practice of law and be ordered to take and pass the Multi-State Professional Responsibility Examination (MPRE). The respondent has excepted to the recommendation as too severe. We disagree, and we accept the recommendation of the hearing panel and hearing board.

I.

The respondent was licensed to practice law in Colorado in 1989. . . .

In December 1994, S.R., a teenager, and her mother, met with the senior partner at the law firm where the respondent was an associate. In August 1994, S.R. attended a party held in the home of third parties. The police were called and they cited several persons at the party with trespassing and underage drinking. S.R. gave the police a driver's license in her possession that had been issued to her friend, S.J. A criminal summons charging trespass was issued to S.R. in the name of her friend, S.J. Since she was not aware of the summons in her name, S.J. failed to attend the first court hearing and a bench warrant was issued in her name. S.R., posing as S.J., later appeared to reset the matter. S.R. was arrested, jailed, and later released under the name of S.J.

After being assigned the case by the senior partner, the respondent wrote to the Colorado Springs City Attorney's Office, and advised the City Attorney, falsely, that he represented S.J., when he actually represented S.R. He requested and obtained discovery using S.J.'s name. He also notified the court clerk of his entry of appearance in the S.J. case. The senior partner "consulted and advised" the respondent, but the hearing board did not make findings as to when this occurred or as to the details of the conversation.

On February 14, 1995, the respondent appeared at a pretrial conference scheduled for S.J. His client, S.R., waited outside during the hearing. Although he spoke with an assistant city attorney about the case, the respondent did not reveal his client's true identity. The assistant city attorney agreed to dismiss the S.J. matter. The respondent presented the city's motion to dismiss the case and the court entered an order of dismissal on February 14, 1995.

Prior to the pretrial conference, S.J. called the respondent about the case. The respondent told her that he intended to get the trespassing charge dismissed, but that S.J. would then have to petition on her own to get the criminal record sealed. He also told S.J. the date and time of the pretrial hearing.

After the case was dismissed, the respondent met with his client and her mother, and S.J. and her stepfather. S.J. was upset that the respondent had spoken with the assistant city attorney outside of S.J.'s presence and she wanted to know if her name had been cleared. The respondent took S.J. and her stepfather outside, and explained that the trespassing charge had been dismissed and that his client would pay the court costs. The respondent admitted that S.J. would nevertheless have a criminal record and that she would have to petition the court to have her criminal record sealed. S.J.'s stepfather subsequently called his lawyer who reported the events to the district attorney.

The respondent stipulated that the foregoing conduct violated Colo. RPC 1.2(d) (counseling a client to engage, or assisting a client, in conduct that the lawyer knows is criminal or fraudulent)[1]; Colo. RPC 3.3(a)(1) (knowingly making a false statement of material fact or law to a tribunal); . . . Colo. RPC 8.4(c) (engaging in conduct involving dishonesty, fraud, deceit or misrepresentation); Colo. RPC 8.4(d) (engaging in conduct prejudicial to the administration of justice). . . .

II . . .

The respondent portrays his situation as involving a close question between the loyalty he owed his client, and his duty to the court. He apparently seeks to invoke the status of a "subordinate lawyer," as addressed in Colo. RPC 5.2. . . .

However, . . . the respondent admits to having violated [Colo. RPC 3.3] . . . [which] applies because of his initial appearance before the court in which he represented, falsely, that he was appearing on behalf of the named defendant, S.J. At the pretrial conference he presented the motion to dismiss to the court resulting in the case being dismissed. The respondent had the duty to disclose to the court that his client was impersonating S.J. in the criminal proceedings.

Further, Colo. RPC 3.3(b) clearly resolves the respondent's claimed dilemma in that it provides that the duty to be truthful to the court applies even if to do so requires disclosure of otherwise confidential information. It is not "arguable" that the respondent's duty to his client prevented him from fulfilling his duty

---

1. Section 18-5-113, 6 C.R.S. (1997), provides in part:

 18-5-113. Criminal impersonation. (1) A person commits criminal impersonation if he knowingly assumes a false or fictitious identity or capacity, and in such identity or capacity he:

 (d) Does an act which if done by the person falsely impersonated, might subject such person to an action or special proceeding, civil or criminal, or to liability, charge, forfeiture, or penalty; or

 (e) Does any other act with intent to unlawfully gain a benefit for himself or another or to injure or defraud another.

(2) Criminal impersonation is a class 6 felony.

to be truthful to the court. The protection afforded by Colo. RPC 5.2(b) for a subordinate who acts in accordance with a supervisory lawyer's direction is not available to the respondent.

While we have determined that Colo. RPC 5.2(b) does not entitle the respondent to immunity, an attempt to obtain guidance from a senior partner and a failure of a senior partner to suggest a reasonable and ethical course of conduct for the respondent could be a factor to be considered in mitigation. . . . Here, the board's finding that the senior partner "consulted and advised" the respondent, without detail about the advice, if any, given is inadequate to allow us to conclude that the consultation is a mitigation factor.

▧ The Bounds of the Law: *Criminal Conduct*

In two previous notes,[1] we addressed the law of fraud and saw that lawyers have no special immunity from that law, either in representing clients or in their own personal conduct outside of law practice. In this chapter, two cases, *Belge* and *Casey,* illustrate several ways that the equally vast scope of the criminal law imposes significant limitations on a lawyer's behavior.[2]

The Model Rules

Appellate decisions regarding lawyer discipline reveal that courts impose severe sanctions on lawyers who commit crimes. Lawyers must be aware of the contours of the criminal law both to avoid committing crimes themselves (as the lawyer avoided in *Belge*) and to avoid counseling or assisting client crimes (as occurred in *Casey*). When either of these dangers arise, Model Rules 8.4(b) and 1.2(d) become relevant. Model Rule 8.4(b) regulates lawyers who commit crimes. When a client engages in or plans conduct that constitutes a crime, Model Rule 1.2(d) comes into play.

Lawyer Crimes

Belge's conduct implies recognition of a significant legal limit on his own action created by New York's hindering prosecution statute. Belge observed, but did not alter, conceal, or destroy, the physical evidence of his client's crime. Note that the court says its work would be much more difficult if the grand jury had indicted Belge under this statute for "obstruction of justice," presumably because in that case, his conduct would have moved beyond merely protecting

---

1. The Bounds of the Law: *Duties to Nonclients, supra* p. 155; The Bounds of the Law: *Client Fraud, supra* p. 252.
2. Although an exact count of criminal prohibitions probably is impossible, one author estimates about 3,600 federal and 985 state crimes in her jurisdiction (Arizona). Susan A. Ehrlich, *The Increasing Federalization of Crime*, 32 Ariz. St. L.J. 825, 826 (2000). *See also* ABA Task Force on the Federalization of Criminal Law, *The Federalization of Criminal Law* (ABA 1998), App. C, which lists more than 3,000 federal crimes.

confidentiality to an active felony cover-up of a client crime.[3] To understand this point, imagine what would have occurred if, when Belge discovered the bodies, he dug a deep hole and buried them to protect his client. His conduct then would have constituted hindering prosecution under the New York statute, because he would have intended to prevent discovery of the physical evidence and would have done so by an act of concealment.

If Belge had violated the hindering prosecution statute, he also would have been subject to professional discipline for violation of Model Rule 8.4(b), which prohibits lawyers from committing crimes "that reflect adversely on the lawyer's honesty, trustworthiness, or fitness as a lawyer in other respects."[4] Several aspects of this rule have been extensively litigated.

First, it has been argued that lawyers who commit crimes do not respect the law and therefore should not be allowed to continue to practice. However, not all crimes fall within the prohibition of this rule. Consider, for example, whether Belge should have been disciplined for failing to provide decent burial of the dead. If every misdemeanor (including traffic offenses) qualified, most of us would be in trouble. On the other hand, professional code provisions and courts hold that most serious crimes (often defined to include most felonies) do reflect on the lawyer's ability to practice law.

Some criminal conduct is so serious and so related to character traits necessary to practice law that courts discipline lawyers involved regardless of whether the conduct constitutes a misdemeanor or felony.[5] Crimes involving dishonesty or lack of trustworthiness, such as fraud and theft, clearly fit this category.[6] The same is true of offenses that involve violence, or serious interference with the

---

3. *See* Bruce A. Green, *The Criminal Regulation of Lawyers*, 67 Fordham L. Rev. 327 (1998).

4. *See, e.g.,* United States v. Cueto, 151 F.3d 620 (7th Cir. 1998) (lawyer/business partner of client who knowingly falsely charged an FBI investigator with soliciting a bribe, and filed false motions that attacked the Federal Bureau of Investigation (FBI) and U.S. Attorney convicted of obstruction of justice; lawyer's personal financial interest was a "corrupt endeavor" to influence the due administration of justice" which protected his client's illegal gambling operation); Cueto v. Attorney Registration & Disciplinary Comm., 2005 U.S. Dist. LEXIS 14636 (recounting the lawyer's subsequent disbarment).

5. Rule 19 of the ABA Model R. for Lawyer Disc. Enforcement (1999) defines "serious crime" to include, generally, any felonies or lesser crimes that reflect adversely on the lawyer's fitness to practice and specifically, those that involve "interference with the administration of justice, false swearing, misrepresentation, fraud, deceit, bribery, extortion, misappropriation, theft, or an attempt, conspiracy or solicitation of another to commit a 'serious crime.'"

6. *E.g.,* Atty. Grievance Comm'n. v. Bereano, 744 A.2d 35 (Md. 2000) (lawyer convicted of mail fraud based on violations of state election fundraising laws disbarred regardless of lack of potential for direct personal gain); In re Moore, 691 A.2d 1151 (D.C. 1997) (lawyer convicted of a misdemeanor for willful failure to file tax returns suspended for three years); Wilson v. Neal, 964 S.W.2d 199 (Ark. 1998) *aff'd,* 16 S.W.3d 228 (Ark. 2000) (lawyer who pleaded guilty to misdemeanors of knowingly disposing of soybeans and rice that were mortgaged and pledged to the Farmers Home Administration and knowingly taking money from a Department of Agriculture bank account and using it for unapproved purposes suspended for five years). *See also* Milton C. Regan, *Eat What You Kill: The Fall of a Wall Street Lawyer* (U. Mich. 2004) (detailing the bankruptcy fraud and perjury convictions and subsequent disbarment of John Gellene); In re Gellene, 182 F.3d 578 (7th Cir. 1999); In re Gellene, 709 A.2d 196 (N.J. 1998).

administration of justice, such as obstruction of justice or bribery.[7] Courts also agree that domestic violence constitutes a ground for professional discipline, not only because of the violent acts involved, but also because the lawyer cannot be trusted with vulnerable or defenseless persons.[8] For similar reasons, courts find sexual misconduct that exploits another indicative of a lack of trustworthiness.[9] On the other hand, Model Rule 8.4, Comment [2] excludes "some matters of personal morality, such as adultery and comparable offenses" that also may be criminal but do not necessarily indicate that the lawyer is incompetent, dishonest, or untrustworthy.[10]

Second, so long as the evidence in a disciplinary proceeding shows that the lawyer committed the requisite criminal act, professional discipline can occur whether or not that lawyer was convicted or even charged with a crime.[11] Professional discipline has even occurred in cases where a jury has acquitted the

---

7. In re LaMartina, 38 So. 3d 266 (La. 2010) (lawyer mother who violated probation by trespassing on school property after conviction of resisting arrest and unauthorized access to a public school must receive mental health treatment to avoid suspension); In re LaMartina, 2012 La. LEXIS 1427 (one-year suspension imposed for same lawyer for shoplifting and failure to appear); In re Convery, 765 A.2d 724 (N.J. 2001) (lawyer who pled guilty to a federal misdemeanor of promising employment in return for political activity, due to his attempts to get zoning variances for a client, suspended for six months); In re Floyd, 527 S.E.2d 357 (S.C. 2000) (lawyer who stole an automobile, robbed bank, and shot a teller disbarred); Disc. Proc. Against Curran, 801 P.2d 962 (Wash. 1990) (lawyer convicted of vehicular homicide of two clients, whom he attempted to drive home after several drinks at lunch, suspended for six months).

8. *E.g.,* Atty. Grievance Comm'n. v. Painter, 739 A.2d 24 (Md. 1999) (lawyer guilty of repeated domestic violence of wife and child disbarred); Iowa S. Ct. Bd. of Prof. Ethics & Conduct v. Polson, 569 N.W.2d 612 (Iowa 1997) (lawyer guilty of domestic abuse suspended from practice two years); In re Walker, 597 N.E.2d 1271, *modified,* 601 N.E.2d 327 (Ind. 1992) (lawyer who assaulted female companion he had previously represented in a divorce and her nine-year-old daughter suspended from practice for 60 days).

9. *E.g.,* Iowa S. Ct. Atty Disc. Bd. v. Templeton, 784 N.W. 2d 761 (Iowa 2010) (lawyer who pled guilty to invasion of privacy—nudity, for his window peeping into a house shared by three women indefinitely suspended); In re Boudreau, 815 So. 2d 76 (La. 2002) (lawyer who pled guilty to possession of child pornography disbarred); Atty. Grievance Comm'n. v. Thompson, 786 A.2d 763 (Md. 2001) (lawyer who pled guilty to stalking a teenage boy suspended indefinitely); In re Parrott, 480 S.E.2d 722 (S.C. 1997) (lawyer convicted of simple assault for pulling down a woman's bathing suit at a beach suspended).

10. *See, e.g.,* In re Nuss, 67 P.3d 386 (Or. 2003) (lawyer convicted of misdemeanor crime of harassment for intentionally reaching into another's car and offensively touching the victim's shoulder not subject to discipline). Some of the most difficult cases concern lawyers who commit alcohol or drug crimes. *See, e.g.,* In re Lock, 54 S.W.3d 305 (Tex. 2001) (lawyer's guilty plea to possession of a controlled substance (cocaine), a third-degree felony, should not subject lawyer to compulsory discipline, but rather to standard disciplinary procedure where mitigating factors can be considered).

11. In re Schaeffer, 2012 Del. LEXIS 272 (lawyer whose actions violated misdemeanor statute prohibiting false police reports publicly reprimanded despite never being charged with the crime); In re Williams, 85 So. 3d 583 (La. 2012) (lawyer who shot and killed a friend permanently disbarred despite reversal of manslaughter conviction and charges later being dismissed); In re Treinen, 131 P.3d 1282 (N.M. 2006) (lawyer placed on supervised probation under conditional discharge after pleading no contest to a misdemeanor count of battery against a household member committed a criminal act and was subject to discipline; any legislative attempt to limit to grounds for professional discipline would be unconstitutional violation of separation of powers).

lawyer,[12] and where the lawyer was later pardoned for the crime.[13] At the same time, a conviction is conclusive evidence that a lawyer committed the crime.[14]

Third, the cases make clear that the criminal conduct need not involve client representation. Criminal acts such as fraud, negligent homicide, and failing to render assistance to children injured in a hit-and-run accident have resulted in successful disciplinary action.[15] Fourth, serious criminal conduct may indicate an immediate risk to clients or the public. For this reason, many states allow for immediate interim suspension of a lawyer following the conviction of a serious crime or a felony.[16] The lawyer remains entitled to a disciplinary hearing at a later date that might provide evidence of mitigation of the sanction.

Client Crimes

Unlike Belge, Casey seemed oblivious to the fact that criminal law placed legal limits on his representation of a client. He was either unaware of Colorado's criminal impersonation statute, or unaware of its application in his client's case. *Casey* illustrates that lawyers must not only avoid criminal acts themselves, but also must understand the criminal law to give competent legal advice to clients. Model Rule 1.2(d) prohibits lawyers from knowingly assisting or counseling client crimes or frauds.[17] Courts focus on whether the lawyer knew about the client's conduct; ignorance of the fact that the client's conduct was a crime is no defense.[18]

This rule first requires that lawyers understand what their clients are doing. Failing to garner all of the relevant facts opens lawyers to allegations of incompetence for failing to provide clients with crucial legal advice. Second, Model

---

12. *E.g.*, In re Segal, 719 N.E.2d 480 (Mass. 1999) (lawyer acquitted of making false statements to a federally insured bank later suspended for two years for the same conduct); People v. Odom, 941 P.2d 919 (Colo. 1997) (lawyer who committed the felony of concealing property to avoid seizure, but who was never charged with the crime, disbarred).

13. In re Abrams, 689 A.2d 6 (D.C. 1997) (en banc) (lawyer who received presidential pardon after pleading guilty to testifying falsely to Congress publicly censured for dishonesty, deceit, and misrepresentation).

14. RLGL § 5, Comment g.

15. *E.g.*, In re Capone, 689 A.2d 128 (N.J. 1997) (lawyer who committed mail fraud by making a false statement on loan application suspended for two years); In re Brown, 674 So. 2d 243 (La. 1996) (lawyer convicted of negligent homicide disbarred); Tate v. St. Bar, 920 S.W.2d 727 (Tex. Crim. App. 1996) (lawyer who fled the scene and failed to stop and render assistance to three injured children disbarred).

16. *E.g.*, N.Y. Jud. Law § 90(4) (McKinney 2003) (interim suspension for "serious crimes" and for failure to file income tax returns); Ohio Gov. Bar R. V § 5 (2003) (interim suspension for felonies and default of child support orders).

17. We discussed the application of this rule to fraud in The Bounds of the Law: *Client Fraud*, *supra* p. 252.

18. *E.g.*, Fla. Bar v. Brown, 790 So. 2d 1081 (Fla. 2001) (lawyer who, at client's request, solicited campaign contribution checks from subordinate lawyers, delivered them to client, and premium-billed client for reimbursement suspended for 90 days for violating Rule 1.2(d) despite his apparent lack of knowledge that client's conduct was criminal); In re Bloom, 745 P.2d 61 (Cal. 1987) (lawyer unsuccessfully argued that he thought helping a client transport plastic explosives to Libya was not unlawful).

Rule 1.2(d) requires that a lawyer properly identify the correct legal character-ization of his client's conduct. For example, the moment Casey learned that his client had given the police an assumed name, he also learned that she was com-mitting another crime. At that point, Casey should have told his client about the legal significance of her conduct and advised her to correct the record; that is, to cease her criminal activity. His incompetence eventually led him to facilitate a client felony (criminal impersonation) that was much more serious than the original misdemeanor charge (trespass).

A lawyer who fails to recognize his client's crime also can fail to properly identify the criminal activity as past, continuing, or future. The crime of Casey's client did not end when she gave someone else's driver's license to the police. She continued her criminal conduct by using the assumed identity in court records and in negotiations with the prosecutor. Casey's failure to understand that his client was engaged in a continuing crime prevented him from recognizing that Model Rule 1.2(d) had been triggered. Failing to appreciate his client's con-tinuing crime further meant that his appearance on behalf of a client with an assumed name assisted her crime. It also meant that he lied to the court.

Accessorial Liability

One issue *Casey* did not discuss was whether the lawyer's conduct went far enough to constitute a violation of Model Rule 8.4(b), as well as 1.2(d). Although Casey did not violate the criminal impersonation statute directly, he might have been guilty of accessorial liability—that is, he might have been an accomplice to his client's crime.

Typical accomplice statutes prohibit intentional "aiding," "abetting," "advis-ing," "assisting," "counseling," or "encouraging" the criminal act of another.[19] Model Rule 1.2(d) loosely incorporates these principles of accessorial liability.[20] The knowledge requirement in Model Rule 1.2(d) roughly parallels the *mens rea* of the crime of accomplice liability[21] and the "counsels or assists" language in the rule tracks the *actus reus* commonly required by most accomplice statutes. Thus, a lawyer like Casey who facilitates a client crime can be disciplined not only for violating Model Rule 1.2(d), but also for violating Model Rule 8.4(b) if that lawyer has acted as a criminal accomplice.

Refco illustrates that lawyers who intend to commit a serious crime (*mens rea*) and agree to aid the client in committing it (*actus reus*)[22] also can become

---

19. Wayne R. LaFave, *Criminal Law* § 6.7 (5th ed., West 2010); Model Penal Code § 2.06.

20. Other specific examples include MR 3.3(a)(3) (knowing presentation of false testimony), 3.4(a) (unlawfully obstructing access to evidence), and 3.4(b) (falsifying evidence, assisting others in fal-sifying evidence). Geoffrey C. Hazard, Jr. & W. William Hodes, *The Law of Lawyering* § 5.12 (3d ed., Aspen Law & Business 2002).

21. The Model Penal Code requires that an accomplice have the "purpose" or conscious desire to facilitate the commission of the offense. Model Penal Code § 2.06(3)(a). *See, e.g.,* In re DeRose, 55 P.3d 126 (Colo. 2002) (lawyer who pled guilty to aiding and abetting a client's illegal structure of financial transactions to evade reporting requirements disbarred).

22. Arnold H. Loewy, *Criminal Law in a Nutshell* § 16.01 (4th ed., West 2003).

co-conspirators of their clients. In many situations, an accomplice is also a co-conspirator.[23] Unlike accomplice liability, however, conspiracy to commit a crime constitutes a separate crime, even if the underlying crime itself is never completed.[24] The lawyer need not actually aid, abet, or assist, so long as she purposely promotes the criminal act and agrees with the others that one of them will commit it.[25] Conspiracy liability also can occur where lawyers claim mere incompetence; that they simply failed to recognize client criminal conduct. Where there is evidence showing that the lawyer assisted the client's crime and the lawyer "deliberately closed his eyes to facts he had a duty to see,"[26] courts have been willing to imply the knowledge or recklessness necessary to make the lawyer legally responsible as a co-conspirator as well as subject to professional discipline. In other words, lawyers who ignore what most lawyers would not ignore can become co-conspirators. Of course, like accomplices, lawyer co-conspirators also have been subject to professional discipline for violating Model Rule 8.4(b).[27]

The Criminal Law and Client Advocacy

Together, *Belge* and *Casey* illustrate the operation of the professional rules involving lawyer and client criminal conduct. Lawyers who commit crimes themselves, or who assist or counsel clients in committing crimes, might not only be indicted and convicted, but they could also lose their license to practice law. As federal and state criminal codes grow to address ever-widening areas of conduct, lawyers in all kinds of practice must be able to identify and respond to applicable criminal limitations on their client's conduct as well as their own.

2. Failure to Disclose Facts

Problems

8-9. Martyn & Fox's client dies of natural causes while the client's personal injury action is pending. Now the likely recovery will be less

---

23. *See, e.g.,* Joshua Dressler, *Understanding Criminal Law* § 30.08 (6th ed., LexisNexis 2012). *See, e.g.,* United States v. Flores, 454 F.3d 149 (3d Cir. 2006) (lawyer who was willfully blind to illegal source of client's money convicted of conspiracy).

24. Ellen S. Podgor & Jerold H. Israel, *White Collar Crime in a Nutshell* 40 (4th ed., West 2009).

25. Model Penal Code § 5.03. The federal conspiracy statute, 18 U.S.C. § 371 (2006), prohibits conspiracies to commit any offense against the United States or to defraud the United States. A number of federal criminal statutes also include conspiracy provisions. For a list of representative provisions, *see* Podgor & Israel, *supra* note 24, at 37.

26. United States v. Benjamin, 328 F.2d 854 (2d Cir. 1964) (conviction of lawyer for conspiracy to commit securities fraud).

27. *E.g.,* Lawyers' Roles: *The Instrumental Lawyer and the Bounds of the Law, supra* p. 243, n. 6, documenting lawyer Joseph Collins's disbarment on consent following his criminal conviction in the *Refco* matters; In re Lee, 755 A.2d 1034 (D.C. App. 2000) (lawyer convicted of conspiracy with client to launder money disbarred); In re Petition of Anderson, 851 S.W.2d 408 (Ark. 1993) (lawyer convicted of conspiracy with client to possess cocaine with intent to distribute failed to gain readmission to the bar).

than half. Can we settle the case before the other side finds out? What if our client died as a result of the injury inflicted by the alleged tortfeasor?

8-10. May (must) Martyn & Fox disclose the presence just outside the courtroom of a witness that we know the other side has been trying to subpoena for weeks?

8-11. Judge: "Since your client has no priors, I will sentence him to probation." Martyn knows that the client has two priors, but neither client nor Martyn causes the judge's material error. What should Martyn do?

> **Consider: Model Rules 1.6(b)(6), 3.3, 3.4, 8.4(c) and (d)**
> **RLGL §§ 63 and 120**

In re Forrest

730 A.2d 340 (N.J. 1999)

PER CURIAM. . . .

I

In 1984, respondent was admitted to the New Jersey bar. At the time the ethics complaint was filed, respondent practiced with the law firm of Lieberman & Ryan in Somerville. In March 1993, Robert and Mary Ann Fennimore, husband and wife, retained Lieberman & Ryan to represent them in a personal injury action resulting from a car accident in which the Fennimores' car had been hit by another vehicle. The Fennimores, both of whom were in the car at the time of the accident, sought to recover from the driver of the other car. Mr. Fennimore claimed that as a result of the accident he suffered a rotator cuff tear, limitation of movement in his right ring finger, limitation of strength in his left shoulder, chronic cervical strain, and headaches. He further claimed that all of his injuries were "permanent . . . ."

On April 5, 1993, Lieberman & Ryan filed a complaint against the driver of the other car on behalf of the Fennimores. Respondent was assigned to work on the Fennimores' file.

Mr. Fennimore died sometime between April 1993 and December 1993, for reasons unrelated to the car accident. . . . Mrs. Fennimore notified respondent of her husband's death.

In December 1993, respondent, knowing of Mr. Fennimore's death, served unsigned answers to interrogatories, entitled "Plaintiff Robert A. Fennimore's Answers to Defendant's . . . Interrogatories," on his adversary, Christopher Walls, Esq. Neither the answers nor the cover letter indicated that Mr. Fennimore had died.

On June 8, 1994, respondent and Mrs. Fennimore appeared at an arbitration proceeding apparently conducted pursuant to Rule 4:21A (mandating arbitration in automobile negligence actions with amount in controversy less than $15,000 and other personal injury actions with amount in controversy less than $20,000). Before the proceeding, respondent advised Mrs. Fennimore that when she testified she should not voluntarily reveal her husband's death. When the arbitrator inquired about Mr. Fennimore's absence, respondent replied that Mr. Fennimore was "unavailable." The arbitrator awarded $17,500 to Mrs. Fennimore and $6000 to Mr. Fennimore. At no time before, during, or after the arbitration proceeding did respondent or Mrs. Fennimore inform the arbitrator that Mr. Fennimore had died.

After the arbitration, respondent contacted Walls to discuss a possible settlement. Again, respondent did not inform Walls of Mr. Fennimore's death.

From January to August 1994, Walls propounded several requests on respondent to produce Mr. Fennimore for a medical examination, but respondent did not reply to those requests. Consequently, Walls filed a motion with the trial court to compel Mr. Fennimore to appear for a medical examination. Respondent did not oppose or otherwise reply to the motion, and the court entered an order on September 9, 1994, that directed Mr. Fennimore to submit to a medical examination on October 4, 1994. After the order was entered, respondent did not disclose Mr. Fennimore's death but nevertheless contacted Walls to further discuss settlement. Only when Mr. Fennimore failed to appear for the court-ordered medical examination did respondent inform Walls of Mr. Fennimore's death.

The DEC [District Ethics Committee] found respondent's conduct in handling the Fennimore matter to be unethical and concluded that respondent violated . . . RPC 3.3(a)[1] (failure to disclose material fact to tribunal), RPC 3.4(a) (obstructing party's access to evidence of potential evidentiary value), and RPC 8.4(c) (engaging in conduct involving dishonesty, fraud, deceit or misrepresentation). . . .

. . . Respondent admits that he acted imprudently when he failed to disclose Mr. Fennimore's death to the court, the arbitrator, and opposing counsel. Respondent argues, however, that certain circumstances mitigate his conduct. Specifically, respondent contends that he acted out of a desire to enhance the recovery for his clients and always had his clients' best interests in mind; that he made no misrepresentations throughout the Fennimore matter but merely withheld certain information, a negotiation technique he describes as "bluffing" and "puffing"; and that he did not knowingly or intentionally violate the Rules of Professional Conduct. Respondent has expressed regret for his misguided conduct in failing to disclose Mr. Fennimore's death.

II

A

The failure to disclose a material fact to a tribunal is an ethical violation under RPC 3.3(a)[1]. Respondent violated that rule when he failed to inform the trial court that opposing counsel's motion to compel Mr. Fennimore to appear for a doctor's examination was moot.

We find guidance in Virzi v. Grand Trunk Warehouse & Cold Storage Co., 571 F. Supp. 507, 512 (E.D. Mich. 1983), in which the court held that, under [Rule 3.3] , plaintiff's attorney had an affirmative duty to disclose the fact of his client's death to the court and his adversary. The attorney in Virzi, after learning of his client's death, appeared before the court at a pretrial conference and entered into a settlement agreement without notifying the court or opposing counsel of plaintiff's death. In setting aside the settlement, the court held that "by not informing the court of plaintiff's death, . . . plaintiff's attorney led this court to enter an order of a settlement for a non-existent party." Acknowledging that an attorney has an affirmative duty to zealously represent a client's interests, the court noted that an attorney "also owes an affirmative duty of candor and frankness to the court and opposing counsel when such a major event as the death of the plaintiff has taken place." See also Toledo Bar Assn. v. Fell, 364 N.E.2d 872, 873 (Ohio 1977) (imposing indefinite suspension from practice of law on Workmen's Compensation attorney who "understood that it had been the long established practice . . . to deny any claim for permanent-total disability benefits upon notice of the death of the claimant, [and] deliberately withheld information concerning his client's death prior to the hearing on the motion concerning the claim"); American Bar Association, Formal Opinion No. 95-397 (1995) (advising that, when client dies in midst of settlement negotiations, lawyer has duty to inform court and opposing counsel of death in first communication to either); In re Jeffers, 1994 WL 715918 (Cal. Review Dept. of State Bar Court Dec. 16, 1994) (imposing two-year probation on attorney who failed to inform court of client's death and represented to court during settlement discussions that he could not communicate with client because "client's brain was not functioning"). . . .

In addition, respondent violated RPC 3.3(a) . . . when he withheld the fact of Mr. Fennimore's death from the arbitrator. The fact that the violation occurred before an arbitrator as opposed to a court does not render the rule inapplicable. Arbitration is "a substitution . . . of another tribunal for the tribunal provided by the ordinary processes of law." . . .

We view respondent's proffer to the arbitrator that Mr. Fennimore was "unavailable" for the arbitration hearing as nothing less than a concealment of the material fact that Mr. Fennimore was deceased. Unquestionably, the arbitrator would have been compelled to consider Mr. Fennimore's death in determining the amount of any monetary award. Additionally, we note that the cause of action originally filed on behalf of Mr. Fennimore—an automobile negligence/personal injury action—would have been transformed into a survivor's action upon Mr. Fennimore's death. See N.J.S.A. 2A:15-3. To withhold information about Mr. Fennimore's death from the arbitrator effectively prevented the arbitrator from properly discharging his responsibilities under the court rules.

B

As did the DEC and the DRB, we find that respondent obstructed opposing counsel's access to potentially valuable evidence, in violation of RPC 3.4(a), by failing to inform opposing counsel that Mr. Fennimore was deceased. Respondent deliberately misled his adversary by serving answers to interrogatories propounded on Mr. Fennimore without disclosing that his client was deceased. Respondent exacerbated that deception by attempting to negotiate a settlement of the claim although his adversary remained uninformed of Mr. Fennimore's death. As the court observed in *Virzi, supra*, the attorney

> did not make a false statement regarding the death of plaintiff. He was never placed in a position to do so because during the . . . settlement negotiations defendants' attorney never thought to ask if plaintiff was still alive. Instead, in hopes of inducing settlement, [he] chose not to disclose plaintiff's death. . . . But the fact of plaintiff's death . . . would have had a significant bearing on defendants' willingness to settle.

We also find that respondent engaged in conduct involving dishonesty, deceit, and misrepresentation, in violation of RPC 8.4(c). Respondent misrepresented to the arbitrator the reasons for Mr. Fennimore's absence at the arbitration proceeding, encouraged Mrs. Fennimore to withhold from the arbitrator the fact of her husband's death, and misled opposing counsel throughout the discovery and negotiation process.

III

The principal goal of disciplinary proceedings is to foster and preserve public confidence in the bar, and to protect the public from an attorney who does not meet the high standards of professional responsibility. . . .

Attorneys must "possess a certain set of traits—honesty and truthfulness, trustworthiness and reliability, and a professional commitment to the judicial process and the administration of justice." . . .

A misrepresentation to a tribunal "is a most serious breach of ethics because it affects directly the administration of justice." . . . Accordingly, we have recognized that "the destructive potential of such conduct to the justice system warrants stern sanctions." . . .

In the instant matter, respondent concealed a material fact from the court and arbitrator. That concealment was compounded by respondent's misrepresenting to the arbitrator the reasons for Mr. Fennimore's absence at the hearing, encouraging Mrs. Fennimore to evade questions about her husband's death, and obstructing Walls's access to the fact of Mr. Fennimore's death. Respondent's misconduct extended far beyond adversarial tactics that might constitute acceptable "puffing" or "bluffing." Respondent's nondisclosure of Mr. Fennimore's death deceived both his adversary and the arbitrator about a fact that was crucial to the fair and proper resolution of the litigation.

. . . Respondent's conduct was not an isolated incident but occurred over a period of at least nine months. Respondent engaged in a continuing course of dishonesty, deceit, and misrepresentation. Respondent's deception of his adversary and the arbitrator is inexcusable, and the contention that it occurred because of a sincere but misguided attempt to obtain a permissible tactical advantage in a lawsuit strains our credibility. Misrepresentation of a material fact to an adversary or a tribunal in the name of "zealous representation" never has been nor ever will be a permissible litigation tactic.

We believe that respondent now understands the gravity of his misdeeds. Nonetheless, respondent's ethical transgressions are serious, and he must be sanctioned accordingly. We conclude that respondent should be suspended from the practice of law for six months. Respondent is also ordered to reimburse the Disciplinary Oversight Committee for appropriate administrative costs.

3. Failure to Disclose Law

Problem

8-12. Martyn is preparing an appellate brief, which argues that the trial court properly dismissed an indictment against her client because the court correctly construed a criminal statute narrowly so as to exclude her client's conduct. Martyn finds only one reported decision citing the statute, a ten-year-old state supreme court case that upheld the statute's constitutionality. The prosecutor's brief does not mention this case, and Martyn doesn't like the case's dicta, which might suggest a broader statutory meaning. Should Martyn cite the case?

Consider: Model Rules 1.6(b)(6), 3.3
             RLGL §§ 63 and 120

Matter of Hendrix
986 F.2d 195 (7th Cir. 1993)

POSNER, Circuit Judge.

This appeal concerns the effect of a discharge in bankruptcy on litigation against the debtor's liability insurer outside of bankruptcy. In re Shondel, 950 F.2d 1301 (7th Cir. 1991), decided well before the appeal briefs were filed yet cited by neither party, dooms the appeal, but we shall not stop with that observation, as there are a few new wrinkles in this case.

On April 6, 1990, an automobile driven by Daniel Hendrix injured Sara Page. Hendrix had liability insurance, but, . . . he and his wife . . . declared bankruptcy under Chapter 7 of the Bankruptcy Code on June 5, 1990. On July 13, Hendrix added to the list of creditors that he had filed in the bankruptcy court the Pages, who at some time . . . between April 6 and July 13 had filed a personal injury suit against Hendrix in an Indiana state court. The Pages, despite being listed and receiving notice, did not file a claim in the bankruptcy proceeding. On September 12, 1990, the bankruptcy court granted Hendrix a discharge from his debts to the listed creditors. . . .

. . . [T]he Pages filed a motion to reopen the bankruptcy proceeding. The motion asked the bankruptcy judge to modify Hendrix's discharge so that they could ask the Indiana state court to reopen their suit for the purpose of proceeding against Hendrix's insurer. The bankruptcy judge granted the relief sought on September 23, 1991, the district judge affirmed, and Hendrix—which is to say Atlanta Casualty Company, for Hendrix has no interest in the matter, his discharge being secure, unmodified, and unchallenged, as far as any effort by the Pages to collect a judgment against him arising from the accident is concerned—appeals. . . .

The discharge had by virtue of 11 U.S.C. §524(a)(2) the force of an injunction against a suit by any holders of listed debts (such as the Pages) to collect those debts from Hendrix. But as to whether such an injunction extends to a suit only nominally against the debtor because the only relief sought is against his insurer, the cases are pretty nearly unanimous that it does not. In re Shondel, *supra*, 950 F.2d at 1306-09; Green v. Welsh, 956 F.2d 30 (2d Cir. 1992); In re Jet Florida Systems, Inc., 883 F.2d 970 (11th Cir. 1989) (per curiam); In re Western Real Estate Fund, Inc., 922 F.2d 592, 601 n.7 (10th Cir. 1990) (per curiam); 3 Collier on Bankruptcy ¶524.01 at pp. 524-16 to 524-17 (Lawrence P. King ed., 15th ed. 1991); *see also* In re Fernstrom Storage & Van Co., 938 F.2d 731, 733-34 (7th Cir. 1991); *contra*, In re White Motor Credit, 761 F.2d 270, 274-75 (6th Cir. 1985). . . . If this is right, the discharge did not in fact prevent the Pages from proceeding in state court against Hendrix, provided they were seeking only the proceeds of his insurance policy. . . .

We recur in closing to the parties' failure to cite *Shondel*. Although the cases are not identical, this appeal could not succeed unless we overruled *Shondel*. Needless to say, the appellant failed to make any argument for overruling *Shondel*, for it failed even to cite the case. This omission by the Atlanta Casualty Company (the real appellant) disturbs us because insurance companies are sophisticated enterprises in legal matters, *Shondel* was an insurance case, and the law firm that handled this appeal for Atlanta is located in this circuit. The Pages' lawyer, a solo practitioner in a nonmetropolitan area, is less seriously at fault for having failed to discover *Shondel*—and anyway his failure could not have been a case of concealing adverse authority, because *Shondel* supported his position. At all events, by appealing in the face of dispositive contrary authority without making arguments for overruling it, Atlanta Casualty filed a frivolous appeal.

This conclusion may seem questionable because, given the intrinsic difficulty of the issues presented by the appeal, and the fact that *Shondel* is the only case on point, the appellant, although it would still have lost, would not have risked sanctions had it urged us to overrule *Shondel*. But that is true in a great many cases in which sanctions are imposed under Fed. R. App. P. 38 for filing a frivolous appeal. The court does not ask whether the appeal might have been nonfrivolous if presented differently, with arguments and authorities to which the appellant in fact never alluded. If the appeal is blocked by authorities that the appellant ignored, the appellant is sanctioned without inquiry into whether the authorities if acknowledged might have been contested.

There is a further point. Although as we noted in Thompson v. Duke, 940 F.2d 192, 196 n.2 (7th Cir. 1991), the circuits are divided (and we have not taken sides) on whether a failure to acknowledge binding adverse precedent violates Fed. R. Civ. P. 11, if Atlanta Casualty's counsel knowingly concealed dispositive adverse authority it engaged in professional misconduct. ABA Model Rules of Professional Conduct Rule 3.3(a)[2]. ⌐The inference would arise that it had filed the appeal for purposes of delay, which would be an abuse of process and thus provide an additional basis for imposition of sanctions under Fed. R. App. P. 38 ("damages for delay"). A frivolous suit or appeal corresponds, at least approximately, to the tort of malicious prosecution, that is, groundless litigation; a suit or appeal that is not necessarily groundless but was filed for an improper purpose, such as delay, corresponds to—indeed is an instance of—abuse of process.⌐ Both, we hold, are sanctionable under Rule 38. We direct Atlanta Casualty's counsel to submit within 14 days a statement as to why it or its client, or both, should not be sanctioned under Rule 38 for failing to cite the *Shondel* case to us.

We are not quite done. Rule 46(c) of the appellate rules authorizes us to discipline lawyers who practice before us. In deciding whether a lawyer has engaged in conduct sanctionable under that rule, we have looked not only to the rules of professional conduct but also to Rule 11 of the civil rules, which makes it sanctionable misconduct for a lawyer to sign a pleading or other paper, including a brief, if he has failed to make a reasonable inquiry into whether his position "is well grounded in fact and is warranted by existing law or a good faith argument for the extension, modification, or reversal of existing law." Reasonable inquiry would have turned up *Shondel*. The lawyer who signed Atlanta Casualty's briefs in this court is therefore directed to submit a statement within 14 days as to why he should not be sanctioned under Rule 46(c). . . .

4. False Evidence

Problem

8-13. Prior to trial, Fox discusses with Client whether he has ever smoked marijuana. Client asks what that has to do with the matter, and Fox tells him, "Nothing, but I am worried the other side just might ask that question." Client admits he smokes marijuana from time to time. At trial, opposing counsel asks Client whether he has ever smoked marijuana, and he immediately responds, "No." Does Fox have any obligation to correct the record? Can we settle the case before the lie is disclosed? What if the same thing happened during Client's deposition?

Consider: Model Rules 1.6(b)(6), 3.3
          RLGL §§ 63 and 120

United States v. Shaffer Equipment Co.
11 F.3d 450 (4th Cir. 1993)

NIEMEYER, Circuit Judge:

In an action brought by the United States Environmental Protection Agency ("EPA") under the Comprehensive Environmental Response, Compensation, and

Liability Act ("CERCLA"), 42 U.S.C. § 9601 et seq., to recover over $5 million in costs incurred in cleaning up a hazardous waste site in Minden, West Virginia, the district court found that the government's attorneys deliberately and in bad faith breached their duty of candor owed to the court during the course of proceedings. The court found that Robert E. Caron, the EPA's on-scene coordinator for the cleanup, had misrepresented his academic achievements and credentials in this and in other cases and that the government's attorneys wrongfully obstructed the defendants' efforts to root out the discrepancies and failed to reveal them once they learned of them.[1] . . .

On appeal, the government contends that the district court adopted an overly broad interpretation of the applicable rules of lawyer conduct and abused its discretion in imposing the most severe sanction by dismissing the action. . . .

I . . .

When the defendants first scheduled the deposition of Caron for September 12, 1991, an EPA assistant regional counsel, Charles Hayden, reviewed Caron's academic credentials. Caron was unable to produce his college diploma (allegedly because his mother failed to mail it to him), but he stated that he had received an undergraduate degree from Rutgers University in 1978 and had taken courses at Drexel University, Trenton State College, and Brookdale Community College. . . .

On the morning of September 12, prior to the deposition, Hayden learned that Caron had not formally received a degree from Rutgers and so advised J. Jared Snyder, a Department of Justice attorney representing the government at the deposition. At the deposition, however, Caron testified, in the presence of Snyder, that he had completed all of the requirements for a degree at Rutgers and that the only reason he had not received his diploma was a question of paperwork. Caron also testified that he had continued taking courses at Drexel for a masters degree. He stated that his bachelors degree work was in environmental science and that his masters degree work was in organic chemistry.

When the deposition was resumed about two months later, on November 27, 1991, Caron was shown a copy of a professional resume on which he had claimed to have received a B.S. degree in environmental science from Rutgers and an M.S. degree in organic chemistry from Drexel. At that point, Snyder directed the witness not to answer any questions about the resume, claiming that the inquiry was not relevant, despite defense counsel's assertion that Caron's credibility was at issue. When counsel for the defendants suggested that the parties obtain a court ruling, Snyder took a recess from the deposition . . . called his superior at the Department of Justice, William A. Hutchins, who called his superior, Bruce Gelber, who called the Deputy Regional Counsel of the EPA, Michael Vaccaro. Following the various calls, Hutchins eventually called Snyder back and

---

1. Caron later resigned from the EPA and pled guilty to the criminal charge of making material false declarations in violation of 18 U.S.C. § 1623.

instructed him to advise Caron of the option to refuse giving further testimony until Caron obtained his own attorney. In addition, Hutchins advised Snyder to permit Caron to answer if Caron so elected and to place any objections on the record. When the deposition resumed, Snyder followed Hutchins' instructions, but he continued to maintain that the questioning was irrelevant. . . .

Two days after the deposition, Snyder researched the question of whether Caron's credibility was relevant to the litigation and concluded that it was relevant as a matter of law. Snyder nonetheless did not supplement the government's response to an earlier interrogatory directed to Caron's credentials (to which the government had objected on the basis of irrelevance) and did not withdraw the relevancy objection to the discovery, despite his conclusion that the inquiry was relevant under current law. . . .

On December 19, 1991, after Vaccaro told the EPA Office of the Inspector General about "the Caron problem," the Inspector General began a criminal investigation. . . .

Hutchins learned in December, during the course of his own investigation, that of the Superfund sites on which Caron had worked six were in litigation. Hutchins then instructed the government attorneys on each of those six cases that the government was not to rely on Caron's testimony. Hutchins also directed the attorneys not to disclose the existence of any investigation because to do so might prejudice the investigation and might also violate Caron's privacy rights.

As the attorney on this case, Snyder received Hutchins' instructions and followed them. Thus, in December 1991, when Snyder prepared the government's motion for summary judgment, he did not cite any testimony from Caron, nor did he include any affidavits executed by Caron. But Snyder did base the summary judgment motion on the administrative record compiled under Caron's direction as the On-Scene Coordinator during the cleanup. The district court found that "Caron [had] played a significant role in the preparation of documents contained in the administrative record."

On January 7, 1992, the defendants, in an effort to learn more facts about Caron's qualifications and credentials, subpoenaed records from the various colleges identified by Caron during his deposition. When Snyder learned of this, he telephoned counsel for the defendants to object because the subpoena was served after December 31, 1991, the discovery cutoff date. Snyder followed up with a letter requesting that the subpoena be withdrawn and that the documents be returned to the various institutions. Drexel University later reported that it had no record of Caron's attendance there, and Snyder was so advised by defense counsel. In response, Snyder wrote a letter of thanks dated January 17, 1992, stating that "we are looking into the matter and will let you know if Mr. Caron's testimony requires correction." While Snyder had also intended, in that letter, to disclose the existence of the criminal investigation and had so drafted the letter, Hutchins and Gelber directed him to delete the reference, and Snyder followed the instruction.

On January 17, 1992, Snyder filed the government's motion for summary judgment which he had started preparing in December. He made no mention of the EPA investigation, the criminal investigation, or the misstatements or mis-representations of Caron's credentials.

Still attempting to discover the extent of the Caron problem after the government filed its summary judgment motion, defense counsel discovered in late January 1992, through independent means, that Caron had testified falsely in another case. Defense counsel decided to bring this evidence to the attention of the Assistant United States Attorney on the case who, following consultation with Snyder and Hutchins, then advised the court for the first time in a letter dated January 31, 1992, of the Caron problem and requested a stay.

Based on these facts, the district court concluded that Snyder and Hutchins violated their general duty of candor to the court as well as the particular duties imposed by West Virginia Rule of Professional Conduct 3.3 (describing the lawyer's duty of candor toward the tribunal) and Federal Rule of Civil Procedure 26(e)(2) (obliging counsel to supplement discovery requests). . . .

. . . Stating that the only sanction appropriate to address the violation was dismissal, the [district] court dismissed the action under its inherent powers and awarded the defendants their attorney's fees incurred in responding to the government's misconduct, under the Equal Access to Justice Act, 28 U.S.C. §2412.

This appeal followed.

II . . .

Our adversary system for the resolution of disputes rests on the unshakable foundation that truth is the object of the system's process which is designed for the purpose of dispensing justice. However, because no one has an exclusive insight into truth, the process depends on the adversarial presentation of evidence, precedent and custom, and argument to reasoned conclusion—all directed with unwavering effort to what, in good faith, is believed to be true on matters material to the disposition. Even the slightest accommodation of deceit or lack of candor in any material respect quickly erodes the validity of the process. As soon as the process falters in that respect, the people are then justified in abandoning support for the system in favor of one where honestly is preeminent.

. . . [I]t is important to reaffirm . . . the principle that lawyers, who serve as officers of the court, have the first line task of assuring the integrity of the process. Each lawyer undoubtedly has an important duty of confidentiality to his client and must surely advocate his client's position vigorously, but only if it is truth which the client seeks to advance. . . . [W]e recognize that the lawyer's duties to maintain the confidences of client and advocate vigorously are trumped ultimately by a duty to guard against the corruption that justice will be dispensed on an act of deceit. . . .

Even limiting our consideration to the provisions of Rule 3.3 which, the government argues, define a lawyer's duty of candor more restrictively, we are nevertheless satisfied that the district court was justified in finding that the government's attorneys breached their duty of candor under that rule. . . .

Addressing first the "actual knowledge" requirement of Rule 3.3, the government contends that, while it may have had suspicions about Caron's misstatements, it did not fully appreciate their falsity until the investigation was completed. While it is true that a mere suspicion of perjury by a client does not carry with it the obligation to reveal that suspicion to the court under Rule 3.3, the government's attorneys in this case cannot find shelter behind any such doubt. Caron admitted to Snyder as early as September 1991 that he did not have a college degree. By December 1991, when an EPA investigation was under way and EPA regional counsel had referred the matter to the Office of Inspector General, the lawyers for the United States had actual knowledge of the discrepancy in Caron's sworn testimony in which he said, on the one hand, that he had no college degree and, on the other, that he had both a bachelor of science degree and a masters degree. At that time, the government's lawyers also had had conversations with Rutgers University which confirmed that no degree had been issued, were aware of misrepresentations on Caron's employment application, and actually possessed a copy of Caron's fraudulent resume. Against this evidence, the government's claim to have held only a suspicion rings hollow.

We move to the government's principal argument under Rule 3.3, that the information which Caron falsified in his credentials was not material to the proceeding. First of all, we find the sincerity of the position undermined because Snyder, the Justice Department attorney in this case, reached the exact opposite conclusion during the course of his independent research in November 1991. . . .

The issue before the district court in this case was whether the defendants are liable to the EPA for costs incurred in cleaning up a hazardous waste site. To establish its case, the government must demonstrate that the release or the threatened release of hazardous wastes caused the EPA to incur "response costs." One method for challenging the appropriateness of the response costs is for the defendant to demonstrate that the methods of cleaning up are not consistent with the National Contingency Plan established by CERCLA. Procedurally, the government relies on the administrative record developed during the cleanup, and the defendant bears the burden of demonstrating that this reliance is arbitrary and capricious. Because this method for establishing its case relies on the administrative record and not testimony, the government argues that Caron's credibility and credentials are not material. . . .

The administrative record in this case is large, consisting of volumes of bills, communications, and authorizations developed primarily from on-site activity. The person placed in overall charge of the site was Robert Caron. While Caron's decisions were subject to approval by superiors, as On-Scene Coordinator he made most of the decisions and, when he sought the approval of superiors, his recommendations were adopted in virtually all of the cases. It was Caron who recommended and obtained approval for the solvent extraction method, side-stepping the traditional method of physically removing the contaminated soil. As it turned out, the pilot process proved unsatisfactory and the traditional method of removing the soil was ultimately utilized. However, the experimental process was abandoned only after over $1 million in costs were incurred, which the EPA now seeks to impose on the defendants. While Caron's role in this litigation relates primarily to supporting response selection, he also had a major role in approving project-related expenditures. Thus, Caron's credentials, capability and credibility are relevant to the examination of the administrative record in this case.

Even where review of a case is confined to the evidence contained in the administrative record, the Supreme Court has concluded that evidence of bad faith or improper behavior by an administrative agency's official in compiling that record justifies inquiry beyond the record compiled. The fact that the government's agent in charge of monitoring expenses and selecting responses filed fraudulent documents with the federal government and perjured himself repeatedly in connection with his federal employment is, we think, of primary relevance to an examination of the integrity and reliability of the administrative record.

It is obviously difficult to assess the impact that Caron's fraud may have had on the development of the record, particularly on the selection of the solvent extraction method, an issue hotly debated by the parties. Would Caron have been given the responsibility for initiating a pilot program if his credentials had not been misrepresented to the EPA in his employment application? Would his recommendations have carried the same weight on review by superiors? To what extent are the defendants saddled in this case with decisions in the administrative record tainted by questions of competence and integrity? . . . Given the great possibility that Caron's deception affected administrative decisions in this case and disguised a weakness in his capabilities, we cannot agree with the government that the sole relevance of the "Caron problem" is with regard to impeachment of Caron's testimony. That approach is too narrow. Moreover, the significance of impeaching the principal EPA witness, who was largely responsible for developing the record, renders impeachment information material. . . .

Once we find the government's attorneys had actual knowledge of Caron's deception and that the deception was material under Rule 3.3, we move to a review of whether Caron's conduct amounted to a fraudulent act of the EPA. . . . Caron's perjury in an attempt to cover up his earlier deception was certainly a fraudulent act. Since Caron was involved in the case as an important agent of the EPA and his misrepresentation was made in the course of his employment with the EPA with the effect of disguising a weakness in the EPA's case, his action is fairly characterized as an act of the EPA.

Distilling the district court's findings, this case reduces to an effort by an important EPA witness to cover up or minimize his long history of fraud. The government's attorneys compounded the problem by obstructing the defendants' efforts to uncover this perjury and in failing themselves to reveal it. When the government's attorneys filed a motion for summary judgment dependent on the administrative record made by Caron and requested a favorable resolution of the case prior to a full documentation of the perjury, these attorneys overstepped the bounds of zealous advocacy, exposing themselves and their employer to sanctions. While this violation was effectively brought to light by opposing counsel, this was not done until after the expenditure of significant time and money.

III

Due to the very nature of the court as an institution, it must and does have an inherent power to impose order, respect, decorum, silence, and compliance with lawful mandates. This power is organic, without need of a statute or rule for its definition, and it is necessary to the exercise of all other powers. Because the inherent power is not regulated by Congress or the people and is particularly subject to abuse, it must be exercised with the greatest restraint and caution, and then only to the extent necessary. . . .

In this case, the government proposed to the district court a lesser sanction to be imposed if a breach of the duty of candor were to be found. It suggested (1) opening for de novo review the administrative record with respect to the selection of the solvent extraction method; (2) allowing discovery by defendants on the EPA's selection of the solvent extraction method; and (3) allowing discovery on any and all matters involving Caron. The district court rejected this offer as a "rather slight sanction." . . .

In doing so, we believe that the district court did not adequately address the broad policies of deciding the case on the merits where the orderly administration of justice and the integrity of the process have not been permanently frustrated, and of exercising the necessary restraint when dismissal is based on the inherent power. Thus, we reverse its dismissal order. ⌐We are confident that the district court's objective of punishing the wrongdoers, deterring similar future conduct, and compensating the defendant can be achieved by a sanction, short of dismissal, tailored more directly to those goals. ⌐

The occasion to consider the disciplining of members of the bar is not a happy one, and the district court's response was understandably stern. We are in full agreement with the district court's expressed concern, and we repeat that our adversary system depends on a most jealous safeguarding of truth and candor. But ⌐we also observe that through an outright dismissal, the defendants receive the benefit of a total release from their obligations under the environmental protection laws. This would provide the defendants relief far beyond the harm caused by the government attorneys' improper conduct and would frustrate the resolution on the merits of a case which itself has strong policy implications. . . . ⌐

Without suggesting a sanction which is appropriate, we point out that in considering the proper role of the administrative record in this case and the respective burdens of proof, the district court may deny the government the benefit of any portion of the record or the right to claim any expense, which may have been tainted by Caron's misconduct, even if it becomes impossible to assess accurately the extent of that taint. Because of the government's misconduct, the benefit of any doubt must be resolved in the defendants' favor. . . .

Accordingly, we affirm the district court's finding that a breach of ethical conduct occurred, but we vacate the judgment of the district court dismissing the case and remand for the imposition of a sanction short of outright dismissal. Since an award of attorney's fees may be part of the district court's overall calculus in selecting a sanction after further proceedings, we leave for later review, if necessary, any question on whether attorney's fees were appropriately awarded.* . . .

5. Criminal Defense

Problem

8-14. How does Martyn & Fox deal with a criminal defendant client who insists, incredibly, he was in Paris, France, the night of the murder in Paris, Texas? What if we know in advance? What if it happens as a surprise? Does it matter that we are convinced our client is innocent?

   Consider: Model Rules 1.6(b)(6), 3.3
                     RLGL §§ 63 and 120

Nguyen v. Knowles

2010 U.S. Dist. Lexis 89894 (E. D. Cal.)
aff'd, 2010 U.S. Dist. Lexis 97816

John F. MOULDS, United States Magistrate Judge.
FACTS

Early in the morning on June 3, 1998, a group of men wearing dark clothing and masks came in through the front door of the Silver Fox Casino. The victims identified the intruders as Asian by their accents and size. One victim recognized an intruder speaking in Vietnamese and using the name "Bao." . . .

A total of $31,400 in cash was taken from the casino [as well as paychecks from the casino to a robbery victim, Sandra Woodsworth] . . . .

On August 25, 1998, police discovered guns at the home of Minh Nguyen, a felon, during an unrelated search. Minh, thinking that he was in trouble for the gun possession, gave the officers information about the robbery. He . . . identified Thanh Do ("Andy"), Johnny Nguyen ("Johnny"), and [petitioner, Hung Nguyen ("Henry")] as involved in the robbery. Minh's information took police to Andy and Johnny's homes, leading to their arrest. . . .

Minh could only identify [petitioner] by his nickname "Henry." However, Minh did take police to [petitioner]'s home. He also informed police that [petitioner] had taken a trip to Vietnam after the robbery.

---

* On remand, the district court ordered lawyers Hutchins and Snyder to pay personal sanctions of $2,000 each and prohibited them from seeking reimbursement from the government. It also accepted a consent decree, which it deemed necessary because of Mr. Caron's misconduct in the case and the government's inability to rely on his testimony. Finally, it vacated its initial award of attorney's fees to the defendants to enhance the value of the consent decree to the government. United States v. Shaffer Equipment Co., 158 F.R.D. 80 (S.D. W. Va. 1994).

A search of [petitioner]'s room on September 1, 1998, produced incriminating evidence. Police recovered a white garbage bag with blood on it. The bag was similar to the moneybag used in the robbery. Additionally, police found ledgers with blood on them and the casino checks to Sandra Woodsworth in [petitioner]'s room. [Petitioner] was arrested two days later in San Francisco.

Johnny Nguyen testified [that] . . . [Petitioner] was present at each meeting [to plan the robbery and] named [petitioner], himself, and two other individuals, Bao and Duong, as participants in the robbery. . . .

Minh's testimony confirmed [petitioner]'s presence at the meetings to plan the robbery. . . . After the robbery, [petitioner], Johnny, and Andy came over to Minh's house. Minh went out with [petitioner] later that night. The guns were eventually brought back to Minh.

Prior to [petitioner]'s testimony, defense counsel met with the trial judge ex parte without the [petitioner] present to discuss an "ethical conflict." Defense counsel felt that [petitioner] was going to present perjurious testimony. Upon questioning from the judge, counsel indicated he had warned [petitioner] that perjury is a crime that poses strategic risks and advised him to testify truthfully. Counsel also indicated he did not file a motion to withdraw and felt he could continue to represent [petitioner]. The court agreed with defense counsel that [petitioner] should present his testimony in a narrative manner.

In his testimony, [petitioner] described himself as a full-time student who likes to go out with his friends. He described Johnny and Minh as gang members. Though [petitioner] said he was not a gang member himself, it was stipulated in rebuttal that a deputy sheriff would testify that [petitioner] stated he was a member of the "TL" (Tenderloin) gang from San Francisco when questioned about housing assignments in the jail. [Petitioner] admitted he heard conversations about the robbery on numerous occasions but dismissed the plans as a display to impress girls. According to the [petitioner], the day before the robbery Minh borrowed $100 to get a motel room to drink beer and invite girls over. Later that evening Minh told [petitioner] Andy had already rented a motel room. [Petitioner] was disappointed to find there were no girls present at the motel and left after one beer. He testified the others discussed the casino robbery at the motel. He left the motel to go to karaoke. . . .

[Petitioner] testified Minh, Johnny, Andy, and Duong arrived at his house the next morning to clean their guns and count their money. Johnny was bleeding. [Petitioner] watched television while the others were in his room and went back to sleep once they left. Minh offered defendant $400 but defendant only accepted the $100 Minh owed him. [Petitioner] cleaned the trash from his room and checked to make sure there was no blood in the house.

Weeks after the robbery Johnny, Johnny's girlfriend, and [petitioner] went to Vietnam together. [Petitioner] estimated that he spent about $4000 there, $2000 of which he claimed was from his sister. His sister corroborated this but had no receipts to show she had given [petitioner] any money. In addition to the trip, [petitioner] brought a pager, a "fake" Movado watch, and spent $775 in car repairs after the robbery. When he went to Vietnam [petitioner] was behind on his rent. He claimed to have paid the landlord's wife but this was contradicted by a stipulation.

ANALYSIS . . .

Petitioner's claims arise from the following facts. Trial commenced on February 23, 1999. Jury selection was completed on March 1, 1999, and the prosecution's case in chief started on the same day. At the start of the afternoon session on March 1, 1999, the court dismissed the jury until the next day. Thereafter, the court took up a few matters with the prosecutor, Mr. Durenberger, and defense counsel, Mr. Salinger. . . . At the conclusion of those matters, the court held a conference with defense counsel to discuss an issue defense counsel had raised with the court ex parte. Neither petitioner nor the prosecutor were present during the conference. Prior to the conference, the following statements were made on the record, in petitioner's presence:

THE COURT: Okay. Mr. Salinger, I need to discuss with you the issue you raised ex parte. I think Mr. Durenberger is leaving the courtroom, and I do not plan to discuss the merits of the case with you, only your professional responsibilities with your client, for the record.

MR. SALINGER: Thank you. With that, perhaps I'll leave it there and make a record about what I'd like to discuss with you. . . .

THE COURT: I think we can probably discuss this without the defendant here. We can probably just return him to his cell, and then I can discuss your professional responsibilities with you, Mr. Salinger. Does that make sense?

MR. SALINGER: Yes, your Honor.

THE COURT: All right. That will conclude these proceedings. Henry [petitioner], we'll see you tomorrow morning at nine o'clock.

MR. SALINGER: All right.

After petitioner left the courtroom, the court made the following statement on the record:

THE COURT: Let's go back on the record. The defendant is no longer in court, and for the record, Mr. Salinger has raised with the Court, ex parte, what he felt was an ethical conflict due to the fact that his client, Henry, has elected to take the stand in this case and to relate to the jury what Mr. Salinger perceives as perjurious testimony.

After an off the record exchange between the court and counsel, the following exchange was recorded:

THE COURT: . . . I have provided Mr. Salinger with what the Court has researched to be the proper things for defense counsel to do in the event of this situation, namely, that his client should be adviced [sic] that perjury is a crime. Have you advised him of that?

MR. SALINGER: Yes.

THE COURT: And you need to also advise him of the strategic risk of perjury.

MR. SALINGER: Yes.

THE COURT: Have you advised him about testifying truthfully and making full disclosure?

MR. SALINGER: Yes.

THE COURT: Have you considered presenting perjury or arguing perjury to the Court or jury?

MR. SALINGER: Yes, I have.

THE COURT: And I don't believe you have asked to withdraw as counsel. You believe you can continue to represent him, provided you don't participate in the perjury?

MR. SALINGER: Correct, your Honor.

THE COURT: And it's your opinion that the defendant wishes to, nevertheless, take the stand against your advice?

MR. SALINGER: Yes, your Honor.

THE COURT: And for lack of a better term, free narrative approach will be used during direct exam?

MR. SALINGER: Yes.

THE COURT: And as I ascertained, Mr. Salinger, what you told me in my chambers and pretty much what you should do legally in this respect, and that is to simply elicit from the defendant who he is. It's very fundamental background questions, and then, essentially, ask him a very large leading question, such as, Can you tell us what happened on June 3rd, 1998, at 6:30 a.m., and let him speak in narrative fashion.

I'm concerned, of course, because of the impact of that on the jury. The jury will see the dichotomy or the difference between the defendant's testimony and all the other witnesses' testimony, but it seems to me he's put himself in that situation by putting you in this conflict situation, so it appears from the case law that this is the proper procedure to follow.

It also indicates, according to points and authorities I shared with you, you should not ask him specific questions that might elicit perjury, and, basically, the only way you can do that is to ask him narrative questions, and, of course, you can't, in your closing argument, make any reference to the jury anything he said that was perjurious.

MR. SALINGER: To clarify that—in my closing argument, I was planning to use only facts that I believe is the truth. Is that permissible?

THE COURT: Yes. . . .

MR. SALINGER: Okay.

THE COURT: In any event, that's what I believe we'll ascertain, and I believe, at the outset, you accurately described your duty to me in chambers, which, frankly, is an issue I hadn't faced as a trial judge for some peculiar reason.

It appears you came to the correct conclusion yourself, and that is, to ask your client leading questions, and you've represented you've done all the things the case law requires, told him about the dangers, told him he could be prosecuted, told him all the other things, including the strategic risk of lying to a jury potentially. And beyond that, you can do nothing else but ask a leading question and hope that the jury doesn't include you, uh, the defendant's false statements to the jury, but I think you pretty much removed yourself by just asking the narrative question.

MR. SALINGER: Very good, your Honor. Just for the record, I'd like to clarify, since you will be the judge that will be imposing sentence, I have no firsthand knowledge, and it's just that he gave me one event of the facts, and now he's wanting to testify to another version of the facts.

THE COURT: If I use the word perjury, I'm using it—it's possible perjury, if that. I'm not accusing your client of perjury, but I think that what you're saying, what he told the jury is so 180 degrees from what he told you, and whether that's perjury or not, when I say perjury, I meant purported or alleged or possible perjury. . . . Do you have any other questions, Mr. Salinger?

MR. SALINGER: No, your Honor. You've covered everything.

THE COURT: Very good. That will conclude these proceedings.

Subsequently, petitioner took the stand in his defense and testified in narrative fashion. Petitioner testified through an interpreter. The prosecutor objected twice to the narrative form of petitioner's testimony; both objections were overruled. . . .

The prosecutor cross-examined petitioner in a question and answer format. On redirect, petitioner's counsel asked him if he had any response to the cross-examination or anything he wanted to add to his testimony. . . . Petitioner made one clarification to his testimony. Thereafter, the court asked petitioner a series of questions concerning events prior to the robbery. At the conclusion of the court's questioning, the prosecution asked three more cross-examination questions.

a. Right To Be Present

Petitioner's first claim is that his exclusion from the conference between the judge and defense counsel violated his rights, guaranteed by the Confrontation Clause and the Due Process Clause, to be present at a critical stage of the proceedings, as well as his right to the assistance of counsel. . . .

In the petition, which is signed under penalty of perjury, petitioner avers that "his testimony at trial was truthful" and that he "knows of no reason why counsel would believe petitioner intended to commit perjury." Petitioner has presented evidence that suggests a language barrier may have affected his communications with his attorney, and the record suggests that, while petitioner understands English, an interpreter was present at trial to assist him. Petitioner also avers that counsel did not advise him that he would have to testify in narrative fashion or that he thought petitioner would commit perjury, did not explain to petitioner what perjury was or how to testify, did not inform petitioner that he was going to tell the trial judge petitioner was going to commit perjury, and never told petitioner about the in camera hearing with the judge.

⌐It is clear that petitioner had a due process right to be present at the in camera hearing⌐ . . . As the Eighth Circuit has held,

> once the possibility of client perjury is disclosed to the trial court, the trial court should reduce the resulting prejudice. It should limit further disclosures of client confidences, inform the attorney of his other duties to his client, inform the defendant of her rights, and determine whether the defendant desires to waive any of those rights. U.S. v. Long, 857 F.2d 436, 446 (8th Cir. 1988).

In the instant case, the trial court took none of those steps and, indeed, took the erroneous view that petitioner's presence was not required. . . .

As a result of the ex parte hearing, petitioner testified in narrative fashion. In his petition, petitioner avers that his trial testimony was truthful and that if he had been present at the hearing he could have clarified any misunderstanding with his counsel. The jury heard petitioner's testimony and ultimately disbelieved it in material part.[8] . . . ⌐[A]ssuming arguendo that petitioner did not receive proper advisements concerning the risks and consequences of giving perjured testimony from either the trial court or his attorney, . . . the court cannot find that this error was harmful.⌐ With the advisements, one of three possible paths would have been before petitioner: to testify truthfully with the assistance of his attorney, to testify in narrative fashion, or to decide not to testify. Since petitioner represents here that his testimony was truthful and his attorney just misunderstood him, there is no basis for concluding that petitioner would have opted not to testify nor, as the court has already observed, is there any basis in the record for finding that the jury's verdict was based on the fact that petitioner's testimony was provided in narrative fashion. . . .

b. Ineffective Assistance of Counsel

Petitioner's second claim is that his trial counsel provided ineffective assistance of counsel by discussing with the trial court "his belief that petitioner intended to perjure himself without possessing a firm factual basis for that belief."

The Sixth Amendment guarantees the effective assistance of counsel. . . . To support a claim of ineffective assistance of counsel, a petitioner must first show that, considering all the circumstances, counsel's performance fell below an objective standard of reasonableness. . . . Strickland v. Washington, 466 U.S. 668 (1984).

Second, a petitioner must establish that he was prejudiced by counsel's deficient performance. Prejudice is found where "there is a reasonable probability that, but for counsel's unprofessional errors, the result of the proceeding would have been different." Id. at 694. . . .

---

8. The record reflects that the trial took five days, and that the jury deliberated for more than five days, sent numerous notes to the trial court over the course of the deliberations, and at one point represented that they were deadlocked. Notwithstanding the apparent rigor of the deliberations, the jury ultimately rejected petitioner's testimony and found him guilty of the charges.

In Nix v. Whiteside, 475 U.S. 157 (1986), the United States Supreme Court addressed what constitutes "'reasonable professional' responses to a criminal defendant client who informs counsel that he will perjure himself on the stand." First among the reasonable responses is the duty "to attempt to dissuade the client from the unlawful course of conduct." This attempt may include the threat to withdraw from representation if the client persists in the desire to commit perjury. Counsel may also move to withdraw from representation prior to the start of trial. When counsel learns of proposed perjury during trial, counsel has the option of allowing his client to take the stand and to testify in narrative fashion, unaided by counsel. Finally, "an attorney's revelation of his client's perjury to the court is a professionally responsible and acceptable response to the conduct of a client who has actually given perjured testimony."

In the instant case, there is no evidence that petitioner told his attorney that he would commit perjury. Instead, counsel told the court that petitioner wanted to testify in a manner that differed from what petitioner had previously told counsel. Precedent in this and other circuits suggests that an attorney should have a "firm factual basis" for believing that a client will testify falsely before acting on such a belief. In the instant case, petitioner's counsel "did not lay out a firm factual basis" for his position. In fact, petitioner's counsel told the court that he had "no firsthand knowledge, and it's just that he gave me one event of the facts, and now he's wanting to testify to another version of the facts." In addition, counsel chose to raise this perceived conflict with the trial court prior to petitioner's testimony at an ex parte hearing without petitioner present. Under the circumstances of this case, that decision fell outside the bounds of reasonably competent professional assistance. For the reasons set forth in Section a *supra*, there is no reasonable probability that the outcome of petitioner's trial would have been different had counsel not erred, and for those reasons petitioner is not entitled to relief from his conviction.

There is, however, a reasonable probability that the outcome of petitioner's sentencing hearing might have been different had counsel not approached the trial court, particularly without petitioner present. At sentencing, the trial court made the following comment after hearing from petitioner's mother:

> And it's very unfortunate that Henry, your youngest child, was involved in this. It's a very sad comment on him, not you. Because you have given him opportunities to succeed. *But he has essentially thrown that in your face by not only committing this offense, but lying to this jury in this courtroom.*

Subsequently, after hearing from petitioner's father, the trial court said:

> . . . [T]his has very little to do with you. In fact, my heart is breaking when I think that Henry would dishonor such wonderful parents as you are. I do not understand his behavior. It is very peculiar. Particularly given the fact that he was offered to resolve this matter by pleading guilty to these charges and doing a much lower sentence. The one that you're asking me to give him now.
>
> Instead, he turned down the People's offer and the Court's offer to resolve this like the other young men, and instead dragged me, the District Attorney,

the defense attorney, through a long, complicated trial. Which agonized this jury. They wrote me letter after letter after letter with legal questions and problems.

Henry got up on the stand and lied. *He perjured himself so badly that his own attorney could not even ask him questions for fear of getting in trouble himself.* That is, with the State Bar, the person who licenses lawyers in California.

So you can see why I would be disappointed at best in Henry's conduct not only in the commission of the robberies in this, case, and being the active instigator of that robbery, but coming to this court and failing to take his punishment early. And rather than taking his punishment early, he waited and dragged this Court and a lot of lawyers and jurors through a long trial. . . .

But that does not change my deep respect and admiration for your family and your daughters and the fact that Henry some day will leave state prison and hopefully be a good citizen. *But he is going to go to prison for a long time based upon his conduct in this case and his conduct in this courtroom.* And I'm so sorry as a judge that I have to treat him this way.

But he has earned every year, every day, every month that I'm going to impose. Because he's dishonored you and he's dishonored this courtroom, where I expect honesty and forthrightness.

Subsequently, the court imposed a sentence of twenty-three years and eight months in state prison, a sentence longer by four years and four months than that recommended by the probation department. . . .

In Lowery v. Cardwell, 575 F.2d 727 (9th Cir. 1978), the United States Court of Appeals for the Ninth Circuit held that a habeas petitioner was entitled to relief on the ground that his right to due process had been violated when his attorney informed the finder of fact that the attorney had formed a belief that his client's defense was based on false testimony. The court of appeals found that the attorney had "disabled the fact finder from judging the merits of the defendant's defense." While the trial court was not the trier of fact as to the criminal charges against petitioner, he was the final arbiter at sentencing. Counsel's decision to seek the court's guidance and to acquiesce in the exclusion of his client from the in camera hearing, disabled the trial court from independently judging petitioner's veracity. It is apparent from the record that the trial court's assessment of petitioner's veracity had a significant impact on the sentencing hearing . . . [and] ultimately added an additional four years and four months to petitioner's sentence.[12]

For the foregoing reasons, this court finds that petitioner was prejudiced at sentencing by his counsel's decision to discuss his concerns about petitioner's testimony with the court in petitioner's absence, and the state court's rejection of this aspect of this claim was an unreasonable application of clearly established

---

12. Petitioner's attorney interposed no objection to the court's reliance on petitioner's alleged perjury. During sentencing, petitioner's counsel made the following statement: "We understand and respect the Court's desire to send a message both for not taking the offer and for Henry's conduct in the courtroom. And I'd just like to point out that the sentence prescribed in the probation report adequately sends that message. It's doubling basically the offer that he got from the prosecution. That's a long time."

United States Supreme Court precedent. Petitioner is entitled to relief from the sentence imposed by the trial court. . . .

In the instant case, the Sixth Amendment violation occurred at the in camera hearing, which took place during trial, and the prejudice occurred at sentencing. Accordingly, the court will recommend that petitioner's application for writ of habeas corpus be granted and that the State of California be given a period of thirty days in which to elect whether to retry petitioner or to resentence him.

■ Lawyers' Roles:
Zealous Representation Within the Bounds of the Law

Several of the cases in the last three chapters in this book provide dramatic examples of lawyers who underidentified or overidentified with clients. Those who apparently underidentified with clients, like the lawyers in *Perez, Anonymous,* and *Pressly,* breached fiduciary duties. The other extreme involved lawyers who apparently overidentified, like the lawyers in *Refco,* and, as a result, were implicated in their client's violations of law. The lawyers in *Casey, Forrest,* and *Shaffer Equipment* also fell into this trap and, as a result, facilitated a client crime (*Casey*) and a fraud on the court (*Forrest* and *Shaffer Equipment*).

But the vast majority of lawyers avoid these extremes by representing their clients zealously within the bounds of the law.[1] These lawyers refrain from directive behavior by fulfilling their fiduciary duties and providing zealous representation. At the same time, these lawyers avoid instrumentalism by maintaining the professional objectivity necessary to provide their clients with good legal advice. They recognize definitive legal norms but remain willing to challenge them openly when significant rights of a client are at stake. This is what Judge Noonan calls the "right relation . . . struck most of the time."[2] It is a relation of collaborator, "wise counselor,"[3] or translator, rather than parent or puppet.

Lawyers as Collaborators

Consider, for example, the lawyer in *Purcell.* He listened to very credible threats of harm from his own client and realized that the third parties who were likely to be harmed by his client's behavior could not protect themselves. He then exercised his discretion to warn authorities to prevent the harm. But when a court later sought his testimony to convict his former client, he protected his client's

---

1. This phrase closely parallels the language in both Canon 31 of the 1908 Canons of Ethics, the title of Canon 7 of the 1969 Code of Professional Responsibility ("A Lawyer Should Represent a Client Zealously Within the Bounds of the Law"), and ¶ 9 of the Preamble to the Model Rules of Professional Conduct.
2. John T. Noonan, Jr., *The Lawyer Who Overidentifies with His Client,* 76 Notre Dame L. Rev. 827, 840 (2001).
3. Lon L. Fuller & John D. Randall, *Professional Responsibility: Report of the Joint Conference,* 44 ABA J. 1159, 1161 (1958).

confidentiality by appropriately asserting the privilege on his client's behalf. The Massachusetts court points out that he, too, acted within the bounds of the law and zealously protected his client's interests. Further, the result in *Purcell* gives lawyers an incentive to prevent serious harm when efforts to dissuade their clients from harmful conduct prove unsuccessful. Lawyers can act to save lives and at the same time avoid betraying their client's confidence in a subsequent proceeding.

Similarly, the lawyers in *Belge* steered clear of obstructing justice by merely observing rather than actively concealing the buried bodies they discovered. The information was disclosed only after their client blurted it out on the stand. The court holds that their apparent violation of a misdemeanor statute had to give way to the client's Fifth Amendment right. These lawyers not only observed the bounds or limits of the law, they also zealously advocated their client's interests throughout the proceeding, by preparing a legally recognized defense (insanity) justified by the facts.

The Collaborative Model

These lawyers acted as collaborators with their clients. They did not control or manipulate their clients and observed all of the fiduciary duties the law demands. They acted competently and loyally, communicated with their clients, enabled them to make decisions about the matter, and kept their confidences. At the same time, they did not shirk from clear explanations to clients when their clients' conduct approached legally unacceptable boundaries. When necessary, these lawyers refused to act instrumentally and told their clients why. They were empathetic but offered objective advice. They identified with their clients enough to do a good job but did not become tools of their client's wrongdoing. When they disagreed with the clients' proposed conduct, they respected the clients enough to remonstrate with the clients about the propriety of the clients' conduct. When legal competence demanded that they draw a line between their clients' behavior and their own, they did so.

Professor James Boyd White invokes another metaphor for this collaborative model, the metaphor of lawyers as translators. Each client-lawyer relationship brings with it the opportunity to translate the client's desires and moral values into legal categories. It also affords a lawyer the opportunity to gain new insight into the impact of the legal system on a client.[4] The client brings a desire to accomplish an objective, which the lawyer must listen to with care. Lawyers advocate for the client, but also advocate to the client, teaching the client about competing moral values or public policy choices that the law has embodied to protect the interests of others.[5]

Ultimately, lawyers, like other professionals, listen to clients' stories, translate these client narratives into legal language, and translate law and legal policy

---

4. Clark D. Cunningham, *The Lawyer as Translator, Representation as Text: Towards an Ethnography of Legal Discourse,* 77 Cornell L. Rev. 1298 (1992).
5. William F. May, *Beleaguered Rulers: The Public Obligation of the Professional* 80 (Westminster John Knox 2001).

back to their clients to offer guidance. In most cases, lawyers can help clients achieve their legal goals. In some instances, they must inform clients that certain actions cannot be taken, or even that certain goals cannot be realized. In each case, they are not only translating the clients' desires to the legal system and back again, but they are also acting as private lawmakers, who both influence and are influenced by the law and legal system in which they function. To do this well, lawyers must respect each client's moral autonomy but also help each client understand the moral values and public policy choices embedded in the law itself. The best lawyers also respect their own moral integrity and are willing to deliberate and, if necessary, argue with clients about their goals and interests.

D.   Detecting Conflicts of Interest

Problem

8-15. Martyn & Fox want to hire a brilliant third-year law student in their litigation department. The student gained litigation experience working in a law school domestic violence & juvenile law clinic. To facilitate the obligatory conflicts check, Martyn & Fox ask the new hire for the names of her clinic clients and a brief description of each case. Does it matter if Martyn & Fox currently represents the county child protective services agency?

Consider: Model Rules 1.6(b)(7), 1.7 Comment [3], 5.1

Chapter 9

Conflicts of Interest: Loyalty and Independent Judgment

"If it pleases the Court, Your Honor, I'd like to quit the defense and join the prosecution."

A. Introduction

This chapter and the next two explore the fiduciary duty of loyalty, which can be traced back several centuries in the law of agency.[1] Fiduciary obligations arise out of relationships where one party must share confidential information with, and trust and depend on, another. Loyalty imposes an obligation on lawyers to act for the benefit of clients by recognizing and responding to any influences (conflicts of interest) that might interfere with loyalty to the client's interest.

In what has been viewed as a classic description of the fiduciary duty of loyalty, then Chief Judge Cardozo explained:

> Many forms of conduct permissible in a workaday world for those acting at arm's length are forbidden to those bound by fiduciary ties. . . . Not honesty alone, but the punctilio of an honor the most sensitive, is then the standard of behavior.[2]

In the last three chapters, we saw that the obligation to maintain client confidences constitutes one facet of this loyalty obligation. This chapter and the next two focus on the principal feature of loyalty: the need to recognize and respond to conflicts of interest created by others, including the lawyer's own interest, the interest of a third person, or the interest of another current or former client of the lawyer or law firm. These chapters also address additional remedies commonly sought to remedy conflicts, including judicial disqualification and injunctive relief, the law of undue influence, and fee forfeiture.

Throughout this material, we find it helpful to address conflicts by following the four-step approach to resolving conflict of interest recommended in Model Rule 1.7 comment [2] and outlined here.

Conflicts of Interest

Step One: Identify the client(s)
Step Two: Determine whether a conflict of interest exists. [Rule 1.7(a)]
           7 categories:
   1. **Personal Interests of a Lawyer:**
      General Rule: 1.7
      Specific Rules: 1.8(a) Business transactions w/clients
                         1.8(b) Use of client information
                         1.8(c) Client gifts to lawyer
                         1.8(d) Literary rights
                         1.8(e) Financial assistance to client
                         1.8(h) Limitation of liability to client
                         1.8(i) Proprietary interest in litigation

---

1. *Restatement (Third) of Agency* § 8.01 (2006).
2. Meinhard v. Salmon, 164 N.E. 545, 546 (N.Y. 1928).

1.8(j) Lawyer/client sexual relationship

3.7 Lawyer as witness

2. Interests of Another Current Client:

General Rule: 1.7

Specific Rules: 1.8(g) Aggregate Settlements

1.13(g) Organizations and Constituents

3. Interests of a Third Person:

General Rule: 1.7

Specific Rules: 1.8(f) Third-person compensation

5.4(c) Third-person direction

1.13(a) Organizations

4. Interests of a Former Client:

General Rule: 1.9

5. Interests of a Prospective Client:

General Rule: 1.18

6. Government Lawyers:

General Rule: 1.11 Former and Current Government Officers and Employees

Specific Rule: 1.12 Former Judge, Arbitrator, Mediator or Other Third-Party Neutral

7. Imputed Conflicts:

General Rule: 1.10

Specific Rules: 1.8(k) Current Clients: Specific Rules

1.11 Former and Current Government Officers and Employees

1.12 Former Judge, Arbitrator, Mediator or Other Third-Party Neutral

Step Three: **Decide whether the conflict is consentable. [Rule 1.7(b)(1)]**

Step Four: **If it is, consult with affected clients and obtain informed consent confirmed in a well-crafted writing. [Rule 1.7(b)(2)]**

General Rules: 1.7, 1.0(b), 1.0(e)

Specific Rules: 1.8 Current Clients: Specific Rules

Problem

9-1.   Local Municipality filed a motion to disqualify Martyn & Fox, claiming that Martyn & Fox cannot represent a developer in an appeal from a zoning decision because we currently represent Local Municipality on some tax collection matters. Martyn, who is handling the zoning appeal, distinctly recalls chatting with the city solicitor and getting a waiver. Is Martyn & Fox safe?

Consider: **Model Rules 1.7, 1.13**

RLGL §§ 97, 121, 122

Maritrans GP Inc. v. Pepper, Hamilton & Scheetz
602 A.2d 1277 (Pa. 1992)

PAPADAKOS, J. . . .

Maritrans is a Philadelphia-based public company in the business of transporting petroleum products along the East and Gulf coasts of the United States by tug and barge. Maritrans competes in the marine transportation business with other tug and/or barge companies, including a number of companies based in New York. Pepper is an old and established Philadelphia law firm. Pepper and Messina represented Maritrans or its predecessor companies in the broadest range of labor relations matters for well over a decade. In addition, Pepper represented Maritrans in a complex public offering of securities, a private offering of $115 million in debt, a conveyance of all assets, and a negotiation and implementation of a working capital line of credit. Over the course of the representation, Pepper was paid approximately $1 million for its labor representation of Maritrans and, in the last year of the representation, approximately $1 million for its corporate and securities representation of Maritrans.

During the course of their labor representation of Maritrans, Pepper and Messina became "intimately familiar with Maritrans' operations" and "gained detailed financial and business information, including Maritrans' financial goals and projections, labor cost/savings, crew costs and operating costs." This information was discussed with Pepper's labor attorneys, and particularly with Messina, for the purpose of developing Maritrans' labor goals and strategies. In addition, during the course of preparing Maritrans' public offering, Pepper was furnished with substantial confidential commercial information in Maritrans' possession—financial and otherwise—including projected labor costs, projected debt coverage and projected revenues through the year 1994, and projected rates through the year 1990. Pepper and Messina, during the course of their decade-long representation of Maritrans, came to know the complete inner-workings of the company along with Maritrans' long-term objectives, and competitive strategies in a number of areas including the area of labor costs, a particularly sensitive area in terms of effective competition. In furtherance of its ultimate goal of obtaining more business than does its competition, including the New York–based companies, Maritrans analyzed each of its competitors with Pepper and Messina. These analyses included an evaluation of each competitor's strengths and weaknesses, and of how Maritrans deals with its competitors.

Armed with this information, Pepper and Messina subsequently undertook to represent several of Maritrans' New York–based competitors. Indeed, Pepper and Messina undertook to represent the New York companies in their labor negotiations, albeit with a different union, during which the New York companies sought wage and benefit reductions in order to compete more effectively with, i.e., to win business away from, Maritrans.

In September, 1987, Maritrans learned from sources outside of Pepper that Pepper and Messina were representing four of its New York–based competitors in their labor relations matters. Maritrans objected to these representations, and voiced those objections to many Pepper attorneys, including Mr. Messina. Pepper and Messina took the position that this was a "business conflict," not a "legal conflict," and that they had no fiduciary or ethical duty to Maritrans that would prohibit these representations.

To prevent Pepper and Messina from taking on the representation of any other competitors, especially its largest competitor, Bouchard Transportation Company, Maritrans agreed to an arrangement proposed by Pepper whereby Pepper would continue as Maritrans' counsel but would not represent any more than the four New York companies it was then already representing. In addition, Messina—the Pepper attorney with the most knowledge about Maritrans—was to act not as counsel for Maritrans but, rather, as counsel for the New York companies, while two other Pepper labor attorneys would act as counsel for Maritrans; the attorneys on one side of this "Chinese Wall" would not discuss their respective representation with the attorneys on the other side. Maritrans represented that it agreed to this arrangement because it believed that this was the only way to keep Pepper and Messina from representing yet more of its competitors, especially Bouchard.

Unbeknownst to Maritrans, however, Messina then "parked" Bouchard and another of the competitors, Eklof, with Mr. Vincent Pentima, a labor attorney then at another law firm, at the same time that Messina was negotiating with Pentima for Pentima's admission into the partnership at Pepper. Moreover, notwithstanding Pepper's specific agreement not to represent these other companies, Messina for all intents and purposes was representing Bouchard and Eklof, as he was conducting joint negotiating sessions for those companies and his other four New York clients. On November 5, 1987, Maritrans executives discussed with Pepper attorneys, inter alia, Maritrans' plans and strategies of an aggressive nature in the event of a strike against the New York companies. Less than one month later, on December 2, 1987, Pepper terminated its representation of Maritrans in all matters. Later that month, on December 23, 1987, Pepper undertook the representation of the New York companies. Then, on January 4, 1988, Mr. Pentima joined Pepper as a partner and brought with him, as clients, Bouchard and Eklof. In February, 1988, Maritrans filed a complaint in the trial court against Pepper and Messina.

Discovery procedures produced evidence as follows: (i) testimony by principals of the New York companies to the effect that the type of information that Pepper and Messina possess about Maritrans is of the type considered to be confidential commercial information in the industry and that they would not reveal that information about their companies to their competitors; (ii) testimony by principals of the New York companies that they were desirous of obtaining Maritrans' confidential commercial information; (iii) testimony by principals of the New York companies that labor costs are the one item that make or break a company's competitive posture; (iv) an affidavit from the United States Department of Labor attesting that, contrary to defendant Messina's sworn testimony at the first preliminary hearing in February, 1988, Maritrans' labor contracts are not on file with the Department of Labor and thus not available under the Freedom of Information Act; and other information as well. . . .

[C]ourts of this Commonwealth and throughout the United States which have imposed civil liability on attorneys for breaches of their fiduciary duties by engaging in conflicts of interest, notwithstanding the existence of professional rules under which the attorneys also could be disciplined.

I. Actionability and Independent Fiduciary Duty at Common Law of Avoiding Conflicts of Interest—Injunctive Relief . . .

Activity is actionable if it constitutes breach of a duty imposed by statute or by common law. Our common law imposes on attorneys the status of fiduciaries vis à vis their clients; that is, attorneys are bound, at law, to perform their fiduciary duties properly. Failure to so perform gives rise to a cause of action. It is "actionable." Threatened failure to so perform gives rise to a request for injunctive relief to prevent the breach of duty.

At common law, an attorney owes a fiduciary duty to his client; such duty demands undivided loyalty and prohibits the attorney from engaging in conflicts of interest, and breach of such duty is actionable. As stated by the United States Supreme Court in 1850:

> There are few of the business relations of life involving a higher trust and confidence than those of attorney and client or, generally speaking, one more honorably and faithfully discharged; few more anxiously guarded by the law, or governed by sterner principles of morality and justice; and it is the duty of the court to administer them in a corresponding spirit, and to be watchful and industrious, to see that confidence thus reposed shall not be used to the detriment or prejudice of the rights of the party bestowing it. Stockton v. Ford, 52 U.S. at 247. . . .

Adherence to those fiduciary duties ensures that clients will feel secure that everything they discuss with counsel will be kept in confidence. . . .

III. Scope of Duties at Common Law

. . . Attorneys have always been held civilly liable for engaging in conduct violative of their fiduciary duties to clients, despite the existence of professional rules under which the attorneys could also have been disciplined.

Courts throughout the country have ordered the disgorgement of fees paid or the forfeiture of fees owed to attorneys who have breached their fiduciary duties to their clients by engaging in impermissible conflicts of interests. . . .

Courts have also allowed civil actions for damages for an attorney's breach of his fiduciary duties by engaging in conflicts of interest.

Courts throughout the United States have not hesitated to impose civil sanctions upon attorneys who breach their fiduciary duties to their clients, which sanctions have been imposed separately and apart from professional discipline. . . .

IV. Equity

Injunctive relief will lie where there is no adequate remedy at law. The purpose of a preliminary injunction is to preserve the status quo as it exists or previously existed before the acts complained of, thereby preventing irreparable injury or gross injustice. A preliminary injunction should issue only where there is urgent necessity to avoid injury which cannot be compensated for by damages. . . .

Pepper and Messina argue that a preliminary injunction was an abuse of discretion where it restrains them from representing a former client's competitors, in order to supply the former client with a "sense of security" that they will not reveal confidences to those competitors where there has been no revelation or threat of revelations up to that point. We disagree. Whether a fiduciary can later represent competitors or whether a law firm can later represent competitors of its former client is a matter that must be decided from case to case and depends on a number of factors. One factor is the extent to which the fiduciary was involved in its former client's affairs. The greater the involvement, the greater the danger that confidences (where such exist) will be revealed. Here, Pepper and Messina's involvement was extensive as was their knowledge of sensitive information provided to them by Maritrans. We do not wish to establish a blanket rule that a law firm may not later represent the economic competitor of a former client in matters in which the former client is not also a party to a law suit. But situations may well exist where the danger of revelation of the confidences of a former client is so great that injunctive relief is warranted. This is one of those situations. . . . It might be theoretically possible to argue that Pepper and Messina should merely be enjoined from revealing the confidential material they have acquired from Maritrans but such an injunction would be difficult, if not impossible, to administer. . . . As fiduciaries, Pepper and Messina can be fully enjoined from representing Maritrans' competitors as that would create too great a danger that Maritrans' confidential relationship with Pepper and Messina would be breached.

Here, the trial court did not commit an abuse of discretion. On these facts, it was perfectly reasonable to conclude that Maritrans' competitive position could be irreparably injured if Pepper and Messina continued to represent their competitors and that Maritrans' remedy at law, that is their right to later seek damages, would be difficult if not impossible to sustain because of difficult problems of proof, particularly problems related to piercing what would later become a confidential relationship between their competitors and those competitors' attorneys (Pepper and Messina). . . . In short, equitable principles establish that injunctive relief here was just and proper. Damages might later be obtained for breach of fiduciary duties and a confidential relationship, but that remedy would be inadequate to correct the harm that could be prevented by injunctive relief, at least until the court could examine the case in greater detail. . . .

The Law Governing Lawyers:
Losing a Client by Disqualification or Injunction

Maritrans identifies multiple remedies that the law of agency has made available to clients whose lawyers breach fiduciary duties of loyalty or confidentiality. When conflicts of interest have caused harm, clients can bring a malpractice or breach of fiduciary duty claim,[1] and seek fee forfeiture as well.[2] They also can seek professional discipline when a violation of the relevant Rule of Professional Conduct occurs.[3] In egregious cases, lawyers have been held criminally accountable as well.[4]

When serious harm is threatened but has not yet occurred, *Maritrans* teaches us that clients or former clients can seek injunctive relief to prevent the representation of other clients in transactional representations outside of court. It also makes clear that the breach of a fiduciary duty by one lawyer vicariously disqualifies the entire law firm based on the principle of imputation. Clients, former clients, and other judicial participants can seek similar relief through a disqualification motion if a matter is pending before a court.[5] In the past half-century, courts have examined most conflicts of interest in this context.

Injunctive Relief

With respect to the equitable remedy of injunctive relief, the *Maritrans* court first makes clear that breaches of statute or common law qualify as actionable activity. Because lawyers are fiduciaries, and fiduciaries owe duties of loyalty and confidentiality, it follows that agency remedies for breach of fiduciary duty should be available. Injunctive relief is such a remedy, but should only be granted when "there is an urgent necessity to avoid injury" and no adequate legal remedy exists. The facts in *Maritrans* presented just such a case. Maritrans should not have been forced to wait until it lost all or part of its business to competitors before claiming a remedy.[6]

Disqualification

Like injunctive relief, disqualification prevents a lawyer or former lawyer (and that lawyer's current law firm) from representing another client. When granted, disqualification can prevent harm to clients or former clients by ensuring that the case will be presented without conflicting loyalties or improper use of confidential information.[7] For example, if Pepper Hamilton had attempted to represent one of Maritrans' competitors against Maritrans in litigation, Maritrans

---

1. Recall dePape v. Trinity Health Systems, Inc., *supra* p. 100, and Perez v. Kirk & Carrigan, *supra* p. 167.

2. *See* The Law Governing Lawyers: *Loss of Fee or Other Benefits*, *infra* p. 364.

3. *See, e.g.,* St. ex rel. Neb. St. Bar Assn. v. Frank, 631 N.W.2d 485 (Neb. 2001) (lawyer who simultaneously represented an insurance company in litigation and another client in a claim against the insurance company publicly reprimanded).

4. *See, e.g.,* United States v. Bronson, 658 F.2d 920 (2d Cir. 1981) (mail fraud conviction based on lawyer's conflict of interest).

5. *See, e.g.,* Richard E. Flamm, *Lawyer Disqualification: Conflicts of Interest and Other Bases* (Banks Jordan 2003); Franklin v. Callum, 782 A.2d 884 (N.H. 2001) (both parties granted disqualification of the other side's lawyer on different legal theories).

6. Of course, if damages had already been caused by the firm's conflict of interest, then Maritrans could seek a remedy at law for the past harm in addition to an equitable remedy to prevent future damage.

7. RLGL § 6, Comment i.

could have asked the court to disqualify its former law firm as a means to prevent the firm's use of its confidential information against it in subsequent litigation. We first encountered this remedy in *Merits Incentives* in Chapter 6 and again in *Meyerhofer* in Chapter 8, and we will see repeated consideration of disqualification as a remedy in the conflict of interest cases in this book.[8]

Disqualification motions originated well over a century ago as requests for court orders,[9] addressed to the inherent power of judges designed to regulate the course of proceedings. Such motions usually are addressed to trial courts but can be raised in any court where a conflict occurs.[10] The motion to disqualify may be made by the lawyer's present or former client, but any other party to the litigation also has standing to raise the issue.[11] Trial judges also are empowered to raise such an issue *sua sponte*.[12] Although a few courts initially thought they had no such power, litigation over the past 50 years has left no doubt that courts can, and should, disqualify lawyers when their conduct threatens the fairness of a judicial proceeding.[13]

Although disqualification provides relief from real or serious threats of breaches of loyalty or confidentiality, it also imposes costs on other parties to a proceeding. When a lawyer is disqualified, the time schedule might need to be adjusted to allow the client who has lost a lawyer time to retain new counsel. When the motion to disqualify comes from opposing counsel or the court, clients can be deprived of their chosen lawyers without their consent. For these reasons, courts recognize that motions to disqualify can be used to tactical advantage by

---

8. *E.g.,* Murray v. Village of Hazel Crest, *infra* p. 314, Sanford v. Commonwealth of Va., *infra* p. 316, Eastman Kodak Co. v. Sony Corp., *infra* p. 335, Cascades Branding Innovation, *infra* p. 398, Martin v. Atlanticare, *infra* p. 409, Neumann v. Tuccio, *infra* p. 558.

9. The first case was Gauden v. Georgia, 11 Ga. 47 (1852). *See* Kenneth L. Penegar, *The Loss of Innocence: A Brief History of Law Firm Disqualification in the Courts,* 8 Geo. J. Legal Ethics 831, 832 (1995).

10. *See, e.g.,* Williams v. State, 805 A.2d 880 (Del. 2002) (appellate counsel disqualified for positional conflict of interest). Appellate courts review disqualification decisions of trial courts using an abuse of discretion standard. *See, e.g.,* People ex rel. Dept. of Corps v. Speedee Oil Change Sys., Inc. 980 P.2d 371, 378 (Cal. 1999).

11. Ronald E. Mallen & Jeffrey Smith, *Legal Malpractice* § 17.15 (2010 ed.). *See also* Foley-Ciccantelli v. Bishop's Grove Condominium Ass'n Inc., 797 N.W. 2d 789 (Wis. 2011) (nonparty has standing to seek disqualification when a prior representation is so connected with current litigation so as to be "likely to affect the just and lawful determination of the non-client party's position").

12. This might be especially likely to occur in criminal cases, where judges assume special responsibility for the fairness of the proceeding. *E.g.,* Fed. R. Crim. P. 44(c) (federal district courts required to inquire into any proposed joint representation); Cuyler v. Sullivan, 446 U.S. 335 (1980) (trial judge has important role in assuring fairness of trial of joint defendants).

13. *E.g.,* Ennis v. Ennis, 276 N.W.2d 341, 348 (Wis. App. 1979). Administrative law judges also exercise this power in appropriate circumstances. *See, e.g.,* Prof. Reactor Operator Socy. v. United States NRC, 939 F.2d 1047 (D.C. Cir. 1991) (Administrative Procedure Act's right to counsel guarantee requires concrete evidence that counsel's presence would impede its investigation to exclude a lawyer from representing a subpoenaed witness); SEC v. Csapo, 533 F.2d 7 (D.C. Cir. 1976) (same standard required for similar SEC rule granting agency authority to disqualify lawyers); In re Scioto Broadcaster, 5 FCC Rcd. 5158 (1990) (FCC review board and Commission will intervene only in cases of clear conflicts of interest).

opposing parties in litigation. Courts have responded to this potential for misuse of the court's power in three ways.

First, courts are careful to scrutinize the facts and law offered in support of disqualification motions. Second, courts increasingly use the doctrines of laches, estoppel, or waiver to deny motions to disqualify when they have not been made on a timely basis.[14] Third, orders granting or denying disqualification usually are not appealable until a final judgment on the merits.[15] This means that where disqualification is denied, the targeted lawyer may continue the representation, but the other side can raise the issue on appeal. On the other hand, if the motion is granted, the client represented by the now-disqualified lawyer is forced to find new counsel.[16] If that client settles or wins the case, the disqualified lawyer has no independent right to appeal. Only if the client loses the case can the issue be raised on appeal.[17]

The Relevance of the Rules of Professional Conduct

In assessing whether a lawyer should be disqualified, courts typically begin with the conflict of interest rules in the applicable rules of professional conduct or common law.[18] If a rule of professional conduct has been violated, disqualification commonly follows, because, as *Maritrans* teaches, the applicable professional rules derive from the lawyer's common law duties. A few courts impose an additional requirement, explicitly limiting disqualification to fiduciary breaches that would "taint" the trial.[19] Perhaps because it has faced the greatest number of disqualification motions, the Second Circuit adopts this "restrained approach" to disqualification motions, both to promote judicial economy and because it prefers "disciplinary machinery" for "less serious allegations of ethical impropriety."[20]

When the Rule of Professional Conduct has been violated, the lawyer should have recognized the conflict and responded by withdrawing from the representation

---

14. *See, e.g.*, Universal City Studios, Inc. v. Reimerdes, 98 F. Supp. 2d 449 (S.D.N.Y. 2000).

15. In the federal courts, an order granting or denying disqualification cannot be appealed until a final judgment on the merits has been reached. Richardson-Merrell Inc. v. Koller, 472 U.S. 424 (1985); Flanagan v. United States, 465 U.S. 259 (1984); Firestone Tire & Rubber v. Risjord, 449 U.S. 368 (1981). State courts are split on this issue. *See* David B. Harrison, *Appealability of State Court's Order Granting or Denying Motion to Disqualify Attorney*, 5 A.L.R. 4th 1251 (1981).

16. Successor counsel will usually be allowed to use the disqualified lawyer's work product if it does not contain impermissible client confidential information. RLGL § 6, Comment i; In re George, 28 S.W.3d 511 (Tex. 2000) (identifying various approaches to making the determination whether the work product contains confidential information).

17. Richardson-Merrell, Inc. v. Koller, 472 U.S. 424 (1985); Firestone Tire and Rubber Co. v. Risjord, 449 U.S. 368 (1981).

18. In some situations such as bankruptcy, statutory provisions impose additional conflict of interest standards. *See, e.g.*, In re Leslie Fay Cos., 175 B.R. 525 (Bankr. S.D.N.Y. 1994).

19 Armstrong v. McAlpin, 625 F.2d 433 (2d Cir. 1980), *vacated on other grounds*, 449 U.S. 1106 (1981).

20 *See* The European Cmty. v. RJR Nabisco, Inc., 134 F. Supp. 2d 297, 303 (E.D.N.Y. 2001) (reviewing Second Circuit decisions).

that created it.[21] Granting a disqualification motion simply requires the lawyer to do what she already should have done—move to withdraw under Model Rule 1.16(a)—to avoid a violation of the relevant conflict of interest rule.[22]

A more difficult situation is presented when a potential or threatened violation of the rules appears in a case. Then, courts look to seriousness of the potential violation and the likelihood that it will affect the fairness of the matter before the court. Relief will be denied unless the possibility of an injury to a party or the fairness of the proceeding can be shown.[23]

Although disqualification motions are the most common remedy sought by clients and former clients to redress conflicts of interest, *Maritrans* illustrates that other remedies, including civil damages, fee forfeiture, dismissal of a claim or defense, and professional discipline also exist.[24] The potential for each of these remedies will be explored throughout the materials in this chapter and the next two. Each remedy has its own legal requirements, and multiple remedies might exist for the same breach of fiduciary duty. One thing is certain: lawyers today have to worry about more than malpractice suits and professional discipline. They also realize that injunctive relief or disqualification may be granted to an opposing party, involuntarily depriving them of the opportunity to represent a client, as well as exposing them to potential tort liability and loss of compensation.

B.   Joint Representations

1. Divorce and Dissolution

Problem

9-2.   Husband and Wife ask Martyn & Fox to prepare the papers for the dissolution of their marriage. May Martyn & Fox represent both spouses? Does it make any difference if the spouses have already agreed to property division, child custody, and support obligations? What if Husband and Wife, to save money and keep peace in the fractured family, ask Martyn to mediate their disputes regarding these issues?

---

21. *See, e.g.,* Schlumberger Tech., Inc. v. Wiley, 113 F.3d 1553, 1561 (11th Cir. 1997).

22. *See, e.g.,* Williams v. State, 805 A.2d 880 (Del. 2002) (trial counsel's motion to withdraw as appellate counsel granted due to a conflict created by previous Supreme Court argument).

23. *See, e.g.,* United States v. Kitchin, 592 F.2d 900, 903 (5th Cir.), *cert. denied,* 444 U.S. 843 (1979) (lawyer may be disqualified "only where there is a reasonable possibility that some specifically identifiable ethical impropriety actually occurred, and, in light of the interests underlying the standards of ethics, the social need for ethical practice outweighs the party's right to counsel of his choice"); Bd. of Educ. v. Nyquist, 590 F.2d 1241, 1246 (2d Cir. 1979) (conflict must "taint the trial"); In re Infotechnology, Inc., 582 A.2d 215, 216 (Del. 1990) (conflict must "adversely affect . . . the fair and effective administration of justice").

24. *See* RLGL § 6. In fact, Pepper Hamilton settled with Maritrans for $3 million following the Pennsylvania Supreme Court decision, an amount slightly less than its legal fees in the matter. *See* James L. Kelly, *Lawyers Crossing Lines: Nine Stories* 79 (Carolina Academic Press 2001).

If the mediation results in agreement on these matters, may Martyn draft the legal papers necessary to effectuate the dissolution?

Consider: Model Rules 1.7, 1.10, 2.4
RLGL §§ 128, 130

The Professional Ethics Committee
for the State Bar of Texas
Opinion No. 583 (2008)

Question Presented

May a lawyer enter into an arrangement to mediate a divorce settlement between parties who are not represented by legal counsel and prepare the divorce decree and other necessary documents to effectuate an agreed divorce if the mediation results in an agreement?

Statement of Facts

A lawyer is hired by the parties in a divorce case to mediate a settlement and prepare all of the documents necessary to effect an agreed divorce if an agreement results from the mediation. Under the proposed arrangement, the lawyer will conduct the mediation and, if an agreement is reached, prepare the decree of divorce and other documents, which may include conveyances of real property, various releases, child support provisions and visitation schedules. The parties to the divorce are not represented at any time by their own separate legal counsel. The lawyer/mediator advises both parties that the lawyer/mediator does not represent either party during the mediation or in the preparation of the documents to implement the agreed terms of the divorce. The parties agree that the fee of the lawyer/mediator will be paid one-half by each.

Discussion

Under the Rules of Professional Conduct, mediation does not constitute the practice of law. [MR 2.4] . . .

[A] lawyer acting as a mediator is subject to the requirements of Rule [1.12]. Since the proposed arrangement for mediation followed by document preparation is to be agreed on by the parties before the mediation begins, the proposed arrangement would be in violation of Rule [1.12(b)], which provides in pertinent part that "[a] lawyer who is an adjudicatory official shall not negotiate for employment with any person who is involved as a party or as attorney for a party in a pending matter in which that official is participating personally and substantially." Thus under Rule [1.12(b)] a lawyer/mediator may not enter into an agreement with the parties to a divorce to provide both mediation and legal services with respect to the divorce. Rule [1.12(a)], which applies to representation in a matter as to which a lawyer has previously acted as an adjudicatory official, would not be applicable to the circumstances here considered since here the mediation and document preparation services are agreed to when the mediation begins.)

Although acting as a mediator with respect to a divorce does not constitute the practice of law, the preparation of documents to implement an agreement for divorce reached in a mediation clearly involves the provision of legal services by the lawyer/mediator. If a lawyer who is also a mediator chooses to act solely as a lawyer with respect to a particular divorce, the lawyer may represent only one of the two parties in preparing documents to implement an agreement for divorce. A divorce, no matter how amicable or uncontested, is a litigation proceeding under Texas law. In the circumstances here considered, the preparation of documents for both otherwise unrepresented parties in a divorce to effect an agreed settlement would constitute representation of both parties in the divorce litigation. Because a divorce in Texas necessarily involves litigation, a lawyer in the case of a divorce could not provide legal services to both parties . . . under Rule [1.7] . . ., which provides without qualification that "[A] lawyer shall not represent opposing parties to the same litigation." Hence, even if a lawyer/mediator did not propose to provide mediation in the case of a particular divorce, the lawyer/mediator could not in any circumstances act as a lawyer representing both parties to prepare documents to effectuate an agreed divorce.

Conclusion

Under the Texas Disciplinary Rules of Professional Conduct, a lawyer may not agree to serve both as a mediator between parties in a divorce and as a lawyer to prepare the divorce decree and other necessary documents to effect an agreement resulting from the mediation. Because a divorce is a litigation proceeding, a lawyer is not permitted to represent both parties in preparing documents to effect the terms of an agreed divorce.

2. Litigation Co-Parties

Problems

9-3. Two defendants are charged with murder arising from a botched bank robbery that resulted in the killing of a customer. If defendants insist on being represented jointly, can Martyn & Fox represent both defendants? Does it matter if only the "shooter" is eligible for the death penalty? Would it be okay if Martyn represents one defendant and Fox represents the other?

9-4. Martyn & Fox is asked to represent driver-son and passenger-father in a lawsuit arising from an auto accident where the driver of the other car has pleaded guilty to speeding. Can we take this case? What happens when before his deposition, Son tells Fox, "I had two drinks before I picked up Dad"?

Consider: Model Rules 1.7, 1.8(b), 1.10
RLGL §§ 128, 129

Murray v. Village of Hazel Crest

2006 U.S. Dist. LEXIS 89388 (N.D. Ill.)

William T. HART, United States District Judge.

Before this court are four related [but] . . . separately pending cases. Each case is brought by a different plaintiff: Patrick Murray, Michael Garofalo, David Nelson, and Mark Peers. Each plaintiff was formerly employed as a sergeant in the Police Department of defendant Village of Hazel Crest. . . . Each plaintiff applied for the position of deputy chief of police and alleges that he suffered discrimination because of race when an allegedly less-qualified African-American patrol officer was promoted to that position effective July 12, 2005. There is only one deputy chief position at the police department. Each plaintiff also alleges that he was constructively discharged as a result of his treatment, Murray and Nelson on December 1, 2005, Garofalo in June 2006, and Peers in March 2006. Each plaintiff alleges in his complaint that his damages include the loss of income that he would have earned had he been promoted to Deputy Chief and each seeks injunctive relief in the form of a promotion. Each plaintiff also alleges lost wages from being forced to resign and damages for emotional injury. Each plaintiff also seeks reinstatement.

Each plaintiff is represented by attorneys Patricia Rummer and Richard Lowell. Defendant Village of Hazel Crest has moved to disqualify counsel from representing any of the plaintiffs on the ground that conflicts of interest exist among the plaintiffs because each plaintiff contends that he should have been the one promoted to deputy chief of police. Counsel contend this is not a conflict and that each client desires to be represented by them.

[The court cites its local version of Model Rule 1.7]

. . . It is a defense to plaintiffs' Title VII failure to promote damages claims, as well as their claims for promotion and reinstatement, that a particular plaintiff would not have been promoted even if there had been no discrimination. 42 U.S.C. § 2000e-5(g)(2). This can be shown by proof that an applicant other than the particular plaintiff would have been selected even if there had been no discrimination. The defense that another person would have instead been selected would also apply to any § 1983 discrimination claim that plaintiffs may ultimately be pursuing. To the extent one plaintiff proves that he was the one that would have been promoted if not for discrimination, he provides a defense against the claims of the other three defendants. Thus, the attorney gathering or presenting evidence as to the qualifications of one plaintiff (which is absolutely necessary in order to pursue that plaintiff's interests) is in direct conflict with the interests of the other three plaintiffs who each want to show he is the most qualified or otherwise most likely to have been promoted.

Plaintiffs contend none of them need show that he would have actually been promoted because each can proceed on a "lost-chance theory." . . . Since the individual probabilities for all applicants must total 100%, any successful proof that a particular applicant had a greater probability of being selected means that the probable hiring of other applicants must decrease. Thus, even under the lost-chance theory, the plaintiffs in the present cases would be in direct competition with each other regarding lost wages. Assuming liability can be proven, any successful showing of greater capability by one plaintiff has a direct negative impact on the other plaintiffs. The corollary is that showing one of the plaintiffs is less capable has a positive impact on the other plaintiffs.[2] Even though plaintiffs also claim some damages that are not based directly on lost wages from not being promoted, they are still in direct and irreconcilable conflict regarding back pay and front pay whether proceeding on a lost-chance theory or simply seeking to prove that each was the only one that would have been promoted.

In their surreply, counsel . . . imply that plaintiffs are willing to forego the possibility of greater damages in the interest of the cost-saving of sharing counsel. There is, however, no indication that plaintiffs have been fully advised of the possibilities and consented after full disclosure. There is also no indication each plaintiff has been advised of the strengths or weaknesses of his individual claim. Given their representation of all four plaintiffs, as well as their own self-interest in continuing to represent all four, counsel have an actual conflict simply trying to give such advice. Additionally, counsel's speculative result of requiring defendants to take away the promotion and hold a new competition for the position is unlikely.

Finding the existence of a direct conflict of interest does not end the matter since it is possible that the conflict is waivable. Plaintiffs' attorneys point to the affidavits they have provided and contend they have satisfied the requirements of [Rule 1.7]. Even ignoring the conclusory nature of the affidavits, they do not show that Rule [1.7] is satisfied. The affidavit from each of plaintiffs' attorneys contains the following identical paragraphs:

> 5. I have carefully examined the applicable law and the facts to determine whether any conflict exists with respect to representing all four of the plaintiffs. I have determined as a result that there is no conflict with respect to my representation of the four individuals with respect to their claims in these cases.

> 6. Each of the four plaintiffs has expressly stated that he desires to be represented by the same counsel.

Despite the assertions by counsel that they have examined the law and facts and have determined that no conflict exists, . . . [t]he fact that all of them have stated that they desire to be represented by the same counsel does not satisfy the requirement of waiver because such consent must occur "after disclosure." The affidavits are silent as to any disclosures that were made. However, before requiring that counsel make full disclosures to their clients and determine if

---

2. It is also possible that one of the four plaintiffs would stand out as the most qualified. In that circumstance, that plaintiff should have a lawyer independent of the other plaintiffs to advise him whether he should proceed on a lost-chance theory or instead go for it all by taking a traditional approach and eschewing the lost-chance theory.

they are willing to continue to consent to representation, it should first be determined whether such a waiver is possible. . . .

Here, the four plaintiffs have a common interest in showing that defendants selected the winning candidate because of his race and in showing the lack of qualifications of the candidate that was selected. There are also likely to be some economies in being represented by the same attorneys. However, plaintiffs are in direct conflict with each other regarding showing who is the most likely to have been selected for the promotion. Each plaintiff has an interest in showing that he is highly qualified as well as an interest in showing that other plaintiffs lacked qualifications. The issues in conflict will have a substantial impact on any damages that are recovered. This is a situation where a disinterested attorney would determine that each plaintiff should have his own attorney. Plaintiffs' attorneys would not be able to vigorously pursue damages on behalf of one plaintiff without coming into direct conflict with the interests of the other plaintiffs. Counsel will be disqualified from representing multiple plaintiffs in this case.

Defendants contend that present counsel should not have the option of remaining in the case by representing only one plaintiff, that they should be disqualified from representing any plaintiff in this case. Rule 1.9 applies to that issue. . . . Whether such representation would be appropriate may depend on whether plaintiffs have already revealed confidential information to the attorneys that would give unfair advantage to one of the other plaintiffs. If counsel desires to continue to represent one of the plaintiffs, counsel must carefully consider whether such representation would be appropriate and must obtain the consent of the other plaintiffs, including after each of the other plaintiffs has retained his new counsel. . . .

3. Employer and Employee

Problem

9-5. Our longtime corporate brokerage client and two of its stockbrokers have been sued for violating know-your-customer regulations. Can Martyn & Fox represent the corporation and both stockbrokers?

**Consider: Model Rules 1.7, 1.8(b), 1.10, 1.13
RLGL §§ 128,129,131**

Sanford v. Commonwealth of Virginia

687 F. Supp. 2d 591 (E.D. Va. 2009)

Robert E. Payne, Senior United States District Judge.

BACKGROUND

This action arises out of the death of John Charles Sanford on December 24, 2006. At the time of his death, Sanford was a patient in the Medical

College of Virginia Main Hospital ["MCV"] who was recovering from surgery, which had been performed on December 20, 2006, in which his kidney was removed. . . .

B. Sanford's Hospitalization and the Events Before December 24, 2006

. . . Sanford was admitted to MCV to have surgery for the removal of a kidney on December 20, 2006. At the time, Sanford was 40 years of age, five feet five inches tall, weighed 150 pounds, and was mentally and physically disabled.

. . . In April 1994, a physician at MCV determined that Sanford was suffering from Biemond's Syndrome, a neurological condition which included cerebellar damage and ataxia (a severe loss of muscular coordination). Sanford's head and body shook almost continuously and, at times, rather violently. He was able to walk only with the assistance of a "walker," and he wore leg braces which extended from knee to foot.

It is alleged that, on December 22, 2006, two days after his surgery, Sanford was found by his brother in the hall outside his room at which time he was naked, delirious, hallucinating, and clinging to a hand rail for support, trying to hold himself upright without the assistance of the walker. It is alleged that Sanford's delirium and hallucinations were the consequence of toxic levels of certain medications prescribed and administered by the MCV medical defendants. The MCV medical staff was aware of Sanford's condition and had summoned the Virginia Commonwealth University Police Department ["VCUPD"] to help in restraining him. However, before the VCUPD officers arrived, Sanford's brother, the lead plaintiff in this case, was successful in penetrating the delirium in returning Sanford to his room and getting him into his bed. It is alleged that, on December 23, 2006, other family members found Sanford delirious and hallucinating and concluded that he was not being attended by any physician or nurse because he was on the floor in his hospital room partially disrobed and cleaning up imaginary blood.

As a consequence of the events of December 22 and 23, the lead plaintiff requested a psychiatric consult and liaison service, asserting that the justification therefore was that Sanford was not acting as he usually acted and that he was not being cared for in the manner consistent with his disability and his postoperative condition.

C. December 24, 2006: Sanford's Death and the Plaintiffs' Claims

On December 24, 2006, it is alleged that Sanford became delirious as a consequence of the medications he had been prescribed and administered by the MCV medical defendants. The nursing defendants (except Chief Nursing Officer ["CNO"] Crosby) summoned the VCUPD officers (except for Colonel Fuller), and the security guard, Lancaster, to the scene. Lancaster and Officer Bailey of the VCUPD responded and allegedly physically seized Sanford, wrestled him to the ground, put his hands behind his back, handcuffed him with metal handcuffs and held him prone. He was kept in that position by Bailey, aided by Lancaster and the other VCUPD officer defendants, for approximately thirty minutes. During that time, one or more of the nursing defendants injected him with Haldol, a sedative. After he had been laying handcuffed and prone for approximately thirty minutes, the VCUPD officers and the nursing staff turned Sanford over and discovered that he was dead. . . .

The same lawyer represents all of the VCUPD officer defendants and Colonel Fuller [the VCUPD officer and supervisor] (the "VCUPD defendants"). Another lawyer represents security guard Lancaster and all of the other MCV employees who are either doctors or nurses (the "MCV defendants"). Thus, each lawyer representing each set of defendants has multiple clients.

DISCUSSION

. . . In this case, the possibility of the conflict was identified at two pretrial conferences . . . . Counsel for both sets of defendants represent that thereafter, each of the lawyers met with their respective clients and, pursuant to Rule 1.7(b), secured the consent of each client to the joint representation. Each lawyer has expressed the view that he will "be able to provide competent and diligent representation to each affected client." . . .

In support of the disqualification motion, the Plaintiffs have identified three types of conflict that must be examined respecting disqualification of counsel for the VCUPD defendants. The Plaintiffs have identified five kinds of conflicts which need to be examined to determine whether disqualification is necessary for the MCV defendants. Each will be considered in turn.

A. VCUPD Officer Defendants

First, there is, according to the Plaintiffs, the conflict between Colonel Fuller and all of the subordinate VCU police officers respecting the adequacy of training for dealing with hospital patients. Colonel Fuller has admitted that VCUPD officers receive no special training about how to deal with restraining hospital patients, [but] that his officers are adequately trained to deal with hospital patients because their general training about how to deal with handcuffed persons includes instruction to check for signs of physical distress and for difficulty in breathing.

. . . Officer Carter's testimony clearly conflicted with Colonel Fuller's testimony on that point. Officer LaVigne's does not. However, LaVigne's testimony would permit an argument that he engaged in no misconduct, and that the lack of training respecting how to deal with hospital patients, not his conduct, was the cause of Sanford's death. Officer Pryor testified that he did not monitor Sanford during the period when he was handcuffed and that places his testimony also at odds with the position of Colonel Fuller respecting the adequacy of training.

Thus, on this topic, the adequacy of training, there appears to be a substantial discrepancy in the testimony of the VCUPD officer defendants and an incompatibility in positions that the VCUPD officer defendants occupy vis-a-vis Colonel Fuller. The possibilities for settlement also appear to be substantially different on the claims and liabilities in question as to Colonel Fuller, on one hand, and the VCUPD officer defendants, on the other.

It is also asserted by the Plaintiffs that there is conflict between the VCUPD officer defendants who initially responded to the summons to Sanford's room and effectuated the seizure by handcuffing Sanford and keeping him facedown on the floor, and those officers who arrived on the scene later. This conflict arises out of the undisputed evidence that the accepted protocol for the VCUPD in situations such as the one here at issue is that the first responding officer provides the lead and that subsequently responding officers follow the instructions of the lead officer. Officer Bailey was the lead responder and the other defendants, Officers Pryor, LaVigne, and Carter, followed his lead, as specified by the departmental protocol. . . . Thus, the objective evidence is that Officer Bailey took the action which resulted in handcuffing Sanford and in maintaining him in a prone position and that Officers Pryor and Carter acted pursuant to his explicit direction in doing what they did and that Officer LaVigne followed Officer Bailey's lead in accord with the departmental protocol.

These largely undisputed facts present a somewhat clearer incompatibility in the positions occupied by Officer Bailey, on the one hand, and Officers Pryor, Carter and LaVigne, on the other. The latter would be able to assert that their conduct was governed by protocol, which had been set in place when they arrived upon the scene and by the instructions of Officer Bailey. Thus, they could argue that the reasonableness of their conduct, which lies at the heart of their ability to defend a number of the claims against them, must be assessed differently than the conduct of Officer Bailey who was the one who first laid hands on Sanford and who also dictated that Sanford be kept in handcuffs and be kept facedown in the prone position. . . .

Lastly, the Plaintiffs point to a conflict created by an order that was issued by Corporal Branch, the superior of all of the other VCU police officers (excepting Colonel Fuller). Corporal Branch arrived after the other officers had arrived and acted. It was undisputed that Sanford was calm by the time that Corporal Branch arrived upon the scene. It was further undisputed that Corporal Branch gave an order to Officer Bailey and the other officers to keep Sanford in the restraints until stronger restraints arrived from the psychiatric ward (such restraints having been sent for by the nursing staff at the direction of the VCU police officer defendants). Corporal Branch has said that he intended his order to mean that Officer Bailey and the others should keep Sanford handcuffed and prone until the stronger restraints arrived. After issuing that order, Corporal Branch left the scene. It also appears that Sanford died during this phase of the restraint. . . .

A lawyer representing the officers other than Corporal Branch might reasonably be expected to argue to the jury that the conduct of those officers was quite reasonable in view of Corporal Branch's instruction. Of course, the mere fact that they were following Corporal Branch's instructions would not present a legal defense, but it would present a significant basis for differentiating the reasonableness of the conduct of Corporal Branch on the one hand and the other officers on the other. . . .

Moreover, the situation confronting Officers LaVigne, Pryor, and Carter must be measured in perspective of Officer Bailey's conduct (handcuffing Sanford and keeping him prone) and Corporal Branch's order (to keep him that way). Thus, it is rather clear that to defend the reasonableness of their conduct, as well as the rightness of their conduct, Officers LaVigne, Carter, and Prior would want to point to the conduct of Officer Bailey and Corporal Branch as the cause of Sanford's death, rather than the action they took in doing what they were told to do by the departmental protocol, by Officer Bailey and Corporal Branch.

B. VCU Medical Defendants

The motion asserts several conflicts among the VCU medical defendants. First, Dr. Meguid diagnosed Sanford's condition as opium withdrawal rather than delirium. . . . Several defense experts (a pharmacist, a toxicologist, and a psychiatrist) have expressed the opinion that Sanford's symptoms were consistent with delirium, not with opium withdrawal. . . .

In other words, the expert opinions of the defense experts will support the conclusion that Dr. Meguid misdiagnosed Sanford. There is a medical malpractice claim against Dr. Meguid and an attorney representing Dr. Meguid would certainly want to present expert testimony that Dr. Meguid's diagnosis was correct. However, there appears to be no such evidence offered on his behalf and, indeed, the defense experts render opinions which make it quite difficult for Dr. Meguid to assert that his diagnosis was a correct one. On this record, there is a significant incompatibility in position between Dr. Meguid and the other medical professionals on this issue. . . .

Second, it is undisputed that Dr. Meguid made a medical note that Haldol should be avoided for Sanford, if possible. Further, Dr. Meguid recognized that Haldol might not be appropriate for a patient with Biemond's Syndrome and that the drug could have adverse cardiac side effects. Dr. Maiberger, however, prescribed Haldol and Nurse Brown or Nurse Ferguson administered Haldol. Neither of the three were aware of Dr. Meguid's cautions respecting the use of Haldol for Sanford. At oral argument on the disqualification motion, counsel for the medical defendants asserted that it was the position of Dr. Maiberger and Nurse Brown that they had no reason to be aware of Dr. Meguid's caution because Dr. Meguid had not entered his note in the computerized system which, in turn, would have alerted the nurses to Dr. Meguid's cautionary advice. That failure is a further indictment of Dr. Meguid.

Quite clearly there are conflicting positions presented by the testimony. Dr. Meguid certainly is entitled to present, as part of his defense, that he cautioned against the use of Haldol. At the same time, Dr. Maiberger and the nurses intend to say that they had no reason to know of this caution because Dr. Meguid did not act in accord with established procedure at the Hospital to take the necessary actions to alert them to his caution. Counsel for Dr. Maiberger and the nurses, therefore, would certainly want to point the finger of fault toward Dr. Meguid as part of the means of defending Dr. Maiberger and the nurses.

Neither Dr. Maiberger nor the nurses have asserted the position (Dr. Meguid's failure to enter the note in the computer) that quite logically might assist in exonerating them from liability, if supported by the evidence and if accepted by the jury. . . .

Third, it is alleged that there exists a conflict between CNO Crosby and Nurse Brown on the issue of training. CNO Crosby asserts that Nurse Brown was properly trained in every respect and, in particular, in the restraint policy that CNO Crosby says that she established. It is beyond dispute that Nurse Brown violated the restraint policy as it is understood by CNO Crosby. Thus, as the Plaintiffs contend, if CNO Crosby properly trained Nurse Brown to follow the policy, then Nurse Brown ignored that training and that fact would certainly be pertinent in making out a defense for Chief Nurse Crosby. On the other hand, if Nurse Brown complied with her training, then a reasonable juror could conclude, and counsel representing Nurse Brown would want to argue, that she was not properly trained and that her actions were reasonable ones. . . .

Fourth, it is alleged that there is a likely conflict between Dr. Grob, the urologist who performed the surgery and under whose care Sanford was at the time of the incident, and Dr. Koo, an attending physician. Dr. Grob was on vacation at the time of Sanford's death, and had delegated the task of post-operatively caring for Sanford to Dr. Koo. Dr. Koo is a newly added defendant, and he has not been deposed so it is uncertain what his position will be. The claims against Dr. Grob include failing to recognize signs of Sanford's delirium, failing to supervise residents, failing properly to communicate with consultant physicians and failing properly to communicate with the attending physician who was covering for Dr. Grob. That physician is Dr. Koo.

Dr. Grob has fastened his defense on the fact that he was on a holiday vacation, and that he had turned all of the responsibility for Sanford's care to Dr. Koo as a covering attendant physician. Thus, it appears rather likely that there is a conflict between Dr. Grob and Dr. Koo. . . .

Finally, it is alleged that Dr. Maiberger was not properly advised of the facts by Nurse Brown at the time that he had prescribed the administration of Haldol for Sanford. Dr. Maiberger prescribed the use of Haldol without seeing Sanford and did so on the basis of a description given by Nurse Brown over the telephone to the effect that Sanford's conduct was such that it took six officers to hold Sanford down. The record simply does not support the version of facts communicated by Nurse Brown to Dr. Maiberger. Indeed, there is evidence that only two people were involved in handcuffing Sanford; that the task was accomplished relatively quickly; and that Sanford was in fact calm well before Haldol was administered. It seems rather clear that the defense of Dr. Maiberger requires a showing that his conduct was reasonable in perspective of the information that he was given by Nurse Brown. And, of course, if that information was wrong, then Dr. Maiberger would have a defense, the existence of which would require the lawyer defending Dr. Maiberger to point at Nurse Brown's inadequate information as a means of exonerating Dr. Maiberger. That evidence would point necessarily, in an inculpatory fashion, to Nurse Brown. . . .

C. The Legal Principles

. . . The [comments] to Rule 1.7 make clear that "[l]oyalty and independent judgment are essential elements in the lawyer's relationship to a client." This assessment ought to be undertaken at the beginning of the representation of multiple clients in the same action, but the rules make clear that if the conflict arises after the representation has been undertaken, it is the obligation of the lawyer to withdraw from the representation.

"Loyalty to a client is also impaired when a lawyer cannot consider, recommend or carry out an appropriate course of action for the client because of the lawyer's other responsibilities or interests. The conflict in effect forecloses alternatives that otherwise would be available to the client." Rule 1.7 [Comment] [8]. It is also important to note that [in situations where] "simultaneous representation of parties whose interests in litigation may conflict, such as coplaintiffs or codefendants, . . . [a] . . . conflict may exist by reason of substantial discrepancy in the parties' testimony, incompatibility in positions in relation to an opposing party or the fact that there are substantially different possibilities of settlement of the claims or liabilities in question." Rule 1.7 [Comment] [23]. . . .

The applicable rule requires disqualification when the independent professional judgment of the lawyer is likely to be affected. Accordingly, some stronger indicator than judicial intuition or surmise on the part of opposing counsel is necessary to warrant the "drastic step of disqualification of counsel."

As explained above, the conflicts that are presented here are real conflicts. They exist now and they have existed throughout the course of the case. They have significant impact on the conduct of the trial respecting how best to serve the interests of the individual defendants who are affected by the extant conflicts.

Furthermore, the conflicts here raise the serious prospect that the trial could fall into disarray. This prospect has actually manifested itself in the motions for summary judgment presented by the defendants and in the presentation of expert testimony, including several contentions of law and opinion favoring the interest of one defendant while presenting the prospect of real harm to others.

It is obvious from reviewing the motions for summary judgment and the expert opinions that counsel, both for the VCUPD officers and the VCU medical defendants, have staked out defensive positions that they think are the best positions for the defense side of the case considered as a whole. It does not appear, however, that counsel have considered, or that they appreciate, how the assertion of those positions could affect the ability of each individual defendant to defend herself or himself by presenting arguments that other defendants are really responsible for Sanford's tragic death even though another defendant may have had some involvement in the circumstances leading up to that death. Nor do the summary judgment papers indicate that these potential individual defenses have been developed or pursued. . . .

The conflicts also present very real risks of serious, adverse consequences for the rights of the litigants, mostly the defendants, but also those of the plaintiffs. . . .

Each defendant is entitled to use the record to exonerate himself or herself even if to do so inculpates another defendant in the same category of defendants (*i.e.*, the same group of clients).

The pleadings, motions and briefs filed thus far afford no indication that such a course in being pursued on behalf of any defendant who, from the record evidence, could take it. . . . Of course, a lawyer who represents all defendants is not free to pursue such a course on behalf of any defendant because to do so would be to act adversely to one or more of his other clients. On the other hand, the failure to pursue such a course compromises the interest of any defendant on whose behalf that approach could be taken at trial. . . .

Counsel for each group of defendants asserts that disqualification is not required because all of the defendants have consented to multiple representations. It is true that Rule 1.7(b) provides that the written consent of the client may allow counsel to represent clients who otherwise would not be representable under Rule 1.7(a)(2). However, [Rule 1.7(b) requires] four conditions to a representation under the consent process. . . . [Here], the Court cannot conclude that any lawyer reasonably could believe, as the first condition requires, that he would be able to provide competent and diligent representation to each of the affected clients identified in the foregoing discussion of conflicts. . . .

The record shows that each of the VCUPD defendants, including the legal guardian for the now incompetent Colonel Fuller, signed documents stating the following:

> I, [Defendant's name], hereby declare that, notwithstanding the existence of any possible conflicts of interest, I knowingly and voluntarily consent to the continued representation by [counsel for the VCUPD Defendants] in this matter. This informed consent is made after consultation with my attorney.

Although counsel for these defendants asserts that the consent was provided knowingly and voluntarily, there is no basis in the record to conclude that the affected defendants had the very real conflicts described to them thoroughly and accurately. And, such a showing is essential especially where, as here, the conflicts are so patent and so numerous and have such potentially adverse consequences for many of the defendant clients. The absence of that showing alone renders the record on consent here insufficient to animate the exception permitted by Rule 1.7(b). . . .

Setting aside the importance of obtaining properly executed written consent, to focus on the particularities of the conflict waivers is to miss the key point. . . . In this case, neither of these counsel were in position to request a waiver because, for the reasons set forth fully above, neither reasonably could have believed that, under the circumstances of this case, they could represent all of the defendants whom they undertook to represent.

CONCLUSION

For the foregoing reasons, the PLAINTIFFS' MOTION TO DISQUALIFY DEFENSE COUNSEL ON THE BASIS OF A CONFLICT OF INTEREST is granted. . . . Considering the complex issues presented in this record and the rather significant nature of the conflict, it appears that this case ought to be one in which counsel, having been disqualified, should not further remain in the case. However, it is appropriate to leave that prospect open and to allow for discussion and further assessment of that issue after each defendant is separately advised by counsel not laboring under conflicts.

4.   Real Estate Transactions

Problem

9-6.   Buyer and Seller of real estate come to Martyn & Fox to handle the deal. They have agreed on the price, date of closing, and identity of the property to be conveyed. Can Martyn & Fox undertake the engagement?

Consider: Model Rules 1.7, 1.8(b), 1.10
RLGL § 130

Anderson v. O'Brien

2005 Conn. Super. Lexis 3365

CARMEN L. LOPEZ, Judge.

I. FACTS:

. . . According to the allegations of the revised complaint, the plaintiff is an elderly, childless widow that was living alone in her home located in a desirable neighborhood of Guilford. Sometime in the year 2002, the O'Brien defendants (who are husband and wife) befriended her with the purpose of convincing her to sell them her home. The plaintiff had no desire to sell her home, as she had previously turned down offers to purchase her home by developers interested in developing a subdivision located to the west of the plaintiff's home. Her lack of desire to sell is evidenced by the fact that she never listed the property for sale.

The O'Briens continued in their efforts to buy the plaintiff's home and eventually included in their offer to purchase, an offer to build a cottage for the plaintiff on the property where she could live out her life and be treated as part of the family. The O'Briens agreed to assume all responsibility for the construction of the cottage. The O'Briens also arranged for their lawyer, the defendant Peter I. Manko, to represent the plaintiff in the real estate transaction.

On May 28, 2003, the plaintiff signed a real estate contract in which she agreed to sell the property to the O'Brien defendants. The contract called for a closing date of August 1, 2003. The contract was drafted by the defendant Manko. . . . On July 3, 2003, the O'Briens came to the plaintiff's home and told her they were picking her up to take her to the closing, which was scheduled for

5:00 that afternoon in Manko's office. The plaintiff was ill on that day and was not expecting to attend a closing.

When she arrived at Manko's office she inquired of both Manko and the O'Briens as to whether she should have her own attorney and she was reassured that Manko was a good lawyer and that he would take care of all of the parties, including the lender. According to the plaintiff, she did not read any of the closing documents that were placed before her, nor were they read to her. Notwithstanding her concerns, she signed the documents. Although the contract contained a clause making reference to the plaintiff's right to remain on the property residing in the cottage, none of the closing documents referred to the plaintiff's life estate in the property.

The plaintiff further alleges that after the closing, the O'Briens changed their treatment of her. They were rude and cruel and kept all details of the construction of her cottage from her. She was constantly reminded that the property did not belong to her anymore but rather to the O'Briens. Although a structure was built for her, it was not a cottage, but rather a small barn like structure that could not accommodate her furnishings.

The plaintiff's revised complaint contains eleven counts. Counts one through six are against the O'Brien defendants and allege fraudulent representation, breach of contract and intentional or negligent infliction of emotional distress.

Counts seven through eleven are against the defendant Peter I. Manko. Count seven alleges legal malpractice, count eight alleges recklessness, count nine alleges fraudulent representation, count ten alleges that Manko violated [the Connecticut Unfair Trade Practices Act] (CUTPA) and count eleven alleges a breach of fiduciary duty by Manko. . . .

IV. DISCUSSION

A.   The Eighth Count: Recklessness

In the eighth count of the complaint, entitled "Recklessness by the defendant Manko," the plaintiff restates the allegations contained in the seventh count, which is entitled "Legal Malpractice by defendant Manko." According to the allegations of the seventh and eighth counts, the defendant Manko prepared a contract for the sale of the plaintiff's property to the O'Brien defendants. He prepared the contract on behalf of both the plaintiff and the O'Brien defendants. According to the allegations in the complaint, the representation of the plaintiff in this transaction created an attorney-client relationship between Manko and the plaintiff. As a result, Manko owed the plaintiff the duty to represent her with reasonable care and diligence.

The plaintiff also alleges, in this count, that Manko knew, or should have known, that the plaintiff, who was ill on the day of the closing, inquired about whether she should have separate counsel and was reassured that Manko could represent all of the parties. The closing of the sale of the plaintiff's property took place in Manko's office at about 5:00 in the afternoon, at least one month before the date specified in the contract. As a result, the plaintiff alleges that she was rushed into the closing.

Furthermore, the plaintiff alleges that Manko failed to inform the lender of her life estate thereby allowing the lender to have an interest in the property superior to hers. In addition, he did not prepare a deed subject to the plaintiff's life estate. As a result, the plaintiff's life estate was not recorded on the land records.

The plaintiff alleges that these facts state a claim for recklessness. Manko objects[,] stating that the facts as alleged merely support a claim for malpractice.

> "While [courts] have attempted to draw definitional [distinctions] between the terms wilful, wanton or reckless, in practice the three terms have been treated as meaning the same thing . . . . A wilful act is one done intentionally or with reckless disregard of the consequences of one's conduct."

After examining the alleged facts, and construing these facts in a light most favorable to the plaintiff, the court concludes that the plaintiff has pled a cause of action sounding in recklessness. The facts demonstrate that not only did Manko fail to exercise due care in the preparation of the legal documents on behalf of the plaintiff, but he also disregarded the consequences of his actions, as well as the rights of the plaintiff.

The allegations of the complaint go beyond asserting that an attorney's conduct fell below that of a reasonable attorney under the same circumstances. Here, the plaintiff, an elderly widow, was picked up at her home on the day of the closing by the buyers, who are clients of Manko. She did not know that the closing was to take place on that particular day since it was one month before the closing date that was designated in the contract. She was ill and it was late in the afternoon on the day of the closing. She questioned the appropriateness of proceeding with only one lawyer. The documents were not read to her before she signed them.

If these facts are proven at trial, they will establish something more than a failure to use the degree of care and skill which the ordinarily prudent attorney would use under similar circumstances. It will establish that this conduct took on the "aspect of highly unreasonable conduct, involving an extreme departure from ordinary care, in a situation where a high degree of danger is apparent . . . . It is at least clear . . . that such aggravated negligence must be more than any mere mistake resulting from inexperience, excitement, or confusion, and more than mere thoughtlessness or inadvertence, or simply inattention." . . .

B. The Tenth Count: CUTPA

In the tenth count, the plaintiff alleges the same facts as those alleged in counts seven and eight. In addition, in paragraph thirty of the tenth count, the plaintiff asserts that the "representation of seller, purchaser and mortgagee in the same real estate sales transaction impacts upon the entrepreneurial aspects of the practice of law" [because "this conduct establishes that Manko was motivated by being able to triple-dip"].

As a result, Manko's conduct allegedly violates CUTPA/Connecticut Unfair Trade Practices Act, General Statutes §42-110a et seq.) in that it is (1) "unlawful, offends public policy as it has been established by . . . Rules of Professional Conduct, (2) immoral, unethical, oppressive or unscrupulous, or (3) causes substantial injury to consumers of legal services."

In the recent case of Anderson v. Schoenhorn 874 A.2d 798 (Conn. App. 2005) the Appellate court stated: "In general, CUTPA applies to attorney conduct, but only as to the entrepreneurial aspects of legal practice. . . . Professional negligence, or malpractice, does not fall under CUTPA. . . . Although many decisions made by attorneys eventually involve personal profit as a factor, but are not considered part of the entrepreneurial aspect of practicing law . . . the conduct of a law firm in obtaining business and negotiating fee contracts does fall within the ambit of entrepreneurial activities."

The facts in this case establish that the defendant Manko's conduct involves allegations which concern "obtaining business and negotiating fee contracts." This conduct must be tested against the "cigarette rule." "It is well settled that in determining whether a practice violates CUTPA we have adopted the criteria set out in the cigarette rule by the federal trade commission for determining when a practice is unfair: (1) Whether the practice, without necessarily having been previously considered unlawful, offends public policy as it has been established by statutes, the common law, or otherwise—in other words, it is within at least the penumbra of some common law, statutory, or other established concept of unfairness; (2) whether it is immoral, unethical, oppressive, or unscrupulous; (3) whether it causes substantial injury to consumers, [competitors or other businesspersons]. . . . All three criteria do not need to be satisfied to support a finding of unfairness. A practice may be unfair because of the degree to which it meets one of the criteria or because to a lesser extent it meets all three."

A careful review of the allegations contained in the tenth count in a manner most favorable to the plaintiff leads the court to conclude that the plaintiff has pled sufficient facts to state a cause of action under CUTPA.

If the facts as alleged are proven, the plaintiff will have established that Manko violated Rule 1.7 of the Rules of Professional Conduct. This in turn would satisfy the first prong of the cigarette rule which requires a determination of whether the practice offends public policy. In this court's opinion the Rules of Professional Conduct are a judicially conceived public policy because "since October 1986, the conduct of attorneys has been regulated . . . by the Rules of Professional Conduct, which were approved by the judges of the Superior Court and which superseded the Code of Professional Responsibility."

Also, the Supreme Court has found clear statements of public policy in the Rules of Professional Conduct in other instances.

Regarding the second and third prongs of the cigarette rule, the court concludes that the allegations within the complaint, if proven, will establish that the conduct was unethical, (thereby satisfying the second prong) as well as a practice that caused substantial injury to consumers and to competitors alike.

C. The Eleventh Count: Breach of a Fiduciary Duty

Manko argues that the plaintiff has failed to allege sufficient facts to support a claim of a breach of a fiduciary duty. It is his position that the facts as alleged in the complaint do not implicate his honesty, loyalty or morality, which are the hallmarks of a fiduciary duty.

"Professional negligence alone, however, does not give rise automatically to a claim for breach of fiduciary duty. Although an attorney-client relationship imposes a fiduciary duty on the attorney; . . . not every instance of professional negligence results in a breach of that fiduciary duty. [A] fiduciary or confidential relationship is characterized by a unique degree of trust and confidence between the parties, one of whom has superior knowledge, skill or expertise and is under a duty to represent the interests of the other . . . . Professional negligence implicates a duty of care, while breach of a fiduciary duty implicates a duty of loyalty and honesty."

The commentary to Rule 1.7 of the Rules of Professional Conduct states, in relevant part, that, "Loyalty is an essential element in the lawyer's relationship to a client." Here, the allegations include a claim that an elderly, and ill person was brought to Manko's office to sign a deed to her home. She was uncomfortable enough with the situation that she asked whether she should have her own attorney. Despite the plaintiff's expression of discomfort, Manko continued with the transaction, acting in the capacity of her attorney. He also presumably accepted the proceeds of the sale as her trustee.

As an attorney, Manko possessed a superior skill and expertise to those of the plaintiff. Pursuant to the Rules of Professional Conduct, he was under a duty of loyalty and trust to the plaintiff. The court concludes that the plaintiff has pled sufficient facts, as read in the light most favorable to the plaintiff, to support a claim of breach of a fiduciary duty.

Accordingly, the defendant's motion to strike counts eight, ten, and eleven of the plaintiff's revised complaint dated April 1, 2005, is hereby, denied.

5. Business and Estate Planning

Problems

9-7. A longtime client of Martyn & Fox asks us to represent three partners in forming a new business: our longtime client, who is the money guy; the new venture's CEO; and the woman who owns the patent that is key to the business plan. May we?

9-8. A corporate client's CEO asks Martyn & Fox to represent his wife and him in drawing up new wills. Can we do so? What if the wife takes Martyn aside and tells her to draft a codicil that diverts a substantial part of her assets to a "friend"? What if later, during divorce proceedings, the wife calls Martyn & Fox to be refreshed as to husband's assets; may (must) Martyn & Fox share that information?

Consider: Model Rules 1.7, 1.8(b), 1.10
RLGL §§ 60, 130

A. v. B.
726 A.2d 924 (N.J. 1999)

Pollock, J.

This appeal presents the issue whether a law firm may disclose confidential information of one co-client to another co-client. Specifically, in this paternity action, the mother's former law firm, which contemporaneously represented the father and his wife in planning their estates, seeks to disclose the existence of the father's illegitimate child to the wife.

A law firm, Hill Wallack, . . . jointly represented the husband and wife in drafting wills in which they devised their respective estates to each other. The devises created the possibility that the other spouse's issue, whether legitimate or illegitimate, ultimately would acquire the decedent's property.

Unbeknown to Hill Wallack and the wife, the husband recently had fathered an illegitimate child. Before the execution of the wills, the child's mother retained Hill Wallack to institute this paternity action against the husband. Because of a clerical error, the firm's computer check did not reveal the conflict of interest inherent in its representation of the mother against the husband. On learning of the conflict, the firm withdrew from representation of the mother in the paternity action. Now, the firm wishes to disclose to the wife the fact that the husband has an illegitimate child. To prevent Hill Wallack from making that disclosure, the husband joined the firm as a third-party defendant in the paternity action. . . .

I . . .

In October 1997, the husband and wife retained Hill Wallack, a firm of approximately sixty lawyers, to assist them with planning their estates. On the commencement of the joint representation, the husband and wife each signed a letter captioned "Waiver of Conflict of Interest." In explaining the possible conflicts of interest, the letter recited that the effect of a testamentary transfer by one spouse to the other would permit the transferee to dispose of the property as he or she desired. The firm's letter also explained that information provided by one spouse could become available to the other. Although the letter did not contain an express waiver of the confidentiality of any such information, each spouse consented to and waived any conflicts arising from the firm's joint representation.

Unfortunately, the clerk who opened the firm's estate planning file misspelled the clients' surname. The misspelled name was entered in the computer program that the firm uses to discover possible conflicts of interest. The firm then prepared reciprocal wills and related documents with the names of the husband and wife correctly spelled.

In January 1998, before the husband and wife executed the estate planning documents, the mother coincidentally retained Hill Wallack to pursue a paternity claim against the husband. This time, when making its computer search for conflicts of interest, Hill Wallack spelled the husband's name correctly. Accordingly, the computer search did not reveal the existence of the firm's joint representation of the husband and wife. As a result, the estate planning department did not know that the family law department had instituted a paternity action for the mother. Similarly, the family law department did not know that the estate planning department was preparing estate plans for the husband and wife.

A lawyer from the firm's family law department wrote to the husband about the mother's paternity claim. The husband neither objected to the firm's representation of the mother nor alerted the firm to the conflict of interest. Instead, he retained Fox Rothschild to represent him in the paternity action. After initially denying paternity, he agreed to voluntary DNA testing, which revealed that he is the father. Negotiations over child support failed, and the mother instituted the present action.

After the mother filed the paternity action, the husband and wife executed their wills at the Hill Wallack office. The parties agree that in their wills, the husband and wife leave their respective residuary estates to each other. If the other spouse does not survive, the contingent beneficiaries are the testator's issue. The wife's will leaves her residuary estate to her husband, creating the possibility that her property ultimately may pass to his issue. Under N.J.S.A. 3C:1-2, :2-48, the term "issue" includes both legitimate and illegitimate children. When the wife executed her will, therefore, she did not know that the husband's illegitimate child ultimately may inherit her property.

The conflict of interest surfaced when Fox Rothschild, in response to Hill Wallack's request for disclosure of the husband's assets, informed the firm that it already possessed the requested information. Hill Wallack promptly informed the mother that it unknowingly was representing both the husband and the wife in an unrelated matter.

Hill Wallack immediately withdrew from representing the mother in the paternity action. It also instructed the estate planning department not to disclose any information about the husband's assets to the member of the firm who had been representing the mother. The firm then wrote to the husband stating that it believed it had an ethical obligation to disclose to the wife the existence, but not the identity, of his illegitimate child. Additionally, the firm stated that it was obligated to inform the wife "that her current estate plan may devise a portion of her assets through her spouse to that child." The firm suggested that the husband so inform his wife and stated that if he did not do so, it would. . . .

II

This appeal concerns the conflict between two fundamental obligations of lawyers: the duty of confidentiality, Rules of Professional Conduct (RPC) 1.6(a), and the duty to inform clients of material facts, RPC 1.4(b). The conflict arises from a law firm's joint representation of two clients whose interests initially were compatible, but now conflict.

Crucial to the attorney–client relationship is the attorney's obligation not to reveal confidential information learned in the course of representation. [The court cites Model Rule 1.6(a).]

A lawyer's obligation to communicate to one client all information needed to make an informed decision qualifies the firm's duty to maintain the confidentiality of a co-client's information. [The Court cites Model Rule 1.4(b).] In limited situations, moreover, an attorney is permitted or required to disclose confidential information. Hill Wallack argues that RPC 1.6 mandates, or at least permits, the firm to disclose to the wife the existence of the husband's illegitimate child. RPC 1.6(b) requires that a lawyer disclose "information relating to representation of a client" to the proper authorities if the lawyer "reasonably believes" that such disclosure is necessary to prevent the client "from committing a criminal, illegal or fraudulent act that the lawyer reasonably believes is likely to result in death or substantial bodily harm or substantial injury to the financial interest or property of another . . . ." Despite Hill Wallack's claim that RPC 1.6(b) applies, the facts do not justify mandatory disclosure. The possible inheritance of the wife's estate by the husband's illegitimate child is too remote to constitute "substantial injury to the financial interest or property of another" within the meaning of RPC 1.6(b).

By comparison, in limited circumstances RPC 1.6(c) permits a lawyer to disclose a confidential communication. RPC 1.6(c) permits, but does not require, a lawyer to reveal confidential information to the extent the lawyer reasonably believes necessary "to rectify the consequences of a client's criminal, illegal or fraudulent act in furtherance of which the lawyer's services had been used." Although RPC 1.6(c) does not define a "fraudulent act," the term takes on meaning from our construction of the word "fraud," found in the analogous "crime or fraud" exception to the attorney-client privilege.

We likewise construe broadly the term "fraudulent act" within the meaning of RPC 1.6(c). So construed, the husband's deliberate omission of the existence of his illegitimate child constitutes a fraud on his wife. When discussing their respective estates with the firm, the husband and wife reasonably could expect that each would disclose information material to the distribution of their estates, including the existence of children who are contingent residuary beneficiaries. The husband breached that duty. Under the reciprocal wills, the existence of the husband's illegitimate child could affect the distribution of the wife's estate, if she predeceased him. Additionally, the husband's child support payments and other financial responsibilities owed to the illegitimate child could deplete that part of his estate that otherwise would pass to his wife.

In effect, the husband has used the law firm's services to defraud his wife in the preparation of her estate. . . .

Under RPC 1.6, the facts support disclosure to the wife. . . .

[T]he husband and wife signed letters captioned "Waiver of Conflict of Interest." These letters acknowledge that information provided by one client could become available to the other. The letters, however, stop short of explicitly authorizing the firm to disclose one spouse's confidential information to the other. Even in the absence of any such explicit authorization, the spirit of the letters supports the firm's decision to disclose to the wife the existence of the husband's illegitimate child.

Neither our research nor that of counsel has revealed a dispositive judicial decision from this or any other jurisdiction on the issue of disclosure of confidential information about one client to a co-client. Persuasive secondary authority, however, supports the conclusion that the firm may disclose to the wife the existence of the husband's child.

The forthcoming Restatement of The Law Governing Lawyers § [60] comment l ("the Restatement") suggests, for example, that if the attorney and the co-clients have reached a prior, explicit agreement concerning the sharing of confidential information, that agreement controls whether the attorney should disclose the confidential information of one co-client to another.

As the preceding authorities suggest, an attorney, on commencing joint representation of co-clients, should agree explicitly with the clients on the sharing of confidential information. In such a "disclosure agreement," the co-clients can agree that any confidential information concerning one co-client, whether obtained from a co-client himself or herself or from another source, will be shared with the other co-client. Similarly, the co-clients can agree that unilateral confidences or other confidential information will be kept confidential by the attorney. Such a prior agreement will clarify the expectations of the clients and the lawyer and diminish the need for future litigation.

In the absence of an agreement to share confidential information with co-clients, the Restatement reposes the resolution of the lawyer's competing duties within the lawyer's discretion:

> [T]he lawyer, after consideration of all relevant circumstances, has the . . . discretion to inform the affected co-client of the specific communication if, in the lawyer's reasonable judgment, the immediacy and magnitude of the risk to the affected co-client outweigh the interest of the communicating client in continued secrecy. [Restatement (Third) The Law Governing Lawyers § [60], comment l.]

Additionally, the Restatement advises that the lawyer, when withdrawing from representation of the co-clients, may inform the affected co-client that the attorney has learned of information adversely affecting that client's interests that the communicating co-client refuses to permit the lawyer to disclose.

In the context of estate planning, the Restatement also suggests that a lawyer's disclosure of confidential information communicated by one spouse is appropriate only if the other spouse's failure to learn of the information would be materially detrimental to that other spouse or frustrate the spouse's intended testamentary arrangement. The Restatement provides two analogous illustrations in which a lawyer has been jointly retained by a husband and wife to prepare reciprocal wills. The first illustration states:

> Lawyer has been retained by Husband and Wife to prepare wills pursuant to an arrangement under which each spouse agrees to leave most of their property to the other. Shortly after the wills are executed, Husband (unknown to Wife) asks Lawyer to prepare an inter vivos trust for an illegitimate child whose existence Husband has kept secret from Wife for many years and about whom Husband had not previously informed Lawyer. Husband states that Wife would be distraught at

learning of Husband's infidelity and of Husband's years of silence and that disclosure of the information could destroy their marriage. Husband directs Lawyer not to inform Wife. The inter vivos trust that Husband proposes to create would not materially affect Wife's own estate plan or her expected receipt of property under Husband's will, because Husband proposes to use property designated in Husband's will for a personally favored charity. In view of the lack of material effect on Wife, Lawyer may assist Husband to establish and fund the inter vivos trust and refrain from disclosing Husband's information to Wife. . . .

The other illustration states:

Same facts as [the prior Illustration], except that Husband's proposed inter vivos trust would significantly deplete Husband's estate, to Wife's material detriment and in frustration of the Spouses' intended testamentary arrangements. If Husband will neither inform Wife nor permit Lawyer to do so, Lawyer must withdraw from representing both Husband and Wife. In the light of all relevant circumstances, Lawyer may exercise discretion whether to inform Wife either that circumstances, which Lawyer has been asked not to reveal, indicate that she should revoke her recent will or to inform Wife of some or all the details of the information that Husband has recently provided so that Wife may protect her interests. Alternatively, Lawyer may inform Wife only that Lawyer is withdrawing because Husband will not permit disclosure of information that Lawyer has learned from Husband. . . .

The Professional Ethics Committees of New York and Florida, however, have concluded that disclosure to a co-client is prohibited. N.Y. St. Bar Assn. Comm. on Prof. Ethics, Op. 555 (1984); Fla. St. Bar Assn. Comm. on Prof. Ethics, Op. 95-4 (1997).

The New York opinion addressed the following situation:

A and B formed a partnership and employed Lawyer L to represent them in connection with the partnership affairs. Subsequently, B, in a conversation with Lawyer L, advised Lawyer L that he was actively breaching the partnership agreement. B preceded this statement to Lawyer L with the statement that he proposed to tell Lawyer L something "in confidence." Lawyer L did not respond to that statement and did not understand that B intended to make a statement that would be of importance to A but that was to be kept confidential from A. Lawyer L had not, prior thereto, advised A or B that he could not receive from one communications regarding the subject of the joint representation that would be confidential from the other. B has subsequently declined to tell A what he has told Lawyer L.

In that situation, the New York Ethics Committee concluded that the lawyer may not disclose to the co-client the communicating client's statement. The Committee based its conclusion on the absence of prior consent by the clients to the sharing of all confidential communications and the fact that the client "specifically in advance designated his communication as confidential, and the lawyer did not demur."

The Florida Ethics Committee addressed a similar situation:

Lawyer has represented Husband and Wife for many years in a range of personal matters, including estate planning. Husband and Wife have substantial individual assets, and they also own substantial jointly-held property. Recently, Lawyer prepared new updated wills that Husband and Wife signed. Like their previous wills, their new wills primarily benefit the survivor of them for his or her life, with beneficial disposition at the death of the survivor being made equally to their children. . . .

Several months after the execution of the new wills, Husband confers separately with Lawyer. Husband reveals to Lawyer that he has just executed a codicil (prepared by another law firm) that makes substantial beneficial disposition to a woman with whom Husband has been having an extra-marital relationship.

Reasoning that the lawyer's duty of confidentiality takes precedence over the duty to communicate all relevant information to a client, the Florida Ethics Committee concluded that the lawyer did not have discretion to reveal the information. In support of that conclusion, the Florida committee reasoned that joint clients do not necessarily expect that everything relating to the joint representation communicated by one co-client will be shared with the other co-client.

In several material respects, however, the present appeal differs from the hypothetical cases considered by the New York and Florida committees. Most significantly, the New York and Florida disciplinary rules, unlike RPC 1.6, do not except disclosure needed "to rectify the consequences of a client's . . . fraudulent act in the furtherance of which the lawyer's services had been used." RPC 1.6(c). Second, Hill Wallack learned of the husband's paternity from a third party, not from the husband himself. Thus, the husband did not communicate anything to the law firm with the expectation that the communication would be kept confidential. Finally, the husband and wife, unlike the co-clients considered by the New York and Florida Committees, signed an agreement suggesting their intent to share all information with each other. . . .

The law firm learned of the husband's paternity of the child through the mother's disclosure before the institution of the paternity suit. It does not seek to disclose the identity of the mother or the child. Given the wife's need for the information and the law firm's right to disclose it, the disclosure of the child's existence to the wife constitutes an exceptional case "for compelling reason clearly and convincingly shown." . . .

C. Simultaneous Representation of Adversaries

Problems

9-9. Viacom and Disney are both competing for an open TV channel in New York before the Federal Communications Commission.

    (a) Can Martyn represent Viacom while Fox represents Disney, if each lawyer seeks his or her client's consent?

    (b) What if Martyn & Fox lawyers feel comfortable taking on the representation of both?

    (c) If Martyn & Fox already represents Viacom in another unrelated matter, can we just take on the representation of Disney seeking the channel?

9-10. Martyn & Fox has been retained by Magnum Industries to defend a products liability action. In-house counsel for Magnum tells Fox that the case is "routine," but she is troubled by the fact that plaintiff's counsel works for a law firm that regularly represents Forest Products, Inc., a wholly owned Magnum subsidiary. Does it make any difference if Forest Products is only a partially owned subsidiary?

Consider: Model Rules 1.7, Comment [34]; 1.10, 1.13
RLGL §§ 121, Comment d, 128

Eastman Kodak Company v. Sony Corporation

2004 U.S. Dist. LEXIS 29883 (W.D.N.Y.)

Jonathan W. FELDMAN, United States Magistrate Judge.

Preliminary Statement

Sometimes a case will present an issue that requires a court to choose between the lesser of two unfair results. This is one of those cases.

Relevant Facts

Founded in Rochester, Eastman Kodak Company (hereinafter Kodak) is the area's largest private employer. Kodak's important and widespread presence in our community inevitably results in the company becoming involved in a myriad of court proceedings in both state and federal courts. These lawsuits run the gamut, from intellectual property cases, to contract actions, to employment discrimination claims. Woods Oviatt Gilman, LLP (hereinafter Woods Oviatt) is one of Rochester's oldest law firms and has an active litigation practice in both state and federal courts. Woods Oviatt's business model intentionally seeks to avoid having Kodak as a client. This business decision has obvious benefits to Woods Oviatt, as it allows the firm to attract and represent clients who may have interests adverse to Kodak, without offending conflict of interest rules associated with the practice of law. The instant dispute pays tribute to the difficult conflict problem created when an otherwise legitimate corporate acquisition by Kodak results in Kodak becoming an uninvited client of Woods Oviatt.

For several years, Woods Oviatt has represented Heidelberg Digital LLC (hereinafter Heidelberg).[1] Indeed, Heidelberg chose Woods Oviatt as their counsel because, among other things, the law firm could represent Heidelberg in its business dealings with Kodak. Among the many matters Woods Oviatt handled

---

1. Woods Oviatt began representing Heidelberg in 1999, shortly after the company was formed. Heidelberg came into existence when its parent company, Heidelberger Druckmaschinen AG ("Druckmaschinen"), acquired Kodak's black and white printing business. Since that time, Woods Oviatt has represented Heidelberg in a variety of matters, including a major construction financing project, an intellectual property dispute, an environmental matter, and employment discrimination cases.

for Heidelberg were two employment discrimination lawsuits, one pending in this Court (Jackson v. Heidelberg) and the other pending in New York State Supreme Court (McEwen v. Heidelberg). The Jackson case has proceeded through discovery and defendant's summary judgment motion is now pending before the Court. In McEwen, New York State Supreme Court Justice Evelyn Frazee has ordered the parties to complete all discovery by January 31, 2005 and file a note of issue by February 15, 2005. Both the Jackson and McEwen cases have been actively litigated by Woods Oviatt on behalf of Heidelberg for several years.

In May 1, 2004 Kodak acquired Heidelberg. There is no dispute that Woods Oviatt was aware of the Kodak-Heidelberg transaction before it occurred. On April 1, 2004, a month before the acquisition closed, Woods Oviatt attorney Andrew J. Ryan, Esq. submitted an affidavit in the Jackson case which confirmed the expectation that Kodak was going to purchase Heidelberg on May 1, 2004. . . . Woods Oviatt also performed legal work for Heidelberg in furtherance of the transaction, although the firm describes their involvement as "peripheral" and limited to "some minor housekeeping matters." In addition, during the pre-closing "due diligence" process, Woods Oviatt maintained Heidelberg's records at their office for Kodak representatives to review. Following Kodak's acquisition of Heidelberg, Woods Oviatt continued to act as defense counsel in the Jackson and McEwen cases and continued to bill for legal services rendered in those cases.[3]

In July 2004, William G. Bauer, a partner at Woods Oviatt, entered an appearance as local counsel in two separate cases currently pending in this Court. In both cases Kodak is the opposing litigant. One of the cases (Kodak v. Sony Corporation) is a patent infringement suit. The other (Employees Committed for Justice ("ECJ") v. Kodak) is a class action complaint alleging, *inter alia*, that "Kodak has engaged in an ongoing pattern and practice of discrimination against its African-American employees." According to Kodak, Ms. McEwen is a putative member of the potential class in the ECJ v. Kodak case.

After the May acquisition of Heidelberg, Kodak's legal department assumed responsibility for all litigation matters involving Heidelberg. In June or July 2004, W. Stephen Tierney, a partner in Woods Oviatt, called Joseph Leverone, an in-house attorney with Heidelberg, to ascertain "what role, if any, Heidelberg wanted [Woods Oviatt] to play in the pending discrimination cases going forward." Tierney did not receive a reply to his phone messages and on August 2, 2004, he sent an e-mail to Heidelberg asking whether "we should continue to work on the [litigation] files, now that [Kodak] has acquired [Heidelberg]."

A week later, on August 9, 2004, Gary Van Graafeiland, General Counsel and Senior Vice President of Kodak, wrote to James P. McElheny, the Managing Partner of Woods Oviatt, stating that Kodak had "recently learned" that Bauer was "representing clients with interests adverse to those of Kodak" in the ECJ v.

---

3. On August 16, 2004, Woods Oviatt filed a motion to withdraw from further representation of Heidelberg in the Jackson case. It has also, consistent with direction from Kodak and its own ethical obligations, continued to prosecute the summary judgment motion and filed Reply papers as recently as November 9, 2004.

Kodak and Sony v. Kodak cases. Because Kodak had acquired Heidelberg, and Woods Oviatt continued to represent Heidelberg in litigation, Van Graafeiland requested that "your firm [Woods Oviatt] remove this conflict of interest by withdrawing from the representation of the plaintiffs in the ECJ action and the defendants in the Sony action." By letter dated August 13, 2004, McElheny responded, asserting that "Heidelberg is our client" and therefore, Woods Oviatt does "not believe the Code of Professional Responsibility is implicated." However, in order to alleviate Kodak's ethical "concerns," McElheny informed Van Graafeiland that Woods Oviatt would withdraw from further representation of Heidelberg in the Jackson and McEwen cases.

By letter dated August 20, 2004, Van Graafeiland responded to McElheny's August 13, 2004 letter. Van Graafeiland rejected Woods Oviatt's request to withdraw from the Jackson and McEwen cases as "not acceptable" because it would cause "substantial prejudice to Heidelberg and Kodak, given the firm's long-term representations in those cases and the level of activity therein." The instant motions to disqualify Woods Oviatt from acting as local counsel in the Sony v. Kodak and ECJ v. Kodak cases followed.

Discussion

Is Kodak a Current Client of Woods Oviatt?: The first issue to be addressed is whether Kodak's acquisition of Heidelberg transformed them into one and the same "client" for conflict purposes. Resolution of this initial issue is critical because if the two entities are to be treated as a single client, then under the Code of Professional Responsibility, Woods Oviatt's representation of ECJ and Sony as local counsel is *"prima facie* improper." Cinema 5, Ltd. v. Cinerama, Inc., 528 F.2d 1384, 1387 (2d Cir. 1976).

Determining the existence and nature of conflicts in the context of "corporate families" and the appropriate remedy upon the finding of a conflict can be a difficult and complicated undertaking. The relevant inquiry centers on whether the corporate relationship between the two corporate family members is "so close as to deem them a single entity for conflict of interest purposes." Discotrade Ltd. v. Wyeth-Ayerst International, Inc., 200 F. Supp. 2d 355, 358 (S.D.N.Y. 2002). *See* JPMorgan Chase Bank v. Liberty Mutual Insurance Co., 189 F. Supp. 2d 20, 21 (S.D.N.Y. 2002) (conflict found where, even though corporations may not be "alter egos" of one another, their relationship was "extremely close and interdependent, both financially and in terms of direction").

The evidence of a "close and interdependent relationship" between Kodak and Heidelberg is compelling here. The Kodak-Heidelberg transaction was neither a merger of equals, nor an attenuated corporate affiliation. Rather, Kodak essentially swallowed Heidelberg. Heidelberg is now wholly owned by Kodak. Heidelberg's "one person" Board of Directors is a Senior Vice President of Kodak. Three-fourths of Heidelberg's eight corporate officers are Kodak employees. After the acquisition, Heidelberg's technology system was integrated with Kodak's. Significantly, Heidelberg shares Kodak's legal department. Indeed, Kodak's Legal Division has direct supervisory responsibility over both the McEwen and Jackson cases. *See* Hartford Accident and Indemnity Co. v. RJR Nabisco, Inc.,

721 F. Supp. 534, 540 (S.D.N.Y. 1989) ("If the parent and subsidiary were in fact distinct and separate entities for representation purposes, then there would have been no need for the parent's general counsel to have retained this supervisory role."). Heidelberg is unquestionably intertwined with Kodak, both in terms of corporate ownership and business management.[6] Hence, for conflict purposes, Kodak and its wholly owned and operationally integrated subsidiary, Heidelberg, are the same client. *See* Stratagem Development Corp. v. Heron International N.V., 756 F. Supp. 789, 792 (S.D.N.Y. 1991) (where "the liabilities of a [wholly owned] subsidiary corporation directly affect the bottom line of the corporate parent," law firm could not simultaneously represent both in adverse actions).

2. *Is There a Conflict?*: Because Kodak and Heidelberg's post-acquisition relationship constitutes a single client for conflict purposes, the applicable conflict analysis is the more exacting "*prima facie* conflict" standard. . . . "The more stringent alternative, known somewhat misleadingly as the '*per se*' rule, pertains to situations where a law firm undertakes to represent two adverse parties, both of which are 'clients in the traditional sense,' and the relationship between the firm and the clients is continuing." University of Rochester, 2000 U.S. Dist. LEXIS 19030. The more stringent test is warranted because the propriety of the lawyer's conduct "must be measured not so much against the similarities in litigation, as against the duty of undivided loyalty which an attorney owes to each of his clients." *Cinema 5, Ltd.*, 528 F.2d at 1386. "Under the Code [of Professional Responsibility], the lawyer who would sue his own client, asserting in justification the lack of 'substantial relationship' between the litigation and the work he has undertaken to perform for that client, is leaning on a slender reed indeed."

Under the foregoing analysis, there is little doubt that a *prima facie* conflict exists here. By accepting employment as local counsel in the Sony v. Kodak and ECJ v. Kodak cases, Woods Oviatt essentially agreed to participate in two lawsuits in which an existing client (Kodak) is an adverse party. Because such concurrent representation could weaken Woods Oviatt's fiduciary and fundamental duty of undivided loyalty owed to Kodak, it is "*prima facie* improper." Moreover, the concurrent representation is *prima facie* improper, irrespective of any substantial relationship among or between the various state and federal cases.

3. *Does the Conflict Require Disqualification?*: A finding that Woods Oviatt is simultaneously representing adverse parties does not end the disqualification analysis. " . . . The decision of whether to grant a motion to disqualify is within the discretion of the Court and the movant bears the burden of demonstrating that disqualification is warranted. However, once the doctrine of concurrent representation is held to apply, the burden of avoiding disqualification shifts to the lawyer to either (1) obtain consent from the client or (2) "show at the very

---

6. A review of Heidelberg's post-acquisition website (*http://www.nexpress.com*) only confirms the close family relationship of the two companies, as well as their integrated business operations and interests. The website describes NexPress as "a Kodak company headquartered in Rochester, New York." The company's web page "logo" includes the following description: "NexPress: A Kodak Company."

least, that there will be no actual or apparent conflict in loyalties or diminution in the vigor of his representation."

Kodak obviously does not consent here, thus Woods Oviatt bears the burden of demonstrating that there will be no actual or apparent conflict in their duty of undivided loyalty owed to Kodak. Aside from proposing that Kodak should, in fairness, waive the conflict, the firm does not argue that it could realistically be Kodak's zealous advocate and champion in defending Kodak's wholly owned subsidiary against employment discrimination charges in federal court, while simultaneously representing a plaintiff suing Kodak on employment discrimination charges in the same federal court. . . . [I]t is difficult to imagine a clearer conflict of interest or an appearance of divided loyalties. And because the stricter "prima facie" test applies to concurrent representation situations, Woods Oviatt's defense of Kodak in the Heidelberg discrimination suits while at the same time defending Sony, Kodak's adversary in the patent case, is similarly problematic, even without factual or legal similarities in the two actions. Put simply, without Kodak's consent, it is ethically impermissible for Woods Oviatt to have a wholly owned and integrated subsidiary of Kodak as a client and simultaneously represent Kodak's adversaries in pending litigation in state and federal court. Case law clearly supports this conclusion.

4. *What is the Appropriate Remedy?*: The foregoing is really a prelude to the crux of the present dispute—what client should Woods Oviatt be disqualified from representing? Kodak contends that given the advanced stages of the Jackson and McEwen litigation, Kodak would be severely prejudiced if Woods Oviatt were to withdraw from either case at this late date. Invoking the so-called "hot potato" principle, Kodak argues that the only ethically acceptable remedy is for the Court to disqualify Woods Oviatt from representing Sony and ECJ. Under the hot potato principle,

> an attorney cannot avoid disqualification under the *Cinema* 5 rule merely by "firing" the disfavored client, dropping the client like a hot potato, and transforming a continuing relationship to a former relationship by way of client abandonment. Indeed, the offense inherent in taking on the conflicting representation is compounded by seeking to "fire" the client in pursuit of the attorney's interest in taking on a new, more attractive representation. If, as one judge has written, "the act of suing one's client is a 'dramatic form of disloyalty,'" what might be said of trying to drop the first client in an effort to free the attorney to pursue his or her self-interest in taking on a newer and more attractive professional engagement?

Universal City Studios, Inc. v. Reimerdes, 98 F. Supp. 2d 449, 453 (S.D.N.Y. 2000) *See* Stratagem Development Corp., 756 F. Supp. at 794 (absent consent, "a firm is to remain with the client in the already-existing litigation and seek new counsel to represent the other, not vice-versa").

Woods Oviatt counters that if Kodak's purchase of Heidelberg made Kodak an uninvited client of their firm, the firm should be permitted to simply withdraw from the Jackson and McEwen cases and continue as local counsel for clients adverse to Kodak in the Kodak v. Sony and ECJ v. Kodak cases. Woods Oviatt points to its longstanding policy of not representing Kodak and argues that the conflict predicament the firm finds itself in was not due to any action on their part, but was created solely by Kodak purchasing their long-time client. Lawyers for Sony and ECJ also appeared before this Court and argued that their clients would be prejudiced if Woods Oviatt, and in particular William Bauer, Esq., were not able to be their local counsel. Based on the foregoing, Woods Oviatt urges the Court not to automatically apply the "hot potato rule". Instead, the firm advocates taking a more "flexible approach" to attorney disqualification where the conflict arises solely due to the business activities of the client. The rationale for the "flexible approach" to disqualification issues was described by the court in Gould, Inc. v. Mitsui Mining and Smelting Co., 738 F.Supp. 1121, 1126 (N.D. Ohio 1990):

> The explosion of merger activity by corporations during the past fifteen years, and the corresponding increase in the possibility that attorney conflicts of interest may arise unexpectedly, make it appropriate for a court to adopt a perspective about the disqualification of counsel in ongoing litigation that conforms to the problem. This means taking a less mechanical approach to the problem, balancing the various interests. The result is that the courts are less likely to order disqualification and more likely to use other, more tailored measures to protect the interests of the public and the parties.

In *Gould*, a conflict arose when several years after litigation had commenced, the defendant acquired a company that plaintiff's counsel represented in unrelated matters. The court held that although plaintiff's counsel . . . represent[ed] conflicting interests, disqualification pursuant to the "hot potato" rule would not be mechanically applied, but rather would be subject to a balancing of competing factors. The relevant factors include: (1) prejudice to the parties, including whether confidential information has been conveyed, (2) costs and inconvenience to the party being required to obtain new counsel, (3) the complexity of the various litigations, and (4) the origin of the conflict. After analyzing the factors, the Court in *Gould* gave the law firm the right to choose which client it wanted to represent and which it wanted to drop. . . .

This court agrees that the "flexible approach" provides a far more practical framework to disqualification issues generated by mergers and acquisitions than the rigid "hot potato rule," but under either analytical model Woods Oviatt's continued representation of Sony or ECJ is ethically problematic. Indeed, most, if not all, of the *Gould* factors favor the disqualification position urged by Kodak.

First, there is no dispute that in purchasing Heidelberg, Kodak's labor department has assumed supervisory responsibility over both the McEwen and the Jackson cases. While Kodak does not refer to any specific confidential information that has been disclosed to Woods Oviatt since the acquisition, given the factual and legal overlap of McEwen and the allegations of race discrimination in ECJ, Kodak's concern is justified. For example, an internal Kodak study of wage and promotion disparity for African-American employees is relied upon by Woods Oviatt's clients in the ECJ complaint. The same Kodak document has been demanded by Woods Oviatt in their defense of Heidelberg in the McEwen action. Moreover, it appears (and is not disputed by Woods Oviatt) that Ms. McEwen is a potential class member in the ECJ v. Kodak case. Allowing Woods Oviatt to assume representation of Ms. McEwen as a member of a class suing Kodak for race discrimination, after having defended Kodak's wholly owned subsidiary on charges of race discrimination filed by Ms. McEwen in which she claims both Heidelberg and Kodak discriminated against her, clearly suggests conflicted loyalties and thus weighs against allowing Woods Oviatt's choice of clients.

The second and third *Gould* factors, the cost and inconvenience of obtaining new counsel in light of the complexity of the litigations involved, also tip in Kodak's favor. The prejudice to Kodak in having to find new counsel to assume the defense of Heidelberg in the Jackson and McEwen cases is not insignificant. In McEwen, Judge Frazee's scheduling order requires Woods Oviatt to complete all discovery by January 31, 2005 and file a note of issue two weeks thereafter. In Jackson, Woods Oviatt has filed and briefed a summary judgment motion now pending before this Court. Allowing Woods Oviatt to drop the Jackson and McEwen cases at this point and forcing Kodak to locate new counsel willing and able to assume representation at crucial junctures in both these cases creates a real potential for prejudice to the client. Kodak complains that if Woods Oviatt is permitted to drop the Heidelberg cases, it may unduly delay the ongoing litigation and increase their legal fees as new counsel gets "up to speed" on each case. Finally, while the complexity of the Sony and ECJ cases would appear to be substantial, the gravity of this factor is offset by the fact that both the Sony and ECJ cases are in the very early stages of litigation and capable lead counsel for both clients would remain in the cases, even if Woods Oviatt were disqualified.

The final *Gould* factor is the origin of the conflict, that is, which party created the conflict? In *Gould*, as in this case, as a result of an acquisition, a law firm found itself representing a subsidiary in one litigated matter, while simultaneously suing the subsidiary's parent in an unrelated matter. In allowing the law firm to choose which client to continue to represent, the *Gould* court emphasized that the creation of the conflict was not due to any "affirmative act" of the law firm. Rather, the conflict spawned the moment the acquisition was consummated, as it was not until that point that the law firm represented conflicting interests.

Here, however, it was Woods Oviatt's decisions to act as local counsel for Sony and ECJ, decisions the firm made with full knowledge of Kodak's intent to acquire their client, Heidelberg, that created the relevant conflicts.[9] In sum,

---

9. Woods Oviatt refers the Court to two other clients (Marie Long and Canon U.S.A.) who have or had interests adverse to Kodak at the time of Kodak's acquisition of Heidelberg. Woods Oviatt argues that Kodak's position would require the firm to "abandon" these clients as well. However, Woods Oviatt's representation of Marie Long and Canon pre-dated the Kodak's acquisition of Heidelberg by a year, whereas their decision to enter an appearance as local counsel for ECJ and Sony occurred after the Heidelberg acquisition. This important distinction brings the Long and Canon situations closer to the facts of Gould, Inc. v. Mitsui Mining and Smelting Co., 738 F.Supp. 1121 (N.D. Ohio 1990). In any event, any potential conflict in the Long and Canon representations is not before this Court and Kodak here has specifically represented it will not waive the conflict with respect to Sony and ECJ cases.

Gould is factually distinguishable from the instant case because here, Woods Oviatt accepted clients with interests adverse to Kodak after Kodak acquired the firm's existing client. Accordingly, the final *Gould* factor also weighs against Woods Oviatt's request to drop the Heidelberg cases and continue to represent Sony and ECJ.

The foregoing is not meant to suggest that Sony, ECJ, or even Woods Oviatt will not be prejudiced if Woods Oviatt is not allowed to choose Sony and ECJ as clients and terminate its defense of Heidelberg in the Jackson and McEwen cases. Woods Oviatt avers that "Kodak's real motive in bring[sic] this motion is to deny the plaintiffs in this [ECJ] case and the defendants in the Sony case access to Mr. Bauer's knowledge and experience." That accusation is one this Court takes very seriously, especially because "courts must guard against tactical use of motions to disqualify counsel." Indeed, during the hearing on the motion to disqualify, this Court inquired whether Kodak intended to discharge Woods Oviatt from the Jackson and McEwen cases should the Court grant its motions to disqualify Woods Oviatt from the ECJ and Sony cases. Kodak's lawyers repeatedly assured this Court that their motions to disqualify Woods Oviatt were not interposed for tactical reasons and that Kodak wanted Woods Oviatt to remain as counsel in order to complete the Jackson and McEwen litigations. I accept counsels' representations as officers of this Court.

Nevertheless, and to be clear, while the "flexible approach" may require Woods Oviatt's disqualification from being local counsel for Sony and ECJ, the approach also mandates flexibility in allowing Woods Oviatt to resume their legitimate business model and avoid having Kodak or any Kodak "family member" as a client of the firm. Nothing in this decision is meant to link Woods Oviatt and Kodak together any longer than necessary to complete the two Heidelberg litigations. Once completed, any attempt by Kodak to use its new-found status as a "former client" of Woods Oviatt as a strategy to preclude the firm from welcoming clients with interests adverse to Kodak would be looked upon with skepticism, at least by this Court.

Conclusion

I began with observing that this case involved the Court having to choose a result that would inevitably involve some degree of unfairness to whichever clients Woods Oviatt would not be representing. In making the choice, "[a] delicate balance must be struck between two competing considerations: the prerogative of a party to proceed with counsel of its choice and the need to uphold ethical conduct in courts of law." After due consideration to the competing interests involved, I conclude that: (1) for conflict purposes, Kodak and Kodak's wholly owned subsidiary, Heidelberg, are to be treated as a single client; (2) absent consent, Woods Oviatt may not simultaneously represent both Kodak and clients with litigation interests adverse to Kodak; and (3) application of the "flexible approach" to disqualification results in Woods Oviatt's disqualification from acting as local counsel to Sony and ECJ. Therefore, Kodak's motions to disqualify Woods Oviatt from representing Sony and ECJ in the instant cases are granted.

D. Positional Conflicts

Problem

9-11. Delaware has passed legislation that makes it very difficult to do a hostile takeover of a public company incorporated in Delaware. Martyn & Fox is hired to defend Colossus against a hostile takeover by enforcing this legislation in a case brought in Delaware Chancery Court. At the same time, Martyn & Fox is hired by Amalgamated Industries to seek a hostile takeover of Apex Corporation, a Delaware corporation headquartered in Ohio. May Martyn & Fox support the takeover of Apex by attacking the same Delaware law as unconstitutional in an action pending in the United States District Court for the Northern District of Ohio?

Consider: Model Rule 1.7
RLGL § 128 comment f

Chapter 10

Conflicts of Interest: Specific Rules

A. Introduction

This chapter addresses specific conflicts of interest governed by Model Rule 1.8. This rule regulates ten particular conflicts identified by courts as creating the potential for compromising the interests of clients, the lawyer's independent professional judgment, or both. In these situations, a client is deemed vulnerable to exploitation by a lawyer's exercise of influence over the client.

Although general conflict of interest rules such as Model Rule 1.7 also might capture these conflicts, these special rules give clients and lawyers additional warning about the particular conflicts, the need to avoid them, or, if consent to these conflicts is sought, the greater disclosure obligations necessary to secure informed consent to waive them. These realities have led to the crafting of Model Rule 1.8, which flatly bans some conflicts as nonconsentable, and heavily regulates the content of disclosure and consent obligations as to others.

In all of these situations, the heightened scrutiny given to these specific conflicts signals their continuing threat to clients, lawyers, and law firms.[1] As a result, lawyers must comply with more significant regulation in addressing them, and clients can count on multiple remedies if their interests are compromised. For example, agency law imposes fiduciary duties on lawyers because clients repose trust in lawyers, who in turn must act solely on the client's behalf. When a lawyer acts on her own behalf as well—in a business transaction with a client, receipt of a client gift, or use of client confidences—agency law provides for a presumption of undue influence to protect client interests.[2] It is difficult to

---

1. MR 1.8(k) imputes all of these lawyer conflicts to the lawyer's firm. The only exception is a lawyer-client sexual relationship, which is governed by Rule 1.10(a).
2. Dan Dobbs, *Law of Remedies* § 10.3 (2d ed. 1993) ("The dominant party's conduct counts as undue influence when he uses his position to sway the judgment of the other by advice or suggestion, or even by implication.").

overcome such a presumption because the lawyer must be able to show that the transaction was completely fair and fully disclosed in writing to the client.[3]

In some situations, the presumption of undue influence is so strong that the conflict has been deemed nonconsentable. For example, Model Rule 1.8(j) bans all sexual relations with clients that did not precede the professional relationship.[4] This absolute prohibition applies to protect clients from "unfair exploitation of the lawyer's fiduciary role,"[5] and "because the client's own emotional involvement renders it unlikely that the client could give adequate informed consent."[6] It also protects lawyers, whose emotional involvement makes impairment of professional judgment a significant risk.[7]

In light of these concerns, it should not be surprising that when clients have been harmed by a sexual relationship with a lawyer, the law governing lawyers provides for a myriad of other legal remedies beyond professional discipline. Clients have successfully recovered for an intentional tort,[8] malpractice,[9] and breach of fiduciary duty.[10] Lawyers also have been disqualified[11] and subject to fee forfeiture.[12]

---

3. *E.g.,* Passante v. McWilliam, 62 Cal. Rptr. 2d 298 (Cal. App. 1997) (lawyer who "came through in the clutch" raising money for a client's company and was promised 3 percent of the firm's stock unable to prevail for breach of oral contract because, if promise was bargained for, it violated the lawyer's ethical duty, which should have included a written waiver and advice to seek outside counsel and, if gratuitous, not legally enforceable); McRentals Inc., v. Barber, 62 S.W.3d 684 (Mo. App. 2001) (lawyer who advised clients that he could not represent them if they wanted to sell their business to lawyer met burden of proving no undue advantage in business transaction with client where client in fact consulted with another lawyer, and transaction was fair to the client).

4. Comment [17] points out that the client-lawyer relationship "is almost always unequal" and that a sexual relationship violates "the lawyer's basic ethical obligation not to use the trust of the client to the client's disadvantage."

5. *Id.*

6. *Id.*

7. *Id.*

8. *See, e.g.,* McDaniel v. Gile, 281 Cal. Rptr. 242 (Cal. App. 1991) (lawyer whose sexual advances were refused by client stopped working on the client's case and gave her incorrect advice about her legal rights liable for intentional infliction of emotional distress); Barbara A. v. John G., 193 Cal. Rptr. 422 (Cal. App. 1983) (lawyer who told client he "couldn't possibly get anyone pregnant" liable for battery and fraud after client suffered a tubal pregnancy that rendered her sterile). When complaints allege negligence or malpractice, they trigger the duty to defend in professional liability policies. However, the same policies specifically exclude intentional acts, such as battery and fraud. Insurers typically are required to provide a defense when both are pleaded. In such cases, the insurer reserves the right to claim later that no duty to indemnify the defendant exists because sexual misconduct is not a covered occurrence. *See, e.g.,* St. Paul Fire & Marine Ins. Co. v. Engelmann, 639 N.W.2d 192 (S.D. 2002).

9. *See, e.g.,* Walter v. Stewart, 67 P.3d 1042 (Utah App. 2003); Doe v. Roe, 681 N.E.2d 640 (Ill. App. 1997).

10. *See, e.g.,* Walter v. Stewart, 67 P.3d 1042 (Utah App. 2003); Tante v. Herring, 453 S.E.2d 686 (Ga. 1994) (lawyer who misused confidential information about client's mental and emotional condition to convince her to engage in sex with lawyer liable to client and husband).

11. *See, e.g.,* Musick v. Musick, 453 S.E.2d 361 (W. Va. 1994) (lawyer who engaged in sexual relationship with client disqualified from further representation on motion of opposing party).

12. Piro v. Sarofim, 80 S.W. 3d 717 (Tex. App. 2002) (lawyer who, *inter alia*, engaged in inappropriate personal relationship with client during divorce forfeited $3 million fee).

The conflicts in this chapter all share this significant potential for client harm. When these situations are recurring, more detailed regulation can be expected.[13] At the same time, the law governing lawyers will continue to offer overlapping remedies for breach of significant loyalty obligations, including professional discipline, damages, fee forfeiture, and disqualification.[14]

B. Client and Lawyer Interests

1. Business Transactions with Clients

Problem

10-1. It is crunch time. The initial public offering (IPO) of Giggle is almost ready to proceed, but the client has run out of cash to pay counsel. Martyn suggests a 3 percent allocation of shares in lieu of the outstanding balance. The client gleefully accepts. The IPO is a success. Martyn, as a major shareholder of Giggle, is asked to serve on the board.

Consider: Model Rules 1.7, 1.8, 1.10
RLGL § 126

Liggett, d/b/a Liggett Construction Company v. Young
877 N.E.2d 178 (Ind. 2007)

DICKSON, Justice.

The plaintiff, Ronald Liggett, d/b/a Liggett Construction Company, brings this appeal to challenge a trial court summary judgment ruling in a contract dispute arising from Liggett's construction of a private residence for his attorney, defendant Dean Young, and Young's wife, Elisabeth. . . .

In 2001, when sued by a supplier of bricks and materials used in the construction of the Youngs' home, Liggett initiated a third-party complaint against the Youngs. The Youngs' answer included a counterclaim against Liggett seeking

---

13. *See* Fla. Rule 1.8(j) (2012); Ohio R. Prof. Conduct 1.8(f)(4) (2012) (detailing disclosures required by insurance defense lawyers who represent policyholders, including selection and direction of the lawyer, fees and costs, litigation guidelines, confidentiality, conflicts of interest, settlement, risk of judgment beyond policy limits, and how to report violations).
14. *See, e.g.,* Iowa S. Ct. Bd. of Prof. Ethics & Conduct v. Fay, 619 N.W.2d 321 (Iowa 2000) (lawyer who advised client on business matters and then leased his own property to client for client's business suspended for 30 days for failing to provide full disclosure and recommend another lawyer, and civilly liable for negligent misrepresentation because client had regularly relied on lawyer for legal services); In re Halverson, 998 P.2d 833 (Wash. 2000) (lawyer who had sexual relationship with client suspended from practice for six months after settling a civil suit by the client for a "substantial sum"); In re Sonnier, 157 B.R. 976 (Bankr. E.D. La. 1993) (lawyer who violated aggregate settlement rule could not discharge his former client's debts in bankruptcy because he breached fiduciary duty by accepting an unauthorized settlement).

damages for allegedly negligent and untimely performance of the work under the building contract. . . . [T]he trial court granted partial summary judgment and . . . entered final judgment in favor of the Youngs and against Liggett as to all of Liggett's claims against the Youngs. . . .

Among Liggett's issues on appeal, we find one to be dispositive: "Whether the trial judge erred in finding no genuine issue of material fact with respect to the enforceability of a contract drafted and entered into between an attorney and his builder/client." . . .

1. Professional Conduct Rule 1.8

Liggett's appeal contends in part that the Youngs failed to carry their burden on summary judgment to prove that the construction contract was not void by reason of Indiana Professional Conduct Rule 1.8, which restricts an attorney's ability to engage in transactions with the attorney's client. Liggett urges that Dean Young violated this rule by drafting the construction contract for the project, and that attorney/client transactions are presumptively invalid as the product of undue influence. In response, the Youngs contend (a) that Liggett's designation of evidence on summary judgment, claiming an entitlement to receive the contract price plus an additional amount, is inconsistent with his claim that the contract should be found void, and (b) that the construction contract was a standard commercial transaction to which Rule 1.8 does not apply. . . .

At all relevant times (from the contract date of July 2, 1999, through the date the Youngs filed their complaint, April 2, 2001), Rule 1.8(a) of the Indiana Rules of Professional Conduct [applied.] . . .

The Comment to Rule 1.8, as relevant to subsection (a), emphasized the general principle that "all transactions between client and lawyer should be fair and reasonable to the client," and added that, "[i]n such transactions a review by independent counsel on behalf of the client is often advisable." But the Comment also noted an exception:

> Paragraph (a) does not, however, apply to standard commercial transactions between the lawyer and the client for products or services that the client generally markets to others, for example, banking or brokerage services, medical services, products manufactured or distributed by the client, and utilities services. In such transactions, the lawyer has no advantage in dealing with the client, and the restrictions in paragraph (a) are unnecessary and impracticable.

The parties disagree regarding whether their transaction falls within this "standard commercial transaction" exception. The Youngs argue that they fall within the exception because the transaction involves a product and/or service that Liggett, a building contractor, generally markets to others. Liggett contends that it does not apply because the dispute centers on the interpretation of the construction contract drafted by his lawyer, Dean Young.

Regardless whether this transaction does not qualify as a standard commercial transaction and thus subjects Dean Young to the requirements of Rule

1.8(a), the Rules of Professional Conduct have limited application outside of the attorney disciplinary process. . . .

We conclude that . . . there exists an independent common law basis, apart from violation of Rule 1.8, on which a client may seek recourse in damages.

2. Common Law Attorney–Client Fiduciary Duty

Claims involving separate attorney-client transactions have long been governed by principles of Indiana law that guide the resolution of this appeal.

> Indiana case law recognizes that transactions entered into during the existence of a fiduciary relationship are presumptively invalid as the product of undue influence. Transactions between an attorney and client are presumed to be fraudulent, so that the attorney has the burden of proving the fairness and honesty thereof.

This statement of general principle does not endeavor to specifically address standard commercial transactions between a lawyer and a client in which the lawyer does not render legal services. But, parallel to the "standard commercial transaction" exception noted in the Comment to Professional Conduct Rule 1.8, such transactions are likewise generally considered as not subject to the common law prohibition against attorney-client transactions. *See* Section 126 of the Restatement (Third) of The Law Governing Lawyers, particularly comment (c). . . .

The parties' construction contract, however, was in the form of a pre-printed "Building, Construction and No-Lien Agreement" approved by the Indiana State Bar Association, the header of which declared: "the selection of a form of instrument, filling in blank spaces, striking out provisions and insertion of special clauses, constitutes the practice of law and should be done by a lawyer." . . . Dean Young drafted Paragraph 12 of the construction contract . . . [and] . . . at the time the contract was entered, Dean Young was serving "as Liggett's personal attorney." The Youngs did not respond to that assertion in the summary judgment proceeding, and acknowledge that at the time of the contract's execution, Dean Young "was acting as the attorney for Liggett on an unrelated matter." . . .

As a preliminary matter, we observe that Liggett did not, by asserting completion of his obligations under the contract, forego his claim that the construction contract was void due to Dean Young's dual status in the transaction. Of greater significance, however, is that Liggett's claims against the Youngs are for materials and labor not included in the original base construction contract but result instead from additional items that Liggett claims were performed at the Youngs' request. These claims derive from custom language drafted by Young and inserted sub-paragraph (b) in paragraph "12. ADDITIONAL COVENANTS" of the preprinted contract. This sub-paragraph 12(b) states: "(b) Subject to changes which from time to time may be made following construction [sic] between Builders and Owners, and, where necessary, following consultation with Owners' construction/mortgage lenders."

With respect to Liggett's contentions regarding the dual status of Dean Young as both a party to the contract with Liggett and as Liggett's attorney at the time, we conclude that the designated evidence on the Youngs' motion for partial summary judgment did not affirmatively establish the absence of a genuine issue of material fact as to whether, in light of Dean Young's fiduciary relationship as Liggett's attorney, the building contract transaction was fair and honest so as to overcome the common law presumption that the contract was fraudulent. Nor was there designated matter showing that the transaction, the centerpiece of which was a contract allegedly prepared and modified by attorney Dean Young, should as a matter of law be treated as a standard commercial transaction to which the common law presumption did not apply. Under such circumstances, the Youngs are not entitled to partial summary judgment foreclosing Liggett's claims against them. . . .

This cause is remanded to the trial court for resolution of the remaining claims of each party in a manner consistent with this opinion.

BOEHM, Justice, concurring in result.

The dispositive issue in this appeal is whether the contract provision bars Liggett's claim to be compensated for unwritten change orders. I agree with the majority that summary judgment in favor of the Youngs must be reversed, and this case should be remanded for trial.

. . . [T]his case boils down to some familiar and relatively simple points. At a time when Dean Young was acting as Liggett's attorney, the Youngs contracted for Liggett to build their home. Liggett had no separate attorney. Liggett claims that the parties agreed to oral change orders and that a variety of change orders added substantially to the cost of the project. He seeks compensation for those. The Youngs respond to Liggett's claims by invoking the provision in their written contract that prohibited unwritten change orders.

As I see it, this is rather simply resolved without regard to whether the written contract was "void" as "fraudulent" or not "fair and honest." First, this is in my view plainly not a "standard" contract contemplated by the exception to Rule of Professional Responsibility 1.8. That exception is designed to permit ordinary, truly "standard" transactions (e.g., a lawyer who represents a telephone company may get telephone service, and a lawyer who represents a bank may have its credit card). It permits these transactions because they are entered into by many others on the same terms, making them presumptively fair. In any event, except for widely used phone service agreements and the like, the exception applies only if the lawyer-consumer does not draft the contract. This exception does not apply to a unique document prepared by the lawyer in question, which is what we have here, unless the other conditions listed in section 126 of the Restatement (Third) of the Law Governing Lawyers are met. These conditions require that the client (Liggett) be aware of the risks, the terms of the transaction be fair and reasonable to the client, and the client be encouraged to seek independent legal advice. This doctrine is one of substantive law, not one derived, except perhaps tangentially, from the Rules of Professional Responsibility.[6]

---

6. I agree that the Rules of Professional Responsibility do not of themselves create civil liability. The Preamble so provides. But the Preamble also provides that the Rules establish standards of conduct that may be evidence of a breach of the standard of conduct required under other legal doctrines. Although this appears explicitly for the first time in the 2005 Preamble to the Rules, I believe it is a statement of a rule of common law that long predated that preamble and the transactions in this case.

The "transaction" at issue as to Liggett's claims is not the original contract, which on its face seems to me to be relatively ordinary and not "unfair." Rather, the change orders are the "transactions" for which Liggett seeks compensation. The Youngs do not deny that changes were requested, and seek to invoke a provision in the contract Dean Young prepared that requires change requests be in writing. The Youngs thus contend that a change order that they made orally and that caused additional cost to the contractor could be put in place without adjustment of the contractor's compensation. That, on its face, is not "fair and reasonable" to the contractor who is also the client. And if there is any doubt on that point it should be resolved against the attorney who elects to deal with a client. Accordingly, the lawyer is precluded from enforcing this provision against the client. This is simply an application of the basic principle that a fiduciary who deals with his beneficiary must look out for the beneficiary's interests above his own. *See* In re Good, 632 N.E.2d 719, 721 (Ind. 1994) ("Transactions entered into during the existence of a fiduciary relationship are presumptively invalid as the product of undue influence. Transactions between an attorney and client are presumed to be fraudulent, and the attorney has the burden of proving that they were fair and honest.") As I see it, under this doctrine, the Youngs' requesting changes and Dean Young's failure to caution against any changes not in writing leaves any resulting loss in the lawyer's lap, not the client's.

It seems that there is no dispute of material fact that the Youngs requested changes, but the amount of damages, if any, from these changes is not established. Accordingly, if the trier of fact accepts Liggett's contentions that he incurred additional expenses as a result of changes in the home made with the Youngs' prior knowledge after the initial contract, Liggett is entitled to recover the fair compensation attributable to those changes, notwithstanding any provision in the attorney's contract requiring change orders to be in writing. . . .

Lawrence J. Fox
Legal Tender: A Lawyer's Guide to Handling Professional Dilemmas
85-96 (ABA 1995)

It Wasn't the Money

It wasn't the money. He was sure it wasn't the money. Though, if he were honest (heaven knew this was no time not to be honest), that part pleased him, too. But there really had been other factors that had prompted him far more than the money. Peter could remember, as if it had just happened, the sense of pride he felt when he received the telephone call from Edward Frazier, the CEO of Hanscom Industries.

Peter met Ed when Peter was a third-year associate at Caldwell & Moore. Ed, at the time, had just been promoted to Sector Manager in the Life Sciences Division of Hanscom, Caldwell & Moore's third-largest client. Life Sciences was planning a joint venture with a Norwegian pharmaceutical firm, and Ed and he had put together their respective teams to conduct the due diligence, negotiate, and then document the transaction. They had worked literally around the clock, made two trips to Oslo together, and become fast friends.

This first business connection was followed by many others as each of them moved up the ladder at their respective places of employment. Ed was the first non–Caldwell & Moore person to call Peter to congratulate him when he made partner. It was not two years later that Ed became a corporate vice president, the level one had to achieve in order to be awarded the much-sought-after Hanscom Industry stock options under a plan that Peter had established for Hanscom with the help of one of his tax department colleagues.

At the time of the call, Peter had tried to remember how many "deals" he had undertaken for Hanscom—five or six, at least. But nothing had been more significant in his work for Hanscom than when Old Man Taylor had come to Peter in 1984 and told Peter he would, henceforth, be in charge of the Hanscom client relationship for Caldwell & Moore. Taylor had placed his hand on Peter's shoulder, looked him in the eye, and emphasized to Peter how the Hanscom–Caldwell & Moore relationship went back 70 years. It was now Peter's to preserve for the next generation of his firm's lawyers.

From that point forward, Peter had become both the point person to receive calls from key personnel at Hanscom and, within Caldwell & Moore, the distributor of the treasured Hanscom work assignments. Being assigned Hanscom matters was a sure sign to associates that their work was viewed as meeting Caldwell & Moore's rather exalted standards.

In early 1987, Ed Frazier had been elected CEO of Hanscom, and only six months after that, Peter reluctantly accepted the chairmanship of his firm. How ironic his ascendancy to this new position had seemed in light of his many talks with Ed in which Peter lorded over Ed how lucky Peter was to work in an enterprise whose management was shared among all 55 or 60 partners, a principle that elicited a high level of skepticism from Ed. Indeed, Ed had offered his view that, at some point, Caldwell & Moore just wouldn't be able to function in the old way, a thought Peter had dismissed out-of-hand at the time.

In any event, when Peter received the call from Ed, he attached no special significance to it. They talked at least once a month, often on business matters (though at that point each seemed to be presiding more than they were working). But this call was different. "Peter," he started, "The board of directors of Hanscom just met in executive session out here in Hatboro. We had some really tough personnel decisions to make, as you probably know. Your partner Carol really helped us. But that's not why I'm calling. Carol's got that covered, as you would expect. What we want to know, Peter, is whether you would go on the Hanscom board of directors?"

Peter immediately interrupted, "You don't need me on your board. I attend the meetings when you need a lawyer and I send my colleagues when you need someone who really knows the law."

"You're right enough about that," responded Ed, "but we don't want you to join our board as a lawyer. We value your judgment and, frankly, when we searched for a replacement for Reg Stevens, everyone agreed you were the best choice. You know us, you used to know the law and, heaven knows, you're independent, too independent if you ask me."

"Well," Peter gathered himself together, "I am deeply flattered by the offer. I would very much like to do it for you, Ed. Caldwell & Moore, however, has an elaborate policy governing these directorships." Turning to a more delicate subject, Peter continued, "I don't want you to think this is an issue, but what are the director fees, Ed? Under our rules I would get to keep the fees. But I'll have to report them to my compensation committee."

"We pay our directors $50,000 per year, $5,000 per board or committee meeting. You get some stock options, too."

"I guess my partner John Mangas knows what your D & O coverage is. I hope you don't still have that Union American policy. My partners will want to know you have real insurance," Peter responded, thinking at the time that extra money might finance the little Porsche he had been admiring.

But it certainly wasn't just the money. He had been honored that the Hanscom board valued his judgment. He had considered how going on the board would cement the relationship between Caldwell & Moore and this valued client. Those poaching competitor law firms, particularly the New York lawyers selling their expertise as if the Philadelphians were country bumpkins, might, at last, back off once they knew Peter was sitting in the inner sanctum.

But these arguments in favor did not forestall considerable discussion when he breathlessly shared with his fellow partners his good news. His partners were hardly enthusiastically endorsing his acceptance of this offer.

There were certain arguments that were stated openly. Hanscom's stock had been particularly volatile over the years. Caldwell & Moore earned giant fees defending two 10b-5 actions when announcements of negative news had caused the share price to drop. Hanscom engaged in risky lines of business—pharmaceuticals, chain saws. The company was a defendant in Superfund litigation. The reasons that made Hanscom a fascinating client hardly commended it as a company on whose board one would willingly serve.

Then there were the arguments that went unspoken, contained in simply a glance or an avoidance in the halls. Peter could feel the resentment, the sense that he was being too uppity, that the last thing he needed with his exalted partnership share was more income.

In the end, the executive committee had approved his going on the board. The approval meeting went more smoothly than he had expected; whatever else could be said, securing the Hanscom Industries client relationship was a priority. These perilous times cried out for preserving existing clients at almost any cost.

It was only minutes later that Peter called Ed. "Caldwell & Moore is thrilled that you asked me to join," he lied. Then, compensating for his unprincipled characterization of the firm's deliberative process, he reminded Ed that he really didn't think it was important that they nominate him, hoping nonetheless that Ed would stick to his resolve.

Peter soon became a regular in the boardroom. Being a director was a genuine high. Peter got to rub elbows with a cluster of prominent fellow

Philadelphians—the CEO of First Philadelphia Trust, the Provost of the University, and the head of the local NAACP chapter.

The seat on the board also more than fulfilled his firm's expectations that it would cement the Hanscom-Caldwell & Moore relationship. Since all major corporate transactions showed up on the board agenda at an early stage, it became politically impossible for discussion to proceed other than on the assumption that Peter's firm would handle each.

Financially, Peter could hardly believe how well his directorship turned out. The $50,000 not only funded the Porsche, but also gave him a chance to make a substantial contribution to his old prep school. More important, his stock options to purchase 10,000 shares of Hanscom had yielded him a six-figure paper profit. Lawyers in their practice certainly had no way of accumulating capital without creating billable hours; yet this nest egg had been created without a single time sheet entry!

Finally, he enjoyed the challenge of deciding the matters that came to the board. Peter particularly loved the opportunity his board membership gave him to pretend he was a businessman, yes, even an entrepreneur, rather than a staid lawyer who was always telling his business clients why they could not do something.

Maybe he would be forced to acknowledge it was the money. But that thought only increased his pain as he tried to sort out the events that prompted this reminiscence. He never imagined he would find himself at such a juncture of crisis, irritated that at least a few of his partners would now view this as a just reward for his hubris in becoming a director.

Peter recalled that he had been as enthusiastic as anyone with the proposal that Hanscom sell limited-partnership interests in their various resort hotels. The idea of splitting away the expected appreciation in the underlying real estate—appreciation that would get lost in the basic evaluations by the market of the price of Hanscom stock—provided an excellent way for Hanscom to secure a much-needed capital infusion to finance expansion of its other lines of business. It also had the not-undelightful side benefit that all of the resources of Caldwell & Moore's excellent business department would have to be mustered to bring the offering to fruition. The icing on the cake, if you will, was the opportunity this offering provided Peter and his partners to buy these limited-partnership interests at a discount (they had to pay no commission to the underwriters, a fact duly disclosed, and of course universally ignored, in the offering material).

The year of the offering turned out to be a banner year for everyone: Hanscom ended up raising $115 million (to be received across five years); Caldwell & Moore broke firm revenue and profits per partner records; Peter had his highest billings ever.

The board meeting of May 21 was held in the usual location, Aronomink Country Club, away from the neurosis that gripped the headquarters every time these monthly meetings occurred. The agenda gave no hint of what was to come.

It was only when Edward moved to the head of the table that Peter noticed the strain in his face. Edward began, "I think, with your indulgence, I will omit the usual preliminaries. We have a matter to address that is so important I think we will need all the time we have scheduled.

"There is no point in beating about the bush. I received a call yesterday from our local U.S. Attorney, Bill Allan. Bill told me that a grand jury has been investigating M.A.I. Appraisal Company and its president, Marvin Hammer. You will recall that M.A.I. appraised our resort properties in Martha's Vineyard, the two in Maine, Padre Island, the Berkshires, and Cape May in connection with the limited-partnership offering. Bill tells me he has uncovered substantial evidence that M.A.I. received bribes."

"Bribes!" shrieked Jay Harris, the university Provost. "Who could have given him bribes?"

"That's the real problem. Bill tells me it was our own CFO, George Sandel; he even knew the amounts."

"But how could that happen?" Peter numbly asked.

"Well, George, as we all recognize, is in charge of our accounting function. Apparently, he was able to code the payments in such a way that they were lumped in with our commission payments to travel agencies."

"But, why would George do such a thing? He's our most conservative executive. My God, he still wears a pocket liner!" interjected another director.

"I was as incredulous as all of you. It appears George got nervous that the appraisals wouldn't come in high enough. Only George really appreciated how much we needed the cash. So he decided to ensure our success by offering a little extra to Marvin."

"I hate to ask — as if it mattered — but . . . how much?" stuttered Peter.

"Bill claims he's documented $100,000; it may be more," replied Ed.

"No," said Peter, not hiding his rising annoyance, "I mean how much did he overstate the appraised amounts?"

"We really don't know. In fact, we don't know whether they were over-appraised or not. All we know at this point is that Marvin received an extra fee. For all we know, the appraisals are the same as they would have been."

"Spoken like a true lawyer," Peter observed wryly.

"How can we ever replace George?" asked the Provost.

"That's the least of our problems," Ed answered. "Bill sounded like he thought we at Hanscom had hired Marvin because he could be bought. Some snide remarks about M.A.I. meaning 'made as instructed.'"

"Well," Peter began, carefully choosing his words, "wearing my lawyer hat, I can tell you we have one immediate problem. The next annual payments from the limited partners are due June 1. We have to tell them about this before that date."

"Tell them!" bellowed Ed. "We can't tell them. If we don't receive that money on June 1, we'll have no cash to pay Chemical Bank our quarterly interest."

"But you can't have our investors making payments when they don't know about these phony appraisals. Our prospectus made all kinds of representations . . . ."

Ed instantly cut him off. "I should never have let you and your partners buy into that deal. Now all you can think of is saving the partners their money."

"You're missing the point," Peter started.

"I am missing nothing of the kind. We don't even know if the appraisals were wrong. They seemed fair to all of us. I was surprised how high Padre Island came in but . . . " Ed trailed off.

"No, the point is that we raised all that money from investors without telling them our appraiser was receiving bribes . . . from us. The prospectus, the Caldwell & Moore prospectus, omitted a material fact."

"Peter, for all we know that was a harmless error. Now you just sound like a lawyer trying to cover his butt. If the appraisals would have been the same anyway, what difference does it make? There's nothing material about a $100,000 expense in a $115 million transaction."

"There is if it involves fraud. Ed, we better think about how we're going to inform our investors," declared Peter, trying to lower the decibel level.

"Peter, you are a director of this company. You must act in the best interests of the company. And I'm telling you the best interest of Hanscom Industries is to publicize nothing. It is *not* to worry about Caldwell & Moore or our investors. In fact, Peter, if you think your firm can't handle the investigation I propose we undertake, I know three law firms that would be glad to help Hanscom out of this difficulty without compromising their loyalty to us."

Peter was stunned. His old friend Ed had never spoken to him in this way. But the predicament was real enough. He could not sort out the issues as they seemed to turn him upside down like ferocious ocean waves the day after a storm.

Hanscom needed the money, and if the payment were not received, a Chapter XI filing was not unlikely. But the liability to the investors if the prospectus contained an omission was clear. And that liability could run to Caldwell & Moore—his firm had drafted virtually every line of the Registration Statement. Letting the investors make yet one more annual payment after all this was known was the type of fact the plaintiffs' class action bar drooled for.

But what if Ed was right? Did they really have to disclose a harmless error? And what of his partners who would be paying over $800,000 of the June 1 payment? What would they say? Worse, what would his wife say when she heard this investment was in jeopardy, she who had urged him to buy zero-coupon bonds with this money, money earmarked for the kids' college education? She would be *ruthless*.

The rest of the meeting passed as a blur. He was sure he had supported Ed's resolution that a special committee of the board conduct an investigation. He was equally certain that he had agreed Caldwell & Moore would be glad to act as counsel to the committee, since he was now convinced that it was in everyone's interest that the matter be investigated before any action were taken. But did he actually make a speech that it was in the best interests of the investors that the circumstances surrounding the appraisals not be disclosed to them? He wasn't positive, but his cotton-filled cranial cavity suggested such a thought as he found himself talking with his trusted counselor and partner, Harry Gill.

"You won't believe what's happened" were his opening words, as he sought counsel as he had so many times in the past from Harry, everyone's first refuge when the pressure became too much. Harry was smart, he was nonjudgmental, and he could be trusted. After Peter recounted the events at Aronomink, even admitting that he might have said a few foolish things in the panic that he was about to lose his directorship, the firm's biggest client, and his investment as a limited partner, Harry looked heavenward, pressed his fingers to his forehead, and spun his chair around, looking for the longest time out his window, saying nothing. The silence was as palpable as in a Friends meeting, as meaningful as an eloquent speech, telling Peter in no uncertain terms that he had reached some pinnacle in challenging Harry. It was every bit as bad as when a physician told you that he had never seen such a condition before, precisely what you didn't want to hear. And now, sitting behind Harry's back, Harry's silence was exactly what Peter didn't want to hear. Answer me, he thought. Tell me there's a solution.

Finally, Harry slowly turned to face Peter, his voice choked with emotion as he began, "Peter, I don't know what to say. You know I didn't want you to take the directorship. I was even more upset when you and the rest of our partners bought into the resort deal. So I don't want you to think this is an 'I told you so.' But the real problem for me, Peter, and the reason I've taken so long staring out the window at Billy Penn, is that I don't think I can advise you on this. I'm a partner at Caldwell & Moore. Our client is Hanscom Industries. The questions you're asking me go to your role as a director, to Hanscom's duties to its investors, some of whom are my partners. The conflicts of interest diagram is like the path of the struck ball in three-cushion billiards. And that doesn't include the interests of Caldwell & Moore; the firm will very likely end up a defendant in a 10b-5 action, an action whose centerpiece is going to be your board membership and our partners' purchasing of these investment interests."

"I feel sick that I would be forced to even say these words to you. But frankly, the best advice I can give you right now is to call up Alan over at White & Mager. If he has no conflicts, maybe you can gain counsel from him, counsel that would preserve whatever confidentiality you will need, counsel who will represent only you. You better just hope that the Union American policy comes through."

Peter was aghast. In the space of two hours he had been attacked by two of his closest friends. He couldn't consult his own partner. He had to start worrying about liability and insurance and defense.

Of course, as usual, Harry was right. But that fact gave him no comfort. As he rose from the chair, he searched helplessly for the right words. Tears welled up as he avoided eye contact with Harry. He mumbled a hapless thank you and slowly, oh so slowly, left the room, knowing he would be forced to admit it was the money.

2. Gifts, Rights, Loans, and Aggregate Settlements

Problems

10-2. Great business development idea! Martyn & Fox should insert a clause in all of its estate planning documents that appoints a Martyn & Fox lawyer as the fiduciary (executor, administrator, or personal representative) of an estate or trustee of a trust. Then, when Martyn & Fox lawyers act as fiduciary, the fiduciary hires Martyn & Fox as counsel for the trust or estate.

10-3. The client's story is in every newspaper. Front page. But the client is broke. Should Martyn & Fox provide free legal services to this criminal defendant in return for the movie rights to his story?

10-4. The offer is ridiculous. But our client, to survive financially, thinks that she must settle her case now. Should Martyn & Fox pay her living expenses through trial?

10-5. A real tragedy. An automobile accident resulting in the death of Wife and serious injuries to Daughter and Grandmother. Martyn & Fox undertook the representation of Daughter and Grandmother, as well as the Estate of Wife. Defendant's insurer offers policy limits of $1,000,000 to settle all claims. Should Martyn & Fox accept the offer?

Consider: Model Rule 1.8
RLGL §§ 6, 37

Burrow v. Arce
997 S.W.2d 229 (Tex. 1999)

Justice HECHT delivered the opinion of the Court.

The principal question in this case is whether an attorney who breaches his fiduciary duty to his client may be required to forfeit all or part of his fee, irrespective of whether the breach caused the client actual damages. Like the court of appeals, we answer in the affirmative and conclude that the amount of the fee to be forfeited is a question for the court, not a jury. . . .

I

Explosions at a Phillips 66 chemical plant in 1989 killed twenty-three workers and injured hundreds of others, spawning a number of wrongful death and personal injury lawsuits. One suit on behalf of some 126 plaintiffs was filed by five attorneys, David Burrow, Walter Umphrey, John E. Williams, Jr., F. Kenneth Bailey, Jr., and Wayne Reaud, and their law firm, Umphrey, Burrow, Reaud, Williams & Bailey. The case settled for something close to $190 million, out of which the attorneys received a contingent fee of more than $60 million.

Forty-nine of these plaintiffs then filed this suit against their attorneys in the Phillips accident case alleging professional misconduct and demanding forfeiture of all fees the attorneys received. More specifically, plaintiffs alleged that the attorneys, in violation of rules governing their professional conduct, solicited business through a lay intermediary, failed to fully investigate and assess individual claims, failed to communicate offers received and demands made, entered into an aggregate settlement with Phillips of all plaintiffs' claims without plaintiffs' authority or approval, agreed to limit their law practice by not representing others involved in the same incident, and intimidated and coerced their clients into accepting the settlement. Plaintiffs asserted causes of action for breach of fiduciary duty, fraud, violations of the Deceptive Trade Practices—Consumer Protection Act, . . . negligence, and breach of contract. The attorneys have denied any misconduct and plaintiffs' claim for fee forfeiture.

The parties paint strikingly different pictures of the events leading to this suit:

The plaintiffs contend: In the Phillips accident suit, the defendant attorneys signed up plaintiffs en masse to contingent fee contracts, often contacting plaintiffs through a union steward. In many instances the contingent fee percentage in the contract was left blank and 33-1/3% was later inserted despite oral promises that a fee of only 25% would be charged. The attorneys settled all the claims in the aggregate and allocated dollar figures to the plaintiffs without regard to individual conditions and damages. No plaintiff was allowed to meet with an attorney for more than about twenty minutes, and any plaintiff who expressed reservations about the settlement was threatened by the attorney with being afforded no recovery at all.

The defendant attorneys contend: No aggregate settlement or any other alleged wrongdoing occurred, but regardless of whether it did or not, all their clients in the Phillips accident suit received a fair settlement for their injuries, but some were disgruntled by rumors of settlements paid co-workers represented by different attorneys in other suits. After the litigation was concluded, a Kansas lawyer invited the attorneys' former clients to a meeting, where he offered to represent them in a suit against the attorneys for a fee per claim of $2,000 and one-third of any recovery. Enticed by the prospect of further recovery with minimal risk, plaintiffs agreed to join this suit, the purpose of which is merely to extort more money from their former attorneys.

These factual disputes were not resolved in the district court. Instead, the court granted summary judgment for the defendant attorneys on the grounds that the settlement of plaintiffs' claims in the Phillips accident suit was fair and reasonable, plaintiffs had therefore suffered no actual damages as a result of any misconduct by the attorneys, and absent actual damages plaintiffs were not entitled to a forfeiture of any of the attorneys' fees. . . .

The Clients contend that the Attorneys' serious breaches of fiduciary duty require full forfeiture of all their fees, irrespective of whether the breaches caused actual damages, but if not, that a determination of the amount of any lesser forfeiture should be made by a jury rather than the court. The Clients also contend that their lack of actual damages has not been established as a matter of law. The Attorneys argue that no fee forfeiture can be ordered absent proof that the Clients sustained actual damages, but even if it could, no forfeiture should be ordered for the misconduct the Clients allege. . . .

II

At the outset we consider whether the Attorneys have established as a matter of law that the Clients have suffered no actual damages as a result of any misconduct by the Attorneys. . . .

. . . [W]e conclude that the Attorneys failed to establish as a matter of law that the Clients did not suffer actual damages, and thus the Attorneys were not entitled to summary judgment dismissing the Clients' claims on that basis.

III

The Attorneys nevertheless argue that the Clients have not alleged grounds that would entitle them to forfeiture of any of the Attorneys' fees. . . . The Clients counter that whether they sustained actual damages or not, the Attorneys, for breach of their fiduciary duty, should be required to forfeit all fees received, or alternatively, a portion of those fees as may be determined by a jury. These arguments thus raise four issues: (a) are actual damages a prerequisite to fee forfeiture? (b) is fee forfeiture automatic and entire for all misconduct? (c) if not, is the amount of fee forfeiture a question of fact for a jury or one of law for the court? and (d) would the Clients' allegations, if true, entitle them to forfeiture of any or all of the Attorneys' fees? We address each issue in turn.

A

To determine whether actual damages are a prerequisite to forfeiture of an attorney's fee, we look to the jurisprudential underpinnings of the equitable remedy of forfeiture. The parties agree that as a rule a person who renders service to another in a relationship of trust may be denied compensation for his service if he breaches that trust. Section 243 of the Restatement (Second) of Trusts states the rule for trustees: "If the trustee commits a breach of trust, the court may in its discretion deny him all compensation or allow him a reduced compensation or allow him full compensation." Similarly, section 469 of the Restatement (Second) of Agency provides:

> An agent is entitled to no compensation for conduct which is disobedient or which is a breach of his duty of loyalty; if such conduct constitutes a willful and deliberate breach of his contract of service, he is not entitled to compensation even for properly performed services for which no compensation is apportioned.

Citing these two sections, section [37] of the . . . Restatement (Third) of The Law Governing Lawyers applies the same rule to lawyers, who stand in a relation of trust and agency toward their clients. Section [37] states in part: "A lawyer engaging in clear and serious violation of duty to a client may be required to forfeit some or all of the lawyer's compensation for the matter."

Though the historical origins of the remedy of forfeiture of an agent's compensation are obscure, the reasons for the remedy are apparent. The rule is founded both on principle and pragmatics. In principle, a person who agrees to perform compensable services in a relationship of trust and violates that relationship breaches the agreement, express or implied, on which the right to compensation is based. The person is not entitled to be paid when he has not provided the loyalty bargained for and promised. . . . Pragmatically, the possibility of forfeiture of compensation discourages an agent from taking personal advantage of his position of trust in every situation no matter the circumstances, whether the principal may be injured or not. The remedy of forfeiture removes any incentive for an agent to stray from his duty of loyalty based on the possibility that the principal will be unharmed or may have difficulty proving the existence or amount of damages. In other words, as comment b to section [37] of the . . . Restatement (Third) of The Law Governing Lawyers states, "forfeiture is also a deterrent."

To limit forfeiture of compensation to instances in which the principal sustains actual damages would conflict with both justifications for the rule. It is the agent's disloyalty, not any resulting harm, that violates the fiduciary relationship and thus impairs the basis for compensation. An agent's compensation is not only for specific results but also for loyalty. Removing the disincentive of forfeiture except when harm results would prompt an agent to attempt to calculate whether particular conduct, though disloyal to the principal, might nevertheless be harmless to the principal and profitable to the agent. The main purpose of forfeiture is not to compensate an injured principal, even though it may have that effect. Rather, the central purpose of the equitable remedy of forfeiture is to protect relationships of trust by discouraging agents' disloyalty. . . .

The Attorneys nevertheless argue that forfeiture of an attorney's fee without a showing of actual damages encourages breach-of-fiduciary claims by clients to extort a renegotiation of legal fees after representation has been concluded, allowing them to obtain a windfall. The Attorneys warn that such opportunistic claims could impair the finality desired in litigation settlements by leaving open the possibility that the parties, having resolved their differences, can then assert claims against their counsel to obtain more than they could by settlement of the initial litigation. The Attorneys urge that a bright-line rule making actual damages a prerequisite to fee forfeiture is necessary to prevent misuse of the remedy. We disagree. Fee forfeiture for attorney misconduct is not a windfall to the client. An attorney's compensation is for loyalty as well as services, and his failure to provide either impairs his right to compensation. While a client's motives may be opportunistic and his claims meritless, the better protection is not a prerequisite of actual damages but the trial court's discretion to refuse to afford claimants who are seeking to take unfair advantage of their former attorneys the equitable remedy of forfeiture. Nothing in the caselaw in Texas or elsewhere suggests that opportunistically motivated litigation to forfeit an agent's fee has ever been a serious problem. . . .

We therefore conclude that a client need not prove actual damages in order to obtain forfeiture of an attorney's fee for the attorney's breach of fiduciary duty to the client.

B

The Clients argue that an attorney who commits a serious breach of fiduciary duty to a client must automatically forfeit all compensation to the client. . . .

. . . [T]o require an agent to forfeit all compensation for every breach of fiduciary duty, or even every serious breach, would deprive the remedy of its equitable nature and would disserve its purpose of protecting relationships of trust. A helpful analogy, the parties agree, is a constructive trust, of which we have observed:

> Constructive trusts, being remedial in character, have the very broad function of redressing wrong or unjust enrichment in keeping with basic principles of equity and justice. . . . Moreover, there is no unyielding formula to which a court of equity is bound in decreeing a constructive trust, since the equity of the transaction will shape the measure of relief granted.

Like a constructive trust, the remedy of forfeiture must fit the circumstances presented. It would be inequitable for an agent who had performed extensive services faithfully to be denied all compensation for some slight, inadvertent misconduct that left the principal unharmed, and the threat of so drastic a result would unnecessarily and perhaps detrimentally burden the agent's exercise of judgment in conducting the principal's affairs.

The . . . Restatement (Third) of The Law Governing Lawyers rejects a rigid approach to attorney fee forfeiture. Section [37] states:

> A lawyer engaging in clear and serious violation of duty to a client may be required to forfeit some or all of the lawyer's compensation for the matter. In determining whether and to what extent forfeiture is appropriate, relevant considerations include the gravity and timing of the violation, its wilfulness, its effect on the value of the lawyer's work for the client, any other threatened or actual harm to the client, and the adequacy of other remedies.

The remedy is restricted to "clear and serious" violations of duty. Comment d to section [37] explains: "A violation is clear if a reasonable lawyer, knowing the relevant facts and law reasonably accessible to the lawyer, would have known that the conduct was wrongful." The factors for assessing the seriousness of a violation, and hence "whether and to what extent forfeiture is appropriate," are set out in the rule. . . . Comment a states: "A lawyer is not entitled to be paid for services rendered in violation of the lawyer's duty to a client, or for services needed to alleviate the consequences of the lawyer's misconduct." And comment e observes: "Ordinarily, forfeiture extends to all fees for the matter for which the lawyer was retained . . . . " But comment e adds: "Sometimes forfeiture for the entire matter is inappropriate, for example when a lawyer performed valuable services before the misconduct began, and the misconduct was not so grave as to require forfeiture of the fee for all services." And comment b expands on the necessity for exercising discretion in applying the remedy:

> Forfeiture of fees, however, is not justified in each instance in which a lawyer violates a legal duty, nor is total forfeiture always appropriate. Some violations are inadvertent or do not significantly harm the client. Some can be adequately

dealt with by the remedies described in Comment a or by a partial forfeiture (see Comment e). Denying the lawyer all compensation would sometimes be an excessive sanction, giving a windfall to a client. The remedy of this Section should hence be applied with discretion. . . .

Section [37] sets out considerations similar to those for trustees in applying the remedy of fee forfeiture to attorneys. . . . The several factors embrace broad considerations which must be weighed together and not mechanically applied. For example, the "willfulness" factor requires consideration of the attorney's culpability generally; it does not simply limit forfeiture to situations in which the attorney's breach of duty was intentional. The adequacy-of-other-remedies factor does not preclude forfeiture when a client can be fully compensated by damages. Even though the main purpose of the remedy is not to compensate the client, if other remedies do not afford the client full compensation for his damages, forfeiture may be considered for that purpose.

To the factors listed in section [37] we add another that must be given great weight in applying the remedy of fee forfeiture: the public interest in maintaining the integrity of attorney-client relationships. . . . The Attorneys' argument that relief for attorney misconduct should be limited to compensating the client for any injury suffered ignores the main purpose of the remedy. . . .

Accordingly, we conclude that whether an attorney must forfeit any or all of his fee for a breach of fiduciary duty to his client must be determined by applying the rule as stated in section [37] of the proposed Restatement (Third) of The Law Governing Lawyers and the factors we have identified to the individual circumstances of each case.

C

The parties agree that the determination whether to afford the remedy of forfeiture must be made by the court. The Clients argue, however, that they are entitled to have the amount of the forfeiture set by a jury. The Attorneys argue, and the court of appeals held, that the amount of any forfeiture is also an issue to be decided by the court.

Forfeiture of an agent's compensation, we have already explained, is an equitable remedy similar to a constructive trust. As a general rule, a jury "does not determine the expediency, necessity, or propriety of equitable relief." Consistent with the rule, whether a constructive trust should be imposed must be determined by a court based on the equity of the circumstances. However, when contested fact issues must be resolved before equitable relief can be determined, a party is entitled to have that resolution made by a jury.

These same principles apply in deciding whether to forfeit all or part of an agent's compensation. Thus, for example, a dispute concerning an agent's culpability—whether he acted intentionally, with gross negligence, recklessly, or negligently, or was merely inadvertent—may present issues for a jury, as may disputes about the value of the agent's services and the existence and amount of any harm to the principal. But factors like the adequacy of other remedies and the public interest in protecting the integrity of the attorney-client relationship, as well as the weighing of all other relevant considerations, present legal policy issues well beyond the jury's province of judging credibility and resolving factual disputes. The ultimate decision on the amount of any fee forfeiture must be made by the court. . . .

Thus, when forfeiture of an attorney's fee is claimed, a trial court must determine from the parties whether factual disputes exist that must be decided by a jury before the court can determine whether a clear and serious violation of duty has occurred, whether forfeiture is appropriate, and if so, whether all or only part of the attorney's fee should be forfeited. Such factual disputes may include, without limitation, whether or when the misconduct complained of occurred, the attorney's mental state at the time, and the existence or extent of any harm to the client. If the relevant facts are undisputed, these issues may, of course, be determined by the court as a matter of law. Once any necessary factual disputes have been resolved, the court must determine, based on the factors we have set out, whether the attorney's conduct was a clear and serious breach of duty to his client and whether any of the attorney's compensation should be forfeited, and if so, what amount. Most importantly, in making these determinations the court must consider whether forfeiture is necessary to satisfy the public's interest in protecting the attorney-client relationship. The court's decision whether to forfeit any or all of an attorney's fee is subject to review on appeal as any other legal issue.

▀ The Law Governing Lawyers:
Loss of Fee or Other Benefits

In *Burrow,* the Supreme Court of Texas explains the jurisprudential underpinnings of another equitable remedy for breaches of fiduciary duty: fee forfeiture. In *Liggett,* the Indiana Supreme Court granted a similar remedy: rescission of a transaction with a client, with concomitant loss of benefits to the lawyer. Both courts also cite the Rules of Professional Conduct, which restate basic fiduciary duties. In this note, we examine some of the details of these well-established remedies to understand their relationship to other legal and equitable remedies provided to clients whose lawyers breach fiduciary duties.

Loss of Contractual Benefits

Lawyer-agents who breach duties of obedience, loyalty, or confidentiality lose their entitlement to fees or other contractual rights because they have violated a basic fiduciary duty essential to the contract. In refusing to enforce such contracts, *Liggett* illustrates that agency rules, such as a presumption of undue influence, require close scrutiny of business transactions between lawyers and clients to give lawyers incentives to preserve fiduciary duties. Similarly, the *Burrow* court typifies the view that the fee forfeiture remedy should be provided both for breaches of fiduciary duty to a particular client and to deter similar conduct in other cases.

Either or both of these remedies can arise as a defensive response when a lawyer sues a client to obtain what would otherwise be a contractual entitlement, such as an unpaid fee, or other benefit, such as Young's counterclaim for damages under the building contract that Young drafted. *Burrow* points out that clients can seek the benefit of such remedies on their own as well. If the fee has already been paid, or the contractual benefit has already been provided, the client can seek return of the benefit through other equitable remedies such as a constructive trust or fee forfeiture.[1] One example involves civil actions to order lawyers or other agents to account for, return, or hold in constructive trust specific property acquired because of the improper use of confidential information.[2] Lawyers who breach fiduciary duties also may be ordered to disgorge profits to the client.[3]

Fee Forfeiture

Although *Burrow* represents a contemporary example of the usefulness of fee forfeiture, the remedy itself, like the constructive trust, is quite old. In a bankruptcy case, Judge Learned Hand traced the lawyer's duty not to represent opposing interests back three centuries, and found that the usual consequence of doing so had been that the lawyer was "debarred from receiving any fee from either, no matter how successful his labors."[4] *Burrow* represents the well-settled view that the forfeiture that follows from breach of the contract does not require proof of other damages and may overlap with other legal remedies.

We have already seen examples of legal relief available to clients who can prove that a lawyer's breach of fiduciary duty caused them harm. For example, Dr. dePape was able to show that his lawyers' failure to inform him about legal options caused him $278,760 in lost income and emotional distress. If pled, he also could have been entitled to punitive damages.[5] Similarly, Mr. Perez was able to state a claim for emotional distress damages due to his lawyers' breach of confidentiality. Both of these clients could have sought fee forfeiture as well, but neither did, probably because third parties paid the fees in their cases.

Further, liability insurance would certainly cover a damage award, but rarely will be available to pay a fee forfeiture award. The Minnesota Supreme Court has analogized fee forfeiture to cases about punitive damages and concluded that the availability of insurance to cover a lawyer's individual breach of fiduciary duty was contrary to public policy, but that coverage for a law firm's vicarious

---

1. When a client seeks a forfeiture of fees already paid, courts sometimes refer to the remedy as "fee disgorgement."

2. RLGL § 6, Comments d, e.

3. *See, e.g.,* In re Estate of Corriea, 719 A.2d 1234 (D.C. App. 1998) (disgorgement of profits insurable as damages, but insurer could justify refusal of coverage if it proved that the lawyer intended to deceive the client by not disclosing his conflict of interest).

4. Silbiger v. Prudence Bonds Corp., 180 F.2d 917, 920 (2d Cir. 1950) (citing cases). *See also* Woods v. City Natl. Bank & Trust Co. of Chic., 312 U.S. 262 (1941).

5. *See also* Anderson v. O'Brien, *supra* p. 324.

responsibility was not.[6] This means that an insurer will be required to pay the fee forfeiture award on behalf of a law firm, but the law firm can seek indemnity against the errant lawyer who breached a fiduciary duty to the client.[7]

Clear and Serious Violations

Although clients do not have to prove causation or actual damages to be entitled to fee forfeiture, they do have to prove a clear and serious violation of a duty owed the client. Breaches of the core agency duties of obedience,[8] disclosure, confidentiality, and loyalty usually qualify, although the source of the duty can be civil law (for example, legal malpractice) or criminal law (for example, fraud) as well.[9] Most common are violations of conflicts of interest obligations[10], such as representing a client's wife in a divorce,[11] failing to disclose that the law firm employed the opposing party's adjuster,[12] or pressuring a client to change a fee contract,[13] all of which evidence clear disloyalty.

The duty breached also must be clear and serious enough to justify fee forfeiture. *Burrow* adopts the Restatement factors to determine whether the breach constituted a clear and serious violation. The first factor, whether the violation was "clear," is determined by an objective standard: whether "a reasonable lawyer, knowing the relevant facts and law reasonably accessible to the lawyer, would have known that the conduct was wrongful."[14] For example, Model Rule 1.8(g)'s regulation of aggregate settlements means that the lawyers in *Burrow* would not be able to claim that they had no idea such a rule existed. The second factor, whether the violation was "serious," can be demonstrated in a number of ways. Some courts hold that a serious breach of duty can be shown only if the client was harmed.[15] *Burrow* represents the modern view, that harm is not necessary so long as the breach of a duty is otherwise clear and serious, such as a representation under a conflict of interest.[16] Isolated, inadvertent breaches, such

---

6. Perl v. St. Paul Fire & Marine Ins. Co., 345 N.W.2d 209 (Minn. 1984).

7. *Id.* at 216-217.

8. Francisco v. Foret, 2002 Tex. App. LEXIS 2610.

9. RLGL § 37, Comment c.

10. Rodriguez v. Disner, 2012 U.S. App. LEXIS 16698 (9th Cir.) (class action fees denied due to conflict of interest created by sliding-scale incentive agreement with class representatives).

11. Jeffry v. Pounds, 136 Cal. Rptr. 373 (Cal. App. 1977).

12. Rice v. Perl, 320 N.W.2d 407 (Minn. 1982).

13. Searcy, Denney, Scarola, Barnhart & Shipley, P.A. v. Scheller, 629 So. 2d 947 (Fla. App. 1993).

14. RLGL § 37, Comment d. *See, e.g.,* Hardison v. Weinshel, 450 F. Supp. 721 (E.D. Wis. 1978) (lawyer who withdrew from case shortly before trial because he mistakenly believed that client would not prevail forfeits all fees).

15. *See, e.g.,* Sealed Party v. Sealed Party, 2006 U.S. Dist. LEXIS 28392 (S.D. Tex.); Frank v. Bloom, 634 F.2d 1245 (10th Cir. 1980); Crawford v. Logan, 656 S.W.2d 360 (Tenn. 1983); Burk v. Burzynski, 672 P.2d 419 (Wyo. 1983).

16. *See, e.g.,* Hendry v. Pelland, 73 F.3d 397 (D.C. Cir. 1996) (lawyers represented property owners with conflicting interests); In re Eastern Sugar Antitrust Litig., 697 F.2d 524 (3d Cir. 1982) (law firm failed to disclose merger negotiations with opposing party's firm); Jackson v. Griffith, 421 So. 2d 677 (Fla. App. 1982) (lawyer coerced client to sign fee contract).

as the failure to explain fully the terms of a settlement when the trial judge in fact explained them to the client, do not rise to the level of a clear and serious breach.[17]

Multiple breaches in the same case are much more likely to qualify. For example, in a Texas case following *Burrow*, a law firm succeeded in getting a client a $56 million divorce settlement, even though she had signed a prenuptial agreement that limited her to about $12 million.[18] Along the way, the firm charged an unjustified contingent fee and changed the fee contract after the representation was underway, all the while knowing that the client's "alcohol and prescription drug problem impaired her ability to agree to the amount of attorney fees."[19] One of the lawyers pursued a romantic relationship with the client that included his acceptance of expensive gifts and use of her credit card. When the client disputed some of the fees, the lawyers failed to keep the disputed portion in a trust account until the dispute was resolved. The court concluded that the serious breaches of duty to the client "did not affect the value of their legal work but would have if the underlying case had not settled," and ordered forfeiture of the $3 million fee.[20]

Total or Partial Forfeiture

When the client has shown a clear and serious breach, *Burrow* relies on the Restatement of the Law Governing Lawyers for the proposition that, normally, fee forfeiture will be total.[21] The court eschews an absolute rule of total forfeiture in all cases, recognizing that other courts have imposed partial fee forfeiture when the misconduct can be separated in time from other valuable services the lawyer has performed. The court cites other factors as well, including the willfulness of the violation, its effect on the client, and the adequacy of other remedies. It then adds a final factor to be given great weight: "the public interest in maintaining the integrity of attorney-client relationships." The court avoids, however, the question of burden of proof. The most logical view seems to be that the client must show the clear and serious breach, at which point total forfeiture is presumed. The burden of proof then shifts to the lawyer to justify less than full forfeiture, by establishing the value of the service rendered apart from the breach.[22] Such an approach parallels the reasoning in *Young*, where the court presumed undue influence because of the lawyer's self-dealing and then shifted

---

17. Hoover v. Larkin, 2001 Tex. App. LEXIS 6313.

18. Angela Ward, *Arce Jeopardizes Family Lawyers' Fee; Jury Awards 6.3 Million Verdict for Breach of Fiduciary Duty,* Texas Lawyer 16 (Nov. 15, 1999).

19. Piro v. Sarofim, 80 S.W.3d 717 (Tex. App. 2002).

20. *Id.* The court also upheld the trial judge's finding that the $6 million verdict, half for compensatory damages and half for fee forfeiture, was made in the alternative, but it added that "the trial court could have rendered judgment against the lawyers on both awards without creating a double recovery." *Id.* at 21.

21. RLGL § 37, Comment e.

22. *See* RLGL § 42(2).

the burden of proof to the lawyer to establish that the transaction was indeed reasonable and fair.

How might these factors play out on remand in *Burrow*? First, note that the aggregate settlement rule that the law firm allegedly breached is a longstanding loyalty rule that protects each client's right to individualized fiduciary duties. If the rule were violated, it is possible that the court could impose total fee forfeiture regardless of the lack of demonstrable harm to the clients. However, it is also possible that the law firm provided valuable services to each client up until the point of settlement. Suppose, for example, that the firm vigorously developed the liability issues in the case and worked up the damage claims of each client individually. It is hardly far-fetched to think that this work prompted the settlement negotiations, which otherwise would not have occurred. At that point, the breach of the aggregate settlement rule, although still a serious matter, might be viewed as less of a breach of all duties owed during the total representation. On the other hand, if the law firm did little of this work and the defendant conceded liability, the breach appears nearly total.

Thus, where the breach of fiduciary duty permeates the entire relationship, the grounds for total fee forfeiture are found.[23] This explains why so many of the full forfeiture cases involve conflicts of interest that tainted the entire representation. On the other hand, where the conflict arises during the representation, the lawyer may be reimbursed for services provided before he should have responded to the conflict.[24] Because so much is unknown and disputed in *Burrow*, the court properly remands for additional development of the facts.

Statutory Fee Forfeiture

Fee forfeiture can occur pursuant to statute as well.[25] Most prominent are criminal statutes that provide for forfeiture of the fruits of criminal activity, including lawyer's fees.[26] Of course, lawyers who know that their clients are paying them with the fruits of the crime also risk other criminal penalties, such as aiding and abetting the crime or receiving stolen property.[27] Forfeiture statutes provide for civil forfeiture of the client's funds traceable to criminal activity, on the theory that they passed to the government at the time of the crime.[28] The government can seize all assets of a defendant at the point of indictment on a showing of

---

23. *E.g.*, Chen v. Chen Qualified Settlement Fund, 552 F.3d 218 (2d Cir. 2009) (lawyer who requested an excessive fee in violation of Rule of Professional Conduct and did not provide adequate documentation to court forfeits entire fee despite successful result in medical malpractice case).

24. *E.g.*, Hill v. Douglas, 271 So. 2d 1 (Fla. 1971) (lawyer did not forfeit fee until he should have known he would be a witness).

25. *See, e.g.*, Federal Trade Comm'n v. Network Services Depot Inc., 617 F.3d 1127 (9th Cir. 2010) (lawyer who failed to diligently review source of client's flat fee was willfully ignorant that funds were derived from client's fraudulent activities and must surrender most of fee to a constructive trust designed to benefit fraud victims).

26. *E.g.*, 21 U.S.C. §§ 848, 853 (2006).

27. *See* The Bounds of the Law: *Criminal Conduct, supra* p. 270.

28. *See* Geoffrey C. Hazard & W. William Hodes, *The Law of Lawyering* § 9.32 (2002).

probable cause to believe that the assets will ultimately be found to be subject to forfeiture.[29] If the criminal case determines that the assets are the proceeds of the crime, they are permanently forfeited to the government, but the statute exempts a "bona fide purchaser for value" of property otherwise subject to forfeiture. [30]

The Supreme Court has held that these statutes are intended to reach lawyer's fees, as well as other assets of the defendant, and that using this statutory power to freeze cash paid to a lawyer does not violate a client's rights.[31] The Court was not persuaded by the argument that this meant that some defendants would be deprived of counsel of their choice. The majority pointed out that the Sixth Amendment guaranteed them a lawyer but gave them no constitutional right "to spend another person's money" for such services. If no untainted sources of money could be found to retain private counsel, appointed counsel would suffice.[32] The practical reality created by these cases is that a lawyer retained by a defendant in a matter in which such a statute applies takes on the risk of nonpayment. Courts also have held that lawyers must essentially audit the source of the client's money to ensure payment.[33]

Overlapping Remedies

Courts have created different equitable remedies to fill gaps in legal relief. Occasionally, these remedies overlap, allowing a client to seek several in the same case. For example, *Burrow* leaves open the possibility of breach of fiduciary duty tort damages in addition to fee forfeiture.[34] Courts also have ordered fee forfeiture as part of a disciplinary sanction.[35] A former client who succeeded in disqualifying his former lawyer from representing his wife in a divorce also was entitled to reversal of the trial court's order to pay his wife's attorney fees.[36] The client later filed a grievance as well, which resulted in a public reprimand

---

29. United States v. Monsanto, 924 F.2d 1186 (2d Cir. 1991) (en banc).

30. A "bona fide purchaser for value" is a person who "was reasonably without cause to believe that the property was subject to forfeiture" when he took the property. 21 U.S.C. § 853(c) (2006).

31. Caplin & Drysdale v. United States, 491 U.S. 617 (1989); United States v. Monsanto, 491 U.S. 600 (1989).

32. *Id.* at 626.

33. *See, e.g.,* United States v. McCorkle, 321 F.3d 1292 (11th Cir. 2002) (burden of proof on lawyer F. Lee Bailey to identify the portion of the fee collected while he was a bona fide purchaser for value).

34. *See also Hendry, supra* note 15; *Piro, supra* note 18.

35. Fla. Bar v. Rodriguez, 959 So. 2d 150 (Fla. 2007) (lawyer suspended for two years and ordered to disgorge fee to client who was the victim of a conflict of interest); Fla. Bar v. St. Louis, 2007 Fla. LEXIS 762 (companion case, lawyer disbarred and ordered to disgorge fee).

36. Ennis v. Ennis, 276 N.W.2d 341 (Wis. 1979). *See also* Newton v. Newton, 955 N.E. 2d 572 (Ill. App. 2011) (law firm that represented wife in divorce after husband consulted with same firm in same matter tainted by conflict of interest that voided entire fee agreement with wife, following disqualification of the firm); Image Tech. Serv. v. Eastman Kodak Co., 136 F.3d 1354 (9th Cir. 1998) (former client not entitled to attorney fees under Clayton Act for work done by lawyer who was later disqualified).

of the lawyer.[37] In an analogous case claiming fee forfeiture under a federal statute, the court disqualified the law firm due to the defendant's statement that he wanted to plead guilty, but could not because such a plea would jeopardize the $103,000 fee he had already paid his lawyer. Following disqualification, the court also ordered fee forfeiture, including a state common law conversion action to recover the money the firm had already spent.[38]

One issue that commonly arises is whether a law firm that defends its own disqualification motion can charge its current client for the defense.[39] If the firm is disqualified, the client might have a partial or complete defense to the payment of legal fees.[40] Such a client also may seek disgorgement of a fee already paid.

Together, the common law agency remedies of fee forfeiture and other loss of contractual benefits, as well as statutes that accomplish the same result, create minefields for unwary lawyers. You can avoid the common law remedies by honoring your fiduciary obligations, including duties of obedience, disclosure, confidentiality, and loyalty.

3. Significant Lawyer Personal Interests

Problems

10-6. We blew it. Don't know how but we did. Martyn & Fox failed to file a client's case within the appropriate statute of limitations. Must Martyn sit down with the client, confess her error, and offer to pay the entire amount of the underlying claims?

10-7. Client tells Martyn & Fox that he is strapped for cash and cannot afford our requested retainer in a divorce case. Martyn & Fox, at Fox's suggestion, has Client sign a promissory note secured by a mortgage on the family home in lieu of the retainer.

10-8. Martyn & Fox represents Big Bank in a wide variety of matters. A colleague tells Fox at lunch, "Did you hear the latest? Sarah Snyder [an associate at Martyn & Fox] is dating the General Counsel of Big Bank. How's that for cementing our relationship?"

10-9. Martyn & Fox represents Acme Corp. in contested litigation against Zenon, Inc. Our senior associate wants to assume a major role in the case, even though he is married to the lead lawyer for Zenon. He says it'll be a great challenge.

Consider: Model Rules 1.7, 1.8, 1.10
RLGL §§ 125, 127

---

37. In re Conway, 301 N.W.2d 253 (Wis. 1981).
38. United States v. Moffitt, Zwerling, & Kemler, P.C., 83 F.3d 660 (4th Cir. 1996), *cert. denied,* 519 U.S. 1101 (1997).
39. Some clients in this position agree to defend the action, but at the law firm's own expense. *See, e.g.,* Padco v. Kinney & Lange, 444 N.W.2d 889 (Minn. App. 1989).
40. *See, e.g.,* In re Bonneville Pacific Corp., 196 B.R. 868 (D. Utah 1996); Goldstein v. Lees, 120 Cal. Rptr. 253 (Cal. App. 1975).

Iowa Supreme Court Attorney Disciplinary Board v. Monroe
784 N.W.2d 784 (Iowa 2010)

TERNUS, Chief Justice.

The complainant, Iowa Supreme Court Attorney Disciplinary Board, filed charges against the respondent, William Monroe, alleging he engaged in a sexual relationship with a client in violation of the Iowa Rules of Professional Conduct. . . .

III. Factual Findings

Monroe was admitted to practice law in Iowa in 1998. In 2007 he was retained by Doe to represent her in a dissolution proceeding that included a child custody issue. Monroe was acquainted with Doe, having represented her in a prior legal matter. In late May 2007, Monroe and Doe commenced a sexual relationship. Monroe continued to represent Doe, and after various misdemeanor criminal charges were filed against Doe in the summer of 2007, Monroe represented her in those matters as well.

The intimate relationship between Monroe and his client ended in mid-August 2007 by mutual agreement. Doe decided she was not interested in having a serious relationship at that time. In addition, they both recognized that their relationship might be detrimental to Doe in the dissolution action and may interfere with Monroe's representation of Doe.

Doe testified at the hearing before the commission, and we find, that she was not coerced by Monroe to engage in an intimate relationship with him, that there was no understanding or anticipation that her attorney fees would be reduced by virtue of their relationship, and that she felt it was her own decision to be in or out of the relationship. Doe harbors no ill will toward Monroe and continues to regard him as a good friend upon whom she can call in times of need.[2]

Eventually, Doe's husband became aware of his wife's relationship with Monroe. He told his attorney, who then reported the situation to the disciplinary authorities in the fall of 2007, resulting in the filing of the charges at issue here.

The attorney representing Doe's husband also contacted the assistant county attorney to share his concerns regarding Monroe's relationship with Doe. The assistant county attorney told Monroe what she had heard and suggested that Monroe should not represent Doe in the criminal matters. Although Monroe withdrew from the dissolution case in early fall 2007, he continued to represent Doe in the criminal matters until they were resolved in October 2007. Even though Monroe no longer represented Doe in the dissolution matter, he periodically injected himself into that case through phone calls to Doe's new attorney

---

2. Doe testified that she and Monroe "were friends before, friends during, and friends after — now."

regarding suggestions and information pertinent to the dissolution proceeding. After Doe was billed for her new attorney's conversations with Monroe, Doe asked Monroe to refrain from contacting her new attorney.

As previously stated, Monroe admitted in the disciplinary case that he had a sexual relationship with Doe. . . .

IV. Ethical Violations

. . . Monroe seems to suggest in his answer that his relationship with Doe was not improper with respect to the public intoxication case because their intimate relationship predated his representation of her on that matter. This suggestion indicates Monroe may misperceive the charges against him. . . .

Monroe's sexual relationship with his client was not legitimized once he withdrew from representing her in the dissolution matter. Rule . . . 1.8(j) provides: "A lawyer shall not have sexual relations with a client . . . unless the person is the spouse of the lawyer or the sexual relationship predates the *initiation* of the client-lawyer relationship." (Emphasis added.) Monroe's client-lawyer relationship with Doe commenced in the spring of 2007. He did not have sexual relations with her until late May 2007. Therefore, the rule's exception for sexual relationships that predate the client-lawyer relationship does not apply here. Monroe's intimate relationship with Doe violated rule . . . 1.8(j) for the entire period it existed because their client-lawyer relationship predated their sexual relationship and Doe continued to be his client during the time they were intimately involved. . . .

V. Sanction

"There is no standard sanction for a particular type of misconduct, and though prior cases can be instructive, we ultimately determine an appropriate sanction based on the particular circumstances of each case." In determining a suitable sanction for an attorney's ethical violations,

> we consider the nature and extent of the respondent's ethical infractions, his fitness to continue practicing law, our obligation to protect the public from further harm by the respondent, the need to deter other attorneys from engaging in similar misconduct, our desire to maintain the reputation of the bar as a whole, and any aggravating or mitigating circumstances.

We think two of these considerations mandate a suspension here: the nature of the ethical infraction and the need to deter other attorneys from engaging in similar misconduct.

Monroe had a sexual relationship with his client that spanned several weeks. There is no gray area with respect to the prohibition of such conduct, no nuance subject to differing interpretations. Therefore, the ethical violation is obvious and should have been obvious to Monroe before he engaged in sex with his client.

This type of misconduct also clearly jeopardizes the client's interests. *See* Iowa R. Prof'l Conduct 1.8(j) cmt. [17] (discussing dangers posed by attorney's sexual relationship with client). The fact that the misconduct occurred while Monroe represented Doe in a dissolution action and in criminal matters is an aggravating circumstance because clients are particularly vulnerable under these circumstances, and the possibility of harm, especially when child custody matters are at stake, is high.[3] *See* 1 Restatement (Third) of the Law Governing Lawyers § 16, cmt. *e* (1998) ("A lawyer may not . . . enter a sexual relationship with a client when that would undermine a client's case, abuse the client's dependence on the lawyer, or create risk to the lawyer's independent judgment, for example, when the lawyer represents the client in a divorce proceeding."). Moreover, Monroe failed to recognize the potential for harm as evidenced by his continuing representation of Doe after their sexual relationship commenced. Finally, Doe suffered from situational depression in reaction to her marital situation, further affecting her capacity to make good choices for herself.[4] It is important to deter other attorneys in similar circumstances from putting their own self-interest ahead of those of the client, the very antithesis of a lawyer's professional duty.

On the other hand, the situation presented by the facts of this case is less egregious than we have encountered with respect to other violations of rule 32:1.8(j). *See, e.g., Marzen,* 779 N.W.2d at 768-69 (finding attorney's sexual relationship with extremely vulnerable client, whom he represented in an involuntary commitment proceeding, warranted six-month suspension); *Morrison,* 727 N.W.2d at 119-20 (imposing three-month suspension on attorney who engaged in sexual relationship with client after he had been previously admonished for making sexual advances toward another client); *McGrath,* 713 N.W.2d at 703-04 (concluding three-year suspension was warranted for attorney who preyed upon dissolution client's vulnerability by obtaining sex in exchange for legal services and who had attempted to do so with another dissolution client); *Furlong,* 625 N.W.2d at 713-14 (imposing eighteen-month suspension on attorney who performed "uninvited and unwelcome" sex acts on client and sexually harassed at least two other clients by making unwanted sexually motivated physical contact with them). In the present case, the misconduct appears to be an isolated occurrence, there being no evidence that Monroe had engaged in similar transgressions in the past. In addition, Monroe's conduct was not predatory, Doe felt she entered the relationship voluntarily and that Monroe had not taken advantage of her, and Doe has seemingly suffered no emotional harm

---

3. We note there was no proof Monroe's sexual relationship with Doe impacted the child custody dispute between Doe and her husband. The board merely argues "the relationship *could have had* negative repercussions on Ms. Doe's custody of her child." (Emphasis added.)

4. Doe had been treated in the past for other mental health problems, but there is no evidence these past problems were active at the time in question or had any influence on Doe's capacity for good decision-making.

from the relationship.[5] We agree with the commission's observation that Monroe "genuinely wanted to assist Ms. Doe, [but] lost sight of the ethical boundaries" governing his relationship with his client. In addition, as the commission noted, Monroe had his own "emotional/personality weaknesses/vulnerabilities."

We also consider Monroe's "fitness to continue practicing law" and "our obligation to protect the public from further harm" by this attorney. Clearly, Monroe needs a better understanding of his ethical obligations, the vulnerability of clients under the stress of a dissolution or facing criminal charges, and the impact a sexual relationship between him and his client has on his client and his own ability to professionally represent that client. Without this knowledge, Monroe poses a risk to the public. We also note, however, that Monroe has contributed a significant amount of time to the representation of clients on a pro bono basis. In addition, members of the bar and of the judiciary testified at the hearing that, other than the matter that brought Monroe to the attention of the disciplinary authorities, he has practiced in an ethical fashion. Taking all of the pertinent factors into consideration, we concur in the commission's recommendation that Monroe's license to practice law in this state be suspended for thirty days.

The commission also recommended that Monroe's license not be reinstated until he has furnished "evidence that he has completed counseling (at his expense), which counseling is focused on [his] current lack of appreciation for how his behavior with Jane Doe was wrong." Shortly before submission of this matter to our court on May 19, 2010, Monroe filed a report from a mental health counselor whom he has been seeing on a weekly basis since February 2010. (Monroe had previously been a client of the same professional when he suffered from depression in 2004.) The counselor stated that she has "identified and processed at length" with Monroe "the issues of unequal power in a relationship with a [p]rofessional," including "the serious repercussions and the risk of harm, both mentally and emotionally, to a client who is in a vulnerable state." The counselor opined that Monroe was keenly aware of the ramifications of such a relationship and had resolved not to let it happen again. She stated she has worked with Monroe to "set up guidelines within his thinking and also within his office to prevent any future reoccurrence."

We are satisfied the May report from Monroe's counselor provides sufficient verification that Monroe has addressed the matters leading to his unethical behavior. Therefore, we decline to require any additional counseling prior to reinstatement. . . .

We suspend Monroe's license to practice law for thirty days. . . .

---

5. Doe was being treated for her situational depression during the time in question, but the board introduced no evidence from Doe or her therapist that Doe's relationship with Monroe adversely affected Doe's mental or emotional state. The only harm shown in the record was attorney fees incurred by Doe that were attributable to Monroe's contact with Doe's new attorney.

C.   Client and Third-Person Interests

Problems

10-10.   Fox is an estate lawyer. One day, he receives a visit from an agitated 50ish man who says, "I need some help for Dad. It is too hard for Dad to travel downtown these days. He needs to change his will to make sure his grandchildren's education is paid for." What should Fox do?

10-11.   Martyn & Fox is hired by Insurance Company to represent several of its insureds.

   (a) Who is our client?

   (b) Can Insurance Company tell Martyn & Fox how many depositions to take? Whether and when to hire an expert witness? What motions to file? To send bills to an outside auditing company for review?

   (c) In the course of investigating our first case, Fox comes across a confidential medical file stating that the insured was told by his physician to stop driving because of his Parkinson's disease. The insured's policy includes standard language that excludes coverage for drivers who have certain medical conditions. What should Fox do with this information?

   (d) The plaintiff's complaint in our second case demands $300,000 in damages resulting from an auto accident. Plaintiff offers to settle the case for the policy limits of $100,000, but Insurance Company tells Martyn, "We'd rather pay you to litigate this case than settle with that malingerer." What should Martyn do?

   (e) In our third case, the insured is a physician accused of medical malpractice. Plaintiff offers to settle well within policy limits, and Insurance Company agrees, but the physician refuses, saying, "Settling this case will destroy my professional reputation." Insurance Company directs Fox to settle. What should Fox do?

Consider: Model Rules 1.7, 1.8(f), 1.14, 5.4(c)
            RLGL § 134

Paradigm Insurance Co. v. The Langerman Law Offices, P.A.

24 P.3d 593 (Ariz. 2001)

FELDMAN, J.

The ultimate question in this case is whether an attorney may be held liable to an insurer, which assigned him to represent an insured, when the attorney's negligence damages only the insurer. . . .

Paradigm issued an insurance policy covering Dr. Benjamin A. Vanderwerf for medical malpractice liability. Vanderwerf, Medical Director of Samaritan Transplant Service, a division of Samaritan Health Service (Samaritan), and another doctor were sued by Renee Taylor, who alleged that Vanderwerf committed malpractice by injuring her during a catheter removal procedure. Taylor included Samaritan as a defendant, alleging that at the time of the negligent act, Vanderwerf was acting as Samaritan's agent or employee. . . .

. . . In due course, Paradigm assigned defense of Taylor's claims to Langerman. Langerman undertook the assignment, with Vanderwerf evidently acquiescing, and appeared in the action as Vanderwerf's counsel. During the course of representation, Langerman advised Paradigm that it believed there was no viable theory of liability against Samaritan. Langerman, however, failed to investigate whether Vanderwerf was covered by Samaritan's liability insurance and, thus, was unable to advise Paradigm whether the defense could be tendered to Samaritan.

After a time, . . . Paradigm terminated Langerman's representation in Taylor and retained new counsel for Vanderwerf.

Vanderwerf's new lawyer discovered that Samaritan had liability coverage through Samaritan Insurance Funding (SIF) that not only covered Vanderwerf for Taylor's claim but probably operated as the primary coverage for the claim. . . . Accordingly, new counsel tendered the claim to SIF, which rejected it on the grounds that the tender was untimely.

Taylor v. Vanderwerf was eventually settled for an amount within Paradigm's policy limits. Thus, Vanderwerf was not injured by Langerman's failure to make a timely tender to SIF. However, Paradigm, compelled to act as Vanderwerf's primary carrier, was forced to settle Taylor's claim with its own funds and without being able to look to SIF for contribution or indemnification.

Langerman then presented Paradigm with its statement for legal services. Paradigm refused to pay, claiming Langerman had been negligent both in failing to advise it of SIF's exposure as the primary carrier and by not promptly tendering the defense. When Langerman sued for fees, Paradigm counterclaimed for damages. . . .

DISCUSSION

A. Whether an Express Agreement Is Necessary to Form an Attorney-Client Relationship

Langerman argues that, before an attorney-client relationship can form between an insurer and the counsel it retains to represent an insured, express mutual consent must be reached among all of the respective parties. We disagree. The law has never required that the attorney-client relationship must be initiated by some sort of express agreement, oral or written. Quite to the contrary, the current rule is described as follows:

> A relationship of client and lawyer arises when: (1) a person manifests to a lawyer the person's intent that the lawyer provide legal services for the person; and

. . . (a) the lawyer manifests to the person consent to do so. *Restatement (Third) of The Law Governing Lawyers* §14.

Indeed, comment c to section 14 indicates that either intent or acquiescence may establish the relationship. . . .

B. Potential and Actual Conflicts of Interest with the Insurer as Client

Langerman contends that absent the consent of the insured, a lawyer assigned by an insurer to represent the insured forms an attorney-client relationship only with the insured and never with the insurer. Any contrary conclusion, asserts Langerman, inherently creates a strong potential conflict of interest for the attorney, weakens his "undivided allegiance" to the insured, and creates "situations rife with opportunities for mistrust and second guessing." Langerman's concern over conflicts of interest between attorney, insurer, and insured is not unfounded. This case presents the typical situation found when defense is provided by a liability insurer: as part of the insurer's obligation to provide for the insured's defense, the policy grants the insurer the right to control that defense—which includes the power to select the lawyer that will defend the claim. But the fact that the lawyer is chosen, assigned, and paid by the insurer for the purpose of representing the insured does not automatically create an attorney-client relationship between the insurer and lawyer. . . .

Thus, because the insured has given the insurer control of the defense as part of the agreement for indemnity, the assigned lawyer more or less automatically becomes the attorney for the insured. But does the assigned lawyer automatically also become the attorney for the insurer in every case? . . . Langerman . . . argu[es] that even in the absence of actual conflict between the insured and insurer, there is always a great potential for it. . . .

. . . There can be no doubt that actual conflicts between insured and insurer are quite common and that the potential for conflict is present in every case. Conflicts may arise over the existence of coverage, the manner in which the case is to be defended, the information to be shared, the desirability of settling at a particular figure or the need to settle at all, and an array of other factors applicable to the circumstances of a particular case. This is especially true in cases involving medical malpractice claims.[1] We have recognized such tensions, holding . . . that when a conflict actually arises, and not simply when it potentially exists, the lawyer's duty is exclusively owed to the insured and not the insurer. Because a lawyer is expressly assigned to represent the insured, the lawyer's primary obligation is to the insured, and the lawyer must exercise independent professional

---

1. For instance, in the ordinary case in which liability is probable, even if somewhat questionable, it would almost always be in the interest of the insurer to make a reasonable settlement offer within policy limits. However, such a settlement might not be in the insured's interest and he or she may prefer to take a chance at trial because any settlement payment will require reporting that physician to the National Practitioner Data Bank, thus potentially affecting the physician's ability to obtain hospital privileges or malpractice insurance in the future.

judgment on behalf of the insured. Thus, a lawyer cannot allow an insurer to interfere with the lawyer's independent professional judgment, even though, in general, the lawyer's representation of the insured is directed by the insurer.

. . . We have, in fact, previously held that an attorney assigned to represent an insured cannot supply the insurer with information that either may be or actually is detrimental to the insured's interests. . . . Where a substantial danger of harming the client does not exist, there is no actual conflict of interest — only the potential of a future conflict. . . .

We agree with Langerman that the potential for conflict between insurer and insured exists in every case; but we note that the interests of insurer and insured frequently coincide. For instance, both insurer and insured often share a common interest in developing and presenting a strong defense to a claim that they believe to be unfounded as to liability, damages, or both. Usually insured and insurer have a joint interest in finding additional coverage from another carrier. Thus, by serving the insured's interests the lawyer can also serve the insurer's, and if no question arises regarding the existence and adequacy of coverage, the potential for conflict may never become substantial. In such cases, we see no reason why the lawyer cannot represent both insurer and insured; but in the unique situation in which the lawyer actually represents two clients, he must give primary allegiance to one (the insured) to whom the other (the insurer) owes a duty of providing not only protection, but of doing so fairly and in good faith.

Perhaps recognizing this, the court of appeals determined that the "majority rule" was "in the absence of a conflict, the attorney has two clients, the insurer and the insured." We believe the court of appeals' characterization of the majority rule is too absolute. A host of potential problems are created by holding that, as a matter of law, a lawyer hired by the insurer to represent an insured always accepts the responsibilities of dual representation until a conflict actually arises — thus always automatically forming an attorney–client relationship with both the insurer and insured. There are many cases in which the potential for conflict is strong enough to implicate ER 1.7 . . . from the very beginning. Think, for example, of a claim with questionable liability against an insured covered by limits much lower than the amount of damages. The potential for conflict is quite substantial unless and until the insurer has committed itself to offering or waiving the policy limits. Thus we do not endorse the view that the lawyer automatically represents both insurer and insured until the conflict actually arises.[3] . . .

C. Duty to a Nonclient . . .

If a lawyer's liability to the insurer depends entirely on the existence of an attorney-client relationship and for some reason the insurer is not a

---

3. To forestall confusion among the bar, we hasten to point out that even when the insurer is not the lawyer's client, it certainly is the insured's agent to prepare and handle the defense. Thus, for instance, communications between the nonclient insurer and the lawyer would generally be entitled to the same degree of confidentiality — as long as the general requirements for privilege are met — as those between the insured client and the lawyer.

client,[6] then the lawyer has no duty to the insurer that hired him, assigned the case to him, and pays his fees. There are many problems with that result: if that lawyer's negligence damages the insurer only, the negligent lawyer fortuitously escapes liability. Or if the lawyer's negligence injures both insurer and insured in a case in which the insured is the only client but refuses to proceed against the lawyer, the insurer is helpless and has no remedy. Such unjust results are not just bad policy but unnecessary. The Restatement holds the view that a lawyer may, in certain circumstances, owe a duty to a nonclient. [The court quotes RLGL §51(3).]

Comment g to this section advises:

> [A] lawyer designated by an insurer to defend an insured owes a duty of care to the insurer with respect to matters as to which the interests of the insurer and insured are not in conflict, whether or not the insurer is held to be a co-client of the lawyer.

In addition, comment f to Restatement section 14 states:

> Because and to the extent that the insurer is directly concerned in the matter financially, the insurer should be accorded standing to assert a claim for appropriate relief from the lawyer for financial loss proximately caused by professional negligence or other wrongful act of the lawyer.

. . . Arizona's courts have long recognized situations in which a professional is under a duty of care to nonclients. In Fickett v. Superior Court, for example, the attorney representing a guardian of an estate was accused of negligence by the ward in failing to discover that the guardian had dissipated the estate by misappropriation, conversion, and improper investing. 558 P.2d 988, 89 (Ariz. 1976). . . . The court of appeals [held] that one could not say, as a matter of law, that the guardian's attorney owed no duty to the ward. . . .

In Napier v. Bertram we recognized that, although the "general rule is that a professional owes no duty to a non-client unless special circumstances require otherwise," there are "special circumstances" where we have "imposed liability on a professional to the extent that a foreseeable and specific third party is injured by the professional's actions." 954 P.2d 1389 (Ariz. 1998). . . . [T]hese circumstances are found in a myriad of contexts. *See, e.g.,* Lombardo v. Albu, 14 P.3d 288 (Ariz. 2000) (purchaser's real estate agent has duty to disclose purchaser's financial difficulties to seller); Hamman v. County of Maricopa, 775 P.2d 1122, 1127-28 (Ariz. 1989) (psychiatrist has duty to exercise reasonable care to protect foreseeable victim of patient); Mur-Ray Mgmt. Corp. v. Founders Title Co., 819 P.2d 1003, 1008-09 (Ariz. App. 1991) (imposing duty of reasonable care for escrow agent's representations to third persons). The

---

6. When, for instance, the insured does not consent to a dual relationship, the potential for conflict is great, or the conflict is real.

"common thread [that] exists between" such cases is that "there was a foreseeable risk of harm to a foreseeable non-client whose protection depended on the actor's conduct."

But Langerman argues that Paradigm need not have depended on it, as every insurer has both the freedom and financial ability to hire separate counsel to protect the insurer's own interests. This, of course, must be done in cases in which a conflict exists or is imminent, but we certainly need not impose such an expense on every insurer in every case just to provide the insurer with protection against malpractice by the lawyer it has chosen to handle the defense. When the interests of insurer and insured coincide, as they often do, it makes neither economic nor practical sense for an insurer to hire another attorney to monitor the actions and decisions of the attorney assigned to an insured. More important, we believe that a special relationship exists between the insurer and the counsel it assigns to represent its insured. The insurer is "in some way dependent upon" the lawyer it hires on behalf of its insureds. For instance, the insurer depends on the lawyer to represent the insured zealously so as to honor its contractual agreement to provide the defense when liability allegations are leveled at the insured. In addition, the insurer depends on the lawyer to thwart claims of liability and, in the event liability is found, to minimize the damages it must pay. Thus, the lawyer's duties to the insured are often discharged for the full or partial benefit of the nonclient. *See Fickett,* 558 P.2d at 990. We reject Langerman's attempt to distinguish the present case from our cases that recognize that a professional has a duty to third parties who are foreseeably injured by the lawyer's negligent actions.

CONCLUSION

. . . [B]ased on a long line of precedent, when an insurer assigns an attorney to represent an insured, the lawyer has a duty to the insurer arising from the understanding that the lawyer's services are ordinarily intended to benefit both insurer and insured when their interests coincide. This duty exists even if the insurer is a nonclient. We hold again today that a lawyer has a duty, and therefore may be liable for negligent breach, to a nonclient under the conditions set forth in previous case law and the Restatement. . . .

The record does not allow us, however, to determine whether, as a matter of law, Langerman actually breached its duty to Paradigm in this case. Thus, our holding does not determine whether the applicable standard of conduct would have required Langerman to investigate the existence of a different primary insurer or advise Paradigm to tender the defense to that other insurer. Although we have decided that an attorney-client relationship is not a prerequisite to Paradigm's maintaining a tort action against Langerman for its alleged negligence, whether Langerman actually breached its duty to Paradigm or caused damage is left for the trial court to decide on remand. Under the circumstances of this case, suffice it to say that absent any conflict or significant risk of conflict that compelled Langerman to act as it did, Langerman had a duty to Paradigm—regardless of whether Paradigm was a client. . . .

Lawyers and Clients:
Insurance Defense

The substantial number of lawyers who provide insurance defense representation live in a triangular world, caught between the routine demands of insurers, who select the lawyers who will receive large groups of cases, and the individual insureds, who represent one lone matter and whose interests might depart from those of the insurer. As a consequence, lawyers in this kind of practice often face pressure from either insured or insurer, or both, to shape, and in some cases cramp, the bounds of fiduciary duty owed clients.

Most of the problems created by insurance defense practice originate in the insurance contract itself. Typical liability policies promise to "defend" when a covered person is sued for a covered event, and to "indemnify" that person up to an insured amount. They also provide that the insured agrees to "cooperate" in the defense of the matter, and usually delegate authority to the insurer "to make such investigation, negotiation, and settlement of any claim or suit as it deems expedient."

These contract provisions can create a conflict between the interests of insured and insurer; for example, when the insured insists on the insurer's duty to defend and the insurer stands on its right to control settlement. Insurance law addresses any such conflict by construing the contract language against the insurer-drafter. Courts read the insurance contract to promote more consistent obligations—for example, to both defend and settle with due consideration for the insured's interests. By requiring due regard for the insured's interests, this insurance law also indirectly supports maintaining the integrity of the lawyers' obligations to their client-insureds.

The Clients

When an insurer hires a lawyer or law firm to defend an insured, all jurisdictions agree that the lawyer represents the insured.[1] Providing a "defense" necessarily includes providing a lawyer, complete with the 5 Cs. Jurisdictions do not agree about whether the lawyer also represents the insurer. Some characterize insurance defense as a one-client/third-party payer situation.[2] Lawyers have only one client, the insured, and must comply with Model Rules 1.8(f) and 5.4(c) by resisting pressure from insurers that might interfere with the lawyer's independent professional judgment. Other jurisdictions, as in *Paradigm*, adopt a joint-client approach, meaning that the defense lawyer represents both the insured and the insurer,[3] and is subject to the rigors of Model Rule 1.7 with respect to

---

1. MR 1.8(f) and Comment [11], 5.4(c); RLGL § 134, Comment f.
2. *Id.; see also* In re R. of Prof. Conduct, 2 P.3d 806 (Mont. 2000). *See* Thomas D. Morgan, *What Insurance Scholars Should Know About Professional Responsibility*, 4 Conn. Ins. L.J. 1 (1997-1998).
3. MR 1.7.

each client.[4] Some courts do not specify, but instead require lawyers to clarify the matter in each representation.[5]

Each of these constructs solves some problems and creates others. First, who can sue for incompetence? *Paradigm* indicates that, at least where the harm was caused to the insurer but not the insured, some jurisdictions find the insurer need not be a client to seek malpractice relief.[6] Some jurisdictions invoke the equitable subrogation doctrine to reach the same result. Others allow the insurer to sue only if it is properly a second client of the lawyer, a situation that necessitates adequate attention to waivers of conflicts of interest by the insured.[7] Similarly, vicarious liability claims against the insurer will turn on the insurer's right to control the details of the lawyer's conduct.[8]

Second, who can invoke and waive the attorney-client and work-product privileges? If both insured and insurer are clients, the co-client privilege[9] protects matters of common interest against third persons, but not between the co-clients. Note 3 in *Paradigm* points to the same result, even when the insurer is not a client if the insurer acts as agent of the insured for the purposes of preparing the defense.[10]

Third, can insurers use inside counsel-employees to represent insureds? Some courts have allowed such a practice,[11] on the grounds that a lawyer/employee owes the same loyalty to the client, whether employed directly by the insured or retained as an independent contractor.[12] Others have specifically

---

4. Stephen Pepper, *Applying the Fundamentals of Lawyers' Ethics to Insurance Defense Practice*, 4 Conn. Ins. L.J. 27 (1997); Charles Silver & Kent Syverud, *The Professional Responsibilities of Insurance Defense Lawyers*, 45 Duke L.J. 255 (1995).

5. *E.g.,* Amend. to R. Regulating the Fla. Bar; In re R. of Prof. Conduct, 838 So. 2d 1140 (Fla. 2003) (adopting new R. Prof. Conduct 4-1.7(e), which requires lawyers to ascertain whether they represent only the insured or both the insured and insurer in insurance defense).

6. *See also* St. & County Mut. Fire Ins. Co. v. Young, 2007 U.S. Dist. Lexis 46395 (N.D. W. Va.).

7. *E.g.,* Pine Is. Farmers Coop v. Erstad & Riemer, P.A., 649 N.W.2d 444 (Minn. 2002) (in the absence of a conflict of interest between the insured and the insurer, the insurer can become a co-client of defense counsel if defense counsel consults with the insured, explains the implications of dual representation and the advantages and risks involved, and the insured gives its express consent to the dual representation); *see also* Zenith Ins. Co v. Cozen O'Connor, 55 Cal. Rptr. 3d 998 (Cal. App. 2007) (lawyer hired by insurance company to defend claim owed no duty to reinsurance carrier).

8. St. Farm Mut. Auto. Ins. Co. v. Traver, 980 S.W.2d 625 (Tex. 1998) (insurer does not have the right, comparable to that of a client, to control defense lawyer). *But see* Givens v. Mullikin, 75 S.W.3d 383 (Tenn. 2002) (insurer might be vicariously liable for abuse of process by independent contractor defense counsel it selected where insurer knowingly authorized or directed the acts in question).

9. RLGL § 75.

10. Palmer by Diacon v. Farmers Ins. Exch., 861 P.2d 895 (Mont. 1993) (in bad-faith cases, the insured is entitled to the entire claim file, but where the insurer denies any coverage, the lawyers represented only the insurer, and, therefore, the files were privileged against the insured).

11. *E.g.,* Unauthorized Practice of Law Comm'n v. American Home Assurance Co., 261 S.W.3d 24 (Tex. 2008); In re Youngblood, 895 S.W.2d 322 (Tenn. 1995).

12. *See* Charles Silver, *The Future Structure and Regulation of Law Practice: When Should Government Regulate Lawyer-Client Relationships?* 44 Ariz. L. Rev. 787 (2002).

prohibited it,[13] on the grounds that an insurer/employer would be able to assert so much pressure on its employee/counsel that insurers would interfere with the exercise of counsel's professional judgment.[14]

In many situations, it might not matter which of these characterizations a jurisdiction has adopted, because when conflicts develop, two-client courts such as *Paradigm* typically assert that the insured becomes the primary client. Similarly, third-party payment/one-client courts often find reason to grant insurers some rights, such as in finding that the insurer is the agent of the insured for purposes of the attorney-client or work-product privilege, or by invoking the doctrine of equitable subrogation to allow a malpractice suit by the insurer against the defense lawyer. Regardless of the characterization that is adopted, the insurance defense lawyer must remain focused on the interests of the insured, despite the reality that the insurer is a repeat player in the world of law firm finance. Neither Rule 1.7 nor Rule 1.8(f) allows lawyers to behave in any other way.[15]

The Five Cs

Control   The typical insurance policy's delegation of the right to control settlement decisions to the insurer creates the potential for a direct conflict between insured and insurer whenever the two do not agree about the response to a settlement offer. The lawyer for the insured should realize that the policy language granting the insured the right to a "defense" includes a lawyer who owes an ordinary fiduciary duty of obedience, as required by Model Rule 1.2(a).

In all situations, the lawyer's representation of the insured continues to be governed by the lawyer's ethical obligations, including the obligation to relay each settlement offer to the insured and to relay each insured's response to the insurer.[16] Any conflict in the decision to settle requires disclosure to the insured. If serious enough, many courts recognize that the policy language that creates the conflict also requires affirmative duties of good faith imposed by insurance law on the insurer.[17] Usually, this will put pressure on the insurer to settle in a manner consistent with the best interests of the insured.

The right to settle has been especially contentious in professional liability cases. *Paradigm* points to medical malpractice defense, where an actual conflict can develop if an insurer wishes to settle a matter rather than pay the cost of

---

13. *E.g.,* Brown v. Kelton, 2011 Ark. 93 (2011); Am. Ins. Assn. v. Ky. Bar Assn., 917 S.W.2d 568 (Ky. 1996) (a lawyer cannot agree to do all of an insurer's defense work for a set fee because it would violate MR 1.7(b) and 1.8(f)).

14. Aviva Abramovsky, *The Enterprise Model of Managing Conflicts of Interest in the Tripartite Insurance Defense Relationship*, 27 Cardozo L. Rev. 193 (2005).

15. ABA Formal Op. 01-421.

16. MR 1.2 (a); RLGL §134, Comment f. *See also* Kent D. Syverud, *The Duty to Settle*, 76 Va. L. Rev. 1113 (1990).

17. Betts v. Allstate Ins. Co., 201 Cal. Rptr. 528 (Cal. App. 1984) (insurer and defense counsel jointly and severally liable for excess verdict, emotional distress, and punitive damages for failing to settle within policy limits where liability was clear).

litigating it, but an insured demands a full defense, complete with expensive expert witnesses, perhaps because his or her professional reputation might be at stake. Some professional insurance policies solve this conflict by specifically assigning the right to decide whether and when to settle to the insured or the insurer. Courts construe ambiguous policies consistent with the insurance law of bad faith against the insurer drafter.[18] In situations where the insurer has the contractual right to settle, the insured who disagrees has another option: to release the insurer of its obligations under the policy and defend the action at the insured's own expense. The lawyer's failure to advise the insured of this option creates liability.[19]

Communication   Model Rule 1.4 applies to a number of recurring circumstances in insurance defense practice. Initially, Rules 1.7 and 1.8(f) require the lawyer to inform the insured that the insurer is a third-party payer or joint client, and explain that certain conflicts might develop during the course of the representation. A few jurisdictions have created required disclosure statements regarding an insured client's rights and have mandated that each insured receive such a statement at the beginning of each representation. Typical required disclosures run the gamut of the 5 Cs, including the lawyer's obligation to keep the client informed; to provide competent service, including the insured's right to control the representation when the interests of the insured and insurer conflict; to maintain confidentiality; and to identify and respond to conflicts of interest.[20]

Competence   The insured client has no incentive to seek anything other than a Cadillac defense. The insurer, however, tends to look at these matters on a macro basis, and therefore includes defense costs among its highest costs of doing business. Insurers may attempt to limit their costs by relying on insurance policy language that cedes substantial control of the representation to the insurer. Decisions about fees and strategy extending to matters such as staffing, motion practice, and the need for expert witnesses, all can be second-guessed, often by nonlawyer auditors.[21] At the very least, insureds are entitled to know when insurers refuse to pay for a service that the defense lawyer deems necessary for the insured's defense. At the same time, the insurance contract cannot provide

---

18. Saucedo v. Winger, 915 P.2d 129 (Kan. App. 1996) (insurance policy that did not specifically give insurer the right to settle without insured physician's consent was ambiguous and interpreted to mean that insurer could not settle without insured's consent).

19. Rogers v. Robson, Masters, Ryan, Brumund & Belom, 392 N.E.2d 1365 (Ill. App. 1979), aff'd, 407 N.E.2d 47 (Ill. 1980) (failure to inform insured of settlement offer and option of releasing insurer from its contractual obligations and defending suit at insured's own expense creates malpractice liability for damages caused by lack of disclosure).

20. E.g., Fla. R. Prof. Conduct 4-1.8(j) (2007); Ohio R. Prof. Conduct 1.8(f) (2007).

21. E.g., Glenn K. Jackson, Inc. v. Roe, 273 F.3d 1192 (9th Cir. 2001) (auditor that found errors in law firm's billings to insurer, which resulted in insurer firing law firm, owed no duty of care to law firm and could not be liable for fraud because the law firm presented no evidence of reasonable reliance; but auditor might be liable for libel or slander if law firm can show reckless disregard of the truth).

the lawyer with a waiver sufficient to compromise the lawyer's judgment as to what is required to provide a competent representation.[22]

Billing audits are another example of the guerilla war between insurance companies and defense counsel, with insurers insisting on these audits of defense fee billings, usually performed by independent contractors paid by contingent fees. Here, the contingent fee paid to third-party, nonlawyer auditors creates an incentive to quibble with each hour billed and causes additional pressure on defense counsel to cut down on expenditures. Courts generally do not prohibit such practices,[23] but do construe Rule 1.6 to require explicit consent by insureds to the confidential disclosures necessitated by such audits.[24]

This conflict about the cost necessary to provide competent representation has led to literally dozens of bar association opinions that often condemn insurers' interference with retained counsel.[25] Many of these opinions hold that lawyers may not ethically comply with any insurer's requirement of prior approval before undertaking research, depositions, or retaining expert witnesses.[26] The Restatement does allow for some outside direction, but only if it is reasonable in scope, does not create interference with the lawyer's independent professional judgment, and the client consents.[27] This means that so long as a defense lawyer reasonably believes that forgoing a deposition, motion, or having an expert testify will not violate his or her duty of competent representation, he or she may comply, but only if the insured consents.[28]

A defense lawyer who does not reasonably believe that cost cutting will allow for competent representation might worry about malpractice liability. *Paradigm* demonstrates the potential for such an action by the insurer, whether or not it is a client. The issue of incompetence has also been raised in the context of wrongful discharge actions filed by former inside counsels, who claimed that they were fired because they unsuccessfully attempted to resist pressure to reduce necessary litigation costs.[29]

---

22. Fla. R. Prof. Conduct 1.8(j).

23. *E.g.*, Bronx Leg. Servs. v. Leg. Serv. Corp., 64 Fed. Appx. 310 (2d Cir. 2003) (LSC authorized by law to audit operations and therefore may require groups that receive federal funding to disclose client names and the nature of the representation to government).

24. In re R. of Prof. Conduct, 2 P.3d 806 (Mont. 2000) (detailed descriptions of professional services can be provided only to third-party auditors after first obtaining contemporaneous, fully informed consent of insureds); Ohio R. Prof. Conduct 1.8(f) (2007).

25. ABA Formal Op. 01-421 cites these state opinions.

26. *Id.*; In re R. of Prof. Conduct, 2 P.3d 806 (Mont. 2000).

27. RLGL § 134(2).

28. *Id.*, ill. 5.

29. *E.g.*, Lewis v. Nationwide Mut. Ins. Co., 2003 U.S. Dist. LEXIS 5126 (D. Conn. 2003) (lawyer who worked as inside counsel for an insurer to defend its insureds stated cause of action for wrongful discharge and intentional infliction of emotional distress when he was demoted and fired for refusing to permit the insurer to interfere with his independent professional judgment); Spratley v. St. Farm Mut. Auto. Ins. Co., 78 P.3d 603 (Utah 2003) (lawyers who quit their jobs as in-house counsel for insurer, claiming that insurer required them to violate ethical duties to insureds, could disclose matters relating to their representation of the insurer so long as disclosures were reasonably necessary).

Confidentiality One-client/third-party payer courts rely on Model Rule 1.8(f), which makes clear that the lawyer who represents the insured cannot share an insured's confidential information without consent. Courts that find that a defense lawyer represents two clients face the same conflict between the lawyer's duty to inform one client under Model Rule 1.4 and the lawyer's duty to maintain confidentiality to the other client under Model Rule 1.6. Recall that the court in *A. v. B.* justified disclosure in such a joint client situation only on the basis of an explicit exception in its state version of Model Rule 1.6. When no such exception exists, the lawyer who discloses confidential information will be liable for breach of fiduciary duty, as were the lawyers in *Perez* who made this mistake in a similar joint client context.

Confidentiality issues also occur when a lawyer discovers facts suggesting that coverage is at issue, such as facts that tend to establish that the insured's conduct was intentional rather than negligent. Most two-client courts require separate counsel for the insured when this occurs. Some jurisdictions allow the insurer to bring a separate declaratory judgment action to determine the issue of coverage, but the insurer cannot use any information relating to the underlying representation of the insured to raise or litigate the issue. Lawyers who learn information that compromises coverage will have to withdraw from representing the insurer, and they will not be able to disclose the insured's confidences or otherwise provide reasons why they are withdrawing.

Lawyers who disclose such information without obtaining the insured's express informed consent will be subject to malpractice or breach of fiduciary liability if the insured is injured by disclosure to the insurer.[30] Further, the insurer will be estopped to deny the policy coverage if this information is used to promote a policy defense before the underlying case is properly defended.[31] An insurer also might be liable for bad faith if it refuses to settle the case due to the leaked policy defense.[32]

Conflict of Interest Resolution Using an insured's confidences to create a policy defense constitutes one of at least four situations that courts have characterized as actual conflicts of interest that require defense lawyers to represent one client only, the insured. *Paradigm* identifies several other actual conflicts that require defense counsel to shift allegiance exclusively to the insured, and if necessary, notify the insurer to retain its own counsel in the matter. In one-client/third-party payer jurisdictions, these same conflicts require special attention to prevent interference with the lawyer's independent professional judgment.

---

30. *See, e.g.,* Perez v. Kirk & Carrigan, *supra* p. 167.

31. Emp'rs. Cas. Co. v. Tilley, 496 S.W.2d 552 (Tex. 1973) (insurer estopped to deny coverage because it attempted to use insured's statements obtained by lawyer hired by insurer to defend insured).

32. Parsons v. Contl. Natl. Am. Group, 550 P.2d 94 (Ariz. 1976) (insurer estopped from denying coverage under its policy when its denial was based on confidential information obtained from insured's lawyer, and insurer's refusal to settle within policy limits after it learned of the policy defense constituted bad faith, resulting in an obligation to pay all of the underlying judgment, which was twice the policy limit).

The second actual conflict occurs when multiple claims are alleged against an insured, some of which may involve conduct that the insurer asserts is not covered by the insurance policy. Here, courts hold that the duty to defend extends beyond the duty to indemnify, which means that the insurer must provide an adequate defense against the allegedly uncovered conduct. Courts have developed two approaches to this issue. Some require defense under a "reservation of rights," which means that the insurer can reserve its right to claim any policy exclusion later, but must provide a conflict-free defense in the meantime. Others allow a declaratory judgment action to be filed by the insurer before any trial on the merits to determine coverage and the obligation to defend.

Providing an adequate defense under a reservation of rights requires defense counsel to ignore the interests of the insurer and focus exclusively on the interests of the insured. For example, a complaint that alleges both intentional and negligent misconduct usually creates an actual conflict between insured, who desires insurance coverage of any liability, and insurer, which prefers a finding of intentional tort that will release it from its contractual obligations. The insurer is entitled to hire its own counsel in the matter, but the lawyer retained to provide the insured's defense must be guided solely by the insured's best interests.[33] Once again, insurance law provides that failure to send a reservation of rights letter or provide independent counsel to an insured estops the insurer from later denying coverage.[34]

The third actual conflict occurs when an insured is sued for an amount in excess of policy limits.[35] When this occurs, insurance law imposes an obligation on the insurer to act in good faith in responding to settlement offers. Where there is a reasonable probability that the insured will be found liable for an excess judgment, the insurer must take the insured's interests into account.[36] This means that the insurer must have an objective legal basis to justify its refusal to settle. If a lawyer representing the insured alone would advise litigating genuine issues of liability or damages, failure to settle within policy limits may have a reasonable basis; if a lawyer representing the insured alone would recommend settlement, and the insured would settle, failure to settle within policy limits constitutes bad faith.[37]

---

33. For a case involving sexual misconduct by a physician where the court found that the lawyer offered a "splendid" defense under a reservation of rights, *see* St. Paul Fire and Marine Ins. Co. v. Engelmann, 639 N.W.2d 192 (S.D. 2002).

34. Beckwith Mach. Co. v. Travelers Indem. Co., 638 F. Supp. 1179 (W.D. Pa. 1986) (where the failure to send a reservation of rights letter or file a declaratory judgment action estopped the insurer from denying coverage and created liability for bad faith and breach of contract).

35. *See* Shaya B. Pacific, LLC v. Wilson, Elser, Moskowitz, Edelman, & Dicker, LLP, 38 A.D.3d 34 (N.Y. App. 2006) (law firm hired to defend an insured may have a duty to investigate issue of excess coverage by another insurer).

36. ABA Formal Op. 96-403.

37. Behn v. Legion Ins. Co., 173 F. Supp. 2d 105 (D. Mass. 2001) (insurer acted reasonably in refusing to settle medical malpractice case where expert witness opined that defendant psychiatrist complied with the standard of care, facts indicated comparative fault of plaintiff, and insured refused consent to settle).

Sanford illustrates another variation of this circumstance: multiple insureds facing damage claims. Here, courts require separate counsel for each insured to guarantee each his or her right to a conflict-free defense.[38] Failure to recognize this conflict can create insurer liability for bad-faith refusal to settle, including the full amount of any eventual judgment against the insured. Lawyers faced with insurers who refuse to settle within policy limits or provide independent counsel must remind insurers about this potential for bad-faith liability.[39]

Insurance Law

In most jurisdictions, insurance law facilitates the work of defense lawyers by creating additional incentives for insurers to abide by their obligation to provide a "defense" free of unwarranted interference in the client-lawyer relationship. Lawyers who represent insurers must explain this law to provide competent representation. Similarly, lawyers who represent insureds need to understand insurance law ramifications to inform and protect their clients.

For example, the tort of bad faith in insurance law is designed to encourage reasonable settlements in the best interests of insureds. Insurance law also includes the remedy of estoppel to prevent the insurer from unfairly relying on a policy defense. Similarly, courts find that conflicts created by the duty to defend and policy limitations necessitate a reservation of rights letter when some claims are made outside of policy coverage. These letters promote a fair response to conflicts by notifying insureds about the contractual limits of their policies, thereby allowing them to seek additional counsel for the uncovered conduct. Insurer's obligations to defend under a reservation of rights also require lawyers to provide a defense for covered events focused on the insured's interests alone.

Conclusion

Understanding the ethical obligations of insurance defense counsel begins with identifying the insured as the primary or sole client of the lawyer. Once this has been done, four conclusions quickly follow:

1. Defense lawyers owe insureds all of the 5 Cs, meaning that they cannot allow insurers to interfere in the exercise of their independent professional judgment. Lawyers who breach any of the 5 Cs will be accountable to the insured. Insurers harmed by incompetence also may be able to obtain relief.

2. Insurers may exert some control over fees and strategy, but only if consistent with the lawyer's independent judgment. However, they cannot impose prior approval requirements on defense counsel. Lawyers can agree to direction that is reasonable in scope, but they must inform insureds about the insurer's imposed limitations and obtain informed consent to any disclosures to the insurer.

---

38. *E.g.*, Wolpaw v. General Accident Ins. Co., 639 A.2d 338 (N.J. Super 1994).
39. Haddick ex rel. Griffith v. Valor Ins., 763 N.E.2d 299 (Ill. 2001) (cause of action for bad-faith refusal to settle found where liability conceded, medical expenses were in excess of policy limits, and insurer did not offer to settle for policy limits until one year after settlement demand initially made).

3. Arrangements with defense counsel that offer insurers more opportunity to control fees and strategy, such as flat fees or inside counsel status, are prohibited in some jurisdictions to prevent interference with independent professional judgment.

4. Insurers may have contractual control over settlement decisions, but insurance law and the ethical responsibilities of defense counsel impose obligations of good faith on both in communicating and responding to settlement offers.

When any conflict over confidentiality, coverage, settlement, or control develops, defense lawyers who understand that the insured is their primary or only client will view that matter through the correct lens of the insured's best interests. They will communicate relevant facts and options, insist on competent defense of the insured's case, keep the insured's confidences, and identify and respond to conflicts of interest. When a conflict is identified, defense lawyers will notify their client(s) about the source and nature of the conflict and determine how counsel without such a conflict would proceed. Insurance law usually assists defense lawyers in fully understanding their obligations because it provides additional incentives for insurers to meet their contractual obligations.

Chapter 11

Conflicts of Interest: Former, Prospective, Imputed, and Government Clients

When a client-lawyer relationship ends, a lawyer's obligations of control, communication, and competence wind down. The lawyer's obligation of confidentiality continues unabated, however, which results in some continuing obligation of loyalty, or conflicts resolution to former clients. Similar confidentiality obligations attach to prospective client consultations. These confidentiality obligations are summarized in the following chart.

Confidentiality Duties to Current, Former, and Prospective Clients

	Current Clients	Former Clients	Prospective Clients
Definition:	RLGL § 14: Client and lawyer agree that lawyer will provide legal services or client agrees and lawyer fails to object and client reasonably relies	1.9(a): Formerly represented a client in a matter	1.18(a): Discusses with a lawyer the possibility of forming a client-lawyer relationship with respect to a matter
Duty:	1.6(a): No disclosure of information relating to the representation AND 1.8(b): No use of such information to the disadvantage of the client.	1.9(a), (b): No subsequent materially adverse representation in the same or substantially related matter AND 1.9(c): No use or disclosure of information relating to the previous representation.	1.18(c): No subsequent materially adverse representation in the same or substantially related matter if information received could be significantly harmful AND 1.18(b): No use or disclosure of information learned in the consultation.
Exceptions:	1.6(b) [Chapters 7 & 8]	Former client consent or 1.9(c) = 1.6(b)	1.18(b) (c) & (d) = 1.9 = Prospective client consent or 1.6(b)

Whether we are addressing a fiduciary duty or a privilege, confidentiality extends to information received from prospective clients and current clients, and continues after the representation ends. Prospective clients repose trust in and must disclose some information to lawyers to determine whether to retain lawyers. The law governing lawyers cloaks this information with the same confidentiality protection that current clients receive. The same protection extends postrepresentation to former clients and extends beyond the client's death. If a lawyer decides not to represent a prospective client, that person or entity becomes essentially a "former client" for purposes of the confidentiality rules. Unlike concurrent and specific conflicts regulated by Model Rules 1.7 and 1.8, former client and prospective client conflicts are always consentable.

When lawyers work in firms, the conflicts of each lawyer are imputed to the firm. Lawyers who move between firms carry conflicts arising from their own matters or knowledge with them, but generally not those of the former firm. Imputation can be waived by a former or a prospective client and such a waiver can be conditioned on the establishment of a screen designed to prevent that tainted lawyer from having any involvement in the subsequent matter. In some prospective and former client situations, these screens may be used without client consent.

A. Former Client Conflicts

Problems

11-1. Three years ago, Martyn & Fox prepared tax returns for Wife's business. Husband now wants Martyn & Fox to represent him in a divorce. Can we? What if we handled an employment discrimination claim for Wife's business?

11-2. Martyn was general counsel for Capital Hospital for ten years before joining Martyn & Fox.

   (a) Can Martyn & Fox represent Small Hospital, a competitor of Capital, in lobbying the state legislature for changes in state Medicaid reimbursement rates?

   (b) Can Martyn & Fox advise Sunshine Hospital and Rehabilitation Center in another county that there are no antitrust ramifications of potential expansion, when Martyn advised Capital that a planned expansion would not be wise under the same law?

   (c) Can Martyn & Fox represent plaintiff, who alleges medical malpractice that occurred while a patient at Capital Hospital during Martyn's tenure there?

11-3. Martyn & Fox signs a joint defense agreement with a law firm representing a co-defendant of Martyn & Fox's client. Plaintiff succeeds in getting the other law firm disqualified because plaintiff is the other firm's former client. What happens to Martyn & Fox?

Consider: Model Rules 1.0(k), 1.9, 1.10
RLGL § 132

Oasis West Realty, LLC v. Goldman

250 P.3d 1115 (Cal. 2011)

Baxter, Justice

In early 2004, plaintiff Oasis embarked on a plan to redevelop and revitalize a nine-acre parcel it owned in Beverly Hills by erecting a five-star hotel and luxury condominiums. A Hilton hotel was already on the property, and the project is often referred to as the Hilton project. The Hilton project required the approval of the Beverly Hills City Council.

On January 26, 2004, Oasis retained defendant Attorney Kenneth A. Goldman (Goldman) and his law firm, defendant Reed Smith, LLP (Reed Smith), to provide legal services in connection with the Hilton project. According to the engagement letter, Goldman was to "have overall responsibility for this matter." Oasis has alleged that it hired Goldman "because, among other things, he was an attorney reputed to be an expert in civic matters and a well-respected, influential leader who was extremely active in Beverly Hills politics." Oasis said it believed that "Goldman's statements and opinions on City development matters bore significant influence on City Council members and the local citizenry," particularly on members of the Southwest Homeowners Association, of which he was the president.

During the representation, Goldman became "intimately involved in the formulation of the plan for Oasis'[s] development of the Property, its overall strategy to secure all necessary approvals and entitlements from the City and its efforts to obtain public support for the Project. Mr. Goldman was a key Oasis representative in dealing with Beverly Hills City Officials, including the Planning Commission and City Council. Throughout the representation, Oasis revealed confidences to Mr. Goldman, which it reasonably believed would remain forever inviolate." Reed Smith, in turn, received about $ 60,000 in fees. In April 2006, Goldman advised Oasis that he and Reed Smith would no longer represent Oasis in connection with the Hilton project.

Oasis's development proposal was presented to the city council in June 2006, after the representation had ended. For the next two years, the council and the city's planning commission reviewed thousands of pages of technical studies, held over 18 hearings, and received input from hundreds of community members. In April 2008, the council certified the environmental impact report and adopted a General Plan Amendment Resolution and the Beverly Hilton Specific Plan Resolution with Conditions of Approval, which paved the way for final approval of the Hilton project.

Shortly thereafter, a group of Beverly Hills residents opposed to the general plan amendment formed the Citizens Right to Decide Committee, with the goal of putting a referendum on the ballot that would allow voters to overturn the city council's approval of the Hilton project. It was at this point that Goldman engaged in the conduct that is of concern in this proceeding.

According to the complaint, Goldman "lent his support" to the group opposing the Hilton project; "campaigned for and solicited signatures for a Petition circulated by said citizen's group that sought to abrogate the City Council's approval of the Project and instead place approval in the hands of the citizenry by proposition vote on November 4, 2008 (Measure 'H')"; and "distributed a letter seeking to cause residents of Beverly Hills to sign the Petition for the purpose of placing a referendum on the ballot, asking Beverly Hills voters to overturn approval of the Project." In a declaration filed in support of the special motion to strike, Goldman confirmed that on or about May 12, 2008, the day the city council provided final approval to the Hilton project, he and his wife walked their street to solicit signatures for the petition to overturn the council's decision. Goldman estimated that they spoke to 10 neighbors and collected five or six signatures over a period of less than an hour and a half, and that he left a note at four or five homes where there was no response.[2] Goldman estimated that through the couple's joint effort on May 12 as well as additional work by his wife, they managed to collect approximately 20 signatures. Goldman insisted that he at no time disclosed confidential information acquired during the representation of Oasis to anyone, and did not believe that he disclosed to anyone that he had ever represented Oasis in connection with the Hilton project.[3]

---

2. The note read as follows:

> "*LORI AND KEN GOLDMAN*
>
> "Dear Neighbor:
>
> "Sorry we missed you when we stopped by.
>
> "We stopped by to see if you would sign the Referendum Petition to overturn the City Council's recent approval of the Hilton plans. The Council approved an additional 15-story Waldorf-Astoria Hotel (where Trader Vic[']s is now), a new 16-story condo tower on the corner of Merv Griffin Way and Santa Monica and a new 6-8 story condo tower on the corner of Wilshire and Merv Griffin Way. At the last minute, the Council also allowed the developer to remove one of the floors of parking that they had previously agreed to add! And all of this in addition to the 232 condos that the Council had just finished approving on the Robinson's-May site. And all of this at one of the busiest intersections on the entire Westside!
>
> "And all this is in the name of more and more revenue. And they don't even make any plans to seriously correct the awful intersection and lines of waiting traffic that will grow and grow.
>
> "So we will sign the Referendum Petition and urge you to do likewise. Please call us at (310) 552- . . . to figure out a convenient time to sign. We have only 2 weeks!
>
> "*Ken and Lori*"

3. Goldman also attended a city council meeting on May 6, 2008, to oppose enforcement, unsuccessfully, of the requirement that persons soliciting signatures for a referendum petition carry the full text of the resolution. . . . Goldman's remarks, in [part], were as follows: "Good evening members of the Council. I am here to speak on a very narrow issue concerning the Hilton that has been discussed and alluded to tonight. It is hard for me to believe that anyone in this Chamber would view it as being fair, whether you're for the Hilton or for the Referendum, to have to carry around 15 1/2 pounds of material from home to home to home to home, whether you're 15 years old or 85 years old. It's never been done. [¶] . . . It's just not necessary. You can take the executive summary, you can take the resolution. [¶] I know every single one of you. I know every single one of you is fair and right and I cannot believe that you would think it is fair and right, whether you're for it or against it, to have someone, to require someone to carry that kind of material around with them when they are trying to seek whatever they are trying to seek. We've never done this before in this city, we shouldn't do it now. It's just not right; again, whether you're for the Hilton or for the Referendum. Don't require it, because it's not fair and each of the five of you knows that. It's not right. It's not necessary to inform the citizenry. There's a lot of material there. Nobody is going to read through that. Nobody that's spoken tonight, I guarantee you, I haven't read through that. Thank you."

In a letter to Reed Smith dated May 14, 2008, Oasis criticized Goldman's conduct as a "manifest violation of both his and your firm's fiduciary obligations as our prior counsel" and demanded that Goldman and Reed Smith "immediately and unconditionally terminate and withdraw from any and all activities that may in any manner be construed as adverse to the Project, its approval or Oasis'[s] interests." Reed Smith responded by letter the same day that pending its review of these allegations, Goldman and the firm had agreed not to "engage in any actions concerning the referendum petition that is being circulated." In a letter sent the next day, Oasis insisted that "remedial action" be taken immediately to minimize further damage and proposed that Goldman and his wife ("as mutual agents of the other") "retract the letter and their support for the petition and referendum."

The citizens' committee collected the necessary signatures to place the proposed general plan amendment on the ballot as Measure H. Measure H, which ratified the city council's decision, was passed by voters on November 2, 2008, by a margin of 129 votes.

On January 30, 2009, Oasis filed the pending lawsuit against Goldman and Reed Smith for breach of fiduciary duty, professional negligence, and breach of contract, seeking damages in excess of $ 4 million. . . .

DISCUSSION

. . . We shall consider the causes of action for breach of fiduciary duty, professional negligence, and breach of contract together, as all three claims are based on Goldman's alleged breach of his duties as former counsel to Oasis. The elements of a cause of action for breach of fiduciary duty are the existence of a fiduciary relationship, breach of fiduciary duty, and damages. The elements of a cause of action for professional negligence are (1) the existence of the duty of the professional to use such skill, prudence, and diligence as other members of the profession commonly possess and exercise; (2) breach of that duty; (3) a causal connection between the negligent conduct and the resulting injury; and (4) actual loss or damage resulting from the professional negligence. And the elements of a cause of action for breach of contract are (1) the existence of the contract, (2) plaintiff's performance or excuse for nonperformance, (3) defendant's breach, and (4) the resulting damages to the plaintiff. . . .

Oasis contends that Goldman, as its lawyer, was "a fiduciary . . . of the very highest character" and bound "to most conscientious fidelity—*uberrima fides*." (*Cox v. Delmas*, 33 P. 836 (Cal 1893).) Among those fiduciary obligations were the duties of loyalty and confidentiality, which continued in force even after the representation had ended. As we have previously explained, "[t]he effective functioning of the fiduciary relationship between attorney and client depends on the client's trust and confidence in counsel. The courts will protect clients' legitimate expectations of loyalty to preserve this essential basis for trust and security in the attorney–client relationship." Accordingly, "an attorney is forbidden to do either of two things after severing [the] relationship with a former client. [The attorney] may not do anything which will injuriously affect [the] former client in any matter in which [the attorney] formerly represented [the client] nor may [the attorney] at any time use against [the] former client knowledge or information acquired by virtue of the previous relationship."

Oasis contends that defendants violated this prohibition in a number of ways. Oasis asserts in particular that Goldman acquired confidential and sensitive information relating to the Hilton project through the course of the representation, particularly during team meetings that discussed matters of strategy with respect to the city council, other city officials, and civic organizations, and that Goldman then *used* this information when he actively opposed the precise project he had been retained to promote. . . . In light of the undisputed facts that Goldman agreed to represent Oasis in securing approvals for the project, acquired confidential information from Oasis during the course of the representation, and then decided to publicly oppose the very project that was the subject of the prior representation, it is reasonable to infer that he did so. Moreover, inasmuch as Goldman was obligated under . . . the State Bar Rules of Professional Conduct to disclose to Oasis any personal relationship or interest that he knew or reasonably should have known could substantially affect the exercise of his professional judgment—but never did so—it is likewise reasonable to infer that Goldman's opposition to the project developed over the course of the representation, fueled by the confidential information he gleaned during it. Oasis further claims that, because of Goldman's overt acts in opposition to the project, it was forced to investigate Goldman's conduct and prepare a letter demanding defendants' adherence to their legal and fiduciary duties, thereby incurring over $3,000 in legal fees. Based on this showing and the inferences therefrom, we conclude that Oasis has demonstrated a likelihood of prevailing on each of its three causes of action. . . .

Defendants argue first that the duty [to former client] should be read to apply in only two specific circumstances: (1) where the attorney has undertaken a concurrent or successive representation that is substantially related to the prior representation and is adverse to the former client, or (2) where the attorney has disclosed confidential information. . . .

It is not difficult to discern that use of confidential information against a former client can be damaging to the client, even if the attorney is not working on behalf of a new client and even if none of the information is actually disclosed. For example, an attorney may discover, in the course of the representation of a real estate developer, that city officials are particularly concerned about the parking and traffic impacts of a proposed development, or that an identifiable population demographic is especially disposed to oppose the proposed development. Under the interpretation proposed by defendants and adopted by the Court of Appeal, the attorney would be free to terminate the representation of the developer and use this information to campaign (quite effectively, one would imagine) against the precise project the attorney had previously been paid to promote. Inasmuch as the harm to the client is the same, the rule appropriately bars the attorney from *both* disclosing *or* using the former client's confidential information against the former client. Indeed, the same rule prevails in most jurisdictions, as evidenced by the Restatement Third of the Law Governing Lawyers, section 60. . . .

Defendants' contention that they were somehow relieved of their duties of loyalty and confidentiality by section 125 of the Restatement Third of the Law Governing Lawyers is mistaken. A comment to that provision explains that "[i]n general, a lawyer may publicly take personal positions on controversial issues without regard to whether the positions are consistent with those of some or all of the lawyer's clients. . . . For example, if tax lawyers advocating positions about tax reform were obliged to advocate only positions that would serve the positions of their present clients, the public would lose the objective contributions to policy making of some persons most able to help. [¶] *However*, a lawyer's right to freedom of expression is modified by the lawyer's duties to clients. . . . *The requirement that a lawyer not misuse a client's confidential information (see § 60) similarly applies to discussion of public issues.*" (Rest.3d Law Governing Lawyers, § 125, com. e, italics added; see also *id.*, § 33(2), ["Following termination of a representation, a lawyer must: [¶] . . . [¶] (d) take no unfair advantage of a former client by abusing knowledge or trust acquired by means of the representation."].)

An illustration in the Restatement discussion of section 125 demonstrates the distinction: "Lawyer represents Corporation in negotiating with the Internal Revenue Service to permit Corporation to employ accelerated depreciation methods for machinery purchased in a prior tax year. At the same time, Lawyer believes that the accelerated depreciation laws for manufacturing equipment reflect unwise public policy. Lawyer has been working with a bar-association committee to develop a policy statement against the allowance, and the committee chair has requested Lawyer to testify in favor of the report and its proposal to repeal all such depreciation allowances. Any new such legislation, as is true generally of such tax enactments, would apply only for current and future tax years, thus not directly affecting Corporation's matter before the IRS. Although the [current] legislation would be against Corporation's economic interests, Lawyer may, without Corporation's consent, continue the representation of Corporation while working to repeal the allowance." (Rest.3d Law Governing Lawyers, § 125, cmt. e, illus. 6) Defendants' alleged conduct here is not analogous to "Lawyer's" efforts to repeal depreciation allowances in the future. What Oasis alleges here, in the terms of the analogy above, is that Lawyer, after obtaining IRS approval of the depreciation allowance, withdrew and then, on Lawyer's own behalf, sought to have "Corporation's" depreciation allowance *for that prior tax year* overturned and used confidential information to make that case. Defendants have not identified any authority to countenance such conduct, and our own research has uncovered none.

Defendants complain that a "broad categorical bar on attorney speech" would lead to a parade of horribles. They warn that a lawyer would be prevented even from voting in an election against the former client's interest and that the prohibition would necessarily extend to every attorney in an international law firm. It seems doubtful that a single vote in a secret ballot in opposition to a client's interest would offer "a reasonable prospect" of "adversely affect[ing] a material interest of the client." (Rest.3d Law Governing Lawyers, § 60(1)(a).) In any event, we are not announcing a broad categorical bar here, nor are we presented with a situation requiring us to articulate how imputed disqualification rules would apply in this context. . . . A claim that Goldman used confidential information acquired during his representation of Oasis in active and overt support of a referendum to overturn the city council's approval of the Hilton project, where the council's approval of the project was the explicit objective of the prior representation [states a cause of action]. . . .

Finally, we conclude that Oasis has set forth a prima facie case of actual injury and entitlement to damages. Oasis asserts that because of Goldman's active and overt opposition to the Hilton project, it was compelled to protect its rights by retaining legal counsel to prepare a letter demanding that Goldman cease and desist from further misconduct. The cost of this remediation exceeded $3,000. It is "the established rule that attorney fees incurred as a direct result of another's tort are recoverable damages." In particular, recoverable damages include "the expense of retaining another attorney" when reasonably necessary to "attempt to avoid or minimize the consequences of the former attorney's negligence." . . .

Cascades Branding Innovation, LLC v. Walgreen Co.
2012 U.S. Dist. LEXIS 61750 (N.D. Ill.)

Harry D. LEINENWEBER, District Judge. . . .

I. BACKGROUND

Plaintiff Cascades Branding Innovation, LLC ("Cascades Branding") is wholly owned by Cascades Ventures, LLC ("Cascades Ventures"). Cascades Ventures, in turn, is wholly owned by Anthony O. Brown ("Brown"). Brown is also the President and Co-Founder of Cascades Branding. As Brown sees it, he and Cascades Ventures were put on this earth to assist inventors and their companies in "overcome[ing] obstacles to effective patent licensing," helping David-like small inventors slay Goliath "giant enterprises" who infringe their patents. Other people call Brown the "original patent troll."

Cascades Branding, an Illinois limited liability company, is the exclusive licensee of the patent in suit, U.S. Patent No. 7,768,395 ("the '395 Patent"). The patent relates to improvements in mobile devices, allowing devices to locate branded products and services in their vicinity. Best Buy and Target each have a mobile device application ("app") that allows mobile devices to locate nearby stores without the user having to enter location information. Plaintiff claims this infringes on the '395 patent and . . . accuses both Defendants of inducing infringement and contributory infringement by making their apps available for customers (among others) to download and use.

Defendants Best Buy and Target are each incorporated in Minnesota and have their principal places of business there also. Best Buy is represented by Robins Kaplan. Specifically, Emmett J. McMahon ("McMahon") of Robins Kaplan has appeared *pro hac vice* on Best Buy's behalf.

Brown, as owner of Cascades Ventures, approached Robins Kaplan partner Ronald J. Schutz ("Schutz") in the summer of 2010 as owner of Cascades Ventures, seeking representation for Cascades Ventures (or a to-be-formed affiliate) in the licensing and enforcement of a patent portfolio (the "Elbrus Portfolio") unrelated to the patent in suit. The two exchanged a series of e-mails which have been submitted to the Court by agreement of both Plaintiff and Robins Kaplan. Schutz declined to represent Cascades, and informally notified him of this in an August 27, 2010 e-mail. More formally, Schutz definitively closed the file on May 20, 2011 and communicated this in an e-mail of the same date.

The parties agree no attorney–client relationship was formed, but dispute whether Schutz learned confidential information during that exchange that could help Best Buy in the current litigation.

Several years ago, Schutz and McMahon represented a company called TechSearch, LLC, which Brown co-founded and headed as President until he sold it lock, stock and barrel in 2005. As part of that representation, Schutz, McMahon and other Robins Kaplan attorneys helped litigate two lawsuits related to a patent portfolio (the "Chan Portfolio") unrelated to the patent at issue in this lawsuit or the patents that were the issue of the 2010 negotiations. As part of the representation, Robins Kaplan represented TechSearch in reaching settlement or licensing agreements with at least eight companies. That relationship lasted from approximately 2002 to 2004.

Cascades contends that, through the two interactions, Robins Kaplan has gained privileged information relating to Brown's (and thus Cascades Branding's) litigation strategy, business model, and approach to negotiating settlements, licenses and reasonable royalties.

Events in this litigation began percolating on April 14, 2011, when attorneys for Cascades Branding notified Best Buy it was infringing on the patent (the same day they filed suit). . . .

III. MOTION TO DISQUALIFY

A. Legal Standard . . .

Disqualification "is a drastic measure which courts should hesitate to impose except when absolutely necessary. A disqualification of counsel, while protecting the attorney-client relationship, also serves to destroy a relationship by depriving a party of representation of their own choosing." Freeman v. Chicago Musical Instrument Co., 689 F.2d 715, 721-722 (7th Cir. 1982) (issue of appealability of disqualification later superseded by Richardson-Merrell, Inc. v. Koller, 472 U.S. 424 (1985).

The parties also cite to the ABA Model Rules of Professional Conduct and seem to agree that they are substantially similar to both Illinois' rules (where Plaintiff is located) and Minnesota's rules (where Robins Kaplan and Best Buy are located). . . . Since the parties agree Illinois rules are applicable, and because questions of client confidences are judged from the perspective of the client (Westinghouse Electric Corp. v. Kerr-McGee Corp., 580 F.2d 1311, 1319-1320

(7th Cir. 1978)), . . . the rules of the state of the purported client in this case (Illinois' rules) will be cited.

Two primary Illinois rules govern: Rule 1.9 (Duties to Former Clients) and Rule 1.18 (Duties to Prospective Client). [The Court cites the black letter of Rule 1.9, and Comments [2] and [3], as well as the black letter of Rule 1.18 and Comments [3] and [6]].

As to whether a substantial relationship exists between a client and an attorney, "a three-level inquiry [should] be undertaken. . . . First, the trial judge must make a factual reconstruction of the scope of the prior legal representation. Second, it must be determined whether it is reasonable to infer that the confidential information allegedly given would have been given to a lawyer representing a client in those matters. Third, it must be determined whether that information is relevant to the issues raised in the litigation pending against the former client." *LaSalle Nat'l Bank v. County of Lake*, 703 F.2d 252, 255-256 (7th Cir. 1983).

In general, "an attorney for a corporate client owes his duty [of loyalty] to the corporate entity rather than a particular officer, director or shareholder." Bd. of Managers of Eleventh Street Loftominium Ass'n. v. Wabash Loftominium, LLC., 876 N.E.2d 65, 72 (Ill. App. Ct. 2007) (hereinafter, *Loftominium*). However, there may be circumstances where the lawyer must consider a subsidiary or other constituent of a corporate client to be a client as well, such as those instances where the subsidiary has the same management group.

B. Analysis

Without a doubt, the first question that must be answered is whether Cascades Branding has any former or prospective relationship with Robins Kaplan.

Cascades Branding says that *Loftominium* decrees it has both. Starting with TechSearch, the Court is confident that Robins Kaplan's relationship with this company imposes no former-client duties in relation to Cascades Branding. The Court finds that *Loftominium*'s extension of the client definition was limited to instances of subsidiaries or other closely-related entities (phrased as "other constituents" of the corporate entity).

Cascades Branding is in no way, shape or form a subsidiary, affiliate, parent or any other permutation of TechSearch. That Brown once ran and owned TechSearch, and now runs and owns Cascades Branding (through the parent company Cascades Ventures) stretches the understanding of *Loftominium* past the breaking point. As Best Buy points out, Brown sold TechSearch, and in doing so, he relinquished all claims to that company. Cascades' only link (either parent or subsidiary) is common personnel (Brown), a link too tenuous to alone confer former client status.

Brown's claim to former client status in regards to TechSearch is further hampered by the comments to Illinois Rule 1.9 regarding the passage of time. Seven years passed between 2004 and the 2011 litigation of this case, a factor that also weighs against crediting the TechSearch relationship as a former client relationship. Further discrediting this argument is Brown's request (as Cascades Ventures owner) for a client–attorney agreement from Robins Kaplan during his 2010 discussions with that firm. It demonstrates that even Brown did not believe that relationship governed his current interactions with the firm, and that a new dynamic governed. In sum, the TechSearch/Cascades Branding connection is just too tenuous.

The question in relation to Brown and Cascades Ventures' interactions with Robins Kaplan in 2010 merits a closer look, however.

Just as in the TechSearch relationship, Cascades Branding was not the party engaging in the relationship with Robins Kaplan. But unlike TechSearch, Cascades Branding is a wholly-owned subsidiary of the party (Cascades Ventures) that had the relationship with Robins Kaplan. It is also clear that the parent company, Cascades Ventures, is directing the current litigation. Cascades Ventures and Plaintiff are managed by the same personnel, are part of the same corporate family and are closely aligned in purpose.

It also appears that Cascades Ventures routinely operates its litigation through subsidiaries created for that purpose. In fact, the litigation which Brown sought to entice Robins Kaplan into filing was eventually filed through a subsidiary, Cascades Computer Innovation.

Loftominium is not the only authority for the proposition that a parent, subsidiary or affiliate company can be a dual, if unsuspected, client. In Discotrade, Ltd. V. Wyeth-Ayerst Int. Inc., 200 F.Supp.2d 355 (S.D.N.Y. 2002) (hereinafter *Discotrade*) plaintiff, a distributor, sued defendant, a supplier, alleging fraud and breach of contract. Wyeth moved to disqualify plaintiff's counsel on the grounds that Discotrade's counsel also represented a subsidiary of Wyeth's parent company in a patent application matter. The court found the corporate relationship between defendant and the parent company "so close as to deem them a single entity for conflict of interest purposes." *Id.* at 358-359. The closeness was based upon both companies being wholly-owned subsidiaries of the parent company, sharing the same board of directors and several senior officers, and using the same computer network, travel department, letterhead and health benefit plan.

The Second Circuit approved of *Discotrade*, but cautioned that it agreed with "the ABA that affiliates should not be considered a single entity for conflicts purposes based solely on the fact that one entity is a wholly-owned subsidiary of the other, at least when the subsidiary is not otherwise operationally integrated with the parent company." GSI Commerce Solutions, Inc. v. BabyCenter, L.L.C., 618 F.3d 204, 210-212 (2nd Cir. 2010) (disqualifying counsel for concurrent representation when the entities shared responsibility for both the provision and management of legal services). *GSI* noted that the focus on legal and management issues "reflects the view that neither management nor in-house legal counsel should, without their consent, have to place their trust in outside counsel in one matter while opposing the same counsel in another." *Id.* The notion even has a home in the Seventh Circuit. *See Westinghouse*, 580 F.2d at 1321 (protecting confidentiality interest of affiliate of client).

These cases dealt with concurrent representation, however, and the situation at hand deals with prospective representation, making it a further step removed.

As Plaintiff points out, prospective representation, at least where confidential information has been shared, is viewed through the prism of Rule 1.9, governing former clients. But that one step of removal does not destroy the logic of parties reasonably expecting confidentiality in their past discussions with lawyers. As Charles W. Wolfram noted,

> Here, too, courts have generously protected reasonable expectations in the confidentiality of information on the part of both the original corporate client and its then affiliates. As with concurrent-representation analogs, the few decisions dealing with the issue in the context of a corporate family have rooted a prohibition against the later representation on the grounds of confidentiality. Again in agreement with concurrent-representation analogs, the duty of the lawyer to avoid such conflicted representations applies whether the lawyer is likely to have learned the linking confidential information in the earlier representation from either the corporate client or from the non-client affiliate. . . .
>
> While the foregoing places important conflict limitations on the right of a lawyer to represent an adverse client, it is important to note that protection of confidentiality exhausts the duties of a lawyer to any former client, and certainly to a non-client to whom the lawyer owes confidentiality duties. In other words, no matter how adverse the later representation may be, if it is not also factually linked to the earlier representation in the way required under the substantial-relationship standard, the later representation is permissible. *Legal Ethics: Corporate-Family Conflicts*, 2 J. Inst. Stud. Leg. Eth. 295, 355-356.

This Court, too, believes that the once-removed analysis does not destroy the expectation of confidentiality. Further, it is apparent that Cascades Ventures (the party that had the prospective-client relationship with Robins Kaplan) is effectively the same party as Cascades Branding for the purpose of conflict-of-interest analysis. This conclusion is based on the fact that Cascades Ventures is the sole owner of Cascades Branding, and due to the fact that Cascades Ventures appears responsible for acquiring and managing the legal representation of its subsidiaries. It is further based on the unique business model of Cascades Ventures, a non-practicing entity ("NPE") seeking to enforce patents through subsidiaries.

No one disputes that the litigation is directly adverse to Cascades Branding. Therefore, under the above analysis, it is directly adverse to Cascades Ventures as well.

The disqualification question, therefore, turns on whether Cascades Ventures had a substantial relationship with Robins Kaplan. Under the first prong of the Seventh Circuit's analysis, the Court must reconstruct the scope of the representation. The parties do not dispute that the current litigation was not discussed. The scope, instead, was Cascades Ventures' disclosure of confidential information in the course of exploring whether the law firm would represent it in the Elbrus patent portfolio matter.

The Court notes that the August 25, 2010 e-mail from attorney Schutz to Brown affirmatively demonstrates that confidential information was disclosed. . . .

The August 25, 2010 communication reflects a distinct litigation strategy with regards to the Elbrus portfolio, and it further reflects that Schutz (e-mailing from an airport) was able to recall this information off the top of his head without the benefit of a file.

Robins Kaplan maintains that this e-mail reflects only strategy specific to one target of the Elbrus litigation, and does not reflect a wider knowledge of Cascades Ventures' "playbook" in regards to reasonable royalties in licensing, settlement thresholds, litigation strategy, Cascades Ventures' business model or other information that would be useful to a lawsuit opponent.

Plaintiff alleges that all of those broader matters were, in fact, communicated.

Robins Kaplan points to the eventual resultant Elbrus litigation (conducted by another firm), which did not necessarily follow the strategy outlined in the August 25, 2010 e-mail. . . .

The e-mail does reflect an exchange on just one patent portfolio, but the Court notes that the second prong of the substantial relationship question does not call for who can prove what information was communicated. It asks merely whether "it is reasonable to infer that the confidential information *allegedly* given would have been given to a lawyer representing a client in those matters." *See LaSalle, infra* (emphasis added).

The Court believes the e-mail at issue not only reflects strategy specific to one target in the Elbrus matter, but is illuminating as to Cascades Ventures' core litigation, licensing, reasonable royalty and business model strategies. Further, the emails reflect that Cascades Ventures and Schutz had other discussions not reflected in the submitted e-mails. It is reasonable to assume that, particularly in the unique context of an NPE, discussions would have necessarily touched on questions of what sort of return Cascades Ventures would accept, what sort of settlements would make litigation profitable, and what sort of royalty and licensing agreements Cascades was looking for. The second prong, therefore, is met.

As to the third prong, it must be determined if the information learned in that consultation is relevant to the current litigation. The Court finds that it is. NPE litigation is dollars-and-cents driven phenomenon, unburdened, usually, by the emotional, bet-the-company patent litigation sometimes seen by practicing entities. Information on an NPE's thresholds for profit, licensing, royalty and litigation, therefore, give a much clearer picture to an opponent of where one might be attacked in litigation, and how an opponent will respond to those attacks.

Outside of the Seventh Circuit's three-prong analysis, the Illinois Rules call for the same result. Robins Kaplan has received information that could be significantly harmful to Cascades Ventures in this litigation, and Rule 1.18 mandates disqualification not only of Schutz, but the entire firm.

The Court is careful to note that it does not intend to impugn Schutz, McMahon or their firm in their conduct thus far revealed. It is simply a fact of life that knowledge, once gained, cannot be completely flushed out of someone's head. This is only further demonstrated by Schutz's ability to recall, without the benefit of any paperwork in front of him, detailed confidential information about the consultation with Brown. It would not be fair to either Cascades

Ventures or Best Buy to ask him to operate without use of that knowledge, and in any case, Rule 1.18 does not allow for it.

The Court does not reach its conclusion lightly, and is cognizant that it deprives Best Buy of its long-term and preferred counsel in this matter. As Plaintiff notes, however, local counsel can continue to represent Best Buy, and this Court is prepared to entertain any and all motions for extended deadlines by Best Buy that are premised on the need to retain new counsel and get them up to speed.

IV. CONCLUSION

Because Robins Kaplan learned confidential information in its prospective client negotiations with Plaintiff that would be harmful to Plaintiff in this litigation, Plaintiff's Motion to Disqualify Robins Kaplan as Best Buy's attorney is granted. . . .

B. Prospective Client Conflicts

Problems

11-4. Martyn & Fox received a call to defend a major accounting firm in a 10b-5 class action involving a dot-com company whose stock has precipitously dropped. The accounting firm sent Fox the pleadings, and Fox met with them for three hours yesterday, explaining the firm's approach and the possible lines of defense the accounting firm might use. The firm promised to get back to Martyn & Fox next week. Today, Martyn circulated a conflicts memo asking whether the firm could take on the representation of the defendant underwriter in the same matter. What should Fox do?

11-5. Small Co. asks Martyn & Fox to bring a huge fraud and RICO claim against Magna Co. Martyn circulates a conflicts memo. The next day, she receives a call from her bankruptcy partner. "We represent Big Bank in a $600 million loan to Magna that is scheduled to close next Tuesday. I'll tell the CEO right away, and we'll be heroes."

Consider: Model Rules 1.0(k), 1.18
RLGL § 15

Lawyer Websites
ABA Formal Opinion 10-457
*American Bar Association Standing Committee
on Ethics and Professional Responsibility*

I. Introduction

Many lawyers and law firms have established websites as a means of communicating with the public. A lawyer website can provide to anyone with

Internet access a wide array of information about the law, legal institutions, and the value of legal services. Websites also offer lawyers a twenty-four hour marketing tool by calling attention to the particular qualifications of a lawyer or a law firm, explaining the scope of the legal services they provide and describing their clientele, and adding an electronic link to contact an individual lawyer.

The obvious benefit of this information can diminish or disappear if the website visitor misunderstands or is misled by website information and features. A website visitor might rely on general legal information to answer a personal legal question. Another might assume that a website's provision of direct electronic contact to a lawyer implies that the lawyer agrees to preserve the confidentiality of information disclosed by website visitors.

For lawyers, website marketing can give rise to the problem of unanticipated reliance or unexpected inquiries or information from website visitors seeking legal advice. This opinion addresses some of the ethical obligations that lawyers should address in considering the content and features of their websites.

II. Website Content . . .

B. Information About the Law

Lawyers have long offered legal information to the public in a variety of ways, such as by writing books or articles, giving talks to groups, or staffing legal hotlines. Lawyer websites also can assist the public in understanding the law and in identifying when and how to obtain legal services. . . .

Legal information, like information about a lawyer or the lawyer's services, must meet the requirements of Rules 7.1, 8.4(c), and 4.1(a). Lawyers may offer accurate legal information that does not materially mislead reasonable readers. . . . Although no exact line can be drawn between legal information and legal advice, both the context and content of the information offered are helpful in distinguishing between the two.

With respect to context, lawyers who speak to groups generally have been characterized as offering only general legal information. With respect to content, lawyers who answer fact-specific legal questions may be characterized as offering personal legal advice, especially if the lawyer is responding to a question that can reasonably be understood to refer to the questioner's individual circumstances. However, a lawyer who poses and answers a hypothetical question usually will not be characterized as offering legal advice. To avoid misunderstanding, our previous opinions have recommended that lawyers who provide general legal information include statements that characterize the information as general in nature and caution that it should not be understood as a substitute for personal legal advice.

Such a warning is especially useful for website visitors who may be inexperienced in using legal services, and may believe that they can rely on general legal information to solve their specific problem. It would be prudent to avoid any misunderstanding by warning visitors that the legal information provided is general and should not be relied on as legal advice, and by explaining that legal advice cannot be given without full consideration of all relevant information relating to the visitor's individual situation.

C. Website Visitor Inquiries

Inquiries from a website visitor about legal advice or representation may raise an issue concerning the application of Rule 1.18 (Duties to Prospective Clients). Rule 1.18 protects the confidentiality of prospective client communications. It also recognizes several ways that lawyers may limit subsequent disqualification based on these prospective client disclosures when they decide not to undertake a matter.

Rule 1.18(a) addresses whether the inquirer has become a "prospective client," defined as "a person who discusses with a lawyer the possibility of forming a client-lawyer relationship." To "discuss," meaning to talk about, generally contemplates a two-way communication, which necessarily must begin with an initial communication. Rule 1.18 implicitly recognizes that this initial communication can come either from a lawyer or a person who wishes to become a prospective client.

Rule 1.18 Comment [2] also recognizes that not all initial communications from persons who wish to be prospective clients necessarily result in a "discussion" within the meaning of the rule: "a person who communicates information unilaterally to a lawyer, without any reasonable expectation that the lawyer is willing to discuss the possibility of forming a client-lawyer relationship, is not a prospective client."

For example, if a lawyer website specifically requests or invites submission of information concerning the possibility of forming a client-lawyer relationship with respect to a matter, a discussion, as that term is used in Rule 1.18, will result when a website visitor submits the requested information.[20] If a website visitor submits information to a site that does not specifically request or invite this, the lawyer's response to that submission will determine whether a discussion under Rule 1.18 has occurred.

A telephone, mail or e-mail exchange between an individual seeking legal services and a lawyer is analogous.[21] In these contexts, the lawyer takes part in a bilateral discussion about the possibility of forming a client-lawyer relationship and has the opportunity to limit or encourage the flow of information. For example, the lawyer may ask for additional details or may caution against providing any personal or sensitive information until a conflicts check can be completed.

Lawyers have a similar ability on their websites to control features and content so as to invite, encourage, limit, or discourage the flow of information to

---

20. Rule 1.18 cmt. 1.
21. *See, e.g.,* Virginia Legal Eth. Op. 1842 (2008) (absent voicemail message that asks for detailed information, providing phone number and voicemail is an invitation only to contact lawyer, not to submit confidential information).

and from website visitors.[22] A particular website might facilitate a very direct and almost immediate bilateral communication in response to marketing information about a specific lawyer. It might, for example, specifically encourage a website visitor to submit a personal inquiry about a proposed representation on a conveniently-provided website electronic form which, when responded to, begins a "discussion" about a proposed representation and, absent any cautionary language, invites submission of confidential information.[23] Another website might describe the work of the law firm and each of its lawyers, list only contact information such as a telephone number, e-mail or street address, or provide a website e-mail link to a lawyer. Providing such information alone does not create a reasonable expectation that the lawyer is willing to discuss a specific client-lawyer relationship.[24] A lawyer's response to an inquiry submitted by a visitor who uses this contact information may, however, begin a "discussion" within the meaning of Rule 1.18.

In between these two examples, a variety of website content and features might indicate that a lawyer has agreed to discuss a possible client-lawyer relationship. A former client's website communication to a lawyer about a new matter must be analyzed in light of their previous relationship, which may have given rise to a reasonable expectation of confidentiality.[25] But a person who knows that the lawyer already declined a particular representation or is already representing an adverse party can neither reasonably expect confidentiality, nor the lawyer wishes to discuss a client-lawyer relationship. Similarly, a person who purports to be a prospective client and who communicates with a number of lawyers with the intent to prevent other parties from retaining them in the same matter should have no reasonable expectation of confidentiality or that the lawyer would refrain from an adverse representation.[26]

---

2. *See, e.g.*, Arizona State Bar Op. 02-04 (2002) (lawyers who maintain websites with e-mail links should include disclaimers to clarify whether e-mail communications from prospective clients will be treated as confidential); Massachusetts Bar Ass'n Op. 07-01 (2007) (lawyer who receives unsolicited information from prospective client through e-mail link on law firm website without effective disclaimer must hold information confidential because law firm has opportunity to set conditions on flow of information).

23. *See, e.g.*, Virginia Legal Eth. Op. 1842 *supra* note 21 (website that specifically invites visitor to submit information in exchange for evaluation invites formation of client-lawyer relationship).

24. E-mails received from unknown persons who send them apart from the lawyer's website may even more easily be viewed as unsolicited. *See, e.g.*, Arizona State Bar Op. 02-04, *supra* note 22 (e-mail to multiple lawyers asking for representation); San Diego County Bar Assn. Op. 2006-1 (inquirer found lawyer's e-mail address on state bar membership records website accessible to the public).

25. *See, e.g.*, Oregon Eth. Op. 2005-146 (2005) (lawyer who sends periodic reminders to former clients risks giving recipients reasonable belief they are still current clients).

26. *See, e.g.*, Virginia Legal Eth. Op. 1794 (2004) (person who meets with lawyer for primary purpose of precluding others from obtaining legal representation does not have reasonable expectation of confidentiality); Ass'n of the Bar of the City of New York Committee on Prof'l and Jud. Eth. Formal Op. 2001-1 (2001) ("taint shoppers," who interview lawyers or law firms for purpose of disqualifying them from future adverse representation, have no good faith expectation of confidentiality).

In other circumstances, it may be difficult to predict when the overall message of a given website communicates a willingness by a lawyer to discuss a particular prospective client-lawyer relationship. Imprecision in a website message and failure to include a clarifying disclaimer may result in a website visitor reasonably viewing the website communication itself as the first step in a discussion.[27] Lawyers are therefore well-advised to consider that a website-generated inquiry may have come from a prospective client, and should pay special attention to including the appropriate warnings mentioned in the next section.

If a discussion with a prospective client has occurred, Rule 1.18(b) prohibits use or disclosure of information learned during such a discussion absent the prospective client's informed consent.[28] When the discussion reveals a conflict of interest, the lawyer should decline the representation,[29] and cannot disclose the information received without the informed consent of the prospective client.[30] For various reasons, including the need for a conflicts check, the lawyer may have tried to limit the initial discussion and may have clearly expressed those limitations to the prospective client. . . .

Rule 1.18(c) disqualifies lawyers and their law firms who have received information that "could be significantly harmful" to the prospective client from representing others with adverse interests in the same or substantially related matters.[31] For example, if a prospective client previously had disclosed only an intention to bring a particular lawsuit and has now retained a different lawyer to initiate the same suit, it is difficult to imagine any significant harm that could result from the law firm proceeding with the defense of the same matter. On the other hand, absent an appropriate warning, the prospective client's prior disclosure of more extensive facts about the matter may well be disqualifying.

Rule 1.18(d) creates two exceptions that allow subsequent adverse representation even if the prospective client disclosed information that was significantly harmful: (1) informed consent confirmed in writing from both the affected and the prospective client, or (2) reasonable measures to limit the disqualifying information, combined with timely screening of the disqualified lawyer from the subsequent adverse matter. Rule 1.18(d)(2) specifically would allow the law firm (but not the contacted lawyer) to "undertake or continue" the representation of someone with adverse interests without receiving the informed consent

---

27. *See, e.g.,* Massachusetts Bar Ass'n Op. 07-01, *supra* note 22 (in absence of effective disclaimer, prospective client visiting law firm website that markets background and qualifications of each lawyer in attractive light, stresses lawyer's skill at solving clients' practical problems, and provides e-mail link for immediate communication with that lawyer might reasonably conclude that firm and its individual lawyers have implicitly "agreed to consider" whether to form client-lawyer relationship).

28. Rule 1.18(b) allows disclosure or use if permitted by Rule 1.9. Rule 1.9(c)(2) and its Comment [7] in turn link disclosure to Rule 1.6, the general confidentiality rule, which requires client informed consent to disclosure.

29. Rule 1.18 cmt. 4.

30. Rule 1.18 cmt. 3.

31. *See also* RESTATEMENT (THIRD) OF THE LAW GOVERNING LAWYERS § 15 (2) (2000).

of the prospective client if the lawyer who initially received the information took reasonable precautions to limit the prospective client's initial disclosures and was timely screened from further involvement in the matter as required by Rule 1.0(k). . . .

C.   Imputed Client Conflicts

Problems

11-6. Martyn & Fox is in a ten-day countdown to trial when one of its associates darkens Fox's door to announce that she is leaving the firm on Friday. When Fox recovers from the shock of losing his right arm in the case on such short notice, the associate tells him that she will be taking a few clients to the firm on the other side of the case, but not to worry—she'll be screened. What should Martyn & Fox do?

11-7. Martyn & Fox's Berlin office represents Volkswagen in a dispute with Chrysler. Under rules applicable to German lawyers, screening of a lateral lawyer is permitted to lift imputation; under the rules applicable to Martyn & Fox in New York, no screening is permitted. Should Martyn & Fox be disqualified?

11-8. Martyn & Fox agrees to staff a hotline for the local legal services project every Tuesday. One Tuesday, a Martyn & Fox associate received a phone call from an individual who has been the victim of predatory lending by The Dollar Store. Without seeing any documents, the associate gave the woman advice about possible remedies, only to learn upon returning to the firm that Big Bank, Martyn & Fox's largest client, owns The Dollar Store. Is Martyn & Fox in trouble?

**Consider: Model Rules 1.0(c), 1.7, 1.9, 1.10, 1.16, 6.5, 8.5
           RLGL § 124**

Martin v. Atlanticare

2011 U.S. Dist. LEXIS 122987 (D. N. J.)

Joel SCHNEIDER, United States Magistrate Judge

After Lisa Grosskruetz, Esquire, did substantial substantive defense work on this case while employed by defendants' law firm, Morgan, Lewis and Bockius, LLP ("Morgan"), she left Morgan and went to work for plaintiffs' law firm, Costello & Mains, P.C. The question before the Court is whether Costello & Mains should be disqualified because it employed a side-switching attorney.[1] Under

---

1. "A side-switching attorney is one who formerly represented a client in a matter and subsequently undertakes representation, or affiliates herself with a firm that has undertaken representation, of an adversary in a related matter." *Pallon v. Roggio,* 2006 U.S. Dist. LEXIS 59881 (D.N.J. 2006).

the circumstances presented herein the answer is an emphatic yes. Accordingly, defendants' Motion to Disqualify Plaintiffs' Counsel is GRANTED. . . .

Fact Background

Plaintiffs Shelly Martin ("Martin"), Karla Mayfield and Donna Davis filed this lawsuit on October 28, 2010 . . . [alleging] that defendants discriminated and retaliated against them because of their race and ethnicity. Plaintiff Martin also alleges that her employer, AtlantiCare Regional Medical Center (ARMC), violated the New Jersey Wage and Hour Law and the Fair Labor Standards Act by not paying her for work in excess of forty hours per week. Martin brings this claim on behalf of herself and as a "collective action" on behalf of similarly situated workers.

Plaintiffs are represented by Costello & Mains ("CM"). The managing partner of the firm is Kevin Costello ("Costello" or "KC"). Defendants are represented by Morgan. . . . At the inception of the case, defendants' defense was coordinated by a three-attorney team at Morgan. The supervising partner-in-charge was Richard Rosenblatt, Esquire ("RR"). The other attorneys on the original defense team were Lisa Grosskruetz, Esquire ("LG") and Prashanth Jayachandran, Esquire, ("PJ"). LG started working for Morgan on November 22, 2010 after having litigated employment matters in New Jersey for 23 years. PJ has been admitted to practice for 12 years and has extensive experience representing employers in wage and hour class and collective actions.

According to her time records LG started working on this case for Morgan on November 24, 2010. LG left Morgan on March 4, 2011. During the approximately 4 1/2 months she was employed at Morgan LG worked 108.2 hours on the case. During the same time period RR worked only 13.1 hours on the case and PJ worked 49.6 hours. This motion to disqualify arises from the fact that after LG left Morgan on March 4, 2011, she started working for CM on March 7, 2011.[4] LG subsequently left CM on April 15, 2011 and is no longer working for the firm.[5] Defendants were not notified of LG's side-switching before LG started working at CM. Defendants first learned that their former defense counsel was employed at their adversary's law firm when PJ noticed LG's name on CM's letterhead.

The parties do not dispute that LG is disqualified from representing plaintiffs pursuant to New Jersey Rule of Professional Conduct ("RPC") 1.9. Defendants argue that since LG is disqualified from representing plaintiffs, the disqualification should be imputed to CM pursuant to RPC 1.10. . . .

---

4. Defendants do not allege that LG worked on the case while she was employed by CM. Defendants also do not allege that LG revealed any privileged information or client confidences to CM.

5. While LG was working for Morgan, Costello initiated the discussions about her coming to work for him. During the call Costello learned that LG was apparently dissatisfied with her work at Morgan.

Motions to Disqualify

In the District of New Jersey, issues regarding professional ethics are governed by L. Civ. R. 103.1(a). This Rule provides that the Rules of Professional Conduct of the American Bar Association as revised by the New Jersey Supreme Court shall govern the conduct of members of the bar admitted to practice in the District. . . .

When determining whether to disqualify counsel the Court must closely and carefully scrutinize the facts to prevent unjust results. . . . New Jersey courts have consistently eschewed per se rules of disqualification, stressing the 'fact-sensitive nature' of a decision to disqualify counsel. Cardona v. Gen. Motors Corp., 942 F.Supp. 968, 976 (D.N.J. 1996). . . .

RPC 1.9 and 1.10(c)

RPC 1.10(c) provides the framework for deciding defendants' motion. This RPC reads:

(c) When a lawyer becomes associated with a firm, no lawyer associated in the firm shall knowingly represent a person in a matter in which that lawyer is disqualified under RPC 1.9 unless,

(1) the matter does not involve a proceeding in which the personally disqualified lawyer had primary responsibility;

(2) the personally disqualified lawyer is timely screened from any participation in the matter and is apportioned no part of the fee therefrom; and

(3) written notice is promptly given to any affected former client to enable it to ascertain compliance with the provisions of this Rule.

As RPC 1.10(c) dictates, the Court must first determine whether LG is disqualified under RPC 1.9, which governs duties to former clients. . . .

LG joined CM immediately after leaving Morgan where she worked on the defense of the present case. Although plaintiffs minimize LG's role while at Morgan, they acknowledge that LG is disqualified from working on the case pursuant to RPC 1.9(a) and (b).

Having determined that LG is disqualified from representing plaintiffs pursuant to RPC 1.9, the pertinent issue becomes whether LG's disqualification is imputed to CM. To make this determination the Court must assess the three elements of RPC 1.10(c). . . .

"Primary Responsibility"

The focus of the parties' arguments centers on whether LG had primary responsibility for the defense of the litigation while she was employed at Morgan. Primary responsibility is defined in the "terminology" section of the RPC's as "actual participation in the management and direction of the matter at the policy-making level or responsibility at the operational level as manifested by the continuous day-to-day responsibility for litigation or transaction decisions." RPC 1.0(h). . . .

If the Court determines that LG had "primary responsibility" while at Morgan its inquiry is complete and defendants' motion must be granted. Pursuant to RPC

1.10(c)(1), an attorney with primary responsibility cannot be screened at her new firm. See In re Gabapentin Patent Litigation ("Gabapentin"), 407 F.Supp.2d 607, 611 (D.N.J. 2005) (screening of individual attorneys from involvement in a case at the firm was insufficient alone to overcome the imputed disqualification, where the individuals had primary responsibility in the same matter while acting as counsel for the opposing party). . . .

If LG did not have primary responsibility, the Court must then analyze RPC 1.10(c)(2) and (3). If LG was adequately screened and is not apportioned a fee from the case, and if adequate written notice was given to her affected former client, e.g., AtlantiCare, then defendants' motion should be denied. ("The attorney's limited, peripheral involvement with the adverse party before switching firms would not prevent the new firm from continuing in the matter if the attorney were properly screened").

Plaintiffs and LG minimize LG's role while at Morgan. LG alleges she "was assigned to perform certain limited tasks with regard to this matter." Plaintiffs argue, "the work Ms. Grosskreutz performed while an associate at Morgan Lewis concerned nothing more than review of mostly irrelevant and/or discoverable documents and interviews of witnesses that elicited discoverable information." . . .

Plaintiff's characterization of LG's role at Morgan as "limited" does not comport with the evidence. This is illustrated by the fact that from November 2010 to March 2011 LG worked 108.2 hours on the case, almost twice as many hours as the combined total of the other two members of the Morgan defense team. Further, . . . LG acknowledges that she prepared all or part of defendants' removal papers and motion to dismiss, reviewed client documents for relevancy, consulted with defendants' in-house counsel, prepared witness outlines, interviewed defendants' witnesses, prepared witness summaries, and spoke with plaintiffs' counsel. LG's contemporaneous time billing entries also contradict her allegation that she only performed "limited tasks." According to her billing entries LG researched relevant legal issues, prepared legal papers, analyzed plaintiffs' complaints, reviewed background investigation materials about plaintiffs provided by the client, exchanged e-mails with the client, reviewed client documents, prepared representation letters, analyzed plaintiffs' discovery directed to defendants, reviewed and analyzed plaintiffs' personnel files with regard to the defense of their discrimination claims, prepared witness outlines, interviewed witnesses, prepared witness summaries, communicated with her clients about plaintiffs, and identified relevant and responsive documents. These are hardly "limited" roles. LG's descriptions evidence that she played a substantial and substantive role in AtlantiCare's defense.

Defendants' Declarations provide further evidence of LG's integral defense role. RR provided Morgan's strategic leadership. RR alleges that LG was "intimately involved in every facet of the defense" and that she "took an active operational role in almost all aspects of [Morgan's] defense of this matter" RR also states that the Morgan team would "make collaborative decisions as to how to address issues arising in the case." In addition, RR stated that LG would make recommendations for how to proceed with AtlantiCare's defense and he would brief LG on his communications with the client. RR's staffing plan was for LG and PJ "to share primary responsibility for the day-to-day operational management of the case with [his] oversight and direction as needed." RR expected that eventually LG "would assume virtually the sole day-to-day lead operational role" by the time PJ became fully involved in another case pending in Boston. RR explained that given LG's experience "the staffing plan was to have [LG] handle the bulk of the day-to-day case handling."

AtlantiCare's in-house counsel corroborates Morgan's Declarations. She swore: . . .

> We sent volumes of documents and materials to Morgan Lewis related to the case, which Ms. Grosskreutz reviewed. Ms. Grosskreutz also interviewed several witnesses. She communicated with me regarding her witness interviews and her review of documents related to this case. I also spoke with Ms. Grosskreutz regarding our legal strategy and our internal efforts to collect relevant documents. In addition, Ms. Grosskreutz is aware of AtlantiCare's investigation into matters raised by the Complaint.

LG's e-mails also evidence her integral defense role. The e-mails demonstrate that the Morgan defense team and AtlantiCare regularly communicated about the status of the case and defense strategies. The e-mails also demonstrate that LG was privy to information protected by the attorney-client privilege and work-product doctrine. In addition, the e-mails show that LG provided her strategic input on different employment related issues.

The foregoing evidence demonstrates to the Court that LG's actions fit squarely within the meaning of the term "primary responsibility" as the term is defined in the RPC's. In order to have primary responsibility it was not necessary for LG to be the supervising attorney on the file or the partner in charge of the file. This is evident by the fact that the applicable definition merely requires "participation" in the "management and direction of the matter at the policy-making level." LG plainly "participated" in the management of the case as she took the "laboring oar" in AtlantiCare's defense and she regularly consulted with the Morgan defense team about defense strategy. Further, as PJ was "out of pocket" in February 2011, and RR's role at the time was minimal, LG was essentially responsible for AtlantiCare's entire defense before she left Morgan. LG also had "responsibility at the operational level" as manifested by the "continuous day-to-day responsibility for litigation or transaction decisions." This is evidenced by LG's regular and continuous work on the file from when she started at Morgan to when she left. Given the breadth of her work and the number of hours she worked on the case, it cannot be reasonably challenged that LG had operational and decisional responsibilities. The Court finds that LG had "primary responsibility" even though she was not the "supervising attorney" on the file and even though she shared defense responsibility with her colleagues. . . .

Based on the evidence presented, plaintiffs' argument that "Ms. Grosskreutz [did] not receive any confidential information while employed at Morgan Lewis" is incredulous. . . .

The Court does not agree with plaintiffs' conclusion that LG played a minimal and unimportant defense role. LG's document reviews, witness interviews, etc. were significant and integrally related to the defense of the case.[15] This work is not, as plaintiffs argue, "mechanical." Document review, preparing briefs and interviewing witnesses are all integral to an effective litigation defense. . . .

The Court discounts plaintiffs' argument that even if CM received information from LG regarding the case, the information would have been discoverable and not subject to any privilege. This argument has been rejected in various decisions. . . .

While some of the information LG had access to may be disclosed in discovery, it is also likely that other materials are privileged and not subject to production. The outcome of defendants' disqualification motion should not be dependent on a document by document analysis of what is and is not discoverable, otherwise:

> A former client seeking to keep a lawyer from side-switching would essentially be required to disclose privileged communications simply to maintain a level playing field and meet its burden of persuasion on a motion to disqualify. Every disqualification motion would have the potential to turn into a subdispute over complex privilege issues relating to documents and communications—all before the case even started. Such a standard would be manifestly unworkable and improper. H20 Plus, LLC v. Arch Pers. Care Prods., L.P., 2010 U.S. Dist. LEXIS 124055 (D.N.J. 2010)

The Court also agrees with defendants' argument that, "[f]ailure to disqualify Plaintiffs' counsel under these circumstances would undermine the confidence that clients have in their outside counsel."

Screening

As noted, since LG had "primary responsibility" at Morgan, her conflict is imputed to CM pursuant to RPC 1.10(c) and defendants' motion to disqualify must be granted. However, even if LG did not have primary responsibility, defendants' motion would still be granted because plaintiffs cannot satisfy the screening requirement in RPC 1.10(c)(2). . . .

RPC 1.10(f) provides some guidance:

> Any law firm that enters a screening arrangement, as provided by this Rule, shall establish appropriate written procedures to insure that: (1) all attorneys and other personnel in the law firm screen the personally disqualified attorney from

---

15. Defendants argue:

   Plaintiffs would have the Court believe that Ms. Grosskreutz was some neophyte junior lawyer playing a bit role sitting in a library researching case law. This is absurd. As Costello & Mains touted on its website while Ms. Grosskreutz was employed by it, she is a lawyer with 23 years of extensive experience representing employers, having "devoted her litigation and trial practice solely to the practice of Labor and Employment law" and worked for "several large law firms with offices in New Jersey and nationwide."

any participation in the matter, (2) the screened attorney acknowledges the obligation to remain screened and takes action to insure the same, and (3) the screened attorney is apportioned no part of the fee therefrom.

In addition, RPC 1.0(l) (Terminology) states:

> "Screened" denotes the isolation of a lawyer from any participation in the matter through the timely adoption and enforcement by a law firm of a written procedure pursuant to RPC 1.10(f) which is reasonably adequate under the circumstances to protect information that the isolated lawyer is obligated to protect under these Rules or other law.

Kevin Costello provided the only evidence as to LG's screening. His Certification states that upon LG's hiring "she was immediately screened from any contact or communication regarding the present matter." The details of the screening were not included in the Certification. However, Costello represented at oral argument that LG was told before she started working for him that she was "not going to work on AtlantiCare." Costello represented that the first day LG came to work he told everyone in his office that LG "can't touch this file," "she can't see this file," she "can't go to that file drawer herself," and she can't "click on AtlantiCare" on the "case management system." Costello also claims he had a reminder meeting with everyone in his office. Costello acknowledges that his firm did not have a written screening policy.

RPC 1.10(f) and 1.0(e) indicate in clear and unmistakable terms that to be adequate a screening procedure must be in writing. CM never established a written procedure and for this reason alone its screening was inadequate. CM argues its screening was adequate because the RPC's do not provide a time frame for when a written screening procedure must be deployed.[18] Therefore, CM argues, even though it did not have a written screening procedure when LG started at CM, nor at any time during the 6–7 weeks she worked there, CM's screening was adequate. This argument defies all notions of common sense. If the purpose of a screening procedure is to protect information the isolated lawyer is required to protect, written procedures should be in place before a disqualified lawyer starts work. At a minimum, the procedures should be in place when the employment starts, not after the disqualified lawyer leaves the firm. It makes no sense for the RPC's to require a written screening procedure but to find that the written procedure can be adopted after the disqualified lawyer leaves the firm. "[T]imely screening arrangements are essential to the avoidance of firm disqualification." LaSalle Nat'l Bank v. County of Lake, 703 F.2d 252, 259 n.3 (7th Cir. 1983).

In addition, even if CM's screening procedure was put in writing, the procedure CM used was inadequate. . . . There is no indication that the AtlantiCare

---

18. Costello argued, "[i]t [RPC's] doesn't say that you can't verbally screen and substantively screen and compellingly and finally and well-donely [sic] screen. And then, by the way, memo it up later and say, by the way, referring back to our meeting on such and such a day, just be reminded, blah, blah, blah."

file was physically separated from CM's other files. In addition, the file was not specially secured or "kept under lock and key," LG and CM's employees did not acknowledge in writing CM's procedures, and LG was not "locked out" of the AtlantiCare file on CM's computer system. These are the sorts of procedures that are put in place in instances where courts have found screens to be adequate.[21]

RPC 1.10(b)

LG left CM on April 15, 2011, which is the same day defendants filed the present motion. Plaintiffs argue that because LG left CM, the present motion should be governed by RPC 1.10(b). . . . [24]

Defendants argue that severing a relationship with a disqualified attorney does not cure imputed disqualification. . . .

This Court agrees, and finds further support for this conclusion in Cardona, 942 F. Supp. at 976, wherein the court found that a rule permitting the cleansing of an imputed conflict by the mere dismissal of a side-switching attorney "would not provide any disincentive to a law firm that contemplates hiring an attorney who has formerly represented an adverse party." Accord Lawler v. Isaac, 592 A.2d 1 (App. Div. 1991) ("The firm must be disqualified even if the associate disclosed none of his previously acquired knowledge and even though he is no longer employed by [the firm.]").

For the reasons discussed, therefore, the Court finds that RPC 1.10(b) is not applicable to the conflict imputation issue before it.

Conclusion

In sum, the Court finds that Costello and Mains must be disqualified because LG's conflict is imputed to the entire firm. Since LG had "primary responsibility" for AtlantiCare's defense while she worked at Morgan, screening cannot prevent the conflict imputation. In addition, even if LG did not have primary responsibility, disqualification is appropriate because CM did not employ an adequate screening procedure. . . .

---

21. In addition to screening, in order for CM to avoid imputation of LG's conflict CM was required to give prompt written notice of LG's employment to defendants. The purpose of the notice is to enable defendants to ensure compliance with the RPC's. See RPC 1.10(c)(3). CM did not give this notice. Instead, Morgan first learned about LG's side-switching when it saw her name on CM's letterhead. This apparently occurred shortly after LG joined the firm. The appropriate course of conduct should have been for CM to notify Morgan before LG started at the firm. This would have enabled defendants to "ascertain compliance" with RPC 1.10(c) sooner rather than later. . . . If CM had time to employ LG and add her name to its letterhead, it certainly had the opportunity to notify defendants of LG's employment before she started at the firm or contemporaneously therewith. Despite CM's actions in this regard, however, the Court does not base CM's disqualification on its failure to give proper notice pursuant to RPC 1.10(c)(2).

24. As aptly put in another opinion, CM urges the Court to adopt a rule whereby the imputed disqualification of a "tainted" lawyer "evaporates" upon the departure of the side-switching attorney. Cardona, *supra*, 942 F. Supp. at 976.

Lawrence J. Fox

Legal Tender: A Lawyer's Guide to Handling Professional Dilemmas
122-125 (ABA 1995)

My Lawyer Switched Sides; Don't Worry, There's a Screen

The litigation department breakfasts always seemed to be scheduled for the wrong day of the week. Just when the key deposition loomed with its 10:00 A.M. start, the chairman insisted everyone meet at 7:30 in the tired windowless conference room on 13, the one with the boring duck prints that were always askew. Obligations and self-interest overcame the need for last-minute deposition preparations. After all, associate reviews were just around the corner. She wondered, as she raced to be on time, why she had ever bothered to switch firms. It was true: they weren't all identical; they were just the same. They made you feel the same—tired and overworked—and the paycheck was delivered with the same heavy resentment. They made you feel the same anxiety that you would not meet the firm's billable hour "targets," the euphemism employed by the chair of each firm to describe her 2,200 hour quota. She had to find a better way, she thought, as she slumped resignedly into the well-worn conference room chair. How many hours had she spent in this room? In these meetings? Being bored?

Barely listening, she maintained her studied attentive pose, one she had mastered to get her through those interminable depositions. She would follow her usual rule: make an attempt at one cogent remark, but otherwise remain silent. Talking at meetings like this could only hurt her chances for partnership (as if she cared), and no one ever made partner because of her "performance" at departmental meetings. Wait, look alert, pick your moment, and then get out as soon as possible.

The conversation turned to privileged documents: something about whether you could withhold internal corporate memos in document discovery on the grounds of privilege when they were addressed to multiple executives as well as in-house general counsel. Her mind wandered back to the practice of one of her clients at the old firm. Suddenly sensing this anecdotal tidbit as "her" moment, she shared with the assembled group, "When I was at Bryans & Putnam, one of our clients, City Trust Company, had a bright line rule: so long as the document had counsel's name or initials on it anywhere—as writer, addressee, copied in or later sent the document—they deemed it privileged. It made it real easy to decide which documents to withhold."

Several minutes later, as the discussion rejected her formulation as far too broad, even unprofessional, it suddenly occurred to her. Of course! The firm had litigation against City Trust Company, she was "screened" from that litigation (she had prepared some early interrogatories for City Trust) and she had suddenly revealed a City Trust confidence to everyone. Panic replaced boredom; nausea gripped her. What should she do? What would her firm colleagues do? Was her career going up in smoke before her eyes? She had broken her trust; she hadn't intended to, she hadn't been thinking. It was just a passing remark. She rose shakily, mumbled an apology, and hurried to the ladies' room.

Her mind raced back to her first thoughts about leaving her old firm. The head-hunter had called and indicated how easy it was to place a young associate practicing in Pennsylvania, one of the few states that provided for screening of private lawyers when they switched firms. It made looking for a job so much simpler. She did not have to worry about whether the possible new employers had cases against her old clients. If the headhunter found a firm that liked her, she could just accept the job without worrying about potential conflicts. If any were discovered, the Pennsylvania rules would simply require that she be screened from those matters.

She felt comfortable with that arrangement. She knew how she viewed client confidences—she would never share them. In fact, it gave her great pride to think of herself as a lawyer of integrity, one who could be trusted with confidential information. Indeed it was one of the things that drove her husband crazy—the way she always knew the best secrets weeks before he would hear about it at a cocktail party or read it in the newspaper. She even felt flattered when, after the two matters from which she had to be screened were identified, the chairman of her new firm's professional responsibility committee said to her that the firm was not going to take any elaborate measures to screen her because the firm had a long tradition of placing substantial trust in their associates.

But now! What could she do? Maybe she shouldn't do anything. If she talked to anyone at her new firm that would just emphasize the importance of her disclosure. Would her new firm then have to resign from handling the City Trust matters? One of them involved Pegasus Construction Company, her new firm's largest litigation client. And did she have to tell City Trust? Or anyone at Bryans & Putnam? So many questions! No one to turn to. She was spinning with concerns. It was too much to handle. She would leave early—it would be her first pre-8:00 P.M. departure in weeks—and maybe she could persuade her husband that dinner at the new Thai restaurant on South Street would be in order . . . she needed a chance to clear her head, to regroup.

The next day dawned early and bright—the kind of day that gave June such a good reputation. The dinner had been close to perfect, perhaps a tad too much wine. And while she hated to admit it, it may have been the wine that permitted her to see the situation clearly.

There was no doubting her mistake; she shouldn't have blurted out those remarks at the meeting the day before, but it was only after the dinner that she recalled how upset she had been originally when she learned that City Trust took this position on the privilege. She recalled with clarity how it had offended her at the time, how surprised she was that the partners at old Bryans & Putnam had so blithely accepted the client's notion of privilege. So was there really anything wrong with what she had said? If City Trust's position were defensible . . . maybe she had an obligation to tell someone, maybe her new firm would be obliged to resign. But since it was her view that City Trust was wrong, there really was no harm. If her colleagues who worked on City Trust matters at her new firm used her information to press a little harder for documents that City Trust withheld on the ground of privilege, it would be for the courts to decide who was right. And it wasn't like she had shared confidential facts about the case.

As she contemplated all of this, she couldn't really tell whether it was the weather, the Cabernet Sauvignon, or the chicken satay that had induced this new sense of calm; the problems of yesterday had been put to rest and, particularly pleasing, she had handled the entire matter herself. Off she went to work with a new lightness in her step, not unlike the way she felt the day she learned she had passed the bar exam. Maybe she would go for partner after all.

Practice Pointers:
Implementing a Conflicts Control System

Chapters 9 through 11 illustrate the need to identify and properly respond to a wide variety of potential conflicts of interest. Model Rule 1.10 imputes individual lawyer conflicts to "lawyers associated in firms."[1] Model Rule 5.1 requires lawyers with managerial authority in law firms to establish policies and procedures "designed to detect and resolve conflicts of interest."[2] MR 5.3 requires the same supervision of nonlawyer personnel. A law firm's policies and procedures therefore must include the development, use, and maintenance of a system of accurate information and the proper resolution of conflicts identified using such a system.

Building a Database

Current law regulating personal, concurrent, third-person, prospective, and former client conflicts requires precise identification of the client, nature of the matter, and the lawyers who work on the case. Because most conflicts are imputed to other lawyers in the firm,[3] a firm-wide database should include the following information about law-firm lawyers and clients to check for conflicts.

Law-Firm Lawyers   Identifying personal conflicts generated by the interests of law-firm lawyers requires information about each lawyer in the law firm, including:

- The name of each lawyer;
- A list of material interests (property, business, and financial) owned by that lawyer; and

---

1. MR 1.0(c); The Law Governing Lawyers: *Actual and Accidental Clients, supra* p. 79.
2. MR 5.1, Comment [2]. In re Columbia Valley Healthcare Sys. LP, 320 S.W.3d 819, 826 (Tex. 2010) (oral screening instructions are ineffective; a firm must adopt "formal, institutionalized screening measures").
3. MR 1.8(h), 1.10, 1.11, and 1.12 generally impute the conflict of one lawyer to others in the firm. MR 1.10(a) exempts prohibitions "based on a personal interest of the prohibited lawyer" if the personal interest "does not present a significant risk of materially limiting the representation of the client by the remaining lawyers in the firm." Of course, a firm will not be able to evaluate whether a personal conflict of one of its lawyers materially limits the client's representation without knowing that it exists.

- Substantial property, business, or financial interests of persons in that lawyer's household.

Law-Firm Clients, Prospective and Former Clients Identifying client conflicts requires information about current, prospective, and former clients, including:

- Accurate identification of the client, including subsidiaries, parents, or other affiliates, and control persons of entity clients, as well as changes or variations in personal or corporate name;[4]
- A description of the subject matter of the client representation, including the identities (with changes when they occur) of actual and potential opposing parties;
- Any third persons or entities, such as insurers, who are paying for or are direct beneficiaries of the representation; and
- The names of law firm lawyers responsible for the matter.

Checking for Conflicts

Once the initial database has been established, new data should be added before any new client matter is opened by the firm, as well as at any time that new personnel join the firm.[5] Any changes in client identity, client status, opposing parties, or lawyers working on the file should be entered on the day that the change occurs or the firm becomes aware of it.[6]

Conflicts should be monitored by timely entries into the database, by timely use of the database to search for relevant matches, and by notification about new client matters through interoffice memoranda, which trigger the memory of all firm lawyers. These procedures help assure that information from each source is supplemented by the other.

Identifying Conflicts

Absent an emergency, a new client file should be opened only after the completion of a conflicts check, including:

1. Checking for any matches between the prospective client's identifying information and the law-firm lawyers' interests, probable opponents and their lawyers, current, and former clients;
2. Circulating a written conflicts memo throughout the firm;
3. Summarizing the results in a writing that finds either that no matches were found or, if they were, that they indicate no conflict or a consentable

---

4. Commercial services make this information available to law firms.

5. MR 1.6 (b)(7); ABA Formal Op. 09-455 (2009) Disclosure of Conflicts Information When Lawyers Move Between Law Firms (conflicts information should not be disclosed until the moving lawyer and prospective new firm have engaged in substantive discussions and should be no greater than reasonably necessary to accomplish the purpose of conflicts detection). *See also* Problems 8-15 p. 299 and 13-5 p. 511.

6. Client status includes changes from prospective to current client, current to former client, former to prospective client, or former to current client.

conflict for which consent has been obtained, or, if permitted as a solution, that a timely and adequate screen has been established; and

4. Review by a neutral person of any information, matches, and explanatory memoranda.

Responding to Conflicts: Obtaining Informed Consent

If a potential conflict is identified, the lawyer and firm must first determine whether the conflict is consentable. If it is, the lawyer and firm next must examine whether they are free to disclose the information necessary to secure an "informed consent" consistent with their confidentiality duties.

When lawyers are able to seek client consent, Model Rules 1.7, 1.9, 1.10, 1.11, and 1.12 require that "each affected client gives informed consent, confirmed in writing."[7] Model Rule 1.0(e) defines "informed consent" as the client's agreement to the representation "after the lawyer has communicated adequate information and explanation about the material risks of and reasonably available alternatives to the proposed course of conduct."[8] A written confirmation of the client's informed consent is designed to clarify the nature of the conflict and "impress on clients the seriousness of the decision."[9]

Although an "informed consent, confirmed in writing"[10] does not require the client's signature or any specific language, it should be viewed as the written culmination of a client's understanding and agreement after the client has been given time to consider the matter and raise questions or concerns.[11] To memorialize such an informed consent, the lawyer is well advised to include a description of both the material risks and reasonably available alternatives to the conflict in the written document. Forms should be used carefully,[12] boilerplate avoided, and the letter should include specific language that adequately describes the client's situation and the nature of the conflict.

For example, describing the material risks of the proposed course of conduct may include conflicts created by the legal rights of the parties involved (such as the legal effect of a counterclaim filed by the opposing party against one of the clients), conflicts created by the individual facts in each representation (such as the fact that the opposing party has limited or unlimited insurance coverage), and conflicts created by any prior or continuing relationship of the lawyer with either party. Clients should also be made aware of changes in circumstance that

---

7. M R 1.7(b)(4). MR 1.8(a) and (g) further require that the client sign the writing.

8. MR 1.0(e). *See also* Woolley v. Sweeney, 2003 U.S. Dist. LEXIS 8110, at *20-23 (N.D. Tex.) (oral waiver with screen invalid even for former "sophisticated" client; "Acquiescence of a client without informed consent is tantamount to no consent at all.").

9. MR 1.7, Comment [20].

10. MR 1.0(b).

11. MR 1.7, Comment [20].

12. A few jurisdictions mandate consent disclosure language for particular conflicts. *See, e.g.,* Ohio R. Prof. Conduct 1.8(f)(4) (2011) (mandating "Statement of Insured Client's Rights").

may require the lawyer to withdraw, and what will happen if the representation of any client ends before the legal service is completed.[13]

Similarly, describing alternatives will always include the possibility of retaining another lawyer or firm without a conflict and the right to discharge the conflicted lawyer at any time. Other alternatives, in the case of joint representations, include options about the sharing of confidential information,[14] as well as an explanation about the nature of the lawyer's role in individual and joint representations, such as the fact that joint representations will require each client to assume greater responsibility for making decisions than might be the case if a lawyer were to advocate individually on their behalf.[15]

Responding to Conflicts: Establishing and Maintaining Effective Screens

Screens may be available to resolve some former-client conflicts,[16] either as part of the informed consent process,[17] or if otherwise recognized by the rules of professional conduct[18] or common law.[19] *Martin* agrees with Model Rule 1.10(a)(2) that even when allowed, a screen will not be deemed legally adequate unless it was timely established and the law firm that established it gave proper written notice to all affected parties.[20]

Model Rule 1.0(k) defines "screened" as "isolation of a lawyer from any participation in a matter through the timely imposition of procedures within a firm that are reasonably adequate under the circumstances to protect information

---

13. *See* MR 1.7, Comment [29]. Absent explicit and still effective consent to the contrary, the lawyer probably will be required to withdraw from some or all of the representations, causing additional expense and effort.

14. *See* MR 1.7, Comment [31].

15. *See* MR 1.7, Comment [32].

16. MR 1.10(a). *See also* D.C. Bar Leg. Eth. Comm'n, Formal Op. 349 (2009) (although joint defense agreements do not create former "clients," such agreement can give rise to a conflict that requires a timely screen to avoid disqualification).

17. *E.g.,* MR 1.7, 1.8, and 1.9; State v. Smith, 761 N.W.2d 63 (Iowa 2009) (the screen was one factor to be considered, along with client's waiver of conflict in deciding whether the conflict was actual or potential, serious or speculative).

18. MR 1.11(b)-(c) (former government employees), 1.12(c) (former judges, arbitrators, and mediators), 1.18(d) (prospective clients).

19. *See, e.g.,* RLGL § 124; Kirk v. First Am. Title Ins. Co., 108 Cal. Rptr. 3d 620 (Cal. Ct. App. 2010) (screening allowed in prospective client case where lawyer was in different office of large law firm and possessed only a small amount of confidential information); Meza v. H. Muhlstein & Co., 98 Cal. Rptr. 3d 422, 429 (Cal Ct. App. 2009) (screening not allowed in a side-switching case, where disqualification is due to lawyer's representation of the opposing side during the same case).

20. Several empirical studies indicate that lawyers do not often understand these requirements. Susan P. Shapiro, *Tangled Loyalties: Conflict of Interest in Legal Practice* 411-412 (U. Mich. Press 2002) (screens do not always meet the specifications found in ethics codes and case law and reinforce a double standard between clients with clout and formerly less powerful clients); Lee A. Pizzimenti, *Screen Verité: Do Rules About Ethical Screens Reflect the Truth About Real-Life Law Firm Practice?* 52 U. Miami L. Rev. 305 (1997) (study found the majority of firms take conflicts seriously, but that they "are hampered by flawed conflicts detection, flawed systems for maintaining screens and to some extent, an adversarial rather than fiduciary analysis of screen issues").

that the isolated lawyer is obligated to protect under these Rules or other law."[21] The New Jersey rule in *Martin* also requires that "effective written procedures" be in place before the screen is established to ensure that the screened lawyer actually is isolated from the matter and all firm lawyers understand the precise details of that isolation.[22]

To meet this standard, a law firm should:

- Determine whether the firm is large enough to establish an effective screen;[23]
- Implement a written screening policy;
- Establish the screen before the screened lawyer joins the firm, or if the lawyer is already in the firm, as soon as the conflict has been timely detected;[24]
- Acknowledge in writing that the screened lawyer will not communicate with any firm lawyers about the matter;
- Notify all law firm personnel about the screen, indicating they may not communicate with the screened lawyer about the matter;
- Quarantine all law firm files about the screened matter. Electronic files should be available only with a proper password, and paper files should be kept in an area that is not available to the screened lawyer;[25]
- Establish bookkeeping procedures that assure the screened lawyer does not share in the fee revenue from the case;[26] and
- Give prompt notification to all clients, former clients, or other parties that the screen has been established.[27]

---

21. MR 1.0(k).

22. *See also* Tucker v. Rossmiller, 569 F. Supp. 2d 834 (W.D. Wis 2008) (implementation of a formal mechanism to isolate the tainted lawyers required to prevent a mere "*de facto* screen that occurred by happenstance").

23. *See, e.g.*, Intelli-Check, Inc. v. Tricom Card Technologies, 2008 U.S. Dist. LEXIS 84435 (E.D.N.Y.) (screen upheld where firm consisted of 420 lawyers and screened lawyers were separated geographically and technologically); United States v. Pelle, 2007 U.S. Dist. LEXIS 13570 (D.N.J.) (ten-lawyer firm too small for effective screen because accidental exposure to the matter is likely).

24. *See, e.g.*, Lutron Elec. Co. v. Crestron Elec., Inc., 2010 U.S. Dist. LEXIS 120864 (D. Utah) (screen created as soon as firm was notified that one of its lawyers had worked for the opposing party at his former firm, timely); Chinese Auto. Distrib. of Am. LLC v. Bricklin, 2009 U.S. Dist. LEXIS 2647 (S.D.N.Y.) (screen set up three months after lateral joined firm when firm knew about conflict at the time that lateral joined but determined there was no conflict, not timely). Lucent Techs., Inc. v. Gateway, Inc., 2007 U.S. Dist. LEXIS 35502 (S.D. Cal.) (lateral listed former client upon joining the firm, but firm did not screen until after it made appearance in new case one month later, not timely).

25. *See* Graham Co. v. Griffing, 2009 U.S. Dist. LEXIS 103222 (E.D. Pa.) (screen should include restrictions on access to billing records of the matter at issue); Papyrus Tech. Corp. v. N.Y. Stock Exch., Inc., 325 F. Supp. 2d 270 (S.D.N.Y. 2004) (sealing of firm's document management system so that only members of the team working on the case could access electronic documents held to be effective).

26. *See* Gerald v. Turnock Plumbing, Heating & Cooling, LLC, 768 N.E.2d 498 (Ind. Ct. App. 2002) (screened lawyer was a partner and would receive a portion of firm's fees; disqualification granted).

27. MR 1.10 (a)(2)(ii) (former clients); 1.11(b)(2) (former government officers and employees), 1.12(c)(2) (former judges, arbitrators, and mediators); 1.18(d)(2)(ii) (prospective clients).

Once screens are timely implemented and carefully established, they also must be maintained. Inadvertent or intentional breaches of screens must be reported to affected clients to prevent further sanctions.[28] Further, screens can proliferate, so that law firms can find themselves with hundreds of them, each one generating the need to notify affected parties, segregate files, prevent communication, and preclude revenue sharing.[29] Keeping track of these details requires a great deal of skill. This is why, once established, law firms should maintain screens by:

- Creating law firm mechanisms that periodically remind screened lawyers of their obligations and inquire about the maintenance of proper screening procedures; and
- Promptly notify the affected clients and former clients if the screen is breached.

Integrating a Conflicts Control System into Law Firm Management

Law firms should establish a committee or designate a partner with responsibility for implementing the conflicts control system. Once a committee or partner is identified as having responsibility for monitoring conflicts within the firm, all conflicts detection and avoidance practices should be made routine by written policies and procedures that require compliance by all law firm personnel. When potential conflicts are discovered, the partner or committee should have the authority to decide how to respond. Law firm policy should include the requirement that any member of a law firm ethics committee potentially involved in any conflict be disqualified from considering its resolution. The partner or committee in charge of conflicts should also make clear that deviations from the firm policy are serious concerns and will result in appropriate sanctions.[30]

Following these procedures will not prevent conflicts, but they do put lawyers in a position to know about them and respond appropriately. Two things are certain. First, lawyers must know both the conflicts rules and the provisions

---

28. *E.g.,* Spur Prod. Corp. v. Stoel Rives LLP, 153 P.3d 1158 (Idaho 2007) (valid malpractice claim presented by client for failure of law firm to inform client of breach in a screen, causing client to agree to settle the underlying litigation client would not otherwise have agreed to if it had known about screen breach); Steel v. Gen. Motors Corp., 912 F. Supp. 724 (D.N.J. 1995) (inadvertent breach in screen required disqualification). *See also* Prince Jefri Bolkiah v. KPMG, 2 A.C. 222 (H.L. 1999) (disqualification required where lawyers in accounting firm disregarded screen in favor of team approach to prelitigation services).

29. Susan R. Martyn, *Visions of the Eternal Law Firm: The Future of Law Firm Screens,* 45 S.C. L. Rev. 937 (1994).

30. *See* Norfolk S. Ry. Co. v. Reading Blue Mt. & N. R.R. Co., 397 F. Supp. 2d 551, 555 (M.D. Pa. 2005) (screen that provided, "All personnel of this law firm are under strict written instruction not to discuss or reference the matter involving [x] with [the screened lawyer]" not adequate because it did not include the prospect of termination or disciplinary proceedings for violators); Elizabeth Chambliss & David B. Wilkins, *The Emerging Role of Ethics Advisors, General Counsel, and Other Compliance Specialists in Large Law Firms,* 44 Ariz. L. Rev. 559 (2002).

about screening if they are to have any hope of convincing a client to consent to a screen or a court to accept an involuntary substitute. Second, the law governing lawyering makes clear that failure to discover a conflict is no defense to discipline, disqualification, fee forfeiture, or other client remedies.[31]

D. Government Client Conflicts

Government lawyers and officials such as judges are governed by special conflicts rules, including Model Rules 1.11 and 1.12, as well as statutes and government regulations that govern conflict of interest. These rules seek to protect former government clients and to prevent lawyers from exploiting public employment for the benefit of others. They differ both in scope of individual disqualification and the situations in which screening is permitted. The basics of these rules are summarized in the following chart.

Former Clients and Former Government Matters		
	Former Clients	**Former Government Representation**	**Former Judge, Arbitrator, Mediator, or Other Third-Party Neutral**
Prior Representation	Formerly represented a client in a matter	Government employee or public officer	Judge, arbitrator, mediator, or other third-party neutral
Subsequent Disqualification	Same or substantially related matter and materially adverse interests	"Matter" [1.11(e)] and personal and substantial participation as government employee/ officer & 1.9(c)	"Matter" and personal and substantial participation as a judge, arbitrator, mediator, or other third-party neutral
Except	Informed consent of former client	Informed consent of agency	Informed consent of all parties to the proceeding
Firm	1.10	1.11(b)	1.12(c)

---

31. *See, e.g.,* In re Guaranty Ins. Serv., Inc., 310 S.W.3d 630, 632 (Tex. App. 2010) (law firm whose conflicts-screening procedures were "thorough" and "exemplary" but failed to reveal that a newly hired paralegal had worked on the case while employed by counsel for the opposing party, disqualified; "[a] firm's screening procedures, however thorough, must actually be effective in order to rebut the presumption of shared information.").

Problems

11-9. Martyn & Fox recently hired Julia Davis, a lawyer who worked for the state attorney general's office for the past six years. Ms. Davis's first case in the AG's office was the successful defense of a race discrimination class action against the State Department of Taxation. In her last case, she served as lead counsel in negotiating a settlement in an antitrust suit on behalf of the State Department of Transportation against General Motors.

    (a) Can Martyn & Fox take on the representation of Paula Pearson, who wishes to bring a race discrimination complaint against the State Department of Taxation based on events that occurred four years after Ms. Davis's defense of the department?

    (b) Can Martyn & Fox take on the representation of Local Municipality against General Motors based on facts identical to the State Department of Transportation case?

11-10. Grayson, the senior partner at Martyn & Fox, has been mediating a dispute between Hydrogen Electric and Steel Company over electric rates for the year 2009. He finished facilitating the participants' agreement last Tuesday. Now Martyn has been called by Steel Company to see if the firm will represent Steel Company against Hydrogen Electric for the year 2010 electric charges. May Martyn take the case?

Consider: Model Rules 1.11, 1.12, 7.6
RLGL § 133

Lawyers and Clients: *Representing Governments*

A substantial group of lawyers provide legal services to federal, state, and local government units in the widest variety of matters.[1] Model Rule 1.13, Comment [9] extends the rule's entity concept of organizations to governmental organizations, but cautions that issues related to client identity and fiduciary obligations may be shaped not only by the government lawyer's general and specific ethical obligations, but also by the client-government's public obligations imposed by constitution, statute, regulation, or common law.

For example, the last problems regarding mediators and government lawyers required you to apply special conflict of interest rules found in Model Rules 1.11 and 1.12. Unlike private lawyers, lawyers who work for governmental units also are subject to additional regulations found in federal and state statutes and

---

1. The federal government employed about 34,000 lawyers, state governments about 37,000, and local governments about 50,000 in 2011. Together, these lawyers account for about 10 percent of all U.S. lawyers. *See* Bureau of Labor Statistics, *Occupational Employment and Wages, May 2011: Lawyers*, available at http://www.bls.gov/oes/current/oes231011.htm (last visited July 7, 2012).

regulations that govern their conduct. Comment [1] to Model Rule 1.11 expressly refers to this other law.[2]

The Clients

At various times, government lawyers have identified their client as an agency official, the agency itself, a branch of government, the government itself, or the people served by the government.[3] Government lawyers work within complex legal structures that authorize their own and their clients' work. Lawyers who work for government agencies typically view their client as the agency, with its policy articulated by the agency officer who has the power to decide a particular matter.[4] On the other hand, lawyers who work in a state attorney general office or the U.S. Department of Justice might define their client as the state or federal government itself, where the public interest is articulated by the person or persons in the office with legitimate authority to direct government policy.[5] Government lawyers such as Judge Advocate General lawyers or public defenders also may be assigned to represent individuals.[6] Prosecutors, on the other hand, do not represent individuals, but are "ministers of justice"[7] who represent a sovereign government, which has an obligation to "govern impartially."[8]

The Restatement adopts a contextual approach, which eschews universal definitions of governmental clients and focuses instead on political and organizational responsibility of government officials, legal organizations within which government lawyers work, and the purpose for which one is identifying the client.[9]

---

2. MR 1.12 generally parallels MR 1.11 and, together with the Code of Judicial Conduct, forms the primary source of rules that regulate the conduct of judges, arbitrators, and mediators. We explore issues of judicial ethics in Chapter 16.

3. Richard W. Painter, *Getting the Government America Deserves: How Ethics Reform Can Make a Difference*, 121-122 (Oxford U. Press 2009).

4. *See* D.C. R. Prof. Conduct 1.6(k) (2007) ("The client of the government lawyer is the agency that employs the lawyer unless expressly provided to the contrary by applicable law, regulation, or order."). *See also* Jeffrey Rosenthal, *Who Is the Client of the Government Lawyer?* in Patricia E. Salkin, ed., *Ethical Standards in the Public Sector: A Guide for Government Lawyers, Clients, and Public Officials* 13 (ABA Sect. of St. and Local Gov. L. 1999).

5. Jonathan R. Macey & Geoffrey P. Miller, *Reflections on Professional Responsibility in a Regulatory State*, 63 Geo. Wash. L. Rev. 1105 (1995).

6. *See* D.C. R. Prof. Conduct 1.6, Comment [39] (2007); D.C. Op. 313 (2002) (whether former Navy JAG lawyer now can continue to represent same defendant in postconviction proceeding in private practice); Kathleen Clark, *Government Lawyering: The Ethics of Representing Elected Representatives*, 61 Law & Contemp. Prob. 31 (1998). We deal with the special ethical dilemma of public defenders and JAG lawyers in Lawyers and Clients: *Criminal Defense, infra* p.118.

7. MR 3.8, Comment [1].

8. Berger v. United States, 295 U.S. 78, 88 (1935). *See* Bruce A. Green & Fred C. Zacharias, *Prosecutorial Neutrality*, 2004 Wis. L. Rev. 837. This obligation to seek justice may be especially complex after conviction. *See* Fred C. Zacharias, *The Role of Prosecutors in Serving Justice After Convictions*, 58 Vand. L. Rev. 171 (2005). *See also* Freeport-McMoRan Oil & Gas Co. v. F.E.R.C., 962 F.2d 45 (D.C. Cir. 1992) (the principle in *Berger* applies equally to the government's civil lawyers, who should have dismissed an appeal when the issue became moot).

9. RLGL § 97 Comment c.

Take, for example, the situation where agencies of the same government feud over governmental policy. Lawyers who work for those agencies typically view their client as the agency. But the client's identity can be further complicated in jurisdictions where the attorney general is charged by constitution or statute with the task of providing representation to each agency. There, legal regulation essentially requires that two lawyers in the same office represent each agency's point of view to the appropriate decision maker; in the alternative, special assistants outside the office might be required to remove control of the attorney general over the matter.[10]

The Five Cs

Control and Communication Like the organization's lawyer, the government lawyer must take direction from duly authorized constituents of the client. When a given constituent or group of constituents propose to engage in unlawful conduct, the lawyer must pursue the matter up the ladder of government authority.[11] For example, when lawyers and constituents disagree, lawyers for executive branch agencies can appeal a matter not only to the political or cabinet head of the agency, but all the way to the executive itself.[12] Lawyers for agencies empowered to make decisions independent of the executive would stop at the agency level.[13] When the disagreement cannot be resolved by such an appeal, the lawyer and constituents may end up asking a court to resolve it.[14]

Some government lawyers have the power to control and decide certain legal matters that ordinarily would be reposed only in the client.[15] For example, the

---

10. *See, e.g.,* Granholm v. PSC Mich. Pub. Serv. Comm'n, 625 N.W.2d 16 (Mich. App. 2000) (when the Attorney General is a party to litigation against a state agency, which is entitled to representation by the attorney general's office, dual representation creates a conflict of interest that must be remedied by appointment of an independent special assistant attorney general for the state agency); EPA v. Pollution Control Bd., 372 N.E.2d 50 (Ill. 1977) (where attorney general is not an actual party, he can represent opposing state agencies in the dispute); Justin G. Davids, *State Attorneys General and the Client-Attorney Relationship: Establishing the Power to Sue State Officers,* 38 Colum. J.L. & Soc. Probs. 365 (2005).

11. MR 1.13(b); RLGL § 97 Comment f.

12. Peter L. Strauss, *Overseer, or "The Decider"? The President in Administrative Law,* 75 Geo. Wash. L. Rev. 696 (2007).

13. Kathleen Clark, *Government Lawyers and Confidentiality Norms,* 85 Wash. U. L. Rev. 1033 (2007).

14. *See, e.g.,* Vaughn v. King, 167 F.3d 347 (7th Cir. 1999) (City of Gary Sanitary District had statutory power to hire independent outside counsel without mayor's signature); State ex rel. McGraw v. Burton, 569 S.E.2d 99 (W. Va. 2002) (Office of Attorney General may not be stripped of its inherent core functions, but in light of long-established statues, practice and precedent, the state executive branch and related entities may in some circumstances employ and use non-employee lawyers); Salt Lake City Comm'n v. Salt Lake City Co. Atty., 985 P.2d 899, 907 (Utah 1999) (in the absence of any contradictory statutes, county attorney represents county as an entity, not individual commissioners, who therefore have no power to hire outside counsel when they disagree with county attorney except when county attorney "refuses to act or is incapable of acting or is unavailable for some other reason"; disagreements about whether this exception has occurred may be settled by appeal to the Attorney General or by seeking a declaratory judgment from a court).

15. Model Rules, Scope ¶[18]; RLGL § 97(1) and Comment g.

client's authority to settle or decide whether to appeal a matter can be exercised by a government lawyer properly empowered by statute, constitution, or common law.[16] When a government lawyer has this responsibility, the lawyer essentially serves as trustee for the government, taking into consideration some version of the public interest in making the decision.[17]

Competence   Some government lawyers face the same huge caseloads that also plague lawyers for private clients.[18] In addition, they obviously must be aware of the often complex body of law that creates and regulates their clients. But they also must be diligent in recognizing special regulations that govern their own conduct, such as restrictions on accepting gifts or outside compensation, as well as recognizing personal financial interests.[19]

For example, current federal government lawyers in all three branches of government are subject to the federal conflict of interest statutes, which limit the ability of all federal employees, including federal lawyers, to represent or receive compensation to represent private parties in a "particular matter" in which the United States is a party or has an interest.[20] Violations of these governmental ethics codes can result in administrative sanctions and criminal prosecution. Many governments administer these codes through an internal administrative process.

Prosecutors exercise substantial power in the criminal justice system. It is regularly observed that they have the duty to seek justice rather than a professional obligation to win.[21] Model Rule 3.8 recognizes this obligation to fairly execute the criminal law by imposing disciplinary rules that reflect constitutional

---

16. *See, e.g.,* 28 U.S.C. §§ 516, 519 (2010) (authorizing the Department of Justice to make and control most litigation decisions—this power varies considerably at the state level). *See* Justin G. Davids, *State Attorneys General and the Client-Attorney Relationship: Establishing the Power to Sue State Officers,* 38 Colum. J.L. & Soc. Probs. 365 (2005); William P. Marshall, *Break up the Presidency? Governors, State Attorneys General, and Lessons from the Divided Executive,* 115 Yale L.J. 2246 (2006).

17. Clark, *supra* note 13.

18. *See, e.g.,* N.Y. St. Bar Op. 751 (2002) (a lawyer who represents a government agency may not undertake more matters than the lawyer can competently handle, but must accept a superior's resolution of the issue if it constitutes an arguable question of professional duty).

19. The U.S. Justice Department administers its regulations through its Office of Professional Responsibility and issues annual reports about the sources and outcomes of its investigations. *See* U.S. Department of Justice Office of Professional Responsibility, *Annual Report* (2005) *available at* http://www.justice.gov/opr/annualreport2005.pdf.

20. 18 U.S.C. §§ 203, 205 (2010). Members of Congress also are prohibited from practicing in the Court of Federal Claims or the Court of Appeals for the Federal Circuit. 18 U.S.C. § 204. *See also* Kathleen Clark, *Do We Have Enough Ethics in Government Yet? An Answer from Fiduciary Theory,* 1996 U. Ill L. Rev. 57.

21. MR 3.8, Comment [1]; ABA, *Standards for Criminal Justice: Prosecution Function and Defense Function,* 3-1.2(c) (3d ed. 1993). *See also* Bruce A. Green, *Why Should Prosecutors Seek Justice* 26 Fordham Urb. L.J. 607 (1999); H. Richard Uviller, *The Virtuous Prosecutor in Quest of an Ethical Standard: Guidance from the ABA,* 71 Mich. L. Rev. 1145 (1973).

requirements; for example, the duty to provide exculpatory evidence to criminal defendants[22] or not to prosecute a case without probable cause.[23]

The American Bar Association, the National District Attorney's Association, and the U.S. Department of Justice all have promulgated guidelines that seek to promote this goal.[24] At the same time, unlike other lawyers, prosecutors have civil immunity for judicial actions,[25] which perhaps explains in part why misconduct in charging, plea bargaining, granting immunity, and suppression of evidence continue to occur.[26] On the other hand, the prosecutor's affirmative obligations to protect the constitutionally protected rights of criminal defendants, such as the obligation to disclose exculpatory evidence, have been made part of Model Rule 3.8, which specifically governs prosecutors.[27] Although professional discipline is not common,[28] it does occur.[29] Beyond discipline, prosecutors obviously need to avoid conduct that results in reversals of criminal

---

22. MR 3.8(d) recognizes (and expands) the constitutionally required rule of Brady v. Maryland, 373 U.S. 83 (1963). *See* ABA Formal Op. 09-454. Cf. RLGL § 97(4) (requiring prosecutors and other government lawyers to "observe applicable restrictions imposed by law").

23. MR 3.3(a); RLGL § 97(3); Fred C. Zacharias & Bruce A. Green, *The Duty to Avoid Wrongful Convictions: A Thought Experiment in the Regulation of Prosecutors*, 89 B.U. L. Rev. 1 (2009).

24. National District Attorney's Association, *National Prosecution Standards* (2d ed. 1991) *available at* http://www.ndaa.org/pdf/NDAA%20NPS%203rd%20Ed.%20w%20Revised%20Commentary.pdf; *United States Attorney's Manual,* Title 9-27.000 "Principles of Federal Prosecution" (1997) *available at* http://www.usdoj.gov/usao/eousa/foia_reading_room/usam/title9/27mcrm.htm.

25. Imbler v. Pachtman, 424 U.S. 409 (1976) (prosecutors who engage in quasi-judicial/advocacy roles such as bringing criminal prosecutions and presenting evidence in court or to a grand jury are absolutely immune from civil liability); Burns v. Reed, 500 U.S. 478 (1991) (prosecutors who engage in nonadvocacy/investigative or administrative roles such as giving erroneous advice to police entitled to only qualified immunity for good-faith actions).

26. *See* Bennett L. Gershman, *Prosecutorial Misconduct* (2d ed., West 2007).

27. The McDade Amendment, 28 U.S.C. § 530B (2010), explicitly makes federal DOJ lawyers and other law enforcement lawyers subject to the lawyer codes in the jurisdictions where they are admitted to practice law. *See also* Ramsey v. Bd. of Prof. Resp. of Tenn. Sup. Ct., 771 S.W.2d 116 (Tenn. 1989) (prosecutors subject to professional discipline despite state constitutional provision that prosecutors can be removed only by impeachment).

28. Fred C. Zacharias, *The Professional Discipline of Prosecutors*, 79 N.C. L. Rev. 721 (2001).

29. *See, e.g.,* Ellen Yaroshefsky & Bruce A. Green, *Prosecutors' Ethics in Context: Influences on Prosecutorial Disclosure* in *Lawyers in Practice: Ethical Decision Making in Context* 269 (U. Chicago Press 2012) (discussing disbarment of District Attorney Michael Nifong for failing to disclose exculpatory evidence and misleading a judge in a rape case and similar misconduct of federal prosecutors in the Ted Stevens prosecution); In re Field, 2010 WL 489505 (Cal.) (prosecutor who intentionally withheld key evidence in two cases, made highly improper closing argument, and obtained evidence in violation of a court order suspended four years); In re Stuart, 803 N.Y.S. 2d 577 (App. Div. 2006) (prosecutor who misrepresented location of critical witness to the court suspended for three years); In re Peasley, 90 P.3d 764 (Ariz. 2004) (prosecutor who deliberately presented false testimony disbarred for violating Rule 3.3); In re Paulter, 47 P.3d 1175 (Colo. 2002) (prosecutor who impersonated a public defender when suspect asked to speak to a lawyer suspended for three months for violating Rules 4.3 and 8.3(c)); State v. Mucklow, 35 P.3d 527 (Colo. 2000) (prosecutor who failed to disclose exculpatory evidence publicly censured for violating Rule 3.8(c)); In re Bonet, 29 P.3d 1242 (Wash. 2001) (prosecutor who offered co-defendant inducement not to testify in co-defendant's case disbarred for violating Rules 3.4(b), 8.4(b), and (d)); In re Howes, 940 P.2d 159 (N.M. 1997) (prosecutor who spoke to represented criminal defendant without permission publicly

convictions.[30] Prosecutors also have been held liable under civil rights statutes for erroneous advice that violates a defendant's constitutional right.[31]

Confidentiality   Like all other lawyers, government lawyers are prohibited from both using confidential information to their client's disadvantage and from disclosing it without adequate informed consent.[32] In addition, the government's power gives its lawyers access to information about not only the government-client, but also about individuals outside of government. Government lawyers also must keep this "confidential governmental information" about individuals confidential because the government client itself has an obligation to keep such information secret.[33]

Government lawyers who seek to disclose confidential information must be attuned to a careful identification of their client to obtain adequate informed consent. For example, a state attorney general was disciplined for disclosing to an environmental group an agency's potential change of position on landfill requirements. The agency had revealed this information to an opposing party in an individual case, but claimed that the subsequent AG's disclosure could have hamstrung its political ability to change course. The fact that the agency's disclosure might have constituted a privilege waiver,[34] or the fact that disclosure might have been required if a FOIA request had been made, were not defenses to the unauthorized disclosure.[35]

---

reprimanded for violating Rule 4.2); In re Howes, 39 A.3d 1 (D.C. App. 2012) (same prosecutor disbarred for improper witness payments).

30. Gershman, *supra* note 26, at 567-579. *See also* United States v. Stein, 495 F. Supp. 2d 390 (S.D.N.Y. 2007) (dismissing indictment against individual corporate officers because in promulgating Thompson Memorandum, DOJ "deliberately or callously prevented many of these corporate defendants from obtaining funds for their defense that they would have had absent the government's interference . . . thereby foreclos[ing them] from presenting the defenses they wished to present and in some cases, even depriv[ing] them of counsel of their choice).

31. *See, e.g.,* Buckley v. Fitzsimmons, 509 U.S. 259 (1993) (prosecutor who made false statements about criminal defendant to the media); Mitchell v. Forsyth, 472 U.S. 511 (1985) (attorney general who participated in illegal wiretapping); McSurely v. McClellen, 697 F.2d 309 (D.C. Cir. 1982) (prosecutor who prepared illegal search warrant and led illegal raid).

32. MR 1.6, 1.8(b); RLGL §§ 16(3), 97, Comment a.

33. MR 1.11(c).

34. The attorney-client privilege and work product doctrine extend to government clients, but courts pay careful attention to proper identification of the client in applying the privilege. RLGL § 74. *See, e.g.,* In re Grand Jury Investigation, 399 F.3d 527 (2d Cir. 2005) (governor's office could invoke attorney-client privilege against United States in investigation of alleged bribery in the state); In re Lindsey, 158 F.3d 1263 (D.C. Cir. 1998) (information that deputy White House counsel learned when acting as intermediary between the president and his private counsel was protected by the president's personal attorney-client privilege but "common interest" doctrine not appropriate to withhold information about possible criminal misconduct obtained in conferring with the president and his private counsel on matters of overlapping concern to the president personally and in his official capacity). For a discussion of the meaning of a range of similar cases, *see* Patricia E. Salkin & Allyson Phillips, *Eliminating Political Maneuvering: A Light in the Tunnel for the Government Attorney-Client Privilege,* 39 Ind. L. Rev. 561 (2006).

35. Law. Disc. Bd. v. McGraw, 461 S.E.2d 850 (W. Va. 1995).

On the other hand, the government's ability to keep information confidential is also shaped by extensive legal regulation, which recognizes that transparency in many government functions is essential to maintaining the government's legitimacy. For example, federal and state whistleblowing statutes allow government employees to disclose government wrongdoing and prohibit retaliation if they do so.[36] Extensive regulation of government information also requires disclosure of some information, such as agency structure and management. Open meeting acts, as well as freedom of information acts, require disclosure of other information when requested. These provisions may increase the scope of permitted government lawyer disclosure, especially if the legislative branch requires such disclosure, which could trigger the "required by law" exception in Model Rule 1.6(b)(6).[37]

Model Rule 1.13(c) creates another ground for discretionary disclosure if a government client is engaged in a clear violation of law that is reasonably certain to result in substantial injury to the organization, and the lawyer has been unsuccessful in remedying it through appropriate channels. No crime or fraud need be involved, as long as the government's violation of law is related to the lawyer's representation.[38] This discretion rests on a lawyer's reasonable belief that substantial harm to the government will result, a belief about which those in power might disagree. Nevertheless, assuming the lawyer has documented a clear violation of law, presumably substantial tort damages or patterns of illegal activity that would substantially undermine public trust may suffice to trigger this exception.[39]

Conflict of Interest Resolution Lawyers working for government clients are subject to both the general conflicts provision in Model Rule 1.7 and the former client conflict provision in Model Rule 1.9.[40] Lawyers currently working for the government and those who leave government service also are subject to the specialized conflicts provisions of Model Rule 1.11.[41] Lawyers who leave government

---

36. Robert T. Begg, *Whistleblower Law and Ethics*, in *Ethical Standards in the Public Sector: A Guide for Government Lawyers, Client, and Public Officials* at 136; James E. Moliterno, *The Federal Government Lawyer's Duty to Breach Confidentiality*, 14 Temp. Pol. & Civ. Rights L. Rev. 633 (2005); Jesselyn Radack, *The Government Attorney-Whistleblower and the Rule of Confidentiality: Compatible at Last*, 17 Geo. J. Legal Ethics 125 (2003); Roger C. Cramton, *The Lawyer as Whistleblower: Confidentiality and the Government Lawyer*, 5 Geo. J. Leg. Ethics 291 (1991).

37. *See, e.g.*, Law. Disc. Bd. v. McGraw, *supra* note 35 (particular disclosure not allowed because it was not required by the state FOIA statute, as no request for the information had been made).

38. MR 1.13, Comment [6].

39. *See, e.g.*, Christopher A. Britt, *The Commissioning Oath and the Ethical Obligation of Military Officers to Prevent Subordinates from Committing Acts of Torture*, 19 Geo. J. Legal Ethics 551 (2006); Kathleen Clark, *Ethical Issues Raised by the OLC Torture Memorandum*, 1 J. Natl. Sec. L. & Policy 455 (2005).

40. MR 1.11(d). Painter, *supra* note 3 at 126-129; In re Jackson, 27 So. 3d 273 (La. 2010) (prosecutor who dismissed drunk driving case after accepting $500 from defendant to represent him in same case disbarred).

41. *E.g.*, In re White, 11 A.3d 1226 (D.C. App. 2011), *cert. denied sub nom.* White v. D.C. Bd. of Prof'l Resp., 131 S. Ct. 2941 (lawyer who as a government lawyer supervised investigation of a claim and subsequently represented same private client in litigation of same claim disbarred).

service are subject to a narrower former client disqualification based on whether the lawyer "participated personally and substantially" in a "matter,"[42] rather than the broader substantially related matter protection for private clients in Model Rule 1.9(a).[43] A few jurisdictions extend this prohibition to substantially related matters as well.[44]

Where a former government lawyer is disqualified, the Model Rule provides for either government agency consent or screening to remove the problem.[45] Screening also has been upheld in moves from one government office to another, such as from a public defender's office to a prosecutor's office.[46]

The Bounds of the Law

Federal Regulation   In addition to the applicable Rules of Professional Conduct, state and federal conflict of interest statutes regulate government lawyers during and after their government service. Officers and employees of the executive branch are subject to provisions concerning financial conflicts of interest.[47] Specific conflict of interest rules also apply to lawyers who serve as trustees in bankruptcy courts.[48] Several agencies add additional requirements that govern who can practice before that agency.[49] Some lawyers, such as special prosecutors, also are subject to particular agency regulations.[50] Former government employees are governed by the Ethics in Government Act, which contains several restrictions that are stricter than those found in the professional codes.[51] Violations of all of these provisions are felonies, punishable with fines and imprisonment for

---

42. MR 1.11(a), (e); RLGL § 133.

43. *E.g.,* Gatewood v. State, 880 A.2d 322 (Md. 2005) (prosecutor who represented defendant on substantially related matter not disqualified); D.C. Op. 315 (2002) (a former EPA lawyer who had no more than official responsibility or participation in litigation substantially related to the drafting status of proposed regulations may represent a private client in challenging the EPA's final rules); N.Y. St. Bar Op. 748 (2001) (a former prosecutor may represent criminal defendants investigated and prosecuted during the former prosecutor's tenure with a district attorney's office if he or she did not participate personally and substantially in the investigation or prosecution of the defendant, and where doing so violated neither the duty to represent the new client zealously nor the duty to protect the former client's confidences).

44. *See, e.g.,* D.C. R. Prof. Conduct 1.11(a) (2007); Jordan v. Phila. Hous. Auth., 337 F. Supp. 2d 666 (E.D. Pa. 2004).

45. MR 1.11(b); RLGL §124(3).

46. St. ex rel. Horn v. Ray, 138 S.W.3d 729 (Mo. App. 2002).

47. 18 U.S.C. §§ 208, 209 (2010).

48. 18 U.S.C. § 154 (2010) imposes criminal liability on trustees and others for certain personal conflicts of interest. Lawyers hired by the trustee also are subject to 11 U.S.C. § 327 (2010), which creates standards for disinterested representation.

49. *See, e.g.,* Practice Before the Internal Revenue Service, 31 C.F.R. § 10.25 (2012) (practice by former government employees, their partners, and their associates).

50. For a discussion of how these regulations affected the work of Kenneth Starr, *see* David Halperin, *Ethics Breakthrough or Ethics Breakdown? Kenneth Starr's Dual Roles as Private Practitioner and Public Prosecutor,* 15 Geo. J. Legal Ethics 231 (2002).

51. 18 U.S.C. § 207 (2010). *See* Thomas D. Morgan, *Appropriate Limits on Participation by a Former Agency Official in Matters Before an Agency,* 1980 Duke L.J. 1 (discussing the history of the Ethics in Government Act).

up to five years.[52] Courts have used the elements of these statutes as the basis for granting disqualification motions.[53] State disciplinary agencies also have relied on these provisions in cases of professional discipline.[54] Like Model Rule 1.11, these statutes governing government employees are sometimes referred to as "revolving door rules," a phrase that refers to the practice of lawyers moving back and forth between government service and private practice. The goal of both sets of rules is to prevent potential abuses, such as use of confidential governmental information or the risk that a lawyer might misuse a government position to benefit herself in later private practice. Most relevant is 18 U.S.C. § 207, which contains three provisions that stringently regulate the conduct of former government lawyers.

The first provision permanently prohibits appearances and communications with any government agency, department, or court in particular matters where the person participated "personally and substantially" while a government employee.[55] The consent of the agency is not a defense (as it would be in Model Rule 1.11). So long as the former employee made the communication or appearance "with the intent to influence" the merits on behalf of another person in a matter in which she formerly participated, the crime is complete. Thus, a lawyer who filed a pro bono amicus brief on behalf of a private client on the same side as the government in a case she worked on as a government lawyer would violate the statute, but, so long as the former agency consented, not Model Rule 1.11. At the same time, 18 U.S.C. § 207 does not bar a former government lawyer from counseling a private client on a matter that the lawyer worked on at the government, but the same lawyer would need the agency's consent to do so under Model Rule 1.11.[56]

The second provision creates a two-year restriction on communications or appearances with any governmental agency, court, or department on behalf of another party in connection with particular matters under that person's official responsibility before she left the government.[57] For example, a high-level employee of the Internal Revenue Service who retired and started a tax service violated this provision when he attended meetings with an IRS officer and three taxpayers whose tax collection had been his responsibility prior to retirement.[58]

---

52. 18 U.S.C. § 216 (2010).

53. *See, e.g.,* In re Rest. Dev. of P.R., Inc., 128 B.R. 498 (Bankr. D.P.R. 1991); Kessenich v. Commodity Futures Trading Comm'n, 684 F.2d 88 (D.C. Cir. 1982).

54. *See, e.g.,* Disc. Counsel v. Eilberg, 441 A.2d 1193 (Pa. 1982) (lawyer who violated 18 U.S.C. § 203(a) suspended from practice for five years).

55. 18 U.S.C. § 207(a)(1) (2010); D.C. Op. 297 (2000) (the Indian Self-Determination Act, 25 U.S.C. § 450i(j), creates an exception to the restrictions in 18 U.S.C. § 207(a) for former government employees retained by Indian Tribes, but Rule 1.6 protects the government's confidentiality).

56. A lawyer acting as an expert witness on behalf of the government may not violate the statute. 18 U.S.C. § 207(j)(6) (2010); EEOC v. Exxon Corp., 202 F.3d 755 (5th Cir. 2000).

57. 18 U.S.C. § 207(a)(2) (2010).

58. United States v. Coleman, 805 F.2d 474 (3d Cir. 1986).

The third provision creates a one-year prohibition on certain senior governmental personnel from appearing before or communicating with the governmental agency for which they worked.[59]

State Provisions The majority of states also have enacted ethics laws that restrict the practice of both current and former lawyers and other governmental employees.[60] State and municipal agencies also regulate the conduct of employees, including lawyers.[61] Like federal lawyers, state lawyers are subject to both these ethics statutes and the relevant professional code.[62] State provisions generally parallel those in the federal law and Model Rule 1.11. For example, many include bans on appearances or representation before the lawyer's former agency for a period of time.[63] Many states also bar representation in matters in which the former government lawyer participated personally and substantially.[64] A few jurisdictions regulate additional matters as well, such as prohibiting former government lawyers from accepting employment with entities that are subject to regulation by their former agency employer or with those that do business with the state.[65] State law also parallels federal law in targeting former employees of particular agencies or commissions.[66] Despite these similarities, each state has

---

59. 18 U.S.C. § 207(c) (2010).

60. *See, e.g.,* National Conference of State Legislators, *The State of State Legislative Ethics: A Look at the Ethical Climate and Ethics Laws for State Legislators* (Ctr. for Ethics in Govt. 2002); Rachel E. Boehm, Student Author, *Caught in the Revolving Door: A State Lawyer's Guide to Post-Employment Restrictions*, 15 Rev. Litig. 525, 532 n.26 (1996), citing statutes in 30 states.

61. *See* Mark Davies, *Considering Ethics at the Local Government Level, in Ethical Standards in the Public Sector, supra* note 36 at 127-155. These provisions generally have withstood constitutional attack. *See, e.g.,* Ortiz v. Taxn. and Revenue Dept., 954 P.2d 109 (N.M. App. 1998) (statute prohibiting former public officers and employees from representing persons for pay before their former government agency employers is constitutional as applied to executive branch employees); Midboe v. Comm'n on Ethics for Pub. Employees, 646 So. 2d 351 (La. 1994) (Code of Governmental Ethics for public servants was not unconstitutional as applied to lawyer because the legislature was not regulating law practice in general). *But cf.,* Shaulis v. Pa. St. Eth. Comm'n, 833 A.2d 123 (Pa. 2003) (Public Official and Employee Ethics Act violated separation of powers because it specifically targeted lawyers who were former government employees).

62. *See, e.g.,* P.J.S. v. Pa. St. Eth. Comm'n, 723 A.2d 174 (Pa. 1999) (lawyer who served as part-time city solicitor subject to both state ethics laws and state lawyer code).

63. *See, e.g.,* Cal. Govt. Code § 87406(d)(1) (2007) (one-year ban on acting as an attorney for any person before the agency that formerly employed the lawyer); N.Y. Pub. Off. Law § 73(8)(a) (i) (2002) (two-year ban on appearing or practicing before state agency that formerly employed the person in any matter).

64. *See, e.g.,* Ark. Code § 19-11-709(b)(1) (2007) (permanent disqualification); Ind. Code § 4-2-6-11(c) (2007) (permanent disqualification).

65. Boehm, *supra* note 60, at 535.

66. *See, e.g.,* Ohio Rev. Code § 102.03(2) (2007) (regulating practice of former commissioners and attorney examiners of the public utilities commission); Tex. Water Code § 26.0283 (2002) (regulating assistance by former employees of the Texas Natural Resource Conservation Commission); Or. Rev. Stat. § 244.045(2) (2001) (regulating former deputy and assistant attorneys general).

enacted its own special mix of prohibitions, often in response to a particular political embarrassment.[67]

Conclusion

All of this legal regulation demands careful attention, especially to several details that many of these rules share. First, each rule makes the role of the government employee relevant to its reach. Second, many of these rules also define the lawyer's role after leaving government service. Finally, each rule creates a distinctive penalty. Some create criminal penalties, others administrative remedies, such as loss of a government contract or benefit.[68] Federal and state governments have found these additional remedies necessary to curb specific abuses of the public trust. Courts also have used these provisions as a guide to other relief, such as disqualification. Wise government lawyers need to remain aware of both professional code provisions and other state and federal law to fully understand their obligations.

---

67. *See, e.g.*, Robert C. Newman, *New York's New Ethics Law: Turning the Tide on Corruption*, 16 Hofstra L. Rev. 319 (1988).

68. *E.g.*, Tex. Water Code, *supra* note 66, provides that the Texas Water Commission "shall deny an application . . . for a permit" if a former employee provides assistance to the applicant.

Chapter 12

Fees and Client Property

"I'm certain I speak for the entire legal profession when
I say that the fee is reasonable and just."

The materials in this chapter represent a very small sample of an enormous body of law that governs the fees that lawyers can contract for and collect from their clients. Disputes over fees are common, and they occur for at least three reasons. First, some lawyers who do a good job of explaining the basis of the fee and who keep more than adequate records of the time they have expended on the matter nevertheless face clients who are unhappy with the lawyer or the result in their case, or are otherwise unwilling to pay for the representation. Second, most lawyers do not intentionally overcharge, but they might fail to explain the fee or the progress in the matter so that clients are unpleasantly taken by surprise when they later receive the bill. Third, some lawyers charge clients unreasonable fees, and a few do so fraudulently.[1]

Although it might appear that lawyers are free to bargain with clients at arm's length regarding fees before they enter into a client-lawyer relationship, notions of fiduciary duty in the law governing lawyers in fact limit the freedom of lawyers to contract for and collect fees. Fee agreements nearly always involve some degree of conflict of interest because the lawyer's personal financial interest potentially conflicts with the client's interests in the representation. As we have seen in prior chapters, the remedy for a potential conflict in loyalty is consultation, communication, and informed consent. For fees, as for other conflicts, the greater the potential for conflict, the greater the legal regulation provided to control it.

The loyalty-based conflict of interest rules discussed in the last three chapters apply only after a lawyer has agreed to represent a client. Model Rule 1.5 nevertheless imposes several fiduciary-like requirements in the context of pre-contractual fee negotiations, such as obligations to communicate the basis of the fee, limitations on the propriety of certain fee arrangements, and the general requirement that fees are subject to an objective standard of reasonableness. This chapter explores these obligations in the context of hourly, contingent, statutory, and flat fees, as well as the lawyer's correlative fiduciary obligation to handle client funds and property.

A. Hourly Fees

Problems

12-1. Martyn flies to San Francisco for a client who has agreed in the retainer letter to pay full hourly rates for travel. If during a six-hour flight, Martyn works on another client's matters for four hours, may she bill the two clients a total of ten hours? What if the work on the plane was *pro bono*?

12-2. May Martyn & Fox charge clients $2/page for all incoming and outgoing faxes? What about billing clients $200/hour for contract lawyers whose agency charges us $150?

Consider: Model Rule 1.5

---

1. Douglas R. Richmond, *For a Few Dollars More: The Perplexing Problem of Unethical Billing Practices by Lawyers,* 60 S.C. L. Rev. 63 (2008).

Billing for Professional Fees, Disbursements, and Other Expenses
ABA Formal Opinion 93-379
American Bar Association Standing Committee
on Ethics and Professional Responsibility

Consistent with the Model Rules of Professional Conduct, a lawyer must disclose to a client the basis on which the client is to be billed for both professional time and any other charges. Absent a contrary understanding, any invoice for professional services should fairly reflect the basis on which the client's charges have been determined. In matters where the client has agreed to have the fee determined with reference to the time expended by the lawyer, a lawyer may not bill more time than she actually spends on the matter, except to the extent that she rounds up to minimum time periods (such as one-quarter or one-tenth of an hour). . . .

It is a common perception that pressure on lawyers to bill a minimum number of hours and on law firms to maintain or improve profits may have led some lawyers to engage in problematic billing practices. These include charges to more than one client for the same work or the same hours, surcharges on services contracted with outside vendors, and charges beyond reasonable costs for in-house services like photocopying and computer searches. Moreover, the bases on which these charges are to be assessed often are not disclosed in advance or are disguised in cryptic invoices so that the client does not fully understand exactly what costs are being charged to him.

The Model Rules of Professional Conduct provide important principles applicable to the billing of clients, principles which, if followed, would ameliorate many of the problems noted above. The Committee has decided to address several practices that are the subject of frequent inquiry, with the goal of helping the profession adhere to its ethical obligations to its clients despite economic pressures.

The first set of practices involves billing more than one client for the same hours spent. In one illustrative situation, a lawyer finds it possible to schedule court appearances for three clients on the same day. He spends a total of four hours at the courthouse, the amount of time he would have spent on behalf of each client had it not been for the fortuitous circumstance that all three cases were scheduled on the same day. May he bill each of the three clients, who otherwise understand that they will be billed on the basis of time spent, for the four hours he spent on them collectively? In another scenario, a lawyer is flying cross-country to attend a deposition on behalf of one client, expending travel time she would ordinarily bill to that client. If she decides not to watch the movie or read her novel, but to work instead on drafting a motion for another client, may she charge both clients, each of whom agreed to hourly billing, for the time during which she was traveling on behalf of one and drafting a document on behalf of the other? A third situation involves research on a particular topic for one client that later turns out to be relevant to an inquiry from a second client. May the firm bill the second client, who agreed to be charged on the basis of time spent on his case, the same amount for the recycled work product that it charged the first client?

The second set of practices involve billing for expenses and disbursements, and is exemplified by the situation in which a firm contracts for the expert witness services of an economist at an hourly rate of $200. May the firm bill the client for the expert's time at the rate of $250 per hour? Similarly, may the firm add a surcharge to the cost of computer-assisted research if the per-minute total charged by the computer company does not include the cost of purchasing the computers or staffing their operation? . . .

Professional Obligations Regarding the Reasonableness of Fees

Implicit in the Model Rules and their antecedents is the notion that the attorney-client relationship is not necessarily one of equals, that it is built on trust, and that the client is encouraged to be dependent on the lawyer, who is dealing with matters of great moment to the client. The client should only be charged a reasonable fee for the legal services performed. Rule 1.5 explicitly addresses the reasonableness of legal fees. The rule deals not only with the determination of a reasonable hourly rate, but also with total cost to the client. The Comment to the rules states, for example, that "[a] lawyer should not exploit a fee arrangement based primarily on hourly charges by using wasteful procedures." The goal should be solely to compensate the lawyer fully for time reasonably expended, an approach that if followed will not take advantage of the client. . . .

The lawyer's conduct should be such as to promote the client's trust of the lawyer and of the legal profession. . . . An unreasonable limitation on the hours a lawyer may spend on a client should be avoided as a threat to the lawyer's ability to fulfill her obligation under Model Rule 1.1 to "provide competent representation to a client." . . .

On the other hand, the lawyer who has agreed to bill on the basis of hours expended does not fulfill her ethical duty if she bills the client for more time than she actually spent on the client's behalf. In addressing the hypotheticals regarding (a) simultaneous appearance on behalf of three clients, (b) the airplane flight on behalf of one client while working on another client's matters and (c) recycled work product, it is helpful to consider these questions, not from the perspective of what a client could be forced to pay, but rather from the perspective of what the lawyer actually earned. A lawyer who spends four hours of time on behalf of three clients has not earned twelve billable hours. A lawyer who flies for six hours for one client, while working for five hours on behalf of another, has not earned eleven billable hours. A lawyer who is able to reuse old work product has not re-earned the hours previously billed and compensated when the work product was first generated. Rather than looking to profit from the fortuity of coincidental scheduling, the desire to get work done rather than watch a movie, or the luck of being asked the identical question twice, the lawyer who has agreed to bill solely on the basis of time spent is obliged to pass the benefits of these economies on to the client. The practice of billing several clients for the same time or work product, since it results in the earning of an unreasonable fee, therefore is contrary to the mandate of . . . Model Rule 1.5.

Moreover, continuous toil on or over-staffing a project for the purpose of churning out hours is also not properly considered "earning" one's fees. One job of a lawyer is to expedite the legal process. Model Rule 3.2. . . . A lawyer should take as much time as is reasonably required to complete a project, and should certainly never be motivated by anything other than the best interests of the client when determining how to staff or how much time to spend on any particular project.

It goes without saying that a lawyer who has undertaken to bill on an hourly basis is never justified in charging a client for hours not actually expended. If a lawyer has agreed to charge the client on this basis and it turns out that the lawyer is particularly efficient in accomplishing a given result, it nonetheless will not be permissible to charge the client for more hours than were actually expended on the matter. When that basis for billing the client has been agreed to, the economies associated with the result must inure to the benefit of the client, not give rise to an opportunity to bill a client phantom hours. This is not to say that the lawyer who agreed to hourly compensation is not free, with full disclosure, to suggest additional compensation because of a particularly efficient or outstanding result, or because the lawyer was able to reuse prior work product on the client's behalf. The point here is that fee enhancement cannot be accomplished simply by presenting the client with a statement reflecting more billable hours than were actually expended. On the other hand, if a matter turns out to be more difficult to accomplish than first anticipated and more hours are required than were originally estimated, the lawyer is fully entitled (though not required) to bill those hours unless the client agreement turned the original estimate into a cap on the fees to be charged.

Charges Other than Professional Fees

In addition to charging clients fees for professional services, lawyers typically charge their clients for certain additional items which are often referred to variously as disbursements, out-of-pocket expenses or additional charges. . . . [W]e believe that the reasonableness standard explicitly applicable to fees under Rule 1.5(a) should be applicable to these charges as well. . . .

A. General Overhead

When a client has engaged a lawyer to provide professional services for a fee (whether calculated on the basis of the number of hours expended, a flat fee, a contingent percentage of the amount recovered or otherwise) the client would be justifiably disturbed if the lawyer submitted a bill to the client which included, beyond the professional fee, additional charges for general office overhead. In the absence of disclosure to the client in advance of the engagement to the contrary, the client should reasonably expect that the lawyer's cost in maintaining a library, securing malpractice insurance, renting of office space, purchasing utilities and the like would be subsumed within the charges the lawyer is making for professional services.

B. Disbursements

At the beginning of the engagement lawyers typically tell their clients that they will be charged for disbursements. When that term is used clients justifiably should expect that the lawyer will be passing on to the client those actual payments of funds made by the lawyer on the client's behalf. Thus, if the lawyer hires a court stenographer to transcribe a deposition, the client can reasonably expect to be billed as a disbursement the amount the lawyer pays to the court reporting service. Similarly, if the lawyer flies to Los Angeles for the client, the client can reasonably expect to be billed as a disbursement the amount of the airfare, taxicabs, meals and hotel room.

It is the view of the Committee that, in the absence of disclosure to the contrary, it would be improper if the lawyer assessed a surcharge on these disbursements over and above the amount actually incurred unless the lawyer herself incurred additional expenses beyond the actual cost of the disbursement item. In the same regard, if a lawyer receives a discounted rate from a third party provider, it would be improper if she did not pass along the benefit of the discount to her client rather than charge the client the full rate and reserve the profit to herself. Clients quite properly could view these practices as an attempt to create additional undisclosed profit centers when the client had been told he would be billed for disbursements.

C. In-House Provision of Services

Perhaps the most difficult issue is the handling of charges to clients for the provision of in-house services . . . [such as] charges for photocopying, computer research, on-site meals, deliveries and other similar items. Like professional fees, it seems clear that lawyers may pass on reasonable charges for these services. Thus, in the view of the committee, the lawyer and the client may agree in advance that, for example, photocopying will be charged at $.15 per page, or messenger services will be provided at $5.00 per mile. However, the question arises what may be charged to the client, in the absence of a specific agreement to the contrary, when the client has simply been told that costs for these items will be charged to the client. We conclude that under those circumstances the lawyer is obliged to charge the client no more than the direct cost associated with the service (i.e., the actual cost of making a copy on the photocopy machine) plus a reasonable allocation of overhead expenses directly associated with the provision of the service (e.g., the salary of a photocopy machine operator).

. . . Any reasonable calculation of direct costs as well as any reasonable allocation of related overhead should pass ethical muster. On the other hand, in the absence of an agreement to the contrary, it is impermissible for a lawyer to create an additional source of profit for the law firm beyond that which is contained in the provision of professional services themselves. The lawyer's stock in trade is the sale of legal services, not photocopy paper, tuna fish sandwiches, computer time or messenger services.

Matter of Fordham
668 N.E.2d 816 (Mass. 1996)

O'CONNOR, J.

This is an appeal from the Board of Bar Overseers' (board's) dismissal of a petition for discipline filed by bar counsel against attorney Laurence S. Fordham . . .

We summarize the hearing committee's findings. On March 4, 1989, the Acton police department arrested Timothy, then twenty-one years old, and charged him with OUI, operating a motor vehicle after suspension, speeding, and operating an unregistered motor vehicle. At the time of the arrest, the police discovered a partially full quart of vodka in the vehicle. After failing a field sobriety test, Timothy was taken to the Acton police station where he submitted to two breathalyzer tests which registered .10 and .12 respectively.

Subsequent to Timothy's arraignment, he and his father, Laurence Clark (Clark) consulted with three lawyers, who offered to represent Timothy for fees between $3,000 and $10,000. Shortly after the arrest, Clark went to Fordham's home to service an alarm system which he had installed several years before. While there, Clark discussed Timothy's arrest with Fordham's wife who invited Clark to discuss the case with Fordham. Fordham then met with Clark and Timothy.

At this meeting, Timothy described the incidents leading to his arrest and the charges against him. Fordham, whom the hearing committee described as a "very experienced senior trial attorney with impressive credentials," told Clark and Timothy that he had never represented a client in a driving while under the influence case or in any criminal matter, and he had never tried a case in the District Court. The hearing committee found that "Fordham explained that although he lacked experience in this area, he was a knowledgeable and hard-working attorney and that he believed he could competently represent Timothy. Fordham described himself as efficient and economic in the use of [his] time. . . .

"Towards the end of the meeting, Fordham told the Clarks that he worked on [a] time charge basis and that he billed monthly. . . . In other words, Fordham would calculate the amount of hours he and others in the firm worked on a matter each month and multiply it by the respective hourly rates. He also told the Clarks that he would engage others in his firm to prepare the case. Clark had indicated that he would pay Timothy's legal fees." After the meeting, Clark hired Fordham to represent Timothy.

According to the hearing committee's findings, Fordham filed four pretrial motions on Timothy's behalf, two of which were allowed. One motion, entitled "Motion in Limine to Suppress Results of Breathalyzer Tests," was based on the theory that, although two breathalyzer tests were exactly .02 apart, they were not "within" .02 of one another as the regulations require. The hearing committee characterized the motion and its rationale as "a creative, if not novel, approach to suppression of breathalyzer results." . . . [T]he trial, which was before a judge without jury, was held on October 10 and October 19, 1989. The judge found Timothy not guilty of driving while under the influence.

Fordham sent . . . bills to Clark . . . [that] totaled $50,022.25, reflecting 227 hours of billed time, 153 hours of which were expended by Fordham and seventy-four of which were his associates' time. Clark did not pay the first two bills when they became due and expressed to Fordham his concern about their amount. Clark paid Fordham $10,000 on June 20, 1989. At that time, Fordham assured Clark that most of the work had been completed "other than taking [the case] to trial." Clark did not make any subsequent payments. Fordham requested Clark to sign a promissory note evidencing his debt to Fordham and, on October 7, 1989, Clark did so. In the October 13, 1989, bill, Fordham added a charge of $5,000 as a "retroactive increase" in fees. On November 7, 1989, after the case was completed, Fordham sent Clark a bill for $15,000.

Bar counsel and Fordham have stipulated that all the work billed by Fordham was actually done and that Fordham and his associates spent the time they claim to have spent. They also have stipulated that Fordham acted conscientiously, diligently, and in good faith in representing Timothy and in his billing in this case. . . .

Four witnesses testified before the hearing committee as experts on OUI cases. One of the experts, testifying on behalf of bar counsel, opined that "the amount of time spent in this case is clearly excessive." He testified that there were no unusual circumstances in the OUI charge against Timothy and that it was a "standard operating under the influence case." The witness did agree that Fordham's argument for suppression of the breathalyzer test results, which was successful, was novel and would have justified additional time and labor. He also acknowledged that the acquittal was a good result; even with the suppression of the breathalyzer tests, he testified, the chances of an acquittal would have been "not likely at a bench trial." The witness estimated that it would have been necessary, for thorough preparation of the case including the novel breathalyzer suppression argument, to have billed twenty to thirty hours for preparation, not including trial time.

A second expert, testifying on behalf of bar counsel, expressed his belief that the issues presented in this case were not particularly difficult, nor novel, and that "the degree of skill required to defend a case such as this . . . was not that high." He did recognize, however, that the theory that Fordham utilized to suppress the breathalyzer tests was impressive and one of which he had previously never heard. Nonetheless, the witness concluded that "clearly there is no way that [he] could justify these kind of hours to do this kind of work." . . .

An expert called by Fordham testified that the facts of Timothy's case presented a challenge and that without the suppression of the breathalyzer test results it would have been "an almost impossible situation in terms of prevailing on the trier of fact." He further stated that, based on the particulars in Timothy's case, he believed that Fordham's hours were not excessive and, in fact, he, the witness, would have spent a comparable amount of time. The witness later admitted, however, that within the past five years, the OUI cases which he had brought to trial required no more than a total of forty billed hours, which encompassed all preparation and court appearances. He explained that, although he had not charged more than forty hours to prepare an OUI case, in comparison to Fordham's more than 200 expended hours, Fordham nonetheless had spent a reasonable number of hours on the case in light of the continuance and the subsequent need to reprepare, as well as the "very ingenious" breathalyzer suppression argument, and the Clarks' insistence on trial. In addition, the witness testified that, although the field sobriety test, breathalyzer tests, and the presence of a half-empty liquor bottle in the car placed Fordham at a serious disadvantage in being able to prevail on the OUI charge, those circumstances were not unusual and in fact agreed that they were "normal circumstances."

The fourth expert witness, called by Fordham, testified that she believed the case was "extremely tough" and that the breathalyzer suppression theory was novel. She testified that, although the time and labor consumed on the case was more than usual in defending an OUI charge, the hours were not excessive. They were not excessive, she explained, because the case was particularly difficult due to the "stakes [and] the evidence." She conceded, however, that legal issues in defending OUI charges are "pretty standard" and that the issues presented in this case were not unusual. . . .

In considering whether a fee is "clearly excessive" within the meaning of S.J.C. Rule 3:07, DR 2-106(B), the first factor to be considered pursuant to that rule is "the novelty and difficulty of the questions involved, and the skill requisite to perform the legal service properly." That standard is similar to the familiar standard of reasonableness traditionally applied in civil fee disputes. Based on the testimony of the four experts, the number of hours devoted to Timothy's OUI case by Fordham and his associates was substantially in excess of the hours that a prudent experienced lawyer would have spent. According to the evidence, the number of hours spent was several times the amount of time any of the witnesses had ever spent on a similar case. We are not unmindful of the novel and successful motion to suppress the breathalyzer test results, but that effort cannot justify a $50,000 fee in a type of case in which the usual fee is less than one-third of that amount.

The board determined that "because [Fordham] had never tried an OUI case or appeared in the district court, [Fordham] spent over 200 hours preparing the case, in part to educate himself in the relevant substantive law and court procedures." Fordham's inexperience in criminal defense work and OUI cases in particular cannot justify the extraordinarily high fee. It cannot be that an inexperienced lawyer is entitled to charge three or four times as much as an experienced lawyer for the same service. A client "should not be expected to pay for the education of a lawyer when he spends excessive amounts of time on tasks which, with reasonable experience, become matters of routine." . . .

[T]he third factor to be considered in ascertaining the reasonableness of the fee is its comparability to "the fee customarily charged in the locality for similar legal services." The hearing committee made no finding as to the comparability of

Fordham's fee with the fees customarily charged in the locality for similar services. However, one of bar counsel's expert witnesses testified that he had never heard of a fee in excess of $15,000 to defend a first OUI charge, and the customary flat fee in an OUI case, including trial, "runs from $1,000 to $7,500." Bar counsel's other expert testified that he had never heard of a fee in excess of $10,000 for a bench trial. In his view, the customary charge for a case similar to Timothy's would vary between $1,500 and $5,000. One of Fordham's experts testified that she considered a $40,000 or $50,000 fee for defending an OUI charge "unusual and certainly higher by far than any I've ever seen before." The witness had never charged a fee of more than $3,500 for representing a client at a bench trial to defend a first offense OUI charge. She further testified that she believed an "average OUI in the bench session is two thousand [dollars] and sometimes less." . . .

Although finding that Fordham's fee was "much higher than the fee charged by many attorneys with more experience litigating driving under the influence cases," the hearing committee nevertheless determined that the fee charged by Fordham was not clearly excessive because Clark "went into the relationship with Fordham with open eyes," [and] Fordham's fee fell within a "safe harbor." . . .

The finding that Clark had entered into the fee agreement "with open eyes" was based on the finding that Clark hired Fordham after being fully apprised that he lacked any type of experience in defending an OUI charge and after interviewing other lawyers who were experts in defending OUI charges. . . . It is also significant, however, that the hearing committee found that "despite Fordham's disclaimers concerning his experience, Clark did not appear to have understood in any real sense the implications of choosing Fordham to represent Timothy. Fordham did not give Clark any estimate of the total expected fee or the number of $200 hours that would be required." . . .

That brings us to the hearing committee's finding that Fordham's fee fell within a "safe harbor." The hearing committee reasoned that as long as an agreement existed between a client and an attorney to bill a reasonable rate multiplied by the number of hours actually worked, the attorney's fee was within a "safe harbor" and thus protected from a challenge that the fee was clearly excessive. . . .

The "safe harbor" formula would not be an appropriate rationale in this case because the amount of time Fordham spent to educate himself and represent Timothy was clearly excessive despite his good faith and diligence. Disciplinary Rule 2-106(B)'s mandate that "[a] fee is clearly excessive when, after a review of the facts, a lawyer of ordinary prudence, experienced in the area of the law involved, would be left with a definite and firm conviction that the fee is substantially in excess of a reasonable fee," creates explicitly an objective standard by which attorneys' fees are to be judged. We are not persuaded by Fordham's argument that "unless it can be shown that the 'excessive' work for which the attorney has charged goes beyond mere matters of professional judgment and can be proven, either directly or by reasonable inference, to have involved dishonesty, bad faith or overreaching of the client, no case for discipline has been established." Disciplinary Rule 2-106 plainly does not require an inquiry into whether the clearly excessive fee was charged to the client under fraudulent circumstances, and we shall not write such a meaning into the disciplinary rule.

Finally, bar counsel challenges the hearing committee's finding that "if Clark objected to the numbers of hours being spent by Fordham, he could have spoken up with some force when he began receiving bills." Bar counsel notes, and we agree, that "the test as stated in the DR 2-106(A) is whether the fee 'charged' is clearly excessive, not whether the fee is accepted as valid or acquiesced in by the client." Therefore, we conclude that the hearing committee and the board erred in not concluding that Fordham's fee was clearly excessive. . . .

The fact that this court has not previously had occasion to discipline an attorney in the circumstances of this case does not suggest that the imposition of discipline in this case offends due process.

In charging a clearly excessive fee, Fordham departed substantially from the obligation of professional responsibility that he owed to his client. The ABA Model Standards for Imposing Lawyer Sanctions §7.3 (1992) endorses a public reprimand as the appropriate sanction for charging a clearly excessive fee. We deem such a sanction appropriate in this case. . . .

Lawrence J. Fox

Raise the Bar: Real World Solutions for a Troubled Profession

15-30 (ABA 2007)

End Billable Hour Goals . . . Now

We are delighted you have selected Austen Dental Services for all your dental needs. We look forward to providing you with high quality cost effective services. Our team of talented young dentists are highly motivated to give you outstanding services not only by virtue of their professional commitment to you, but also because the very best of them will be offered partnership in our great organization. To that end, we are sure you will be pleased to learn that we will charge for our services on an hourly basis. To demonstrate their dedication, we require our young dentists to record at least 2,000 billable hours per year, with bonuses if the dentist should achieve benchmarks of hourly dedication beyond 2,000.

* * *

Hourly billing has been with the legal profession a very long time. The evolution from one line bills "for professional services" to billing on the basis of precise calculation of time began when clients, particularly those with in-house counsel, as well as insurance companies that hire lawyers to represent insureds, looked for greater accountability and precision in the way they were charged for lawyer services. What started as an innovation grudgingly accepted by law firms, soon became the gold standard, applied almost universally to this day, despite numerous objections and staunch advocates in favor of alternative billing methods.

From accepting hourly billing, it was not very long before the tracking of time became not only a basis for preparing invoices but also a welcomed, even celebrated, management tool. Raise the hourly rate $5 or $10 and the revenue went right to the bottom line. Get each lawyer to add one billable hour per month, per week or per day, and you achieved the same results. Review time accounting records and you could rank order not just associates, but all lawyers, in terms of their commitment to the enterprise. Lawyers went from being professionals evaluated on their excellence to being full time equivalent timekeepers ("FTE's") evaluated on the basis of numbers. . . .

The next step in the march of the billable hour was the adoption by firms of billable hour goals—just like those describing so many affirmative action initiatives. And not, heaven forefend, to be confused with billable hour quotas or requirements. Just a gentle nudge directed at all lawyers that the firm had expectations. But it was not long before these goals became much more than that. Firms told their lawyers, especially the associates, that the firms would provide bonuses to those lawyers whose billable hour production exceeded certain thresholds, perhaps $25,000 for 2,000 hours, another $10,000 for the next 200 and so on, bonuses cascading without limit. It is these billable hour requirements, with both their attendant bonuses and the unspoken but inevitable negative effects of failing to meet the firm's expectations, that prompt this ethical rumination, addressing the question of whether what we are doing with billable hours violates principles of professional responsibility, if not the professional responsibility rules themselves. . . .

THE CONFLICT—COMPOUNDED

Though hourly billing is universally employed, and has many characteristics that recommend it, hourly billing certainly has one huge ethical deficit. The client has a very real interest in limiting the client's legal fees; the lawyers get rewarded, at least in the short run, for an increased number of hours. In short, hourly billing is a great incentive for the lawyer to undertake more tasks and to complete them more slowly, perhaps contrary to the interests of the client.

The imposition of specific goals, quotas or requirements for billable hours by law firms only heightens this conflict and, as the fictional disclosure in the preface to this article makes clear, they are hard to justify as serving any legitimate client interest. Simply ask yourself how you would feel if your dentist made that disclosure to you before you underwent a painful root canal. While the pain the young dentist might be inclined to prolong to add to her hour total may be more stinging than any a lawyer can inflict, any incentive to inflict pain on clients by delaying resolution of their matters or increasing their fees is something our profession should stamp out, not encourage.

DISTORTIONS

Think about the distortions that are introduced by this system. The affected lawyers are always asking two questions: What are my hours? What goal can I achieve? As the year drags on the lawyer either falls behind the goal or realizes that yet a higher goal (and its resulting additional bonuses) is achievable. Either way the obsession with these statistics only grows. . . .

Think also about the likely effect of this system on the recording of time. In the brave new world of lawyer time accounting, hours are measured in tenths (a mere six minutes), an absurd construct that . . . has placed virtually every lawyer in America in a position in which he or she is guilty of multiple mini-frauds every day. If one really kept track of every hour every work day in six minute increments, that is, in fact, all one would have time to do. . . .

Given this reality—that when most lawyers put down their time they are doing so based on estimates—the question arises whether it is likely that the presence of billable hour punishments and rewards has any distortive effect on how these estimates are made. Do we suppose that estimates high and estimates low are essentially equivalent, making the use of estimates mere harmless error that comes out in the wash? Or do we think that the special incentives built into the system by billable hour rewards might, just might, encourage lawyers to estimate and record on the high side the number of six minute increments dedicated to any given task? . . .

All of which says nothing about the unspeakable possibilities. Short on hours? Need a few to achieve the minimum requirement? The next highest goal? Who can really say all the research for this memorandum only required three hours? I'll just read a few more cases to make sure I've got it right. Or see if there are any law review articles on point. Or maybe I can draft a memorandum to the client. Write a few letters. Prepare a memo to the file documenting my work. I am just being careful, precise, conscientious, avoiding malpractice—all admirable goals worthy of nothing but high praise.

And then there is the most unspeakable effect of all. No one follows me around. No one really knows how much time I spent reviewing these documents in a lonely warehouse. Yet since I worked so efficiently isn't it fair to record an extra hour or two? No, not an even hour. How about 1.3 hours? Or that last memorandum took two point four hours but was worth so much more. What an insight I had! It's clearly worth, shall we say, 8.6? Or while I traveled for, and billed Client A, I was working on Client B's matters. Shouldn't they both pay for my six hour flight to L.A.? Twelve added billable hours credited to my account. . . .

BAD POLICY

Even if billable hours were scrupulously and honestly kept for only those tasks efficiently performed and essential to serving the best interests of the client, it still would be the wrong way to award bonuses to associates for a number of different reasons. . . .

Put simply, looking at a chart of associate annual hours does provide a method of awarding bonuses with apparent precision, but its simplicity of application belies the fact that not all similar billable hour statistics reflect similar situations—or anything close to it. For that reason, it is critical that the firm embarked on such a billable hour reward and punishment enterprise must go behind the stark numbers on the computer printout to understand why the numbers are what they are, whether they reflect sloth or some failure on the part of the firm to provide sufficient work, allocate work fairly, or otherwise give the affected associate appropriate opportunities. A failure to take this nuanced approach, while surely reducing administrative time, breeds resentment among the associate corps, directed at both their "fortunate" colleagues pocketing the extra bonuses and the partners who use such a mechanical measure for allocating rewards.

The use of billable hour bonuses also only focuses on one narrow dimension of an associate's total performance. Think for a moment about the questionnaire we know Caldwell & Moore uses to evaluate associates. It certainly asks questions about the associate's ability to research and write, to be responsive, to deal with clients, to follow instructions, to accept increasing responsibility, to take the initiative and to succeed at myriad other activities. Yet when it comes to bonuses, Caldwell & Moore only rewards associates on the basis of billable hours. Where is the bonus for the brilliant brief, the riveting oral argument, the call the associate got directly from the client with new business for the firm, the imaginative idea that saved the client thousands of dollars? To make judgments like these certainly takes more familiarity with what associates are doing and how they are doing it than to look at the billable hour chart, but surely Caldwell & Moore owes its associates the awarding of bonuses (if any there shall be) on qualitative factors at least as much (I would say far more) as it does on raw billable hour totals. Far more important, Caldwell & Moore owes its clients the knowledge that when the client's law firm rewards its professionals for work done on behalf of the firm's clients, it values excellence, imagination, cost-savings, efficiencies and speed at least as much (again, I would say far more) as it values the accumulation of hour upon hour of professional services. In fact, should not clients be assured that if Caldwell & Moore is going to reward the achievement of billable hour thresholds, those rewards will only be granted if the hours are not just calculated but also evaluated for their necessity and competence?

Think for a moment, moreover, about what a billable hour reward and punishment system says about where the law firm's real values are. The hiring literature, the firm web-site, the summer associate presentations all may talk about a balanced life. . . . The real message—the one that counts—is that Caldwell & Moore is a sweat shop and the more you sweat the more you will be rewarded with bonuses now and with the fruits of the bonus-striving of associates later if you bill enough hours to become a partner.

DOES IT COUNT?

No. The answer to the question is no. Does [fill in the blank non-billable activity] count as billable hours for purposes of bonuses? That is the question out of every naïve associate's mouth. The sophisticated already know—whatever the activity, no matter how important to the health of the firm or the good of the poor—it doesn't really count. Hiring, pro bono, bar association work, writing an article, attending a CLE. . . .

THE SOLUTION

In fact, all of these activities must count. In the long run, Caldwell & Moore will only succeed if its lawyers dedicate themselves with real quality time to hiring and retaining the very best talent, training the firm's lawyers to perform at the highest professional level, mentoring associates to become partners, developing a real diversity program that recruits, retains and promotes women and minorities. Moreover, the profession of law will only survive if lawyers—including Caldwell & Moore lawyers—dedicate themselves to pro bono, bar association work, continuing legal education and the greater civic good of the community.

But, instead of making these "non-productive" hours count in a billable hour bonus system, the entire rewards and punishments for billable hours method should be jettisoned in favor of a system of rewards and punishments that rewards excellence, innovation, imagination, savings for the client, pro bono dedication, bar association commitment, hiring, mentoring and training, diversity, and all of the other characteristics that yield a rich fulfilling professional life. . . .

ANTICIPATING THE CRITICS

This diatribe has already drawn considerable dissent. Perhaps it will draw more. I certainly welcome the dialogue. But permit me to answer in advance a few of my critics.

It has been asserted that my concern about the recording of billable hours is slanderous, that I am accusing the profession of wholesale fraud. That is certainly not my intent. But we also cannot blind ourselves to four things. First, there have been far too many documented cases of billable hour abuse. From the case of the celebrated Chicago law firm partner billing over 6,022 hours in one year,[2] to Lisa Lerman's catalogue of over-billing, expense padding and other criminal conduct by sixteen high profile lawyers at prestigious *American Lawyer 200* law firms,[3] to think our profession is pristine is to ignore the facts. Second, I am much more focused on the subtle effects that billable hour quotas and rewards create than I am on out-and-out fraud. To suggest that these effects are not likely is to assume lawyers are not human beings, when we know all too well that they are. Third, even if lawyers were perfect, it is impossible to think that we are carrying the right message to our firm colleagues—when we employ billable hour requirements and provide billable hour bonuses—about the importance we place on non-billable activities. Fourth, and most important, we are a profession that owes all these duties to our clients; they are our raison d'étre, and how must they feel if they know this is the basis on which lawyers working on their matters are rewarded? Consider again the mythical three-hour root canal procedure to capture the point.

It has also been argued that associates really want to be rewarded this way, they like the certainty of knowing that if they put in exactly 2,103 hours they

---

2. *Chapman & Cutler Axes 17 Firm Staff*, Chicago Daily Law Bulletin, March 22, 1995.
3. Lisa G. Lerman, *Blue-Chip Bilking: Regulation of Billing and Expense Fraud by Lawyers*, 12 Geo. J. Legal Ethics 205 (1999); *See Bill Padding Happens*, Legal Times, Oct. 18, 2004.

will achieve the 2,000 bonus and the 2,100 extra bonus. This argument proves my point. While there is so much associates hate about our billable hour culture, of course they do like certainty. Everyone likes certainty. And knowing that I've got a lock on an extra $15,000 so long as I spend New Year's Eve in front of a CRT reviewing documents for privilege—guaranteeing compensation that will pay for far more than my midnight champagne makes me feel warm and fuzzy all over. But the certainty that arises from no more than the writing down of a pre-stipulated number of hours is not a desired result. Rather an associate should know that his or her lawyers' hours will be evaluated for quantity for sure, but also for quality, for innovation, for benefit to the client, and that the associate's non-billable hours will be evaluated too, and then—no certainty here—the associate may get a bonus if this overall review yields the conclusion that the associate is entitled to a bonus. Is it subjective? To be sure. But we are lawyers, producing legal work, running law firms, preserving a threatened profession, and there is no way a lawyer's contribution to those goals should be evaluated in other than a qualitative, albeit subjective, way. Leave it to the production line employees installing windshields and rearview mirrors to get compensated by purely objective criteria.

Last I have been confronted by those who say that far too many firms operate this way to change things now. Indeed, I have been accused of systematically seeking to change virtually the whole big firm business model.

To this I plead guilty. My experience with the Raise the Bar Project has convinced me of two things. First, our problems are profound and deeply troubling. Any enterprise that loses 78% of its new hires in the first three years is in a state of crisis. Second, we must change the way we do business other than incrementally if we are going to turn the ship of state around. Half-measures will not work. Maybe this idea will not either. But in our search for solutions we will have to develop ideas that change in some dramatic way the manner in which we do business, that overcome the litany of problems—too long to repeat here—that started the Section of Litigation to declare, enough of decrying the current state of affairs, let us find solutions, the goal of the project and this article.

B. Contingent Fees

Problems

12-3. Martyn & Fox entered into a one-third contingent fee agreement with Client, who has been seriously injured by Drunk Driver, who everyone believed was uninsured. Two months later, after we have spent about 10 hours drafting and filing a complaint, it turns out Drunk Driver was insured and her insurer offers the policy limits of $150,000, which Client accepts as a total settlement of the matter. Client threatens to file a disciplinary complaint unless we agree to reduce our fee to $5,000 ($500/hour). What should we do?

12-4. Massachusetts, after competitive bidding, hired Martyn & Fox to sue the tobacco companies at a time when the suit seemed hopeless. The fee agreement, signed for Massachusetts by the Attorney General, called for a 25 percent contingent fee. Two years later, as part of an overall settlement with 40 states, Massachusetts was awarded $8.3 billion. Should Martyn & Fox collect $2.075 billion?

12-5. Martyn & Fox's client is sued for $10 million, to be trebled as part of an alleged antitrust conspiracy among drug companies. May Martyn & Fox negotiate a fee agreement that would award the firm 25 percent of everything the client saves below $30 million?

12-6. Martyn & Fox routinely refers medical malpractice actions to Hastie & Moore, in exchange for one fourth of Hastie & Moore's 40 percent contingent fee. Fox just discovered that Hastie & Moore has not paid us our share after settling the last two cases we referred. What should we do?

Consider: Model Rule 1.5

Contingent Fees
ABA Formal Opinion 94-389
American Bar Association Standing Committee
on Ethics and Professional Responsibility

B. Contingent Fees Are Employed in Multiple Situations

It should be recognized at the outset that when we address contingent fees we are talking about a wide variety of situations. Contingent fees are no longer, if ever they were, limited to personal injury cases. Nor are contingent fees limited to suits involving tortious conduct. Contingent fees are now commonly offered to plaintiff-clients in collections, civil rights, securities and anti-trust class actions, real estate tax appeals and even patent litigation.

Nor is this compensation arrangement limited to plaintiffs. In this Committee's recent Formal Opinion 93-373, the Committee considered the ethical issues raised by the increasingly employed so-called "reverse contingent fees," in which defendants hire lawyers who will be compensated by an agreed upon percentage of the amount the client saves. The Committee concluded that as long as the fee arrangement reached between the lawyer and client realistically estimates the exposure of the defendant client, such a fee is consistent with the Model Rules.

Moreover, contingent fees are not limited to litigation practice. Fees in the mergers and acquisitions arena are often either partially or totally dependent on the consummation of a takeover or successful resistance of such a takeover. Additionally, fees on public offerings are often tied to whether the stocks or bonds come to market and to the amount generated in the offering. Banks are also hiring lawyers to handle loan transactions in which the fee for the bank's lawyers is dependent in whole or part on the consummation of the loan.

The use of contingent fees in these areas, for plaintiffs and defendants, impecunious and affluent alike, reflects the desire of clients to tie a lawyer's compensation to her performance and to give the lawyer incentives to improve returns to the client. The trend also may reflect a growing dissatisfaction with hourly rate billing. Because of the growing importance and widespread use of contingent fees, the Committee will first address in detail the factors that should be considered before a lawyer and client enter into such a fee arrangement, and then address the specific questions occasioning this opinion.

C. The Decision by the Client to Enter Into a Contingent Fee Agreement Must Be an Informed One

Nothing in the Model Rules expressly prohibits a lawyer from entering into a contingent fee agreement with any client. Nevertheless, the lawyer must recognize that not all matters are appropriate for a contingent fee. For example, Model Rule 1.5(d) makes it clear that a contingent fee may never be agreed to, charged or collected in a criminal matter or divorce proceeding. More to the point, in Informal Opinion 86-1521 this Committee concluded that, "when there is any doubt whether a contingent fee is consistent with the client's best interest," and the client is able to pay a reasonable fixed fee, the lawyer "must offer the client the *opportunity* to engage counsel on a reasonable fixed fee basis before entering into a contingent fee arrangement." (Emphasis added.) . . .

In other words, regardless of whether the lawyer, the prospective client, or both, are initially inclined towards a contingent fee, the nature (and details) of the compensation arrangement should be fully discussed by the lawyer and client before any final agreement is reached.

The extent of the discussion, of course, will depend on whether it is the lawyer or the client who initiated the idea of proceeding with the contingent fee arrangement, the lawyer's prior dealings with the client (including whether there has been any prior contingent fee arrangement), and the experience and sophistication of the client with respect to litigation and other legal matters. . . .

E. In a Case in Which Liability Is Clear and Some Recovery Is Certain, a Fee Based on a Percentage of the Recovery Can Be Ethically Proper . . .

. . . [E]ven in cases where there is no risk of non-recovery, and the lawyer and client are certain that liability is clear and will be conceded, a fee arrangement contingent on the amount recovered may nonetheless be reasonable. As the increasing popularity of reverse contingent fees demonstrates, for almost all cases there is a range of possible recoveries. Since the amount of the recovery will be largely determined by the lawyer's knowledge, skill, experience and time expended, both the defendant and the plaintiff may best be served by a contingency fee arrangement that ties the lawyer's fee to the amount recovered.

Also, an early settlement offer is often prompted by the defendant's recognition of the ability of the plaintiff's lawyer fairly and accurately to value the case and to proceed effectively through trial and appeals if necessary. There is no ethical reason why the lawyer is not entitled to an appropriate consideration for this value that his engagement has brought to the case, even though it results in an early resolution. . . .

That having been said, there may nonetheless be special situations in which a contingent fee may not be appropriate. For example, if in a particular instance a lawyer was reasonably confident that as soon as the case was filed the defendant would offer an amount that the client would accept, it might be that the only appropriate fee would be one based on the lawyer's time spent on the case since, from the information known to the lawyer, there was little risk of non-recovery and the lawyer's efforts would have brought little value to the client's recovery.[15] And even if, in such circumstances, after a full discussion, it were agreed between lawyer and client that a contingent fee was appropriate, the fee arrangement should recognize the likelihood of an early favorable result by providing for a significantly smaller percentage recovery if the anticipated offer is received and accepted than if the case must go forward through discovery, trial and appeal. . . .

In re Everett E. Powell, II
953 N.E.2d 1060 (Ind. 2011)

PER CURIAM. . . .

Prior to Respondent's representation of T.G., another attorney, Mark E. Ross ("Ross"), had represented T.G. in obtaining a settlement of a personal injury action. T.G. had a history of drug and alcohol abuse, and she was in an apparently abusive and controlling relationship with J.S., the father of her six children. In August 2004, Ross created, with T.G.'s consent, a "special needs trust" to hold $42,500 from the settlement to preserve T.G.'s eligibility for public assistance and to prevent rapid depletion by T.G. and those who may not be acting in her best interests, including J.S. Ross agreed to become the trustee because he was unable to find any other qualified individual or institution to serve.

T.G. soon began demanding access to the trust money, pressured, Ross believed, by J.S. and his mother. Ross sent a series of letters to T.G. reminding her of the purposes of the special needs trust, expressing willingness to surrender his position to a qualified successor trustee, saying that he was, in fact, very close to resigning as trustee (in which case, he told her a court would appoint a successor), and suggesting she contact some smaller banks to see if any would be willing to take over as trustee.

---

15. Similar reasoning has led many courts to find that it is inappropriate to charge a contingent fee in cases involving first party insurance benefits where there is no risk of non-recovery and the lawyer merely submits the claim on behalf of the client. But courts have also found that contingent fees may be appropriate in these types of cases, if the lawyer performs additional services relating to the recovery by the client. *See* In re Doyle, 581 N.E.2d 669 (Ill. 1991).

On October 27, 2004, T.G. (accompanied by J.S.) consulted Respondent about getting access to the funds in the trust. During this consultation, Respondent reviewed documents provided by T.G., which showed the amount of money placed in the trust and indicated Ross's willingness to step aside as trustee. Because T.G. did not have funds to pay a fee upfront, Respondent suggested that he could take the case on a contingent basis. On the same day, the parties entered into an agreement under which Respondent would "provide legal services concerning removal of Mark E. Ross as trustee of your Special Needs Trust" for a fee of "1/3 of whatever was in the trust." The agreement also stated:

- T.G. and her family have sought legal representation for some time and no attorney is willing to take on this case.
- T.G. had been given the option of paying for Respondent's services on an hourly basis.
- The agreement could result in a substantial fee for Respondent for little work.
- The parties agreed that the one-third fee was reasonable under the circumstances.
- J.S. attested to all the statements and signed as a witness.

The following day, October 28, 2004, Respondent faxed a letter to Ross telling him of T.G.'s dissatisfaction and asking him to dissolve the trust. Ross sent a return fax saying that he was glad T.G. had consulted an attorney and that he had offered to have the trust pay for one or two hours for legal work. Ross told Respondent of the reasons the trust was created and expressed concern that the assets would be quickly depleted if T.G. got unfettered access to them. On the same day, Respondent and Ross reached an agreement by phone that Respondent would take over as successor trustee.

Respondent prepared a short "Resignation and Replacement of Trustee" document, which T.G., Respondent, and Ross signed on October 29. Having become the successor trustee at this point, Respondent executed documents terminating the trust, in accordance with T.G.'s wishes [and accompanied] T.G. went to the downtown branch of Fifth Third Bank and showed employees there the trust termination documents. They refused to allow Respondent to sign anything allowing T.G. to withdraw any money from the trust account. Respondent and T.G. then went to another branch of Fifth Third Bank. Without showing the employees there the trust termination documents, he executed a signature card for the trust account in his purported capacity as trustee. . . .

Later on October 29, Respondent prepared an accounting of funds to be distributed from the trust, showing $14,815.55 as his fee, $200 to be held for any tax and accounting fees, and $29,429.62 for T.G. . . .

The hearing officer rejected any justification for a one-third contingent fee Respondent collected for his services and calculated that a reasonable fee for Respondent's services was $3,000, based on 15 hours of work at $200 per hour.

Discussion . . .

Even if a fee agreement is reasonable under the circumstances at the time entered into, subsequent developments may render collection of the fee unreasonable. In Matter of Gerard, 634 N.E.2d 51 (Ind. 1994), an elderly, hospitalized woman (Randolph) retained the respondent to prepare a will and help recover certificates of deposit she believed were lost or stolen. The fee agreement stated that the respondent was to receive "as a retainer an amount equal to one-third of all assets recovered." He charged $250 for preparing a will, and during the following month, he located 23 certificates of deposit, all safely deposited under the client's name, with a value of over $450,000. He retained a fee of nearly $160,000. The respondent's actions were largely administrative and required no specific legal skill. He claimed he spent 160 hours in this effort. After the client died, her estate filed suit against him to recover the allegedly excessive fee. The respondent then renegotiated his fee and retained just $28,000 for his services (for 160 hours at his customary rate of $175.00 per hour).

> [T]he Hearing Officer found no evidence Respondent knew collection of Randolph's assets would be a simple, uncontested matter until after Randolph signed the contingency fee agreement. However, a more important fact is that **Respondent did not renegotiate his fee after realizing his client's entitlement to the certificates was not seriously in doubt, but instead nonetheless accepted the inflated contingency fee.** . . .
>
> . . . Respondent's acts in securing the inflated fee represent greedy overreaching. His proper course of action would have been to renegotiate his fee after it became apparent that collection of Randolph's assets was a simple, uncontested matter. His failure to immediately do so indicates a conscious attempt to secure an excessive fee, which imparts added culpability to Respondent's acts. Id. at 53-54 (emphasis added).

In the current case, Respondent may have reasonably believed at the outset that removing Ross as trustee would be contested (despite documentation indicating Ross was willing to step aside in favor of a qualified successor). He may have even reasonably questioned the amount of money in the trust upon which his fee would be calculated and collected (despite documentation that $42,500 had been deposited in it just a few months earlier). But within two or three days, Ross agreed to resign as trustee in favor of Respondent, and Respondent had assumed control over the trust, knew the balance in the trust account, had gained access to those funds, and had cut himself a check for his fee. At this point, he knew the case did not involve any complex issues, prolonged time commitment, risk of no recovery, or even any opposition. . . .

We do not suggest that a contingent fee must be reduced every time a case turns out to be easier or more lucrative than contemplated by the parties at the outset. But collection of a fee under the original agreement is unreasonable when it gives the attorney an unconscionable windfall under the totality of the circumstances. On the evidence before us in this case, we conclude that

Respondent violated the Indiana Professional Conduct Rule 1.5(a) by collecting a fee that was clearly excessive and unreasonable under the totality of the circumstances. . . .

We agree with the hearing officer's finding of the following facts in aggravation: (1) Respondent is not remorseful; (2) he lacks insight into his misconduct; (3) he made disingenuous, contradictory, unsupported, and evasive assertions during the proceedings; (4) he did not cooperate fully with the Commission's investigation; (5) he was on notice that his client was vulnerable and took an indifferent attitude; (6) he made misrepresentations to Ross (that he intended to act as trustee when he intended to terminate the trust) and to Fifth Third Bank (that he was acting as trustee when he had already terminated the trust); and (7) he has not made restitution. We find the following facts in mitigation: (1) Respondent has no disciplinary history; and (2) at the time of the misconduct, he was newly admitted to the bar. . . .

Exploitive overreaching in misconduct involving fees is even more culpable when the client is particularly vulnerable. In Matter of Gerard, discussed above, the Court imposed a suspension of one year without automatic reinstatement for collecting an unreasonable fee from an elderly, hospitalized woman. In the current case, Respondent was on notice from the outset of the circumstances that prompted T.G. herself to agree a special needs trust just two months earlier--her history of drug and alcohol abuse, her apparently abusive and controlling relationship with J.S., the need to preserve her eligibility for public assistance, and the danger of rapid depletion if she had unfettered access to the funds. Respondent not only dissolved the special needs trust that was meant to protect her assets from dissipation, but he actually began the dissipation by retaining an unreasonable fee from those assets.

In light of Respondent's collection of an unreasonable fee from a vulnerable client, his lack of insight into his misconduct, and the other aggravating circumstances described above, we conclude that Respondent should be suspended for 120 days without automatic reinstatement.

C.   Flat Fees

Problems

12-7. Insurance company offers to hire Martyn & Fox to represent all of its insured physicians in medical malpractice cases for $200,000 per case. Can Martyn & Fox accept this arrangement? What if the offer is for $20,000 per case?

12-8. Martyn & Fox take on a breach of contract case for a fixed fee of $50,000. After two years of difficult litigation, Martyn & Fox asks client if the firm can switch to a contingent fee of 40 percent of any recovery. "It's taken us a lot more time than we expected," Fox intones.

12-9. Martyn & Fox agrees to defend Client's breach of contract action for a flat fee of $20,000. Six months later, Client fires us, saying, "I just like the lawyers down the block better," and demands a refund of $15,000. What should Martyn & Fox do?

Consider: Model Rules 1.5, 1.15
RLGL §§ 18, 38, 40, 44

In re Sather

3 P.3d 403 (Colo. 2000)

Justice BENDER delivered the Opinion of the Court.

I. INTRODUCTION

In this attorney regulation proceeding, we address the conduct of the attorney-respondent, Larry D. Sather, who spent and failed to place into a trust account $20,000 he received as a "non-refundable" advance fee for a civil case. Because Sather treated these funds as his own property before earning the fee, Sather's conduct violated Colo. RPC 1.15(a). Sather labeled the $20,000 fee "nonrefundable" even though he knew that the fee was subject to refund under certain circumstances, thereby violating Colo. RPC 8.4(c). After being discharged by his client, Sather failed to return all of the unearned portion of the $20,000 promptly, in violation of Colo. RPC 1.16(d). . . .

II. FACTS AND PROCEDURAL BACKGROUND

. . . Sather agreed to represent Franklin Perez in a lawsuit against the Colorado State Patrol and certain individual troopers. Perez alleged that the troopers violated his civil rights during a traffic stop on December 7, 1995. Almost a year after the stop, on November 15, 1996, Sather and Perez entered into a written agreement for legal services, captioned "Minimum Fee Contract." Sather drafted the agreement, the terms of which required Perez to pay Sather $20,000 plus costs to represent Perez in the case against the State Patrol. Sather testified that he had never charged this large an amount as a flat fee in a civil case.

The contract referred to the $20,000 alternatively as a "minimum fee," a "non-refundable fee," and a "flat fee." The contract stated that Perez understood his obligation to pay this fee "regardless of the number of hours attorneys devote to [his] legal matter" and that no portion of the fee would be refunded "regardless of the time or effort involved or the result obtained." The contract acknowledged Perez's right to discharge Sather as his attorney, but the contract informed Perez that in no circumstance would any of the funds paid be refunded:

IN ALL EVENTS, NO REFUND SHALL BE MADE OF ANY PORTION OF THE MINIMUM FEE PAID, REGARDLESS OF THE AMOUNT OF TIME EXPENDED BY THE FIRM.

The client has been advised that this is an agreed flat fee contract. The client acknowledges that the minimum flat fee is the agreed upon amount of $20,000, regardless of the time or effort involved or the result obtained.

Thus, the contract stipulated that Perez pay Sather $20,000 for his legal services; that he pay all legal costs incurred by Sather in the case; and that no funds would be refundable after Perez paid Sather the flat fee of $20,000.[3]

Perez paid Sather $5,000 of the minimum fee on November 17, 1996. He paid the remaining $15,000 on December 16th. Sather spent the $5,000 soon after receiving the money. Sather kept the second payment of $15,000 for approximately one month before spending these funds. Sather did not place any of these funds in his trust account before spending them. Sather testified that he spent Perez's $20,000 because he believed he earned the fees upon receipt. Sather stated that while he could not cite a specific rule for this opinion, he thought it was a common practice in the legal community to treat flat fees as being earned on receipt.

Less than a month after agreeing to represent Perez, on December 6, 1996, Sather filed suit in Denver District Court on behalf of Perez against the State Patrol and three troopers. In addition to claims for tort and civil rights injuries, the complaint included a claim for attorney's fees. The Attorney General's Office, which represented the State Patrol and three troopers, negotiated with Sather and offered Perez a $6,000 settlement, which Perez refused. Sather then requested an extension of time to respond to a pretrial motion, which the court granted.

On April 21, 1997, in a matter unrelated to the Perez case, this court suspended Sather from the practice of law for thirty days, effective May 21, 1997. *See* People v. Sather, 936 P.2d 576, 579 (Colo. 1997). As required, Sather notified Perez of his suspension and Perez responded on May 23, requesting an accounting of the hours Sather worked on his case. Perez requested that Sather provide the accounting by May 30, but Sather replied that he would be unable to provide this information until the third week of June. Thereafter, on June 4, 1997, Perez faxed Sather notice discharging him from his case because of the suspension.

Acting pro se, Perez received an extension of time to file a response to the State Patrol's motion after informing the court that he was seeking replacement counsel to handle the case. Then, on August 21, 1997, Perez wrote a letter to the Attorney General's Office, accepting the offer of $6,000 to settle all of his claims against the State Patrol and the troopers. . . .

Sather provided the accounting requested by Perez on June 27, 1997. Sather claimed that his fees, his paralegal assistant's fees, costs and expenses in Perez's case as of the date of discharge totaled $6,923.64. At that time, Sather acknowledged that he should refund $13,076.36, the balance of the $20,000 paid by Perez.

---

3. In contrast to the contract's language, Sather testified that he knew that the fees were subject to refund and that he "never treated the fees as non-refundable."

Despite acknowledging his duty to return the unearned $13,076.36 to Perez, Sather did not refund any money to Perez because at the time of discharge he had spent Perez's funds. On September 3, 1997 — three months after Perez discharged him — Sather paid Perez $3,000. Sather paid the remaining $10,076.36 on November 2, 1997. The hearing board found that this delay prejudiced Perez because he did not have access to his funds for almost five months.

At the time Sather and Perez entered into the flat fee agreement, Sather was involved in personal bankruptcy proceedings. Sather filed a Chapter 7 bankruptcy proceeding in U.S. Bankruptcy Court in March 1995, over a year before agreeing to represent Perez. Sather later converted this case to a Chapter 13 proceeding, and then attempted to reconvert the case to a Chapter 7 filing. At the time of the hearing, the bankruptcy case was still pending. During the representation, Sather never told Perez that he had declared bankruptcy. After discharging Sather, Perez hired an attorney to pursue a claim against Sather in the bankruptcy proceeding for a refund of the fees ($6,923.64) Sather charged for work on Perez's suit.

Much later, in June 1998, Perez and Sather agreed to an arbitration by the Colorado Bar Association concerning the amount of fees charged by Sather for his work. The arbitrator awarded Perez $2,100.00, which represented the cost to Perez to bring the arbitration action. The arbitrator did not award Perez any recovery of the fees Sather charged for work performed. Shortly before the hearing in this case, on November 17, 1998, Sather paid Perez the award. . . .

III.   DISCUSSION . . .

A. Colo. RPC 1.15 Requires Segregation of Attorney and Client Property

. . . Colo. RPC 1.15(a) and [c] indicate that an attorney has an obligation to keep clients' funds separate from his own, and that advance fees remain the property of the client until such time as the fees are "earned."

The rule requiring that an attorney segregate funds advanced by the client from the attorney's own funds serves important interests. As a fiduciary to the client, one of an attorney's primary responsibilities is to safeguard the interests and property of the client over which the attorney has control. *See Restatement (Third) of the Law Governing Lawyers* § [44] cmt. (b). Requiring the attorney to segregate all client funds — including advance fees — from the attorney's own accounts unless and until the funds become the attorney's property protects the client's property from the attorney's creditors and from misuse by the attorney. Thus, Colo. RPC 1.15(a) and (f) further the attorney's fiduciary obligation to protect client property.

In addition to protecting client property, requiring an attorney to keep advance fees in trust until they are earned protects the client's right to discharge an attorney. Upon discharge, the attorney must return all unearned fees in a timely manner, even though the attorney may be entitled to quantum meruit recovery for the services that the attorney rendered and for costs incurred on behalf of the client.

If an attorney suggests to a client that any pre-paid or advance funds are "non-refundable" or constitute the attorney's property regardless of how much or how little work the attorney performs for the client, then the client may fear loss of the funds and may refrain from exercising his right to discharge the attorney. . . .

B. An Attorney Earns Fees by Conferring a Benefit on or Providing a Service for the Client

. . . We hold that an attorney earns fees only by conferring a benefit on or performing a legal service for the client. Unless the attorney provides some benefit or service in exchange for the fee, the attorney has not earned any fees and, with a possible exception in very limited circumstances, the attorney cannot treat advance fees as her property.

Funds given by clients to attorneys as advance fees or retainers benefit attorneys and clients. Some forms of advance fees or retainers appropriately compensate an attorney when the fee is paid because the attorney makes commitments to the client that benefit the client immediately. Such an arrangement is termed a "general retainer" or "engagement retainer," and these retainers typically compensate an attorney for agreeing to take a case, which requires the attorney to commit his time to the client's case and causes the attorney to forego other potential employment opportunities as a result of time commitments or conflicts. Although an attorney usually earns an engagement retainer by agreeing to take the client's case, an attorney can also earn a fee charged as an engagement retainer by placing the client's work at the top of the attorney's priority list. Or the client may pay an engagement retainer merely to prevent the attorney from being available to represent an opposing party. In all of these instances, the attorney is providing some benefit to the client in exchange for the engagement retainer fee.

In contrast to engagement retainers, a client may advance funds — often referred to as "advance fees," "special retainers," "lump sum fees," or "flat fees" — to pay for specified legal services to be performed by the attorney and to cover future costs. We note that unless the fee agreement expressly states that a fee is an engagement retainer and explains how the fee is earned upon receipt, we will presume that any advance fee is a deposit from which an attorney will be paid for specified legal services.

Advance fees present an attractive option for both the client and the attorney. Like engagement retainers, advance fees allow clients to secure their choice of counsel. Additionally, some forms of advance fees, e.g., "lump sums" or "flat fees," benefit the client by establishing before representation the maximum amount of fees that the client must pay. . . . So long as the fees are reasonable, such arrangements do not violate ethical rules governing attorney fees.

Advance fees benefit the attorney because the attorney can secure payment for future legal services, eliminating the risk of non-payment after the attorney does the work. . . .

C. "Non-Refundable" Fees

. . . Because fees are always subject to refund under certain conditions, labeling a fee "non-refundable" misleads the client and may deter a client from exercising their rights to refunds of unearned fees under Colo. 1.16(d). Thus, we hold that attorneys cannot enter into "non-refundable" retainer or fee agreements. . . .

In the limited circumstances in which an attorney earns fees before performing any legal services (i.e., engagement retainers) or where an attorney and client agree that the attorney can treat advance fees as the attorney's property before the attorney earns the fees by supplying a benefit or performing a service, the fee agreement must clearly explain the basis for this arrangement and explain how the client's rights are protected by the arrangement. In either of these situations, however, an attorney's fees are always subject to refund if excessive or unearned, and an attorney cannot communicate otherwise to a client. . . .

IV. DISCIPLINE OF ATTORNEY-RESPONDENT SATHER . . .

. . . [W]e agree with the board's conclusion that Sather violated Colo. RPC 1.16(d) by only partially repaying Perez's advance fee three months after being discharged and paying the balance of the refund five months after being discharged. . . . A discharged attorney must refund unearned fees in a timely fashion and failure to do so is a violation of Colo. RPC 1.16(d). . . . Because Sather only partially returned the unearned fees three months after being discharged and did not return the remainder of the unearned fees until five months after being discharged, we agree with the board that his conduct violated Colo. RPC 1.16(d).

We also agree with the board's determination that Sather violated Colo. 8.4(c) by materially misrepresenting to Perez the nature of the fee he paid. Colo. RPC 8.4(c) prohibits attorneys from engaging in conduct that involves "dishonesty, fraud, deceit, or misrepresentation." The fee agreement Sather drafted clearly expressed that the $20,000 was non-refundable, irrespective of the number of hours Sather spent on the case, and that "*In All Events, No Refund Shall Be Made Of Any Portion*" of the $20,000. (Emphasis in original.) Despite this strong language of the contract he drafted, Sather testified that he understood his ethical obligation to return any unearned portion of the fees in the event of discharge. We approve of the board's finding that Sather knowingly used misleading language to describe the fee arrangement and knowingly made a material misrepresentation to his client concerning the $20,000 advance fee. Thus, we accept the board's finding that Sather's conduct involved dishonesty, deceit, fraud and misrepresentation in violation of Colo. RPC 8.4(c). . . .

▣ Practice Pointers:
Trust Fund Management

The Colorado Supreme Court disciplined lawyer Sather for failing to repay his client's advance fee after being discharged and for materially misrepresenting the nature of the fee as "nonrefundable." Lawyers also have repayment obligations when clients discharge them, as occurred in *Malonis*, set out below.

Until the turn of the twentieth century, lawyers commonly commingled their clients' funds with their own, and could have repaid these amounts from any account. Stock market crashes in both England and America led to a reexamination of professional accounting requirements, then to requirements that lawyers could not commingle client funds with lawyer operating accounts,[1] and eventually to specific regulations such as those in Model Rule 1.15, discussed in *Sather*. These provisions obviously are intended to protect client funds and property, but they also prohibit lawyers from using trust accounts to shield their own money from personal or business creditors.[2] In short, lawyers may not deposit their own funds in a client trust account (except to cover bank charges), nor may they deposit client funds, such as advance payment of fees and retainers, in their own business account. Lawyers also must notify clients and third parties whenever the lawyer receives property or funds to which the client or third party has an interest, promptly deliver the funds to the appropriate party, and provide an accounting of funds upon request.[3]

These rules mandate separation of client and lawyer funds, identification and safeguarding of other client property, complete and accurate recordkeeping, as well as the retention of any disputed fees or funds in the trust account,[4] and prompt distribution of all portions of the property not in dispute. Violating these provisions creates strict liability. *Sather* represents the view shared by nearly every jurisdiction: Knowing violations of rules that require segregation of client funds will result in severe discipline, even when client's interests are

---

1. ABA Canons of Prof. Ethics, Canon 11 *Dealing with Trust Property* (1908).
2. In re Valasquez, 507 A.2d 145 (D.C. 1986) (lawyer who deposited personal business funds in client trust account to avoid creditors disbarred in two jurisdictions).
3. St. ex rel. Okla. Bar Assn. v. Taylor, 71 P.3d 18 (Okla. 2003) (lawyer who failed to understand applicable law regarding distribution of client funds to third-party medical providers publicly reprimanded); In re Haar, 698 A.2d 412 (D.C. 1997) (lawyer who withdrew disputed legal fee from client's trust account negligently misappropriated funds despite lawyer's legal entitlement to the amount because client did not agree to the withdrawal); cf. Rielgeman v. Krieg, 679 N.W.2d 857 (Wis. App. 2004) (lawyer who sent letter to client's medical provider promising to pay medical bill out of settlement proceeds personally liable for the bills because lawyer released all funds to client without protecting medical lien).
4. Model Rule 1.15(a) also applies to funds held for third parties. *See* Atty. Grievance Comm'n v. Clark, 767 A.2d 865 (Md. 2001) (lawyer who repeatedly failed to pay state income withholding taxes violated Rule 1.15 by failing to remit money that belonged to the state).

not otherwise compromised.[5] Courts also agree that inadvertent commingling violates these rules, even if temporary and without harm to a client.[6]

Yet, in spite of these requirements, so many clients have been the victims of lawyers who have "borrowed" or stolen client funds that many jurisdictions have adopted additional specific rules that govern trust account management. By 1976, nearly every jurisdiction had created a client protection fund, financed by assessments on all lawyers, which reimburses clients who have been the victims of lawyer theft. In addition, some jurisdictions also require that lawyers keep specific records such as a ledger for each client showing the source of all funds deposited, the name and description of payees, and the amount of all deposits and payments,[7] and journals, which record receipts and disbursements from all law practice bank accounts.[8] Others require banks to notify disciplinary authorities of any overdrafts in a trust account.[9] A few even require audits of trust accounts.[10]

To meet the requirement of a separate account for client funds, most lawyers today establish an Interest on Lawyer Trust Account (IOLTA) with a local bank. All client funds that cannot earn net interest are kept in this account, and the interest is paid to a central fund that is used to fund legal services for those unable to pay.[1111] Local rules additionally might require that some client funds, such as those that are significant in size or held for a long period of time or

---

5. *See, e.g.,* Iowa S. Ct. Disc. Bd. v. Ries, 812 N.W. 2c 594 (Iowa 2010) (lawyer who failed to refund client's inadvertent fee overpayment suspended for 30 days); Douglas' Case, 809 A.2d 755 (N.H. 2002) (lawyer who improperly withdrew funds from client trust account in the "startlingly erroneous" belief that withdrawal was proper suspended from practice for six months); Atty. Grievance Comm'n v. Hayes, 789 A.2d 119 (Md. 2002) (lawyer who operated practice for 30 years using only a trust account suspended for 90 days for commingling and misusing funds despite otherwise spotless record).

6. Atty Grievance Comm'n v. Jeter, 778 A.2d 390 (Md. 2001) (inexperienced lawyer who failed to deposit client personal injury funds in trust account suspended for six months despite lawyer's remorse and lack of intent to defraud).

7. Ariz. S. Ct. R. 43(d)(2) (2007); Cal. R. Prof. Conduct 4-100(C) (2007); Colo. R. Prof. Conduct 1.15(j) (2007); Conn. R. Super. Ct. Gen. §2-24(b) (2007); Fla. Bar R. 5-1.2 (2006); Haw. R. Prof. Conduct 1.15(g) (2007); Ind. Admis. & Disc. R. 23, §29(a) (2007); Minn. R. Prof. Conduct 1.15(h) (2005), *id.,* at App. 1; N.J. R. Prof. Conduct 1.15 (2006); N.J. R. Gen. Application 1:21-6(c) (2007); N.Y. Code Prof. Resp. DR 9-102(D) (2007); Ohio R. Prof. Conduct 1.15 (2007); R.I. R. Prof. Conduct 1.15 (2007); Vt. R. Prof. Conduct 1.15(e) (2007); Va. R. Prof. Conduct 1.15A(a) (2007).

8. Cal., Colo., Conn., Haw., Ind., Minn., N.J., N.Y., R.I., Va.

9. *See, e.g.,* Fla. Bar R. 5-1.2(c)(4) (2006); Ind. Admis. & Disc. R. 23, § 29(b) (2007); Mass. R. Prof. Conduct 1.15(h) (2007).

10. *See, e.g.,* N.J. R. Gen. Application 1:21-6(h) (2007); Vt. R. Prof. Conduct 1.15A(b) (2007). For a compilation of the ABA Model Rules governing these subjects, *see* ABA, Model Rules for Client Protection (1999).

11. In Brown v. Leg. Found. of Wash., 123 S. Ct. 1406 (2003), the Supreme Court upheld the constitutionality of state IOLTA programs so long as client funds held in the accounts do not earn net interest for the client.

those for trusts or estates, be kept in another separate account where the interest accrues to that client.

How do lawyers avoid inadvertent breach of these trust account obligations? First, just as law firms should not allow any one lawyer carte blanche in billing clients, law firms also should make at least two lawyers responsible for administration of law firm trust accounts.[12] Second, all trust accounts should adhere to certain fundamental rules designed to prevent inadvertent breaches. Jay Foonberg has written an entire book on the subject, and summarizes his advice in what he calls "The Ten Commandments of Good Trust Accounts."[13]

Rule 1: Have a trust account.

Rule 2: Never let anyone else sign your trust account.

Rule 3: Obtain and understand your IOLTA (Interest on Lawyers' Trust Account) rules.

Rule 4: Immediately notify the client every time something is added to the client's account balance and every time something is taken from the account balance.

Rule 5: Unearned fees and unexpended costs belong in the trust account until earned or spent.

Rule 6: Do not commingle your funds with the client funds in the trust account.

Rule 7: Be sure you understand the exact nature of the item deposited or credited to the trust account.

Rule 8: Reconcile the bank trust account monthly.

Rule 9: Reconcile and examine the individual client trust account balances monthly, and do not delay giving the clients their money.

Rule 10: Be alert to third-party claims.

In addition, Foonberg recommends that all lawyers maintain specific records required by the ABA Model Rules on Trust Account Records and by a growing number of jurisdictions.[14] Most important is a journal, which records all deposits, checks, dates, and amounts, and explains each item, and a client ledger, or running balance, by client, of all checks, disbursements, dates, amounts, and explanations. Lawyers and law firms also should keep all bank statements and records, as well as copies of each month's or quarter's reconciliation of the lawyer's accounts with the bank's statements.

Easy access to client funds continues to tempt lawyers. If history is any guide, you should expect increasing regulation of your bookkeeping practices to prevent further loss to clients.

---

12. *See, e.g.,* In re Fonte, 905 N.Y.S. 2d 173 (N.Y. App. 2010) (lawyer who failed to supervise and discover partner's theft of $17 million in trust accounts suspended for three years).

13. Jay G. Foonberg, *How to Start and Build a Law Practice* 491-496 (ABA L. Prac. Mgt. Sec. L. Student Div. 2004).

14. *Model Rules for Client Trust Account Records*, Aug. 9, 2010, *available at* http://www.american-bar.org/content/dam/aba/migrated/cpr/clientpro/adopted_8_10_10.authcheckdam.pdf.

D. Fees on Termination

Problem

12-10.   Martyn & Fox agreed to take on Plaintiff's malpractice suit for a
fixed fee of $30,000, plus a contingent fee equal to 50 percent of
all amounts recovered in excess of $500,000. After Martyn & Fox
spent $100,000 on the matter, Plaintiff hired Caldwell & Moore,
which settled the suit for $500,000. What fee is Martyn & Fox
entitled to collect, and from whom?

Consider: Model Rule 1.5
RLGL §§ 40, 43, 44

Malonis v. Harrington
816 N.E.2d 115 (Mass. 2004)

Greaney, J.

We transferred this case here on our own motion to review a judgment entered
in the Superior Court holding the defendant, Attorney Robert W. Harrington,
liable to the plaintiff, Attorney George C. Malonis, for Malonis's reasonable
attorney's fees and expenses. The fees and expenses were incurred by Malonis
in his representation of Marc J. Loiselle, under a contingent fee agreement, in
a personal injury action against Browning-Ferris Industries, Inc. (BFI). Loiselle
discharged Malonis and retained Harrington, also under a contingent fee agreement, to represent him. Harrington settled the case with BFI and refused to pay
Malonis's claim for attorney's fees and expenses. . . .

Loiselle suffered injuries on April 26, 1991, in a motor vehicle accident.
The operator of the other vehicle was an employee of BFI. Within a few days
of the accident, Loiselle retained Malonis to represent him in a personal injury
action against BFI for a contingent fee of one-third the amount of any recovery
received by Loiselle. Malonis secured a tape of the accident scene from the
police; obtained Loiselle's medical bills and records; communicated with BFI (a
self-insurer); obtained payment for Loiselle of personal injury protection (PIP)
benefits; and sent Loiselle's medical bills and records to BFI. In early 1993, BFI
made a settlement offer of $7,500, which Loiselle rejected. Malonis then pre-
pared and sent a demand letter to BFI, to which BFI responded by extending a
settlement offer of $30,000 (including the PIP benefits already paid). This offer
also was rejected by Loiselle.

In June, 1993, Malonis filed a complaint in the Superior Court against
BFI on Loiselle's behalf. Written discovery was exchanged, and Loiselle was
deposed and underwent an independent medical examination. As the litigation continued, Loiselle still complained of back pain. In April, 1994, on
Malonis's recommendation, Loiselle was examined by an orthopedic surgeon,
who recommended disc surgery. Malonis forwarded the surgeon's report to
BFI. As a consequence of receiving the report, BFI decided to increase its

settlement offer to $57,500, although it did not communicate that offer to Malonis. Settlement discussions that continued between Malonis and BFI focused on figures in the $60,000-$80,000 range, but no agreement was reached.

On September 14, 1994, Loiselle discharged Malonis and engaged Harrington to represent him under a contingent fee agreement calling for one-third of the gross amount of the recovery. Harrington requested that Malonis forward his case file to him, and Malonis complied. On September 21, Malonis gave written notice to Loiselle, Harrington, and BFI, that he would seek to establish an attorney's lien, pursuant to G. L. C. 221, § 50, on any recovery in the case. Between December 16, 1994, and March 27, 1995, Harrington sent Malonis four written requests for an itemized bill for his legal services performed for Loiselle with respect to the BFI case. . . .

In early April, Harrington completed a settlement with BFI for $57,500 (the figure that BFI had determined to offer the preceding year, but had not communicated to Malonis). Having received notice of Malonis's attorney's lien, and anticipating that Malonis expected to receive a portion of the settlement proceeds, counsel for BFI reminded Harrington of the issue of Malonis's payment. Harrington assured BFI's counsel that he "would take care of Mr. Malonis."

On April 4, BFI issued two checks: the first in the sum of $40,000, payable to Loiselle's wife, and the second in the sum of $17,500, payable to Harrington as attorney for Loiselle. Harrington subsequently paid the $40,000 to Loiselle's wife and retained the $17,500 as a legal fee. On April 4, the same day that the checks were issued, Malonis sent Harrington an itemized statement of his hours and costs, claiming $10,320 in hourly fees and $1,035.80 in costs, for a total of $11,355.80. Harrington viewed this amount as "ridiculous" and responded to a demand letter from Malonis with the words, "I will not tender one cent in settlement." Malonis offered to submit the dispute to fee arbitration, but Harrington refused. To date, Malonis has not been compensated for his legal services or expenses by either Loiselle or Harrington.

On July 31, Malonis filed a complaint in the Superior Court asserting claims against Loiselle, . . . and Harrington, with respect to his entitlement to payment for legal services performed for Loiselle in connection with the BFI case. . . .

Loiselle was entirely within his rights to discharge Malonis. The discharge terminated Malonis's right to recover on the contingent fee contract. Thereafter, Loiselle had an obligation to compensate Malonis for the fair and reasonable value of services and skills expended on Loiselle's behalf, on the theory of quantum meruit. The underlying basis for this legal obligation is derived from principles of equity and fairness, to prevent unjust enrichment of one party (the windfall of free legal services to the client) at the expense of another (the discharged attorney who expended time and resources for the client's benefit).

However, the record clearly establishes that, by the time settlement was reached with BFI, it was the reasonable expectation of all of the parties in this case that Harrington had assumed responsibility to pay Malonis. Loiselle, in his pro se answer to the complaint, stated that the case was settled "with the knowledge and understanding that Attorney Harrington was to see to [Malonis] at no cost to [Loiselle] whatsoever." BFI's counsel testified as to Harrington's specific assurance that he would "take care of" Malonis . . . Malonis testified that, although at the time of his discharge he had no direct communications with Harrington or Loiselle on the matter of his payment, he assumed (based in part on past interaction with Harrington), that discussions with Harrington would follow if and when the case settled. Finally, there is no question that Harrington himself understood that Malonis was entitled to payment, as shown by four written requests for an itemized bill for his legal services. Whatever his actual belief, Harrington's own words communicated to BFI's counsel an intention to pay Malonis a portion of his contingency fee. As noted by the judge, it is doubtful that BFI would have disbursed the settlement checks to Harrington without the latter's commitment to "take care of" Malonis.

Harrington is now obligated to compensate Malonis in quantum meruit for the value of his legal services. Given the expectations of the parties in this case, to conclude otherwise would allow Harrington to be unjustly enriched, by permitting him to retain the entire fee, when he, admittedly, was not the major force in obtaining the settlement. . . .

We now consider the fair value of Malonis's quantum meruit recovery, mindful that "the question of what is fair and reasonable compensation for legal services rendered is one of fact for a trial judge to decide." The judge assessed the fees ($10,320) and expenses ($1,035.80) set forth in Malonis's invoice and, quite properly, accepted them as fair and reasonable. The record demonstrates that Malonis invested substantial time and funds in the case, and his efforts contributed materially to the resulting $57,500 settlement.[10] . . . BFI's counsel estimated that Malonis had performed fully eighty per cent of the pretrial work and the settlement negotiations at the time of his discharge, and Harrington does not contradict that estimate. . . .

We comment now on the broader question raised by the case. When a client discharges one attorney before settlement is reached and retains another on a contingent fee basis, who bears the cost of paying the discharged attorney the fair value of his legal services and expenses, the client or successor counsel?[11] Our resolution of this issue recognizes the highly fiduciary nature

---

10. The judge pointed out that Malonis's invoice, reconstructed from his copy of the BFI case file and not from contemporaneous time records, set forth more conservative estimates of time expended on various tasks than ordinarily might be reflected in an attorney's file.

11. The parties have suggested that courts elsewhere are divided on the answer. Our own reading of the cited cases reveals that other courts have resolved similar disputes much as we do today, by reference to governing rules of professional responsibility and application of equitable principles to the specific facts of each case.

of the attorney-client relationship and duties on counsel imposed by the Massachusetts Rules of Professional Conduct . . . .

There is no question that a client must have absolute trust in the integrity, the judgment, and the ability of his or her attorney. When a client, for whatever reason, loses faith in his or her attorney, the client has the unqualified right to change lawyers. "But the right of a client so to do has not much value if the client is put at risk to pay the full contract price for services not rendered and to pay a second lawyer as well." The general rule in Massachusetts is that, on discharge, an attorney has no right to recover on the contingent fee contract, but, thereafter, the attorney may recover the reasonable value of his services on a theory of quantum meruit.

In withdrawing from a case, a discharged attorney must take all reasonable steps to protect the client's interests, including surrendering papers and property to which the client is entitled, and discussing with the client the consequences of the discharge, including his or her expectation of being compensated for work performed. *See* Mass. R. Prof. C. 1.16 (c) and (d). To the extent that the discharge is followed by the retention of another attorney on a contingent fee basis, the successor attorney also should discuss this expectation with the client and make clear, by specific agreement, who will be responsible to pay former counsel's reasonable fee. *See* Mass. R. Prof. C. 1.4 (b), and 1.5. The agreement, no doubt, will depend on the circumstances of each case. In the words of the Superior Court judge, "if the case is an attractive one, successor counsel [may be] willing to commit to sharing his fee on some equitable basis with his predecessor; if he is not willing, the client may be able to find someone who is."

The significant point is that the matter should be resolved by express agreement with the client, based on a frank discussion of the matter, thus allowing an intelligent decision as to which course is in the client's best interests. Absent such express discussion, it is likely (as occurred here) that the client will simply assume that both lawyers will be paid out of the single contingency fee, and will fail to appreciate the potential that fee claims above that amount may be made. Protection of the client's interests—and the client's ability to make a reasoned decision with respect to any settlement offers—requires that this important subject be addressed with clarity and specificity. Any fees to the client ultimately charged by either attorney, of course, whether or not contingent on the outcome, must be reasonable. Mass. R. Prof. C. 1.5 (a). A client should never be made to pay twice. To avoid disputes in the future, we would advise successor counsel, before he or she receives the case, to confer with the client on the issue and to execute a written agreement unambiguously identifying the party responsible for payment of former counsel's reasonable attorney's fees and expenses.

This position is not cast in stone. We recognize some potential for a conflict of interest to arise when the burden of advising a client of the obligation to pay a former attorney, and the need to identify the source of payment, falls on the shoulders of the only alternate candidate, or when an attorney approaches settlement negotiations knowing that a portion of his fee (fixed or, as here, as yet undetermined) is owed to one no longer involved with the case. Attorneys in this situation should never lose awareness that, in matters of fees, attorneys "are fiduciaries who owe their clients greater duties than are owed under the general law of contracts." *Restatement (Third) of the Law Governing Lawyers* §[34] comment b. . . .

E.   Statutory Fees

Problem

12-11.   Martyn & Fox agrees to a one-third contingent fee contract with Client and spends 2,000 hours on Client's federal civil rights action alleging police brutality against Local Municipality, resulting in injunctive relief and a jury verdict of $21,000. What fee will Martyn & Fox receive? What if Local Municipality offers to settle for injunctive relief in exchange for Client's agreement not to seek statutory attorney fees?

Consider: Model Rule 1.5
RLGL § 38

Perdue v. Kenny A.

130 S. Ct. 1662 (2010)

Justice ALITO delivered the opinion of the Court.

This case presents the question whether the calculation of an attorney's fee, under federal fee-shifting statutes, based on the "lodestar," *i.e.*, the number of hours worked multiplied by the prevailing hourly rates, may be increased due to superior performance and results. We have stated in previous cases that such an increase is permitted in extraordinary circumstances, and we reaffirm that rule. But as we have also said in prior cases, there is a strong presumption that the lodestar is sufficient; factors subsumed in the lodestar calculation cannot be used as a ground for increasing an award above the lodestar; and a party seeking fees has the burden of identifying a factor that the lodestar does not adequately take into account and proving with specificity that an enhanced fee is justified. Because the District Court did not apply these standards, we reverse the decision below and remand for further proceedings consistent with this opinion.

I

A

Respondents (plaintiffs below) are children in the Georgia foster-care system and their next friends. They filed this class action on behalf of 3,000 children in foster care and named as defendants the Governor of Georgia and various state officials (petitioners in this case). Claiming that deficiencies in the foster-care system in two counties near Atlanta violated their federal and state constitutional and statutory rights, respondents sought injunctive and declaratory relief, as well as attorney's fees and expenses.

The United States District Court for the Northern District of Georgia eventually referred the case to mediation, where the parties entered into a consent decree, which the District Court approved. The consent decree resolved all pending issues other than the fees that respondents' attorneys were entitled to receive under 42 U.S.C. §1988.

B

Respondents submitted a request for more than $14 million in attorney's fees. Half of that amount was based on their calculation of the lodestar—roughly 30,000 hours multiplied by hourly rates of $200 to $495 for attorneys and $75 to $150 for non-attorneys. In support of their fee request respondents submitted affidavits asserting that these rates were within the range of prevailing market rates for legal services in the relevant market.

The other half of the amount that respondents sought represented a fee enhancement for superior work and results. Affidavits submitted in support of this request claimed that the lodestar amount "would be generally insufficient to induce lawyers of comparable skill, judgment, professional representation and experience" to litigate this case. . . .

The District Court awarded fees of approximately $10.5 million. The District Court found that the hourly rates proposed by respondents were "fair and reasonable," *id.*, at 1285, but that some of the entries on counsel's billing records were vague and that the hours claimed for many of the billing categories were excessive. The court therefore cut the non-travel hours by 15% and halved the hourly rate for travel hours. This resulted in a lodestar calculation of approximately $6 million.

The court then enhanced this award by 75%, concluding that the lodestar calculation did not take into account "(1) the fact that class counsel were required to advance case expenses of $1.7 million over a three-year period with no on[-]going reimbursement, (2) the fact that class counsel were not paid on an on-going basis as the work was being performed, and (3) the fact that class counsel's ability to recover a fee and expense reimbursement were completely contingent on the outcome of the case." The court stated that respondents' attorneys had exhibited "a higher degree of skill, commitment, dedication, and professionalism . . . than the Court has seen displayed by the attorneys in any other case during its 27 years on the bench." The court also commented that the results obtained were "'extraordinary'" and added that "[a]fter 58 years as a practicing attorney and federal judge, the Court is unaware of any other case in which a plaintiff class has achieved such a favorable result on such a comprehensive scale." The enhancement resulted in an additional $ 4.5 million fee award. . . .

II

The general rule in our legal system is that each party must pay its own attorney's fees and expenses, see Hensley v. Eckerhart, 461 U.S. 424, 429 (1983), but Congress enacted 42 U.S.C. § 1988 in order to ensure that federal rights are adequately enforced. Section 1988 provides that a prevailing party in certain civil rights actions may recover "a reasonable attorney's fee as part of the costs."[3] Unfortunately, the statute does not explain what Congress meant by a "reasonable" fee, and therefore the task of identifying an appropriate methodology for determining a "reasonable" fee was left for the courts.

One possible method was set out in Johnson v. Georgia Highway Express, Inc., 488 F.2d 714, 717-719 (CA5 1974), which listed 12 factors that a court should consider in determining a reasonable fee. This method, however, "gave very little actual guidance to district courts. Setting attorney's fees by reference to a series of sometimes subjective factors placed unlimited discretion in trial judges and produced disparate results."

An alternative, the lodestar approach, . . . "achieved dominance in the federal courts" after our decision in *Hensley.* Gisbrecht v. Barnhart, 535 U.S. 789, 801 (2002). "Since that time, '[t]he "lodestar" figure has, as its name suggests, become the guiding light of our fee-shifting jurisprudence.'" *Ibid.*

Although the lodestar method is not perfect, it has several important virtues. First, in accordance with our understanding of the aim of fee-shifting statutes, the lodestar looks to "the prevailing market rates in the relevant community." Developed after the practice of hourly billing had become widespread, the lodestar method produces an award that *roughly* approximates the fee that the prevailing attorney would have received if he or she had been representing a paying client who was billed by the hour in a comparable case. Second, the lodestar method is readily administrable, and unlike the *Johnson* approach, the lodestar calculation is "objective," and thus cabins the discretion of trial judges, permits meaningful judicial review, and produces reasonably predictable results.

III

Our prior decisions concerning the federal fee-shifting statutes have established six important rules that lead to our decision in this case.

First, a "reasonable" fee is a fee that is sufficient to induce a capable attorney to undertake the representation of a meritorious civil rights case. Section 1988's aim is to enforce the covered civil rights statutes, not to provide "a form of economic relief to improve the financial lot of attorneys."

---

3. Virtually identical language appears in many of the federal fee-shifting statutes. See *Burlington v. Dague*, 505 U.S. 557, 562 (1992).

Second, the lodestar method yields a fee that is presumptively sufficient to achieve this objective. Indeed, we have said that the presumption is a "strong" one. *Dague, supra,* at 562.

Third, although we have never sustained an enhancement of a lodestar amount for performance, we have repeatedly said that enhancements may be awarded in "'rare'" and "'exceptional'" circumstances.

Fourth, we have noted that "the lodestar figure includes most, if not all, of the relevant factors constituting a 'reasonable' attorney's fee," and have held that an enhancement may not be awarded based on a factor that is subsumed in the lodestar calculation. We have thus held that the novelty and complexity of a case generally may not be used as a ground for an enhancement because these factors "presumably [are] fully reflected in the number of billable hours recorded by counsel." We have also held that the quality of an attorney's performance generally should not be used to adjust the lodestar "[b]ecause considerations concerning the quality of a prevailing party's counsel's representation normally are reflected in the reasonable hourly rate."

Fifth, the burden of proving that an enhancement is necessary must be borne by the fee applicant.

Finally, a fee applicant seeking an enhancement must produce "specific evidence" that supports the award. (An enhancement must be based on "evidence that enhancement was necessary to provide fair and reasonable compensation"). This requirement is essential if the lodestar method is to realize one of its chief virtues, *i.e.*, providing a calculation that is objective and capable of being reviewed on appeal.

IV

A

In light of what we have said in prior cases, we reject any contention that a fee determined by the lodestar method may not be enhanced in any situation. The lodestar method was never intended to be conclusive in all circumstances. Instead, there is a "strong presumption" that the lodestar figure is reasonable, but that presumption may be overcome in those rare circumstances in which the lodestar does not adequately take into account a factor that may properly be considered in determining a reasonable fee.

B

In this case, we are asked to decide whether either the quality of an attorney's performance or the results obtained are factors that may properly provide a basis for an enhancement. We treat these two factors as one. When a plaintiff's attorney achieves results that are more favorable than would have been predicted based on the governing law and the available evidence, the outcome may be attributable to superior performance and commitment of resources by plaintiff's counsel. Or the outcome may result from inferior performance by defense counsel, unanticipated defense concessions, unexpectedly favorable rulings by the court, an unexpectedly sympathetic jury, or simple luck. Since none of these latter causes can justify an enhanced award, superior results are relevant only to the extent it can be shown that they are the result of superior attorney performance. . . . And in light of the principles derived from our prior cases, we inquire whether there are circumstances in which superior attorney performance is not adequately taken into account in the lodestar calculation. We conclude that there are a few such circumstances but that these circumstances are indeed "rare" and "exceptional," and require specific evidence that the lodestar fee would not have been "adequate to attract competent counsel."

First, an enhancement may be appropriate where the method used in determining the hourly rate employed in the lodestar calculation does not adequately measure the attorney's true market value, as demonstrated in part during the litigation. . . . But in order to provide a calculation that is objective and reviewable, the trial judge should adjust the attorney's hourly rate in accordance with specific proof linking the attorney's ability to a prevailing market rate.

Second, an enhancement may be appropriate if the attorney's performance includes an extraordinary outlay of expenses and the litigation is exceptionally protracted. As Judge Carnes noted below, when an attorney agrees to represent a civil rights plaintiff who cannot afford to pay the attorney, the attorney presumably understands that no reimbursement is likely to be received until the successful resolution of the case, and therefore enhancements to compensate for delay in reimbursement for expenses must be reserved for unusual cases. In such exceptional cases, however, an enhancement may be allowed, but the amount of the enhancement must be calculated using a method that is reasonable, objective, and capable of being reviewed on appeal, such as by applying a standard rate of interest to the qualifying outlays of expenses.

Third, there may be extraordinary circumstances in which an attorney's performance involves exceptional delay in the payment of fees. An attorney who expects to be compensated under § 1988 presumably understands that payment of fees will generally not come until the end of the case, if at all. Compensation for this delay is generally made "either by basing the award on current rates or by adjusting the fee based on historical rates to reflect its present value." Missouri v. Jenkins, 491 U.S. 274, 282. But we do not rule out the possibility that an enhancement may be appropriate where an attorney assumes these costs in the face of unanticipated delay, particularly where the delay is unjustifiably caused by the defense. In such a case, however, the enhancement should be calculated by applying a method similar to that described above in connection with exceptional delay in obtaining reimbursement for expenses.

We reject the suggestion that it is appropriate to grant performance enhancements on the ground that departures from hourly billing are becoming more common. . . .

We are told that, under an increasingly popular arrangement, attorneys are paid at a reduced hourly rate but receive a bonus if certain specified results are obtained, and this practice is analogized to the award of an enhancement such as the one in this case. The analogy, however, is flawed. An attorney who agrees, at the outset of the representation, to a *reduced hourly rate* in exchange for the opportunity to earn a performance bonus is in a position far different from an attorney in a § 1988 case who is compensated at the *full prevailing rate* and then seeks a performance enhancement in addition to the lodestar amount after the litigation has concluded. Reliance on these comparisons for the purposes of administering enhancements, therefore, is not appropriate.

V

In the present case, the District Court did not provide proper justification for the large enhancement that it awarded. The court increased the lodestar award by 75% but, as far as the court's opinion reveals, this figure appears to have been essentially arbitrary. Why, for example, did the court grant a 75% enhancement instead of the 100% increase that respondents sought? And why 75% rather than 50% or 25% or 10%?

The District Court commented that the enhancement was the "minimum enhancement of the lodestar necessary to reasonably compensate [respondents'] counsel." But the effect of the enhancement was to increase the top rate for the attorneys to more than $866 per hour, and the District Court did not point to anything in the record that shows that this is an appropriate figure for the relevant market.

The District Court pointed to the fact that respondents' counsel had to make extraordinary outlays for expenses and had to wait for reimbursement, but the court did not calculate the amount of the enhancement that is attributable to this factor. Similarly, the District Court noted that respondents' counsel did not receive fees on an ongoing basis while the case was pending, but the court did not sufficiently link this factor to proof in the record that the delay here was outside the normal range expected by attorneys who rely on § 1988 for the payment of their fees or quantify the disparity. Nor did the court provide a calculation of the cost to counsel of any extraordinary and unwarranted delay. And the court's reliance on the contingency of the outcome contravenes our holding in *Dague*.

Finally, insofar as the District Court relied on a comparison of the performance of counsel in this case with the performance of counsel in unnamed prior cases, the District Court did not employ a methodology that permitted meaningful appellate review. Needless to say, we do not question the sincerity of the District Court's observations, and we are in no position to assess their accuracy. But when a trial judge awards an enhancement on an impressionistic basis, a major purpose of the lodestar method—providing an objective and reviewable basis for fees—is undermined.

Determining a "reasonable attorney's fee" is a matter that is committed to the sound discretion of a trial judge but the judge's discretion is not unlimited. It is essential that the judge provide a reasonably specific explanation for all aspects of a fee determination, including any award of an enhancement. Unless such an explanation is given, adequate appellate review is not feasible, and without such review, widely disparate awards may be made, and awards may be influenced (or at least, may appear to be influenced) by a judge's subjective opinion regarding particular attorneys or the importance of the case. In addition, in future cases, defendants contemplating the possibility of settlement will have no way to estimate the likelihood of having to pay a potentially huge enhancement.

Section 1988 serves an important public purpose by making it possible for persons without means to bring suit to vindicate their rights. But unjustified enhancements that serve only to enrich attorneys are not consistent with the statute's aim.[8] In many cases, attorney's fees awarded under § 1988 are not paid by the individuals responsible for the constitutional or statutory violations on which the judgment is based. Instead, the fees are paid in effect by state and local taxpayers, and because state and local governments have limited budgets, money that is used to pay attorney's fees is money that cannot be used for programs that provide vital public services. . . .

Justice BREYER, with whom Justice STEVENS, Justice GINSBURG, and Justice SOTOMAYOR Join, Concurring in Part and Dissenting in Part. . . .

As the Court explains, the basic question that must be resolved when considering an enhancement to the lodestar is whether the lodestar calculation "adequately measure[s]" an attorney's "value," as "demonstrated" by his performance "during the litigation." While I understand the need for answering that question through the application of standards, I also believe that the answer inevitably involves an element of judgment. . . .

This case well illustrates why our tiered and functionally specialized judicial system places the task of determining an attorney's fee award primarily in the district court's hands. The plaintiffs' lawyers spent eight years investigating the underlying facts, developing the initial complaint, conducting court proceedings, and working out final relief. The District Court's docket, with over 600 entries, consists of more than 18,000 pages. Transcripts of hearings and depositions, along with other documents, have produced a record that fills 20 large boxes. Neither we, nor an appellate panel, can easily read that entire record. Nor should we attempt to second-guess a district judge who is aware of the many intangible matters that the written page cannot reflect.

My own review of this expansive record cannot possibly be exhaustive. But those portions of the record I have reviewed lead me to conclude, like the Court of Appeals, that the District Judge did not abuse his discretion when awarding an enhanced fee. I reach this conclusion based on four considerations.

First, the record indicates that the lawyers' objective in this case was unusually important and fully consistent with the central objectives of the basic federal

---

8. Justice BREYER's opinion dramatically illustrates the danger of allowing a trial judge to award a huge enhancement not supported by any discernible methodology. That approach would retain the $4.5 million enhancement here so that respondents' attorneys would earn as much as the attorneys at some of the richest law firms in the country. These fees would be paid by the taxpayers of Georgia, where the annual per capita income is less than $34,000, and the annual salaries of attorneys employed by the State range from $48,000 for entry-level lawyers to $118,000 for the highest paid division chief. Section 1988 was enacted to ensure that civil rights plaintiffs are adequately represented, not to provide such a windfall.

civil-rights statute, 42 U.S.C. § 1983. Moreover, the problem the attorneys faced demanded an exceptionally high degree of skill and effort. Specifically, these lawyers and their clients sought to have the State of Georgia reform its entire foster-care system—a system that much in the record describes as well below the level of minimal constitutional acceptability. . . .

The upshot is that the plaintiffs' attorneys did what the child advocate could not do: They initiated this lawsuit. They thereby assumed the role of "a 'private attorney general'" by filling an enforcement void in the State's own legal system, a function "that Congress considered of the highest priority," and "meant to promote in enacting § 1988".

Second, the course of the lawsuit was lengthy and arduous. The plaintiffs and their lawyers began with factual investigations beyond those which the child advocate had already conducted. They then filed suit. And the State met the plaintiffs' efforts with a host of complex procedural, as well as substantive, objections. . . . All told, in opposing the plaintiffs' efforts to have the foster-care system reformed, the State spent $ 2.4 million on outside counsel (who, because they charge the State reduced rates, worked significantly more hours than that figure alone indicates) and tapped its own law department for an additional 5,200 hours of work.

Third, in the face of this opposition, the results obtained by the plaintiffs' attorneys appear to have been exceptional. The 47-page consent decree negotiated over the course of the mediation sets forth 31 specific steps that the State will take in order to address the specific deficiencies of the sort that I described above. And it establishes a reporting and oversight mechanism that is backed up by the District Court's enforcement authority. As a result of the decree, the State agreed to comprehensive reforms of its foster-care system, to the benefit of children in many different communities. And informed observers have described the decree as having brought about significant positive results

Fourth and finally, the District Judge, who supervised these proceedings, who saw the plaintiffs amass, process, compile, and convincingly present vast amounts of factual information, who witnessed their defeat of numerous state procedural and substantive motions, and who was in a position to evaluate the ultimate mediation effort, said:

1. the "mediation effort in this case went far beyond anything that this Court has seen in any previous case,";
2. "based on its personal observation of plaintiffs' counsel's performance throughout this litigation, the Court finds that . . . counsel brought a higher degree of skill, commitment, dedication, and professionalism to this litigation than the Court has seen displayed by the attorneys in any other case during its 27 years on the bench,";
3. the Consent Decree "provided extraordinary benefits to the plaintiff class . . . . " "[T]he settlement achieved by plaintiffs' counsel is comprehensive in its scope and detailed in its coverage. . . . After 58 years as a practicing attorney and federal judge, the Court is unaware of any other case in which a plaintiff class has achieved such a favorable result on such a comprehensive scale."

Based on these observations and on its assessment of the attorneys' performance during the course of the litigation, the District Court concluded that "the evidence establishes that the quality of service rendered by class counsel . . . was far superior to what consumers of legal services in the legal marketplace . . . could reasonably expect to receive for the rates used in the lodestar calculation."

On the basis of what I have read, I believe that assessment was correct. I recognize that the ordinary lodestar calculation yields a large fee award. But by my assessment, the lodestar calculation in this case translates to an average hourly fee per attorney of $249. . . .

At $249 per hour, the lodestar would compensate this group of attorneys—whom the District Court described as extraordinary—at a rate *lower* than the *average* rate charged by attorneys practicing law in the State of Georgia, where the average hourly rate is $268. Accordingly, even the majority would seem to acknowledge that some form of an enhancement is appropriate in this case. . . .

In any event, the circumstances I have listed likely make this a "rare" or "exceptional" case warranting an enhanced fee award. And they certainly make clear that it was neither unreasonable nor an abuse of discretion for the District Court to reach that conclusion. Indeed, if the facts and circumstances that I have described are even roughly correct, then it is fair to ask: If this is not an exceptional case, what is? . . .

I would hold that the principles upon which we agree—including the applicability of abuse-of-discretion review to a District Court's fee determination—require us to affirm the judgment below.

■ Practice Pointers:
Fee Agreements

The materials in this chapter demonstrate that the reasonableness requirement in Model Rule 1.5 applies to every kind of lawyer fee.[1] Statutes, case law, administrative regulation, and court rules all assume that lawyers may bargain for charge and collect fees, but only within limits. This reasonableness limit essentially becomes an implied term in every lawyer-client fee agreement. When it is exceeded, lawyers cannot collect the fee they bargained for, and they may be subject to professional discipline as well.[2]

Legal Regulation of Lawyer's Fees

Although professional discipline is not common in fee cases, *Fordham* and *Powell* illustrate that it is possible whenever a fee is found unreasonable. Statutes and regulations also control the amount of the fee in an increasing numbers of

---

1. RLGL § 34.
2. *See, e.g.,* Robert L. Rossi, *Attorneys' Fees* (2d ed., Thomson 1995).

cases.[3] Some statutes, like the Social Security Act, directly control the amount and calculation of the fee.[4] Others, such as the federal Equal Access to Justice Act, provide for fee shifting; that is, the statute specifically entitles a prevailing plaintiff to recover "reasonable fees and expenses of attorneys" directly from an unsuccessful defendant.[5]

Fee-shifting provisions typically are found in statutes such as the civil rights act in *Perdue* that encourage private attorneys general to assist in enforcing a statutory policy, such as securities, antitrust, environmental, and civil rights laws.[6] The Supreme Court has equated "reasonable" with a lodestar method of calculation (reasonable hourly rate times reasonable number of hours expended) under federal fee-shifting statutes. *Perdue* illustrates that the Court firmly believes the lodestar to be "presumptively sufficient."[7] Although the Court states that contingency enhancements might be "permitted in extraordinary circumstances," the Court has never sustained such an increase.

Every state has similar statutes, regulations, and case law that control lawyers' fees, both in certain kinds of representations such as workers' compensation, and by providing for fee shifting in statutory actions such as consumer or securities fraud.[8] Each jurisdiction has developed its own jurisprudence about the definition of a "reasonable attorney's fee" under these statutes. Beyond these specific statutes, many states now limit the amount of all contingent fees, providing that a lawyer who charges more than the regulated amount will be deemed to have charged an unreasonable fee within the meaning of Model Rule 1.5.[9] Violations of these provisions not only subject a lawyer to discipline, but also create the basis for the client to argue that the fee contract is illegal and therefore unenforceable.[10]

---

3. *See* Rossi, *supra* note 2, at Chapter 10.

4. Gisbrecht v. Barnhart, 535 U.S. 789 (2002) (statutory "reasonable fee . . . not in excess of 25% of . . . the past due benefits" allows for lawyer-client contingent fees subject court review of reasonableness).

5. *Id.*

6. For a list of federal statutes with fee-shifting provisions, *see* John W. Toothman & William G. Ross, *Legal Fees: Law and Management* 351-407 (Carolina Academic Press 2003).

7. Burlington v. Dague, 505 U.S. 557, 562 (1992).

8. *See, e.g.,* Roa v. Lodi Med. Group, 695 P.2d 164 (Cal. 1985) (citing representative statutes); Rossi, *supra* note 2, §§ 11:79-11:87.

9. *E.g.,* N.J. Ct. R. 1:21-7 (2007); N.Y. Jud. L. § 474-a (2007); Fla. R. Prof. Conduct 1.5(f) (2006). Some states also require a prescribed closing statement that regulates the calculation of the contingent fee. *See, e.g.,* Ohio Rev. Code § 4705.15 (2007).

10. *See, e.g.,* Fourchon Docks, Inc. v. Milchem Inc., 849 F.2d 1561 (5th Cir. 1988) (limiting a liquidated damages clause of $216,000 for lawyer's fees in a lease to a reasonable fee of $57,750); Starkey, Kelly, Blaney, & White v. Estate of Nicholaysen, 796 A.2d 238 (N.J. 2002) (oral contingent fee contract not enforceable, but recovery allowed in quantum meruit); White v. McBride, 937 S.W.2d 796 (Tenn. 1996) (lawyer who charged excessive contingent fee loses both contractual rights and quantum meruit recovery); Am. Home Assurance Co. v. Golomb, 606 N.E.2d 793 (Ill. App. 1992) (lawyer who charged fee in excess of that allowed by state statute in medical malpractice cases barred from recovering any fee, including quantum meruit).

Another aspect of the *Perdue* litigation also illustrates the potential for courts to gain jurisdiction over lawyers' fees because of common law and rule-based obligations. *Perdue* was a class action, where court approval is required for fees if the fee is part of a common fund settlement.[11] The Supreme Court has not yet resolved a circuit split in class-action, common fund cases. State and federal courts employ a variety of methodologies from a multifactor approach to a strict lodestar calculation.[12] Bankruptcy law also requires judicial approval of lawyers' fees because the court supervises the costs of administering the estate.[13] In state courts, lawyers who serve as fiduciaries are subject to the power of a probate court to examine and approve expenditures against an estate.[14] In cases that involve juveniles or other persons who lack legal capacity, courts also have a responsibility to approve fees as part of their *parens patriae* power to protect the ward.[15]

Apart from statutory and common law powers, courts have no general ability to supervise lawyer fees.[16] But courts adjudicate fee disputes brought to them in suits by lawyers to recover unpaid fees,[17] or client suits or counterclaims that claim refunds or disgorgement of fees already paid. Model Rule 1.6(b)(5) recognizes the right of a lawyer to use confidential information to bring such a suit, and many lawyers successfully recover sums from clients who unjustly refuse to pay.[18]

---

11. *See also* Morris A. Ratner, *Achieving Procedural Goals Through Indirection: The Use of Ethics Doctrine to Justify Contingency Fee Caps in MDL Aggregate Settlements,* 25 Geo. J. Legal Ethics (2012).

12. *See, e.g.,* Nilsen v. York County, 400 F. Supp. 2d 266 (D. Me. 2005) (cataloguing various federal circuit tests); Lealao v. Beneficial Cal., Inc., 97 Cal. Rptr. 2d 797 (Cal. App. 2000) (trial court had discretion to adjust lodestar in successful $14 million consumer class action by applying a multiplier where necessary to ensure that the fee awarded would be within the range of fees freely negotiated in the legal marketplace in comparable litigation). For a discussion of particular applications of the common fund doctrine, see Rossi, *supra* note 2, at Chapter 6.

13. *See, e.g.,* Watkins v. Sedberry, 261 U.S. 571 (1923); Lynn M. LoPucki & Joseph W. Doherty, *Professional Fees in Corporate Bankruptcies* (Oxford U. Press 2011).

14. Rossi, *supra* note 2, §§ 11:39-11:60.

15. *E.g.,* Hoffert v. General Motors Corp., 656 F.2d 161 (5th Cir. 1981) (upholding trial court's reduction of 40 percent contingent fee contract for a minor to 20 percent of the recovery). Recall that in Spaulding v. Zimmerman, *supra* p. 215, the court relied on this same *parens patriae* power to justify reopening the judgment under the Minnesota equivalent of Fed. R. Civ. P. 60.

16. Gagnon v. Shoblom, 565 N.E. 2d 775 (Mass. 1991) (trial judge has no power to raise issue of excessive fee *sua sponte*).

17. *See, e.g.,* Jane Massey Draper, *Excessiveness or Inadequacy of Attorney's Fees in Matters Involving Commercial and General Business Activities,* 23 A.L.R.5th 241 (1994); Jane Massey Draper, *Excessiveness or Adequacy of Attorneys' Fees in Domestic Relations Cases,* 17 A.L.R.5th 366 (1994); John E. Theuman, *Excessiveness or Adequacy of Attorneys' Fees in Matters Involving Real Estate—Modern Cases,* 10 A.L.R.5th 448 (1993).

18. One constant problem with fee suits is procedural: Any invocation of the court's jurisdiction can result in a counterclaim for other behavior that the client might not otherwise have contested. For example, clients have raised claims about sexual misconduct in the context of a fee suit, and counterclaims for malpractice also are common. *See, e.g.,* Barbara A. v. John G., 193 Cal. Rptr. 422 (Cal. App. 1983); McDaniel v. Gile, 281 Cal. Rptr. 242 (Cal. App. 1991); Ronald E. Mallen & Jeffrey M. Smith, *Legal Malpractice* § 15.9 (West 2007 ed.).

All of this legal regulation means that many fees routinely are reviewed by courts or are subject to explicit legal regulation by statute or court rule. Beyond this specific oversight, any fee also can come to a court's attention by virtue of a suit to recover a promised or already paid fee. Many jurisdictions have established fee arbitration systems to promote alternatives to formal lawsuits.[19] Like the judges called on in lawsuits to decide when fees are payable or refundable, the arbitrators who rule or make recommendations in these cases also rely on the factors set forth in Model Rule 1.5.

Fee Agreements

The best way to avoid fee disputes is to communicate the basis or rate of the fee and the client's responsibility for costs and expenses in a written document. Model Rule 1.5 requires written contingent fees agreements,[20] but only prefers rather than requires a writing for other fee agreements. Some jurisdictions go further, requiring that *all* fee agreements be reduced to a writing.[21] This is because fee disputes are not uncommon, and written documents not only may avoid them, but also clarify the respective rights of both client and lawyer if they do occur. For example, one case upheld a jury verdict of breach of fiduciary duty against a lawyer who failed to reduce a fee agreement to writing after his client requested a written document. The lack of documentation cost the lawyer all but $11,000 of the $100,000 fee to which he claimed entitlement.[22] Thus, the best practice is to provide your clients with a written document that communicates both "the scope of the representation and the basis or rate of the fee and expenses for which the client will be responsible."[23] The effort that you invest in providing such a writing will more than be repaid in client understanding and goodwill, and if necessary, in forming the basis for the resolution of a fee dispute.[24]

A written fee agreement also gives clients and lawyers the opportunity to consider alternative fee structures. This chapter focuses primarily on the common fee arrangements: hourly, contingent, and flat fees. Lawyers and clients are

---

19. *See, e.g.*, ABA Model Rules for Fee Arbitration (1995); Fla. Bar Reg. Rule 14-5 (2007). *See also* Disc. Counsel v. McCord, 770 N.E.2d 571 (Ohio 2002) (lawyer who failed to return fee following an arbitration award to his client suspended for six months for conduct prejudicial to the administration of justice); Guralnick v. N.J. S. Ct., 747 F. Supp. 1109 (D.N.J. 1990) (N.J. system of compulsory binding arbitration for lawyer-client fee disputes not unconstitutional).

20. Other countries such as Canada heavily regulate contingent fees. The European Union (EU) generally disapproves. *See* James Moliterno & George Harris, *Global Issues in Legal Ethics*, 59-64 (Thomson West 2007).

21. Alaska R. Prof. Conduct 1.5(b) (2012) (over $500); Cal. Bus. & Prof. Code § 6147 (2012); Colo. R. Prof. Conduct 1.5(b) (2012); Conn. R. Prof. Conduct 1.5(b) (2007); D.C. R. Prof. Conduct 1.5(b) (2012); N.J. R. Prof. Conduct 1.5(b) (2012); N.Y. DR 2-106(c)(2)(ii) (domestic relations matters); Pa. R. Prof. Conduct 1.5(b) (2006); R.I. R. Prof. Conduct 1.5(b) (2012); Utah R. Prof. Conduct 1.5(b) (2012) (over $750).

22. Frazier v. Boyle, 206 F.R.D. 480 (E.D. Wis. 2002).

23. MR 1.5(b).

24. *See, e.g.*, Ziolkowski Patent Solutions Grp. SC v. Great Lakes Dart Mfg. Inc., 794 N.W. 2d 253 (Wis. App. 2010) (law firm not entitled to collect interest on unpaid bill unless retainer agreement so provides).

becoming increasingly creative in modifying these options. Some adopt blended hourly fees, where the client pays a set rate regardless of which lawyer performs the work. Others prefer retainer plus fees, which supplement monthly retainers with an hourly fee when the lawyer works more than an agreed-on number of hours per month. Task-based fees, which break or unbundle a representation into different legal tasks, such as complaint drafting, negotiation, or interrogatories also are becoming more common, along with work-unit fees, which allocate flat fees by a client-determined unit such as number of lots sold.[25]

Finally, lawyers who amend fee contracts after the representation has commenced are subject to conflict of interest rules, including the law of undue influence designed to enforce their fiduciary obligations to clients. This means that changes to initial agreements are presumed the product of undue influence by the lawyer and voidable by the client.[26]

Fee Collection

Of course, lawyers not only must provide clients with clear fee agreements, but also abide by their provisions in charging and collecting their fees, and provide clarifications where necessary.[27]

Lawyers who execute otherwise valid fee contracts sometimes engage in what ABA Opinion 93-379 called "problematic billing practices." Unfortunately, some of these practices include fraud. For example, Professor Lerman has documented the practices of 16 well-respected lawyers who engaged in blatant billing and expense fraud.[28] Another survey finds that more subtle deception, ranging from performing unnecessary work and "estimating" billable hours to deliberately padding bills or expenses, occurs more than occasionally.[29] Of course, if deliberate, these practices constitute fraud,[30] and if done repeatedly, may rise to

---

25. *ABA Panelists Look into Whys and Hows of Moving to Different Fee Arrangements*, 18 ABA/BNA Lawyers' Manual on Prof. Conduct 485 (2002).

26. Brown & Sturm v. Frederick Rd. Ltd. Partn., 768 A.2d 62 (Md. Ct. Spec. App. 2001); Mallen & Smith, *supra* note 18.

27. Cox's Case, 813 A.2d 429 (N.H. 2002) (lawyer who failed to respond to client's request for accounting data reprimanded for violating MR 1.4 and 1.15(b)).

28. Lisa G. Lerman, *Blue-Chip Bilking: Regulation of Billing and Expense Fraud by Lawyers,* 12 Geo. J. Legal Ethics 205 (1999). For example, one judge described the practices of one of these lawyers as "almost fictional," because they included nearly $100,000 billed for services that were never performed, nearly $500,000 for work done by paralegals that was actually performed by secretaries and a receptionist, and $66,000 for legal research that cost the firm $395. His partners helped cover up the fraud when complaints were made. *Id.* at 238. *See also* Toledo Bar Ass'n v. Stahlbush, 933 N.E. 2d 1091 (Ohio 2010) (lawyer who submitted bills to local courts for more than 24 hours a day suspended for two years).

29. *See* William G. Ross, *The Honest Hour: The Ethics of Time-Based Billing by Attorneys* 23-38 (Carolina Academic Press 1996); Lisa G. Lerman, *Lying to Clients,* 138 U. Penn. L. Rev. 659, 705 (1990). The bill padding was accomplished by billing for hours not actually worked, or by "premium billing," which adds lump sums to a bill based on the lawyer's subjective determination of its value. *Id.* at 709-715.

30. *See, e.g.,* Ratcliff v. Boydell, 674 So. 2d 272 (La. App. 1996) (lawyer who misrepresented amount of client's annuity at settlement to increase his contingent fee and later sued client for defamation

the level of mail or wire fraud under state and federal criminal statutes.[31] We have seen that a clear and serious violation of a lawyer's duty to a client also constitutes grounds for total or partial fee forfeiture.[32] Further, sloppy or negligent billing that does not accurately reflect the agreement or the time spent may be grounds for a breach of contract, malpractice, or breach of fiduciary duty claim.[33]

Lawyers and law firms must monitor the accuracy of fee billings to prevent both intentional and inadvertent wrongdoing. The power of clients to discharge lawyers at any time discussed in *Malonis* and *Sather* means that regardless of the nature of the fee agreement, every lawyer must keep records of time actually spent on each matter to be able to establish the alternative basis for quantum meruit recovery.[34] Billing systems should include efficient and nearly simultaneous recording of time. Good recordkeeping also serves to document adherence to contractual terms, and provides the basis for lawyers to recover fees against clients who refuse to honor their own obligations. In law firms, no lawyer should have carte blanche to send out any bill he or she wishes.[35] Lawyers who lose their fees or are subject to damages in civil actions usually bind their law firms as well. Model Rule 5.1 also makes supervisory lawyers responsible for violations by other lawyers in their firms.[36]

Many jurisdictions recognize retaining or charging liens to secure a lawyer's fee. Retaining liens are nonconsensual and allow lawyers to retain a client's papers and funds in the lawyer's possession until the client pays the bill.[37] The Restatement adopts the minority view, which recognizes retaining liens only where legitimated by statute, because the lawyer's refusal to turn over the client's files may harm the client's interests, including the client's right to fire the lawyer.[38] The Restatement does recognize the legitimacy of charging liens,

---

and malicious prosecution, liable for fraud, intentional infliction of emotional distress, and abuse of process); Cantu v. Butron, 921 S.W.2d 344 (Tex. App. 1996) (lawyers who increased fee from 40 to 45 percent liable for fraud and breach of fiduciary duty, including punitive damages).

31. Lerman, *supra* note 26, at 263-271 (detailing criminal prosecutions of nine lawyers for billing fraud); *id.* at 282-287 (detailing civil penalties in 16 cases of billing fraud).

32. *E.g.,* Am. Home Assurance Co. v. Golomb, 606 N.E.2d 793 (Ill. App. 1992) (total fee forfeiture of illegal fee that violated state statute); The Law Governing Lawyers: *Loss of Fee or Other Benefits, supra* p. 364.

33. *See, e.g.,* Lerman, *supra* note 27, at 696-698; Cripe v. Leiter, 703 N.E.2d 100 (Ill. 1998) (citing cases).

34. RLGL § 40.

35. Ross, *supra* note 27, at 249-260.

36. *E.g.,* In re Fonte, 905 N.Y.S. 2d 173 (N.Y. App. 2010) (lawyer who failed to supervise and discover partner's theft of $17 million in trust accounts suspended for three years).

37. The lien does not include any property held in safekeeping for the client. Ronald D. Rotunda & John S. Dzienkowski, *Legal Ethics: The Lawyer's Deskbook on Professional Responsibility* § 1.8-10(a) (West 2012).

38. RLGL § 43. *See also* Sage Realty Corp. v. Proskauer Rose Geotz & Mendlesohn L.L.P., 689 N.E.2d 879 (N.Y. 1997) (client presumptively entitled to entire file, but law firm may charge for cost of assembling and delivering documents to client). RLGL § 43 does allow a lawyer to withhold a particular document (such as a will) drafted for the client until the client pays for it, so long as retaining the document would not harm the client unreasonably.

because they are created by contract with a client, and provide for the lawyer's right to a fee out of funds recovered for the client.[39] Lawyers also may secure a client payment by taking a security interest in other client property, so long as they remember that in doing so, they are engaging in a business transaction with a client subject to the stringent requirements of Model Rule 1.8(a).[40]

To sum up: Lawyers have every right to be compensated for their work, so long as the compensation is reasonable. To protect yourself, and increase your chances of avoiding or winning a fee dispute, you should reduce fee agreements to a writing or include them in written retainer agreements,[41] and you should keep accurate records of the time you spend on each client matter. The time these tasks take will more than repay you in client goodwill,[42] and eventual recovery of adequate compensation.

---

39. RLGL § 43(2).
40. RLGL § 43(4).
41. *See* Practice Pointers: *Engagement, Nonengagement, and Disengagement Letters, supra* p. 77.
42. *See, e.g.,* Avi Azrieli, *Your Lawyer on a Short Leash: A Survivor's Guide to Dealing with Lawyers* 125-138 (Bridge St. 1997).

Chapter 13

Ending the Client-Lawyer Relationship

We have seen that fiduciary duties generally do not attach until a lawyer agrees to represent a client. So, also, when a lawyer completes a client matter, most, but not all, fiduciary duties, end. In Chapters 6, 7, and 8, we addressed the continuing duties of confidentiality to former clients. In Chapters 9, 10, and 11, we identified specific rules that govern conflicts of interest concerning former clients. In Chapter 12, we saw that the lawyer's fee agreement may be invalidated when a client fires a lawyer. In this chapter, we review the various ways that a client representation can end, including termination by the client and withdrawal from the matter by the lawyer. We also focus here on situations where the client's activity could force the lawyer to resign, and whether the lawyer, faced with such a circumstance, can seek any remedy.

A. Voluntary Withdrawal

1. Unpaid Fees

Problem

13-1. Martyn & Fox has been handling a litigation matter for a client for several years. Last September, the client stopped paying Martyn & Fox's bills, giving one excuse after another. Threats to drop the client have only elicited pleas of cash flow problems and other "check is in the mail" statements. May Martyn & Fox resign?

Consider: Model Rules 1.16
RLGL §§ 32, 33

Gilles v. Wiley, Malehorn & Sirota
783 A.2d 756 (N.J. App. 2001)

PRESSLER, P.J.A.D.

Plaintiff Denise Gilles appeals from a summary judgment dismissing her legal malpractice complaint against defendants, the law firm of Wiley, Malehorn & Sirota, and its partner, Arthur L. Raynes, who had represented her. The gravamen of her complaint is that Raynes, voluntarily and without good cause attributable to her, terminated the representation without adequately protecting her against the running of the statute of limitations, thus causing her to lose her medical malpractice cause of action. . . .

. . . Plaintiff's asserted medical malpractice cause had its genesis in a colonoscopy she underwent on February 26, 1996, to determine the cause of occult bleeding. . . . The gravamen of the asserted medical malpractice was that the physician who performed the . . . colonoscopy perforated her colon, requiring her to undergo an emergency surgical repair that day. During her week-long hospital stay following the surgery, she developed a right hydropneumothorax that retarded her recovery. She apparently did, however, fully recover.

Persuaded by advice she had received from a physician family member that the perforation resulting in the emergency surgery was caused by malpractice, she consulted Raynes in early April 1996. . . .

. . . At Raynes's instruction, plaintiff obtained and delivered to him the relevant medical records. Raynes explained to her that before suit could be commenced, he would need a report from a medical expert opining that she had been the victim of malpractice. Accordingly, he sought an opinion from a forensic gastroenterologist, Dr. Andrew Lo of Beth Israel Medical Center in New York, who reported to him that he believed there had not been malpractice. By letter dated March 24, 1997, Raynes advised plaintiff of Dr. Lo's opinion but added that:

> Let me make clear that the above opinions on your care are those of Dr. Lo, and not of this office. We are willing to pursue your case further. However, in order to make this case viable, we will need to find an expert witness who can testify authoritatively that the care you received did not meet acceptable medical standards. If we do proceed with your case, we will need to lay out additional monies to potential witnesses in order to find one who agrees that you have received substandard treatment. This means that you will incur several hundred more dollars of expenses.

The letter concluded with Raynes's request that plaintiff telephone him to "discuss this further and decide whether you want us to continue to search for an independent expert." Plaintiff communicated her desire to proceed and agreed to pay the expenses involved.

A little over three months later, Raynes received a report dated July 3, 1997, from Dr. Lawrence B. Stein, a board-certified gastroenterologist, who opined that . . . [The medical technique used] . . . "greatly increased the likelihood of creating a colonic perforation and is a deviation from acceptable medical practice." Raynes mailed a copy of Dr. Stein's report to plaintiff on July 18, 1997, under cover of letter simply referring to it and making no further comment thereon.

On October 20, 1997, Raynes wrote to plaintiff again complaining that she had not yet paid the $1,204 she had been billed to cover expenses. The letter noted that the last payment he had received from her was the previous May. He then went on to say that:

> I understand that you want us to continue representing you in this matter; if that has changed, please advise us accordingly. In any event, you must reimburse us for the monies we have disbursed in working on your case thus far, as well as any expenses which may result from future work on your case. We cannot continue as your attorneys unless you fulfill that responsibility.
>
> I would ask that you pay us in full by no later than October 31, 1997. If we do not receive payment from you by that time, we may reconsider our representation of you in this matter. . . .

Although there was some dispute as to when that $1,204 was paid and as to just what the installment arrangements, if any, had been, Raynes agreed in his deposition testimony that by the beginning of January 1998 the balance due had been reduced to something just under $125.

Despite the favorable report from Dr. Stein, Raynes did not file a medical malpractice complaint. Some six months had gone by after his receipt of that report, when, on January 6, 1998, Raynes wrote the following letter to plaintiff:

> This is to advise that our firm has taken a new direction, away from most plaintiffs' malpractice cases. I therefore need to tell you that we will not be in a position to file suit on your behalf.
>
> The work that we have done for you, in obtaining a report from a reputable expert, Dr. Stein, will be useful to you with your next attorney. I enclose a copy of that report for you. Your next attorney will know to obtain the required affidavit from Dr. Stein.
>
> You have two years from the incident of malpractice to file suit. This should afford you sufficient time to obtain another attorney. Failure to file suit within the two year period will likely result in your losing your right to sue. I suggest that you contact another attorney immediately to protect your rights.
>
> There are numerous attorneys who handle medical malpractice cases. I recommend Tom Chesson of Porzio, Bromberg and Newman, whose telephone number is (973) 538-4006, or Adrian Karp, whose telephone number is (973) 267-7787.
>
> We have not charged you at all for our legal time. We have only charged you for reimbursement to us of our expenses.
>
> Best of luck to you.

Several comments must be made about that letter. First, at his deposition, Raynes explained that the firm had had some financially negative experience with contingent fee cases and while some were retained and some new ones being undertaken, they were not regarded as a desirable type of business. He then went on to explain that plaintiff's case was not as good—presumably in terms of damages—as he had originally thought and that Dr. Stein's report was not as strong as he had hoped for. He also suggested that plaintiff's failure to make prompt payment of the bill for expenses played a part in his decision to terminate the representation, although this had not been expressed to her and although her balance at the time of the termination was relatively insignificant.

In any event, the letter, which referred to the two-year statute of limitations but did not expressly state the date on which it would expire, came as a complete surprise to plaintiff, who, as she testified, was away on a trip when it was sent and did not believe that she actually received it until the end of January 1998. She did not, upon its receipt, immediately attempt to communicate with another lawyer, either one of the lawyers mentioned by Raynes or anyone else. As she testified on her deposition, she thought that if Raynes were sending her to another lawyer, then he should have made the referral himself and that in any event, she was so upset when she did receive his letter that she was unable to mobilize herself to take further steps although she did see another lawyer after the statute ran, some three or four weeks later. . . .

. . . Plaintiff asserts that Raynes breached his duty to her by unreasonably terminating the attorney-client relationship so soon before the running of the statute of limitations and without adequately protecting her interests in preserving her cause of action.

The Rules of Professional Conduct (R.P.C.s) speak to termination of the representation. And while we recognize that a cause of action for malpractice cannot be based exclusively on the asserted breach of an R.P.C., nevertheless it is clear that the R.P.C.s may be relied on as prescribing the requisite standard of care and the scope of the attorney's duty to the client. . . .

[The court cites Model Rule 1.16(b)(1) and (d).] The issue then, as we view it, is whether in the totality of the circumstances, Raynes's withdrawal, considering both the manner in which it was done and its timing, was accomplished without "material adverse effect" on plaintiff's interests in that it was attended by those steps "reasonably practicable" to protect her interests.

The trial judge concluded that Raynes had, beyond any question of material fact, acted reasonably. The sole basis of that conclusion was our decision in Fraser v. Bovino, 721 A.2d 20 (N.J. App. 1998), in which we held that in the circumstances there an attorney's termination of the attorney-client relationship "several weeks" before the statute of limitations had run was reasonable in that it afforded plaintiff adequate time to obtain another lawyer. We did not, however, in *Fraser* establish a bright-line rule that a withdrawal several weeks before the running of the statute of limitations is reasonable as a matter of law. We reached that conclusion there based on the operative facts in that case including the plaintiff's sophistication as a business man having regular dealings with lawyers, including such dealings with respect to the basic transactions in controversy; his having failed to raise the issue of possible litigation with defendant attorney until five years and nine months of the six-year statute of limitations had elapsed; and the brief period, some three months, during which the defendant-lawyer reviewed and studied the file. We note further that the defendant-lawyer there had denied that he had ever undertaken the representation.

Clearly the determination of reasonableness is ordinarily circumstantially dependent, and we are satisfied that a finder of fact would be justified in finding from the circumstances here that the timing and method of withdrawal were not reasonable. The facts here are very different from those in *Fraser*. Here, unlike *Fraser*, there was never a disavowal during a twenty-one month period of representation that Raynes represented plaintiff. As he said in his deposition, "I was her lawyer." For a six-month period he had all the information he needed not only to commence an action but also to have reached the conclusion that he eventually did reach respecting the probable unprofitability of the representation, a conclusion that evidently was the primary reason for the withdrawal. Plaintiff, on the other hand, was an unsophisticated lay person unaccustomed to legal dealings. The letter of termination, moreover, while it referred to the two-year statute of limitations and "suggested" plaintiff contact another lawyer immediately, did not specify the critical date. Finally, a fact-finder could also conclude that the period of time left to plaintiff before the statute of limitations had run was unreasonably short, particularly in view of the preceding six-month period following Raynes's receipt of Dr. Stein's favorable report. In this regard, we note that medical malpractice cases are ordinarily difficult representations and are not lightly or casually undertaken by serious and responsible lawyers. It is by no means clear that plaintiff could have obtained a new lawyer who, in three weeks, would have been able to review her file, make the necessary evaluations, and agree to file a complaint, particularly after knowing that her previous lawyer, who had represented her for twenty-one months, had suddenly declined to continue. After all, it apparently took Raynes six months after having reviewed the medical records and experts' reports to decide that he was no longer interested. Finally, and most significantly, a finder of fact could have found that Raynes failed to take those steps "reasonably practicable" to protect her interests, a matter we address hereafter.

Plaintiff supported her resistance to the summary judgment motion by submission of a report from an expert, a member of the bar of this State. The report opined that defendant, after his almost two years of representation, should not have terminated the relationship by a letter sent by ordinary mail but rather should have explained the situation and its imperatives to the client or, at the least, sent her his withdrawal by certified mail both to assure its timely receipt and to impress upon her the urgency of the situation. He also opined that considering the late withdrawal, reasonable steps to protect her interests would have required him to prepare for her a pro se complaint which she could have filed to avoid the danger of the statute running. . . .

The point, of course, is that plaintiff perceived herself as having been abandoned by defendant too late in the day to enable her to protect herself, and we do not regard that perception as prima facie unreasonable. We addressed the issue of abandonment in Kriegsman v. Kriegsman, 375 A.2d 1253 (N.J. App. 1977). Although we were there dealing with an attorney's motion for leave to withdraw from a matter already in litigation, what we said there is equally apt to an attorney's pre-litigation obligations. Thus, in affirming the denial of that motion, we started from the premise that "when a firm accepts a retainer to conduct a legal proceeding, it impliedly agrees to prosecute the matter to a conclusion. The firm is not at liberty to abandon the case without justifiable or reasonable cause, or the consent of its client." . . . [O]ur rationale in *Kriegsman* remains as relevant today as it was then in defining the attorney's duty. As we explained:

> We are not unmindful of the fact that the Rose firm has performed substantial legal services for plaintiff and clearly is entitled to reasonable compensation therefor. Nevertheless, an attorney has certain obligations and duties to a client once representation is undertaken. These obligations do not evaporate because the case becomes more complicated or the work more arduous or the retainer not as profitable as first contemplated or imagined . . . .

Whether Raynes's withdrawal afforded plaintiff a reasonable opportunity in the circumstances to protect her cause of action was, in our view, at least a question of fact precluding summary judgment dismissing the complaint. . . .

2. Client Misconduct

Problem

13-2. Client admits she doesn't pay Social Security for her daughter's "wonderful" nanny because nanny is an undocumented immigrant who might then get in trouble. "I'm trying to protect her job," Client unabashedly announces. Martyn & Fox informs Client, "If you don't report her income and pay the tax, the firm can't prepare and sign your income tax return." "That's okay," says Client. "You just prepare it; I'll sign it. Then the risk's on me." Are we safe?

[handwritten margin note: no; should recuse the firm. by preparing the document, firm is knowingly assisting the client break the law]

Consider: Model Rules 1.2(d), 1.16
RLGL § 32

In the Matter of Steven T. Potts

158 P.3d 418 (Mont. 2007)

. . . FACTUAL AND PROCEDURAL BACKGROUND

This disciplinary action arises from Potts's representation in a will contest involving the estate of Ernestine Stukey (Ernestine). Ernestine died March 8, 2001. Ernestine was survived by her daughter, Evon Leistiko (Evon), her six grandchildren, including Tyson Leistiko (Tyson), and her niece, Charlene Howard (Charlene).

Ernestine executed a will on January 14, 1998, disinheriting Evon and bequeathing most of her estate to Charlene. The will designated Charlene and Ernestine's friend, Verna Kessner (Verna), as co-personal representatives of her estate.

Ernestine's mental health deteriorated over the next two years, and she was involuntarily committed to the Montana State Hospital at Warm Springs. Evon petitioned the Third Judicial District [Court] to become Ernestine's conservator. . . .

Evon filed an initial inventory (initial inventory) with the district court in the conservatorship proceedings, reporting Ernestine's net worth as $1,254,795. The initial inventory included several accounts with a total worth of approximately $270,000, that Evon held in joint tenancy ownership with Ernestine or in which Evon was named as a beneficiary to the accounts (joint tenancy accounts). Ernestine established these joint tenancy accounts with Evon in 1967 and 1991.

As Ernestine's conservator and guardian, Evon petitioned the court to distribute gift money totaling $160,000 from Ernestine's estate to family members. The district court denied the petition on January 24, 2001, and authorized Ernestine's attorneys to investigate Evon's conduct as conservator. Ernestine's attorneys petitioned the court to remove Evon as conservator as a result of the investigation. . . . Ernestine's attorneys alleged that Evon had misappropriated $10,000 of Ernestine's money and engaged in other mismanagement of Ernestine's funds while Ernestine was incapacitated.

Without notifying the district court or Ernestine's attorneys, Evon moved Ernestine to an assisted living facility in the state of Washington. Ernestine purportedly executed a second will (second will) with assistance of Washington counsel on February 12, 2001, while staying in the Alzheimer's Unit of the facility. The second will appointed Evon as personal representative and bequeathed the bulk of the estate to Evon and Evon's family.

Ernestine died on March 8, 2001. A will contest ensued. . . .

Evon retained Potts to represent her and the six grandchildren, including Tyson, in the will contest in the Eighth Judicial District [Court]. Evon's attorney in the conservatorship proceeding provided Potts with Evon's legal file. . . .

Potts attended the settlement conference on November 12 and 13, 2001, with his clients, Evon and Tyson. At that time, Evon already had claimed a fraction of the joint tenancy accounts and was working to obtain the rest of the $270,000. Evon never disclosed this fact at the mediation, even though the other parties apparently assumed that they were negotiating based on the $1.2 million total estate value that included the joint tenancy accounts. Potts also remained silent as to whether the settlement included the joint tenancy accounts.

The parties reached an agreement during the second day of the mediation. They drafted a memorandum of understanding (memorandum) [that] purported to resolve both the will contest and conservatorship dispute. . . . The memorandum referred to the division of "the Estate," but failed to assign a particular dollar value to the total settlement. . . .

In the week following the settlement conference, [Glenn] Tremper [one of the attorneys representing Ernestine's estate] suspected that Evon was attempting to secure the joint tenancy accounts [and asked] Potts to confirm that the parties had reached the settlement in the mediation "based upon the good faith assumption that Ernestine's estate includes the assets identified by Evon as belonging to Ernestine in her proposed Final Accounting before Judge Mizner," in the conservatorship proceeding, [which] included the joint tenancy accounts and valued the total estate at $1.2 million. Tremper's letter requested that Potts let him know "immediately" if his clients had a different understanding of the settlement.

Potts showed Tremper's letter to his client, Tyson. Potts testified that he advised Tyson that any questions concerning what assets were included in the estate "will get cleared up," but that he would prefer to resolve any such dispute "sooner rather than later." Tyson instructed Potts not to respond because he wanted to deal only with a personal representative to be appointed later by the court. Potts did not answer the letter. Tremper construed Potts's silence as confirmation that the parties had based the settlement on the $1.2 million total estate value that Evon had reported to the courts in the initial, second, and final inventories.

One week later, Potts drafted and circulated a stipulation that purported to resolve "all" disputes regarding the division of Ernestine's "estate" as stated in the memorandum. . . .

A battle soon erupted over the meaning and effect of the stipulation and the memorandum. . . . We affirmed the district court's determination that, although the memorandum was ambiguous, the parties intended the $1.2 million total estate value, including the joint tenancy accounts, to be included in the memorandum and the settlement. *In* re Estate of Stukey, 100 P.3d 114 (Mont. 2004), (*Stukey I*). We later affirmed the personal representative's request to distribute the estate according to the formula set forth in *Stukey I. See In re Estate of Stukey,* 126 P.3d 507 (Mont. 2005). (*Stukey II*).

The Office of Disciplinary Counsel of the State of Montana (ODC) received a complaint regarding Potts's conduct surrounding the settlement. . . .

DISCUSSION

. . . Potts argues that Rule 1.6, M.R.P.C., prevented him from disclosing his clients' allegedly fraudulent conduct to anyone, including the court. . . . [because] his clients never consented to revealing such information. . . .

Rule 1.6(b)(1), M.R.P.C. . . . provides no exception for disclosing fraudulent conduct of a client to prevent, rectify, or mitigate fraud [as the rules existed in 2001]. Potts could not have disclosed his clients' confidences under Rule 1.6, M.R.P.C.

Rule 1.6, does not stand alone, however, and thus our analysis does not end here. Rule 1.2(d), prohibits the lawyer from counseling or assisting a client to engage in conduct that the lawyer knows is criminal or fraudulent. . . .

Rule 1.16, requires a lawyer to withdraw from representing a client if such representation will result in violation of the rules of professional conduct. Potts should have withdrawn from representation as soon as his clients' demands for nondisclosure of information propelled his services into the realm of assisting in his clients' fraudulent behavior. We concede that Rule 1.6, M.R.P.C., prevented Potts from disclosing the information against his clients' wishes. We will not endorse legitimate nondisclosure under Rule 1.6, M.R.P.C., however, as an excuse for noncompliance with Rule 1.2(d). . . .

Potts argues that the Commission's finding that his clients engaged in fraud rests on the erroneous conclusion that the joint tenancy accounts were included in Ernestine's estate. Potts contends that his clients, Evon and Tyson, never engaged in fraudulent conduct because the joint tenancy accounts passed as a matter of law to Evon upon Ernestine's death and as a result could not have been included as a part of the settlement basis. . . .

The allegedly fraudulent conduct in this case surrounds Evon's representations of the basis of the settlement value. Settlement agreements are contracts and subject to the provisions of contract law. Under contract principles, a party's conduct rises to the level of actual fraud when he acts with the intent to deceive another to induce him to enter into the contract. . . .

The evidence shows that Evon represented in three inventories to the courts that $1.2 million constituted the total value of Ernestine's estate. These inventories made no distinction between probate and nonprobate assets, such as the joint tenancy accounts. By the time the parties met for mediation, Evon had taken a fraction of the joint tenancy accounts from the $1.2 million estate and was working to secure the rest.

By all accounts in the record, Evon never disclosed to the other parties at the mediation her intent to take part of the $1.2 million estate. . . . Evon knew, however, at the time of the mediation that the $1.2 million value did not represent an accurate settlement basis because she already had taken a fraction of that money and had intended to secure several hundred thousand dollars in the days after the mediation. Evon's misrepresentation of the value of the estate fraudulently induced the other parties to enter into the settlement agreement. The settlement agreement benefited Evon in that it included a stipulation to dismiss the conservatorship action against her and the potential liability associated with it.

Tyson also engaged in fraud by suppressing the truth that the settlement value could not have included the full $1.2 million. . . . After mediation, Tremper informed Potts and his clients, including Tyson, that Evon's final inventory comprised the basis of the settlement. Tremper requested that Potts notify him immediately if there had been a different understanding of the settlement. Tyson instructed Potts not to respond. Tyson's suppression of this relevant fact caused Tremper to believe that the settlement basis included the joint tenancy accounts. . . .

Potts maintains he had no duty to correct opposing counsel's error. We disagree.

Rule 4.1 prohibits Potts from knowingly making a false statement of fact to a third party. Comment 1 provides that a lawyer, while having no affirmative duty to inform an opposing party of relevant facts, must be truthful when dealing with others on a client's behalf. Comment 1 also warns that "a misrepresentation can occur if the lawyer incorporates or affirms a statement of another person that the lawyer knows is false . . . or by omissions that are the equivalent of affirmative false statements." . . .

Similarly, Potts knew that the parties held different understandings as to the settlement basis and he failed to correct the mistake. Tremper's letter raised the question of whether $1.2 million represented the total value of the estate. The letter specifically requested Potts to respond if his clients had a different understanding as to the basis of the settlement. . . . Potts's testimony that he advised Tyson that the problem would have to be "cleared up" at some point shows that he knew the settlement basis was at issue. Potts's omission constituted a misrepresentation that assisted in his clients' fraudulent purpose of taking the joint tenancy accounts outside of the settlement agreement, a violation of Rule 1.2(d). Potts could have avoided this situation by withdrawing from representation under Rule 1.16. . . .

Potts did more than acquiesce to his client's demands of silence in the face of Tremper's inquiries. Potts assisted in his clients' fraud by drafting, circulating, and filing with the court a stipulation, stating that all disputes had been settled, when he knew that the other parties had relied on Evon's misrepresentation of the settlement basis in reaching the agreement. We agree with the Commission's conclusion that Potts violated Rule 1.2(d). . . .

Rule 3.3(a) sets forth the duty of candor toward the tribunal and prohibits a lawyer from knowingly failing "to disclose a material fact to a tribunal when disclosure is necessary to avoid assisting a criminal or fraudulent act by the client." . . . Potts's clients engaged in fraudulent conduct that intended to deceive the other parties as to the scope of the settlement. Potts assisted in their deception.

Potts also violated the duty of candor toward the tribunal when he failed to disclose to the court the material fact that, contrary to what the parties believed, Evon planned on taking the joint tenancy accounts. Tremper's letter notified Potts that the settlement basis was at issue. Potts acknowledged the fact that the value of the settlement would have to be cleared up "sooner or later." At his client's request, Potts said nothing to Tremper about the potential misunderstanding. Knowing that this ambiguity existed in the memorandum, Potts nevertheless proceeded to misrepresent in the signed stipulation to the court that "all" disputes had been settled, when in fact they were just beginning to brew under the surface. The stipulation caused the parties to forge ahead with the settlement, even though Potts and his clients knew that no agreement had been reached on the settlement amount. . . .

This level of misconduct ordinarily would draw punishment in the form of suspension from the practice of law or disbarment. . . . Though we do not condone Potts's conduct in this matter, we recognize that the other parties could have resolved the question of the basis and scope of the settlement by specifically assigning a dollar amount to the estate value in the memorandum. . . .

In light of these mitigating factors, especially Potts's history of compliance with the rules of professional conduct and his character and good reputation to this point, we conclude that a public censure will apprise Potts sufficiently of the gravity of his misconduct under the given circumstances. Moreover, a public censure will alert the public that the Court will not tolerate such misconduct from a lawyer.

Justice Jim RICE, John C. McKEON and Holly BROWN concur in part and dissent in part.

[We] concur with the Court's resolution of the issues related to the professional conduct rule violations and the evidentiary questions raised herein. [We] dissent, however, from the Court's determination [of] the sanction. . . .

[We] would [impose] a thirty-day suspension . . .

B. Wrongful Discharge

1. Inside Counsel

Problem

13-3. Martyn & Fox have counseled Big Pharma that it must disclose recent problems with defibrillators manufactured and implanted five years ago. Big Pharma refuses: "It will cause a panic, and the global risk to patients in rectifying the problem is greater in undergoing surgery to have the defibrillators replaced than just living with a few defective ones." What should Martyn & Fox do? Does it matter if Martyn is inside counsel to Big Pharma?

Consider: Model Rules 1.2(d), 1.6, 1.13, 1.16
RLGL § 32

Heckman v. Zurich Holding Company of America
242 F.R.D. 606 (D. Kan. 2007)

Kathryn H. VRATIL, United States District Judge.

Mary Ann Heckman brings suit against Zurich Holding Company of America ("Zurich") and Universal Underwriters Insurance Company d/b/a Universal Underwriters Group ("UUG") alleging retaliatory discharge and defamation under Kansas law. . . .

Factual Background*

In August of 1995, Zurich hired plaintiff as a research attorney primarily to perform tax work for Universal Underwriters Group (UUG). Plaintiff served under and reported to UUG executives. At the time Zurich hired plaintiff, UUG was significantly overcharging its customers through incorrect rating plans and Curt Starnes, then UUG's general counsel, and others at UUG began to develop a comprehensive compliance program to cure UUG's rating problems.

. . . In 1998, defendants directed plaintiff to assume partial responsibility for distributing compliance reports to certain UUG officers and employees, including acting Presidents and Chief Executive Officers. . . . These compliance reports detailed UUG violations identified through the audits and proposed corrective

---

* The court refers to its earlier opinion at 2007 U.S. Dist. LEXIS 14720 (D. Kan.).

action plans. UUG's board of Directors, which included Zurich's [CEO, CFO, and CLO] received notice of the compliance violations through its annual board meeting.

From 1995 until 2005, defendants' executives, supervisors and business entities charged with correcting compliance violations repeatedly ignored the corrective action plans proposed in the compliance reports.[3] The violations continued despite yearly briefing on such violations and continued attempts by the UUG legal department to implement corrective action plans.

In December of 2004, the Kansas Department of Insurance ("KDI") performed a Market Conduct Exam which revealed UUG's compliance and pricing violations . . . and ordered UUG to refund to customers the overcharges discovered during the examination. . . .

On July 7, 2005, UUG placed Starnes (UUG's general counsel) on administrative leave and promoted plaintiff to interim general counsel. Dave Bowers (Zurich's highest ranking legal officer) promised plaintiff that he would recommend she be named UUG's general counsel if Starnes did not return.

After KDI released its report, Zurich hired the law firm of LeBoeuf, Lamb, Greene and MacRae LLP ("LeBoeuf) to provide an opinion as to UUG's self-reporting requirements and conduct an investigation into the compliance violations . . . Plaintiff willingly participated in efforts to assist LeBoeuf, including coordinating the logistics of the investigation. During the investigation, LeBoeuf attorneys and Zurich internal auditors interviewed plaintiff, focusing on the violations and plaintiff's efforts to rectify them. Plaintiff informed LeBoeuf that Zurich had been aware of UUG's violations for years.

In August of 2005, plaintiff met with LeBoeuf attorneys [and senior level managers at UUG] to discuss UUG's violations and self-reporting obligations. During the meeting, LeBoeuf recommended that UUG report that its violations were the result of a computer glitch. Plaintiff immediately expressed to all meeting participants her unwillingness to advance such a lie. After plaintiff refused to advance the computer glitch excuse, LeBoeuf and attorneys for Zurich Financial Services decided that LeBoeuf attorneys would represent UUG before state insurance regulators regarding the violations. In September of 2005, LeBoeuf attorneys falsely represented to the Pennsylvania insurance regulator that UUG made the decision to overcharge customers without the knowledge of Zurich.

During a de-briefing of the meeting between LeBoeuf and the Pennsylvania insurance regulator, plaintiff informed UUG's president and chief executive officer and Zurich's highest ranking legal officer that LeBoeuf had told the state insurance regulator that Zurich had no knowledge of UUG's violations. Plaintiff

---

3. Plaintiff suggests that the compliance violations were ignored because the proposed corrective action plans would cause defendants to fall short of annual profitability goals, resulting in the loss of substantial distributions of money. Plaintiff alleges that the same individuals who set annual profitability goals were also aware of compliance problems.

also informed [them] that LeBoeuf's representation was false and that she would not support the story. Shortly thereafter, defendants prohibited plaintiff from engaging in direct communication with any state insurance regulator without first filtering such communication through LeBoeuf.

[During the next year and a half, plaintiff reported her concerns regarding LeBoeuf's investigation to various executives and UUG and] . . . also made clear that LeBoeuf was conducting a sham investigation and that she would not be made a scapegoat for UUG's compliance violations. [UUG's CEO] assured plaintiff that she would not be made a scapegoat and offered to prepare a positive evaluation of her work performance to entice her to remain as UUG's interim general counsel. . . .

On February 27, 2006, [UUG's CEO] fired plaintiff, stating that the LeBoeuf investigation report indicated that plaintiff had failed to report the violations and had requested that all UUG compliance audits be suspended. . . . During the termination, [the CEO] gave plaintiff a letter demanding that she refrain from sharing information learned or gleaned as a result of her position as in-house counsel for UUG with anyone, including her own personal counsel, and prevented her from using her company telephone or accessing her computer. Within 15 minutes of her termination, UUG forced plaintiff to exit its premises and leave behind her personal effects and other files, which it later shipped to her house. After plaintiff's termination, UUG sent an email to approximately 1,900 UUG employees informing them that plaintiff had left UUG to pursue other interests. Many of the employees knew that UUG had actually terminated plaintiff's employment, and word soon spread around UUG to almost all of the 1,900 employees that UUG had fired plaintiff.

Analysis

Plaintiff served as defendants' in-house counsel from August of 1995 until February of 2006, when defendants allegedly terminated her employment in retaliation for blowing the whistle on their illegal activity. Kansas subscribes to the doctrine of employment at will. Absent an express or implied contract of fixed duration, or where recognized public policy concerns are raised, employment is terminable at the will of either party. One exception to this general rule is termination in retaliation for whistleblowing. . . .

I. Defendants' Motion For Judgment on the Pleadings

. . . Kansas courts have not considered whether an in-house attorney may maintain a retaliatory discharge claim against her former employer/client. Some courts have refused to extend the tort of retaliatory discharge to in-house counsel. See Balla v. Gambro, Inc., 584 N.E.2d 104, 108 (Ill. 1991) (in-house counsel generally do not have claim under tort of retaliatory discharge). The overwhelming majority of courts which have considered the issue, however, have permitted in-house attorneys to bring retaliatory discharge claims against their former employers/clients so long as they do not run afoul of their duty of confidentiality. *See* O'Brien v. Stolt-Nielson Transp. Group, 838 A.2d 1076, 1084 (Conn. Super. Ct. 2003) (no persuasive per se rationale for barring wrongful termination suits by in-house attorneys); Crews v. Buckman Labs. Int'l, Inc., 78 S.W.3d 852, 857, 863-64 (Tenn. 2002) (in-house counsel may sue for retaliatory discharge in violation of public policy subject to applicable confidentiality restrictions); Burkhart v. Semitool, Inc., 5 P.3d 1031, 1042 (Mont. 2000) (in-house counsel may bring employment claims contemplated under rules of professional conduct); Willy v. Coastal States Mgmt. Co., 939 S.W.2d 193, 200 (Tex. App. 1997) (plaintiff's status as in-house counsel does not preclude wrongful termination claim if it can be proved without violation of confidentiality obligation); GTE Prods. Corp. v. Stewart, 653 N.E.2d 161, 166-67 (Mass. 1995) (wrongful discharge claim of in-house counsel recognized where claim respects client confidences and secrets); Gen. Dynamics Corp. v. Superior Court, 876 P.2d 487, 490 (Cal. 1994) (balanced considerations favor recognition of wrongful discharge claim for in-house counsel unless suit cannot proceed without breach of attorney-client privilege); *see also* Willy v. Admin. Review Bd., 423 F.3d 483, 500 (5th Cir. 2005) (in-house counsel pursuing wrongful discharge claim must comply with duty of confidentiality); Hoffman v. Baltimore Police Dep't, 379 F. Supp.2d 778, 784 (D. Md. 2005) (recognizing that courts permit retaliation claims by in-house counsel, but that such claims do not obliterate client's right to confidences); Meadows v. Kindercare Learning Ctrs., Inc., 2004 U.S. Dist. LEXIS 8770 (D. Or. 2004) (permitting wrongful discharge claim where client confidences ancillary to such claim); Wise v. Consol. Edison Co. of N.Y., 723 N.Y.S.2d 462, 463 (N.Y. App. Div. 2001) (dismissing wrongful discharge claim of in-house counsel which could not be maintained without improper disclosures of client confidences).

. . . [D]efendants argue that the Kansas Supreme Court opinion in Crandon v. State, 897 P.2d 92 (Kan. 1995), suggests that Kansas courts would not recognize such a claim. *Crandon* noted that closeness and trust are essential to the proper function of the relationship between an in-house attorney and her employer/client. Borrowing heavily from *Balla,* an Illinois case, defendants argue that recognition of a retaliatory discharge claim by in-house counsel would effectively chill the attorney–client relationship. This notion has been soundly rejected by many courts. *See, e.g., O'Brien,* 838 A.2d at 1084 (right of action would not unduly impair attorney–client relationship already likely in considerable disarray); *Crews,* 78 S.W.3d at 861 (no discernable impact on attorney–client relationship unless employer expects counsel to blindly follow mandates in contravention of ethical duties). The Court finds nothing in *Crandon* which suggests that Kansas courts would refuse to allow in-house counsel to maintain retaliatory discharge claims.

Defendants further argue that permitting in-house counsel to maintain retaliatory discharge claims does not serve the public policy concerns underlying the cause of action. In this regard, *Balla* notes that retaliatory discharge claims for in-house counsel are unnecessary because attorneys are ethically obligated to report certain wrongful conduct of their clients, which adequately protects the public interest. This idea has also been widely rejected. *See, e.g., Crews,* 78 S.W.3d at 860 (sole reliance on mere presence of ethical rules to protect public policy gives too little weight to economic pressures designed to tempt in-house counsel to subordinate ethical standards to corporate misconduct); *GTE Prods. Corp,* 653 N.E.2d at 166 (public interest better served where in-house counsel's resolve to comply with ethical obligations is strengthened through availability of judicial recourse).

Defendants further argue that imposing liability on employers/clients for discharging in-house counsel is inconsistent with Rule 1.16 of the Kansas Rules of Professional Conduct, which recognizes a client's unlimited right to terminate the attorney-client relationship. Even if Rule 1.16 grants a client the seemingly absolute right to discharge his attorney, this right may not necessarily be "invoked under all circumstances *without consequence.*" *Gen. Dynamics Corp.,* 876 P.2d at 493. Discussing the right of discharge in the context of in-house counsel, *O'Brien,* 838 A.2d at 1084, stated as follows:

> While the principle that a client has the right to terminate an attorney is sound when the attorney–client relationship is the sole relationship between the parties, even then it is not a completely unfettered right, as the discharged attorney has a right to earned fees. . . . When there is a concomitant relationship . . . of employer–employee, the right to discharge an attorney must be balanced with rights emanating from the second relationship. This court sees no rational basis for denying an employee–attorney the right available to other employees to sue for wrongful or constructive discharge when the suit is premised on protecting a well defined public interest.

The Court does not believe that Rule 1.16 cloaks defendants in absolute immunity against plaintiff's retaliatory discharge claim. To hold that Rule 1.16 affords an employer/client absolute immunity from liability for wrongful termination of in-house counsel would be inconsistent with other areas of employment discrimination law. *See* Kachmar v. Sungard Data Sys., Inc., 109 F.3d 173, 179 (3d Cir. 1997) (generally, in-house counsel not barred from suing former employer/client under Title VII of the Civil Rights Act of 1964 ("Title VII"), 42 U.S.C. §2000e *et seq.*); Golightly-Howell v. Oil, Chem. & Atomic Workers Int'l Union, 806 F. Supp. 921, 924 (D. Colo. 1992) (no authority for proposition that Title VII does not protect in-house counsel).

In the light of the overwhelming authority which permits in-house counsel to sue for retaliatory discharge under state law, the Court does not believe that Kansas courts would prohibit plaintiff from maintaining her whistleblower claim under Kansas law. . . . As noted above, however, plaintiff's retaliatory discharge claim must be established within the confines of her duty of confidentiality.

Here, plaintiff's duty of confidentiality is shaped by Rule 1.6 of the Kansas Rules of Professional Conduct . . .

Rule 1.6 is designed to "facilitate[] the full development of facts essential to proper representation of the client," by encouraging the client "to communicate fully and frankly with the lawyer even as to embarrassing or legally damaging subject matter." *Id.* cmt. The Kansas Supreme Court has noted that "[t]he ethical requirement of confidentiality is . . . interpreted broadly, with the exceptions being few and narrowly limited." In re Bryan, 61 P.3d 641, 656 (Kan. 2003).

Plaintiff argues that Rule 1.6(b) [5] permits the disclosure of otherwise confidential information to establish her retaliatory discharge claim, which she argues is "a claim or defense on behalf of the lawyer in a controversy between the lawyer and the client." Defendants respond that the claim or defense exception contemplates only fee disputes between a lawyer and her client. . . .

The ABA's formal opinion supports the conclusion that the claim or defense exception applies to plaintiff's retaliatory discharge claim. ABA Comm. on Ethics and Prof'l Responsibility, Formal Op. 01-424 (2001) (in-house attorney's retaliatory discharge action constitutes "claim" for purpose of claim or defense exception to duty of confidentiality under Model Rule 1.6). Further, courts which have interpreted Model Rule 1.6 within the context of retaliatory discharge claims by in-house counsel have concluded that the claim or defense exception permits plaintiff to disclose otherwise confidential information which is necessary to establish such claim. *See Crews,* 78 S.W.3d at 863 (Rule 1.6 allows in-house counsel to reveal confidences essential to support retaliatory discharge claim); *Burkhart,* 5 P.3d at 1041 (Rule 1.6 extremely broad; contemplates that lawyer may reveal confidential information to establish employment-related claim); *see also* Spratley v. State Farm Mut. Auto. Ins. Co., 78 P.3d 603, 610 (Utah 2003) (reversing order prohibiting in-house counsel from disclosing confidential information in prospective suit against employer based on Rule 1.6).

In light of the authority set forth above, the Court finds that plaintiff is entitled to maintain her retaliatory discharge claim against defendants and is entitled to reveal confidential information under Rule 1.6(b)[5] to the extent necessary to establish such claim. Accordingly, the Court overrules defendants' motion for judgment on the pleadings under Rule 12(c).

Ii. Defendants' Motion for Protective Order

Defendants argue that if the Court permits plaintiff to maintain her retaliatory discharge claim, it should enter a protective order to control the unnecessary disclosure of confidential information. Courts which permit retaliatory discharge claims by in-counsel have recognized the importance of equitable measures, including protective orders, "to permit the attorney plaintiff to attempt to make the necessary proof while protecting from disclosure client confidences subject to [] privilege." *Burkhart,* 5 P.3d at 1041 (quoting *Gen. Dynamics Corp.,* 876 P.2d at 504); *see also Spratley,* 78 P.3d at 610 (disclosure of confidential information under Rule 1.6 should proceed carefully and under close court supervision). . . .

Because this case involves the potential disclosure of confidential information, the Court finds that a protective order which limits the unnecessary disclosure of such information is appropriate. Accordingly, the Court sustains in part defendants' motion for protective order. . . .

2. Law Firm Employees

Problem

13-4. Associate tells Fox that he has discovered that Martyn has been sending bills to clients charging them for Martyn's services at Martyn's hourly rate for services actually performed by Associate. Fox investigates and tells Associate that it's all taken care of, that Martyn will not repeat the conduct because she is now on medication for her depression and seeking psychiatric counseling as well, and that Fox considers the matter satisfactorily resolved. "Don't you worry," Fox soothingly tells Associate. What should Associate do?

Consider: Model Rules 5.1, 5.2, 8.3, 8.4
                RLGL § 32

Pane v. Goffs

2009 Mass. App. Unpub. LEXIS 930;
review denied, 914 N.E. 2d 331

By the Court (KAFKER, GRAHAM & WOLOHOJIAN, JJ.) . . .

The plaintiff, a lawyer formerly employed by the defendant law firm, commenced an action against the law firm and a partner of the law firm asserting a claim for wrongful termination in violation of public policy. . . .

Stripped to the bare essentials, the plaintiff asserts that certain partners of the law firm asked him to research the firm's obligations upon inadvertently finding possible child pornography on the computer of an important client or the computer of an executive of an important client. The plaintiff researched the issue and advised the partners that they were obligated to report the materials to law enforcement authorities. Thereafter, the firm sought an opinion from outside counsel who orally provided the same advice. Rather than report the material to law enforcement, the partners instructed the plaintiff to find an entity that could permanently erase the images. Although the plaintiff proceeded to contact such a company, he admittedly failed to have the images at issue promptly erased, hoping to convince the partners to report the images to authorities. Some months later, in December of 2005, the partners discovered that the images had not been erased and terminated the plaintiff's employment with them in January of 2006.

The plaintiff, who received strong performance evaluations, a raise, and a merit increase from the firm in December of 2005, commenced an action in Superior Court contending in count I that he was wrongfully terminated in violation of public policy for persistently advising the partners to report the existence of the images to law enforcement authorities and for failing to destroy evidence of a crime.[6] The defendants . . . asserted that disclosure of the details of the alleged child pornography along with the process undertaken by the law firm as to its duties upon discovering the images including related conversations among the firm's lawyers, legal analysis, consultation with outside counsel, and actions taken by the law firm violated the plaintiff's duty of confidentiality under Mass. R. Prof. C. 1.6. . . .

Although the plaintiff was an employee at will subject to termination for any reason or no reason at all, where an employee at will has been discharged in violation of a clearly defined public policy, the employee may sue the former employer for wrongful discharge.[8] GTE Products, Inc. v. Stewart, 653 N.E.2d 161 (Mass. 1995) (recognizing judicial recourse for in-house counsel's claim of wrongful termination in violation of public policy). Here, upon the law firm's motion, the judge dismissed the claim not because it failed to state a cause of action, but because of a perceived inability of the plaintiff to succeed without revealing confidential information in violation of Mass. R. Prof. C. 1.6. We think the judge's conclusion was premature. . . .

Rule 1.6 contains a limited number of exceptions. The conclusion that the plaintiff cannot succeed without revealing confidential information, therefore, requires us to find as a matter of law that images of possible child pornography inadvertently discovered on a computer, or its executive, constitute "confidential information related to the representation," that disclosing the details of the images without disclosing the law firm's client's identity would "reveal" confidential information, and that no exception to Rule 1.6 allows disclosure of the law firm's investigation into its duties upon discovery of the images in the context of the plaintiff's action against the law firm. We cannot draw those conclusions from the complaint alone.

The Law Firm's Client. We first address the alleged confidential information of the law firm's client, the details of the images. We are aware of no exception to rule 1.6 which would allow the plaintiff to reveal the law firm's client's confidential information in order to pursue a wrongful termination claim against the law firm. . . . The concept of "confidential information relating to representation," however broad, is not unlimited. The circumstances surrounding the discovery of the alleged pornography are not apparent from the

---

6. Prior to commencing the action, the plaintiff learned that a copy of the images still existed and he reported it to Federal authorities.

8. "Redress is available for employees who are terminated for asserting a legally guaranteed right (e.g., filing workers' compensation claim), for doing what the law requires (e.g., serving on a jury), or for refusing to do what the law forbids (e.g., committing perjury). Smith-Pfeffer v. Superintendent of the Walter E. Fernald State Sch., 533 N.E.2d 1368 (Mass. 1989)." *GTE Prod. Corp.,* 653 N.E.2d 161. "In limited circumstances, we also have permitted redress 'for employees terminated for performing important public deeds even though the law does not absolutely require the performance of such a deed,'" such as employees terminated for cooperating with a criminal investigation of the employer or, perhaps, "whistleblowers." *Ibid.* (internal citation omitted). See also Shea v. Emmanuel College, 682 N.E.2d 1348 (Mass. 1997) (public policy protects at-will employee who reports criminal activity to superiors).

complaint, other than they were unexpectedly encountered while assisting the client on a litigation matter. There is no suggestion in the complaint that the images were related in any way to the client's business or to the underlying matter the law firm was handling for the client. Further, it is not clear that the client authorized such use of the computer or whether the law firm's duty of confidentiality extended to the person or persons responsible for putting the images on the computer. The complaint simply does not establish that the images were either "confidential" or "related to the representation," as those terms are used in rule 1.6.

Moreover, even if the images constitute confidential information related to the representation, it is not clear to us that they need be "revealed" as that term is used in rule 1.6. In *GTE Products Corp.*, 653 N.E.2d 161, the Supreme Judicial Court recognized the difficulty inherent in an attorney's effort to prove a wrongful termination claim without revealing client secrets and confidences. The court noted that "confidentiality concerns may to some degree be ameliorated by a trial court's use of protective orders and other protective devices." Before determining that an attorney's claim cannot succeed without revealing client confidences, a judge should examine whether appropriate orders of the court will adequately protect the client. At this stage of the litigation, the extent to which the details of the images will be at issue is unclear. The law firm has not filed an answer and its reasons for terminating the plaintiff may be unrelated to the details of the images.

To the extent that the case does revolve around the details of the images, we note that to a large degree, protective orders already in place serve to safeguard the law firm's client. The order of impoundment protects the client's identity. No business information, trade secrets, or other information from which it could be possible to identify the client need be revealed in order to proceed with the plaintiff's claim. None of the advice given to the client is at issue or need be explored. Indeed, there is no allegation that the plaintiff ever communicated with the client or that the law firm advised the client with respect to the discovered images. While it very well may be that the client would want the existence of child pornography on its computer to remain a secret, with appropriate orders of the court, it is not apparent on the face of the complaint that the plaintiff cannot succeed without revealing client secrets.

The Law Firm. The law firm assumes that disclosing any discussions that the law firm had regarding its responsibilities upon discovering the images also would reveal client secrets. . . .

[T]he Massachusetts Rules of Professional Conduct, . . . like the modified ABA Rules . . . , provide that a lawyer may reveal client confidences "to the extent the lawyer reasonably believes necessary to establish a claim or defense on behalf of the lawyer in a controversy between the lawyer and the client . . . ." Mass. R. Prof. C. 1.6(b)(2). Other jurisdictions have interpreted this rule as allowing in-house counsel to reveal an employer's confidences in order to pursue a claim for wrongful discharge claim against an employer. Spratley v. State Farm Mut. Auto. Ins. Co., 78 P.3d 603, 608-609 (Utah 2003). Crews v. Buckman Labs.

Intl., Inc., 78 S.W.3d 852, 863-864 (Tenn. 2002). Burkhart v. Semitool, Inc., 5 P.3d 1031 (Mont. 2000). We agree with this interpretation.

We perceive the plaintiff's position with regard to matters concerning the law firm and its obligations upon discovering the images as no different from that of in-house counsel. Much like in-house counsel, the law firm asked the plaintiff to advise the law firm with regard to its obligations. The plaintiff's complaint does not raise any issue concerning advice provided to the law firm's client. To the extent the details of the images are determined to be outside the information protected by rule 1.6 or that court orders adequately will protect the law firm's client, we discern on this limited record no impediment in the rules of professional conduct to revealing those facts related to the law firm's obligations upon discovering the images that are reasonably necessary to pursue the plaintiff's wrongful termination claim against the defendants, the law firm and the partners.[13] . . .

The plaintiff chose to file a prolix complaint with largely unnecessary detail. . . . In the circumstances of this case where confidential information is at risk of disclosure, the judge was well within his discretion to strike those portions of the complaint that were overly descriptive of the computer images or were redundant and unnecessary. Where client confidences are involved, an attorney plaintiff is well advised to reveal only those facts essential to fulfill the requirements of Mass. R. Civ. P. 8(a)(1). . . .

■ Practice Pointers:
Wrongful Discharge

In the last chapter, we saw that an implied condition of every client-lawyer contract is the client's right to discharge the lawyer at any time, for any reason. *Heckman*, on the other hand, tells us that one group of lawyers—those who are employees of the client they serve—can bring claims for wrongful discharge similar to those of other employees under certain circumstances. *Pane* recognizes a similar cause of action against a law firm employer.

Employment-at-Will

Most lawyers are independent contractors. When a client hires a lawyer to perform legal services, the lawyer becomes an agent, but not a servant or employee of the client. Most lawyers also serve a multiple client base.

---

13. That is not to say that the parties and the court may ignore the confidential nature of attorney-client communications even where a controversy arises between the lawyer and the client. . . . Under no circumstances may facts that could lead to the disclosure of the law firm's client's identity be revealed. In addition, the plaintiff and the judge must respect the confidentiality of the law firm whenever possible. All practicable efforts to limit disclosure of confidential information, including sealing orders, protective orders, orders limiting admissibility of evidence, orders restricting the use of testimony in successive proceedings, and, where appropriate, in camera proceedings, should be utilized.

After World War II, corporations began to follow the lead of government units by hiring more inside lawyers as employees.[1] Unlike lawyers in their own practices, these inside lawyers had only one client and were full-time employees who depended on a corporation or government for benefits and terms of employment. For the most part, they performed legal tasks similar to lawyers in outside practices, but often concentrated on providing advice and counsel to prevent or solve legal issues rather than litigation services after a controversy arose.[2] As the value of these services to large organizations increased, more and more legal work has been moved inside organizations. Today, inside lawyers often manage nearly all of the legal matters that confront the organization, and usually decide when to hire outside lawyers for specific tasks.

While this move to inside counsel was developing, courts in most jurisdictions were beginning to develop exceptions to the employment-at-will doctrine. Developed in the latter part of the nineteenth century, this doctrine provided that absent contractual agreements to the contrary, both employer and employee were free to terminate the employment relationship at any time.[3]

Wrongful Discharge

In 1959, a California court created the first exception to the employment-at-will doctrine, in a case where an employee was fired for refusing to commit perjury when his employer ordered him to do so. The court provided the employee with a cause of action for wrongful discharge, holding that the at-will doctrine was limited by important public policies.[4] Today, both common law and statutes protect employee-whistleblowers. Courts have recognized the rights of employees to sue in tort for retaliatory discharge, wrongful termination, and wrongful discharge,[5] and in contract for breach of express and implied provisions in employment contracts,[6] as well as for violation of an implied covenant of good

---

1. In 1951, about 3 percent of all lawyers worked directly for private industry, and 10 percent worked for various levels of the government. *See* Reginald Heber Smith, *The Second Statistical Report on the Lawyer of the United States* 2 (ABA 1951). By 1960, 10 percent of all lawyers worked for private industry. *See* Barbara A. Curran, *The Lawyer Statistical Report: A Statistical Profile of the U.S. Legal Profession in the 1980s*, at 12 (Am. Bar Found. 1985). Since then, these percentages have remained about the same for both private industry and government lawyers (both about 8 percent in 2000). *See ABA Lawyer Demographics*, March 2011, *available at* http://www.americanbar.org/content/dam/aba/migrated/marketresearch/PublicDocuments/lawyer_demographics_2011.authcheckdam.pdf.
2. E. Norman Veasey & Christine T. DiGuglielmo, *Indispensable Counsel: The Chief Legal Officer in the New Reality* 27-34 (Oxford U. Press 2010).
3. Mark A. Rothstein et al., *Employment Law* § 9.1 (4th ed., West 2009).
4. Petermann v. Teamsters Local 396, 344 P.2d 25 (Cal. App. 1959).
5. *See Restatement of the Law (Third) Employment Law*, Chapter 4 (Tentative Draft No. 2 2009).
6. *E.g.*, Wieder v. Skala, 609 N.E. 2d 105 (N.Y. 1992) (an implied term in the employment contract between associate and the firm is that each will conduct themselves according to the governing rules of professional conduct).

faith.[7] Federal and state statutes create similar rights for employees in both the public and private sectors.[8]

Public Policy

The public policy exception to the at-will employment doctrine recognizes that employers are not free to fire employees because they report or refuse to engage in illegal activity, exercise a statutory or constitutional right, or perform a duty required by law.

Some states construe the "illegal activity" exception narrowly, limiting it to situations such as *Pane*, where the employer instructs the employee to commit a crime.[9] Others extend it to tortious acts as well,[10] and some grant the cause of action to employees who refuse to commit a violation of administrative regulations.[11] Jurisdictions differ on whether the unlawful activity must relate to public health and safety, and whether the employee must actually report the activity outside the organization.[12]

Statutes and case law also recognize that employees who exercise a statutory right, such as the right to seek workers' compensation for a workplace injury, also are protected from retaliatory discharge.[13]

Finally, many courts and statutes create a public policy exception for the performance of a public duty required by law. Very few public reporting obligations create mandatory duties. Nevertheless, the courts have not hesitated to protect employees who were fired because they were called to jury service, or insisted on obeying a subpoena, or reported child or elder abuse.[14]

Professional Code Violations

Many courts also have recognized that refusal to violate a professional ethics code could qualify as an important public policy.[15] To establish such an exception to the at-will doctrine, Heckman and other discharged counsel have to cite the relevant rule and establish that it embodies a clear and important public policy with a clear mandate to act. *Heckman* cites decisions from other jurisdictions,

---

7. *See* Rothstein, *supra* note 3, at §§ 9.2-9.6; *See* Lionel J. Postic, *Wrongful Termination: A State-by-State Survey* (BNA 1994).

8. *See* Daniel P. Westman & Nancy M. Modesitt, *Whistleblowing: The Law of Retaliatory Discharge* (BNA 2d ed., 2004); Van Asdale v. Int'l Game Tech., 2011 U.S. Dist LEXIS 56715 (upholding $2 million verdict plus $2.4 million in fees, costs, and prejudgment interest on behalf of two lawyers wrongfully discharged under Sarbanes-Oxley whistleblower provisions).

9. *See, e.g.,* Sabine Pilot Service v. Hauck, 687 S.W.2d 733 (Tex. 1985).

10. *See, e.g.,* Delaney v. Taco Time Int'l. Inc., 681 P.2d 114 (Or. 1984) (potential defamation).

11. *See, e.g.,* Minn. Stat. § 181.932 (2003); N.Y. Lab. Law § 740 (2003); Tenn. Code § 50-1-304 (2003).

12. Rothstein, *supra* note 3, at §§ 8.10-8.11.

13. *See* Theresa Ludwig Kruk, *Recovery for Discharge from Employment in Retaliation for Filing Workers' Compensation Claim,* 32 A.L.R.4th 1221 (1984).

14. Rothstein, *supra* note 3, at § 8.13.

15. *See* Genna H. Rosten, *Wrongful Discharge Based on Public Policy Derived from Professional Ethics Codes,* 52 A.L.R.5th 405 (1997).

which have found such clear public policies in the Model Rule's various prohibitions against fraudulent conduct.[16] Reporting lawyer misconduct also qualifies.[17] Of course, Heckman will be required to prove that she was fired for refusing to participate in and blowing the whistle on her client's lie to regulators as required by a relevant professional rule (perhaps Rules 1.2(d), 4.1(a) or 8.3(c)).

Discharge: Actual and Constructive

The plaintiff in a wrongful discharge case must prove not only that she sought to vindicate an important public policy, but also that she was fired for doing so. When an employee resigns or quits his job, the implication is that the employer did not discharge him. If the facts indicate that the plaintiff did not voluntarily leave her job but felt compelled to resign because of the employer's actions, courts recognize the doctrine of constructive discharge in such a situation. Most courts agree that intolerable employment conditions created by the employer, which essentially force the employee to quit, constitute constructive discharge.[18] On the other hand, single instances of demotion, unfavorable performance reviews, or dissatisfaction with assignments are not enough.[19]

Are Lawyers Different?

When lawyer employees initially sought court recognition of a wrongful discharge cause of action, courts reasoned that the right of clients to fire lawyers at any time should trump any contrary employment law doctrine. *Heckman* and *Pane* illustrate how state courts over the past decade have moved away from that notion and have begun to emphasize the similarity between lawyer-employees and other employees protected by the wrongful discharge doctrine.

The real policy debate in these cases is whether the right of clients to fire lawyers should override other employment protections. *Heckman* begins by pointing out that inside counsel do not forfeit other statutory employment rights simply because they are lawyers.[20] *Pace* also makes clear that lawyers have to

---

16. Burkhart v. Semitool, Inc., 5 P.3d 1031 (Mont. 2000) (refusing to prepare fraudulent patent applications); Kelly v. Hunton & Williams, 1999 U.S. Dist. Lexis 9139 (E.D.N.Y.) (associate fired in retaliation for reporting partner's fraud to the firm; "Billing for hours not worked is fraud."); Brown v. Hammond, 810 F. Supp. 644 (E.D. Pa. 1993) (fraudulent billing prohibited by Rules 1.5, 7.1, and 8.4(c)); Paralegal v. Law., 783 F. Supp. 230 (E.D. Pa. 1992) (paralegal fired for notifying her employer's lawyer that her employer submitted false evidence in violation of Rules 3.3 and 3.4); Parker v. M & T Chemicals, Inc., 566 A.2d 215 (N.J. Super. 1989) (objecting to "unlawful and fraudulent conduct" of client).

17. Wieder v. Skala, 609 N.E. 2d 105 (N.Y. 1992).

18. *See, e.g.,* Crews v. Buckman Laboratories Int'l Inc., 78 S.W.3d 852 (Tenn. 2002) (inside counsel whose employer confiscated her computer, placed her on temporary leave, and gave her a notice of termination fairly raised allegation of constructive discharge, as she did not leave voluntarily and a reasonable person would have felt compelled to resign).

19. *See, e.g.,* GTE Prod. Corp. v. Stewart, 653 N.E.2d 161 (Mass. 1995) (inside counsel quit after one distressing interview with a supervisor).

20. *See, e.g.,* EEOC v. Sidley Austin LLP, 437 F.3d 695 (7th Cir. 2006), *cert. denied,* 549 U.S. 815 (age discrimination suit by thirty-two equity partners against partnership); In re Newark, 788 A.2d

comply with the criminal law. Once a court recognizes these legal obligations, the public policies inherent in other employment laws, such as federal and state whistleblower statutes, become equally easy to follow.

Heckman indicates that the early cases rejected any cause of action for wrongful discharge by lawyer-employees, even where another professional employee, such as an engineer, would be granted a cause of action if fired for making the same disclosure.[21] These courts reasoned that a lawyer who discovers that a client insists on pursuing illegal activity must either convince the client to stop or leave the employment. Lawyers could disclose if allowed or required by a rule of professional conduct, but could not disclose the same client confidences to create a cause of action against their employer. These decisions stressed the need for organizations to be able to trust their lawyers, the need for confidentiality to foster that trust, and the social value of encouraging organizations to seek legal advice. Recognizing a cause of action for wrongful discharge ultimately would lead organizations to avoid sharing information about sensitive or questionable activity with their legal staffs. This avoidance would in turn erase opportunities for inside lawyers to counsel their clients about better means of complying with legal requirements.

Heckman and *Pane* represent the opposite and emerging point of view: that conduct giving rise to a cause of action by organizational employees also ought to extend to a cause of action for wrongful discharge by lawyer-employees.[22] The law firm or corporation remains free to discharge the lawyer but might have to suffer a monetary penalty for punishing lawyers who refuse to violate clear legal mandates, including those in their professional rules. This parallels the situation of other employee-whistleblowers, who are permitted to use confidential information to prove that they had a good-faith belief that their employer was engaged in wrongful activity.[23]

One thing is certain. Competent lawyering requires any lawyer who disagrees with a decision by management (whether corporate or law firm) first to determine the basis for the disagreement. The lawyer who can articulate a clear public policy, embodied in a specific statute, regulation, professional code, or constitutional provision should communicate that policy to responsible decision makers. If at that point the professional loses her job, she will have created a

---

776 (N.J. App. 2002) (unionization of nonmanagerial lawyers employed by city permitted under state public employment law). Federal and state whistleblower statutes provide protection mainly for public sector employees who disclose illegal acts of their government employers.

21. *See, e.g.,* Balla v. Gambro, 584 N.E.2d 104 (Ill. 1991).

22. *See, e.g.,* Alexander v. Tandem Staffing Solutions, Inc., 881 So. 2d 607 (Fla. App. 2004); Spratley v. St. Farm Mut. Auto. Ins. Co., 78 P.3d 603 (Utah 2003). *See also* Gen. Dynamics v. Sup. Ct., 876 P.2d 487, 503 (Cal. 1994) (relying on the statutory exceptions to the attorney-client privilege to provide the basis for a cause of action); Fox Searchlight Pictures, Inc. v. Paladino, 106 Cal. Rptr. 2d 906 (Cal. App. 2001) (lawyer who seeks legal advice about whether to bring a wrongful discharge suit may disclose relevant facts to her own lawyer, including employer confidences and privileged communications).

23. *See* Westman and Modesitt, *supra* note 8, at 22-44.

record that her discharge was caused by her insistence that the organization not violate the articulated public policy.

C. Finding New Employment

Problem

13-5. Star associate at Martyn & Fox is fed up. Outstanding work. Loved by clients. Unappreciated. One day, she darkens Fox's door. "Smith & Wolfman opens on Monday. I have letters from 55 clients asking for their files to be sent to my new firm. You should have given me that raise!"

Consider: Model Rules 1.1, 1.3, 1.4, 1.15, 1.16, 5.6, 7.1, 7.3, 7.4, 8.4(c)
RLGL §§ 31, 32

Ethical Considerations in the Dissolution of a Law Firm or a Lawyer's Departure from a Law Firm
Formal Ethics Opinion No. 116 (2007)
Colorado Bar Association Ethics Committee

I. Introduction and Scope

Many ethical issues arise in connection with the dissolution of a law firm or a lawyer's departure or withdrawal from a firm. Such issues often arise in the context of determining who will represent particular clients following the break-up. The departing lawyer and the responsible members of the firm with [whom] the lawyer has been associated have ethical obligations to clients on whose legal matters they worked. These ethical obligations sometimes can be at odds with the business interests of the law firm or the departing lawyer. In such circumstances, all involved lawyers must hold the obligations to the client as paramount. The ethical considerations discussed in this opinion include the duty to keep the client reasonably informed about the status of the legal matter and to explain a matter to the extent reasonably necessary to permit the client to make informed decisions regarding the representation, pursuant to *Colo. RPC 1.4(a)* and (b); the duty to provide competent representation to the client, pursuant to *Colo. RPC 1.1*; avoiding neglect of client matters because of a break-up, in violation of *Colo. RPC 1.3*; taking appropriate steps upon withdrawal from representation, in accordance with *Colo. RPC 1.16(d)*; ensuring that any funds in which a client or a third party may claim an interest are maintained separate from the lawyers' own property, in accordance with *Colo. RPC 1.15(a)*; refraining from any solicitation or efforts to retain clients that would violate the provisions of *Colo. RPC 7.1* or *Colo. RPC 7.3*; restrictions on a lawyer's right to practice after leaving a firm that might violate *Colo. RPC 5.6(a)*; and generally refraining from any conduct involving dishonesty, fraud, deceit or misrepresentation, in violation of *Colo. RPC 8.4(c)*.

The primary focus of this opinion is on the ethical obligations of lawyers to the clients they represent at the time of the dissolution or the lawyer's departure. The opinion also touches upon the actions of lawyers toward each other in these circumstances. The ethical obligations of the lawyers involved are the same whether the departing lawyer is a partner/shareholder, an associate, or some other category of lawyer such as one designated as of counsel. However, the opinion does not address the legal obligations owed to clients, or the legal duties arising from the relationship between and among the lawyers. It also does not address circumstances in which lawyers who are not in the same firm represent, as co-counsel, a common client.

This opinion substantially adopts and endorses Formal Opinion 99-414 (1999) issued by the Standing Committee on Ethics and Professional Responsibility of the American Bar Association (ABA) . . . [and] focuses on application of the Colorado Rules of Professional Conduct . . . on issues that warrant comment beyond that in ABA Formal Opinion 99-414.

II. Analysis

A. The Client's Right to Choose Counsel

It is now uniformly recognized that the client-lawyer contract is terminable at will by the client. *Colo. RPC 1.16(a)(3)* codifies this principle. When a lawyer who has had primary responsibility for a client matter withdraws from a law firm, the client's power to choose or replace the lawyer borders on the absolute.[4] Neither the firm nor any of its members may claim a possessory interest in clients. In other words, clients do not belong to lawyers.

A lawyer or law firm may not, therefore, take action that impermissibly impairs a client's right to choose counsel. For example, a dispute between attorneys in a law firm over a fee that is due or may come due should not impact the client's right to freely choose counsel.

Nevertheless, the client's right to choose is subject to certain limitations. Generally, a lawyer shall not represent a client, or where representation has commenced, shall withdraw from the representation of a client, if the representation will result in violation of the Rules of Professional Conduct or other law[7] or if the lawyer's physical or mental condition materially impairs the lawyer's ability to represent the client.[8] For example, the departing lawyer may be the only lawyer in the firm with experience in a specialized area of law applicable to a particular client matter. In such circumstances, the law firm from which the lawyer is departing may be unable to continue the representation, except on a limited basis. On the other hand, the departing lawyer may lack the support and resources necessary to handle a complex matter properly after leaving the firm. The departing lawyer may also be prohibited from representing the client if he

---

4. Robert W. Hillman, Hillman on Lawyer Mobility, ("Hillman"), Chapter 2, § 2.3.1 (2000 Supplement).
7. *Colo. RPC 1.16(a)(1)*.
8. *Colo. RPC 1.16(a)(2)*.

or she is associating with a firm that would be precluded from representation due to a conflict of interest. In some situations, the right of a client to select the lawyer may be limited under the provisions of an insurance contract.

In any event, a client represented by a particular lawyer or law firm will have to choose counsel again if the firm breaks up or the responsible lawyer departs from the firm during the course of the representation. In order to make appropriate choices, the client must have sufficient information.

B. Notice to Clients

In Colorado, a lawyer has a duty to keep a client reasonably informed about the status of a matter and to explain a matter to the extent reasonably necessary to permit the client to make informed decisions regarding the representation.[12] When a lawyer plans to cease practice at a law firm, or when a law firm plans to terminate the lawyer's association with the firm, both the lawyer and the firm have responsibility for providing timely notification to clients affected by the lawyer's departure and providing such clients with information sufficient to allow informed choice.

Not only are the remaining and departing lawyers permitted to contact clients about an impending change in personnel, they are required to provide the client with at least enough information to determine the future course of the representation. It is highly preferable that any affected client be notified by a joint communication from the departing lawyer and the firm and that the joint notice be transmitted sufficiently in advance of the lawyer's anticipated departure to allow the client to make decisions about who will represent it and communicate that decision before the lawyer departs. An "affected client" is one for whose active matters the departing lawyer currently is responsible or plays a principal role in the current delivery of legal services.[14]

The joint and advance notice helps ensure an orderly transition that will best protect the interests of the affected client. . . .

In some limited circumstances joint, advance notice is not practicable.[15] If either the departing lawyer or the firm fails or refuses to participate in providing

---

12. *Colo. RPC 1.4.*

14. . . . . [T]he lawyer and the firm also should consider whether the client reasonably would believe itself to be affected by the lawyer's departure, for example, where a lawyer is specifically named in an engagement letter as being expected to provide services to the client. Even if a client is not an affected client, the departing lawyer may choose to notify the client of his or her departure if such notification complies with *Colo. RPC 7.1* and *7.3*. Restrictions purporting to prohibit such contact likely would violate the prohibition of *Colo. RPC 5.6* on restrictions of the right of a lawyer to practice after termination of his or her relationship with a firm.

15. There will be situations in which a departing lawyer will be unable to represent the client, and the notice to the client would not present representation by the departing lawyer as an option. For example, the departing lawyer would be unable to represent the client if the lawyer were suspended from the practice of law or placed on disability inactive status. However, a difference of opinion between the firm and the departing lawyer regarding the competence or ability of one or the other to represent the client does not, standing alone, justify failure or refusal to extend to the client a choice in representation.

timely and appropriate joint notice, unilateral notice is necessary. If unilateral notice is given, it should impartially and fairly provide the same type of information as would have been included in the joint notice.

Consistent with *Colo. RPC 7.1, 7.3* and *7.4*, as applicable, both the departing lawyer and the firm may solicit professional employment from clients or former clients of the firm. In doing so, however, the departing lawyer should be mindful that such solicitation may give rise to a civil claim for damages or other relief under the substantive law, especially while the departing lawyer is still employed by or associated with the law firm.[17] Pursuant to *Colo. RPC 7.3*, . . . [d]eparting lawyers having a "family or prior professional relationship with the prospective client" are not subject to the 30-day waiting period for soliciting clients in personal injury or wrongful death matters . . . and also may solicit clients in person or by telephone without running afoul of *Colo. RPC 7.3*.[18]

If a client or potential client inquires of the firm seeking to contact a lawyer who has departed the firm, the firm must provide the lawyer's new business address and telephone number, if known. Failure to do so may be a violation of *Colo. RPC 1.4* or may reflect a lack of candor.[19] However, after providing information as described above, the firm may inquire whether the call is regarding a legal matter and, if so, may ask whether someone at the firm may help instead.

---

17. *See e.g., Siegel v. Arter & Hadden*, 707 N.E.2d 853 (Ohio. 1999) (unresolved fact issues precluded summary judgment on unfair competition and trade secret counts because of departing lawyer's use of client list with names, addresses, telephone numbers and matters and fee information, despite notice to firm before notice to clients); *Shein v. Myers*, 576 A.2d 985, 986 (Pa. 1990), *appeal denied*, 617 A.2d 1274 (Pa. 1991) ("breakaway" lawyers tortiously interfered with contract between their former firm and its clients by taking 400 client files, making scurrilous statements about the firm, and sending misleading letters to firm clients). *But see, Graubard Mollen v. Moskovitz*, 653 N.E.2d 1179 (N.Y.1995) (departing lawyer's efforts to locate alternative space and affiliations would not violate his fiduciary duties to his firm because those actions obviously require confidentiality and informing firm clients with whom the departing lawyer has a prior professional relationship about his impending withdrawal and reminding them of their right to retain counsel of their choice was permissible).

18. The Committee concurs with the ABA view that a lawyer does not have a prior professional relationship with a client sufficient to permit in-person or live telephone solicitation solely by having worked on a matter along with other lawyers in a way that afforded little or no direct contact with the client. "Prior professional relationship" also may apply to the constituents of an organizational client with whom the lawyer has had substantial contact, who in their individual capacity never were clients of the firm or lawyer.

19. *Colo. RPC 8.4(c)* provides that it is professional misconduct for a lawyer to engage in conduct involving dishonesty, fraud, deceit, or misrepresentation. To the extent such inquiries are handled by non-lawyers employed or associated with the firm, partners or principals in the firm, or those lawyers having direct supervisory authority over the non-lawyer, shall make reasonable efforts to insure that the firm has in effect measures giving reasonable assurance that the non-lawyer's conduct will be compatible with the professional obligations of the lawyer, or shall make reasonable efforts to insure that the person's conduct is compatible with those professional obligations. *Colo. RPC 5.3(a)* and *(b)*.

C. Proper and Continuous Handling of Client Matters

Amid the turmoil of a firm break-up, attorneys should never forget that they have clients and that they continue to owe those clients ethical and legal duties. While an affected client is choosing between the departing lawyer and the law firm, both have a duty to ensure that the client's matter is handled properly. A lawyer shall act with reasonable diligence and promptness in representing a client, and shall not neglect a legal matter entrusted to that lawyer.[22] Unless the relationship between a lawyer and client is terminated as provided in *Colo. RPC 1.16*, a lawyer should carry through to conclusion all matters undertaken for a client.[23]

Absent a special agreement, the client employs the firm and not a particular lawyer, and the firm has responsibility, along with the departing attorney, for the cases being handled by the departing attorney. Therefore, subject to the contrary wishes of an affected client, a law firm is obligated to continue to handle matters that were handled by a departing lawyer. The affected client, however, may continue to view the departing lawyer as the client's representative despite the lawyer's withdrawal from the firm. The attorney-client relationship is an ongoing relationship that gives rise to a continuing duty to the affected client unless and until the client clearly understands, or reasonably should understand, that the relationship is one on which he, she or it can no longer depend.

D. Withdrawal by the Law Firm or Attorney

A lawyer's departure from a law firm generally leads to withdrawal of either the firm or the departing lawyer as counsel for one or more affected clients. In matters in which a lawyer or firm has entered an appearance in a court proceeding, a formal motion to withdraw may be required. *Colo. RPC 1.16(d)* provides that upon termination of representation, a lawyer shall take steps to the extent reasonably practicable to protect a client's interests, such as giving reasonable notice to the client, allowing time for employment of other counsel, surrendering papers and property to which the client is entitled and refunding any advance payment of fee that has not been earned.

When the law firm and the departing lawyer provide proper notice as discussed above, the affected client's matter is handled with diligence and competence during the withdrawal and selection of counsel, and the client chooses to be represented by one or the other (or chooses another lawyer or firm), the interests of the client will have been protected to a large extent. However, client papers and property still can be an issue. In any client matter, files generally

---

22. *Colo. RPC 1.3.*

23. Comment, *Colo. RPC 1.3.* Even after the attorney-client relationship has terminated, the firm and the departing lawyer have an obligation to avoid harming the client's interests. For example, where a client has terminated the client's relationship with a firm, the firm nonetheless has the obligation to make sure that communications coming to the client through the firm are promptly communicated to the client. See *Restatement (Third) The Law Governing Lawyers,* § 33(2)(c).

are created while the departing lawyer is associated with the firm. The proper handling of these client files is discussed below.

The affected client may have paid an advance retainer for representation in a particular matter. Typically, such retainers are paid to the firm rather than an individual lawyer. These funds must be held separate from the lawyers' own property.[28] If the lawyer or law firm holding the client funds is withdrawing from representation, and neither the lawyer nor any third person claims any interest in the funds, the lawyer or firm holding the funds must promptly pay the remaining trust balance to the client or otherwise apply the funds as directed by agreement with the client.[29] If the departing lawyer will be representing the affected client, the client funds held by the firm may, with the client's consent, be transferred to an appropriate trust account established by the departing lawyer.

In some circumstances neither the departing lawyer nor the law firm wants to continue representing the affected client. In this situation, the obligations of the lawyers are no different than in any other situation in which a lawyer wishes to withdraw from representation. The departing lawyer and the firm must bear in mind the responsibilities imposed under *Colo. RPC 1.3* (diligent representation), *Colo. RPC 1.4* (communication), and *Colo. RPC 1.16* (termination of representation).

E. Client Files

With limited exceptions, the client is entitled to the client file. The departing lawyer may remove client files only with the consent of the affected client. If the affected client so requests, the firm must provide the files to the departing lawyer, subject to the limitations discussed in CBA Formal Opinion 104. Pending receipt of instructions from the client, both the departing lawyer and the law firm should have reasonable access to the file in order to protect the interests of the client, which remains the paramount obligation of both. Even if the client has requested that the file be transferred to the departing lawyer, the file should not be removed without giving the firm notice and opportunity to copy the file. Likewise, if the affected client requests that the firm continue the representation, the departing lawyer should be given the opportunity to copy the file. The contents of such client files remain confidential pursuant to the provisions of *Colo. RPC 1.6*.

In some circumstances, a client wishing to have a file transferred to the departing lawyer may owe the firm for past services or for costs advanced on the client's behalf. It is this Committee's view that such situations should be treated the same as any other in which a client discharges a lawyer without fully satisfying his or her financial obligations to the lawyer. The firm may, under certain limited circumstances, assert a retaining lien against client property in its possession.

---

28. *Colo. RPC 1.15(a)*.

29. *See Colo. RPC 1.15(b)*. For proper handling of funds in a lawyer's possession in which the lawyer or another person claims an interest, see *Colo. RPC 1.15(c)*.

The law firm may possess client files in legal matters that are inactive or have been closed. Both the departing lawyer and the firm should consider any ethical obligations they may have with respect to such files insofar as they pertain to client matters for which the departing lawyer was responsible or played a principal role.

F. Conflicts of Interest Arising Out of the Departing Lawyer's New Affiliation

The departing lawyer must also be aware of and avoid conflicts of interest that may arise out of his or her affiliation with another law firm. While lawyers are associated in a firm, none of them shall knowingly represent a client when any one of them practicing alone would be prohibited from doing so by *Colo. RPC 1.7, 1.8(c)*, [or] *1.9.* . . . [35] The rule of imputed disqualification flows from the premise that a firm of lawyers is essentially one lawyer for purposes of the rules governing loyalty to the client. Thus, when the departing lawyer brings clients to his or her new firm, they become the new firm's clients. Likewise, the new firm's clients become the departing lawyer's clients.

Because of the rules concerning imputed disqualification, the departing lawyer and the new firm must perform a thorough conflicts check. This conflicts check should be designed to determine whether the departing lawyer's association with the new firm may involve conflicts of interest based on consideration of the departing lawyer's current and former clients. The process of checking for conflicts of interest may, in some circumstances, be undertaken prior to the departing lawyer's affiliation with the new firm.[38]

G. Restrictions on the Right to Practice

Colo. RPC 5.6(a) provides that a lawyer shall not participate in offering or making a "partnership or employment agreement that restricts the right of a lawyer to practice after termination of the relationship, except an agreement concerning benefits upon retirement or as permitted by Rule 1.17 [regarding the sale of a law practice]." The comment to Rule 5.6 provides that such an agreement "not only limits the lawyer's professional autonomy but also limits the freedom of clients to choose a lawyer."

In Colorado, an agreement prohibiting a departing lawyer from soliciting clients after departure from a firm impermissibly impairs the client's right to discharge and choose counsel, and may lead to discipline for the offending attorney.

---

35. *Colo. RPC 1.10(a)*.

38. The Committee recognizes that there is an inherent tension between the new firm's need to obtain information concerning the departing lawyer's former and current clients in order to comply with the conflict rules, and the departing lawyer's obligations under *Colo. RPC 1.6(a)* not to reveal information relating to representation of clients . . . . [T]he departing lawyer may seek the consent of former or current clients to disclose information to permit a conflict check and under some circumstances it may be possible to check for conflicts of interest without disclosing information relating to the representation of former clients.

Courts in many other jurisdictions have refused to enforce agreements between lawyers and law firms that they viewed as anti-competitive. While a departing lawyer must be mindful of the lawyer's fiduciary obligations to the firm and of the existing contractual relations between the firm and affected clients, the lawyer may not agree to, and the firm must not impose, conditions that might inhibit a client's right to choose counsel.

H. Duty of Candor

Regardless of the nature of the departure, a departing lawyer and firm each have a duty to act with candor toward the other.[41] . . . The duty of candor, as well as Rule 8.4(c), may be breached by a lawyer who misrepresents the lawyer's status or intentions to others at the firm, and vice versa.

While a discussion of the legal, as opposed to ethical, duties of lawyers is beyond the scope of this opinion, lawyers and firms contemplating a dissolution or departure should give careful consideration to their respective legal duties, including potential obligations based on their contractual, agency, or fiduciary relationships. A departing lawyer should consider the consequences that may arise from contacting clients and attempting to obtain consent to transfer matters to the departing lawyer in advance of notifying the firm, or in denying to the firm the lawyer's intention to depart. Firms likewise should consider the consequences of similar actions prior to the contemplated departure of a lawyer who is not yet aware of impending change.[42] Such actions by a departing lawyer or a firm may reflect a lack of candor.

▪ Lawyers' Roles:
Finding Your Own Way

In Chapter 1, we defined legal ethics as the study of what is required for a lawyer to provide a professional service to another. Lawyers' roles are complicated by the facts that clients simultaneously empower lawyers to act and then become subject to the power of the lawyer created by the lawyer's specialized knowledge and ability to access the legal system. Several notes and cases in Chapters 6 and 7 commented on lawyers who apparently assumed directive or instrumental roles, which

---

41. This committee agrees with the Oregon Bar Association and the Oregon Supreme Court that a lawyer has a duty of candor to her or his firm. Or. Bar Assn. Formal Op. No. 2005-70. ("Regardless of contractual, fiduciary, or agency relationship between Lawyer and Firm A, however, it is clear under Oregon RPC 8.4(3) that Lawyer may not misrepresent Lawyer's status or intentions to others at Firm A. *See In re Smith*, 315 Or. 260, 843 P.2d 449 (1992); *In re Murdock*, 328 Or. 18, 968 P.2d 1270 (1998) (although not expressly written, implicit in disciplinary rules and in duty of loyalty arising from lawyer's contractual or agency relationship with his or her law firm is a duty of candor toward that law firm)").

42. *See, e.g., Meehan, et al. v. Shaughnessy*, 535 N.E.2d 1255 (Mass. 1998); *Adler, Barish, Daniels, Levin and Creskoff v. Epstein*, 393 A.2d 1175 (Pa. 1978); *In re Smith, supra* note 41; *In re Murdock, supra*, note 41. at n. 7.

caused them to risk violating legal norms designed to protect clients or the public.[1] At the end of Chapter 8, we pointed out that most lawyers get it right most of the time by zealously representing their clients within the bounds of the law.[2] The cases and materials in the second half of this book illustrate these same themes. Some of the lawyers in these cases acted in directive roles, serving the interests of third persons or their own interests before those of their clients. Others got into trouble by overidentifying with their clients, by seeing themselves as instrumental cogs in the machinery of a legal system that exalts client wishes over all.

Directive Self-Servers

Chapters 9, 10, and 11 offered numerous examples of lawyers who breached fiduciary duty by failing to recognize or respond properly to conflicts of interest. These lawyers underidentified with their clients and fell short of providing zealous representation. They neglected the fiduciary duty lessons that lawyers serve client interests, not their own, another client's or the interests of a third party.[3] Chapter 12 also offered examples of lawyers who placed profit maximization above fiduciary duty to their clients. These lawyers failed to recognize that lawyering is a regulated market, and that clients have absolute rights to discharge them at will.[4] Similarly, *Gilles* in this chapter illustrates a lawyer and law firm that failed to view fiduciary duty from the client's point of view, incorrectly thinking they could abandon the client's case without assuring that the client had ample opportunity to find replacement counsel.

Instrumental Cogs

At the same time, Chapter 14 will offer new and serious examples of lawyers who understood their role in largely instrumental terms. These lawyers provided zealous advocacy, but like the lawyers in *Greycas* and *Cruze,* failed to recognize a clear legal limit to their representation of client interests, whether found in common law, statute, or court rule. They overidentified with their clients and suffered civil liability, sanctions, discipline, and disqualification as a result.[5]

---

1. Lawyers' Roles: *The Directive Lawyer and Fiduciary Duty, supra* p. 170; Lawyers' Roles: *The Instrumental Lawyer and the Bounds of the Law, supra* p. 243.

2. Lawyers' Roles: *Zealous Representation Within the Bounds of the Law, supra* p. 297.

3. *See* Maritrans GP Inc. v. Pepper Hamilton & Scheetz, *supra* p. 304; Murray v. Village of Hazel Crest, *supra* p. 314; Sanford v. Commonwealth of Virginia, *supra* p. 316; Anderson v. O'Brien, *supra* p. 324; Eastman Kodak Co. v. Sony Corp., *supra* p. 335; Liggett v. Young, *supra* p. 347; Burrow v. Arce, *supra* p. 358; Iowa Supreme Court Disciplinary Bd. v. Monroe, *supra* p. 371; Oasis West Realty, LLC v. Goldman, *supra* p. 393; Cascades Branding Innovations, LLC v. Walgreen Co., *supra* p. 398; Martin v. Atlanticare, *supra* p. 409.

4. *See* Matter of Fordham, *supra* p. 443; In re Sather, *supra* p. 459, Malonis v. Harrington, *supra* p. 467.

5. *See* Christian v. Mattel, Inc., *infra* p. 534; Surowiec v. Capital Title Agency, Inc., *infra* p. 541.

Dual Difficulties

Several lawyers in the cases in this book suffered from the excesses of both directive and instrumental role behavior at the same time. Recall for example, *Antioch Litigation Trust,* where the law firm's joint representation of the organization and some of its constituents favored the latter over the former. Similarly, the insurance defense firms in *Perez*[6] and *Spaulding*[7] acted instrumentally toward the insurer that hired them and paid the bill, and inappropriately directed the primary client, the insured, who was entitled to representation complete with the full array of fiduciary duties. In serving one client, the lawyers in both of these cases breached duties to the other, and, at the same time, aided the insurer in neglecting its contractual obligations to the insured.

Getting It Right

At the end of Chapter 8, we noted that most lawyers avoid both of these extremes by acting as collaborators with their clients.[8] Many of the lawyers in the second half of this book also found the right course. For example, the law firm in *A. v. B.* sought the discretion to disclose material information learned from one client to another.[9] These lawyers did not favor one client over another by automatically disclosing, as occurred in *Perez.* Instead, they recognized that some strong policy must justify limiting their fiduciary duty to one client, then sought and won court approval to rely on an explicit confidentiality exception to legitimate the disclosure.

Consider further the actions of the lawyers in *Heckman* and *Pane.*[10] Each understood that lawyers with whom they were associated were engaging in violations of the rules of professional conduct, both understood their own obligation to speak up, and both did so, first to supervisors and eventually to others. Each encountered significant economic, personal, and professional incentives not to speak, or to defer to supervisors who told them that the matter was being handled. Like the lawyer in *Meyerhofer,*[11] both carefully documented the continuing rule violations, and both suffered job loss as a result. Neither had any assurance that any legal relief would later be available to them for doing the right thing, yet each persevered.

All of these lawyers got it right. They realized that the rules of professional conduct allowed them a great deal of professional discretion to do the right thing. We have seen, for example, that lawyers are free to participate in pro bono and law reform cases, an option open to lawyers in a case when client financial limitations might otherwise prevent full judicial consideration of an important legal issue. Further, lawyers are free to choose the kind of practice

---

6. Perez v. Kirk & Carrigan, *supra* p. 167.
7. Spaulding v. Zimmerman, *supra* p. 215.
8. *See* Lawyers' Roles: *Zealous Representation Within the Bounds of the Law, supra* p. 297.
9. *A. v. B., supra* p. 329.
10. Heckman v. Zurich Holding Co. of America, *supra* p. 497; Pane v. Goffs, *supra* p. 503.
11. Meyerhofer v. Empire Fire & Marine Ins. Co., *supra* p. 260.

they prefer and to decide which cases to take.[12] Lawyers also can limit the scope of the engagement and have a great deal of discretion to counsel clients about moral as well as legal limits to conduct. If a client insists on advocacy arguably or clearly outside of legal limits, lawyers also may or must end the representation.[13] Ultimately, lawyers, like all other professionals, have the option of changing jobs, as *Meyerhofer, Heckman,* and *Pane* demonstrate.

Each of these lawyers learned from the law of lawyering to avoid the extremes of both instrumental and directive behavior. They avoided instrumental thinking by being aware of the bounds or limits of the law and by refusing to "exclude their own personal values from all professional decisionmaking."[14] At the same time, they avoided directive thinking by recalling the dictates of fiduciary duty and by checking their personal beliefs against their professional obligations to represent clients zealously within the bounds of the law. In other words, they relied on both their personal values and their professional obligations "to signal an ethical quandary," and drew on these values to construct a personal goal. In this process, they were continually informed by their responsibilities to clients and the bounds of the law to assure them that the action they took was well within the scope of professional discretion "relegated to the lawyer's ungrounded discretion."[15]

Law and Life

In an earlier note, we introduced the idea that lawyers who represent clients zealously within the bounds of the law act as translators or mediators between the private world of clients and the public world of law. The lawyers in these materials who got it right did the same thing for themselves, mediating between their own personal values and the public world of law. They translated the law for themselves, as well as for their clients, and translated their own values into the law. This insight leads us to consider a fuller meaning of the lawyer as translator metaphor, and we defer here to Professor James Boyd White, who created it:

> What I suggest, briefly, is this: that the lawyer is not, as we sometimes think, only a cog in a system of social administration, nor simply a profit-maximizing service provider, but a person who meets, who can learn to meet, the moment at which the language of the law—a language that has justice as its aim—is applied to experience, the moment at which it must confront other languages . . . . The lawyer or judge live constantly at the edge of language, the edge of meaning, where the world can be, must be, imagined anew; to do this well is an enormous achievement; to do it badly, a disaster of real importance, not only for the lawyer or judge

---

12. *See, e.g.,* Patrick J. Schilt, *On Being a Happy, Healthy, and Ethical Member of an Unhappy, Unhealthy, and Unethical Profession,* 52 Vand. L. Rev. 871 (1999).

13. *See* Nathan M. Crystal, *Developing a Philosophy of Lawyering,* 14 Notre Dame J.L., Ethics & Pub. Pol'y 75 (2000).

14. Bruce A. Green, *The Role of Personal Values in Professional Decisionmaking,* 11 Geo. J. Legal Ethics 19, 56 (1997).

15. *Id.*

but for the social world of which they are a part, including the particular people whose lives they affect. . . .

I might sum it up in this way: Of course the lawyer usually knows more than his client about the law, and in some sense has thus already thought about the issue his client presents; but there is always, or almost always, something new and distinctive and problematic about what the client brings him that requires further thought, and often thought of a deep and uncertain kind. . . .

One way to think about the law, in fact, is as an intervention into a world that works largely in nonlegal terms, and for the most part well enough, but that has now suffered a crisis or breakdown calling for its help. . . .

In each case we begin with the life of the world that precedes the lawyer's involvement, where the parties are competent at shaping their own existences; there is then an event that leads one, then the other, to go to a lawyer; there then ensues a lot of activity, mainly in language—followed by an action, or a refusal to act, by the court or by the lawyers in negotiation, and a return to the world of ordinary life, either changed by what has happened, or unchanged. It thus always is—or should be—a question for the lawyer what relation exists or can exist between the language of the law, the language in which he talks and functions, and the experience and life of the world. . . .

[T]he lawyer must perpetually face the relation between legal language and other languages—other ways of representing the situation or the actors in it, other ways of imagining human motive and experience, other ways of shaping the future. In the courtroom and negotiation alike other languages and voices are regularly translated into the law, always with some distortion, sometimes to good effect, sometimes to bad. Sometimes the law itself changes as a result, but in the end it systematically excludes voices, narratives, languages—ways of thinking and talking that it finds irrelevant to its concerns or of which it does not approve. It is thus a constant question for the lawyer how to manage the relation between law and other languages. . . .

Think for example what it would be like to have someone come to you and describe the collapse of a commercial deal, perhaps a partnership or a long-term contract, for which he had once had great hopes, but which has now proven a disaster. How completely could you capture in your own mind what happened in the world, what its significance was, and how would you think about what ought to happen next? How adequate do you suppose the legal language of partnerships or contracts would be to this situation? The language of accounting or economic theory? What place would the voices of languages of the parties, or of outside experts on technical issues, have in what you said or did? This set of questions could be asked about virtually any case—a divorce, an accident, a crime—and they are present not only when the law looks back on past experience, as it does here, but when it tries to shape experience for the future, by drafting a partnership agreement, for example, or a prenuptial contract, or a divorce settlement. . . .

The law is among other things a system for attracting our attention to difficult questions, and holding it there; for stimulating thought of a disciplined and often creative kind, and feelings too, especially . . . the desire for justice that is called into existence by the questions the case presents, by the contrasting views of the lawyers on each side, and by our own inner sense of the reality and importance of what is at stake. The process of legal thought simultaneously resists simplicity and appeals to the side of us that wants to imagine the world, and ourselves and others within it, in a coherent way. A case is a bright moment, at which we have the opportunity to face at once the language we are given to use and the particulars of the case before us, and in both directions we are drawn into real struggles of mind and imagination. The object of law is justice; but the law teaches us, over and over again, that we do not have unmediated access to the pure idea of justice in the heavens, which we can apply directly and with confidence, but rather live in a world in which everything has to be thought about, argued out, and reimagined afresh. It is a lesson in the difficulty of imagining the world, and the self and others within it, in such a way as to make possible coherent speech and meaningful action.[16]

Your Way

Of course, you might not agree with all Professor White has to say, or with our characterization of the lawyers in this book. At the very least, we hope that these materials illustrate for you the wide latitude that you will have in practice to establish your own role with clients, as well as the clear dangers that you will face if you operate too far toward either end of the behavioral spectrum.

The materials in this book demonstrate that the law governing lawyers has responded to both the instrumental and directive extremes with concrete incentives that steer lawyers away from the minefields of violating fiduciary duty and exceeding the bounds of legitimate advocacy. If you favor or tend toward an instrumental role, you need to be especially alert to the bounds of the law that apply to your own conduct as well as that of your client. The lawyers in this book who ignored those limits suffered tort liability, sanctions for violations of procedural rules, criminal liability, disqualification, and professional discipline. If you favor or tend to lean toward a directive role, you will be wise to recall the lawyers in this book who ignored fiduciary duty and suffered malpractice liability, disqualification, loss of a fee or contractual benefit, and professional discipline.

Ultimately, these legal rules spring from and dictate ethics: how we ought to respond to those we chose to serve.[17] They require concrete action, not just intent or thought. They also prod you to assess risk realistically. Beyond understanding these rules and assessing the obligations they create, however, the materials in this book also ask you to consider how your life as a lawyer will influence the rest of your life, and how the rest of your life will influence your practice of law. Most people and most lawyers want to reconcile their personal values with their professional life. To do so requires continuing dialogue between your personal beliefs and your professional practice.[18] Just as representing clients well requires translation of their personal beliefs into the professional language of the law and translation of the moral fabric of legal rules to your client's situation, so

---

16. James Boyd White, *The Edge of Meaning* 223-226, 250-251 (U. Chi. Press 2001).
17. *See, e.g.,* Anthony E. Cook, *Forward: Towards a Postmodern Ethics of Service,* 81 Geo. L.J. 2457 (1993).
18. *See* George W. Kaufman, *The Lawyers' Guide to Balancing Life and Work: Taking the Stress Out of Success* (ABA 1999).

also does your sense of self require continuing translation of your professional to your personal self and back again.

In the end, if you hope to develop the ability to serve clients' interests well, to invent and articulate plans for them, or to grease the bearings of social justice by translating their stories into the language of the law, you will need to develop and maintain the ability to mediate between the ordinary world of everyday life and the legal system.[19] If you want to find guidance for the exercise of your own professional discretion, you also will need to mediate between your personal self and the legal world you work in.[20] As you do this, we wish you the blessing of a life that allows you to integrate your personal and professional self. The lawyers able to discover this connection will be most capable of practicing what they advise their clients: moving on with their lives, perhaps with a renewed sense of vision, influenced both by the ordinary world and the lessons of law that support it.

19. *See* Lawrence S. Krieger, *What We're Not Telling Law Students—and Lawyers—That They Really Need to Know: Some Thoughts-in-Action Toward Revitalizing the Profession from Its Roots,* 13 J. L. & Health 1 (1998-1999).

20. *See, e.g.,* Joseph Allegretti, *Lawyers, Client, and Covenant: A Religious Perspective on Legal Practice and Ethics,* 66 Fordham L. Rev. 1101 (1998).

Part III

Lawyers and Justice: The Limits of Advocacy

Up to this point, we have been traversing the ethical minefield of fiduciary duty. We have examined the contours of each of the 5 Cs: control, competence, communication, confidentiality, and conflict of interest resolution. Along the way, we have encountered a number of legal constraints that impose equally important limits on a lawyer's fiduciary duty or advocacy on behalf of a client.

Every legal representation requires that a lawyer knows these relevant bounds of the law. Agency law rests on the premise that both client and lawyer are autonomous persons who remain responsible for the consequences of their actions. Although it is obvious that a lawyer cannot bribe a judge or shoot a juror on behalf of a client, many other legal limits are less clear. These bodies of law create additional minefields waiting for the lawyer unaware of their existence or unclear about their relevance in a given case.

Chapter 14

The Bounds of the Law

"*If you want justice, it's two hundred dollars an hour.
Obstruction of justice runs a bit more.*"

A.   Introduction

Problems

14-1. Martyn & Fox's real estate department is helping Express Construction develop a shopping center in Montgomery County. The vote will be close. Martyn & Fox is asked by Express to buy a table at the Lincoln Day dinner "to smooth the skids."

14-2. Martyn & Fox's client, an alleged drug dealer, brings an $11,000 cash retainer into the office. "You'll keep this confidential, right?" the client states.

Consider: Model Rules 1.2(d), 1.6, 8.4
18 U.S.C. § 201

▓ The Bounds of the Law:
A Reprise

In previous notes and cases, we have identified some of the limits or bounds of the law that restrain unfettered client allegiance.[1] We begin this chapter by recalling the kinds of legal constraints that can limit a lawyer's advocacy on behalf of a client:

1. The law of **tort**, such as the law of **fraud** that created a duty to a third party in Greycas v. Proud and Thomas H. Lee Equity Fund V, L.P. v. Mayer Brown, Rowe, & Maw LLP; or, the law of negligence, which can create a duty to third parties in cases such as Cruze v. Handler.
2. The law of **evidence**, which can create exceptions to confidentiality enforced through court orders, like the crime-fraud exception to the attorney-client privilege, discussed in Purcell v. District Attorney and United States v. Chen.
3. **Court orders**, issued pursuant to the **inherent power** of a court, that can require a lawyer to provide representation, as discussed in Bothwell v. Republic Tobacco; enjoin a lawyer from further representation, as occurred in Maritrans GP Inc. v. Pepper, Hamilton, & Sheetz; disqualify a lawyer whose representation will taint the trial, as in Murray v. Village of Hazel Crest, Sanford v. Commonwealth of Va., Eastman Kodak Co. v. Sony Corp, Cascades Branding Innovation, LLC v. Walgreen Co., and Martin v. Atlanticare; provide for contempt if a lawyer refuses to obey an order, as occurred in Hughes v. Meade; or, impose sanctions against lawyers who disregard their obligations of candor to the court, as occurred in United States v. Shaffer Equipment Co.
4. Rules of **civil or appellate procedure**, which provided the basis for relief against an opposing party in Matter of Hendrix.

---

1. The Bounds of the Law: *Duties to Nonclients, supra* p. 155; The Bounds of the Law: *Court Orders, supra* p. 208; The Bounds of the Law: *Client Fraud, supra* p. 252; The Bounds of the Law: *Criminal Conduct, supra* p. 270.

5. Civil and criminal provisions in state and federal **securities law**, such as the provisions that afforded relief to third parties in Meyerhofer v. Empire Fire & Marine Ins. Co. and In re Refco Securities Litigation.
6. General **criminal statutes**, such as the prohibition against criminal impersonation, which created a limit on the lawyer's advocacy in People v. Casey; the federal securities fraud conviction described in In re Refco Securities Litigation; or the prohibition against obstruction of justice, which was not transgressed by the lawyers in People v. Belge.[2]
7. The provisions of **insurance law**, which enforce contractual duties to insured persons, such as the law discussed in Paradigm Insurance Co. v. The Langerman Law Offices, P.A.[3]

All of this generally applicable law served as the basis for limiting what a lawyer was able to do on behalf of a client. Each legal provision also created substantial penalties or other consequences for the lawyers unaware of the relevant limit.

In some instances, the lawyer or law firm involved paid substantial damages to third parties or a court for violating relevant legal prohibitions.[4] Several of the cases just listed also illustrate that a lawyer who ignores a relevant limit on advocacy often buys that client extended future litigation. For example, the insurance company that hired the lawyers in *Spaulding* probably ended up paying more than if it initially had disclosed the fact of Spaulding's injury. Or consider the extent to which the clients in *Meyerhofer* would have been better off disclosing the law firm's fee in the first place.

In other cases, such as *Casey* and *Refco*, the lawyer's violation of a criminal statute resulted in discipline for an indictable offense. On the other hand, acceding to the appropriate limit on advocacy resulted in quashing the criminal indictment in *Belge*.

And finally, consider the consequences to the lawyers in *Murray, Sanford, Eastman Kodak, Cacades,* and *Martin*. From the client's perspective, was it worth the time and money to litigate the question of whether they or their law firms should be disqualified due to a conflict of interest?

Lawyers as Gatekeepers

The application of general legal provisions to lawyers continues in many areas. For example, the court in Anderson v. O'Brien held the defendant lawyer responsible for damages under the state unfair trade practices act. Other prominent

---

2. *See also* Lawyers and Clients: *Representing Governments, supra* p. 426 (describing criminal laws that limit the practice of former government lawyers).

3. *See also* Lawyers and Clients: *Insurance Defense, supra* p. 381 (describing insurance law bad-faith remedies).

4. *E.g.,* Greycas v. Proud, *supra* p. 145 (judgment against an opposing party's lawyer for $833,760); United States v. Shaffer Equip. Co., *supra* p. 282 (lawyers ordered to pay personal sanctions for violating Rule 3.3).

examples involve federal law, some of the provisions of which seek to make lawyers gatekeepers of their client's behavior.[5]

Form 8300   In 1984, Congress imposed an IRS reporting rule on a "trade or business" that receives more than $10,000 in cash.[6] A number of federal courts also have considered the effect of this federal anti-money-laundering statute on the practice of criminal defense lawyers. These cases agree that, absent very narrow special circumstances,[7] lawyers who accept more than $10,000 in cash from clients must report the transaction to the Treasury Department, may not withhold the client's name, and are liable for substantial fines up to $25,000 per violation.[8] Similarly, lawyers hired to foreclose on mortgages have been held to be "debt collectors" within the meaning of the Fair Debt Collection Practices Act.[9]

The USA Patriot Act   The USA Patriot Act was passed after September 11, 2001 to respond to terrorist activities. One goal of the law was to strengthen the previously existing Financial Action Task Force on Money Laundering (FATF), an intergovernmental body designed to promote national and international policies to combat money laundering.[10] A new undertaking of this group, called the Gatekeeper Initiative, is directed at professionals, including lawyers, whose clients engage in domestic and international financial transactions and business. Should this initiative become law, lawyers could be required to submit Suspicious Activities Reports (now required of financial institutions)[11] regarding client activities, and lawyers would be prohibited from telling their clients that they had done so. In the United Kingdom, such obligations already apply to lawyers who manage client money or who assist in the planning or execution of transactions for clients concerning any financial or real estate transaction.[12] In other places, such as Canada and Australia, they do not.[13]

---

5. Fred Zacharias, *Lawyers as Gatekeepers*, 41 San Diego L. Rev. 1387 (2004).

6. 26 U.S.C. § 6050I (2006); 26 C.F.R. § 301.6721.

7. Very few cases have found such special circumstances; United States v. Sindel, 53 F.3d 874 (8th Cir. 1995). The courts seem to agree that the statutory filing must amount to something like the facts in *Belge,* a coerced confession of criminal activity, disclosure of which would violate the client's Fifth Amendment right against self-incrimination. *See, e.g.*, Gerald B. Lefcourt, P.C. v. United States, 125 F.3d 79 (2d Cir. 1997).

8. *Id.; See also* In re Vanderveen, 211 P.3d 1008 (Wash. 2009) (lawyer who accepted $20,000 in cash for his fee and later pleaded guilty to willfully violating federal cash reporting laws disbarred).

9. Sayyed v. Wolpoff & Abramson, 485 F.3d 226 (4th Cir. 2007). *See also* Evon v. Law Offices of Sidney Mickell, 2012 Y.S. App. Lexis 15861 (9th Cir.) (lawyer who sent dunning letter to client in "care of" her employer violated Fair Debt Collection Practices Act).

10. *See, e.g.,* U.S. Department of Justice, *Report to Congress on Implementation of Section 1001 of the USA PATRIOT Act*, March 8, 2006, *available at* http://www.justice.gov/oig/special/s0603/final.pdf.

11. 31 U.S.C. § 5318(g) (2011).

12. *See* International Bar Association, *Anti-Money Laundering Forum, available at* http://www.anti-moneylaundering.org/europe/united_kingdom.aspx (last visited July 3, 2012).

13. Federation of Law Soc. of Law Societies of Canada v. Canada (Attorney General), 339 D.L.R. 4th 48 (B.C. 2011) (criminal statutes designed to control money laundering and funding of terrorist

The ABA House of Delegates has taken the position that requiring law-yers who receive or transfer funds on behalf of clients "to verify the identity of clients, maintain records on domestic and international transactions, and develop training programs that would help attorneys identify potential money laundering schemes" was appropriate.[14] The same group strongly opposed the so-called tip-off provisions, which would require lawyers to submit Suspicious Transaction Reports to government authorities based on a mere suspicion that the funds involved in the client's transaction stemmed from illegal activity, and also opposed preventing lawyers from telling their clients that they had done so.

Sarbanes-Oxley The Enron financial meltdown resulted in the passage of the Sarbanes-Oxley Act (SOX) in 2002.[15] Although much of this law aims to regu-late corporate governance, one part of the statute and corresponding regulations add a layer of regulation to lawyers who give advice to public companies about matters that are described or should be described in SEC filings. Many of these obligations parallel those in Model Rule 1.13, but the triggers for up-the-ladder disclosure and the kind of reports that must be made are far more specific. SOX does not require disclosure outside of the organization, but does specify a lawyer's obligations within it. Violations can result in discipline by the SEC, including disbarment.[16]

The Bounds of the Law and Client Advocacy

Proposals like these are not likely to end the debate about the appropriate scope of client advocacy.[17] Taken together, these requirements remind lawyers that neither they nor their clients are exempt from general legal requirements, some of which create limitations on client advocacy. This is not an unfamiliar role, as lawyers have always been in the business of advising clients to avoid illegality. We probably should be most wary of these efforts, however, when the govern-ment seeks to make lawyers agents of its law enforcement efforts. On the other

---

activities unconstitutional as applied to lawyers because the underlying purpose put client's liberty interests at stake and violated the solicitor-client privilege; the federal government should regulate banks and other professions, but the law societies should regulate lawyers, thereby minimizing interference in the client-lawyer relationship).

14. *See* American Bar Association, *ABA Task Force on Gatekeeper Regulation and the Profession on the Financial Action Task Force Consultation Paper*, 10 (2002), *available at* http://apps.americanbar. org/intlaw/committees/public_II/money_laundering/104.pdf. The ABA Task Force on Gatekeeper Regulation and the Profession website has links to current information about anti-money-laundering efforts. American Bar Association, *Task Force on Gatekeeper Regulation and the Profession, available at* http://www.americanbar.org/groups/criminal_justice/pages/TaskForce.html (last visited July 9, 2012).

15. 15 U.S.C. § 7245 (2012); 17 C.F.R. Part 205.

16. *See* Lawrence J. Fox & Susan R. Martyn, *The Ethics of Representing Organizations: Legal Fictions for Client* 255-261 (Oxford U. Press 2009).

17. Empirical evidence is slim, but suggests that in about 15 percent of money laundering convic-tions in one circuit, a lawyer's services "likely were used to launder money." Lawton P. Cummings & Paul T. Stepnowsky, *My Brother's Keeper: An Empirical Study of Attorney Facilitation of Money Laundering through Commercial Transactions*, 2011 J. Prof. L. 1, 36.

hand, we probably should welcome limits on advocacy when they seek to provide a fair and accessible justice system.

This chapter sheds light on additional examples of these legal limits on client advocacy that can ensnare an unenlightened lawyer. These bodies of law create the potential for criminal, civil, disciplinary, or procedural sanctions. We begin by considering a variety of procedural rules and inherent powers that provide the basis for monetary sanctions against lawyers who file frivolous lawsuits or evade discovery obligations. We then turn to consider limitations imposed on lawyers by laws that prohibit bias, such as civil rights provisions and the Americans with Disabilities Act (ADA). Near the end of the chapter, we focus on additional professional rules that prohibit or limit communication with represented and unrepresented persons, judges, and jurors. Finally, we examine the scope and application of professional code provisions that prohibit lawyers from appearing as witnesses in clients' cases.

B. Frivolous Claims

Problem

14-3. Martyn & Fox filed a lawsuit against Chemco one week before the statute of limitations ran, a delay caused by tardy consultation with the firm. The suit was brought on behalf of three children born with birth defects, alleging that the birth defects were caused in utero by their mother's exposure to poisonous chemicals that Chemco emitted into the air near their homes. Ten months later, Martyn & Fox consulted an expert for the first time, who told the firm that there was no way to prove that Chemco's chemicals caused the birth defects in question. Martyn & Fox then voluntarily dismissed the claim, but not until after Chemco had spent thousands of dollars on its own experts. Any concerns for Martyn & Fox?

Consider: Model Rules 3.1, 3.4
Federal Rule of Civil Procedure 11

Christian v. Mattel, Inc.
286 F.3d 1118 (9th Cir. 2002)

McKeown, Circuit Judge:

It is difficult to imagine that the Barbie doll, so perfect in her sculpture and presentation, and so comfortable in every setting, from "California girl" to "Chief Executive Officer Barbie," could spawn such acrimonious litigation and such egregious conduct on the part of her challenger. In her wildest dreams, Barbie could not have imagined herself in the middle of Rule 11 proceedings. But the intersection of copyrights on Barbie sculptures and the scope of Rule 11 is precisely what defines this case.

James Hicks appeals from a district court order requiring him, pursuant to Federal Rule of Civil Procedure 11, to pay Mattel, Inc. $501,565 in attorneys' fees that it incurred in defending against what the district court determined to be a frivolous action. Hicks brought suit on behalf of Harry Christian, claiming that Mattel's Barbie dolls infringed Christian's Claudene doll sculpture copyright. In its sanctions orders, the district court found that Hicks should have discovered prior to commencing the civil action that Mattel's dolls could not have infringed Christian's copyright because, among other things, the Mattel dolls had been created well prior to the Claudene doll and the Mattel dolls had clearly visible copyright notices on their heads. After determining that Hicks had behaved "boorishly" during discovery and had a lengthy rap sheet of prior litigation misconduct, the district court imposed sanctions.

We hold that the district court did not abuse its discretion in determining that the complaint filed by Hicks was frivolous under Rule 11. In parsing the language of the district court's sanctions orders, however, we cannot determine with any degree of certainty whether the district court grounded its Rule 11 decision on Hicks' misconduct that occurred outside the pleadings, such as in oral argument, at a meeting of counsel, and at a key deposition. This is an important distinction because Rule 11 sanctions are limited to misconduct regarding signed pleadings, motions, and other filings. Consequently, we vacate the district court's orders and remand for further proceedings consistent with this opinion. In so doing, we do not condone Hicks' conduct or suggest that the district court did not have a firm basis for awarding sanctions. Indeed, the district court undertook a careful and exhaustive examination of the facts and the legal underpinnings of the copyright challenge. Rather, the remand is to assure that any Rule 11 sanctions are grounded in conduct covered by Rule 11 and to ensure adequate findings for the sizeable fee award.

BACKGROUND

I. Prior Litigation Between Mattel and CDC

Mattel is a toy company that is perhaps best recognized as the manufacturer of the world-famous Barbie doll. Since Barbie's creation in 1959, Mattel has outfitted her in fashions and accessories that have evolved over time. In perhaps the most classic embodiment, Barbie is depicted as a slender-figured doll with long blonde hair and blue eyes. Mattel has sought to protect its intellectual property by registering various Barbie-related copyrights, including copyrights protecting the doll's head sculpture. Mattel has vigorously litigated against putative infringers.

In 1990, Claudene Christian, then an undergraduate student at the University of Southern California ("USC"), decided to create and market a collegiate cheerleader doll. The doll, which the parties refer to throughout their papers as "Claudene," had blonde hair and blue eyes and was outfitted to resemble a USC cheerleader.

Mattel soon learned about the Claudene doll . . . [and] commenced a federal court action in 1997 in which it . . . alleged that CDC infringed various of

Mattel's copyrights. At the time, Claudene Christian was president of CDC and Harry Christian was listed as co-founder of the company and chief financial officer. CDC retained Hicks as its counsel. After the court dismissed CDC's multiple counter-claims, the case was settled. Mattel released CDC from any copyright infringement liability in exchange for, among other things, a stipulation that Mattel was free to challenge CDC's alleged copyright of the Claudene doll should CDC "or any successor in interest" challenge Mattel's right to market its Barbie dolls.

II. The Present Action

Seizing on a loophole in the parties' settlement agreement, within weeks of the agreement, Harry Christian, who was not a signatory to the agreement, retained Hicks as his counsel and filed a federal court action against Mattel. In the complaint, which Hicks signed, Christian alleged that Mattel obtained a copy of the copyrighted Claudene doll in 1996, the year of its creation, and then infringed its overall appearance, including its face paint, by developing a new Barbie line called "Cool Blue" that was substantially similar to Claudene. Christian sought damages in the amount of $2.4 billion and various forms of injunctive relief. In an apparent effort to demonstrate that the action was not a sham, Claudene Christian and CDC were also named as defendants. . . .

Two months after the complaint was filed, Mattel moved for summary judgment. In support of its motion, Mattel proffered evidence that the Cool Blue Barbie doll contained a 1991 copyright notice on the back of its head, indicating that it predated Claudene's head sculpture copyright by approximately six years. Mattel therefore argued that Cool Blue Barbie could not as a matter of law infringe Claudene's head sculpture copyright. . . .

At a follow-up counsel meeting required by a local rule, Mattel's counsel attempted to convince Hicks that his complaint was frivolous. During the videotaped meeting, they presented Hicks with copies of various Barbie dolls that not only had been created prior to 1996 (the date of Claudene's creation), but also had copyright designations on their heads that pre-dated Claudene's creation. Additionally, Mattel's counsel noted that the face paint on some of the earlier-created Barbie dolls was virtually identical to that used on Claudene. Hicks declined Mattel's invitation to inspect the dolls and, later during the meeting, hurled them in disgust from a conference table.

Having been unsuccessful in convincing Hicks to dismiss Christian's action voluntarily, Mattel served Hicks with a motion for Rule 11 sanctions. In its motion papers, Mattel argued, among other things, that Hicks had signed and filed a frivolous complaint based on a legally meritless theory that Mattel's prior-created head sculptures infringed Claudene's 1997 copyright. Hicks declined to withdraw the complaint during the 21-day safe harbor period provided by Rule 11, and Mattel filed its motion.

Seemingly unfazed by Mattel's Rule 11 motion, Hicks proceeded with the litigation and filed a motion pursuant to Federal Rule of Civil Procedure 56(f) to obtain additional discovery. . . . The district court summarily denied the motion. . . .

Hicks then began filing additional papers that were characterized by frequency and volume. Following official completion of the summary judgment briefing schedule, Hicks filed what was styled as a "supplemental opposition." In those papers, Christian asserted for the first time that the head sculpture of Mattel's CEO Barbie (which was created in 1998) infringed Christian's copyright in the Claudene doll. He did not, however, move for leave to amend the complaint.

Hicks later filed additional papers alleging that several additional Barbie dolls infringed the Claudene sculpture. . . . [N]o motion for leave to amend the complaint was filed. . . .

III. The District Court's Orders

The district court granted Mattel's motions for summary judgment and Rule 11 sanctions. The court ruled that Mattel did not infringe the 1997 Claudene copyright because it could not possibly have accessed the Claudene doll at the time it created the head sculptures of the Cool Blue (copyrighted in 1991). . . .

Having rejected Hicks' reasons for eschewing a fees award, the district court made the following observations and findings:

> The court has considered whether an award of monetary sanctions less than the fees actually incurred would represent an appropriate sanction. The court has concluded that it would not. There is no dispute that Mr. Hicks was directly responsible for filing and pursuing this frivolous suit. Nor is there any dispute that the fees sought were actually incurred and paid. *Moreover, the court is satisfied from the documentation provided by Mattel's counsel that the fees incurred were reasonable.* While recognizing the significant burden this award imposes, the court has concluded that in light of Mr. Hicks' failure to respond to lesser sanctions and his continuing disregard for the most basic rules governing an attorney's professional conduct, the costs of his unacceptable behavior should fall squarely on him. Finally, while the court may reimburse an adverse party for expenses incurred in disposing of frivolous litigation, it can never compensate the judicial system for the time spent to dispose of an action that should never have been brought. The court can only hope that a sanction of this size will, at last, put a stop to Mr. Hicks' continuing pattern of abuse. Emphasis added. . . .

The court is satisfied that the other attorneys' fees Mattel has claimed are both reasonable and proximately caused by Mr. Hicks' pursuit of this frivolous action. [T]he Court *grants* Mattel its attorneys' fees in the amount of $501,565.00.

DISCUSSION . . .

II. Imposition of Rule 11 Sanctions . . .

A. *General Rule 11 Principles*

Filing a complaint in federal court is no trifling undertaking. An attorney's signature on a complaint is tantamount to a warranty that the complaint is well grounded in fact and "existing law" (or proposes a good faith extension of the existing law) and that it is not filed for an improper purpose.

Rule 11 provides in pertinent part:

(a) Signature. Every pleading, written motion, and other paper shall be signed by at least one attorney of record in the attorney's individual name. . . .

(b) Representations to Court. By presenting to the court (whether by signing, filing, submitting, or later advocating) a pleading, written motion, or other paper, an attorney or unrepresented party is certifying to the best of the person's knowledge, information, and belief, formed after an inquiry reasonable under the circumstances . . .

(2) the claims, defenses, and other legal contentions therein are warranted by existing law or by a nonfrivolous argument for the extension, modification, or reversal of existing law or the establishment of new law;

(3) the allegations and other factual contentions have evidentiary support or, if specifically so identified, are likely to have evidentiary support after a reasonable opportunity for further investigation or discovery[.]

The attorney has a duty prior to filing a complaint not only to conduct a reasonable factual investigation, but also to perform adequate legal research that confirms whether the theoretical underpinnings of the complaint are "warranted by existing law or a good faith argument for an extension, modification or reversal of existing law." Golden Eagle Distrib. Corp. v. Burroughs Corp., 801 F.2d 1531, 1537 (9th Cir. 1986). One of the fundamental purposes of Rule 11 is to "reduce frivolous claims, defenses or motions and to deter costly meritless maneuvers, . . . [thereby] avoiding delay and unnecessary expense in litigation." Nonetheless, a finding of significant delay or expense is not required under Rule 11. Where, as here, the complaint is the primary focus of Rule 11 proceedings, a district court must conduct a two-prong inquiry to determine (1) whether the complaint is legally or factually "baseless" from an objective perspective, and (2) if the attorney has conducted "a reasonable and competent inquiry" before signing and filing it.

B. The District Court's Findings Regarding the Meritless Claim

1. Did Hicks Have an Adequate Legal or Factual Basis for Filing the Complaint?

Hicks filed a single claim of copyright infringement against Mattel. The complaint charges that the Cool Blue Barbie infringed the copyright in the Claudene doll head. . . . Hicks cannot seriously dispute the district court's conclusions that, assuming the applicability of the doctrine of prior creation, Christian's complaint was legally and factually frivolous.

Indeed, as a matter of copyright law, it is well established that a prior-created work cannot infringe a later-created one. *See* Grubb v. KMS Patriots, L.P., 88 F.3d 1, 5 (1st Cir. 1996) (noting that "prior creation renders any conclusion of access or inference of copying illogical").

Copyright infringement requires proof that a plaintiff owns a valid copyright in the work and that the defendant copied the work. . . . By simple logic, it is impossible to copy something that does not exist. Thus, if Mattel created its doll sculptures before CDC created Claudene in 1994, it is factually and legally impossible for Mattel to be an infringer.

The record of creation is telling and conclusive. The Cool Blue Barbie doll uses the Neptune's Daughter doll head which was created in 1991, some six years before the Claudene doll. . . . Hicks should have been well aware of the prior creation, not to mention that the copyright notice (including date of creation) appears prominently on the back of the dolls' heads. . . .

Consequently, in the face of undisputed evidence concerning the prior creation of the Barbie dolls, the district court did not abuse its discretion by ruling that the complaint was frivolous.

2. Did Hicks Conduct an Adequate Factual Investigation?

The district court concluded that Hicks "filed a case without factual foundation." Hicks, having argued unsuccessfully that his failure to perform even minimal due diligence was irrelevant as a matter of copyright law, does not contest that he would have been able to discover the copyright information simply by examining the doll heads. Instead he argues that the district court did not understand certain "complex" issues. Simply saying so does not make it so. The district court well understood the legal and factual background of the case. It was Hicks' absence of investigation, not the district court's absence of analysis, that brought about his downfall.

The district court did not abuse its discretion in concluding that Hicks' failure to investigate fell below the requisite standard established by Rule 11.

III. The District Court's Additional Findings Regarding Misconduct

Hicks argues that even if the district court were justified in sanctioning him under Rule 11 based on Christian's complaint and the follow-on motions, its conclusion was tainted because it impermissibly considered other misconduct that cannot be sanctioned under Rule 11, such as discovery abuses, misstatements made during oral argument, and conduct in other litigation.

Hicks' argument has merit. While Rule 11 permits the district court to sanction an attorney for conduct regarding "pleadings, written motions, and other papers" that have been signed and filed in a given case, Fed. R. Civ. P. 11(a), it does not authorize sanctions for, among other things, discovery abuses or misstatements made to the court during an oral presentation. . . .

In its January 5, 2000, order, the district court cited multiple bases for its Rule 11 findings. . . .

In connection with the conclusion on boorish behavior, the court cited Hicks' conduct ("tossing Barbie dolls off a table") at a meeting of counsel and his interruption of a deposition following a damaging admission by his client. The charge of misrepresentation of facts was based on a statement made at oral argument that he had never seen a particular catalogue while a videotape of exhibit inspections showed him" leisurely thumbing through the catalogue." Hicks' conflicting representations in pleadings as to the identity of allegedly infringing Barbie dolls was an additional example of misrepresentation noted by the court. Finally, the court determined that Hicks made misrepresentations in his briefs concerning the law of joint authorship in the copyright context. . . .

The laundry list of Hicks' outlandish conduct is a long one and raises serious questions as to his respect for the judicial process. Nonetheless, Rule 11 sanctions are limited to "papers" signed in violation of the rule. Conduct in depositions, discovery meetings of counsel, oral representations at hearings, and behavior in prior proceedings do not fall within the ambit of Rule 11. Because we do not know for certain whether the district court granted Mattel's Rule 11 motion as a result of an impermissible intertwining of its conclusion about the complaint's frivolity and Hicks' extrinsic misconduct, we must vacate the district court's Rule 11 orders.

We decline Mattel's suggestion that the district court's sanctions orders could be supported in their entirety under the court's inherent authority. To impose sanctions under its inherent authority, the district court must "make an explicit finding [which it did not do here] that counsel's conduct constituted or was tantamount to bad faith." We acknowledge that the district court has a broad array of sanctions options at its disposal: Rule 11, 28 U.S.C. § 1927,[11] and the court's inherent authority. Each of these sanctions alternatives has its own particular requirements, and it is important that the grounds be separately articulated to assure that the conduct at issue falls within the scope of the sanctions remedy. . . . On remand, the district court will have an opportunity to delineate the factual and legal basis for its sanctions orders.

IV. The District Court's Decision to Award Attorneys' Fees

Hicks raises various challenges to the quantum of attorneys' fees. Because we are vacating the district court's Rule 11 orders on other legal grounds, we express no opinion at this stage about the particular reasonableness of any of the fees the district court elected to award Mattel. We do, however, encourage the district court on remand to ensure that the time spent by Mattel's attorneys was reasonably and appropriately spent in relation to both the patent frivolousness of Christian's complaint and the services directly caused by the sanctionable conduct.[12] See Fed. R. Civ. P. 11, advisory committee notes, 1993 Amendments, Subdivisions (b) and (c) (noting that attorneys' fees may only be awarded under Rule 11 for those "services directly and unavoidably caused" by the sanctionable conduct).

---

11. Section 1927 provides for imposition of "excess costs, expenses, and attorneys' fees" on counsel who "multiplies the proceedings in any case unreasonably and vexatiously."

12. For example, because the action was frivolous on its face, why would Mattel's attorneys need to spend 700 hours ($173,151.50 in fees) for the summary judgment motion and response? Although Hicks clearly complicated the proceedings through multiple filings, Mattel's theory and approach was stunningly simple and required little explication: (1) Mattel's Barbie dolls and face paint were prior copyright creations that could not infringe the after-created Claudene doll and (2) Christian was neither a contributor to nor owner of the copyright. This is not to say that Hicks' defense of the motion necessarily called for a timid response, but neither does it compel a bazooka approach.

Conclusion

We vacate the district court's Rule 11 orders and remand for further proceedings consistent with this opinion. . . .

C. Discovery Abuse

Problem

14-4. In a product liability case, an associate at Martyn & Fox notes that the client cannot produce certain damaging documents brought to her attention by the head of the lab because they have been destroyed pursuant to the client company's routine document retention procedures that were drafted by Martyn & Fox. Fox replies, "Well, I'm very pleased to learn that our client will now prevail."

Consider: Model Rules 3.2, 3.4, 5.2
Federal Rules of Civil Procedure 26, 37

Surowiec v. Capital Title Agency, Inc.
790 F. Supp. 2d 997 (D. Ariz 2011)

David G. CAMPBELL, United States District Judge. . . .

In November 2006, Plaintiff James Surowiec purchased a condominium unit located in Scottsdale, Arizona from developer Shamrock Glen, LLC. Scott Romley, an employee with Capital Title Agency, Inc. ("Capital"), served as escrow agent for the transaction. Plaintiff alleges, among other things, that Romley failed to disclose before closing that the property would remain encumbered by deeds of trusts held by certain investors in the Shamrock Glen development. Plaintiff claims that those junior liens and related foreclosure actions brought by the investors have prevented him from selling the condominium, resulting in financial loss. . . .

For the reasons that follow, . . . the Court will grant in part . . . [plaintiff's] motions for sanctions.

IV. Spoliation of Evidence.

"The failure to preserve electronic or other records, once the duty to do so has been triggered, raises the issue of spoliation of evidence and its consequences." Thompson v. U.S. Dep't of Housing & Urban Dev., 219 F.R.D. 93, 100 (D. Md. 2003). Spoliation is the destruction or material alteration of evidence, or the failure to otherwise preserve evidence, for another's use in litigation. *See* Ashton v. Knight Transp., Inc., 772 F. Supp. 2d 772 (N.D. Tex. 2011). Plaintiff seeks various sanctions against Defendants for spoliation of emails and other electronic records concerning, among other things, Romley's involvement with title and escrow problems in the sale of Shamrock Glen properties.

"A party seeking sanctions for spoliation of evidence must prove the following elements: (1) the party having control over the evidence had an obligation to preserve it when it was destroyed or altered; (2) the destruction or loss was accompanied by a 'culpable state of mind;' and (3) the evidence that was destroyed or altered was 'relevant' to the claims or defenses of the party that sought the discovery of the spoliated evidence[.]" Goodman v. Praxair Servs., Inc., 632 F. Supp. 2d 494, 509 (D. Md. 2009) (quoting *Thompson,* 219 F.R.D. at 101); *see* In re Napster Copyright Litig., 462 F. Supp. 2d 1060, 1070-78 (N.D. Cal. 2006); Zublake v. UBS Warburg LLC ("*Zublake IV*"), 220 F.R.D. 212, 216 (S.D.N.Y. 2003). . . .

A. Duty to Preserve – The Trigger Date.

It is well established that the "duty to preserve arises when a party knows or should know that certain evidence is relevant to pending or future litigation." *Ashton,* at 800. Stated differently, the duty to preserve is triggered "not only during litigation, but also extends to the period before litigation when a party should reasonably know that evidence may be relevant to anticipated litigation." Morford v. Wal-Mart Stores, Inc., 2011 U.S. Dist. LEXIS 21039 (D. Nev.); *see Zublake IV,* 220 F.R.D. at 216.

Capital was on notice of reasonably foreseeable litigation concerning title and escrow deficiencies in the sale of Shamrock Glen properties, as well as Romley's direct involvement in those deficiencies, no later than April 28, 2007, when an attorney for Shamrock Glen sent a letter to Capital's in-house counsel, Lawrence Phelps. The letter explained that in response to inquiries from homeowners about outstanding liens on their properties, Shamrock Glen investigated the matter and was surprised to learn that while there had been more than twenty units sold, Capital had recorded only four releases from the investors. The threat of future litigation was clear: the letter informed Phelps that some investors "have sought independent legal advice and are anticipated to claim approximately two million dollars in damages," warned that Capital "faces significant potential exposure" in the matter, requested that Phelps provide Shamrock Glen with a copy of Capital's title insurance policy for the property, and advised that it may be prudent for him to provide the insurer with "written notification of these *anticipated claims.*"

The likelihood of litigation was underscored by other related events. Romley sought legal advice with respect to his involvement in Shamrock Glen in December of 2006 or January of 2007, and apparently sought it from Phelps. Phelps testified that by February 1, 2007, he knew litigation was "certainly possible." On April 30, 2007, an email sent to Romley and copied to Phelps asserted, in bold and underscored language, that "[t]his matter must get cleared up immediately or I can assure you that litigation is imminent." . . .

But the duty to preserve evidence "is a duty owed to the *court,* not to the party's potential adversary[.]" *Ashton* at 800 (citing *Victor Stanley II,* 269 F.R.D. at 525-26). . . .

Where a "letter openly threatens litigation, then the recipient is on notice that litigation is reasonably foreseeable and the duty to preserve evidence relevant to that dispute is triggered." *Goodman,* 632 F. Supp. 2d at 511. "'The preservation obligation runs first to counsel, who has 'a duty to advise his client of the type of information potentially relevant to the lawsuit and of the necessity of preventing its destruction.'" *See* Richard Green (Fine Paintings) v. McClendon, 262 F.R.D. 284, 290 (S.D.N.Y. 2009).

When Mr. Phelps, as in-house counsel for Capital, received the April 28, 2007 letter, he was "obligated to suspend [Capital's] document retention/ destruction policy and implement a 'litigation hold' to ensure the preservation of relevant documents." *Goodman,* 632 F. Supp. 2d at 511 (quoting *Thompson,* 219 F.R.D. at 100). He did not. Mr. Phelps testified that he issued no litigation hold and did not otherwise takes steps to suspend Capital's routine destruction of emails more than 30 days old. Nor did he seek to preserve the emails then existing on Mr. Romley's computer. . . .

Once a party knows that litigation is reasonably anticipated, the party owes a duty to the judicial system to ensure preservation of relevant evidence.

B. Culpability.

"Courts have not been uniform in defining the level of culpability—be it negligence, gross negligence, willfulness, or bad faith—that is required before sanctions are appropriate[.]" *Ashton,* 2011 U.S. Dist. LEXIS 17569. Nor is there consensus as to how the level of culpability is to be determined, or what prejudice, if any, may be presumed from culpable conduct. At least one court has concluded that, once the duty to preserve is triggered, the failure to issue a written litigation hold constitutes gross negligence per se and prejudice may be presumed "because that failure is likely to result in the destruction of relevant information." Pension Committee of Univ. of Montreal Pension Plan v. Banc of America Sec. ("*Pension Committee*"), 685 F. Supp. 2d 456, 465 (S.D.N.Y. 2010). Other courts have found the failure to implement a litigation hold to be an important factor in determining culpability, but not per se evidence of culpable conduct giving rise to a presumption of relevance and prejudice. *See, e.g., Victor Stanley II,* 269 F.R.D. at 524, 529-31 (discussing how courts differ in the fault they assign where a party fails to implement a litigation hold).

The Court disagrees with *Pension Committee*'s holding that a failure to issue a litigation hold constitutes gross negligence per se. Per se rules are too inflexible for this factually complex area of the law where a wide variety of circumstances may lead to spoliation accusations. An allegedly spoliating party's culpability must be determined case-by-case.

In this case, Capital has provided no reasonable explanation for its failure to preserve. It does not claim that the April 28 letter was overlooked or misunderstood, that preservation was not feasible, or that it undertook some preservation efforts and innocently failed to take others. . . . Capital's complete failure to suspend its ongoing destruction of emails and to capture the evidence on

Mr. Romley's computer was more than negligent. The Court finds it constituted gross negligence.

C. Scope of the Duty to Preserve—Relevant Evidence.

Some courts have concluded that the scope of the duty to preserve is coextensive with disclosure obligations and available discovery under Rule 26 of the Federal Rules of Civil Procedure. *See, e.g., Zublake IV,* 220 F.R.D. at 217-18. The Court need not determine the outer contours of the duty in this case. Whatever those outer boundaries, they clearly encompassed ongoing emails to and from Romley and information on Romley's computer. *See Zublake IV,* 220 F.R.D. at 218 (duty to preserve certainly extends to "key players").

In Rimkus Consulting Group, Inc. v. Cammarata, 688 F. Supp. 2d 598 (S.D. Tex. 2010), the court declined to follow the approach taken in *Pension Committee* of presuming relevance and prejudice when the spoliating party is grossly negligent, noting that requiring "a showing that the lost information is relevant and prejudicial is an important check on spoliation allegations and sanctions motions." 688 F. Supp. 2d at 616-17. *Rimkus* also made clear, however, that when "the evidence in the case as a whole would allow a reasonable fact finder to conclude that the missing evidence would have helped the requesting party support its claims or defenses, that may be a sufficient showing of both relevance and prejudice to make [sanctions] appropriate." *Id.* at 617. The Court has no doubt that this standard is satisfied here. . . .

[T]he facts and evidence in this case, . . . when considered as a whole and in light of Plaintiff's claims, permits the reasonable inference that Capital's failure to put a litigation hold in place resulted in the loss of relevant evidence. As of April 2007, Capital routinely deleted electronic records pursuant to its 30-day retention policy. Although Capital asserts that it began preserving all emails as a matter of course in October of 2007, its failure to stop email destruction in April of 2007 resulted in the loss of emails between March and September of 2007, not to mention older emails on Romley's computer. The year 2007 was a period of intense communication and negotiation concerning the Shamrock Glen problem, and the Court has no doubt that preserving emails exchanged in March through September of that year would have provided valuable information to Plaintiff. Similarly, acting in April of 2007 to preserve the older emails then on Romley's computer surely would have preserved valuable evidence for Plaintiff. One example is the February 1, 2007 email that managed to survive and provided very helpful evidence to Plaintiff. Plaintiff has shown relevance and prejudice.

D. Appropriate Sanction.

Because spoliation is considered an abuse of the judicial process, courts may impose sanctions "as part of their inherent power to 'manage their own affairs so as to achieve the orderly and expeditious disposition of cases.'" *Morford,* 2011 U.S. Dist. LEXIS 21039 (quoting *Napster,* 462 F. Supp. 2d at 1066). Courts in this

Circuit have suggested that a "finding of fault or simple negligence is a sufficient basis on which a [c]ourt can impose sanctions against a party that has destroyed documents." Melendres v. Arpaio, 2010 U.S. Dist. LEXIS 20311 (D. Ariz. Feb. 12, 2010) (citing Unigard Sec. Ins. Co. v. Lakewood Eng'g & Mfr'g Corp., 982 F.2d 363, 369 n.2 (9th Cir. 1992)). The Court need not determine whether sanctions may be imposed for mere negligence given the finding of gross negligence on the part of Capital. "Sanctions that a federal court may impose for spoliation include assessing attorney's fees and costs, giving the jury an adverse inference instruction, precluding evidence, or imposing the harsh, case-dispositive sanctions of dismissal or judgment." *Victor Stanley II,* 269 F.R.D. at 533. While the court has discretion to impose spoliation sanctions, it "must determine which sanction best (1) deters parties from future spoliation, (2) places the risk of an erroneous judgment on the spoliating party, and (3) restores the innocent party to their rightful litigation position." *Ashton,* 2011 U.S. Dist. LEXIS 17569, (citing *Victor Stanley II,* 269 F.R.D. at 533-34).

Plaintiff primarily seeks the entry of a default judgment against Defendants. Plaintiff alternatively seeks a sanction of preclusion but does not identify what evidence should be precluded. This Circuit has established a five-part test to determine whether a terminating sanction is just: "'(1) the public's interest in expeditious resolution of litigation; (2) the court's need to manage its dockets; (3) the risk of prejudice to the party seeking sanctions; (4) the public policy favoring disposition of cases on their merits; and (5) the availability of less drastic sanctions.'" Valley Eng'rs Inc. v. Elec. Eng'g Co., 158 F.3d 1051, 1057 (9th Cir. 1998) (citation omitted).

The first two factors favor a default judgment. Because the Court and the public have a strong interest in judicial efficiency and the prompt resolution of litigation, Capital's failure to preserve evidence, and the resulting delay caused by multiple discovery disputes and the instant motion for sanctions, weigh in favor of default judgment. The fourth factor, as always, weighs against a terminating sanction. The fifth factor also weighs against a case-dispositive sanction as the lesser sanction of an adverse inference instruction is available. The third factor—prejudice—"looks to whether the spoliating party's actions impaired the non-spoliating party's ability to go to trial or threatened to interfere with the rightful decision of the case." *Leon,* 464 F.3d at 959. While it is apparent that Plaintiff has been prejudiced by the spoliation of emails and other communications concerning Romley's involvement with the Shamrock Glen development, the Court cannot conclude that the spoliation will force Plaintiff to rely on "'incomplete and spotty'" evidence at trial. Applying the five-factor test, the Court finds entry of default judgment to be unwarranted. *See Goodman,* 632 F. Supp. 2d at 519 (finding terminating sanction inappropriate where the spoliating party did not act in bad faith); *Napster,* 462 F. Supp. 2d at 1078 (the court should "impose the 'least onerous sanction' given the extent of the offending party's fault and the prejudice to the opposing party").

Alternatively, Plaintiff seeks an adverse inference jury instruction. "When a party is prejudiced, but not irreparably, from the loss of evidence that was destroyed with a high degree of culpability, a harsh but less extreme sanction than dismissal or default is to permit the fact finder to presume that the destroyed evidence was prejudicial." *Rimkus,* 688 F. Supp. 2d at 618. The Court finds an adverse inference instruction to be warranted in this case. The parties shall submit proposed adverse inference instructions with the other jury instructions to be filed before trial.

Plaintiff's motion for sanctions for spoliation of evidence will be denied with respect to the requests for default judgment or preclusion, but granted as to the request for an adverse inference instruction.

V. Plaintiff's Motion for Sanctions Under Rule 37 and Inherent Powers.

Plaintiff seeks sanctions for alleged discovery abuses on the part of Capital under Rule 37 and the Court's inherent powers. According to Plaintiff, Capital has acted in bad faith by misrepresenting that document searches were ongoing and electronic data was lost during data migration, by using only literal search terms and thereby ensuring that no documents would be found, and by identifying no specific responsive document in a "last minute data dump." Plaintiff seeks severe sanctions, including an *in camera* examination of Mr. Phelps' conduct for disciplinary purposes, an order striking Defendants' expert witness report and testimony, and an order declaring that all privilege claims have been waived. Plaintiff also seeks monetary sanctions, including attorneys' fees and costs. The Court finds that monetary sanctions are warranted.

"Because of their very potency, inherent powers must be exercised with restraint and discretion." Chambers v. NASCO, Inc., 501 U.S. 32, 44, (1991). The imposition of sanctions under a federal court's inherent powers is warranted where a party has acted in bad faith, that is, "vexatiously, wantonly, or for oppressive reasons." *Id.* at 45-46. Rule 37 sanctions are appropriate only where the discovery violation is "due to willfulness, bad faith, or fault of the party." Fair Housing of Marin v. Combs, 285 F.3d 899, 905 (9th Cir. 2002).

The Court . . . finds that Capital acted willfully in connection with its response (or lack thereof) to Plaintiff's initial request for production of documents served in February 2010. Those requests sought all emails from Romley regarding the failure to follow title commitment instructions and all communications of Romley, from the date Capital began serving as the title agency for Shamrock Glen until the date of Romley's termination, including written correspondence and emails directed to the investor lienholders or otherwise pertaining to the Shamrock Glen development. Capital responded in March 2010 by asserting boilerplate objections and producing no documents.

Plaintiff's requests specifically sought communications of Romley pertaining to the Shamrock Glen development, but the search parameters designed by Mr. Phelps included only Plaintiff's name and escrow number—"James M. Surowiec" and "20060669." Those terms were not calculated to capture communications to or from Romley as sought in the document request. Not surprisingly, they produced "zero results."

The Court ordered a new search in August 2010, which resulted in the production of more than 4,000 documents. This substantial production was made only three days before the close of discovery, and required a second-round of depositions of Defendant Romley, Mr. Phelps, and Mr. Brightly.

"Selection of the appropriate search and information retrieval technique requires careful advance planning by persons qualified to design effective search methodology," and the "implementation and methodology selected should be tested for quality assurance[.]" Victor Stanley, Inc. v. Creative Pipe, Inc., 250 F.R.D. 251, 262 (D. Md. 2008). Capital's unreasonably narrow search for documents using only Plaintiff's name and escrow number, and its assertion of unfounded boilerplate objections to document requests 3, 4, and 5, are inexcusable. Given that thousands of responsive documents were discovered once a proper search was performed, and in light of the late production of those documents, the Court concludes that Capital acted willfully in failing timely and adequately to respond to the document requests.

District courts are given "particularly wide latitude" to issue Rule 37 sanctions. Similarly, pursuant the inherent power to control their dockets, district courts have discretion to impose a variety of sanctions for discovery abuses. The Court concludes that Capital's conduct warrants an award of monetary sanctions, but no harsher sanction.

Plaintiff requests an award of attorneys' fees and costs incurred as a result of Capital's misconduct. Under Rule 37(d)(3), an offending party may be ordered to pay the other party's "reasonable expenses" caused by the discovery abuse. With respect to pro se litigants, including those that are licensed attorneys, the general rule is that attorneys' fees are not a payable "expense" under Rule 37 "as there is no direct financial cost or charge associated with the expenditure of one's own time." Pickholtz v. Rainbow Techs., Inc., 284 F.3d 1365, 1375 (Fed. Cir. 2002). The "reasonable expenses" awardable under Rule 37 do include, however, "actual costs incurred as a result of misconduct[.]" *Fosselman*, 2010 U.S. Dist. LEXIS 47137.

"Fees to pro se litigants are awardable under the court's inherent power." Jacobs v. Scribner, 2011 U.S. Dist. LEXIS 4297 (E.D. Cal. Jan. 12, 2011). A rule to the contrary "would place a pro se litigant at the mercy of an opponent who might engage in otherwise sanctionable conduct." *Pickholtz*, 284 F.3d at 1375.

As a sanction for Capital's discovery abuses, the Court, pursuant to Rule 37 and its inherent powers, will require Capital to (1) reimburse the actual expenses Plaintiff incurred as a result of the misconduct, including the expense for the second-round of depositions, and (2) pay reasonable attorneys' fees to compensate Plaintiff for the time he spent challenging the misconduct, preparing for and taking the additional depositions, and bringing the instant motion.

The parties are directed to confer in good faith to resolve any disputes concerning the amount of reasonable expenses and fees. If the parties are unable to agree, Plaintiff may file a motion pursuant to Local Rule 54.2.

D. Bias

Problem

14-5. Martyn is furious with opposing counsel, who happens to be one of the most highly regarded male lawyers in town. In the course of a recent deposition, this lawyer referred to Martyn as "office help," repeatedly called her "sweetheart," and "dear," and raised his voice to drown her out, requiring Martyn to stop talking until he was finished and then inquire if she could be heard. What do you advise?

Consider: Model Rules 4.4, 8.4
Model Code of Judicial Conduct Rule 2.3

In re Charges of Unprofessional Conduct
Contained in Panel Case No. 15976
653 N.W.2d 452 (Minn. 2002)

PER CURIAM.

. . . Respondent's client sustained serious permanent physical injuries that disabled him when a school bus hit and ran over him with a rear tire while he was riding a bicycle in South Minneapolis. The accident crushed his pelvis, and left him in a coma for approximately 1 month. By the time of trial, the client was able to walk with the assistance of a cane. Before the accident, the client was employed as a checker and bagger at a grocery store and as a greeter at a restaurant. His employment background consisted of similar unskilled and physical labor positions. At trial, the client asserted that his permanent injuries prevented him from performing physical-labor-type jobs and that he did not qualify educationally or intellectually for other types of employment. Therefore, he sought damages for future loss of wages and future diminished earning capacity.

[Judge Franklin J. Knoll, the complainant in this disciplinary proceeding,] presided over the personal-injury action and assigned one of his two law clerks to assist with the action. The clerk assigned by complainant to assist in this case is physically disabled. He is paralyzed from his mouth down and has difficulty breathing and speaking. He performed his duties as a law clerk with the assistance of a large wheelchair, respirator and full-time attendant. The disabled clerk was present in the courtroom at the outset of the personal-injury trial, assisted with jury selection, and remained in the courtroom throughout the trial.

On the first day of trial, respondent's client expressed reservations about his ability to receive a fair trial grounded on the fact that if the disabled law clerk continued to work in the courtroom, the jury would compare the clerk who was more severely disabled yet able to work, to himself, who was less severely disabled and claiming an inability to work. Later that same day respondent made an oral motion outside the presence of the jury, "for a mistrial and another panel of jurors without your law clerk present or in the alternative that this case be assigned to another judge." Respondent gave the following explanation for his motion:

I will be asking the jury to award future loss of wages, future diminished earning capacity. I do not believe a jury when they look at the comparison with your
law clerk, who's obviously gainfully employed, working in the courtroom under
great handicap and great duress, will be able to award anything to my client under
those circumstances.

Respondent stated that he brought the motion with "great reluctance" and
acknowledged that the motion was "outrageous and distasteful for the court."
He did not support his motion with any legal authority. Stating that the motion
was "un-American," complainant denied the motion.

The jury found in favor of the defendant on the issue of liability. Subsequently,
respondent brought a written motion for a new trial. Respondent asserted the
presence of the disabled clerk in the courtroom as one basis for the motion.
Respondent again stated that his objection to the clerk's presence in the courtroom was made with "the greatest reluctance," but he argued that the jury would
compare the disabilities of the law clerk with the injuries of his client. Again,
respondent failed to cite any legal authority in support of his position. . . .

In In re Panel File 98-26, 597 N.W.2d 563 (Minn. 1999), we issued an
admonition to a prosecutor for making a motion to exclude a public defender
from participating in a trial based solely on his race. After accepting a position
as a special assistant county attorney, the prosecutor was assigned to take over
the prosecution of an African-American male charged with two counts of felony
robbery of a Caucasian couple. The prosecutor previously assigned to the case
left a memorandum in the case file explaining that the public defender felt race
was an issue in the case and planned to recruit an African-American public
defender to try the case. Subsequently, the prosecutor brought a motion in limine requesting:

> An Order from this Court prohibiting counsel for the defendant to have a per-
> son of color as co-counsel for the sole purpose of playing upon the emotions of
> the jury.

Two workdays after filing the motion, the prosecutor realized the gravity of
her mistake, withdrew the motion, and apologized to both public defenders. She
also implemented measures to prevent reoccurrence of the misconduct. . . .

On review, we rejected the Panel's determination that the prosecutor's conduct was "non-serious" and unequivocally held that race-based misconduct is
inherently serious. Moreover, we emphasized that race-based misconduct committed by an officer of the court is especially destructive because it "undermine[s]
confidence in our system of justice [and] erode[s] the very foundation upon
which justice is based." . . .

. . . [W]e emphasized that race should never be used as a basis for limiting an
attorney's participation in a court proceeding. We extend this holding to encompass situations where disability is used to limit a court employee's participation
in a court proceeding. Neither race nor disability should be used as a means of
limiting participation in our courts. Minnesota has adopted legislation prohibiting discrimination against individuals with disabilities. *See* Minnesota Human

Rights Act (MHRA), Minn. Stat. §§363.01-363.20 (2000). The MHRA prohibits discrimination against individuals with disabilities in employment, housing, public accommodations, public services and education; the MHRA also prohibits race-based discrimination in these same areas. . . . Therefore, we conclude that the Panel's determination that respondent violated Rule 8.4(d) is not clearly erroneous. . . .

. . . A disabled court employee has a right to perform his job in the courtroom. But here we have the perceived rights of two disabled persons potentially in conflict with one another. Respondent's client also suffers from a disability. Respondent's client was concerned that the jury would compare the law clerk's more severe disability with his less severe disability and that comparison would unduly influence the jury to decide against him on his claims and deprive him of a fair trial. Ironically, the concern of respondent's client, as argued by respondent, was not that the law clerk's disability prevented him from capably performing his job, but that the law clerk's demonstrated capability would diminish the client's disability claim. Respondent's motion can be viewed as an inappropriate attempt to address the respective rights of two disabled persons, rather than elevating the rights of one over the rights of another. If respondent was concerned that the jury might make improper comparisons, respondent could have addressed those concerns during voir dire. Nonetheless, when viewed in context, we conclude that the Panel did not act arbitrarily, capriciously or unreasonably by finding that respondent's conduct in this particular situation was non-serious.

Any discriminatory effect from the motion was indirect because respondent did not exercise any authority or control over the disabled clerk. In contrast, the prosecutor in In re Panel File 98-26 misused the power of the state by interfering with a defendant's right to counsel in seeking to prevent the public defender from representing the defendant based solely on the public defender's race. Taking into consideration the unique circumstances of this case, we conclude that the Panel did not act arbitrarily, capriciously, or unreasonably by issuing an amended admonition to respondent. . . .

E. Communication with Unrepresented and Represented Clients and Nonclients

Problems

14-6.   Negotiations have been going on for months, with Martyn & Fox representing the Seller. Buyer's lawyer has been obstreperous, to say the least. Then Martyn receives a call from the potential buyer: "With my lawyer involved, we'll never reach agreement. Let's talk—just you and me. I don't need a lawyer." What if buyer announces, "I fired my lawyer"?

14-7.   Martyn & Fox's client is totally frustrated. "I'll bet our overly generous settlement offers are not even being passed on to the plaintiff by that shyster lawyer of his. Why don't you just call the plaintiff up yourself and tell him our latest?" What if the client simply asks us to write the lawyer on the other side, with a copy to the plaintiff? What if our client asks us to write a letter for the client to send to the plaintiff telling him that he is a fool not to settle? How about preparing a contract that the client can get the adversary to sign?

14-8.   Martyn & Fox's client has a petition for a variance pending. Client tells Fox, "I think if you meet with the Zoning Board chairman and explain our position, the hearing will go a lot better. That's what the Democratic committee person told me." What may Fox do?

14-9.   An Assistant U.S. Attorney gets a call from a defendant whose trial is now scheduled in six weeks. "I can't stand it," defendant exclaims, "That guy [from Martyn & Fox] the company hired to represent me couldn't care less about my case. All he wants is to make sure the company gets off scot-free. Can we talk? I'll meet you at Local Pub at 11:00 P.M. OK?"

14-10.   Martyn & Fox has been representing a corporate client in a Securities and Exchange Commission (SEC) investigation, a fact known to the SEC. One Saturday morning, Fox gets a panicked telephone call from our client's sales manager. The cause: this morning, Justice Department lawyers visited at least ten brokers, two secretaries, and an internal auditor employed by our client. What should Fox do?

14-11.   Can Martyn & Fox send a memorandum to all our client's corporate employees directing them not to talk to anyone from the Justice Department?

14-12.   The trial is a week away. Can Martyn visit with the other side's expert witness? How about a former officer of the party on the other side? What if the officer was separately represented at her deposition?

14-13.   Martyn & Fox's client, an activist vegetarian group, thinks that a national chain is using beef tallow in processing its French fries. They believe the only way to prove this is to get someone hired to work at the national chain's French fry processing center. They ask Martyn & Fox if we will get one of our paralegals to apply for employment at the plant. What should we say?

Consider: Model Rules 4.1, 4.2, 4.3, 5.3
RLGL §§ 99-103

Messing, Rudavsky & Weliky, P.C. v. President & Fellows of Harvard College

764 N.E.2d 825 (Mass. 2002)

COWIN, J.

The law firm of Messing, Rudavsky & Weliky, P.C. (MR&W), appeals from an order of the Superior Court sanctioning the firm for violation of Mass. R. Prof. C. 4.2 . . . [which] prohibits attorneys from communicating with a represented party in the absence of that party's attorney. This appeal raises the issue whether, and to what extent, the rule prohibits an attorney from speaking ex parte to the employees of an organization represented by counsel. . . .

. . . From the stipulated facts, we distill the following. In August of 1997, MR&W filed a complaint against President and Fellows of Harvard College (Harvard) with the Massachusetts Commission Against Discrimination (commission) on behalf of its client, Kathleen Stanford. Stanford, a sergeant with the Harvard University police department (HUPD), alleged that Harvard and its police chief, Francis Riley, discriminated against her on the basis of gender and in reprisal for earlier complaints of discrimination. MR&W represented Stanford, and Harvard was represented before the commission by in-house counsel, and thereafter by a Boston law firm. Following the institution of the suit, MR&W communicated ex parte with five employees of the HUPD: two lieutenants, two patrol officers, and a dispatcher. Although the two lieutenants had some supervisory authority over Stanford, it was not claimed that any of the five employees were involved in the alleged discrimination or retaliation against her or exercised management authority with respect to the alleged discriminatory or retaliatory acts.

In response to a motion by Harvard, the commission [and later, the Superior Court] ruled that MR&W's ex parte contacts with all five employees violated rule 4.2, [and] . . . prohibit[ed] MR&W from using the affidavits it had procured during the interviews, and award[ed] Harvard the attorney's fees and costs it had expended in litigating the motion, in a later order calculated as $94,418.14.[3]

. . . [R]ule [4.2.] has been justified generally as "preserving the mediating role of counsel on behalf of their clients . . . protecting clients from overreaching by counsel for adverse interests," and "protecting the attorney-client relationship."

. . . When the represented person is an individual, there is no difficulty determining when an attorney has violated the rule; the represented person is easily identifiable. In the case of an organization, however, identifying the protected class is more complicated.

Because an organization acts only through its employees, the rule must extend to some of these employees. However, most courts have rejected the position that the rule automatically prevents an attorney from speaking with all employees of a represented organization. . . .

According to comment [7] to rule 4.2, an attorney may not speak ex parte to three categories of employees: (1) "persons having managerial responsibility on behalf of the organization with regard to the subject of the representation"; (2) persons "whose act or omission in connection with that matter may be imputed to the organization for purposes of civil or criminal liability"; and (3) persons "whose statement may constitute an admission on the part of the organization."

---

3. Harvard claimed fees of $152,255.96. The judge reduced this amount after deducting fees incurred in the proceedings before the commission, and subtracting a portion of the billing rate as excessive.

. . . The [Superior Court] judge held that all five employees interviewed by MR&W were within the third category of the comment. He reached this result by concluding that the phrase "admission" in the comment refers to statements admissible in court under the admissions exception to the rule against hearsay. The Commonwealth's version of this rule . . . is identical to Fed. R. Evid. 801(d)(2)(D). Because the comment includes any employee whose statement may constitute an admission, this interpretation would prohibit an attorney from contacting any current employees of an organization to discuss any subject within the scope of their employment. This is, as the Superior Court judge admitted, a rule that is "strikingly protective of corporations regarding employee interviews." . . .

Some jurisdictions have adopted the broad reading of the rule endorsed by the judge in this case. *See, e.g.,* Weibrecht v. Southern Ill. Transfer, Inc., 241 F.3d 875 (7th Cir. 2001); Cole v. Appalachian Power Co., 903 F. Supp. 975 (S.D. W. Va. 1995); Brown v. St. Joseph County, 148 F.R.D. 246, 254 (N.D. Ind. 1993). Courts reaching this result do so because, like the Superior Court, they read the word "admission" in the third category of the comment as a reference to Fed. R. Evid. 801(d)(2)(D) and any corresponding State rule of evidence. This rule forbids contact with practically all employees because "virtually every employee may conceivably make admissions binding on his or her employer." . . .

At the other end of the spectrum, a small number of jurisdictions have interpreted the rule narrowly so as to allow an attorney for the opposing party to contact most employees of a represented organization. These courts construe the rule to restrict contact with only those employees in the organization's "control group," defined as those employees in the uppermost echelon of the organization's management. *See* Johnson v. Cadillac Plastic Group, Inc., 930 F. Supp. 1437, 1442 (D. Colo. 1996); Fair Automotive Repair, Inc. v. Car-X Serv. Sys., Inc., 471 N.E.2d 554 (Ill. App. 1984) (applying rule only to "top management persons who had the responsibility of making final decisions"); Wright v. Group Health Hosp., 691 P.2d 564 (Wash. 1984) (applying rule only to "those employees who have the legal authority to 'bind' the corporation in a legal evidentiary sense, i.e., those employees who have 'speaking authority' for the corporation").

Other jurisdictions have adopted yet a third test that, while allowing for some ex parte contacts with a represented organization's employees, still maintains some protection of the organization. The Court of Appeals of New York articulated such a rule in Niesig v. Team I, 558 N.E.2d 1030 (N.Y. 1990), rejecting an approach that ties the rule to Fed. R. Evid. 801(d)(2)(D). Instead, the court defined a represented person to include "employees whose acts or omissions in the matter under inquiry are binding on the corporation . . . or imputed to the corporation for purposes of its liability, or employees implementing the advice of counsel." Other jurisdictions have subsequently adopted the *Niesig* test. In addition, the Restatement (Third) of the Law Governing Lawyers [§ 100 comment e] endorses this rule.

. . . We adopt a test similar to that proposed in Niesig v. Team I, *supra.*

We . . . interpret the rule to ban contact only with those employees who have the authority to "commit the organization to a position regarding the subject matter of representation." Restatement (Third) of Law Governing Lawyers, at §100 comment e. *See also* Model Rule 4.2 cmt. [7] . . . .

This interpretation, when read in conjunction with the other two categories of the comment, would prohibit ex parte contact only with those employees who exercise managerial responsibility in the matter, who are alleged to have committed the wrongful acts at issue in the litigation, or who have authority on behalf of the corporation to make decisions about the course of the litigation. This result is substantially the same as the *Niesig* test because it "prohibits direct communication . . . 'with those officials . . . who have the legal power to bind the corporation in the matter or who are responsible for implementing the advice of the corporation's lawyer . . . or whose own interests are directly at stake in a representation.'"

Our test is consistent with the purposes of the rule, which are not to "protect a corporate party from the revelation of prejudicial facts," but to protect the attorney-client relationship and prevent clients from making ill-advised statements without the counsel of their attorney. . . .

While our interpretation of the rule may reduce the protection available to organizations provided by the attorney-client privilege, it allows a litigant to obtain more meaningful disclosure of the truth by conducting informal interviews with certain employees of an opposing organization. Our interpretation does not jeopardize legitimate organizational interests because it continues to disallow contacts with those members of the organization who are so closely tied with the organization or the events at issue that it would be unfair to interview them without the presence of the organization's counsel. Fairness to the organization does not require the presence of an attorney every time an employee may make a statement admissible in evidence against his or her employer. The public policy of promoting efficient discovery is better advanced by adopting a rule which favors the revelation of the truth by making it more difficult for an organization to prevent the disclosure of relevant evidence. . . .

Our decision may initially result in some increased litigation to define exactly which employees fall within the bounds of the rule. Although "a bright-line rule" in the form of a "control group" test or a blanket ban on all employee interviews would be easier to apply, the rule we adopt is, as discussed above, fair, and will allow for ex parte interviews without prior counsel's permission when an employee clearly falls outside of the rule's scope.

. . . The five Harvard employees interviewed by MR&W do not fall within the third category of the comment as we have construed it. As employees of the HUPD, they are not involved in directing the litigation at bar or authorizing the organization to make binding admissions. In fact, Harvard does not argue that any of the five employees fit within our definition of this category.

The Harvard employees are also not employees "whose act or omission in connection with that matter may be imputed to the organization for purposes of civil or criminal liability." Stanford's complaint does not name any of these employees as involved in the alleged discrimination. In fact, in an affidavit she states that the two lieutenants "had no role in making any of the decisions that are the subject of my complaint of discrimination and retaliation," and Harvard does not refute this averment. All five employees were mere witnesses to the events that occurred, not active participants.

We must still determine, however, whether any of the interviewed employees have "managerial responsibility on behalf of the organization with regard to the subject of the representation." Although the two patrol officers and the dispatcher were subordinate to Stanford and had no managerial authority, the two lieutenants exercised some supervisory authority over Stanford. However, not all employees with some supervisory power over their coworkers are deemed to have "managerial" responsibility in the sense intended by the comment. "Supervision of a small group of workers would not constitute a managerial position within a corporation."

Even if the two lieutenants are deemed to have managerial responsibility, the Massachusetts version of the comment adds the requirement that the managerial responsibility be in "regard to the subject of the representation." Thus, the comment includes only those employees who have supervisory authority over the events at issue in the litigation. There is no evidence in the record that the lieutenants' managerial decisions were a subject of the litigation. The affidavits of the two lieutenants indicate that they did not complete any evaluations or offer any opinions of Stanford that Chief Riley considered in reaching his decisions.

. . . Because we conclude that rule 4.2 did not prohibit MR&W from contacting and interviewing the five HUPD employees, we vacate the order of the Superior Court judge and remand the case for the entry of an order denying the defendant's motion for sanctions. . . .

F.   Communication with Judges and Jurors

Problem

14-14.   Martyn lost a jury verdict that Fox assured her she was certain to win. In an effort to understand what happened, Martyn phoned three jurors at home after the trial, and she hopes to catch the trial judge tomorrow morning in chambers to chat about the case. Any problem?

Consider: Model Rules 3.3(d), 3.5
Model Code of Judicial Conduct Rule 2.9

Disciplinary Counsel v. Stuard
901 N.E.2d 788 (Ohio 2009)

PER CURIAM.

We must decide in this case the appropriate sanctions for a judge who asked an assistant county prosecutor to prepare a sentencing order via ex parte communications, the assistant county prosecutor who prepared the order, and a second assistant county prosecutor, who reviewed it. . . .

Respondent John M. Stuard . . . was admitted to the practice of law in Ohio in 1965 and has served as a judge of the Trumbull County Court of Common

Pleas since 1991. Respondent Christopher D. Becker . . . was admitted to the
Ohio bar in 1990. Respondent Kenneth N. Bailey . . . was admitted to the Ohio
bar in 1971. . . .

Misconduct

In May and June 2003, Judge Stuard presided over the capital murder trial
of Donna Roberts. Veteran prosecutors Becker and Bailey represented the state,
and J. Gerald Ingram and John Juhasz, also experienced practitioners, represented the defendant. A jury found Roberts guilty of two counts of aggravated
murder, among other crimes, and recommended a sentence of death.

Between the penalty-phase hearing of Roberts's trial in early June and the
sentencing hearing later that month, Judge Stuard engaged in ex parte communications four times with Becker about the sentencing opinion in Roberts's case.
The first communication consisted of a brief conversation on June 18, 2003,
when the judge asked Becker to prepare the court's opinion sentencing Roberts
to death. Judge Stuard gave Becker two pages of notes on the aggravating circumstances and mitigating factors that he had weighed in deciding that the
death sentence was appropriate. The notes did not relate the history and facts
of the Roberts case beyond the discussion of aggravating circumstances and
mitigating factors. For these portions of the sentencing opinion, Judge Stuard
instructed Becker to refer to the sentencing opinion in the companion case of
Nathaniel Jackson, Roberts's codefendant. Becker agreed to write the opinion.

The second ex parte communication occurred in writing the next day, when
the judge found on his desk a 17-page draft of a sentencing opinion in the Roberts
case. Judge Stuard reviewed the draft, which set forth five sections recounting
the case history, facts, aggravating circumstances, mitigating factors, and conclusions of law. He then noted one or more corrections to be made.

In a third ex parte communication, Judge Stuard asked Becker later that
day to make the corrections. Becker made the corrections and also incorporated
Bailey's editorial suggestions, made after Bailey's review of the draft opinion.
The fourth communication occurred when Judge Stuard received the corrected
version of what became his opinion sentencing Roberts to death.

Judge Stuard had had an informal practice of enlisting prosecutorial assistance in drafting journal entries in criminal cases. He employed that practice
in preparing the sentencing opinion in the Roberts case but failed to include
defense counsel in the process. Ingram and Juhasz did not learn until Roberts's
sentencing hearing, on June 20, 2003, that the prosecution had assisted in preparing the court's opinion. They discovered what had happened when Judge
Stuard read his opinion from the bench, and defense counsel, who did not have
a copy of the sentencing order, noticed that one of the prosecutors seemed to be
silently "reading along" with the judge, turning pages of a document in unison.

Ingram objected. In the sidebar discussion that followed, Judge Stuard
acknowledged that he had given his notes to the prosecution and instructed
counsel to draft the sentencing order. Ingram then challenged the process by
which the court had prepared the order sentencing Roberts to death as an impermissible collaboration and ex parte communication.

Judge Stuard concedes and the board found that his ex parte communications with Becker, engaged in without the knowledge or consent of opposing counsel, violated [Code of Judicial Conduct Rules 1.1 and 1.2] (requiring a judge to " . . . comply with the law and * * * act at all times in a manner that promotes public confidence in the integrity of the judiciary") and [Rule 2.9] (providing that, except in situations not relevant here, "[a] judge shall not initiate, receive, permit, or consider communications [as to substantive matters or issues on the merits] made to the judge outside the presence of the parties or their representatives concerning a pending or impending proceeding * * *"). Becker initially defended his actions, but the board found him in violation of [Rule of Professional Conduct 8.4(d)] (prohibiting a lawyer from engaging in conduct that is prejudicial to the administration of justice) and [Rule 3.5(b)] (prohibiting, with exceptions not relevant here, ex parte communication on the merits of a cause with a judge before whom the proceeding is pending). Becker has not objected to the board's report.

Clear and convincing evidence supports that Judge Stuard and Becker committed the cited misconduct. Indeed, in the appeal that followed Judge Stuard's order sentencing Roberts to death, we held that the court committed prejudicial error by delegating responsibility for the content and analysis of its sentencing opinion. We vacated the death sentence and remanded the cause with instructions for Judge Stuard to personally review and evaluate the appropriateness of the death penalty. State v. Roberts, 850 N.E.2d 1168 (OH 2006). We also observed in *Roberts* that the ex parte collaboration between the judge and prosecution to prepare the court's sentencing opinion was "wholly inconsistent" with the ethical constraints of [The Code of Judicial Conduct and the Rules of Professional Conduct].

In contrast to the ex parte communications between Judge Stuard and Becker, Bailey did not exchange any information about the merits of Roberts's case with the presiding judge. He merely reviewed the sentencing order and pointed out typographical errors. The charges of misconduct against Bailey are therefore dismissed.

Sanction

In recommending the public reprimands, the board considered the aggravating and mitigating factors listed in Section 10 of the Rules and Regulations Governing Procedure on Complaints and Hearings Before the Board of Grievances and Discipline. . . .

Neither Judge Stuard nor Becker has a record of prior discipline. Both cooperated appropriately in the disciplinary process. With either letters of recommendation or testimony from members of the community, bench, and bar, Judge Stuard established his excellent character, distinguished service as a judge, reputation for honesty and fairness, and commitment to public service. With letters of recommendation or testimony from members of law enforcement, the bench, and the bar, including both opposing counsel in the Roberts case, Becker has similarly shown his reputation for honesty, good character, and professional competence.

Judge Stuard has complied with our mandate in *State v. Roberts*, 850 N.E.2d 1168 (OH 2006). Both he and Becker have acquiesced in the board's recommendation, assuring that they have recognized their wrongdoing and will not repeat it. A public reprimand is therefore appropriate. . . .

G. Lawyer as Witness

Problem

14-15. Martyn actively negotiates a business deal for Client with Third Party. Two years later, Third Party sues Client to rescind the deal, alleging that Client committed fraud during the negotiations.

    (a) Can Martyn defend Client in the rescission action? Does it matter if Client is now terminally ill? Can Martyn do pretrial work only?

    (b) Can Fox represent Client in the rescission action? Does it matter if Martyn's recollection of the facts might not support Client's position?

    (c) What if Third Party unexpectedly calls Martyn to the stand during the trial? Can Martyn & Fox continue the representation?

Consider: Model Rule 3.7

Neumann v. Tuccio

2009 Conn. Super. LEXIS 2016

DAN SHABAN, J.

On June 26, 2007, the plaintiff, Harry Neumann, Jr., commenced this vexatious litigation action against the defendant, Edward Tuccio. . . . The plaintiff is a real estate agent for Neumann Real Estate, LLC. The defendant is a developer-builder in the construction industry. On September 6, 2005, the defendant initiated a slander lawsuit against the plaintiff. Prior to serving the complaint on the plaintiff, the defendant had information, from an alleged witness, that the allegations in the complaint were incorrect. Specifically, the plaintiff alleges that the defendant "forwarded a copy of his proposed complaint to Robert Tuccio, Jr., his alleged witness, and received numerous communications from Robert Tuccio, Jr. that the allegations of the complaint were incorrect, and that the statements which were alleged in the complaint to have been made by Harry Neumann, Jr. were never in fact made." Despite this, the defendant proceeded with service of the writ, summons and complaint, which commenced the underlying action. That action went to trial, where the court, Frankel, J., granted the plaintiff's motion for a directed verdict, as the defendant had failed to establish a prima facie case. The plaintiff now brings the present action seeking damages stemming from vexatious litigation.

On February 23, 2009, the defendant, represented by his attorney, John R. Williams (Williams), in his individual capacity, filed an answer and raised the special defense of advice of counsel. In response to the special defense, on April 29, 2009, the plaintiff filed a motion to disqualify Williams and his law firm, John R. Williams and Associates, LLC (the law firm), on the ground that Williams and the "attorneys, members, and/or employees" of the law firm will be necessary witnesses to the vexatious litigation action. . . .

In his motion to disqualify attorney Williams and Williams' law firm, the plaintiff states that both should be prohibited from representing the defendant at trial because Williams and "the attorneys, members, and/or employees" of the firm will be necessary witnesses to the defendant's special defense of advice of counsel.[3] In support of this proposition, the plaintiff cites to Rule 3.7 of the Rules of Professional Conduct, which prohibits an attorney from acting as an advocate at a trial in which he is likely to be a necessary witness, except in limited circumstances. The plaintiff further argues that "Defendant will not suffer substantial hardship because Defendant was aware of the Special Defense from the commencement of this case and chose to delay asserting the Special Defense until this close to trial." In opposition, the defendant contends that his counsel should not be disqualified because he would suffer prejudice as a result, he did not use any delaying tactics, and because the plaintiff should have known that the defendant would assert the advice of counsel special defense as it is commonly used in vexatious litigation suits. . . .

A. DISQUALIFICATION OF THE INDIVIDUAL ATTORNEY

Connecticut's Rules of Professional Conduct address the issue of disqualification of a party's counsel. . . . Pursuant to Rule 3.7, "[w]henever counsel for a client reasonably foresees that he will be called as a witness to testify on a material matter, the proper action is for that attorney to withdraw from the case." State v. Webb, 417, 680 A.2d 147 (Conn. 1996). "An attorney is not absolutely prohibited from testifying on behalf of a client, but should only do so when the testimony concerns a formal matter, or the need for the testimony arises from an exigency not reasonably foreseeable . . . Where, however, an attorney does not withdraw, a court exercising its supervisory power can . . . disqualify the attorney." Enquire Printing & Publishing Co. v. O'Reilly, 477 A.2d 648 (Conn. 1984).

Under Rule 3.7, the first relevant inquiry is whether the attorney whose disqualification is sought is a necessary witness in the matter. A necessary witness is not just someone with relevant information, however, but someone who has material information that no one else can provide. Whether a witness ought to testify is not alone determined by the fact that he has relevant knowledge or was involved in the transaction at issue. Disqualification may be required only

---

3. "Advice of counsel is a complete defense to an action of . . . vexatious suit when it is shown that the defendant . . . instituted his civil action relying in good faith on such advice, given after a full and fair statement of all facts within his knowledge, or which he was charged with knowing." *Vandersluis v. Weil*, 407 A.2d 982 (Conn. 1978). Once advice of counsel has been raised as a defense, that party has been deemed to waive the attorney-client privilege.

when it is likely that the testimony to be given by the witness is necessary. . . . There is a dual test for necessity. First the proposed testimony must be relevant and material. Second, it must be unobtainable elsewhere. Quinebaug Valley Engineers Assn., Inc. v. Colchester Fish and Game Club, Superior Court, judicial district of New London at Norwich, Docket No. CV 08 4008053 (July 25, 2008, Abrams, J.).

Attorney Williams' testimony is clearly relevant and material, and therefore satisfies the first element of "necessity." The defense of advice of counsel is a matter of central importance to the determination of a vexatious litigation claim. The testimony the plaintiff seeks to elicit regards the advice and information Williams gave the defendant, including strategy and tactics discussed between them for the prosecution of the action against Neumann. This testimony is not informal or insubstantial, but rather, it is decidedly relevant and material.[5] In fact, the testimony regarding Williams' advice to Tuccio may very well be dispositive of the case.

With regard to the second element, the defendant argues that the testimony is obtainable elsewhere, as the defendant himself can testify as to what advice or information was given by Williams. This argument is unpersuasive. . . .

In the present matter, the defendant's special defense states in full: "The defendant instituted his civil action relying in good faith on the advice of counsel, given after a full and fair statement of all facts within his knowledge or which he was charged with knowing." This assertion does not establish the existence of any other individual who would be able to testify to the truth of the special defense, aside from the defendant himself, and Williams. Given the expertise an attorney has over a lay witness in answering questions relative to decisions regarding legal procedure, theory and technique, it is unlikely that the defendant could completely relay the same depth of information, analysis and advice as could be presented by Williams. Moreover, . . . the defendant's ability to testify as to the advice Williams gave him, and the information he gave Williams, does not render Williams' testimony as evidence that is obtainable elsewhere. Accordingly, Williams' testimony is necessary to shed full light on material matters regarding his representation of the defendant in the underlying case and fairness dictates that the plaintiff should be able to present Williams' testimony at trial given the special defense that has been raised.

As the plaintiff has demonstrated that attorney Williams' testimony is both relevant and necessary, the court concludes that he is a necessary witness who may be disqualified from representing the defendant as an advocate at trial

---

5. A court may hold an evidentiary hearing to determine what facts the attorney knows and whether they are necessary to the disposition of the matter. In this case, such a hearing is unnecessary because Williams' knowledge of the nature of the advice and information provided to the defendant in the underlying case is apparent and undisputed by the defendant. Cf. Jean v. Angle, 2008 Conn. Super. LEXIS 1110 (evidentiary hearing, pursuant to a motion to disqualify, was required to determine whom the attorney represented in the sale of a limousine company, and material matters regarding the purchase transaction of the limousine company and financial payments to the parties, as that information was not readily apparent from the pleadings and motions).

pursuant to Rule 3.7, subject to the three exceptions set forth therein. The defendant argues, however, that his counsel should not be disqualified because the circumstances satisfy the exception in Rule 3.7(a)(3), that "[d]isqualification of the lawyer would work substantial hardship on the client." The court disagrees with the defendant's contention. . . .

[I]n this case, the plaintiff did not unreasonably delay filing the motion to disqualify. Moreover, the fact that the issue of disqualification has been addressed by the court merely four weeks before the trial date is, at least in part, the result of defendant's own delay in waiting to raise the special defense. By doing so, the defendant has effectively created the very hardship he now claims would be prejudicial to him. Finally, because the court has not disqualified the law firm, . . . the defendant should have minimal difficulty retaining new counsel to represent him at trial.

Under the circumstances of this case, the court finds that Williams is a necessary witness and that prohibiting him from representing the defendant at trial would not cause the defendant to suffer undue hardship or prejudice. Accordingly, the plaintiff's motion to disqualify Williams is granted.

B. DISQUALIFICATION OF THE ENTIRE FIRM . . .

. . . "Rule 3.7(b) eliminates the blanket imputed disqualification which previously existed . . . If either the lawyer-advocate or the lawyer-witness (both of the same law firm) has a conflict of interest pursuant to Rule 1.7 (General Conflict) or Rule 1.9 (Former Client) the lawyer-advocate may be precluded from the representation under Rule 1.10. However, absent those specific conflict situations, even if a lawyer is called to testify, another lawyer from the firm may now try the case." 2002 Conn. Super. LEXIS 1415 at *5. . . .

Although there exists a possibility, particularly before a jury, that the firm's participation as trial counsel in a case in which the trial counsel's colleagues are witnesses will raise skepticism, courts have found this concern to be an insufficient ground for disqualifying a firm. . . .

There has been no showing by the plaintiff that there has been, or is, a conflict between the defendant's position and the lawyers' or the law firm's responsibilities to some other client or its own interests in the matter at issue. In that the plaintiff has failed to supply the court with sufficient reason to disqualify the law firm of John R. Williams and Associates, LLC from this matter, it declines to do.

Part IV

Lawyers and Society: The Profession

Part IV of this book offers us an opportunity to examine additional issues about the structure, function, and regulation of the legal profession itself. We address here subjects that raise the question of whether the legal professional fairly can be considered self-governing, and, if so, whether its regulation serves the public interest. We begin by examining a key aspect of self-regulation, the lawyer's duty to report professional misconduct. We next look at restrictions on the ability of lawyers to organize their practices. We move on to consider the impact of constitutional law on the business practices of lawyers. We then reexamine the inherent powers of courts, this time with a focus on whether the judicial branch can prevent the regulation of lawyers by other branches of government. We end the chapter by considering unauthorized practice restrictions that exclude both nonlawyers from legal practice and lawyers from practicing across state and country boundaries.

Chapter 15

Professional Regulation

A. Restrictions on Practice

Problems

15-1. Martyn & Fox is worried about the firm's new lease obligation. What if the firm says that "any lawyer who leaves the firm and practices within 100 miles must pay the firm his last year's draw"? "Forfeits his pension"? "Owes the firm 25 percent of all fees generated by former Martyn & Fox clients"?

15-2. Martyn & Fox's manufacturing client is fed up with repetitive products liability suits over allegedly defective forklift trucks brought by one law firm over the last decade. "Tell them we'll settle with their latest client for an extra $100,000, if they promise never to sue us again," CEO tells our lawyer. Is this a great idea? What if the law firm comes back and says: "We'll agree not to sue again, if you hire us as safety consultants for $200,000 per year?

Consider: Model Rules 1.17, 5.6

Cardillo v. Bloomfield 206 Corp.
988 A.2d 136 (N.J. Super. 2010)

The opinion of the court was delivered by CHAMBERS, J.A.D.

This appeal arises out of an agreement between plaintiff Cathy C. Cardillo, Esq. and defendants Bloomfield 206 Corporation (Bloomfield), James Stathis and Steven Silverman (the Cardillo Agreement). In the Cardillo Agreement, Cardillo, an attorney, agreed not to represent parties in litigation adverse to the defendants. At the same time that she was negotiating the Cardillo Agreement on her own behalf with defendants, she was also negotiating an agreement to settle litigation she had brought on behalf of clients against defendant Bloomfield. Cardillo and counsel for defendants exchanged emails relating their mutual understanding that the two agreements were being negotiated separately.

Cardillo thereafter brought this action to seek a court determination that the Cardillo Agreement was void, contending that it violated *RPC* 5.6(b) which prohibits an attorney from agreeing to restrict the attorney's practice as "part of the settlement of a controversy between private parties." The trial court granted her application, and defendants appealed. We affirm. Attorneys may not circumvent the import of *RPC* 5.6(b) by stating that the settlement of litigation is separate from the agreement to restrict the practice of law where the agreements were negotiated contemporaneously and are interconnected.

I

The path that led to this suit began in 2000, when Cardillo provided legal advice to Liberty Realty, L.L.C. (Liberty) and was paid for those services. The three principals of Liberty were Joseph Covello and defendants Stathis and Silverman.

Thereafter, Cardillo represented Jay Rubinstein and Gary Rubinstein in *Rubinstein v. Bloomfield 206 Corp.* (the *Rubinstein* litigation). Bloomfield was owned by Stathis and Silverman. Since Stathis and Silverman were also owners of Liberty when Cardillo had previously represented that entity, Bloomfield moved to disqualify Cardillo from representing the Rubinsteins.

While this motion was pending, Cardillo and counsel for Bloomfield negotiated a settlement of the *Rubinstein* litigation. Contemporaneously with those negotiations, Cardillo also negotiated with counsel for Bloomfield and its principals, Stathis and Silverman, for the Cardillo agreement whereby she would refrain from representing clients adverse to defendants. On August 28, 2007, the settlement agreement for the *Rubinstein* litigation was executed. The next day, August 29, 2007, after some further negotiation regarding the language in the confidentiality provision, the parties executed the Cardillo Agreement which included the following provision limiting Cardillo's practice:

> Cardillo expressly agrees not to take any position adverse to, represent or participate in the representation of any party in any future action against Stathis, Silverman, Bloomfield 206 or any corporation, limited liability company or other legal entity in which Stathis or Silverman has an existing ownership interest, at the time of her initial representation or participation in the representation of any party. Cardillo represents that as of August 29, 2007, the date of her execution of this agreement, she does not represent any individual or other entity in any pending or contemplated action against Stathis, Silverman, Bloomfield 206 or any corporation, limited liability company or other legal entity in which Stathis or Silverman have an ownership interest.

The Cardillo Agreement further provided that defendants Bloomfield, Stathis and Silverman waived any conflicts of interest that may have arisen due to Cardillo's representation of any parties in the *Rubinstein* litigation or any other action, and they agreed to withdraw any action pending before the court asserting such a conflict of interest.

On January 28, 2009, Cardillo commenced this lawsuit . . . seeking injunctive relief. She sought a ruling that the Cardillo Agreement was void and unenforceable as a violation of *RPC* 5.6(b). She wanted this relief in order to represent a client against another corporation owned by Silverman and Stathis. . . .

II

At the outset, we note that under *RPC* 5.6(b) "[a] lawyer shall not participate in offering or making: . . . (b) an agreement in which a restriction on the lawyer's right to practice is part of the settlement of a controversy between private parties." *RPC* 5.6(b) is modeled after the American Bar Association's (ABA) Model Rule of Professional Conduct 5.6(b). The rationale for the Model Rule has been explained as follows:

> First, permitting such agreements restricts the access of the public to lawyers who, by virtue of their background and experience, might be the very best available talent to represent these individuals. Second, the use of such agreements may provide clients with rewards that bear less relationship to the merits of their claims than they do to the desire of the defendant to "buy off" plaintiff's counsel. Third, the offering of such restrictive agreements places the plaintiff's lawyer in a situation where there is conflict between the interests of present clients and those of potential future clients. While the [*Model Rules*] generally require that the client's interests be put first, forcing a lawyer to give up future representations may be asking too much, particularly in light of the strong countervailing policy favoring the public's unfettered choice of counsel. ABA Comm. Ethics and Prof'l Responsibility, Formal Op. 93-371 (1993) (discussing *RPC* 5.6 in the context of settlement of mass tort litigation)].

Thus, if Cardillo agreed to restrict her practice as part of the settlement of the *Rubinstein* litigation, *RPC* 5.6(b) was violated.

Defendants maintain that *RPC* 5.6(b) is inapplicable because the Cardillo Agreement was not "part of the settlement of a controversy between private parties." Defendants argue that the settlement with the Rubinsteins was separate from the Cardillo Agreement, citing email exchanges by the parties at the time of the negotiations stating that the two matters were separate and the fact that the *Rubinstein* settlement agreement was executed first.

We reject this argument because it ignores the fact that the two agreements were being negotiated simultaneously and were intertwined. Defendants, including Bloomfield, were negotiating the Cardillo Agreement at the same time that Cardillo was representing and negotiating a settlement agreement with Bloomfield on behalf of her clients, the Rubinsteins. Further, during the time period in which the Cardillo Agreement was negotiated, Bloomfield's motion to disqualify Cardillo was pending in the *Rubinstein* litigation.

Indeed, the Cardillo Agreement is expressly tied to the *Rubinstein* litigation, because in the Cardillo Agreement, defendants agreed to waive any conflict Cardillo had in the *Rubinstein* litigation and to withdraw any conflict of interest application pending in court against her. . . . The parties cannot circumvent the import of *RPC* 5.6(b), and the reality of their transaction by expressly claiming during the negotiations that they are negotiating the two agreements separately and then by executing two separate agreements. Nor may they defeat application of the *RPC* by the device of arranging to execute the agreements on different days or with minor negotiations in the interim.

The Cardillo Agreement violates *RPC* 5.6(b) because it restricts Cardillo's right to practice law and it was part of the settlement of the *Rubinstein* litigation. A contract that violates the Rules of Professional Conduct is void and unenforceable as a violation of public policy. Because the Cardillo Agreement violates *RPC* 5.6(b), it is not enforceable. Of course, Cardillo is still bound by *RPC* 1.9 which sets forth the obligations of attorneys to their former clients and limits their ability to participate in litigation involving former clients. . . .

[W]e conclude that the trial court correctly upheld its earlier ruling that the Cardillo Agreement violated *RPC* 5.6(b) and is void and unenforceable.

B. Advertising and Solicitation

Problems

15-3. Can Martyn & Fox advertise their new phone number as "1-800-HonestL"? What about "1-800-PITBULL"?

15-4. Can Martyn & Fox use *www.superlawyers.com* as its URL or website address?

15-5. Can Martyn & Fox e-mail families of recent accident victims to inform them of their need for counsel? Can Fox follow up on e-mail responses with phone calls? Can he discuss the tragedy on a blog or in a chat room?

15-6. Can Martyn & Fox advertise "Law for You" seminars, where Martyn touts the advantage of living trusts? Can Martyn hand out business cards to those who attend the seminars? Advertising brochures? Sample forms?

15-7. Can Martyn ask those who attend the seminar to hire the firm to draft a living trust? Does it matter if the seminar is sponsored by a local not-for-profit organization?

15-8. While visiting her father at a local hospital, Martyn warns the person in the next bed not to sign an insurance settlement form until she speaks to a lawyer. The patient, in gratitude, asks Martyn to be her lawyer.

Consider: Model Rules 7.1-7.5, 8.5

Florida Bar v. Went For It, Inc.
515 U.S. 618 (1995)

Justice O'CONNOR delivered the opinion of the Court.

Rules of the Florida Bar prohibit personal injury lawyers from sending targeted direct-mail solicitations to victims and their relatives for 30 days following an accident or disaster. This case asks us to consider whether such Rules violate the First and Fourteenth Amendments of the Constitution. We hold that in the circumstances presented here, they do not.

I

In 1989, the Florida Bar (Bar) completed a 2-year study of the effects of lawyer advertising on public opinion. After conducting hearings, commissioning surveys, and reviewing extensive public commentary, the Bar determined that several changes to its advertising rules were in order. In late 1990, the Florida Supreme Court adopted the Bar's proposed amendments with some modifications. Two of these amendments are at issue in this case. Rule 4-7.4(b)(1) provides that "[a] lawyer shall not send, or knowingly permit to be sent, . . . a written communication to a prospective client for the purpose of obtaining professional employment if: (A) the written communication concerns an action for personal injury or wrongful death or otherwise relates to an accident or disaster involving the person to whom the communication is addressed or a relative of that person, unless the accident or disaster occurred more than 30 days prior to the mailing of the communication." Rule 4-7.8(a) states that "[a] lawyer shall not accept referrals from a lawyer referral service unless the service: (1) engages in no communication with the public and in no direct contact with prospective clients in a manner that would violate the Rules of Professional Conduct if the communication or contact were made by the lawyer." Together, these rules create a brief 30-day blackout period after an accident during which lawyers may not, directly or indirectly, single out accident victims or their relatives in order to solicit their business.

In March 1992, G. Stewart McHenry and his wholly owned lawyer referral service, Went For It, Inc., filed this action for declaratory and injunctive relief in the United States District Court for the Middle District of Florida challenging Rules 4-7.4(b)(1) and 4-7.8 as violative of the First and Fourteenth Amendments to the Constitution. . . .

The District Court . . . entered summary judgment for the plaintiffs, relying on Bates v. State Bar of Ariz., 433 U.S. 350 (1977), and subsequent cases. The Eleventh Circuit affirmed on similar grounds. . . . We granted certiorari, 512 U.S. 1289 (1994), and now reverse.

II

A

Constitutional protection for attorney advertising, and for commercial speech generally, is of recent vintage. Until the mid-1970's, we adhered to the broad rule laid out in Valentine v. Chrestensen, 316 U.S. 52, 54 (1942), that, while the First Amendment guards against government restriction of speech in most contexts, "the Constitution imposes no such restraint on government as respects purely commercial advertising." In 1976, the Court changed course. In Virginia Bd. of Pharmacy v. Virginia Citizens Consumer Council, Inc., 425 U.S. 748, we invalidated a state statute barring pharmacists from advertising prescription drug prices. At issue was speech that involved the idea that "'I will sell you the X prescription drug at the Y price.'" . . . Striking the ban as unconstitutional, we rejected the argument that such speech "is so removed from 'any exposition of ideas,' and from 'truth, science, morality, and arts in general, in its diffusion of liberal sentiments on the administration of Government,' that it lacks all protection."

. . . In Bates v. State Bar of Arizona, *supra,* the Court struck a ban on price advertising for what it deemed "routine" legal services: "the uncontested divorce, the simple adoption, the uncontested personal bankruptcy, the change of name, and the like." Expressing confidence that legal advertising would only be practicable for such simple, standardized services, the Court rejected the State's proffered justifications for regulation.

Nearly two decades of cases have built upon the foundation laid by *Bates.* It is now well established that lawyer advertising is commercial speech and, as such, is accorded a measure of First Amendment protection. *See, e.g.,* Shapero v. Kentucky Bar Assn., 486 U.S. 466, 472 (1988); Zauderer v. Office of Disciplinary Counsel of Supreme Court of Ohio, 471 U.S. 626, 637 (1985); In re R. M. J., 455 U.S. 191, 199 (1982). Such First Amendment protection, of course, is not absolute. We have always been careful to distinguish commercial speech from speech at the First Amendment's core. "'Commercial speech [enjoys] a limited measure of protection, commensurate with its subordinate position in the scale of First Amendment values,' and is subject to 'modes of regulation that might be impermissible in the realm of noncommercial expression.'" Board of Trustees of State Univ. of N.Y. v. Fox, 492 U.S. 469, 477 (1989), quoting Ohralik v. Ohio State Bar Assn., 436 U.S. 447, 456 (1978). . . .

Mindful of these concerns, we engage in "intermediate" scrutiny of restrictions on commercial speech, analyzing them under the framework set forth in Central Hudson Gas & Elec. Corp. v. Public Serv. Comm'n of N.Y., 447 U.S. 557 (1980). Under *Central Hudson,* the government may freely regulate commercial speech that concerns unlawful activity or is misleading. Commercial speech that falls into neither of those categories, like the advertising at issue here, may be regulated if the government satisfies a test consisting of three related prongs: First, the government must assert a substantial interest in support of its regulation; second, the government must demonstrate that the restriction on commercial speech directly and materially advances that interest; and third, the regulation must be "'narrowly drawn.'"

B

. . . The Florida Bar asserts that it has a substantial interest in protecting the privacy and tranquility of personal injury victims and their loved ones against intrusive, unsolicited contact by lawyers. . . . Because direct mail solicitations in the wake of accidents are perceived by the public as intrusive, the Bar argues, the reputation of the legal profession in the eyes of Floridians has suffered commensurately. The regulation, then, is an effort to protect the flagging reputations of Florida lawyers by preventing them from engaging in conduct that, the Bar maintains, "'is universally regarded as deplorable and beneath common decency because of its intrusion upon the special vulnerability and private grief of victims or their families.'"

We have little trouble crediting the Bar's interest as substantial. . . .

Under *Central Hudson*'s second prong, the State must demonstrate that the challenged regulation "advances the Government's interest 'in a direct and material way.'" . . . That burden, we have explained, "'is not satisfied by mere speculation or conjecture; rather, a governmental body seeking to sustain a restriction on commercial speech must demonstrate that the harms it recites are real and that its restriction will in fact alleviate them to a material degree.'" In Edenfield v. Fane, 507 U.S. 761, 768 (1993), the Court invalidated a Florida ban on in-person solicitation by certified public accountants (CPA's). We observed that the State Board of Accountancy had "presented no studies that suggest personal solicitation of prospective business clients by CPA's creates the dangers of fraud, overreaching, or compromised independence that the Board claims to fear." Moreover, "the record [did] not disclose any anecdotal evidence, either from Florida or another State, that validated the Board's suppositions." In fact, we concluded that the only evidence in the record tended to "contradict, rather than strengthen, the Board's submissions." Finding nothing in the record to substantiate the State's allegations of harm, we invalidated the regulation.

The direct-mail solicitation regulation before us does not suffer from such infirmities. The Florida Bar submitted a 106-page summary of its 2-year study of lawyer advertising and solicitation to the District Court. That summary contains data—both statistical and anecdotal—supporting the Bar's contentions that the Florida public views direct-mail solicitations in the immediate wake of accidents as an intrusion on privacy that reflects poorly upon the profession. As of June 1989, lawyers mailed 700,000 direct solicitations in Florida annually, 40% of which were aimed at accident victims or their survivors. A survey of Florida adults commissioned by the Bar indicated that Floridians "have negative feelings about those attorneys who use direct mail advertising." Fifty-four percent of the general population surveyed said that contacting persons concerning accidents or similar events is a violation of privacy. A random sampling of persons who received direct-mail advertising from lawyers in 1987 revealed that 45% believed that direct-mail solicitation is "designed to take advantage of gullible or unstable people"; 34% found such tactics "annoying or irritating"; 26% found it "an invasion of your privacy"; and 24% reported that it "made you angry." Significantly, 27% of direct-mail recipients reported that their regard for the legal profession and for the judicial process as a whole was "lower" as a result of receiving the direct mail.

The anecdotal record mustered by the Bar is noteworthy for its breadth and detail. With titles like "Scavenger Lawyers" and "Solicitors Out of Bounds," newspaper editorial pages in Florida have burgeoned with criticism of Florida lawyers who send targeted direct mail to victims shortly after accidents. . . .

In light of this showing . . . we conclude that the Bar has satisfied the second prong of the *Central Hudson* test. . . .

In reaching a contrary conclusion, the Court of Appeals determined that this case was governed squarely by Shapero v. Kentucky Bar Assn., 486 U.S. 466

(1988). Making no mention of the Bar's study, the court concluded that "'a targeted letter [does not] invade the recipient's privacy any more than does a substantively identical letter mailed at large. The invasion, if any, occurs when the lawyer discovers the recipient's legal affairs, not when he confronts the recipient with the discovery.'" In many cases, the Court of Appeals explained, "this invasion of privacy will involve no more than reading the newspaper."

While some of *Shapero*'s language might be read to support the Court of Appeals' interpretation, *Shapero* differs in several fundamental respects from the case before us. First and foremost, *Shapero*'s treatment of privacy was casual. . . . Second, in contrast to this case, *Shapero* dealt with a broad ban on all direct-mail solicitations, whatever the time frame and whoever the recipient. Finally, the State in *Shapero* assembled no evidence attempting to demonstrate any actual harm caused by targeted direct mail. The Court rejected the State's effort to justify a prophylactic ban on the basis of blanket, untested assertions of undue influence and overreaching. Because the State did not make a privacy-based argument at all, its empirical showing on that issue was similarly infirm. . . .

Here . . . the harm targeted by the Florida Bar cannot be eliminated by a brief journey to the trash can. The purpose of the 30-day targeted direct-mail ban is to forestall the outrage and irritation with the state-licensed legal profession that the practice of direct solicitation only days after accidents has engendered. The Bar is concerned not with citizens' "offense" in the abstract, but with the demonstrable detrimental effects that such "offense" has on the profession it regulates. Moreover, the harm posited by the Bar is as much a function of simple receipt of targeted solicitations within days of accidents as it is a function of the letters' contents. Throwing the letter away shortly after opening it may minimize the latter intrusion, but it does little to combat the former. . . .

Passing to *Central Hudson*'s third prong, we examine the relationship between the Florida Bar's interests and the means chosen to serve them. With respect to this prong, the differences between commercial speech and noncommercial speech are manifest. [We have] made clear that the "least restrictive means" test has no role in the commercial speech context. "What our decisions require," instead, "is a 'fit' between the legislature's ends and the means chosen to accomplish those ends,' a fit that is not necessarily perfect, but reasonable; that represents not necessarily the single best disposition but one whose scope is 'in proportion to the interest served,' that employs not necessarily the least restrictive means but . . . a means narrowly tailored to achieve the desired objective. . . .

III

Speech by professionals obviously has many dimensions. There are circumstances in which we will accord speech by attorneys on public issues and matters of legal representation the strongest protection our Constitution has to offer. *See, e.g.,* Gentile v. State Bar of Nevada, 501 U.S. 1030 (1991); In re Primus, 436 U.S. 412 (1978). This case, however, concerns pure commercial advertising, for which we have always reserved a lesser degree of protection under the First Amendment. Particularly because the standards and conduct of state-licensed lawyers have traditionally been subject to extensive regulation by the States, it is all the more appropriate that we limit our scrutiny of state regulations to a level commensurate with the "'subordinate position'" of commercial speech in the scale of First Amendment values.

We believe that the Florida Bar's 30-day restriction on targeted direct-mail solicitation of accident victims and their relatives withstands scrutiny under the three-pronged *Central Hudson* test that we have devised for this context. The Bar has substantial interest both in protecting injured Floridians from invasive conduct by lawyers and in preventing the erosion of confidence in the profession that such repeated invasions have engendered. The Bar's proffered study, unrebutted by respondents below, provides evidence indicating that the harms it targets are far from illusory. The palliative devised by the Bar to address these harms is narrow both in scope and in duration. The Constitution, in our view, requires nothing more.

The judgment of the Court of Appeals, accordingly, is *Reversed*.

Justice KENNEDY, with whom Justice STEVENS, Justice SOUTER, and Justice GINSBURG join, Dissenting.

Attorneys who communicate their willingness to assist potential clients are engaged in speech protected by the First and Fourteenth Amendments. That principle has been understood since Bates v. State Bar of Arizona, 433 U.S. 35 (1977). The Court today undercuts this guarantee in an important class of cases and unsettles leading First Amendment precedents, at the expense of those victims most in need of legal assistance. With all respect for the Court, in my view its solicitude for the privacy of victims and its concern for our profession are misplaced and self-defeating, even upon the Court's own premises.

I take it to be uncontroverted that when an accident results in death or injury, it is often urgent at once to investigate the occurrence, identify witnesses, and preserve evidence. Vital interests in speech and expression are, therefore, at stake when by law an attorney cannot direct a letter to the victim or the family explaining this simple fact and offering competent legal assistance. Meanwhile, represented and better informed parties, or parties who have been solicited in ways more sophisticated and indirect, may be at work. Indeed, these parties, either themselves or by their attorneys, investigators, and adjusters, are free to contact the unrepresented persons to gather evidence or offer settlement. This scheme makes little sense. As is often true when the law makes little sense, it is not first principles but their interpretation and application that have gone away.

Although I agree with the Court that the case can be resolved by following the three-part inquiry we have identified to assess restrictions on commercial speech, Central Hudson Gas & Elec. Corp. v. Public Serv. Comm'n of N.Y., 447 U.S. 557, 566 (1980), a preliminary observation is in order. Speech has the capacity to convey complex substance, yielding various insights and interpretations depending upon the identity of the listener or the reader and the context of its transmission. It would oversimplify to say that what we consider here is commercial speech and nothing more, for in many instances the banned communications may be vital to the recipients' right to petition the courts for redress of grievances. The complex nature of expression is one reason why even so-called commercial speech has become an essential part of the public discourse the First Amendment secures. If our commercial speech rules are to control this case, then, it is imperative to apply them with exacting care and fidelity to our precedents, for what is at stake is the suppression of information and knowledge that transcends the financial self-interests of the speaker. . . .

While disrespect will arise from an unethical or improper practice, the majority begs a most critical question by assuming that direct-mail solicitations constitute such a practice. The fact is, however, that direct solicitation may serve vital purposes and promote the administration of justice, and to the extent the bar seeks to protect lawyers' reputations by preventing them from engaging in speech some deem offensive, the State is doing nothing more . . . than manipulating the public's opinion by suppressing speech that informs us how the legal system works. The disrespect argument thus proceeds from the very assumption it tries to prove, which is to say that solicitations within 30 days serve no legitimate purpose. This, of course, is censorship pure and simple; and censorship is antithetical to the first principles of free expression. . . .

It is telling that the essential thrust of all the material adduced to justify the State's interest is devoted to the reputational concerns of the Bar. It is not at all clear that this regulation advances the interest of protecting persons who are suffering trauma and grief, and we are cited to no material in the record for that claim. . . .

. . . The accident victims who are prejudiced to vindicate the State's purported desire for more dignity in the legal profession will be the very persons who most need legal advice, for they are the victims who, because they lack education, linguistic ability, or familiarity with the legal system, are unable to seek out legal services. *Cf.* Trainmen v. Virginia ex rel. Virginia State Bar, 377 U.S. 1, 3-4 (1964).

The reasonableness of the State's chosen methods for redressing perceived evils can be evaluated, in part, by a commonsense consideration of other possible means of regulation that have not been tried. Here, the Court neglects the fact that this problem is largely self-policing: Potential clients will not hire lawyers who offend them. And even if a person enters into a contract with an attorney and later regrets it, Florida, like some other States, allows clients to rescind certain contracts with attorneys within a stated time after they are executed. *See, e.g.*, Rules Regulating the Florida Bar, Rule 4-1.5 (Statement of Client's Rights) (effective Jan. 1, 1993). . . . The very fact that some 280,000 direct-mail solicitations are sent to accident victims and their survivors in Florida each year is some indication of the efficacy of this device. . . .

It is most ironic that, for the first time since Bates v. State Bar of Arizona, the Court now orders a major retreat from the constitutional guarantees for commercial speech in order to shield its own profession from public criticism. Obscuring the financial aspect of the legal profession from public discussion through direct-mail solicitation, at the expense of the least sophisticated members of society, is not a laudable constitutional goal. There is no authority for the proposition that the Constitution permits the State to promote the public image of the legal profession by suppressing information about the profession's business aspects. If public respect for the profession erodes because solicitation distorts the idea of the law as most lawyers see it, it must be remembered that real progress begins with more rational speech, not less. . . .

Opinion Number 2010-6
Philadelphia Bar Association Professional Guidance Committee

. . . This inquiry poses questions raised by the ongoing development of different kinds of social interactive media and the propriety of using those to solicit clients. Rule[s] 7.3, Direct Contact with Prospective Clients, [and 7.2, dealing with Advertising, apply]. . . .

The current structure and interpretation of the Rule 7.3 is also affected to some degree by constitutional limitations on exercise of commercial speech. In *Shapero v. Kentucky Bar Association*, 486 U.S. 466 (1988), the Supreme Court held that the first amendment to the United States Constitution prohibited a ban on a lawyer engaging in commercial speech by sending targeted, direct mail solicitations to prospective clients. The opinion distinguished between overbearing solicitation of an interpersonal nature that might be conducted in person from targeted, direct mail solicitations, as follows:

> "In assessing the potential for overreaching and undue influence, the mode of communication makes all the difference. Our decision in *Ohralik* that a State could categorically ban all in-person solicitation turned on two factors. First was our characterization of face-to-face solicitation as 'a practice rife with possibilities for overreaching, invasion of privacy, the exercise of undue influence, and outright fraud'. . . . Second, 'unique . . . difficulties,' . . . would frustrate any attempt at state regulation of in-person solicitation short of an absolute ban because such solicitation is 'not visible or otherwise open to public scrutiny.' . . . Targeted, direct-mail solicitation is distinguishable from the in-person solicitation in each respect.
>
> Like print advertising, petitioner's letter—and targeted, direct-mail solicitation generally—'poses much less risk of overreaching or undue influence' than does in-person solicitation . . . Unlike the potential client with a badgering advocate breathing down his neck, the recipient of a letter and the 'reader of an advertisement . . . can effectively avoid further bombardment of [his] sensibilities simply by averting [his] eyes,' . . .

Shapero was decided in 1988, generations ago in the development of electronic modes of communication. There are now many more methods of communication available that lend themselves to solicitation. Among the different modes of interaction are the following:

E-mail is electronic communication which appears instantly the moment it is sent in the inbox of the recipient. The recipient, of course, need not be sitting at his or her desk at the time it is sent, and indeed it might be days, weeks or months, before it is even looked at. Furthermore, even assuming that the recipient is sitting at his or her desktop when the e-mail comes in, he or she can exercise a choice of whether or not to open it; once opened, whether or not to read it carefully; and once read, to either respond at the moment, or later, or never.

Blogging is a different mode of interaction. It occurs on a "website" at which "posts" are selectively placed for reading by the person who maintains the blog. There is a host that maintains the content of the blog and decides what is "posted" on the blog. That might be done by posting content sent to the host by a blog reader or from any other source. Depending upon the attentiveness of the host, it is possible that something sent by a lawyer to the blog host, with a suggestion that it be posted, could be received by the host and posted in "real-time," and that if other blog readers were watching the blog when it was posted, then that blog reader could immediately respond and effectively have a real-time communication with the lawyer. However, as with e-mail, which can also be "real-time," the participant watching a blog controls the response. He or she can read it, or not, and, after having read it, decide to respond, or not, and when.

Chat rooms are electronic forums where individuals generally participate simultaneously with each other having a kind of typed out "conversation" in real-time. An electronic chat room, however, where the individuals participate by typing in their messages and having them appear on a screen, requires each individual to affirmatively type out a message and then hit the send button thereby exercising the choice to either respond or not. Like simultaneous e-mail and blogs, it offers protection not present in a personal interaction in real-time because a participant is separated with an electronic "wall" and has the ability to simply leave the chat room at any time, solely within the participant's discretion. By definition, there is no in-person or telephonic presence of any other individuals participating in the chat.

In this respect, each of these kinds of electronic communication is different from in-person direct communication and telephone calls. . . .

The Committee believes that the rationale of the prohibition on direct solicitation, both as explained in the Rule itself and the accompanying comments, and by the Supreme Court's opinion in *Shapero*, lead to the conclusion that usage of these kinds of social media for solicitation purposes is acceptable under Rule 7.3. All of these kinds of social interactions are characterized by an ability on the part of the prospective client to "turn off" the soliciting lawyer and respond or not as he or she sees fit, and an ability to keep a record of its contents.

We do recognize that Rule 7.3 does specifically refer to "real-time electronic communication," and that the ABA Reporter's Explanation states that those words were intended to refer to "chat rooms." But we do not feel bound to apply them as the Reporter's Explanation may have intended. First, we think it significant that the writers of the revised Rule did not choose to refer specifically to "chat rooms" in the Rule itself or to any other mode of electronic communication, and thereby recognized that Rule would be applied, or not, to such modes of communication as they developed and their usages and susceptibility for abuse became more settled. They established in the Rule the principle that real-time electronic communications are covered by the Rule, but left to others the issue of what that means, given the technology of the day and the purposes behind the Rule. Second, even assuming that the technological abilities of chat rooms are the same today as they were in 2000, we think it also relevant that the social attitudes and developing rules of internet etiquette are changing. It seems to us that with the increasing sophistication and ubiquity of social media, it has become readily apparent to everyone that they need not respond instantaneously to electronic overtures, and that everyone realizes that, like targeted mail, e-mails, blogs and chat room comments can be readily ignored, or not, as the recipient wishes.

. . . Under this view of Rule 7.3, "real-time electronic communication" is limited to electronic modes of communication used in a way in which it would be socially awkward or difficult for a recipient of a lawyer's overtures to not respond in real time. The Committee also concludes that even on line chat rooms of the sort where discussion occurs by typed communications do not constitute real-time electronic media.

. . . [T]he Committee finds that it is appropriate for a lawyer who encounters persons "blogging" about complaints, indicating they might need legal assistance, to attempt to communicate with them via the blog or via any other electronic method, provided it is not real-time electronic communication in which the prospective clients are compelled to respond immediately. This would mean, for example, that the lawyer observing this discussion via a blog could submit a "post" to the blog or could send an e-mail if the posters to the blog have supplied their e-mails, and the lawyer could invite the bloggers to visit the lawyer's firm's website.

A few cautionary notes are necessary, however.

First, there might be some types of social media, not directly involved in this inquiry, that are so similar to an in-person communication or telephone call that use of them for solicitation is barred. For example, it is possible to conduct chat rooms over the internet in which the participants communicate in real-time by voice over IP. That could be, and likely is, real-time electronic communication.

Second, simply because use of e-mail blogs or chat rooms for solicitation is not categorically barred by Rule 7.3(a) does not mean it might not be utilized in an ethically inappropriate way, where the lawyer suggests by the content of his writing or other methods that the recipient should or must immediately respond. That is, we believe that if the recipient has the ability to not respond, it is not real-time electronic communication, but if the sender of the e-mail suggests in the content of what he sends that it is important or critical to the recipient's interests that he or she immediately respond in real-time and then they do so, that could become a factor that would lead us to believe that the lawyer would be using a mechanism that is not necessarily a realtime electronic communication as one that is in fact a real-time electronic communication in the specific manner of its use.

Third, the contents of communications, whether sent by real-time electronic communication or otherwise, are of course subject to a whole array of important Rules of which the inquirer must be watchful. Those Rules include 7.1, 7.2 and 7.4 (regarding content of communications), 7.3(b) (limitations on solicitations), 4.2 (admonishment against communicating with persons already represented) and 1.7 (conflicts of interest). . . .

▪ The Bounds of the Law:
The Constitution

In previous notes, we have examined legal restraints that limit a lawyer's advocacy on behalf of a client, such as the law of fraud, the criminal law, court orders, and procedural sanctions. *Went For It* illustrates another legal limit. There, lawyers claimed that the federal or state constitution created a decisive limit on the law governing lawyers itself. They argued that constitutional provisions protected their advocacy on behalf of clients and prevented state regulation or limitation of lawyer behavior.

The First Amendment: Lawyer Speech and Prospective Clients

The result in *Went For It* belies the vitality of the First Amendment as a means of overturning state regulation of lawyer speech. In a series of cases over the past four decades, the Supreme Court has forced the rewriting of traditional rules that prevented advertising and solicitation by applying the First Amendment to lawyer speech.[1] In doing so, the Court has labeled some lawyer speech "political," some "commercial," and some as "unprotected." The following table categorizes these cases and the current professional rules that these cases have shaped.

FIRST AMENDMENT REGULATION OF LAWYER ADVERTISING AND SOLICITATION

Level of Constitutional protection	Traditional First Amendment protection	Commercial Speech (intermediate level scrutiny)	Unprotected Speech (no Constitutional protection)
Kind of speech	Political speech, speech that seeks access to the courts	Speech that proposes a commercial transaction	Speech that proposes an illegal activity; misleading commercial speech
Governmental interest necessary to justify regulation	Compelling govt. interest; regulation must be the least restrictive means to promote governmental interest (no prior restraints)	Substantial govt. interest; speech restriction must directly and materially advance govt. interest and regulation must be narrowly drawn (prior restraints allowed)	Govt. interest presumed; complete ban allowed
Cases	NAACP v. Button, 371 U.S. 415 (1963); Bhd. of R.R. Trainmen v. Va., 377 U.S. 1 (1964); United Mine Workers v. Ill. St. Bar Assn., 389 U.S. 217 (1967); United Trans. Union v. St. Bar of Mich., 401 U.S. 576 (1971); In re Primus, 436 U.S. 412 (1978)	Bates v. St. Bar. of Ariz., 433 U.S. 350 (1977); In re RMJ, 455 U.S.191 (1982); Zauderer v. Disc. Counsel of S. Ct. of Ohio, 471 U.S. 626 (1985); Shapero v. Ky. Bar Assn., 486 U.S. 466 (1988); Peel v. Atty. Registration & Disc. Commn., 496 U.S. 91 (1990); Fla. Bar v. Went For It, Inc. 515 U.S. 618 (1995)	Ohralik v. Ohio St. Bar Assn., 436 U.S. 447 (1978)
Challenged	MR 7.3;	MR 7.1, 7.2, 7.4;	MR 7.3(a);
Rules	DR 2-103, 2-104	DR 2-101, 102, 105	DR 2-103, 104

---

1. Other countries more severely restrict lawyer advertising and solicitation. James Moliterno & George Harris, *Global Issues in Legal Ethics* 174-179 (Thomson West 2007).

Political Speech   The left column of the table includes cases in which the Supreme Court has afforded lawyer speech the highest level of First Amendment protection. Here, the Court allows an overbreadth analysis and requires a compelling interest to justify the restriction on speech. In addition, the regulation must be the least restrictive means to promote the governmental interest, and, to prevent chilling fragile First Amendment interests, no prior restraints are allowed.

In *Button*, for example, the court overturned a Virginia antisolicitation regulation that had been applied to prohibit NAACP lawyers from general solicitation of persons to serve as plaintiffs in constitutional challenges by the NAACP to segregated education. The Court held that the regulation violated the NAACP's First and Fourteenth Amendment rights by "unduly inhibiting protected freedoms of expression and association." It characterized the NAACP's litigation activity as "political expression," which "may well be the sole practicable avenue open to a minority to petition for redress of grievances."[2]

In the next three cases, the court applied the same level of constitutional protection to the activities of labor unions that sought to provide low-cost legal services to their members. These decisions culminated with the statement in *United Transportation Union*: "the common thread running through our decisions in NAACP v. Button, Trainmen, and United Mine Workers is that collective activity undertaken to obtain meaningful access to the courts is a fundamental right within the protection of the First Amendment."[3]

In *Primus,* the Court returned to a distinction that it had first made in *Button* between private pecuniary gain and political expression to overturn an attempt by South Carolina to prohibit an ACLU lawyer from soliciting civil rights plaintiffs. The Court found that the ACLU, like the NAACP, used litigation as a "form of political expression," not as a means to resolve private differences. Responding to the state's argument that the ACLU's policy of requesting attorney's fees took the case outside of political expression, the Court found that such a possibility was not sufficient to equate the work of these lawyers "with that group that exist for the primary purpose of financial gain through the recovery of counsel fees."[4]

Commercial Speech   The middle column of the table includes a line of cases in which commercial, rather than political speech, is at stake. Here, the speech proposes a purely commercial transaction. *Went For It* points to the common-sense differences between political and commercial speech that justify a different level of constitutional scrutiny. Thus, a substantial, rather than compelling, governmental interest, must be shown to uphold the regulation. Further, the regulation need not be the least restrictive means of promoting the governmental interest so long as it directly and materially advances the interest and is narrowly drawn. Prior restraints (such as requiring a bar ethics opinion before

---

2. NAACP v. Button, 371 U.S. 415, 429-430 (1963).
3. United Transp. Union v. St. Bar of Mich., 401 U.S. 576, 585 (1971).
4. In re Primus, 436 U.S. 412, 428, 431 (1978).

releasing an advertisement)[55] are allowed. Further, to prevent fraud, states can require lawyers to add disclaimers to their communications, such as "Advertising Material."[66] Finally, constitutional challenges to professional advertising can be made only as applied to the conduct of the person regulated. An overbreadth analysis is not available to challenge every conceivable application of the regulation because the commercial motive makes such speech likely to recur.[7]

This extensive line of cases means that states cannot completely prohibit advertising but can regulate it to prevent false, fraudulent, or misleading statements. *RMJ* and *Shapero* made clear that "advertising" includes targeted mail as well as mass media communications. *Peel* addressed claims of certification in a letterhead, holding that states could not categorically ban lawyers from honestly advertising a certification granted by a national organization, but they were free to prevent potentially misleading certifications from private organizations by creating official state specialty designations.[8] In the context of a partial, time-based prohibition, *Went For It* adds the protection of personal privacy and, where empirical evidence exists, the reputation of the profession as justifiable state interests.

Unprotected Speech   Despite its extensive application of the First Amendment to lawyer speech, the Supreme Court has characterized one form of lawyer speech—in-person solicitation for pecuniary gain—as unprotected by the First Amendment. The right column of the table summarizes this decision, referred to in *Went For It*. When lawyers seek employment by speaking face to face with potential clients, the state may presume harm to prevent it. In *Ohralik*, the court upheld a complete ban on in-person solicitation by lawyers, finding that that type of speech was a subordinate part of a purely commercial transaction. Unlike media advertising, the pressure of in-person solicitation often demands an immediate response, not leaving the recipient free to evaluate the speech. The evils of fraud, undue influence, intimidation, and overreaching in such a circumstance can be presumed as so likely to occur that the state can prohibit all in-person solicitation by lawyers to prevent them. No actual injury need be shown to justify a complete ban on speech in this circumstance.[9]

Although it is now clear that the First Amendment applies to lawyer advertising and solicitation, the Philadelphia Bar Opinion illustrates that some issues remained unresolved. The Supreme Court has not yet addressed radio and television or e-mail, but the Model Rules include them in the advertising category.[10] On the other hand, because it demands a more immediate response similar to in-person solicitation, real-time electronic or telephone contact is included in the

---

5. C. Hudson Gas & Elec. Corp. v. Pub. Serv. Comm'n of N.Y., 447 U.S. 557, 571 (1980).
6. MR 7.3(c).
7. Bates v. St. Bar of Ariz., 433 U.S. 350, 380-381 (1977).
8. MR 7.4 represents the ABA response to *Peel*.
9. Ohralik v. Ohio St. Bar Assn., 436 U.S. 447, 466 (1978).
10. MR 7.2.

ban on solicitation in Model Rule 7.3.[11] Future developments in electronic and social media contact will necessitate continued attention to this distinction.

Other First Amendment Issues

The First Amendment also has been instrumental in a number of other challenges to regulations of lawyer speech, including advising clients, restrictions on pretrial publicity, criticism of judges, judicial elections, the use of mandatory bar dues, and gag rules on the litigation activity of legal services lawyers.

Advising Clients In two recent cases, the Supreme Court has narrowly construed statutory bans on lawyer advice to avoid First Amendment concerns. In Milavetz, Gallop, & Milaveta, P.A. v. United States, the Supreme Court ruled that lawyers are "debt relief agencies" within the meaning of the bankruptcy statute.[12] It then read the prohibition against advice to incur more debt in contemplation of bankruptcy narrowly, to prevent lawyers from advising clients against "loading up" on debt, an illegal purpose, leaving lawyers free to advise about other valid purposes (such as refinancing a mortgage or making other purchases reasonably necessary for support).[13] In Holder v. Humanitarian Law Project, the Court similarly upheld a provision in the Antiterrorism and Effective Death Penalty Act that banned "material support or resources to a foreign terrorist organization" by construing these provisions to distinguish "independent advocacy for a cause from providing a service to a group that is advocating for a cause."[14]

Pretrial Publicity In Gentile v. St. Bar of Nevada,[15] the Court unanimously upheld most of Model Rule 3.6, but a majority found that part of the rule was void for vagueness as applied to *Gentile,* because its provisions failed to give him adequate warning or principle for determining "when his remarks pass from the safe harbor of the general to the forbidden sea of the elaborated." As a result, the ABA rewrote Model Rule 3.6 in 1994 to eliminate the qualifying terms that the Court found misleading and to authorize a lawyer to respond to adverse publicity initiated by others.

Lawyer Criticism of Judges Free speech also collides with the integrity and fairness of the judicial system when lawyers criticize judges. Model Rule 8.2 recognizes that judges are public officials by restating the First Amendment standard required in defamation cases: a lawyer can be disciplined only for making a false statement (not opinion) about a judge if he or she knows the statement is false

---

11. MR 7.3; Fla. St. Bar Assn., Op. A-00-1 (2000).
12. 130 S. Ct. 1324, 1333 (2010).
13. *Id.* at 1335.
14. 130 S. Ct. 2705, 2721 (2010). *See also* Renee Newman Knake, *Attorney Advice and the First Amendment,* 68 Wash. & Lee L. Rev. 639 (2011) (arguing that these cases fail a required strict scrutiny analysis).
15. 501 U.S. 1030 (1991).

or acts in reckless disregard of the truth.[16] Untrue statements have resulted in discipline, however, where the criticism could have been investigated first, or raised with judicial disciplinary authorities rather than in court proceedings or with the press.[17] Similarly, a number of courts have upheld discipline where lawyers have made repeated false and derogatory statements about judges.[18]

Mandatory Bar Dues   The First Amendment further has played a role in reining in the power of state bar associations that use mandatory dues structures to promote political viewpoints with which individual members may disagree. In Keller v. State Bar of California, the Supreme Court held that the State Bar's compulsory dues could only be used to fund activities "justified by the State's interest in regulating the legal profession and improving the quality of legal services."[19] Although the precise line might not be easy to ascertain, ideological activities such as lobbying for or against state legislation or funding state initiatives not reasonably related to legitimate state goals violates the First Amendment.[20] Subsequent cases have determined that bar dues may fund nonideological activities such as an award for journalists writing on law-related topics.[21]

Legal Services Gag Orders   In Legal Services Corp. v. Velazquez, the Supreme Court invalidated a gag rule that restricted Legal Service Corporation lawyers from challenging existing welfare laws when representing clients seeking welfare benefits.[22] The court held that the LCS Act funded constitutionally protected expression, including welfare representation, and that this restriction on speech was an attempt to "exclude from litigation those arguments and theories Congress finds unacceptable but which by their nature are within the province of the courts to consider."[23] In invalidating the restriction, the Court relied not only on the First Amendment, but also on constitutional separation of powers principles. The legislation threatened "serious impairment of the judicial

---

16. For a discussion of the constitutional application of this rule, *see* In re Shearin, 765 A.2d 930, 937-938 (Del. 2000); In re Palmisano, 70 F.3d 483, 487-488 (7th Cir. 1995); Standing Comm. on Disc. v. Yagman, 55 F.3d 1430, 1438 (9th Cir. 1995).

17. *See, e.g.,* In re Becker, 620 N.E.2d 691 (Ind. 1993); Matter of Holtzman, 577 N.E.2d 30 (N.Y. 1991); In re Lacey, 283 N.W.2d 250 (S.D. 1979).

18. *See, e.g.,* Comm. on Leg. Eth. of W. Va. v. Farber, 408 S.E.2d 274 (W. Va. 1991); St. ex rel. Neb. Bar Assn. v. Michaelis, 316 N.W.2d 46 (Neb. 1982).

19. 496 U.S. 1, 13-14 (1990).

20. Morrow v. St. Bar of Cal., 188 F.3d 1174 (9th Cir. 1999) (requiring membership in State Bar that takes positions on public issues is not unconstitutional, so long as members who dissent can obtain a refund of the portion of their mandatory dues used for that purpose).

21. Thiel v. St. Bar of Wis., 94 F.3d 399 (7th Cir. 1996); Alper v. Fla. Bar, 771 So. 2d 523 (Fla. 2000) (upholding funding of a campaign urging voter support of merit selection of judges). *Cf.* Liberty Counsel v. Florida Bar Bd. of Governors, 12 So.3d 183 (Fla. 2009) (Florida Bar's decision to allow family law section to file an amicus brief supporting the rights of homosexuals to adopt children did not violate objecting member's First Amendment rights because advocacy was not being funded with mandatory dues).

22. 531 U.S. 533 (2001).

23. *Id.* at 546.

function" because it prohibited "expression upon which the courts must depend for the proper exercise of the judicial power."[24]

Beyond the First Amendment

Other fundamental constitutional provisions have played a role in shaping the legal regulation of lawyers. We have seen, for example, how the Supreme Court has interpreted the Privileges and Immunities Clause to overturn residency requirements that limit bar admission.[25]

The Supremacy Clause The Supremacy Clause is the focus of litigation when federal law clearly preempts state provisions to the contrary. For example, a lawyer licensed to practice before the United States Patent Office successfully opposed a state's claim that he was engaged in the unauthorized practice of law. The Supreme Court held that the state unauthorized practice law must yield to incompatible federal legislation, and that the Commissioner of Patents was well within his statutory authority to license nonlawyer patent practitioners.[26] The Supremacy Clause also has played a role in several bankruptcy cases where lawyers have discharged debts such as loans or malpractice judgments that later become relevant in bar admission or disciplinary proceedings. Several cases have held that the Supremacy Clause prevents the imposition of conditions on admission or readmission that require a lawyer to repay debts discharged in bankruptcy.[27] On the other hand, some courts have avoided the Supremacy Clause problem by finding that the debt was not the sole cause for the denial of admission,[28] or the repayment was for some purpose other than penalizing the lawyer for discharging a debt, such as protecting the public.[29]

Although Congress has the power to preempt contrary state legislation, it must be clear about its intent. So, for example, when the Department of Justice relied on a general federal "housekeeping statute" that authorizes executive department officials to set up offices and file governmental documents to justify a substantive regulation of lawyer conduct contrary to an existing state court rule, the Eighth Circuit held that the Department lacked "valid statutory authority" to exempt its lawyers from state professional regulation.[30] Shortly thereafter, Congress passed the McDade Amendment, which specifically requires federal prosecutors to abide by state ethics rules.[31]

---

24. *Id.* at 545.
25. *See* The Law Governing Lawyers: *Admission and Discipline, supra* p. 44.
26. Sperry v. Fla. ex rel. Fla. Bar, 373 U.S. 379 (1963).
27. *See, e.g.,* Cleveland Bar Assn. v. Gay, 763 N.E.2d 585 (Ohio 2002); In re Batali, 657 P.2d 775 (Wash. 1983).
28. In re Gahan, 279 N.W.2d 826 (Minn. 1979).
29. *See, e.g.,* People v. Sullivan, 802 P.2d 1091 (Colo. 1990); Brookman v. St. Bar of Cal., 760 P.2d 1023 (Cal. 1988).
30. United States ex rel. O'Keefe v. McDonnell Douglas Corp., 132 F.3d 1252, 1257 (8th Cir. 1998).
31. 28 U.S.C. § 530B (2006). *See, e.g.,* MR 3.8.

Due Process   In cases where lawyers have been admitted to the bar and have a vested right to practice law, courts impose procedural due process requirements on limitations of the right. We considered the contours of these guarantees in detail in Chapter 2.[32] In Chapter 6, we encountered similar due process guarantees when lawyers or others are held in criminal contempt.[33]

In cases where lawyers seek admission, however, courts are much less likely to impose procedural due process guarantees. So, for example, when a lawyer who is not admitted in a jurisdiction seeks leave of a court for admission *pro hac vice*, the Supreme Court has held that a lawyer has no right to appear and need not be afforded any procedural due process if the motion to appear is denied.[34] Some jurisdictions have created more exacting standards that require a judge to provide substantial justifications for refusing *pro hac vice* admission.[35] In criminal cases where the rights of the defendant rather than the interests of the lawyer are at stake, many courts are more likely to require a judge to provide a legitimate reason why the defendant should be deprived of his choice of counsel,[36] but it is enough if the judge provides notice and an opportunity to show cause why the admission should not be allowed.[37]

Constitutional Power and Client Advocacy

It should come as no surprise that the Constitution, which provides the framework for all law, also has shaped the law governing lawyers. Other notes in this series entitled "The Bounds of the Law" have discussed the limits created by general law that restrict a lawyer's ability to advocate on behalf of a client. In this note, by contrast, we have seen lawyers who seek to expand their right to advocate on behalf of their clients by invoking constitutional rights to restrict the application of other general law, such as professional rules, court procedures, or legislative enactments. In pursuing your law practice, you should be alert to other occasions when state or federal constitutional rights might help you promote legitimate client advocacy.

---

32. *See* The Law Governing Lawyers: *Admission and Discipline, supra* p. 44.

33. The Bounds of the Law: *Court Orders, supra* p. 208.

34. Leis v. Flynt, 439 U.S. 438 (1979). A California court rule prohibiting *pro hac vice* admission by California residents also has withstood a privileges and immunities challenge because the state's requirement that residents take and pass the bar examination simply ensures that all residents are treated alike. Paciulan v. George, 229 F.3d 1226 (9th Cir. 2000).

35. *See, e.g.,* St. ex rel. H.K. Porter Co. v. White, 386 S.E.2d 25 (W. Va. 1989); Hahn v. Boeing Co., 621 P.2d 1263 (Wash. 1980).

36. *See, e.g.,* Panzardi-Alvarez v. United States, 879 F.2d 975, 980 (1st Cir. 1989); Fuller v. Diesslin, 868 F.2d 604, 607-608 (3d Cir. 1989); Herrmann v. Summer Plaza Corp., 513 A.2d 1211, 1214 (Conn. 1986).

37. *See, e.g.,* United States v. Collins, 920 F.2d 619 (10th Cir. 1990).

C. Referrals

Problem

15-9. Martyn tells Fox that she has joined a business referral club. "For only $350 per year, I get to be the only lawyer member of the group, along with one each of various other professionals and businesspeople. All I have to do is attend weekly meetings, give 60-second 'commercials' to the group, and provide referrals to other members." Fox checks the Club's website, which says:

> Joining us is like having dozens of salespeople working for you because all of our members carry several copies of your business card around with them. When they meet someone who could use your products or services, they hand out your card and recommend you. It's as simple as that!

Consider: Model Rules 5.4, 7.2

The Applicability of Colo. RRC 7.2 to Internet-Based Lawyer Marketing Program
Formal Ethics Opinion No. 122 (2010)
Colorado Bar Association Ethics Committee

Introduction and Scope

With the acceleration of technology, Colorado lawyers are exposed to a proliferation of private companies offering internet-based services designed to market legal services. Rule 7.2 of the Colorado Rules of Professional Conduct (Colorado Rules or Colo. RPC) governs lawyer advertising and addresses the propriety and contours of both advertising in internet directories and the use of referral services. . . .

The pivotal point is the distinction between "on-line directory listings" and a for-profit "referral service." The lawyer must evaluate the program under consideration to ascertain that it is in the nature of a listing-type directory rather than a for-profit program that provides referrals to specific lawyers, regardless of the purported criteria for such referrals.

Analysis

A lawyer in Colorado is generally permitted to advertise as long as the lawyer complies with the Colorado Rules. Colo. RPC 7.2(a). A lawyer in Colorado is generally not permitted to pay another person (or entity) in exchange for a recommendation of that lawyer's services. Colo. RPC 7.2(b). Two exceptions to Colo. RPC 7.2(b) are pertinent here: (1) under Colo. RPC 7.2(b)(1), a lawyer may pay the reasonable costs of communications permitted by Colo. RPC 7.2; and (2) under Colo. RPC 7.2(b)(2), a lawyer may pay the usual charges of a not-for-profit lawyer referral service or a qualified lawyer referral service. The Committee quotes Model Rule 7.2 comments [5] & [6].]

Comment [6] also cites the American Bar Association's Model Supreme Court Rules Governing Lawyer Referral Services and Model Lawyer Referral and Information Service Quality Assurance Act (ABA Model Lawyer Referral Rules) as guidance with regard to the definition of a referral service. The ABA Model Lawyer Referral Rules do not specifically define a referral service, but instead articulate the functions of such services. On this point, the ABA Model Lawyer Referral Rules provide the following guidance:

- Lawyer referral services have been in operation in this country for more than 50 years, and were first established in response to requests by middle-income people for assistance in obtaining appropriate legal counsel.
- Lawyer referral and information services are designed to assist persons who are able to pay normal attorney fees but whose ability to locate appropriate legal representation is frustrated by a lack of experience with the legal system, a lack of information about the type of service needed, or a fear of the potential costs of seeing a lawyer.
- Lawyer referral programs offer two important services to the public. First, they help the client determine if the problem is truly of a legal nature by screening inquiries and referring the client to other service agencies when appropriate. The second, and perhaps more important function of a lawyer referral service is to provide the client with an unbiased referral to an attorney who has experience in the area of law appropriate to the client's needs.
- The public has come to equate the function of lawyer referral programs with consumer-oriented assistance, and expects that the loyalty of the program will lie with the consumer, and only secondarily with the participating attorney. Thus, the analysis of whether an online marketing program is permissible under Colo. RPC 7.2 seems to be based on the dichotomy between, on one hand, permissible legal service plans or not-for-profit or qualified lawyer referral services, and, on the other hand, a for-profit referral service that is not an approved lawyer referral service. . . .

I. Types of Programs

The Committee has observed that many of the existing on-line marketing programs being offered to Colorado lawyers fall on a spectrum between a clearly permissible directory and a clearly impermissible for-profit referral service. This opinion examines two hypothetical programs, one from each of these modes.

A. Online Lawyer Directories

FictitiousLegalDirectory.com (a fictional name) re-creates traditional forms of advertising, such as telephone directories and printed lawyer directories, but is adjusted for use on websites. In general, this service provides a directory listing much like that of the Colorado Bar Association's Find-A-Lawyer online directory. The information is free to the user and the user contacts the lawyer directly. The engagement occurs between the user and the lawyer. A lawyer participating in FictitiousLegalDirectory.com must pay for the advertising, typically a monthly fee.

FictitiousLegalDirectory.com groups lawyers, and is searchable, on the bases of practice area and geographical area. This program also provides an opportunity for lawyers to increase their visibility in the directory by paying a larger fee for a more prominent listing. The program prominently explains that it is an advertisement and that it is not recommending a specific lawyer to a client.

B. Online Legal Referral Services

A prospective client submits a description of his or her legal problem to FictitiousLegalReferral.com Any member lawyer in the client's geographic area who is interested in working with that client submits a return message through FictitiousLegalReferral.com that is then forwarded to the client. The lawyer pays a fee for each client contact.

In addition to a per contact fee, to participate in FictitiousLegalReferral. com, an attorney must pay a fee based on the size of the geographic area in which the attorney's listing will appear. A lawyer may pay an additional fee to be the "recommended" lawyer in a limited geographic area. . . . The site does not disclose that "recommended" status is based solely on the payment of a fee.

FictitiousLegalReferral.com nonetheless describes the "pairing" process as one that will pair the prospective client with the "right" lawyer, one who is "specifically qualified" to handle the client's case and is located in the desired geographic area. FictitiousLegalReferral.com also makes representations about the quality of the lawyers with whom prospective clients will be paired, claiming that they are "knowledgeable," and "competent."

FictitiousLegalReferral.com requires only that the attorney be licensed and in good standing in the jurisdictions in which he or she practices. FictitiousLegalReferral.com limits membership in each geographic and practice area. FictitiousLegalReferral.com guarantees members that it will limit participation by geographic area and practice area such that members will recoup at least the amount of their membership fee via clients obtained through the site.

FictitiousLegalReferral.com is a for-profit entity. It has not been approved by any regulatory authority in Colorado.

II. Directory vs. For-Profit Referral Service

FictitiousLegalDirectory.com fits within the delineation of permissible advertising set out in Comment [5] to Colo. RPC 7.2 in that it clearly identifies itself as an advertisement. Further, fees charged to participating lawyers are fixed rather than based on "leads" generated. Finally, FictitiousLegalDirectory. com provides information about lawyers only in a ministerial fashion based on non-substantive criteria such as geographic location and practice area.

By contrast, FictitiousLegalReferral.com does not comply with the standards established by Colo. RPC 7.2. First, it charges lawyers based on the actual number of people who hire the lawyer. Further, and crucially, FictitiousLegalReferral. com purports to recommend a lawyer who will meet the inquiring client's needs. It does this without making clear to the client that (a) the recommended lawyer's information is being provided because the lawyer advertised on

FictitiousLegalReferral.com and paid a fee for "recommended" status, and (b) FictitiousLegalReferral.com is not substantively recommending the services of that lawyer.[3]

FictitiousLegalDirectory.com and FictitiousLegalReferral.com represent extreme examples of permissible and impermissible services. In light of the variety of internet advertising programs, the Committee has determined that it is appropriate to identify criteria for evaluating whether a program is an advertising service or a referral service under Colo. RPC 7.2.

III. Criteria for Evaluating Internet Marketing Programs

It is likely that the proliferation of online attorney marketing programs will continue and that new programs will arise with various permutations of the characteristics identified in this opinion. For future guidance to Colorado lawyers, the Committee sets out the following characteristics that must be present in such a program for it to be an advertising program in which a lawyer is permitted to participate:

A. The selection of lawyers for a potential client identified in response to the potential client's information is a non-subjective process performed by a software program or, in any event, performed without exercise of any discretion, based on the information provided by the potential client and the information provided by participating lawyers.[4]

B. The program takes sufficient steps to ensure that a reasonable potential client understands that (1) only lawyers who have paid a fee to be included in the service will be given the opportunity to respond to the potential client and (2) the service makes no assertion about the quality of the lawyers included in the service without an objective basis for such assertion. The service must not state that it is making referrals of lawyers and must not describe itself in a way that would cause a reasonable potential client to believe the program is selecting, referring, and recommending the participating lawyers. The service should disclose whether the program is open to all licensed lawyers or, if there are limits on the number or qualifications of lawyers who may participate in the program, it should disclose the nature of those limits.

C. The fee charged by the program is a reasonable fee for the advertising and public relations services provided.

D. The program does not limit or restrict, whether directly or by means of a high fee structure, finely drawn geographic and legal practice areas, or otherwise, the number of lawyers it allows to participate for a given geographic area or legal practice area to such an extent that the program

---

3. Ethics opinions from other states have reached conflicting conclusions on whether certain services constitute permissible advertising or improper recommendations. . . .

4. Permissible factors include information about the practice areas, the jurisdictions and courts where the attorney is admitted or regularly practices, years of experience, and hourly rates. Impermissible factors include payment of a fee for preference in referrals or payment of a fee for all referrals in a geographic area.

in effect recommends particular types of potential clients to a particular lawyer.

E. Every initial communication sent by the lawyer to a potential client that is identified through the program complies with Colo. RPC 7.3(d).

Conclusion

The existing lawyer marketing programs in Colorado vary widely with respect to the characteristics that bear on the distinction between "online directory listings" and a for-profit "referral service." The lawyer must evaluate the program under consideration to ascertain that it is in the nature of a listing-type directory rather than a program that purports to provide unbiased referrals to specific lawyers based on criteria such as expertise and experience.

D. Inherent Power

So far in this casebook, we have encountered at least eight examples of the inherent power of the judicial branch of government:

1. *Converse* (bar admission);
2. *Walker* (bar discipline);
3. *Bothwell* (inherent power to compel an unwilling lawyer to accept a civil appointment);
4. *Chen* (contempt power);
5. *Shaffer Equipment* (sanctions against lawyers for failing to mitigate client perjury);
6. The *Murray, Sanford, Eastman Kodak, Cascades,* and *Martin* cases (disqualification);
7. *Mattel* (sanctions for frivolous lawsuit); and
8. *Surowiec* (sanctions for discovery abuse).

These are all examples of *positive* inherent powers; that is, power that the judicial branch of government finds necessary to perform its constitutionally required functions.

This section examines a different but related facet of the inherent powers doctrine: *negative* inherent powers. When a court exercises a negative inherent power, it finds the judicial branch's constitutional power to regulate the bar sufficiently powerful to nullify another branch of government's exercise of the same power. Courts exercise a negative inherent power when they declare a legislative enactment unconstitutional because it infringes on a judicial prerogative.[1]

---

1. *See, e.g.,* Gmerek v. St. Ethics Comm'n, 807 A.2d 812 (Pa. 2002) (evenly divided court upheld trial court's decision that lobbying disclosure act controlled the conduct of lawyer when rendering legal services and therefore infringed on the supreme court's exclusive jurisdiction to regulate lawyers); Irwin v. Surdyk's Liquor, 599 N.W.2d 132 (Minn. 1999) (legislative amendment invalid because it set a "maximum permissible fee" in workers' compensation cases and repealed a prior

Problem

15-10. The State Trial Lawyers' Association recently retained Martyn & Fox. It wants to challenge recent tort reform legislation that caps contingent fees in state medical malpractice and workers' compensation actions. What advice should Martyn & Fox give its new client?

Consider: Model Rule 1.5

Campbell v. Asbury Automotive, Inc.
2011 Ark. 157 (2011)

Paul E. DANIELSON, Associate Justice.

. . . On December 31, 2002, . . . a class-action complaint [was filed] against Asbury Automotive ("Asbury"), . . . alleg[ing] that Asbury "charged Plaintiffs and other similarly situated members of the Plaintiff class, an illegal document preparation fee for preparing the vehicle installment contract (a legal instrument) for the purchase of a vehicle." The [complaint] asserted that the fee itself was illegal, constituting the unauthorized practice of law, and that the retention of the fee violated the Arkansas Deceptive Trade Practices Act ("ADTPA"), Ark. Code Ann. §§ 4-88-101 to -804 (Repl. 2001 & Supp. 2009), resulting in unjust enrichment. . . .

A. Arkansas Deceptive Trade Practices Act . . .

In Preston v. Stoops, 285 S.W.3d 606 (Ark. 2008), the Estate of the Prestons sued their former attorneys from an Oklahoma law firm (collectively, "Stoops"), alleging a violation of the ADTPA and breach of the covenant of good faith and fair dealing. The action stemmed from Mr. Preston's prior medical malpractice suit that was dismissed with prejudice due to Stoops's failure to be licensed as an attorney in Arkansas. Stoops sought summary judgment on the basis that the ADTPA did not apply to the practice of law. . . . We affirmed, stating,

> Stoops undertook legal representation of the Prestons when Stoops was not authorized to practice law in Arkansas. Thus, the unauthorized practice of law is at issue. The unauthorized practice of law falls within this court's constitutional authority to control and govern the practice of law. The suggestion that the practice of law can be regulated by an act of the General Assembly is without merit. Oversight and control of the practice of law is under the exclusive authority of the judiciary. Under Ark. Const. amend. 28, "The Supreme Court shall make

---

provision that had allowed judicial review of lawyer's fees and departure from a statutory contingent fee formula in cases involving medical benefits); Succession of Wallace, 574 So. 2d 348 (La. 1991) (statute that provided that an estate executor could discharge a lawyer designated in the testator's will "only for just cause" invalid because it directly conflicted with MR1.16, which grants clients the right to discharge lawyers for any reason).

rules regulating the practice of law and the professional conduct of attorneys at law." That responsibility could not be discharged if it were dependent upon or controlled by statutes enacted by the General Assembly. Further, any action by the General Assembly to control the practice of law would be a violation of the separation-of-powers doctrine. *See* Ark. Const. art. 4, §§ 1 & 2. We affirm the circuit court's finding that the ADTPA does not apply to the practice of law. *Stoops,* 285 S.W.3d at 609.

Stoops thus stands for the proposition that the unauthorized practice of law is not cognizable under the ADTPA, where an *attorney* not licensed in Arkansas attempts to practice law in Arkansas.

That being said, this court has also recognized another facet of the unauthorized practice of law—the attempt to practice law by a nonlawyer. This is the type of unauthorized practice of law alleged by Campbell, and we must determine whether the General Assembly is precluded from creating a cause of action for the unauthorized practice of law by a nonlawyer, such as under the ADTPA. We hold that it is not. . . .

We have . . . recognized . . . that "[s]tatutes which provide a penalty for unauthorized practice of law by a nonresident of the forum state have been held to be cumulative to the powers of the courts to punish." *McKenzie v. Burris,* 500 S.W.2d 357, 365 (Ark. 1973). Statutes relating to the practice of law are merely in aid of, but do not supersede or detract from the power of the judicial department to define, regulate, and control the practice of law, and the legislative branch may not, in any way, hinder, interfere with, restrict, or frustrate the powers of the courts. Moreover, we have "chosen to recognize and apply certain statutes which are not necessarily inconsistent with, or repugnant to, court rules, and do not hinder, interfere with, frustrate, pre-empt or usurp judicial powers, at least when the statutes were, at the time of enactment, clearly within the province of the legislative branch and when the courts have not acted in the particular matter covered by the statute." *Id.*

Based on the foregoing, it is clear that neither *Stoops* nor Amendment 28 has foreclosed any and all legislative foray into the unauthorized practice of law *by a nonlawyer,* such as under the ADTPA, despite Asbury's contention to the contrary. There can be no doubt that the power of the judicial department, acting through this court to regulate the practice of law, is "exclusive and supreme" under Amendment 28. Yet, nonlawyers engaging in what we exclusively define as the practice of law are currently beyond its purview for purposes of meaningful sanction.[3] Therefore, we hold that, where the General Assembly has seen fit to

---

3. While this court does have a committee that was created to deal with the unauthorized practice of law, we have observed that the rules creating the Supreme Court Committee on the Unauthorized Practice of Law (CUPL) make it plain that, although the Committee is vested with the authority to investigate claims relating to the unauthorized practice of law, . . . CUPL does not have the authority to enforce its opinions without filing a complaint in circuit court, where it can obtain a declaration finding a person is unlawfully practicing law and an injunction to force that person to stop the unauthorized practice . . . .

provide a cause of action when warranted for such activity by a nonlawyer, such as under the ADTPA, neither *Stoops* nor Amendment 28 precludes such action, as long as the legislation in no way hinders, interferes with, restricts, or frustrates the powers of the judiciary to define, regulate, and control the practice of law. We, therefore, reverse the circuit court's grant of summary judgment on this issue and remand. . . .

[B]. Unauthorized Practice of Law

Asbury . . . asserts that its completion of standardized forms, necessary to the purchase of motor vehicles, did not require the training, skill, or judgment of an attorney and was not the practice of law. It avers that it did not hold itself out as providing legal services and did not give legal advice or counsel. It further states that the public benefited by its completion of the forms and that its charging of a separate fee did not transform completion of the forms into the practice of law. . . .

With regard to the practice of law, this court has noted that "[i]t is uniformly held that many activities, such as writing and interpreting wills, contracts, trust agreements and the giving of legal advice in general, constitute practicing law."[4] [We have] held that the completion "by filling in the blank spaces" of "standardized and approved prepared forms of" instruments constituted the practice of law and included warranty deeds; disclaimer deeds; quitclaim deeds; joint tenancy deeds; options; easements; loan applications; promissory notes; real estate mortgages; deeds of trust; assignments of leases or rentals; contracts of sale of real estate; releases and satisfactions of real estate mortgages; agreements for the sale of real estate; bills of sale; contracts of sale; mortgages; pledges of personal property; notices and declarations of forfeiture; notices requiring strict compliance; releases and discharges of mechanic's and materialmen's liens; printed forms approved by attorneys, including the various forms furnished by title insurance companies to real estate brokers for use by them as agents of title insurance companies; actions as closing agent for mortgage loans and completion by filling in the blanks therein with factual data such instruments as are furnished to brokers and are necessary, incidental, and ancillary to the closing of the transaction between the mortgagee for whom they act as agent and the mortgagor; and leases. In that same vein, this court held, in Beach Abstract & Guaranty Co. v. Bar Ass'n of Arkansas, 326 S.W.2d 900 (Ark. 1959), that title examination and curative work, when done for another, constituted the practice of law in its strictest sense.

Notwithstanding those holdings, this court, in Creekmore v. Izard, 367 S.W.2d 419 (Ark. 1963), [and] . . . Pope County Bar Ass'n, Inc. v. Suggs, 624

---

4. We have further recognized that

   when one appears before a court of record for the purpose of transacting business with the court in connection with any pending litigation or when any person seeks to invoke the processes of the court in any matter pending before it, that person is engaging in the practice of law. . . . *Union Nat'l Bank,* 273 S.W.2d at 411.

S.W.2d 828 (Ark. 1981), . . . held that it was in the public interest to permit the limited, outside use of standard, printed forms "in connection with simple real estate transactions, provided they had been previously prepared by a lawyer" and provided:

(1)   That the person for whom the broker is acting has declined to employ a lawyer to prepare the necessary instruments and has authorized the broker to do so; and

(2)   That the forms are approved by a lawyer either before or after the blanks are filled in but prior to delivery to the person for whom the broker is acting; and

(3)   That the forms shall not be used for other than simple real estate transactions which arise in the usual course of the broker's business; and

(4)   That the forms shall be used only in connection with real estate transactions actually handled by such brokers as a broker; and

(5)   That the broker shall make no charge for filling in the blanks; and

(6)   That the broker shall not give advice or opinions as to the legal rights of the parties, as to the legal effects of instruments to accomplish specific purposes or as to the validity of title to real estate. 624 S.W.2d at 829.

The court noted that, standing alone, the completion of the forms at issue fell readily within the practice of law; but . . . [n]onetheless . . . permitted the use of the forms under the restrictions it set forth.

. . . [I]t is clear to this court that the restrictions set forth in *Suggs* have equal application to the forms used in the motor-vehicle-sales business. Asbury admits that the forms are legally binding,[6] but avers that such business dealings are common and simply incidental to the motor-vehicle-dealer business. While that may be true, this court has taken such argument into account and has remained steadfast, as in *Creekmore* and *Suggs,* that the completion of forms legal in nature by nonlawyers, while ordinarily the practice of law, may be permitted, but only within very certain, specific parameters. . . .

The question is, then, did Asbury comply with those requirements? The record in this case makes clear that it did not. . . .

Here, it is abundantly clear that Asbury charged a documentary fee in relation to its completion of legal forms.[7] Because it did so, the circuit court was

---

6. In its November 30, 2006 order, the circuit court found that the following forms used by Asbury were legal documents that affected the legal rights of the consumer: (1) a retail buyer's order; (2) the credit sale disclosure statement; (3) the truth-in-lending statement; (4) the bill of sale; and (5) the purchaser's order. It further found that the following were legal documents in its subsequent order of February 12, 2008: (1) a power of attorney; (2) a warranty contract; (3) a motor-vehicle-lease agreement; (4) a rider amending a sales contract; (5) a promissory note; and (6) a letter of permission. Asbury does not challenge either finding by the circuit court.

7. Asbury also argues that prohibiting it from filling in blanks on routine agreements would unduly hamper commerce and harm the public. However, our case law in no way prohibits Asbury from completing such forms for the benefit of its customers; it simply prohibits Asbury from charging a fee for doing so.

correct in finding that Asbury engaged in the unauthorized practice of law, in contravention of this court's decisions in *Creekmore* and *Suggs*. For this reason, we hold that the circuit court did not err in granting summary judgment to Campbell.

[C]. Finding of a Fiduciary Relationship

Asbury argues, for its second point on cross-appeal, that the circuit court erred in finding that car dealers that prepare or complete legal documents are held to the same standards as a licensed attorney. Specifically, it claims that the unauthorized practice of law in no way creates a fiduciary relationship. . . .

This court has previously held that the standard of care to be applied to one who improperly assumes the function of a lawyer shall be, at a minimum, no less than that required of a licensed attorney. We have further held that a fiduciary relationship exists between attorney and client, and the confidence that the relationship begets between the parties makes it necessary for the attorney to act in utmost good faith. Here, Asbury, by virtue of its unauthorized practice of law, was held to the same standard of care as a licensed attorney, and that would include having a fiduciary relationship with its customers. Accordingly, we cannot say that the circuit court erred in so concluding. . . .

Robert L. BROWN, Justice, dissenting. . . .

[T]he majority now concludes that practicing attorneys, including out-of-state attorneys unauthorized to practice in Arkansas shall be regulated solely by this court while nonlawyers engaged in the unauthorized practice shall not be. . . .

What *Stoops* and *Born* manifestly prohibit is a legislative foray into regulating the practice of law via the ADTPA, period. The majority, though, chooses to draw an artificial distinction between an Oklahoma lawyer unauthorized to practice in Arkansas, which was the situation in *Stoops,* and a lay person who attempts to practice law in this state. The client damaged by the unauthorized attorney in *Stoops* had no recourse under the ADTPA. . . .

E. Unauthorized Practice

Problems

15-11. Martyn & Fox represents mortgagees in lending transactions. Martyn & Fox is approached by a group of investors who want to set up a new business, make Martyn & Fox minority shareholders, and enter into a ten-year contract with Martyn & Fox that provides that Martyn & Fox will have the new enterprise undertake all of the nonlegal aspects of Martyn & Fox's practice (title searches, service of process, advertising foreclosure sales, filing papers, photocopying, messenger services) for the next ten years. "Your clients won't even have to know."

15-12. Martyn & Fox represents a Norwegian company that has subsidiaries in two distant states. Martyn & Fox lawyers travel to both states to negotiate collective bargaining agreements. Has Martyn & Fox engaged in unauthorized practice? Does it matter if the Norwegian company has an office in Martyn & Fox's state?

15-13. A new proposal before the ABA would permit any foreign lawyer to serve as inside counsel or be admitted *pro hac vice* in any proceeding where such admission is available to lawyers from other states. How will you vote?

Consider: Model Rules 5.4, 5.5, 5.7, 7.2, 8.5

Birbrower, Montalbano, Condon & Frank P.C. v. Superior Court

949 P.2d 1 (Cal. 1998), cert. denied, 525 U.S. 920 (1998)

CHIN, J.

Business and Professions Code section 6125 states: "No person shall practice law in California unless the person is an active member of the State Bar . . . ." We must decide whether an out-of-state law firm, not licensed to practice law in this state, violated section 6125 when it performed legal services in California for a California-based client under a fee agreement stipulating that California law would govern all matters in the representation. . . .

I. BACKGROUND

The facts with respect to the unauthorized practice of law question are essentially undisputed. Birbrower is a professional law corporation incorporated in New York, with its principal place of business in New York. During 1992 and 1993, Birbrower attorneys, defendants Kevin F. Hobbs and Thomas A. Condon (Hobbs and Condon), performed substantial work in California relating to the law firm's representation of ESQ. Neither Hobbs nor Condon has ever been licensed to practice law in California. None of Birbrower's attorneys were licensed to practice law in California during Birbrower's ESQ representation.

ESQ is a California corporation with its principal place of business in Santa Clara County. In July 1992, the parties negotiated and executed the fee agreement in New York, providing that Birbrower would perform legal services for ESQ, including "All matters pertaining to the investigation of and prosecution of all claims and causes of action against Tandem Computers Incorporated [Tandem]." The "claims and causes of action" against Tandem, a Delaware corporation with its principal place of business in Santa Clara County, California, related to a software development and marketing contract between Tandem and ESQ dated March 16, 1990 (Tandem Agreement). The Tandem Agreement stated that "The internal laws of the State of California (irrespective of its choice of law principles) shall govern the validity of this Agreement, the construction of its terms, and the interpretation and enforcement of the rights and duties of the parties hereto." Birbrower asserts, and ESQ disputes, that ESQ knew Birbrower was not licensed to practice law in California.

While representing ESQ, Hobbs and Condon traveled to California on several occasions. . . .

ESQ eventually settled the Tandem dispute, and the matter never went to arbitration. But before the settlement, ESQ and Birbrower modified the contingency fee agreement. The modification changed the fee arrangement from contingency to fixed fee, providing that ESQ would pay Birbrower over $1 million. The original contingency fee arrangement had called for Birbrower to receive "one-third (1/3) of all sums received for the benefit of the Clients . . . whether obtained through settlement, motion practice, hearing, arbitration, or trial by way of judgment, award, settlement, or otherwise . . . . "

In January 1994, ESQ sued Birbrower for legal malpractice and related claims in Santa Clara County Superior Court. Birbrower removed the matter to federal court and filed a counterclaim, which included a claim for attorney fees for the work it performed in both California and New York. The matter was then remanded to the superior court. . . . ESQ argued that by practicing law without a license in California and by failing to associate legal counsel while doing so, Birbrower violated section 6125, rendering the fee agreement unenforceable. . . .

II. DISCUSSION

A. The Unauthorized Practice of Law

The California Legislature enacted section 6125 in 1927 as part of the State Bar Act (the Act), a comprehensive scheme regulating the practice of law in the state. . . . Since the Act's passage, the general rule has been that, although persons may represent themselves and their own interests regardless of State Bar membership, no one but an active member of the State Bar may practice law for another person in California. The prohibition against unauthorized law practice is within the state's police power and is designed to ensure that those performing legal services do so competently.

A violation of section 6125 is a misdemeanor. Moreover, "No one may recover compensation for services as an attorney at law in this state unless [the person] was at the time the services were performed a member of The State Bar."

Although the Act did not define the term "practice law," case law explained it as "'the doing and performing services in a court of justice in any matter depending therein throughout its various stages and in conformity with the adopted rules of procedure.'" (People v. Merchants Protective Corp., 209 P. 363, 365 (Cal. 1922).) *Merchants* included in its definition legal advice and legal instrument and contract preparation, whether or not these subjects were rendered in the course of litigation. . . .

In addition to not defining the term "practice law," the Act also did not define the meaning of "in California." In today's legal practice, questions often arise concerning whether the phrase refers to the nature of the legal services, or restricts the Act's application to those out-of-state attorneys who are physically present in the state.

Section 6125 has generated numerous opinions on the meaning of "practice law" but none on the meaning of "in California." In our view, the practice of law "in California" entails sufficient contact with the California client to render the nature of the legal service a clear legal representation. In addition to a quantitative analysis, we must consider the nature of the unlicensed lawyer's activities in the state. Mere fortuitous or attenuated contacts will not sustain a finding that the unlicensed lawyer practiced law "in California." The primary inquiry is whether the unlicensed lawyer engaged in sufficient activities in the state, or created a continuing relationship with the California client that included legal duties and obligations.

Our definition does not necessarily depend on or require the unlicensed lawyer's physical presence in the state. Physical presence here is one factor we may consider in deciding whether the unlicensed lawyer has violated section 6125, but it is by no means exclusive. For example, one may practice law in the state in violation of section 6125 although not physically present here by advising a California client on California law in connection with a California legal dispute by telephone, fax, computer, or other modern technological means. Conversely, although we decline to provide a comprehensive list of what activities constitute sufficient contact with the state, we do reject the notion that a person automatically practices law "in California" whenever that person practices California law anywhere, or "virtually" enters the state by telephone, fax, e-mail, or satellite. . . .

Exceptions to section 6125 do exist, but are generally limited to allowing out-of-state attorneys to make brief appearances before a state court or tribunal. They are narrowly drawn and strictly interpreted. For example, an out-of-state attorney not licensed to practice in California may be permitted, by consent of a trial judge, to appear in California in a particular pending action.

In addition, with the permission of the California court in which a particular cause is pending, out-of-state counsel may appear before a court as counsel *pro hac vice*. A court will approve a *pro hac vice* application only if the out-of-state attorney is a member in good standing of another state bar and is eligible to practice in any United States court or the highest court in another jurisdiction. The out-of-state attorney must also associate an active member of the California Bar as attorney of record and is subject to the Rules of Professional Conduct of the State Bar.

The Act does not regulate practice before United States courts. Thus, an out-of-state attorney engaged to render services in bankruptcy proceedings was entitled to collect his fee.

Finally, California Rules of Court, rule 988, permits the State Bar to issue registration certificates to foreign legal consultants who may advise on the law of the foreign jurisdiction where they are admitted. These consultants may not, however, appear as attorneys before a California court or judicial officer or otherwise prepare pleadings and instruments in California or give advice on the law of California or any other state or jurisdiction except those where they are admitted.

The Legislature has recognized an exception to section 6125 in international disputes resolved in California under the state's rules for arbitration and conciliation of international commercial disputes. This exception states that in a commercial conciliation in California involving international commercial disputes, "The parties may appear in person or be represented or assisted by any person of their choice. A person assisting or representing a party need not be a member of the legal profession or licensed to practice law in California." (Code Civ. Proc., §1297.351.) Likewise, the Act does not apply to the preparation of or participation in labor negotiations and arbitrations arising under collective bargaining agreements in industries subject to federal law.

B. The Present Case

The undisputed facts here show that neither *Baron*'s definition nor our "sufficient contact" definition of "practice law in California" would excuse Birbrower's extensive practice in this state. Nor would any of the limited statutory exceptions to section 6125 apply to Birbrower's California practice. As the Court of Appeal observed, Birbrower engaged in unauthorized law practice in California on more than a limited basis, and no firm attorney engaged in that practice was an active member of the California State Bar. As noted, in 1992 and 1993, Birbrower attorneys traveled to California to discuss with ESQ and others various matters pertaining to the dispute between ESQ and Tandem. Hobbs and Condon discussed strategy for resolving the dispute and advised ESQ on this strategy. Furthermore, during California meetings with Tandem representatives in August 1992, Hobbs demanded Tandem pay $15 million, and Condon told Tandem he believed damages in the matter would exceed that amount if the parties proceeded to litigation. Also in California, Hobbs met with ESQ for the stated purpose of helping to reach a settlement agreement and to discuss the agreement that was eventually proposed. Birbrower attorneys also traveled to California to initiate arbitration proceedings before the matter was settled. As the Court of Appeal concluded, " . . . the Birbrower firm's in-state activities clearly constituted the [unauthorized] practice of law" in California.

Birbrower contends, however, that section 6125 is not meant to apply to any out-of-state attorneys. Instead, it argues that the statute is intended solely to prevent nonattorneys from practicing law. This contention is without merit because it contravenes the plain language of the statute. Section 6125 clearly states that no person shall practice law in California unless that person is a member of the State Bar. The statute does not differentiate between attorneys or nonattorneys, nor does it excuse a person who is a member of another state bar. . . .

Birbrower next argues that we do not further the statute's intent and purpose—to protect California citizens from incompetent attorneys—by enforcing it against out-of-state attorneys. Birbrower argues that because out-of-state attorneys have been licensed to practice in other jurisdictions, they have already demonstrated sufficient competence to protect California clients. But Birbrower's argument overlooks the obvious fact that other states' laws may differ substantially from California law. Competence in one jurisdiction does not necessarily guarantee competence in another. By applying section 6125 to out-of-state attorneys who engage in the extensive practice of law in California without becoming licensed in our state, we serve the statute's goal of assuring the competence of all attorneys practicing law in this state. . . .

Birbrower alternatively asks us to create an exception to section 6125 for work incidental to private arbitration or other alternative dispute resolution proceedings. Birbrower points to fundamental differences between private arbitration and legal proceedings, including procedural differences relating to discovery, rules of evidence, compulsory process, cross-examination of witnesses, and other areas. As Birbrower observes, in light of these differences, at least one court has decided that an out-of-state attorney could recover fees for services rendered in an arbitration proceeding. . . . (*See* Williamson v. John D. Quinn Const. Corp., 537 F. Supp. 613, 616 (S.D.N.Y. 1982).)

In *Williamson*, a New Jersey law firm was employed by a client's New York law firm to defend a construction contract arbitration in New York. It sought to recover fees solely related to the arbitration proceedings, even though the attorney who did the work was not licensed in New York, nor was the firm authorized to practice in the state. In allowing the New Jersey firm to recover its arbitration fees, the federal district court concluded that an arbitration tribunal is not a court of record, and its fact-finding process is not similar to a court's process. The court relied on a local state bar report concluding that representing a client in an arbitration was not the unauthorized practice of law. But . . . in the instant case, it is undisputed that none of the time that the New York attorneys spent in California was spent in arbitration; *Williamson* thus carries limited weight. . . .

We decline Birbrower's invitation to craft an arbitration exception to section 6125's prohibition of the unlicensed practice of law in this state. Any exception for arbitration is best left to the Legislature, which has the authority to determine qualifications for admission to the State Bar and to decide what constitutes the practice of law. Even though the Legislature has spoken with respect to international arbitration and conciliation, it has not enacted a similar rule for private arbitration proceedings. Of course, private arbitration and other alternative dispute resolution practices are important aspects of our justice system. Section 6125, however, articulates a strong public policy favoring the practice of law in California by licensed State Bar members. In the face of the Legislature's silence, we will not create an arbitration exception under the facts presented. . . .

Finally, Birbrower urges us to adopt an exception to section 6125 based on the unique circumstances of this case. Birbrower notes that "Multistate relationships are a common part of today's society and are to be dealt with in common-sense fashion." . . .

Although, as discussed, we recognize the need to acknowledge and, in certain cases, to accommodate the multistate nature of law practice, the facts here show that Birbrower's extensive activities within California amounted to considerably more than any of our state's recognized exceptions to section 6125 would allow. Accordingly, we reject Birbrower's suggestion that we except the firm from section 6125's rule under the circumstances here.

C. Compensation for Legal Services

Because Birbrower violated section 6125 when it engaged in the unlawful practice of law in California, the Court of Appeal found its fee agreement with ESQ unenforceable in its entirety. Without crediting Birbrower for some services performed in New York, for which fees were generated under the fee agreement, the court reasoned that the agreement was void and unenforceable because it included payment for services rendered to a California client in the state by an unlicensed out-of-state lawyer. . . . The Court of Appeal let stand, however, the trial court's decision to allow Birbrower to pursue its fifth cause of action in quantum meruit.[5] We agree with the Court of Appeal to the extent it barred Birbrower from recovering fees generated under the fee agreement for the unauthorized legal services it performed in California. We disagree with the same court to the extent it implicitly barred Birbrower from recovering fees generated under the fee agreement for the limited legal services the firm performed in New York.

It is a general rule that an attorney is barred from recovering compensation for services rendered in another state where the attorney was not admitted to the bar. The general rule, however, has some recognized exceptions. . . .

We agree with Birbrower that it may be able to recover fees under the fee agreement for the limited legal services it performed for ESQ in New York to the extent they did not constitute practicing law in California, even though those services were performed for a California client. Because section 6125 applies to the practice of law in California, it does not, in general, regulate law practice in other states. . . .

■ Practice Pointers:
The Globalization of Law Practice

Unauthorized practice rules are one example of practice restrictions that are under comparative scrutiny around the world. Technology, market forces, and the needs of clients have pressured lawyers to reconsider the practice of law in a global context.

We have already seen a number of examples of comparative legal ethics in this casebook. For example, we noted that many countries provide some legal services to their citizens who cannot afford to pay.[1] We also have seen that the EU differs from U.S. courts about whether the attorney-client privilege extends to inside counsel,[2] and on the extent to which lawyers can screen to remedy conflicts of interest.[3] England and Canada disagree about the extent to

---

5. We observe that ESQ did not seek (and thus the court did not grant) summary adjudication on the Birbrower firm's quantum meruit claim for the reasonable value of services rendered. Birbrower thus still has a cause of action pending in quantum meruit.

1. *See* Lawyers and Clients: *Service Pro Bono Publico, supra* p. 64 n. 2, 4.

2. *See* Lawyers and Clients: *Representing Organizations, supra* p. 187.

3. *See* Practice Pointers: *Implementing an Effective Conflicts Control System, supra* p. 419; Janine Griffiths-Baker & Nancy J. Moore, *Regulating Conflicts of Interest in Global Law Firms: Peace in Our Time?* 80 Fordham L. Rev. 2541 (2012).

which lawyers should be subject to criminal reporting provisions in anti-money-laundering statutes.[4] Some of the most significant differences in regulation occur in bar regulation, including multijurisdictional and multidisciplinary practice.[5]

Multijurisdictional Practice

Unauthorized practice rules combine with Model Rule 5.5(a) to keep lawyers jurisdiction-specific and prevent multijurisdictional practice. *Birbrower* illustrates the fact that lawyers risk a number of penalties if they represent clients in a jurisdiction (or country) where they are not admitted to practice law. Current U.S. restrictions on the unauthorized practice of law originated about a century ago and apply to both nonadmitted lawyers and laypersons. In many states, statutes define the restriction and provide for criminal (usually misdemeanor) penalties.[6] *Campbell* illustrates the other option: courts enforce the restriction through discipline and injunctive relief rather than criminal penalty.[7] *Campbell* and *Birbrower* also typify the practice of all states that rely on judicial definition for the exact meaning of "unauthorized practice" of law.

Yet, as both individual and corporate clients have become more mobile, they often confront legal problems in many jurisdictions. Individuals can live in several jurisdictions and might want a trusted lawyer to provide legal services in all of them. Entity clients can do business throughout the world and might wish to concentrate their legal work with only a few law firms. Some are affected by international, federal, and state environmental, labor, securities, antitrust, or patent laws. Clients or law firms also might prefer to outsource some legal tasks to providers in another jurisdiction.[8]

Model Rule 5.5 allows some, but not all, multijurisdictional practice. The basic rule articulated in *Birbrower* remains the same: A lawyer is not allowed to establish an office or "other systematic and continuous presence" in a jurisdiction where he or she is not admitted to practice. *Birbrower* also illustrates that some jurisdictions have developed exceptions or safe harbors (such as representation

---

4. *See* The Bounds of the Law: *A Reprise, supra* p. 528.

5. *See* Laurel S. Terry, Steve Mark, & Tahlia Gordon, *Adopting Regulatory Objectives for the Legal Profession,* 80 Fordham L. Rev. 2685 (2012); Deborah L. Rhode & Alice Woolley, *Comparative Perspectives on Lawyer Regulation: An Agenda for Reform in the United States and Canada,* 80 Fordham L. Rev. 2761 (2012).

6. *E.g.,* Cal. Bus. & Prof. Code § 6126 (2007); Minn. Stat. § 481.02 (2006); N.Y. Jud. L. § 478 (2007); Tex. Penal Code § 38.123 (2007); Va. Code § 54.1-3904 (2007).

7. *See, e.g.,* Disc. Counsel v. Shrode, 766 N.E.2d 597 (Ohio 2002) (nonlawyer enjoined from filing court documents for a corporation as a "statutory agent"); Fla. Bar v. Furman, 376 So. 2d. 378 (Fla. 1979) (nonlawyer enjoined from providing legal advice about marriage dissolutions and adoptions).

8. *See* MR 1.1 Comment [6], MR 5.3 Comment [3], MR 5.5 Comment [1]; ABA Formal Op. 08-451 (2008) (Lawyer's Obligations When Outsourcing Legal and Nonlegal Support Services); Council of Bars and Law Societies of Europe, *CCBE Guidelines on Legal Outsourcing* (2010) *available at* http://www.ccbe.eu/fileadmin/user_upload/NTCdocument/EN_Guidelines_on_leg1_1277906265. pdf (last visited July 12, 2012).

in arbitration matters) that are recognized in one jurisdiction, but might not excuse similar conduct in another jurisdiction.

Rule 5.5 carves out two groups of exceptions. The first hinges on temporary presence in a jurisdiction to accomplish some specific purpose, such as *pro hac vice* admission, reciprocal admission by motion, the licensing of legal consultants, and temporary practice of foreign law by foreign lawyers. This group of exceptions also includes temporarily associating with another lawyer admitted in the jurisdiction, practice reasonably related to a matter where the lawyer is admitted to practice, and alternative dispute resolution proceedings that are reasonably related to practice where the lawyer is admitted. Note that these exceptions would not have legitimated the California practice of the New York lawyers in *Birbrower* because they were not associated with California counsel, the matter apparently was not related to their New York practice,[9] and ADR was not the primary focus of their efforts to resolve the contract dispute.

The second group of exceptions does not rest on temporary presence, but instead acknowledges a competing policy, such as the need for multijurisdictional services to some clients. Thus, in some, but not all states, entities can hire inside counsel who do not need to be admitted in the jurisdiction where their office is located, and legal services can be provided in any jurisdiction if they are either authorized by federal law[10] or the law of that jurisdiction.

The development of differing exceptions by different jurisdictions parallels the current EU practice that provides a common set of rules for cross-border practice,[11] but also allows each member state to determine foreign practice rules.[12] Similar issues arise among states in this country, which in turn raise issues about the power to discipline lawyers. Model Rule 8.5 clarifies that each jurisdiction where law practice occurs has the ability to discipline both admitted and nonadmitted lawyers.[13] It also provides a choice of law provision.

Multidisciplinary Practice

Multidisciplinary practice (MDP) occurs when lawyers and nonlawyers collaborate to provide clients legal and nonlegal services. Examples include mental

---

9. The lawyers had, however, provided legal services to a sister company, Esq. N.Y. This might explain why the California court leaves open the possibility that the firm can recover for legal services provided in New York to the California affiliate. *See* Birbower v. Sup. Ct., 949 P.2d 1, 14 (1998) (Kennard, J. dissenting).

10. *See, e.g.*, In re Desilets, 291 F.3d 925 (6th Cir. 2002) (lawyer licensed to practice in Texas and admitted in a Michigan federal court may practice law in a federal bankruptcy court in Michigan).

11. James Moliterno & George Harris, *Global Issues in Legal Ethics* 35 (Thomson West 2007).

12. For a chart that details some of these provisions, *see* Conditions for the admission of lawyers from non-EU Member States to the title of the local legal profession in each EU Member State and conditions under which lawyers from non-EU Member States can perform temporary services in each Member State under their own home title, *available at* http://www.ccbe.eu/fileadmin/user_upload/NTCdocument/gats_questionnaire_e1_1182259979.pdf (last visited July 12, 2012).

13. The EU has a similar rule. James Moliterno & George Harris, *Global Issues in Legal Ethics* 23-24 (Thomson West 2007).

health counselors teamed with divorce lawyers, real estate brokers and title insurance providers working with lawyers, or social workers associated with criminal defense lawyers. Clients in complex business transactions might benefit from the combined services of investment bankers, lawyers, accountants, and other associated consultants. Under current rules, these associations are perfectly acceptable so long as lawyers and nonlawyers do not share legal fees or work in an organization in which lawyers and nonlawyers share managerial control.[14] In other words, lawyers can hire nonlawyers but cannot be hired by for-profit organizations owned in whole or part by nonlawyers to provide legal services to third parties.[156] These restrictions protect clients from harm by preventing economic coercion by nonlawyers that will inevitably lead to the compromising of clients' interests.

The ABA has steadfastly refused to change these provisions, despite the recommendation of several groups over the past 30 years.[16] New York, for example, mandates that a "Statement of Client's Rights in Cooperative Business Arrangements" be signed by clients to protect them.[17] Its amended Rule of Professional Conduct also declares: "Multi-disciplinary practice between lawyers and nonlawyers is incompatible with the core values of the legal profession" and therefore requires "strict division between services provided by lawyers and those provided by nonlawyers."[18] Yet some UK and EU countries have rather aggressively changed their regulatory structures for lawyers, allowing some shared ownership or management.[19]

States and countries considering MDP reform must face a number of issues. First, empirically, do clients want diversified professional services from one company or firm? Second, if client demand is present, will clients benefit from MDPs? Third, does any benefit outweigh the harm? Fourth, if demand occurs and clients seem well-served, what will happen when a client who receives MDP services claims competence, confidentiality, or loyalty obligations from such an integrated firm? Finally, if lawyers are members of the MDP firm, will courts

---

14. MR 5.4, 5.5.

15. *Lawline v. ABA*, 956 F.2d 1378 (7th Cir. 1992) (unincorporated association of lawyers, paralegals, and laypersons that answered legal questions and provided assistance in pro se representation without charge subject to Model Rules 5.4 and 5.5, which bear a rational relation to proper state goals; defendants who promulgated the rule were immune from antitrust and civil rights liability).

16. The Kutak Commission in 1980 and the Multidisciplinary Practice Commission in 2002 recommended that these prohibitions be repealed in favor of multidisciplinary practice, including the sharing of fees and management control. Both were defeated. Similar recommendations have been scuttled from the Ethics 20/20 proposals to be presented to the House of Delegates in 2012. *But see* D.C. Rule of Prof. Conduct 5.4(b) (2012) (allowing multidisciplinary practice so long as lawyers in such an enterprise remained free to exercise their independent professional judgment and to adhere to all of their professional obligations under the Model Rules).

17. N.Y. Rule of Prof. Conduct 5.8, Comment [5] (2012).

18. N.Y. Rule of Prof. Conduct 5.8(a) (2012).

19. *See* James Moliterno & George Harris, *Global Issues in Legal Ethics* 42-44 (Thomson West 2007); Ted Schneyer, *Thoughts on the Compatibility of Recent UK and Australian Reforms with U.S. Traditions in Regulating Law Practice*, 2009 J. Prof. Lawyer 13 (2009); Steven Mark, *Views from an Australian Regulator*, 2009 J. Prof. Lawyer 45 (2009).

impose lawyers' fiduciary duties on the firm's nonlegal services (as the Court did in *Campbell*), even if other professionals offer a large part of the service?

Lawyers differ tremendously over the answers to these questions. Some dream of "an unregulated marketplace," where "clients would have the choice of hiring a single firm that provided all of these services or multiple firms that specialized in some subset." These proponents for change also argue that MDPs offer an opportunity to avoid lawyer fiduciary duties such as confidentiality and loyalty.[20] With respect to confidentiality, they maintain that clients can decide when the attorney-client privilege is important enough not to risk an MDP.[21] As for loyalty, MDPs offer a great opportunity to avoid imputed conflicts rules that restrict law firms from growing to their efficient size.[22]

Those who oppose MDPs argue that social welfare promoted by the entire law governing lawyers assures that client interests curb lawyer economic advantage.[23] Loyalty rules including imputed disqualification mean that lawyers must say "no" to some clients to protect the interests of others.[24] Association with other service providers easily could compromise the confidentiality obligations of lawyers because MDPs need shared information among professionals to thrive. Worst of all, lawyers might be tempted to cheat on their independent professional judgment and competence if their part of the package needs to be subordinated to some other service, such as the sale of securities or insurance, to maximize profit.[25] The market does not always provide more consumer choice, but it can lead to monopoly power that robs consumers of bargaining power. Witness the former Big 8 accounting firms, which, without limitations on concentration, soon became the Big 5 and, after further losing their way, are now the regulated Final 4.[26]

The Future

Campbell typifies the incremental way in which most jurisdictions consider change in unauthorized practice rules.[27] Key issues such as profit sharing and management control continue to persist.[28] Ultimately, if MDPs grow and

---

20. Daniel R. Fischel, *Multidisciplinary Practice*, 55 Bus. Law. 951, 957 (2000).

21. *Id.* at 964.

22. *Id.* at 965-967.

23. Lawrence J. Fox, *Dan's World: A Free Enterprise Dream; An Ethics Nightmare*, 55 Bus. Law. 1533 (2000).

24. *Id.* at 1557-1559.

25. *Id.* at 1546-1547.

26. Lawrence J. Fox, *MDPs Done Gone: The Silver Lining in the Very Black Enron Cloud*, 44 Ariz. L. Rev. 547 (2002).

27. *See* Susan Poser, *Main Street Multidisciplinary Practice Firms: Laboratories for the Future*, 37 U. Mich. J.L. Reform 95 (2003).

28. In Wouters v. Algemene Raad de Nederlandse Orde van Advocaten, 2002 ECR I-1577 (2002), the European Court of Justice of the European Communities upheld a ban on partnerships between lawyers and other professionals adopted by the Bar of the Netherlands. The Court held that despite its restrictive effects on competition, the regulation was "necessary for the proper practice of the legal profession," even though other EU member states allowed MDPs. *See also* In re Evans, 902 A.2d 56 (D.C. App. 2006) (lawyer who owned title insurance company took several shortcuts and

multiply, the courts will eventually face other issues. An aggrieved MDP client will bring a malpractice suit or seek some other remedy, such as professional discipline, disqualification, fee forfeiture, or injunctive relief. At that point, courts will have to decide first whether the law governing lawyers applies, and if so, whether it also creates remedies against the entire MDP.

A British case offers us a glimpse of other litigation that might ensue. There, an accounting firm hired lawyers to offer prelitigation services in teams with other professionals. They later took on an audit of a matter adverse to the former prelitigation services client in a substantially related matter. The House of Lords applied the substantial relationship test applicable to lawyers in deciding a loyalty dispute, even though the accounting firm argued that such a standard was not required by accounting profession rules for audit matters.[29] The reasonable expectations of the client, who understood that lawyers were part of the prelitigation services team, trumped the accounting firm's assumption that it could define loyalty and confidentiality obligations by the standards of another profession.

Should more cases produce similar results, nonlawyer professionals on MDP teams will have to face the prospect that confronted the car dealers in *Campbell*: fiduciary protections in the law governing lawyers will control their conduct as well. MDPs then will need to reassess whether the expanded liability and range of remedies opened to clients of the firm are worth the prospect of increased profits.

---

erred in significant ways in handling the probate matter to gain title insurance income suspended for six months because his personal financial conflict of interest was a "central factor" in his misconduct).

29. Prince Jefri Bolkiah v. KPMG, 2 A.C. 222, 2 W.L.R. 215 (H.L. 1998).

Chapter 16

Judicial Ethics

A. Introduction

Judicial ethics is an important topic for lawyers, both because most judges are lawyers, and because lawyers interact with judges, and are thereby "indirectly governed" by the law that governs judicial conduct.[1] A short survey of judicial conduct rules thus provides an opportunity to review similar concepts in the law governing lawyers.

1. Sources of Law

Like lawyers, judges are governed by codes of conduct promulgated by the highest courts. These codes apply to all the activities of full-time and some activities of part-time judges,[2] including justices of the peace, magistrates, court commissioners, special masters, referees, and administrative law judges. Like state lawyer rules of professional conduct, state codes of judicial conduct follow national models that have been drafted and recommended by the American Bar Association.[3] Federal judges are subject to the Code of Conduct for United States Judges, adopted by the United States Judicial Conference.[4] The models

---

1. Ronald D. Rotunda & John S. Dzienkowski, *Legal Ethics: The Lawyer's Deskbook on Professional Responsibility* § 10.0-1 (West 2012).

2. *See* ABA Model Code of Judicial Conduct (2007), Application, Parts II (Retired Judge Subject to Recall), III (Continuing Part-Time Judge), IV (Periodic Part-Time Judge), and V (Pro Tempore Part-Time Judge).

3. The first model, the 1924 Canons of Judicial Ethics, was promulgated in response to a scandal created by Judge Kenesaw Mountain Landis, who earned six times his federal judicial salary in the private practice of law while sitting as a federal judge. Rotunda & Dzienkowski, *supra* note 1, at § 10.0-2. For a compendium of past Codes and Reporter's explanation of changes, *see* ABA Center for Prof. Responsibility, *Model Code of Judicial Conduct* (2007 ed.), Lisa L. Milord, *The Development of the ABA Judicial Code* (ABA 1992).

4. *Available at* http://www.uscourts.gov/rulesandpolicies/codesofconduct/codeconductunitedstates-judges.aspx (last visited July 12, 2012). Supreme Court Justices are not governed by these rules. *See 2011 Year-End Report on the Federal Judiciary* (2011) *available at* http://www.supremecourt.gov/publicinfo/year-end/2011year-endreport.pdf.

for these Codes have been updated and revised over the past 80 years, culminating in the most recent Model Code of Judicial Conduct adopted by the ABA House of Delegates in 2007.

Like executive and legislative branch employees, state and federal judges also are subject to statutory regulations, and, as *Caperton* in this chapter makes clear, constitutional limitations on their exercise of discretion. For example, federal statutes prohibit the practice of law by federal judges[5] and create standards for disqualification.[6] Judges can be disqualified from sitting on a case if they violate these provisions. Both state and federal judges also are subject to criminal sanctions for violation of applicable statutory regulations.[7]

Unlike lawyers, however, judges are absolutely immune from civil liability for their official duties, even if they act from improper motives.[8] Judicial immunity extends to intentional torts such as defamation and malicious prosecution, as well as statutory civil rights actions.[9] The Supreme Court has created this common law immunity to protect judicial independence and to encourage judges to decide all contested and controversial cases without fear of later legal retribution from the parties. An independent judiciary also promotes public confidence in the courts and the rule of law.[10]

Judges who leave the bench are subject, not only to lawyer code provisions such as Model Rule 1.12, but also to court rules that regulate their subsequent practice.[11] Model Rule 1.12 regulates the conduct of former arbitrators and mediators, as well as that of former judges. Lawyers who serve in these capacities also may be subject to more stringent standards under state law or the code of ethics of a private organization, such as the American Arbitration Association.[12]

2. Procedural Remedies

Judicial conduct is controlled primarily by two procedures, also familiar to lawyers: recusal or disqualification motions,[13] and judicial disciplinary sanctions.

---

5. 28 U.S.C. § 454 (2006).

6. 28 U.S.C. § 144 (2006) (bias or prejudice of a judge); §455 (2000) (disqualification).

7. Jeffrey M. Shaman, Steven Lubet, & James J. Alfini, *Judicial Conduct and Ethics* §14.11 (4th ed. LexisNexis 2007).

8. Mireles v. Waco, 502 U.S. 9 (1991); Stump v. Sparkman, 433 U.S. 349 (1978); Pierson v. Ray, 386 U.S. 547 (1967).

9. O'Brien v. Chandler, 352 F.2d 776 (10th Cir. 1965), *cert. denied* 384 U.S. 926 (1966); Garfield v. Palmieri, 297 F.2d 526 (2d Cir. 1962), *cert. denied* 369 U.S. 871 (1962).

10. Shaman, Lubet, & Alfini, *supra* note 7, at § 14.01.

11. U.S. Sup. Ct. R. 7 (2012); *see also* John Paul Jones, *Some Ethical Considerations for Judicial Clerks*, 4 Geo. J. Legal Ethics 771 (1991).

12. *See* MR 1.12, Comment [2]; MR 2.4, Comment [2]; Model Standards of Conduct for Mediators (2005) *available at* http://www.americanbar.org/content/dam/aba/migrated/dispute/documents/model_standards_conduct_april2007.authcheckdam.pdf.

13. *See* Lawyers' Roles: *Judicial Ethics*, *infra* p. 635.

Nearly every state has created a judicial disciplinary commission empowered by constitutional amendment or statute to discipline sitting judges.[14] Judicial disciplinary procedures begin with the filing of a complaint by another judge, lawyer, or any member of the public. Lawyer and judicial codes create an obligation to report another lawyer's or judge's impairment or misconduct to the appropriate authority.[15] Disciplinary sanctions range from private and public reprimands to deprivation of salary to removal from office.

In the federal courts, Article III judges can be removed from office only by impeachment, a seldom-used remedy.[16] In 1980, Congress created judicial councils in each circuit and empowered them to take disciplinary action short of removal from office.[17] Disciplinary sanctions range from private and public censure to temporary suspension of a judge's caseload. Judicial councils also can ask judges to retire and recommend impeachment to the Senate.[18]

Problems

16-1. Martyn is representing a client in an appeal to Judge Jones from an adverse Mt. Carmel zoning hearing board decision. Martyn's client calls her up in a panic. Client's family was out to dinner in Puerto Rico last week, escaping the cold. As the family went to their assigned table in the dining room, they passed a table where Judge Jones, the solicitor for Mt. Carmel Township, and what appeared to be their spouses were seated, clinking champagne flutes. As Client walked past, Judge Jones awkwardly explained they were attending a county association annual meeting. "We're high school classmates, y'know."

16-2. In a local candidate forum for next fall's county elections, the moderator asked the judicial candidates, "What is your opinion on abortion?" "If I had the right case come before me," the Republican candidate replied, "I'd overturn Roe v. Wade in a minute. Worst decision in history," she continued, as the applause from half the attendees drowned out the rest of her speech.

16-3 Fox has a huge contingency practice. When he is nominated to go on the bench, Fox hands off his cases to an old friend, with the understanding Fox will receive a referral fee. "Don't worry," Fox tells his friend, "I'll help you with these cases since I know them so well."

---

14. Shaman, Lubet, & Alfini, *supra* note 7, at § 1.03.

15. Code of Judicial Conduct Rules 2.14, 2.16. *Cf.* MR 8.3.

16. *See* Mary L. Volcansek, *Judicial Impeachment: None Called for Justice* (U. Ill. Press 1993).

17. Judicial Councils Reform and Judicial Conduct and Disability Act of 1980, 28 U.S.C. §§ 331, 332, 372, 604 (2006).

18. Shaman, Lubet, & Alfini, *supra* note 7, at § 1.04. A recent study committee chaired by Associate Justice Stephen Breyer reported on the effectiveness of these procedures in regulating the ethics of federal judges. The committee concluded that the vast majority of complaints filed against federal judges were properly reviewed and resolved, but it did recommend additional procedures to reduce a higher error rate in high-visibility cases. Judicial Conduct and Disability Study Committee, *Implementation of the Judicial Conduct and Disability Act of 1980: A Report to the Chief Justice* (2006).

Three of the cases are pending in the same county court where Fox will sit as a judge.

Consider: Model Code of Judicial Conduct Rules 1.2, 2.9, 2.10, 2.11, 3.1, 3.7, 4.1 28 U.S.C. § 455

Cheney v. United States District Court for the District of Columbia
541 U.S. 913 (2004)

Memorandum of Justice SCALIA.

I have before me a motion to recuse in these cases consolidated below.

I

The decision whether a judge's impartiality can "'reasonably be questioned'" is to be made in light of the facts as they existed, and not as they were surmised or reported. The facts here were as follows:

For five years or so, I have been going to Louisiana during the Court's long December-January recess, to the duck-hunting camp of a friend whom I met through two hunting companions from Baton Rouge, one a dentist and the other a worker in the field of handicapped rehabilitation. The last three years, I have been accompanied on this trip by a son-in-law who lives near me. Our friend and host, Wallace Carline, has never, as far as I know, had business before this Court. He is not, as some reports have described him, an "energy industry executive" in the sense that summons up boardrooms of Exxon Mobil or Con Edison. He runs his own company that provides services and equipment rental to oil rigs in the Gulf of Mexico.

During my December 2002 visit, I learned that Mr. Carline was an admirer of Vice President Cheney. Knowing that the Vice President, with whom I am well acquainted (from our years serving together in the Ford administration), is an enthusiastic duck-hunter, I asked whether Mr. Carline would like to invite him to our next year's hunt. The answer was yes; I conveyed the invitation (with my own warm recommendation) in the spring of 2003 and received an acceptance (subject, of course, to any superseding demands on the Vice President's time) in the summer. The Vice President said that if he did go, I would be welcome to fly down to Louisiana with him. (Because of national security requirements, of course, he must fly in a Government plane.) That invitation was later extended—if space was available—to my son-in-law and to a son who was joining the hunt for the first time; they accepted. The trip was set long before the Court granted certiorari in the present case, and indeed before the petition for certiorari had even been filed.

We departed from Andrews Air Force Base at about 10 a.m. on Monday, January 5, flying in a Gulfstream jet owned by the Government. We landed in Patterson, Louisiana, and went by car to a dock where Mr. Carline met us, to take us on the 20-minute boat trip to his hunting camp. We arrived at about 2 p.m., the 5 of us joining about 8 other hunters, making about 13 hunters in all; also present during our time there were about 3 members of Mr. Carline's staff, and, of course, the Vice President's staff and security detail. It was not an intimate setting. The group hunted that afternoon and Tuesday and Wednesday mornings; it fished (in two boats) Tuesday afternoon. All meals were in common. Sleeping was in rooms of two or three, except for the Vice President, who had his own quarters. Hunting was in two- or three-man blinds. As it turned out, I never hunted in the same blind with the Vice President. Nor was I alone with him at any time during the trip, except, perhaps, for instances so brief and unintentional that I would not recall them—walking to or from a boat, perhaps, or going to or from dinner. Of course we said not a word about the present case. The Vice President left the camp Wednesday afternoon, about two days after our arrival. I stayed on to hunt (with my son and son-in-law) until late Friday morning, when the three of us returned to Washington on a commercial flight from New Orleans.

II

Let me respond, at the outset, to Sierra Club's suggestion that I should "resolve any doubts in favor of recusal." That might be sound advice if I were sitting on a Court of Appeals. There, my place would be taken by another judge, and the case would proceed normally. On the Supreme Court, however, the consequence is different: The Court proceeds with eight Justices, raising the possibility that, by reason of a tie vote, it will find itself unable to resolve the significant legal issue presented by the case. Thus, as Justices stated in their 1993 Statement of Recusal Policy: "[W]e do not think it would serve the public interest to go beyond the requirements of the statute, and to recuse ourselves, out of an excess of caution, whenever a relative is a partner in the firm before us or acted as a lawyer at an earlier stage. Even one unnecessary recusal impairs the functioning of the Court." Moreover, granting the motion is (insofar as the outcome of the particular case is concerned) effectively the same as casting a vote against the petitioner. The petitioner needs five votes to overturn the judgment below, and it makes no difference whether the needed fifth vote is missing because it has been cast for the other side, or because it has not been cast at all.

Even so, recusal is the course I must take—and will take—when, on the basis of established principles and practices, I have said or done something which requires that course. I have recused for such a reason this very Term. See Elk Grove Unified School District v. Newdow, 540 U.S. 945 (2003). I believe, however, that established principles and practices do not require (and thus do not permit) recusal in the present case.

A

My recusal is required if, by reason of the actions described above, my "impartiality might reasonably be questioned." 28 U.S.C. § 455(a). Why would that result follow from my being in a sizable group of persons, in a hunting camp with the Vice President, where I never hunted with him in the same blind or had other opportunity for private conversation? The only possibility is that it would suggest I am a friend of his. But while friendship is a ground for recusal of a Justice where the personal fortune or the personal freedom of the friend is at issue, it has traditionally *not* been a ground for recusal where *official action* is at issue, no matter how important the official action was to the ambitions or the reputation of the Government officer.

A rule that required Members of this Court to remove themselves from cases in which the official actions of friends were at issue would be utterly disabling. Many Justices have reached this Court precisely because they were friends of the incumbent President or other senior officials—and from the earliest days down to modern times Justices have had close personal relationships with the President and other officers of the Executive. John Quincy Adams hosted dinner parties featuring such luminaries as Chief Justice Marshall, Justices Johnson, Story, and Todd, Attorney General Wirt, and Daniel Webster. Justice Harlan and his wife often "'stopped in'" at the White House to see the Hayes family and pass a Sunday evening in a small group, visiting and singing hymns. Justice Stone tossed around a medicine ball with members of the Hoover administration mornings outside the White House. Justice Douglas was a regular at President Franklin Roosevelt's poker parties; Chief Justice Vinson played poker with President Truman. A no-friends rule would have disqualified much of the Court in Youngstown Sheet & Tube Co. v. Sawyer, 343 U.S. 579 (1952), the case that challenged President Truman's seizure of the steel mills. Most of the Justices knew Truman well, and four had been appointed by him. A no-friends rule would surely have required Justice Holmes's recusal in Northern Securities Co. v. United States, 193 U.S. 197 (1904), the case that challenged President Theodore Roosevelt's trust-busting initiative. *See* S. Novick, Honorable Justice: The Life of Oliver Wendell Holmes 264 (1989) ("Holmes and Fanny dined at the White House every week or two . . . ").

It is said, however, that this case is different because the federal officer (Vice President Cheney) is actually a *named party*. That is by no means a rarity. At the beginning of the current Term, there were before the Court (excluding habeas actions) no fewer than 83 cases in which high-level federal Executive officers were named in their official capacity—more than 1 in every 10 federal civil cases then pending. That an officer is named has traditionally made no difference to the proposition that friendship is not considered to affect impartiality in official-action suits. Regardless of whom they name, such suits, when the officer is the plaintiff, seek relief not for him personally but for the Government; and, when the officer is the defendant, seek relief not against him personally, but against the Government. That is why federal law provides for *automatic substitution* of the new officer when the originally named officer has been replaced. . . .

Richard Cheney's name appears in this suit only because he was the head of a Government committee that allegedly did not comply with the Federal Advisory Committee Act (FACA), and because he may, by reason of his office, have custody of some or all of the Government documents that the plaintiffs seek. If some other person were to become head of that committee or to obtain custody of those documents, the plaintiffs would name that person and Cheney would be dismissed. Unlike the defendant in United States v. Nixon, 418 U.S. 683 (1974), or Clinton v. Jones, *supra,* 520 U.S. 681, Cheney is represented here, not by his personal attorney, but by the United States Department of Justice in the person of the Solicitor General. And the courts at all levels have referred to his arguments as (what they are) the arguments of "the government."

The recusal motion, however, asserts the following:

> "Critical to the issue of Justice Scalia's recusal is understanding that this is not a run-of-the-mill legal dispute about an administrative decision . . . . Because his own conduct is central to this case, the Vice President's 'reputation and his integrity are on the line.'"

I think not. Certainly as far as the legal issues immediately presented to me are concerned, this *is* "a run-of-the-mill legal dispute about an administrative decision." I am asked to determine what powers the District Court possessed under FACA, and whether the Court of Appeals should have asserted mandamus or appellate jurisdiction over the District Court.[1] Nothing this Court says on those subjects will have any bearing upon the reputation and integrity of Richard Cheney. Moreover, even if this Court affirms the decision below and allows discovery to proceed in the District Court, the issue that would ultimately present itself *still* would have no bearing upon the reputation and integrity of Richard Cheney. That issue would be, quite simply, whether some private individuals were *de facto* members of the National Energy Policy Development Group (NEPDG). It matters not whether they were caused to be so by Cheney or someone else, or whether Cheney was even aware of their *de facto* status; if they *were de facto* members, then (according to D.C. Circuit law) the records and minutes of NEPDG must be made public.

The recusal motion asserts, however, that Richard Cheney's "reputation and his integrity are on the line" because

> "respondents have alleged, *inter alia,* that the Vice President, as the head of the Task Force and its sub-groups, was responsible for the involvement of energy industry executives in the operations of the Task Force, as a result of which the Task Force and its sub-groups became subject to FACA."

As far as Sierra Club's *complaint* is concerned, it simply is not true that Vice President Cheney is singled out as having caused the involvement of energy executives. But even if the allegation had been made, it would be irrelevant to

---

1 The Questions Presented in the petition, and accepted for review, are as follows:

"1. Whether the Federal Advisory Committee Act (FACA), 5 U.S.C. App. §§ 1 *et seq.*, can be construed . . . to authorize broad discovery of the process by which the Vice President and other senior advisors gathered information to advise the President on important national policy matters, based solely on an unsupported allegation in a complaint that the advisory group was not constituted as the President expressly directed and the advisory group itself reported.

2. Whether the court of appeals had mandamus or appellate jurisdiction to review the district court's unprecedented discovery orders in this litigation."

the case. FACA assertedly requires disclosure if there were private members of the task force, *no matter who* they were—"energy industry executives" or Ralph Nader; and *no matter who* was responsible for their membership—the Vice President or no one in particular. I do not see how the Vice President's "reputation and integrity are on the line" any more than the agency head's reputation and integrity are on the line in virtually all official-action suits, which accuse his agency of acting (to quote the Administrative Procedure Act) "arbitrar[ily], capricious[ly], [with] an abuse of discretion, or otherwise not in accordance with law." 5 U.S.C. §706(2)(A). Beyond that always-present accusation, there is nothing illegal or immoral about making "energy industry executives" members of a task force on energy; some people probably think it would be a good idea. If, in doing so, or in allowing it to happen, the Vice President went beyond his assigned powers, that is no worse than what every agency head has done when his action is judicially set aside.

To be sure, there could be political consequences from disclosure of the fact (if it be so) that the Vice President favored business interests, and especially a sector of business with which he was formerly connected. But political consequences are not my concern, and the possibility of them does not convert an official suit into a private one. That possibility exists to a greater or lesser degree in virtually all suits involving agency action. To expect judges to take account of political consequences—and to assess the high or low degree of them—is to ask judges to do precisely what they should not do. It seems to me quite wrong (and quite impossible) to make recusal depend upon what degree of political damage a particular case can be expected to inflict.

In sum, I see nothing about this case which takes it out of the category of normal official-action litigation, where my friendship, or the appearance of my friendship, with one of the named officers does not require recusal.

B

The recusal motion claims that "the fact that Justice Scalia and his daughter [sic] were the Vice President's guest on Air Force Two on the flight down to Louisiana" means that I "accepted a sizable gift from a party in a pending case," a gift "measured in the thousands of dollars."

Let me speak first to the value, though that is not the principal point. Our flight down cost the Government nothing, since space-available was the condition of our invitation. And, though our flight down on the Vice President's plane was indeed free, since we were not returning with him we purchased (because they were least expensive) round-trip tickets that cost precisely what we would have paid if we had gone both down and back on commercial flights. In other words, none of us saved a cent by flying on the Vice President's plane. The purpose of going with him was not saving money, but avoiding some inconvenience to ourselves (being taken by car from New Orleans to Morgan City) and considerable inconvenience to our friends, who would have had to meet our plane in New Orleans, and schedule separate boat trips to the hunting camp, for us and for the Vice President's party. (To be sure, flying on the Vice President's jet was more comfortable and more convenient than flying commercially; that accommodation is a matter I address in the next paragraph.)[22]

The principal point, however, is that social courtesies, provided at Government expense by officials whose only business before the Court is business in their official capacity, have not hitherto been thought prohibited. Members of Congress and others are frequently invited to accompany Executive Branch officials on Government planes, where space is available. That this is not the sort of gift thought likely to affect a judge's impartiality is suggested by the fact that the Ethics in Government Act of 1978, 5 U.S.C. App. §101 et seq., which requires annual reporting of transportation provided or reimbursed, excludes from this requirement transportation provided by the United States. I daresay that, at a hypothetical charity auction, much more would be bid for dinner for two at the White House than for a one-way flight to Louisiana on the Vice President's jet. Justices accept the former with regularity. While this matter was pending, Justices and their spouses were invited (*all* of them, I believe) to a December 11, 2003, Christmas reception at the residence of the Vice President—which included an opportunity for a photograph with the Vice President and Mrs. Cheney. Several of the Justices attended, and in doing so they were fully in accord with the proprieties.

III

When I learned that Sierra Club had filed a recusal motion in this case, I assumed that the motion would be replete with citations of legal authority, and would provide some instances of cases in which, because of activity similar to what occurred here, Justices have recused themselves or at least have been asked to do so. In fact, however, the motion cites only two Supreme Court cases assertedly relevant to the issue here discussed,[33] and nine Court of Appeals cases. Not a single one of these even involves an official-action suit.[44] And the motion gives

---

2. As my statement of the facts indicated, by the way, my daughter did not accompany me. My married son and son-in-law were given a ride—not because they were relatives and as a favor to me; but because they were other hunters leaving from Washington, and as a favor to them (and to those who would have had to go to New Orleans to meet them). Had they been unrelated invitees to the hunt, the same would undoubtedly have occurred. Financially, the flight was worth as little to them as it was to me.

3. The motion cites a third Supreme Court case, Public Citizen v. Department of Justice, 491 U.S. 440, (1989), as a case involving FACA in which I recused myself. It speculates (1) that the reason for recusal was that as Assistant Attorney General for the Office of Legal Counsel I had provided an opinion which concluded that applying FACA to presidential advisory committees was unconstitutional; and asserts (2) that this would also be grounds for my recusal here. My opinion as Assistant Attorney General addressed the precise question presented in *Public Citizen:* whether the American Bar Association's Standing Committee on Federal Judiciary, which provided advice to the President concerning judicial nominees, could be regulated as an "advisory committee" under FACA. I concluded that my withdrawal from the case was required by 28 USC §455(b)(3), which mandates recusal where the judge "has served in governmental employment and in such capacity . . . expressed an opinion concerning the merits of the particular case in controversy." I have never expressed an opinion concerning the merits of the present case.

4. United States v. Murphy, 768 F.2d 1518 (7th Cir. 1985), at least involved a judge's going on vacation—but not with the named defendant in an official-action suit. The judge had departed for

not a single instance in which, under even remotely similar circumstances, a Justice has recused or been asked to recuse. Instead, the Argument section of the motion consists almost entirely of references to, and quotations from, newspaper editorials.

The core of Sierra Club's argument is as follows:

> "Sierra Club makes this motion because . . . damage [to the integrity of the system] is being done right now. As of today, 8 of the 10 newspapers with the largest circulation in the United States, 14 of the largest 20, and 20 of the 30 largest have called on Justice Scalia to step aside . . . . Of equal import, there is no counterbalance or controversy: not a single newspaper has argued against recusal. Because the American public, as reflected in the nation's newspaper editorials, has unanimously concluded that there is an appearance of favoritism, any objective observer would be compelled to conclude that Justice Scalia's impartiality has been questioned. These facts more than satisfy Section 455(a), which mandates recusal merely when a Justice's impartiality 'might reasonably be questioned.'"

The implications of this argument are staggering. I must recuse because a significant portion of the press, which is deemed to be the American public, demands it.

The motion attaches as exhibits the press editorials on which it relies. Many of them do not even have the facts right. The length of our hunting trip together was said to be several days (San Francisco Chronicle), four days (Boston Globe), or nine days (San Antonio Express-News). We spent about 48 hours together at the hunting camp. It was asserted that the Vice President and I "spent time alone in the rushes," "huddled together in a Louisiana marsh," where we had "plenty of time . . . to talk privately" (Los Angeles Times); that we "spent . . . quality time bonding together in a duck blind" (Atlanta Journal-Constitution); and that "[t]here is simply no reason to think these two did not discuss the pending case" (Buffalo News). As I have described, the Vice President and I were never in the same blind, and never discussed the case. (Washington officials know the rules, and know that discussing with judges pending cases—their own or anyone else's—is forbidden.) The Palm Beach Post stated that our "transportation was provided, appropriately, by an oil services company," and Newsday that a "private jet . . . whisked Scalia to Louisiana." The Vice President and I flew in a Government plane. The Cincinnati Enquirer said that "Scalia was Cheney's guest at a private duck-hunting camp in Louisiana." Cheney and I were Wallace Carline's guest. Various newspapers described Mr. Carline as "an energy company official" (Atlanta Journal-Constitution), an "oil industrialist," (Cincinnati Enquirer), an "oil company executive" (Contra Costa Times), an "oilman" (Minneapolis Star Tribune), and an "energy industry executive" (Washington Post). All of these descriptions are misleading.

---

a vacation with the prosecutor of Murphy's case, immediately after sentencing Murphy. Obviously, the prosecutor is personally involved in the outcome of the case in a way that the nominal defendant in an official-action suit is not.

And these are just the inaccuracies pertaining to the *facts*. With regard to the *law*, the vast majority of the editorials display no recognition of the central proposition that a federal officer is not ordinarily regarded to be a personal party in interest in an official-action suit. And those that do display such recognition facilely assume, contrary to all precedent, that in such suits mere political damage (which they characterize as a destruction of Cheney's reputation and integrity) is ground for recusal. Such a blast of largely inaccurate and uninformed opinion cannot determine the recusal question. It is well established that the recusal inquiry must be "made from the perspective of a *reasonable* observer who is *informed of all the surrounding facts and circumstances.*" Microsoft Corp. v. United States, 530 U.S. 1301 (2000) (Rehnquist, C.J.)

IV

While Sierra Club was apparently unable to summon forth a single example of a Justice's recusal (or even motion for a Justice's recusal) under circumstances similar to those here, I have been able to accomplish the seemingly more difficult task of finding a couple of examples establishing the negative: that recusal or motion for recusal did *not* occur under circumstances similar to those here.

Justice White and Robert Kennedy

The first example pertains to a Justice with whom I have sat, and who retired from the Court only 11 years ago, Byron R. White. Justice White was close friends with Attorney General Robert Kennedy from the days when White had served as Kennedy's Deputy Attorney General. In January 1963, the Justice went on a skiing vacation in Colorado with Robert Kennedy and his family, Secretary of Defense Robert McNamara and his family, and other members of the Kennedy family. (The skiing in Colorado, like my hunting in Louisiana, was not particularly successful.) At the time of this skiing vacation there were pending before the Court at least two cases in which Robert Kennedy, in his official capacity as Attorney General, was a party. In the first of these, moreover, the press might have said, as plausibly as it has said here, that the reputation and integrity of the Attorney General were at issue. There the Department of Justice had decreed deportation of a resident alien on grounds that he had been a member of the Communist Party. (The Court found that the evidence adduced by the Department was inadequate.)

Besides these cases naming Kennedy, another case pending at the time of the skiing vacation was argued to the Court *by Kennedy* about two weeks later. *See* Gray v. Sanders, 372 U.S. 368 (1963). That case was important to the Kennedy administration, because by the time of its argument everybody knew that the apportionment cases were not far behind, and *Gray* was a significant step in the march toward Reynolds v. Sims, 377 U.S. 533 (1964). When the decision was announced, it was front-page news. Attorney General Kennedy argued for affirmance of a three-judge District Court's ruling that the Georgia Democratic Party's county-unit voting system violated the one-person, one-vote principle. This was Kennedy's only argument before the Court, and it certainly put "on the line" his reputation as a lawyer, as well as an important policy of his brother's administration.

Justice Jackson and Franklin Roosevelt

The second example pertains to a Justice who was one of the most distinguished occupants of the seat to which I was appointed, Robert Jackson. Justice Jackson took the recusal obligation particularly seriously. Nonetheless, he saw nothing wrong with maintaining a close personal relationship, and engaging in "quite frequen[t]" socializing with the President whose administration's acts came before him regularly.

In April 1942, the two "spent a weekend on a very delightful house party down at General Watson's in Charlottesville, Virginia. I had been invited to ride down with the President and to ride back with him." Pending at the time, and argued the next month, was one of the most important cases concerning the scope of permissible federal action under the Commerce Clause, Wickard v. Filburn, 317 U.S. 111 (1942). Justice Jackson wrote the opinion for the Court. Roosevelt's Secretary of Agriculture, rather than Roosevelt himself, was the named federal officer in the case, but there is no doubt that it was important to the President.

I see nothing wrong about Justice White's and Justice Jackson's socializing—including vacationing and accepting rides—with their friends. Nor, seemingly, did anyone else at the time. (The Denver Post, which has been critical of me, reported the White-Kennedy-McNamara skiing vacation with nothing but enthusiasm.) If friendship is basis for recusal (as it assuredly is when friends are sued personally) then activity which suggests close friendship must be avoided. But if friendship is *no* basis for recusal (as it is not in official-capacity suits) social contacts that do no more than evidence that friendship suggest no impropriety whatever.

Of course it can be claimed (as some editorials have claimed) that "times have changed," and what was once considered proper—even as recently as Byron White's day—is no longer so. That may be true with regard to the earlier rare phenomenon of a Supreme Court Justice's serving as advisor and confidant to the President—though that activity, so incompatible with the separation of powers, was not widely known when it was occurring, and can hardly be said to have been generally approved before it was properly abandoned. But the well-known and constant practice of Justices' enjoying friendship and social intercourse with Members of Congress and officers of the Executive Branch has *not* been abandoned, and ought not to be.

V

Since I do not believe my impartiality can reasonably be questioned, I do not think it would be proper for me to recuse. That alone is conclusive; but another consideration moves me in the same direction: Recusal would in my judgment harm the Court. If I were to withdraw from this case, it would be because some of the press has argued that the Vice President would suffer political damage *if* he should lose this appeal, and *if*, on remand, discovery should establish that energy industry representatives were *de facto* members of NEPDG—and because some of the press has elevated that possible political damage to the status of an impending stain on the reputation and integrity of the Vice President. But since political damage often comes from the Government's losing official-action suits; and since political damage can readily be characterized as a stain on reputation and integrity; recusing in the face of such charges would give elements of the press a veto over participation of any Justices who had social contacts with, or were even known to be friends of, a named official. That is intolerable.

My recusal would also encourage so-called investigative journalists to suggest improprieties, and demand recusals, for other inappropriate (and increasingly silly) reasons. The Los Angeles Times has already suggested that it was improper for me to sit on a case argued by a law school dean whose school I had visited several weeks before—visited not at his invitation, but at his predecessor's. The same paper has asserted that it was improper for me to speak at a dinner honoring Cardinal Bevilaqua given by the Urban Family Council of Philadelphia because (according to the Times's false report) that organization was engaged in litigation seeking to prevent same-sex civil unions, and I had before me a case presenting the question (whether same-sex civil unions were lawful?—no) whether homosexual sodomy could constitutionally be *criminalized. See* Lawrence v. Texas, 539 U.S. 558 (2003). While the political branches can perhaps survive the constant baseless allegations of impropriety that have become the staple of Washington reportage, this Court cannot. The people must have confidence in the integrity of the Justices, and that cannot exist in a system that assumes them to be corruptible by the slightest friendship or favor, and in an atmosphere where the press will be eager to find foot-faults.

As I noted at the outset, one of the private respondents in this case has not called for my recusal, and has expressed confidence that I will rule impartially, as indeed I will. Counsel for the other private respondent seek to impose, it seems to me, a standard regarding friendship, the appearance of friendship, and the acceptance of social favors, that is more stringent than what they themselves observe. Two days before the brief in opposition to the petition in this case was filed, lead counsel for Sierra Club, a friend, wrote me a warm note inviting me to come to Stanford Law School to speak to one of his classes. (Available in Clerk of Court's case file.) (Judges teaching classes at law schools normally have their transportation and expenses paid.) I saw nothing amiss in that friendly letter and invitation. I surely would have thought otherwise if I had applied the standards urged in the present motion.

There are, I am sure, those who believe that my friendship with persons in the current administration might cause me to favor the Government in cases brought against it. That is not the issue here. Nor is the issue whether personal friendship with the Vice President might cause me to favor the Government in cases in which *he* is named. None of those suspicions regarding my impartiality (erroneous suspicions, I hasten to protest) bears upon recusal here. The question, simply put, is whether someone who thought I could decide this case impartially despite my friendship with the Vice President would reasonably believe that I *cannot* decide it impartially because I went hunting with that friend and accepted an invitation to fly there with him on a Government plane. If it is reasonable to think that a Supreme Court Justice can be bought so cheap, the Nation is in deeper trouble than I had imagined.

As the newspaper editorials appended to the motion make clear, I have received a good deal of embarrassing criticism and adverse publicity in connection with the matters at issue here—even to the point of becoming (as the motion cruelly but accurately states) "fodder for late-night comedians." If I could have done so in good conscience, I would have been pleased to demonstrate my integrity, and immediately silence the criticism, by getting off the case. Since I believe there is no basis for recusal, I cannot. The motion is denied.

Lawrence J. Fox
The Professional Lawyer
15 No. 2 (*ABA 2004*)

I Did Not Sleep with That Vice-President

. . . Justice Antonin Scalia was the subject of a motion to recuse filed by respondent Sierra Club in an action against one Richard B. Cheney, Vice President of the United States, arising out of the Vice President's role as Chair of the National Energy Policy Development Group. The motion was prompted by the disclosure that Vice President Cheney and Justice Scalia had journeyed together and spent two days duck hunting in Louisiana.

In apparent conformity with Supreme Court practice, the motion was referred to Justice Scalia himself who, on March 18, 2004, issued an extraordinary 21-page memorandum denying the motion. . . .

Why is the Scalia memorandum extraordinary? First, there is the question of its length. . . . Me thinks the gentleman doth protest too much.

The tone of the memorandum does not help. Justice Scalia is known for his rapier pen. . . . But with his own integrity on the line, one would have hoped—as it turns out, against hope—that Justice Scalia would have adopted a less belligerent, cynical and dismissive voice in defending his willingness to sit on this important case. Instead we get a strident brief, dripping with annoyed sarcasm that anyone would question his rectitude and, as it turns out, one that raises far more questions than it answers, one that highlights the infirmities of the good Justice's self-assured stance. . . .

Justice Scalia addresses the issue of his host, Wallace Carline, a magnanimous gentleman, who has been inviting Justice Scalia to Louisiana for years. On this occasion Mr. Carline agreed, at Justice Scalia's request, to invite the Vice-President, an avid duck hunter, as well, an invitation the host permitted Justice Scalia to extend personally.

Justice Scalia tells us a lot more about what the host is not, than what he is. But this must be very important because twice in the memorandum Justice Scalia addresses the issue of how his host makes his less than modest living.

The host is not:

"an energy industry executive,"
"an oil company executive,"
"an oil man,"
"an energy company official," or
"an oil industrialist." . . .

What Justice Scalia apparently wanted to make clear was that his host was not an "ExxonMobil" or "Con Ed" executive; he apparently was not a Halliburton executive either, though the host's wholly-owned company does sound an awful lot like a competitor of Halliburton. I guess Justice Scalia is asserting that these oil field supply folks, unlike the BP Unocal gang, are totally indifferent to the administration's energy policy, not caring one way or the other whether the Bush-Cheney administration allows off-shore or North Slope drilling for petroleum.

Justice Scalia then tells us — a real confidence builder here — that the trip was set even before certiorari was granted, and was completed long before the case is to be argued. Justice Scalia does not, however, cite any authority for the remarkable proposition that it would be okay to preside over a case involving a litigant with whom you spent the weekend before oral argument, but not okay to arrange for same thing after cert. is granted.

Only then does Justice Scalia address the trip on Air Force Two, the Vice President's personal jet that whisked Scalia and party to Louisiana. One of the most interesting aspects of this disquisition is what Scalia does not address. While later we learn who was with whom during the duck hunt, in the section of the opinion dealing with the sumptuous air travel arrangements, that subject is studiously not discussed. From the opinion, all one learns is that the complement included the Vice President and his staff and security detail, Justice Scalia and his son and son-in-law, quite a cozy group for a multiple-hour plane ride on a Gulfstream jet. Perhaps the cabin was too noisy for any conversation, unlike a duck blind. But we will never know, though somehow we doubt it. In any event, we receive no assurance that the justice was sequestered from the litigant. . . .

Finally, Justice Scalia addresses the duck hunting itself. We are told there were 13 hunters in all, a group Justice Scalia characterizes as "not intimate," even "sizable," perhaps because he found the flight down so much more *intime*. We learn they took meals together. One day they went fishing — in two boats. And though Justice Scalia studiously fails to tell us whether he was in the Vice President's fishing boat, we know that is where he fished because when it came to the duck hunting, Justice Scalia makes it quite clear that Mr. Cheney and he never shared a duck blind, as it sadly turns out. Finally, lest you were worried about the Vice President having a Clinton problem, we are told that, although virtually everyone shared sleeping rooms, this sharing did not include the Vice President, who was not forced to sleep with Justice Scalia, his son or his son-in-law.

I make light of Justice Scalia's exegesis of the facts. I might even be accused of adopting a Scalia-like tone. But the fact that Justice Scalia spends all this time arguing the facts is really quite informative. Taking the time to share them with us, Justice Scalia must feel that they are critical, if not dispositive to dismissing any allegations that he should recuse himself. But what is he really saying?

If I had been introduced to my host by an oil man, not someone—tears now—who works with the handicapped, then I would have been forced to recuse.

If the host was an oil man and not an oil rig man, then I would have been forced to recuse.

If certiorari had been granted before the trip was set, then I would have been forced to recuse.

If I took a round trip on Air Force Two—and saved the cost of a round-trip ticket—then I would have been forced to recuse.

If I had been in the same duck blind—like he was in the same small plane and same small fishing boat—I would have been forced to recuse.

If I had shared a room with the Vice President, I would have been forced to recuse.

Why *is* Justice Scalia telling us all this? In my view, it demonstrates the weakness of his position. Should any motion to recuse turn on the facts to which Justice Scalia so tenaciously clings? The fact is Justice Scalia spent this huge amount of time with a litigant with a present matter before the court. No amount of tap dancing about who introduced who to whom, whether the host was an oil man or an oil rig man, or whether they were in the same duck blind changes the substance of what occurred. Justice Scalia engaged in conduct vis-à-vis the Vice President that required him to recuse himself. From the point of view of the adverse litigants this situation is intolerable. And no argument about how oblivious Justice Scalia was to the trappings of flying on Air Force Two with his son and son-in-law can change that.

Justice Scalia knows this. He knows that his neutrality was compromised by his sojourn with the Vice President, even if he didn't have to worry whether the Vice President snores. But his memorandum grabs on to one passing lifesaver. For sure if this case were personal to Richard Cheney, he would recuse, Justice Scalia admits. But this case is a suit against Mr. Cheney in his official capacity. And therefore Justice Scalia was certainly required, in his humble opinion, to stay in the case.

It is true that different standards might apply in personal versus official capacity law suits. The Social Security Administrator might well be indifferent to the fact that he or she is sued hundreds of times a month. And the idea that a judge played golf with that administrator while hearing some poor soul's social security appeal might not raise serious questions of judicial ethics. But to analogize such an unremarkable prosaic circumstance to *this* lawsuit against *this* vice president is surely to exalt form above substance.

It is also certainly true, as Justice Scalia repeatedly observes, that the Vice President has been sued in his official capacity. But the concept of official capacity-private capacity cannot be an on-off switch for deciding when a justice must recuse himself. Some official capacity lawsuits are far more personal than lawsuits that are classified as personal. Despite Justice Scalia's naked assertion to the contrary, this lawsuit raises an issue that has garnered significant attention for years—the highly charged question of who was sitting down in secret with the former CEO of Halliburton to decide our country's energy policy. Who were these oil industrialists? Oil men? Energy industry executives? It is an issue on which the Vice President has literally staked his reputation, one that might even affect the Vice President's re-nomination or re-election. And to assert that the Vice President does not have a deep, abiding and personal interest in whether he is going to be forced to share this information with an inquisitive world is to ignore the dozens of editorials that have been written on the topic. . . .

But I have spent too much time addressing Justice Scalia on his own terms (this is all about the Vice President and me) and not nearly enough confronting the very serious ethical lapse his failure to recuse creates. Imagine you are a law-yer. You are handling a major case for a distraught client. The case will be tried next month to a judge. Your client, on your advice, takes a weekend of rest and relaxation at the Homestead. The client enters the elegant dining room with his wife and, as they are escorted to their table, they notice the judge, the adversary and the adversary's wife hoisting martini glasses filled with a silver liquid, laugh-ing boisterously. As your client passes their way, there is an embarrassed silence followed by the judge's halting comment, "Great to see you, Mr. Jones. Just down here for some trout fishing. Of course, we haven't discussed that little matter."

How does that client feel? How do you feel? What has this done to the system of justice? Can the client ever be convinced that the judge will still be impartial? Should there be a need to convince the client of that fact? Even if you know the judge will be impartial, the appearance of bias is both profound and destructive. There is no place for judges fraternizing with litigants who have matters before them. And that is precisely what Justice Scalia brazenly and insensitively did and yet, when called on it, instead of curing the problem by graciously acknowledg-ing the conflict of interest, he launches a rhetorical broadside that only fans the flames.

This Homestead scenario also highlights how useless is Justice Scalia's reli-ance on the matter being one in which Cheney is sued in his official capacity. If at our dining room scene our dismayed client had also been told, "Don't worry. The case I'm deciding next week is against my olive-loving friend in his official capacity," do you suppose the client would feel relieved, any lingering concerns evaporating once those words were uttered by the convivial judge? You see the problems with the personal-official distinction, are that (a) the offended party, a layman, will not understand the distinction and (b) even if he did, in the eyes of the offended party the betrayal looks identical. While the judge may think it is perfectly alright to go duck hunting with a litigant whose case is pending before him (so long as he does not occupy the same duck blind) because the matter involves the litigant in the litigant's official capacity, that fact is of no conse-quence to the litigant who was not invited to join the hunting party.

What does all of this teach us? I think there are two lessons here. First, Supreme Court practice apparently provides that the Justice who is the subject of a recusal motion decides whether the motion should be granted. Thus, we are the recipients of Justice Scalia's twenty page pronuncimento. How much better would it be if every justice but the justice who is the object of attention were to decide this matter? These other justices are fully cognizant of the special con-siderations that must inform a Supreme Court motion to recuse, given the fact if one Justice steps down there is no one to take her place. Moreover, they are objective in a way that any judge who is the subject of such a motion cannot be. You can be sure that if the present eight Justices, without Scalia participating, had decided this motion, the world would have been treated, in the best sense of that word, to a far shorter and more persuasive opinion—even if the Court decided to deny the motion—than the one Scalia handed down. And the world would also have far more confidence that the result that was reached was a fair one.

Second, we could not find a better poster child than Justice Scalia's conduct and his defense for the importance of maintaining an appearance standard, if not the current appearance of impropriety standard, in our canons of judicial conduct. Since Justice Scalia may be completely unaffected by his sojourn with Dick Cheney, some of us might agree with Justice Scalia's assertion that if a Justice of the Supreme Court could be corrupted by this little fishing adventure then the nation is in real trouble. On the other hand, the appearance that Justice Scalia would be biased as a result of his Louisiana sojourn is something our canons of judicial ethics cannot condone or ignore. . . .

In the world of judging, appearances count and anyone who thinks that a requirement that judges be unfettered, honest and erudite in all things is enough, if what the judges appear to be doing goes unregulated, is failing to recognize how fragile is the trust the American public is currently willing to repose in our judiciary. . . .

What is it then that we don't want our judges to appear to be doing, even if they are not in fact doing it? We don't want them to engage in conduct that might lead the public to question their impartiality. We don't want them to engage in conduct that might lead the public to question their independence. We don't want them to engage in conduct that might lead the public to question their honesty. And we don't want them to engage in conduct that might lead the public to question their competence. . . .

Justice Scalia's adventure with Vice President Cheney not only reflected an appearance of impropriety, but also reflected an appearance that Justice Scalia was not impartial. . . .

One final observation: it has been said that Justice Scalia finds being a Supreme Court Justice not all that splendid an occupation, an overrated position that is not quite enough of a challenge for this larger than life intellectual giant, though we notice with interest that Justice Scalia would rather complain than give up the position to cure the problem. But even if he does have a dim view of his job, this should not give him permission to cast a shadow of the court. For so many of us, the Supreme Court is the most important symbol of both the separation of powers and the rule of law. Maintaining the Court's dignity is critical to both of its symbolic roles. Gentle reader, please read Justice Scalia's 21 page tirade again. Has Justice Scalia enhanced the dignity of the Court by providing us with this? Do we feel better about the Court knowing that this Justice did not recuse himself because he did not sleep with Vice President Cheney? I don't think so and I'll bet you don't either.

Caperton v. A. T. Massey Coal Company, Inc.
556 U.S. 868 (2009)

Justice KENNEDY delivered the opinion of the Court.

In this case the Supreme Court of Appeals of West Virginia reversed a trial court judgment, which had entered a jury verdict of $ 50 million. Five justices heard the case, and the vote to reverse was 3 to 2. The question presented is whether the Due Process Clause of the Fourteenth Amendment was violated when one of the justices in the majority denied a recusal motion. The basis for the motion was that the justice had received campaign contributions in an extraordinary amount from, and through the efforts of, the board chairman and principal officer of the corporation found liable for the damages.

Under our precedents there are objective standards that require recusal when "the probability of actual bias on the part of the judge or decisionmaker is too high to be constitutionally tolerable." *Withrow v. Larkin*, 421 U.S. 35, 47 (1975). Applying those precedents, we find that, in all the circumstances of this case, due process requires recusal.

I

In August 2002 a West Virginia jury returned a verdict that found respondents A. T. Massey Coal Co. and its affiliates (hereinafter Massey) liable for fraudulent misrepresentation, concealment, and tortious interference with existing contractual relations. The jury awarded petitioners Hugh Caperton, Harman Development Corp., Harman Mining Corp., and Sovereign Coal Sales (hereinafter Caperton) the sum of $50 million in compensatory and punitive damages.

In June 2004 the state trial court denied Massey's post-trial motions challenging the verdict and the damages award, finding that Massey "intentionally acted in utter disregard of [Caperton's] rights and ultimately destroyed [Caperton's] businesses because, after conducting cost-benefit analyses, [Massey] concluded it was in its financial interest to do so." In March 2005 the trial court denied Massey's motion for judgment as a matter of law.

Don Blankenship is Massey's chairman, chief executive officer, and president. After the verdict but before the appeal, West Virginia held its 2004 judicial elections. Knowing the Supreme Court of Appeals of West Virginia would consider the appeal in the case, Blankenship decided to support an attorney who sought to replace Justice McGraw. Justice McGraw was a candidate for reelection to that court. The attorney who sought to replace him was Brent Benjamin.

In addition to contributing the $1,000 statutory maximum to Benjamin's campaign committee, Blankenship donated almost $2.5 million to "And For The Sake Of The Kids," a political organization formed under 26 U.S.C. § 527. The § 527 organization opposed McGraw and supported Benjamin. Blankenship's donations accounted for more than two-thirds of the total funds it raised. This was not all. Blankenship spent, in addition, just over $500,000 on independent expenditures—for direct mailings and letters soliciting donations as well as television and newspaper advertisements—"to support . . . Brent Benjamin.'"

To provide some perspective, Blankenship's $3 million in contributions were more than the total amount spent by all other Benjamin supporters and three times the amount spent by Benjamin's own committee. Caperton contends that Blankenship spent $1 million more than the total amount spent by the campaign committees of both candidates combined.

Benjamin won. He received 382,036 votes (53.3%), and McGraw received 334,301 votes (46.7%).

In October 2005, before Massey filed its petition for appeal in West Virginia's highest court, Caperton moved to disqualify now-Justice Benjamin under the Due Process Clause and the West Virginia Code of Judicial Conduct, based on the conflict caused by Blankenship's campaign involvement. Justice Benjamin denied the motion in April 2006. He indicated that he "carefully considered the bases and accompanying exhibits proffered by the movants." But he found "no objective information . . . to show that this Justice has a bias for or against any litigant, that this Justice has prejudged the matters which comprise this litigation, or that this Justice will be anything but fair and impartial." In December 2006 Massey filed its petition for appeal to challenge the adverse jury verdict. The West Virginia Supreme Court of Appeals granted review.

In November 2007 that court reversed the $50 million verdict against Massey. The majority opinion, authored by then-Chief Justice Davis and joined by Justices Benjamin and Maynard, found that "Massey's conduct warranted the type of judgment rendered in this case." It reversed, nevertheless, based on two independent grounds—first, that a forum-selection clause contained in a contract to which Massey was not a party barred the suit in West Virginia, and, second, that res judicata barred the suit due to an out-of-state judgment to which Massey was not a party. Justice Starcher dissented, stating that the "majority's opinion is morally and legally wrong." Justice Albright also dissented, accusing the majority of "misapplying the law and introducing sweeping 'new law' into our jurisprudence that may well come back to haunt us."

Caperton sought rehearing, and the parties moved for disqualification of three of the five justices who decided the appeal. Photos had surfaced of Justice Maynard vacationing with Blankenship in the French Riviera while the case was pending. Justice Maynard granted Caperton's recusal motion. On the other side Justice Starcher granted Massey's recusal motion, apparently based on his public criticism of Blankenship's role in the 2004 elections. In his recusal memorandum Justice Starcher urged Justice Benjamin to recuse himself as well. He noted that "Blankenship's bestowal of his personal wealth, political tactics, and 'friendship' have created a cancer in the affairs of this Court." Justice Benjamin declined Justice Starcher's suggestion and denied Caperton's recusal motion.

The court granted rehearing. Justice Benjamin, now in the capacity of acting chief justice, selected Judges Cookman and Fox to replace the recused justices. Caperton moved a third time for disqualification, arguing that Justice Benjamin had failed to apply the correct standard under West Virginia law—*i.e.*, whether "a reasonable and prudent person, knowing these objective facts, would harbor doubts about Justice Benjamin's ability to be fair and impartial." Caperton also included the results of a public opinion poll, which indicated that over

67% of West Virginians doubted Justice Benjamin would be fair and impartial. Justice Benjamin again refused to withdraw, noting that the "push poll" was "neither credible nor sufficiently reliable to serve as the basis for an elected judge's disqualification."

In April 2008 a divided court again reversed the jury verdict, and again it was a 3-to-2 decision. Justice Davis filed a modified version of his prior opinion, repeating the two earlier holdings. She was joined by Justice Benjamin and Judge Fox. Justice Albright, joined by Judge Cookman, dissented. . . .

Four months later—a month after the petition for writ of certiorari was filed in this Court—Justice Benjamin filed a concurring opinion. He defended the merits of the majority opinion as well as his decision not to recuse. He rejected Caperton's challenge to his participation in the case under both the Due Process Clause and West Virginia law. Justice Benjamin reiterated that he had no "'direct, personal, substantial, pecuniary interest' in this case." Adopting "a standard merely of 'appearances,'" he concluded, "seems little more than an invitation to subject West Virginia's justice system to the vagaries of the day—a framework in which predictability and stability yield to supposition, innuendo, half-truths, and partisan manipulations."

II

It is axiomatic that "[a] fair trial in a fair tribunal is a basic requirement of due process." As the Court has recognized, however, "most matters relating to judicial disqualification [do] not rise to a constitutional level." The early and leading case on the subject is Tumey v. Ohio, 273 U.S. 510 (1927). There, the Court stated that "matters of kinship, personal bias, state policy, remoteness of interest, would seem generally to be matters merely of legislative discretion."

The *Tumey* Court concluded that the Due Process Clause incorporated the common-law rule that a judge must recuse himself when he has "a direct, personal, substantial, pecuniary interest" in a case. . . .

As new problems have emerged that were not discussed at common law, however, the Court has identified additional instances which, as an objective matter, require recusal. These are circumstances "in which experience teaches that the probability of actual bias on the part of the judge or decisionmaker is too high to be constitutionally tolerable." To place the present case in proper context, two instances where the Court has required recusal merit further discussion.

A

The first involved the emergence of local tribunals where a judge had a financial interest in the outcome of a case, although the interest was less than what would have been considered personal or direct at common law.

This was the problem addressed in *Tumey*. There, the mayor of a village had the authority to sit as a judge (with no jury) to try those accused of violating a state law prohibiting the possession of alcoholic beverages. Inherent in this structure were two potential conflicts. First, the mayor received a salary supplement for performing judicial duties, and the funds for that compensation derived from the fines assessed in a case. No fines were assessed upon acquittal. The mayor-judge thus received a salary supplement only if he convicted the defendant. Second, sums from the criminal fines were deposited to the village's general treasury fund for village improvements and repairs.

The Court held that the Due Process Clause required disqualification "both because of [the mayor-judge's] direct pecuniary interest in the outcome, and because of his official motive to convict and to graduate the fine to help the financial needs of the village." It so held despite observing that "[t]here are doubtless mayors who would not allow such a consideration as $12 costs in each case to affect their judgment in it." The Court articulated the controlling principle:

> "Every procedure which would offer a possible temptation to the average man as a judge to forget the burden of proof required to convict the defendant, or which might lead him not to hold the balance nice, clear and true between the State and the accused, denies the latter due process of law."

The Court was thus concerned with more than the traditional common-law prohibition on direct pecuniary interest. It was also concerned with a more general concept of interests that tempt adjudicators to disregard neutrality. . . .

The Court in Aetna Life Ins. Co. v. Lavoie, 475 U.S. 813 (1986), further clarified the reach of the Due Process Clause regarding a judge's financial interest in a case. There, a justice had cast the deciding vote on the Alabama Supreme Court to uphold a punitive damages award against an insurance company for bad-faith refusal to pay a claim. At the time of his vote, the justice was the lead plaintiff in a nearly identical lawsuit pending in Alabama's lower courts. His deciding vote, this Court surmised, "undoubtedly 'raised the stakes'" for the insurance defendant in the justice's suit.

The Court stressed that it was "not required to decide whether in fact [the justice] was influenced." The proper constitutional inquiry is "whether sitting on the case then before the Supreme Court of Alabama '"would offer a possible temptation to the average . . . judge to . . . lead him not to hold the balance nice, clear and true.'" The Court underscored that "what degree or kind of interest is sufficient to disqualify a judge from sitting 'cannot be defined with precision.'" In the Court's view, however, it was important that the test have an objective component.

The *Lavoie* Court proceeded to distinguish the state court justice's particular interest in the case, which required recusal, from interests that were not a constitutional concern. For instance, "while [the other] justices might conceivably have had a slight pecuniary interest" due to their potential membership in a class-action suit against their own insurance companies, that interest is "'too remote and insubstantial to violate the constitutional constraints.'"

B

The second instance requiring recusal that was not discussed at common law emerged in the criminal contempt context, where a judge had no pecuniary interest in the case but was challenged because of a conflict arising from his participation in an earlier proceeding. This Court characterized that first proceeding (perhaps pejoratively) as a "'one-man grand jury.'" In re Murchison, 349 U.S. 133 (1955).

In that first proceeding, and as provided by state law, a judge examined witnesses to determine whether criminal charges should be brought. The judge called the two petitioners before him. One petitioner answered questions, but the judge found him untruthful and charged him with perjury. The second declined to answer on the ground that he did not have counsel with him, as state law seemed to permit. The judge charged him with contempt. The judge proceeded to try and convict both petitioners.

This Court set aside the convictions on grounds that the judge had a conflict of interest at the trial stage because of his earlier participation followed by his decision to charge them. The Due Process Clause required disqualification. The Court recited the general rule that "no man can be a judge in his own case," adding that "no man is permitted to try cases where he has an interest in the outcome." It noted that the disqualifying criteria "cannot be defined with precision. Circumstances and relationships must be considered." These circumstances and the prior relationship required recusal: "Having been a part of [the one-man grand jury] process a judge cannot be, in the very nature of things, wholly disinterested in the conviction or acquittal of those accused." That is because "[a]s a practical matter it is difficult if not impossible for a judge to free himself from the influence of what took place in his 'grand-jury' secret session."

The *Murchison* Court was careful to distinguish the circumstances and the relationship from those where the Constitution would not require recusal. It noted that the single-judge grand jury is "more a part of the accusatory process than an ordinary lay grand juror," and that "adjudication by a trial judge of a contempt committed in [a judge's] presence in open court cannot be likened to the proceedings here." The judge's prior relationship with the defendant, as well as the information acquired from the prior proceeding, was of critical import. . . .

III

Based on the principles described in these cases we turn to the issue before us. This problem arises in the context of judicial elections, a framework not presented in the precedents we have reviewed and discussed.

Caperton contends that Blankenship's pivotal role in getting Justice Benjamin elected created a constitutionally intolerable probability of actual bias. Though not a bribe or criminal influence, Justice Benjamin would nevertheless feel a debt of gratitude to Blankenship for his extraordinary efforts to get him elected. That temptation, Caperton claims, is as strong and inherent in human nature as was the conflict the Court confronted in *Tumey* and *Monroeville* when a mayor-judge (or the city) benefited financially from a defendant's conviction, as well as the conflict identified in *Murchison* and *Mayberry* when a judge was the object of a defendant's contempt.

Justice Benjamin was careful to address the recusal motions and explain his reasons why, on his view of the controlling standard, disqualification was not in order. In four separate opinions issued during the course of the appeal, he explained why no actual bias had been established. He found no basis for recusal because Caperton failed to provide "objective evidence" or "objective information," but merely "subjective belief" of bias. Nor could anyone "point to any actual conduct or activity on [his] part which could be termed 'improper.'" In other words, based on the facts presented by Caperton, Justice Benjamin conducted a probing search into his actual motives and inclinations; and he found none to be improper. We do not question his subjective findings of impartiality and propriety. Nor do we determine whether there was actual bias. . . .

The difficulties of inquiring into actual bias, and the fact that the inquiry is often a private one, simply underscore the need for objective rules. Otherwise there may be no adequate protection against a judge who simply misreads or misapprehends the real motives at work in deciding the case. The judge's own inquiry into actual bias, then, is not one that the law can easily superintend or review, though actual bias, if disclosed, no doubt would be grounds for appropriate relief. In lieu of exclusive reliance on that personal inquiry, or on appellate review of the judge's determination respecting actual bias, the Due Process Clause has been implemented by objective standards that do not require proof of actual bias. In defining these standards the Court has asked whether, "under a realistic appraisal of psychological tendencies and human weakness," the interest "poses such a risk of actual bias or prejudgment that the practice must be forbidden if the guarantee of due process is to be adequately implemented."

We turn to the influence at issue in this case. Not every campaign contribution by a litigant or attorney creates a probability of bias that requires a judge's recusal, but this is an exceptional case. We conclude that there is a serious risk of actual bias—based on objective and reasonable perceptions—when a person with a personal stake in a particular case had a significant and disproportionate influence in placing the judge on the case by raising funds or directing the judge's election campaign when the case was pending or imminent. The inquiry centers on the contribution's relative size in comparison to the total amount of money contributed to the campaign, the total amount spent in the election, and the apparent effect such contribution had on the outcome of the election.

Applying this principle, we conclude that Blankenship's campaign efforts had a significant and disproportionate influence in placing Justice Benjamin on the case. Blankenship contributed some $3 million to unseat the incumbent and replace him with Benjamin. His contributions eclipsed the total amount spent by all other Benjamin supporters and exceeded by 300% the amount spent by Benjamin's campaign committee. Caperton claims Blankenship spent $1 million more than the total amount spent by the campaign committees of both candidates combined.

Massey responds that Blankenship's support, while significant, did not cause Benjamin's victory. In the end the people of West Virginia elected him, and they did so based on many reasons other than Blankenship's efforts. Massey points out that every major state newspaper, but one, endorsed Benjamin. It also contends that then-Justice McGraw cost himself the election by giving a speech during the campaign, a speech the opposition seized upon for its own advantage. . . .

Whether Blankenship's campaign contributions were a necessary and sufficient cause of Benjamin's victory is not the proper inquiry. Much like determining whether a judge is actually biased, proving what ultimately drives the electorate to choose a particular candidate is a difficult endeavor, not likely to lend itself to a certain conclusion. This is particularly true where, as here, there is no procedure for judicial factfinding and the sole trier of fact is the one accused of bias. Due process requires an objective inquiry into whether the contributor's influence on the election under all the circumstances "would offer a possible temptation to the average . . . judge to . . . lead him not to hold the balance nice, clear and true." *Tumey,* at 532. In an election decided by fewer than 50,000 votes (382,036 to 334,301), Blankenship's campaign contributions—in comparison to the total amount contributed to the campaign, as well as the total amount spent in the election—had a significant and disproportionate influence on the electoral outcome. And the risk that Blankenship's influence engendered actual bias is sufficiently substantial that it "must be forbidden if the guarantee of due process is to be adequately implemented."

The temporal relationship between the campaign contributions, the justice's election, and the pendency of the case is also critical. It was reasonably foreseeable, when the campaign contributions were made, that the pending case would be before the newly elected justice. The $50 million adverse jury verdict had been entered before the election, and the Supreme Court of Appeals was the next step once the state trial court dealt with post-trial motions. So it became at once apparent that, absent recusal, Justice Benjamin would review a judgment that cost his biggest donor's company $50 million. Although there is no allegation of a *quid pro quo* agreement, the fact remains that Blankenship's extraordinary contributions were made at a time when he had a vested stake in the outcome. Just as no man is allowed to be a judge in his own cause, similar fears of bias can arise when—without the consent of the other parties—a man chooses the judge in his own cause. And applying this principle to the judicial election process, there was here a serious, objective risk of actual bias that required Justice Benjamin's recusal.

Justice Benjamin did undertake an extensive search for actual bias. But, as we have indicated, that is just one step in the judicial process; objective standards may also require recusal whether or not actual bias exists or can be proved. Due process "may sometimes bar trial by judges who have no actual bias and who would do their very best to weigh the scales of justice equally between contending parties." The failure to consider objective standards requiring recusal is not consistent with the imperatives of due process. We find that Blankenship's significant and disproportionate influence—coupled with the temporal relationship between the election and the pending case—"'offer a possible temptation to the average . . . judge to . . . lead him not to hold the balance nice, clear and true.'" *Lavoie,* 475 U. S. at 825, (quoting *Monroeville,* 409 U.S., at 60, in turn quoting *Tumey*, 273 U.S., at 532, 236). On these extreme facts the probability of actual bias rises to an unconstitutional level.

IV

Our decision today addresses an extraordinary situation where the Constitution requires recusal. Massey and its *amici* predict that various adverse consequences will follow from recognizing a constitutional violation here—ranging from a flood of recusal motions to unnecessary interference with judicial elections. We disagree. The facts now before us are extreme by any measure. The parties point to no other instance involving judicial campaign contributions that presents a potential for bias comparable to the circumstances in this case.

It is true that extreme cases often test the bounds of established legal principles, and sometimes no administrable standard may be available to address the perceived wrong. But it is also true that extreme cases are more likely to cross constitutional limits, requiring this Court's intervention and formulation of objective standards. This is particularly true when due process is violated. . . .

[I]t is worth noting the effects, or lack thereof, of the Court's prior decisions. Even though the standards announced in those cases raised questions similar to those that might be asked after our decision today, the Court was not flooded with *Monroeville* or *Murchison* motions. That is perhaps due in part to the extreme facts those standards sought to address. Courts proved quite capable of applying the standards to less extreme situations.

One must also take into account the judicial reforms the States have implemented to eliminate even the appearance of partiality. Almost every State—West Virginia included—has adopted the American Bar Association's objective standard: "A judge shall avoid impropriety and the appearance of impropriety." ABA Annotated Model Code of Judicial Conduct, Canon 2 (2004). The ABA Model Code's test for appearance of impropriety is "whether the conduct would create in reasonable minds a perception that the judge's ability to carry out judicial responsibilities with integrity, impartiality and competence is impaired." Canon 2A, Commentary; (2009).

The West Virginia Code of Judicial Conduct also requires a judge to "disqualify himself or herself in a proceeding in which the judge's impartiality might reasonably be questioned." Canon 3E(1); see also 28 U.S.C. § 455(a) ("Any justice, judge, or magistrate judge of the United States shall disqualify himself in any proceeding in which his impartiality might reasonably be questioned"). Under Canon 3E(1), "'[t]he question of disqualification focuses on whether an objective assessment of the judge's conduct produces a reasonable question about impartiality, not on the judge's subjective perception of the ability to act fairly.'" Indeed, some States require recusal based on campaign contributions similar to those in this case. See, *e.g.*, Ala. Code §§ 12-24-1, 12-24-2 (2006); Miss. Code of Judicial Conduct, Canon 3E(2) (2008).

These codes of conduct serve to maintain the integrity of the judiciary and the rule of law. The Conference of the Chief Justices has underscored that the codes are "[t]he principal safeguard against judicial campaign abuses" that threaten to imperil "public confidence in the fairness and integrity of the nation's elected judges." This is a vital state interest:

> "Courts, in our system, elaborate principles of law in the course of resolving disputes. The power and the prerogative of a court to perform this function rest, in the end, upon the respect accorded to its judgments. The citizen's respect for judgments depends in turn upon the issuing court's absolute probity. Judicial integrity is, in consequence, a state interest of the highest order." *Republican Party of Minn. v. White*, 536 U.S. 765, 793(2002) (Kennedy, J., concurring). It is for this reason that States may choose to "adopt recusal standards more rigorous than due process requires." . . .

Because the codes of judicial conduct provide more protection than due process requires, most disputes over disqualification will be resolved without resort to the Constitution. Application of the constitutional standard implicated in this case will thus be confined to rare instances.

* * *

The judgment of the Supreme Court of Appeals of West Virginia is reversed, and the case is remanded for further proceedings not inconsistent with this opinion.

Chief Justice ROBERTS, with whom Justice SCALIA, Justice THOMAS, and Justice ALITO join, dissenting.

I, of course, share the majority's sincere concerns about the need to maintain a fair, independent, and impartial judiciary—and one that appears to be such. But I fear that the Court's decision will undermine rather than promote these values.

Until today, we have recognized exactly two situations in which the Federal Due Process Clause requires disqualification of a judge: when the judge has a financial interest in the outcome of the case, and when the judge is trying a defendant for certain criminal contempts. Vaguer notions of bias or the appearance of bias were never a basis for disqualification, either at common law or under our constitutional precedents. Those issues were instead addressed by legislation or court rules.

Today, however, the Court enlists the Due Process Clause to overturn a judge's failure to recuse because of a "probability of bias." Unlike the established grounds for disqualification, a "probability of bias" cannot be defined in any limited way. The Court's new "rule" provides no guidance to judges and litigants about when recusal will be constitutionally required. This will inevitably lead to an increase in allegations that judges are biased, however groundless those charges may be. The end result will do far more to erode public confidence in judicial impartiality than an isolated failure to recuse in a particular case. . . .

But there are other fundamental questions as well. With little help from the majority, courts will now have to determine:

1. How much money is too much money? What level of contribution or expenditure gives rise to a "probability of bias"?

2. How do we determine whether a given expenditure is "disproportionate"? Disproportionate *to what*?

3. Are independent, non-coordinated expenditures treated the same as direct contributions to a candidate's campaign? What about contributions to independent outside groups supporting a candidate?

4. Does it matter whether the litigant has contributed to other candidates or made large expenditures in connection with other elections?

5. Does the amount at issue in the case matter? What if this case were an employment dispute with only $10,000 at stake? What if the plaintiffs only sought non-monetary relief such as an injunction or declaratory judgment?

6. Does the analysis change depending on whether the judge whose disqualification is sought sits on a trial court, appeals court, or state supreme court?

7. How long does the probability of bias last? Does the probability of bias diminish over time as the election recedes? Does it matter whether the judge plans to run for reelection?

8. What if the "disproportionately" large expenditure is made by an industry association, trade union, physicians' group, or the plaintiffs' bar? Must the judge recuse in all cases that affect the association's interests? Must the judge recuse in all cases in which a party or lawyer is a member of that group? Does it matter how much the litigant contributed to the association?

9. What if the case involves a social or ideological issue rather than a financial one? Must a judge recuse from cases involving, say, abortion rights if he has received "disproportionate" support from individuals who feel strongly about either side of that issue? If the supporter wants to help elect judges who are "tough on crime," must the judge recuse in all criminal cases?

10. What if the candidate draws "disproportionate" support from a particular racial, religious, ethnic, or other group, and the case involves an issue of particular importance to that group?

11. What if the supporter is not a party to the pending or imminent case, but his interests will be affected by the decision? Does the Court's analysis apply if the supporter "chooses the judge" not in *his* case, but in someone else's?

12. What if the case implicates a regulatory issue that is of great importance to the party making the expenditures, even though he has no direct financial interest in the outcome (*e.g.*, a facial challenge to an agency rulemaking or a suit seeking to limit an agency's jurisdiction)?

13. Must the judge's vote be outcome determinative in order for his non-recusal to constitute a due process violation?

14. Does the due process analysis consider the underlying merits of the suit? Does it matter whether the decision is clearly right (or wrong) as a matter of state law?

15. What if a lower court decision in favor of the supporter is affirmed on the merits on appeal, by a panel with no "debt of gratitude" to the supporter? Does that "moot" the due process claim?

16. What if the judge voted against the supporter in many other cases?

17. What if the judge disagrees with the supporter's message or tactics? What if the judge expressly *disclaims* the support of this person?

18. Should we assume that elected judges feel a "debt of hostility" towards major *opponents* of their candidacies? Must the judge recuse in cases involving individuals or groups who spent large amounts of money trying unsuccessfully to defeat him?

19. If there is independent review of a judge's recusal decision, *e.g.*, by a panel of other judges, does this completely foreclose a due process claim?

20. Does a debt of gratitude for endorsements by newspapers, interest groups, politicians, or celebrities also give rise to a constitutionally unacceptable probability of bias? How would we measure whether such support is disproportionate?

21. Does close personal friendship between a judge and a party or lawyer now give rise to a probability of bias?

22. Does it matter whether the campaign expenditures come from a party or the party's attorney? If from a lawyer, must the judge recuse in every case involving that attorney?

23. Does what is unconstitutional vary from State to State? What if particular States have a history of expensive judicial elections?

24. Under the majority's "objective" test, do we analyze the due process issue through the lens of a reasonable person, a reasonable lawyer, or a reasonable judge?

25. What role does causation play in this analysis? The Court sends conflicting signals on this point. The majority asserts that "[w]hether Blankenship's campaign contributions were a necessary and sufficient cause of Benjamin's victory is not the proper inquiry." But elsewhere in the opinion, the majority considers "the apparent effect such contribution had on the outcome of the election," and whether the litigant has been able to "choos[e] the judge in his own cause," If causation is a pertinent factor, how do we know whether the contribution or expenditure had any effect on the outcome of the election? What if the judge won in a landslide? What if the judge won primarily because of his opponent's missteps?

26. Is the due process analysis less probing for incumbent judges — who typically have a great advantage in elections — than for challengers?

27. How final must the pending case be with respect to the contributor's interest? What if, for example, the only issue on appeal is whether the court should certify a class of plaintiffs? Is recusal required just as if the issue in the pending case were ultimate liability?

28. Which cases are implicated by this doctrine? Must the case be pending at the time of the election? Reasonably likely to be brought? What about an important but unanticipated case filed shortly after the election?

29. When do we impute a probability of bias from one party to another? Does a contribution from a corporation get imputed to its executives, and vice-versa? Does a contribution or expenditure by one family member get imputed to other family members?

30. What if the election is nonpartisan? What if the election is just a yes-or-no vote about whether to retain an incumbent?

31. What type of support is disqualifying? What if the supporter's expenditures are used to fund voter registration or get-out-the-vote efforts rather than television advertisements?

32. Are contributions or expenditures in connection with a primary aggregated with those in the general election? What if the contributor supported a different candidate in the primary? Does that dilute the debt of gratitude?

33. What procedures must be followed to challenge a state judge's failure to recuse? May *Caperton* claims only be raised on direct review? Or may such claims also be brought in federal district court under 42 U.S.C. § 1983, which allows a person deprived of a federal right by a state official to sue for damages? If § 1983 claims are available, who are the proper defendants? The judge? The whole court? The clerk of court?

34. What about state-court cases that are already closed? Can the losing parties in those cases now seek collateral relief in federal district court under § 1983? What statutes of limitation should be applied to such suits?

35. What is the proper remedy? After a successful *Caperton* motion, must the parties start from scratch before the lower courts? Is any part of the lower court judgment retained?

36. Does a litigant waive his due process claim if he waits until after decision to raise it? Or would the claim only be ripe after decision, when the judge's actions or vote suggest a probability of bias?

37. Are the parties entitled to discovery with respect to the judge's recusal decision?

38. If a judge erroneously fails to recuse, do we apply harmless-error review?

39. Does the *judge* get to respond to the allegation that he is probably biased, or is his reputation solely in the hands of the parties to the case?

40. What if the parties settle a *Caperton* claim as part of a broader settlement of the case? Does that leave the judge with no way to salvage his reputation? . . .

To its credit, the Court seems to recognize that the inherently boundless nature of its new rule poses a problem. But the majority's only answer is that the present case is an "extreme" one, so there is no need to worry about other cases. . . .

Extreme cases often test the bounds of established legal principles. There is a cost to yielding to the desire to correct the extreme case, rather than adhering to the legal principle. That cost has been demonstrated so often that it is captured in a legal aphorism: "Hard cases make bad law." . . .

And why is the Court so convinced that this is an extreme case? It is true that Don Blankenship spent a large amount of money in connection with this election. But this point cannot be emphasized strongly enough: Other than a $1,000 direct contribution from Blankenship, *Justice Benjamin and his campaign had no control over how this money was spent.* Campaigns go to great lengths to develop precise messages and strategies. . . .

Moreover, Blankenship's independent expenditures do not appear "grossly disproportionate" compared to other such expenditures in this very election. "And for the Sake of the Kids"—an independent group that received approximately two-thirds of its funding from Blankenship—spent $3,623,500 in connection with the election. But large independent expenditures were also made in support of Justice Benjamin's opponent. "Consumers for Justice"—an independent group that received large contributions from the plaintiffs' bar—spent approximately $2 million in this race. . . .

It is also far from clear that Blankenship's expenditures affected the outcome of this election. Justice Benjamin won by a comfortable 7-point margin (53.3% to 46.7%). Many observers believed that Justice Benjamin's opponent doomed his candidacy by giving a well-publicized speech that made several curious allegations; this speech was described in the local media as "deeply disturbing" and worse. Justice Benjamin's opponent also refused to give interviews or participate in debates. All but one of the major West Virginia newspapers endorsed Justice Benjamin. Justice Benjamin just might have won because the voters of West Virginia thought he would be a better judge than his opponent. Unlike the majority, I cannot say with any degree of certainty that Blankenship "cho[se] the judge in his own cause." I would give the voters of West Virginia more credit than that.

It is an old cliche, but sometimes the cure is worse than the disease. I am sure there are cases where a "probability of bias" should lead the prudent judge to step aside, but the judge fails to do so. Maybe this is one of them. But I believe that opening the door to recusal claims under the Due Process Clause, for an amorphous "probability of bias," will itself bring our judicial system into undeserved disrepute, and diminish the confidence of the American people in the fairness and integrity of their courts. I hope I am wrong.

I respectfully dissent. . . .

Lawyers' Roles:
Judicial Ethics

The Judge's Role

We have seen that the lawyer's role is partisan: to represent the client's interests zealously, within the bounds of the law.[1] The touchstone ethic for judges is the opposite: impartiality, not partisanship. Like lawyers, judges have obligations of communication, competence, confidentiality, and conflict remediation, but these judicial obligations are intended to promote confidence in the "independence, integrity, and impartiality" of a public tribunal.[2] These "three Is" recur

---

1. Model Rules Preamble [8].

2. ABA Code of Judicial Conduct Canon 1. The same "three Is" inform judicial standards around the world. James Moliterno & George Harris, *Global Issues in Legal Ethics* 190-201 (Thomson West 2007).

as foundational values throughout The Model Code of Judicial Conduct, which begins and ends with them and promotes them by requiring compliance with the law,[3] avoiding impropriety and the appearance of impropriety[4] (yet another "I"), and prohibiting abuse of the power of the judicial office.[5]

Judicial Behavior

While performing judicial duties, judges must be mindful of their obligations to act impartially, competently, and diligently. Competence and diligence require that judges give priority to judicial duties,[6] exercise necessary skill in a prompt and timely manner,[7] and properly hire and supervise court staff.[8]

To promote impartiality, Canon 2 of the Model Code requires judges to "uphold and apply the law";[9] act without bias, prejudice, or harassment;[10] prevent external influence on judicial conduct;[11] ensure each person the right to be heard;[12] act in a patient, courteous manner;[13] and avoid *ex parte* contact with parties,[14] as well as extrajudicial statements on pending matters.[15]

Impartiality also requires that judges disqualify or recuse[16] themselves whenever their "impartiality might reasonably be questioned."[17] Rule 2.11, which identifies a number of recurring circumstances in which this general standard applies, is used as the standard for both judicial discipline and disqualification.[18] A majority of states and the federal government also have adopted statutory standards for judicial disqualification.[19] Although a minority of states allow

---

3. CJC Rule 1.1.

4. CJC Rule 1.2.

5. CJC Rule 1.3. *Cf.* MR 3.5.

6. CJC Rule 2.1.

7. CJC Rules 2.5, 2.7. *Cf.* MR 1.1, 1.3.

8. CJC Rule 2.12, 2.13. *Cf.* MR 5.1, 5.3.

9. CJC Rule 2.2. *Cf.* MR 8.4.

10. CJC Rule 2.3. *Cf.* MR 8.4, Comment [3].

11. CJC Rule 2.4. *Cf.* MR 1.8(f), 5.4(c).

12. CJC Rule 2.6. Part (B) of this rule distinguishes between encouraging and coercing parties to settle a matter. *See, e.g.,* Problem 8-6, *supra* p. 267.

13. CJC Rule 2.8. *Cf.* MR 4.4.

14. CJC Rule 2.9. *Cf.* MR 3.5(b).

15. CJC Rule 2.10. *Cf.* MR 3.6.

16. "Disqualification" and "recusal" are used interchangeably in the Code of Judicial Conduct. CJC Rule 2.11, Comment [1]. Historically, however, recusal meant voluntary withdrawal from a case, and disqualification referred to removal of a judge following the motion of a party. Richard E. Flamm, *Judicial Disqualification: Recusal and Disqualification of Judges* §1.1 (2d ed., Banks & Jordan Law Pub. 2007).

17. CJC Rule 2.11. The federal disqualification statute uses the same "impartiality might reasonably be questioned" standard. 28 U.S.C. § 455 (2006). For an analysis of the federal cases, *see* Alan Hirsch & Kay Loveland, *Recusal: Analysis of Case Law Under 28 U.S.C. §§ 455 and 144* (Fed. Jud. Center 2002).

18. Jeffrey M. Shaman, Steven Lubet, & James J. Alfini, *Judicial Conduct and Ethics* § 4.01 (4th ed. LexisNexis 2007).

19. Flamm, *supra* note 16 at § 2.4.

for peremptory disqualification based on the simple motion of any party, most jurisdictions require that good cause be shown to require disqualification.[20]

Substantively, good cause for disqualification requires a determination that a judge's impartiality "might reasonably be questioned."[21] This standard has been construed in hundreds of cases, the general nature of which is identified in Rule 2.11 of the Code of Judicial Conduct. Although the impartiality standard is not limited only to these categories, a judge's impartiality might reasonably be questioned in these specific circumstances:

- Personal bias or prejudice concerning a party, the party's lawyer, or personal knowledge of the facts in dispute.[22] Many courts add that the source of bias must be extrajudicial (that is, personal), rather than originating in the judicial proceeding itself.[23]
- Relatives of the judge who are parties, managers of parties, lawyers in the proceeding, likely to be a material witness, or who have more than a *de minimis* interest that could be substantially affected by the outcome of the matter.[24]
- Economic interests of the judge or judge's household in the subject matter of the proceeding.[25]
- Receipt of donations to the judge's election campaign made by parties or their lawyers in excess of a stated amount[26] (which *Caperton* raises to a constitutional issue in "extraordinary situations").

---

20. Debra Lyn Bassett & Rex R. Perschbacher, *The Elusive Goal of Impartiality*, 97 Iowa L. Rev. 1, 44-45 (2011) (18 jurisdictions allow preemptory challenges at the trial court level; 28 U.S.C. § 144 both read as and was originally intended to be preemptory as well).

21. CJC Rule 2.11(A). *Cf.* MR 1.7(a).

22. CJC Rule 2.11(A)(1).

23. *E.g.,* Farmer v. State, 770 So. 2d 953 (Miss. 2000) (trial judge who took guilty plea overturned on appeal not disqualified from case on remand absent showing of extrajudicial source of partiality or bias). The Supreme Court prefers to call the extrajudicial source doctrine a "factor" in determining whether bias or partiality was present. Liteky v. United States, 510 U.S. 540 (1995) (judge's opinions did not amount to bias or partiality unless they displayed a deep-seated favoritism or antagonism that would make fair judgment impossible). *See also* United States v. Microsoft Corp., 253 F.3d 34 (D.C. Cir. 2001) (judge who gave private interviews to reporters that were very critical to the defense disqualified for lack of impartiality; extrajudicial source rule inapplicable). *See also* Flamm, *supra* note 16, at § 4.6; Shaman, Lubet, & Alfini, *supra* note 18, at § 14.05.

24. CJC Rule 2.11(A)(2); *e.g.,* Matter of Johnson, 532 S.E.2d 883 (S.C. 2000) (judge who failed to disqualify herself in grandson's criminal case publicly reprimanded).

25. CJC Rule 2.11 (A)(3); *e.g.,* Huffman v. Arkansas Jud. Disc. & Disability Commn., 42 S.W.3d 386 (Ark. 2001).

26. CJC Rule 2.11(A)(4); *e.g.,* Mackenzie v. Super Kids Bargain Store, Inc., 565 So. 2d 1332 (Fla. 1990) (reasonable persons would not perceive judge biased in favor of litigants based solely on fact litigants made a campaign contribution in a jurisdiction where state constitution requires election of certain judges); Barber v. Mackenzie, 762 So. 2d 755 (Fla. App. 1990) (judge's disqualification required where counsel who represented party in matrimonial action before judge were members of the committee to re-elect the judge, whose campaign was vigorously opposed).

- Prior public statements by the judge that appear to commit him or her to reach a particular result or rule in a particular way in a proceeding or controversy.[27]
- Prior service as a lawyer, judge, material witness, or government employee or agent in the same matter.[28]

All but the first of these categories is easy to document and prove. *Caperton* and *Cheney* illustrate how the personal bias standard differs.[29] First, it requires interpretation (usually by the judge whose disqualification is sought). Second, that judge likely will suffer from a cognitive bias—that he or she is unbiased or will not be influenced.[30] Together, these two factors invite "interpretive manipulations," such as the holding that actual bias was necessary, even though recusal is mandatory once the judge's "impartiality might reasonably be questioned."[31]

Once a judge is subject to disqualification, two events can override such a result. First, the rule of necessity—that no judge has the requisite impartiality to decide the matter—can prevail over an otherwise substantive basis for disqualification.[32] Second, a disqualification not based on personal bias can be waived by the parties, so long as they make such a decision to waive outside the presence of the judge.[33]

Extrajudicial Conduct

A judge's impartiality obligation reaches into his or her extrajudicial life. Judges must avoid participating in activities that can often lead to disqualification, or

---

27. CJC Rule 2.11(A)(5); *e.g.,* United States v. Norton, 700 F.2d 1072 (6th Cir. 1983) (judge who opposed racism of Ku Klux Klan and Nazi Party not disqualified from actions where those groups are parties). *Cf.* Public Utilities Comm'n v. Pollak, 343 U.S. 451, 467 (1952) (*sua sponte* recusal by Justice Frankfurter in a case involving radio programs played on public transit in Washington, D.C., because his feelings were "so strongly engaged as a victim of the practice in controversy").

28. CJC Rule 2.11(A)(6); *e.g.,* Lee v. State, 735 N.E.2d 1169 (Ind. 1999) (judge who gained information from prior proceeding involving accomplice not required to recuse). *Cf.* Village of Exeter v. Kahler, 606 N.W.2d 862 (Neb. App. 2000) (judge who gained information from an earlier proceeding involving the same party disqualified).

29. *See* Jed Handelsman Shugerman, *In Defense of Appearances: What Caperton v. Massey Should Have Said,* 59 DePaul L. Rev. 529 (2010).

30. Bassett & Perschbacher, *supra* note 20, at 35-39 (describing various forms of cognitive bias); W. Bradley Wendel, *The Behavioral Psychology of Judicial Corruption: A Response to Judge Irwin and Daniel Real,* 42 McGeorge L. Rev. 35 (2010).

31. *Id.* at 40-41. *See also* Steven Lubet, "Ducks in a Row," in *The Importance of Being Honest,* 127-133 (N.Y.U. Press 2008).

32. For example, if all members of an appellate court would be disqualified in a case that challenges legislative pay raises for judges, utility rate increases, or state bar actions, the rule of necessity would override disqualification. Shaman, Lubet, & Alfini, *supra* note 18, at § 4.03. *See* Williams v. United States, 48 F. Supp. 2d 52 (D.D.C. 1999) (recusal not required where federal judge ruled on meaning of statute that affected federal judicial salaries).

33. CJC Rule 2.11(C). *Cf.* MR 1.7(b), 1.0(e); *e.g.,* Matter of Platt, 8 P.3d 686 (Kan. 2000) (judge whose waiver procedure required nonconsenting parties to fire counsel or seek statutory disqualification publicly censured for improper coercive procedures).

undermine their independence, integrity, or impartiality.[34] For example, judges cannot appear voluntarily before a legislative body or accept governmental appointments, except in connection with matters concerning the legal system or administration of justice.[35] Nor may they affiliate with discriminatory organizations.[36] To avoid misuse of judicial power or prestige, judges cannot voluntarily testify as character witnesses[37] or use nonpublic information for a purpose unrelated to judicial duties.[38] To avoid disqualification, judges cannot accept fiduciary appointments,[39] serve as arbitrators or mediators,[40] practice law,[41] serve as an officer or director of any for-profit business entity, or engage in any other financial activities that will interfere with their proper performance of judicial duties.[42] Service on nonprofit boards is allowed, so long as the organization's activities do not frequently come before the judge or the court of which the judge is a member, or circumstances otherwise undermine the judge's impartiality.[43] To maintain judicial independence, a number of rules regulate extrajudicial compensation, basically limiting it to reasonable honoraria, reimbursement of expenses, or the acceptance of "ordinary social hospitality."[44] Public reporting of extrajudicial compensation also is required.[45]

Judicial Selection

Judicial selection is governed by federal and state constitutional and statutory provisions. The United States Constitution requires that federal judges be appointed for life, with the advice and consent of the Senate.[46] Alexander Hamilton recommended life tenure as a means to insulate judges from the "encroachments" of Congress and the "occasional ill humors in the society."[47] States have preferred two other methods: merit selection and judicial election.[48]

Canon 4 of the Code of Judicial Conduct regulates a judge's campaign activity in the majority of jurisdictions where judicial election is a reality. It allows

---

34. CJC Rule 3.1.
35. CJC Rules 3.2, 3.4. *Cf.* MR 3.9.
36. CJC Rule 3.6.
37. CJC Rule 3.3. *Cf.* MR 3.7.
38. CJC Rule 3.5. *Cf.* MR 1.6, 1.8(b), 1.9, & 1.11(c).
39. CJC Rule 3.8.
40. CJC Rule 3.9.
41. CJC Rule 3.10.
42. CJC Rule 3.11.
43. CJC Rule 3.7.
44. CJC Rules 3.12-3.14.
45. CJC Rule 3.14.
46. *See* Lee Epstein & Jeffrey A. Segal, *Advice and Consent: The Politics of Judicial Appointments* (Oxford Press 2005); Sheldon Goldman, *Picking Federal Judges: Lower Court Selection from Roosevelt Through Reagan* (Yale Press 1997).
47. Alexander Hamilton, *Federalist Papers No. 78*, *available at* http://thomas.loc.gov/home/histdox/fed_78.html (last visited July 12, 2012).
48. *See generally* Daniel R. Pinello, *The Impact of Judicial-Selection Method on State-Supreme-Court Policy* (Greenwood Press 1995).

judges to participate in legally approved campaign committees and activities,[49] but it requires judges who become candidates for nonjudicial offices to resign.[50]

In campaigning for judicial office, judges are prohibited from using court staff to campaign or raise money, from seeking endorsements from or making speeches on behalf of political organizations, and most controversially, from making "pledges, promises, or commitments that are inconsistent with the impartial performance" of judicial office.[51]

This "pledges, promises, and commitments" clause language has been more narrowly interpreted since the Supreme Court relied on the First Amendment to overturn a state rule of judicial ethics that prohibited judicial candidates from announcing their views on disputed legal and political issues.[52] The Court found the state prohibition was not sufficiently cabined to serve an otherwise legitimate state interest in the impartiality of judges, defined as lack of bias for or against particular parties to particular proceedings.

Comments [11] through [15] to CJC Rule 4.1 are intended to "encourage adoption of an appropriately narrow interpretation" of the clause, meaning that a judicial candidate does not compromise impartiality by announcing personal views so long as the announcement does not "demonstrate a closed mind on the subject" or include "a pledge or a promise to rule in a particular way if the matter comes before the court."[53] However, a judge who "commits or appears to commit" to a particular result about issues that later come before the court will be subject to disqualification.[54]

The Future

The ideals of impartiality, independence, and integrity remain the primary goal of judicial ethics, embodied in both codes of judicial conduct and relevant statutory regulations. Judges should suspend judgment until all of the evidence has been introduced and, if they cannot act in an unbiased manner, they should disqualify themselves from the case. Yet, the last eight decades have shown that the obligation of avoiding bias and promoting impartiality and independence are not self-executing. Like the law that governs lawyer conduct, the law governing judicial conduct has continually been refined and will continue to evolve in the future.

---

49. CJC Rule 4.2-4.5.
50. CJC Rule 4.5.
51. CJC Rule 4.1.
52. Republican Party of Minn. v. White, 536 U.S. 765 (2002).
53. ABA Center for Prof. Responsibility, *Model Code of Judicial Conduct* 147 (2007 ed.); *see also* Citizen's United v. Fed. Election Comm'n 130 S. Ct. 876, 910 (2010) (upholding *Caperton's* rule that Due Process might require the judge must be recused, but clarifying that the litigant's political speech could not be banned).
54. CJC Rule 2.11(A)(5).

Appendix

Applying the Law Governing Lawyers

A. Problems

Select one of the following problems as the basis for your research following the guidelines in this appendix:

A-1. Martyn & Fox has decided to open a new office in the jurisdiction where you intend to practice law. Select any problem in this book, and research the answer to that problem in that jurisdiction.

A-2. Interview a practicing lawyer, asking him or her to identify an ethics issue he or she has faced in practice. Research the answer to the lawyer's problem in the jurisdiction where that lawyer practices, or in the jurisdiction where you intend to practice law.

A-3. Videotape a legal ethics problem presented in a movie or television program. Research the answer to that problem in the jurisdiction where the lawyers in the program practice law or in the jurisdiction where you intend to practice.

B. Written Assignment

Goals:

Your ultimate goal should be to produce a paper sufficiently informative that a lawyer could rely on your advice in practice.

1. To do this, you will need to select a problem, identify issues, learn some advanced research techniques, and use and improve your analytical and writing ability.
2. Your grade will be based on the quality of your research, organization, use of authority, analysis, and writing.

Writing and Analysis Outline:

1. Use an interoffice research memo format. Direct the memo to the senior partner in Martyn & Fox who asked you for advice.
2. Begin by describing the facts of the problem you have selected. Next, discuss the relevant law in the following order:

A. The professional rules that govern in your jurisdiction.

B. The case law in your jurisdiction.

C. Any state or ABA ethics opinions that address the issue.

D. The rules, case law, and other authorities in other jurisdictions. Here, you should focus on whether and how your jurisdiction's result is consistent with the rules and case law in most other jurisdictions.

You can learn more about any or all of these Research Resources in the introduction to your Law Governing Lawyers supplement.

Overall Requirements:

1. *Length:* Your paper should be about 10–20 double-spaced pages including footnotes, which should be used for citations to authorities. Footnotes can appear at the bottom of each page, or at the end of the paper.

2. *Citations:* Use the ALWD, Bluebook, or local rules for citation form. When referring to primary source material (statutes, cases, court rules, etc.) always go to the material itself. Do not rely on quotations from other authors.

3. *Plagiarism:* When you quote, paraphrase, rely on, or are influenced by someone else's ideas, cite that author. Ideas taken from another source, even if expressed in your own words, also must be cited to avoid mis- representing the work as your own. As a rule, if you are in doubt, footnote the material.

Table of Cases

Table of Model Rules, Restatements, and Other Regulations

Index